The **Rough Guide** to

Denmark

written and researched by

**Lone Mouritsen, Roger E. Norum
and Caroline Osborne**

ROUGH
GUIDES

NEW YORK · LONDON · DELHI

www.roughguides.com

Contents

Danish food and drink
colour section following
p.216

The great outdoors
colour section following
p.312

◄◄ Operæn at dusk, Copenhagen ◄ Bellevue beach, Copenhagen

Introduction to

Denmark

When Denmark topped a 2006 survey of the world's happiest places to live, it didn't come as a shock to most Danes. Poised between Scandinavia proper and mainland Europe and spread over the islands of Zealand and Funen and the Jutland peninsula, this relatively small country (roughly the same size as Switzerland) has always punched above its weight – historically, artistically and politically. What's more, Denmark continues to offer its residents one of the highest standards of living in the world, a social welfare system that's second to none and a smooth-running infrastructure typified by its excellent public transport system. Add to that a confident, cool, uncongested capital, a bevy of picturesque historic towns and an unspoilt natural environment of stunning beaches, forests and rolling meadows, and it's clear why the locals take such pride in showing off their country to visitors. Danes tend to be friendly and welcoming folk, and their ingrained sense of sociability is evident at any gathering, where a plentiful supply of home-grown food and drink, candlelight and open fires are all part of creating the unique atmosphere summed up by the term *hygge*. The English translation ("cosiness") doesn't really do it justice, but more than anything else, it's *hygge* that sums up Denmark's appeal.

This is a conservative and very traditional country: Denmark's immigration policies are some of the toughest in Europe, and its royal family are still held in high regard, their status unquestioned. But it's also a progressive nation, with legendarily liberal social values and forward-thinking attitudes that have made it one of the most environmentally conscious nations in the world.

And although Denmark's **history** is inevitably associated with the exploits of the Vikings, the country has long played a significant role in wider European affairs. Under the Vikings and their descendants, the Danish crown conquered England and drove out the Swedes to rule Norway for nearly five hundred years, as well as maintaining colonial strongholds in South Asia, West Africa and the Caribbean until the early twentieth century. Since then, the country's energies have been turned inwards, toward the development of a well-organized yet hardly over-bureaucratic society

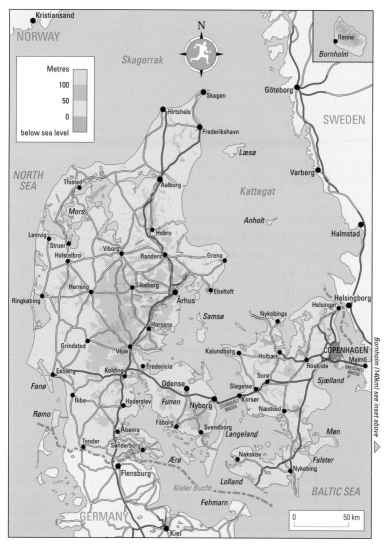

that does much to encourage national pride in culture and the arts, and which strongly fosters the freedoms of the individual.

Denmark is the easiest of the Scandinavian countries to explore in terms of travelling costs and distances: you can drive from Copenhagen in the east to Esbjerg in the west in well under three hours. The bulk of visitors are drawn to the principal **cities** of Copenhagen, Odense and Århus – historic places that combine a lively social and cultural life with a welcoming and homely charm, and whose stylish hotels, shops, cafés and public buildings are living museums of Denmark's outstanding credentials in design and architecture. But it would be a shame never to venture away from the cities. The Danes are justifiably proud of their country's **great outdoors**, and although the landscape isn't hugely dramatic, the gently undulating hillsides, vast meadows and forested valleys are beautifully unspoiled, dotted with picturesque villages – and the 7300km of coastline means you're never far from the sea. Indeed, the Danish **coast** is perhaps the jewel in the country's crown, a bewitching mix of sandy beaches, glimmering chalk cliffs and placid fjords, with over four hundred islands and skerries just off its shores. Furthermore, as Denmark's countryside is criss-crossed by thousands of miles of cycling trails, it's a brilliant place to explore by bike.

Where to go

M ost visitors get their first glimpse of Denmark at the sleek international airport, just outside **Copenhagen** on the island of **Zealand**. One of the most cosmopolitan and culturally alive cities in Europe, it would be downright criminal to visit

Denmark without seeing its capital – and given that it's the only real transportation hub in the country, rather difficult besides. Boasting a wealth of public buildings characterized by cutting-edge design, comely Copenhagen offers an alluring array of cultural attractions that include major national museums and art galleries and an enticing range of entertainment, from cosy cafés and bars to intimate clubs, rocking live music venues and, in the summer, a bevy of outstanding arts and music festivals. Away from the urban zip, and within easy reach of the capital, northern Zealand offers beguiling royal castles and a string of superb beaches, long strands of windswept, sandy shoreline that

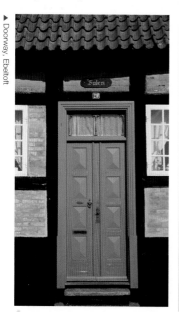

◀ Doorway, Ebeltoft

Fact file

• Denmark is one of the five Nordic nations, and with a total land area of 43,560 square kilometres, it's by far the smallest. The population stands at just over 5.45 million, some 8.5 percent of which are foreign-born citizens and their descendants – a fairly high number for the Scandinavian countries and one which has made immigration a major bone of political contention. Unemployment averages 5.5 percent.

• The standard of living in Denmark is one of the highest in the world – but income tax ranges from 45 percent to 59 percent, and 25 percent VAT is levied on most goods. In return Danes receive free, comprehensive social welfare, while the working week averages 30.6 hours.

• Though granted independence (in 1978 and 1948 respectively), the former colonies of Greenland and the Faroe Islands still have Danish as an official language alongside their native tongues, and the Danish government still provides them with total subsidies of some US$150 million each year.

• Denmark became a constitutional monarchy in 1849, and has been a parliamentary democracy since 1901; 36 percent of MPs are women.

• Denmark has more than twice the amount of bicycles than cars, with 4.2 million cycles and 1.8 million cars.

• Denmark's 950 bakeries churn out fresh bread and the nation's eponymous pastries each night – but pressure from supermarkets combined with the unpopularity of baking as a career means (to the horror of purists) that 35–40 of them are predicted to close annually over the coming years.

• Scandinavians are the world's highest per-capita consumers of coffee, with Danes (who drink four cups a day) coming third after Sweden and Finland.

are blissful spots for summer swimming and winter walking, and hold a smattering of posh bistros and restaurants to boot. South of the capital, picturesque and chipper **Roskilde** is best known for its unforgettable summer

> **Denmark is a progressive nation, with legendarily liberal social values and forward-thinking attitudes that have made it one of the most environmentally conscious nations in the world.**

music festival, but is well worth a stop for its imposing Gothic cathedral and Viking ship museum. The brick towers, stucco palaces and ruined fortresses of southern Zealand's medieval-era towns attest to a rich royal

Royal footprints

As the home of the world's oldest monarchy, it's little surprise that Denmark holds over six hundred grand castles, palaces, manors and estates, which together showcase all the major styles of European architecture, from Renaissance, Baroque and Rococo to Neoclassical and Romantic. Historically, the majority of them belonged to royal or high-ranking noble families, but most passed into state hands when the Danish constitution was ratified in 1849; a great many have been opened up to the public, and have become some of Denmark's most popular visitor attractions. Touring their opulent interiors provides an intimate view of the day-to-day lives of their former inhabitants, while the defensive features – from moats to ramparts – stand testament to Denmark's former strategic importance. The grounds that surround the stately homes, meanwhile, offer endless opportunities for walking, picnicking or simply lazing in the sun, with English-style gardens dotted with sculptures, manicured mazes and tree-lined avenues as well as wilder parklands where you can spot deer and other wildlife.

▲ Langeland beach

history, while the trio of large islands connected to the south coast by road and train links offer an appealing mix of lively beach towns and sleepy lakeside villages. Some 100km off Zealand's eastern coast in the middle of the Baltic Sea, **Bornholm** is a gorgeous and subdued place, its forests and winsome coastline bathed in a breathtaking light – it's easy to see why the locals pledge allegiance first to their island and then to the Danish crown. With fetching harbour towns, white-sand beaches and hundreds of miles of cycling paths, tourism is on the up-and-up here, and it's a great place to revel in the great outdoors.

> **Denmark's stylish public buildings are living museums of the country's outstanding credentials in design and architecture.**

Linked to Zealand by the awe-inspiring Storebælt bridge, **Funen** is Denmark's third largest – and definitely its greenest – landmass, the countryside interspersed with fairytale castles, manicured gardens and small coastal outposts that, in the summertime at least, maintain a warm and friendly atmosphere that's animated by festivals, concerts and a prevailing sensation of bonhomie. The main urban draw is **Odense**, which makes much of its connections with locally-born Hans Christian Andersen and holds a pair of superb art galleries, some excellent restaurants and a sizeable student population who ensure that its many bars and clubs rarely close before dawn. There's yet more rural appeal in the islands of the **south Funen archipelago**, with their gorgeous beaches, scenic cycling routes and opulent old estates.

West by bridge across the Lille Bælt is the expansive **Jutland** peninsula, jutting off from northern Germany in between the squally North Sea and the tranquil Baltic. Given its distance from Copenhagen, the island has an appealingly no-nonsense, bucolic flavour that's evident even in the laid-back city of **Århus**, whose cultural delights rival those of the capital.

▼ ARoS, Århus

Control of southern Jutland, which shares the border with Germany, was tossed back and forth between Denmark and Germany for centuries, a fact evident in the numerous castles built to stave off the invaders. The many bird species that inhabit the marshland and tidal flats of the **south-west coast** are a big draw for those of an avian bent, while the rolling hills of the east end at craggy, nose-shaped **Djursland**, and give way to some of the country's most spectacular white-sand beaches. The unrelenting winds that pummel the remote and rural **western coast** have thrashed the migrating sand dunes about for millennia, creating harsh living conditions for local farmers and fishermen as well as an incredibly striking coastline – and some of the world's best spots for windsurfing. Denmark's longest river, the lithe **Gudenå** bisects the pretty **Lake District** from south to north, and canoeing is the perfect way to explore. North of the river, Denmark's largest forest provides picture-perfect hiking and mountain biking, while valleys and fjord basins rich in Viking history terminate at atmospheric **Skagen**, whose magical oceanic light has attracted painters for decades.

Birdwatching

Denmark is one of Europe's key destinations for birdwatching, and it's a very popular pastime for many Danes, too, who make good use of the tall, sturdy observation towers that you'll see in many of the country's nature reserves. The best birding site in the country is the Wadden Sea marshes and tidal flats on Jutland's southwest coast, where the receding tides provide a muddy refuge for flocks of wild geese, eider ducks and other aquatic birds. There are also regular visits from migratory species such as the red-breasted goose and barred warbler, while sundown and sunrise see well near half a million starlings performing awe-inspiring aerial displays as they gather to roost. Throughout the country, the best time for birding is April, when many species don their handsome mating plumage – great crested grebes, ringed plovers and kingfishers are particularly eye-catching.

When to go

Denmark has the least extreme **climate** of the Scandinavian countries, and though temperatures vary little across the country, wind conditions and proximity to the sea shake things up a bit – you'll notice the stiff breezes along Jutland's west coast in particular. Rainfall levels are more or less constant throughout the year, with an annual average of 61cm; the west tends to be wetter than the east, however.

Though **spring** usually brings bright sunlight and cloudless skies, the best time to visit Denmark is during the **summer** months of June, July and August, when the climate is warmest and the blossoming landscape at its prettiest, and when tourist facilities and transport services are operating at full steam. Bear in mind, though, that July is vacation month for Danes, who head en masse to the countryside or the coast – though even then, only the most popular areas are uncomfortably crowded. Summer is almost always

▲ Coastal farmlands, Funen

sunny and clear, with temperatures rarely stifling: the warmest month is July, which averages 20°C (68°F), though highs of 26°C (78°F) are not unheard of. Copenhagen attracts visitors all year round and is a bit of a law unto itself; as the intake peaks during July and August, the best times to visit the capital are May, early June and September, though you'll find plenty going on throughout the year.

Autumn can also be a good time to visit, with the falling leaves providing a gorgeous golden show – though bear in mind that the coastal waters can get downright chilly as early as September, and that most sights and attractions maintain reduced hours outside of high season, from mid-September onwards.

Cold but rarely severe, Denmark's **winters** are decidedly less frigid than those of its northerly Scandinavian

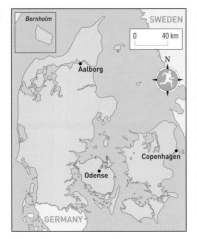

neighbours. Although temperatures can drop as low as minus 15°C (5°F), they usually hover around freezing, with the tail-end of the Gulf Stream keeping the frost off in the coastal towns. Although the possibilities for outside pursuits are limited, winter isn't off–limits for visitors. During the darkest months, when daylight is in short supply, slugs of *snaps* and hot *gløgg* help to keep the cold at bay, and the Danish *hygge* comes into its own.

Average daytime temperature (in centigrade) and rainfall

	Jan	Feb	Mar	Apr	May	Jun	Jul	Aug	Sep	Oct	Nov	Dec
Copenhagen												
°C	1.9	2.0	4.8	9.5	15.0	19.2	20.4	20.3	16.7	12.1	7.1	3.7
mm	46	30	39	39	42	52	68	64	60	56	61	56
Aalborg												
°C	1.7	2.0	4.9	9.8	15.2	19.0	20.1	20.0	16.2	11.9	6.8	3.4
mm	54	35	44	38	49	54	64	67	72	76	75	62
Odense												
°C	2.3	2.5	5.5	10.2	15.6	19.4	20.5	20.7	17.0	12.5	7.3	3.9
mm	52	36	41	38	46	53	62	61	60	62	69	58
Bornholm												
°C	1.9	1.7	3.7	8.0	13.8	18.0	19.5	19.7	16.1	11.9	7.3	3.8
mm	51	32	40	37	37	42	55	55	63	60	76	62

26

things not to miss

It's not possible to see everything that Denmark has to offer in a single trip – and we don't suggest you try. What follows is a selective taste of the country's highlights (in no particular order), from imposing castles and and world-class museums to unspoilt countryside and beautiful beaches. They're arranged in five colour-coded categories with a page reference to take you straight into the guide, where you can find out more.

01 **Cycling** Pages **35 & 44** With over 10,000km of well-maintained, waymarked cycling paths traversing coast, fjord and meadow – not to mention the cities – a bike is the best way to get around this relatively flat and small country.

03 Hans Christian Andersen museums, Odense
Pages **208 & 210** • The museums dedicated to Denmark's most famous writer offer some intriguing insight into the father of the modern fairy tale.

02 Vikingeskibsmuseet, Zealand
Page **148** • Denmark's most famous museum showcases five of the world's most magnificent Viking vessels, dredged up from the fjord bottom where they lay for nearly a thousand years.

04 Møns Klint, Zealand
Page **168** • Easily one of the most popular destinations in the country for Danish holidaymakers, on the forested fringes of the island and looking straight out into the azure Baltic Sea.

05 **Ny Carlsberg Glyptotek, Copenhagen** Page **93** • The Winter Garden of this fine art gallery holds an impressive collection of Egyptian and Roman sculptures.

06 Smørrebrød Page **39** This traditional open sandwich of dark rye bread topped with anything from smoked salmon or shellfish to herring or salami is delectable and delicious.

07 Louisiana Museum of Modern Art, Zealand Page **126** • An outstanding collection of art, housed in a nineteenth-century villa and with a sculpture garden overlooking the Øresund.

08 Koldinghus, Jutland Page **254** • The spectacular restoration of this former royal castle is one of Jutland's must-sees, with imaginative lighting used to distinguish the old from the new.

09 Christiania, Copenhagen Page **85** • Although currently under threat of being "normalized", this self-governing hippie city, with its array of excellent restaurants and nightlife venues, also excels in quirky public art.

10 **Århus nightlife** Page **332** • With a host of excellent venues, Denmark's cultural capital is one of the country's best places for a night on the town.

11 **Gudenå river canoeing, Jutland** Page **320** • Let the world float by as the current pulls you gently along Denmark's longest river.

12 **Kronborg Slot, Zealand** Page **135** • Better known as the Elsinore of Shakespeare's Hamlet, and majestically located on a grassy promontory looking out to the sea.

14 Street sculptures, Holstebro Page 292 •

As West Jutland's centre for the arts, Holstebro is scattered with magnificent sculptures such as Bjørn Nørgaard's *People of Holstebro*.

13 The Queen's Tapestries, Copenhagen Page 78 •

Denmark's history in its entirety, colourfully depicted on these beautiful tapestries displayed at Christiansborg's Royal Reception Rooms.

15 Jutland beaches Page 380 •

The persistent westerly winds that thrash the western coast make for some wonderfully wild beaches and stunning vistas.

16 **Tivoli, Copenhagen** Page **92** • No trip to the capital is complete without a day at the world's oldest amusement park, slap bang in the centre of the city and offering daredevil rides, top-notch entertainment and beautiful landscaped gardens.

17 **Designer shopping, Copenhagen** Page **117** • Head for the streets around Kronprinsensgade and you'll find legions of shops selling clothes by big-name local designers such as Munthe plus Simonsen and Stig P.

18 **Rundkirke, Bornholm** Page **191** • These unique round churches served as defensive strongholds as well as places of worship.

19 Marmorkirken, Copenhagen Page **88** • Built by Frederik V, the impressively huge Marmorkirken is northern Europe's answer to St Peter's in Rome.

20 Viking fortresses Page **352**, **354** & **159** • Built within a twenty year period by Harald Bluetooth, these perfectly circular ring forts are amazing examples of Viking ingenuity.

21 **Sort Sol over the Wadden Sea, Jutland** Page **266** • During spring and autumn, the skies above the Wadden Sea marshes see starlings perform their poetic pre-roosting aerial ballet.

22 **Frederiksborg Slot, Zealand** Page **142** • Denmark's most grandiose castle, its marble and stucco rooms and ornate chapel complemented by gorgeous Baroque grounds replete with canals, fountains and a placid lake.

23 **Fast food** Page **40** • Highly addictive, the Danish hotdog – with all the trimmings – is sold from wagons parked in public places throughout the country.

24 **Summer jazz, Copenhagen** Page **43** • Summer sees the Danish capital come alive with hundreds of jazz concerts at venues all across the city, featuring local and international names.

25 Valdemars Slot, Funen Page **232** • Check out the lavish, over-the-top interiors of this stunning Baroque palace in a picturesque waterside setting.

26 Roskilde Festival, Zealand Page **146** • One of the best music festivals in Europe, with over 100,000 music fans gathering for a long, drunken weekend of peace, love and lots of rock and roll.

Basics

Basics

Getting there

The most convenient way to get to Denmark from the UK and Ireland is to fly to Copenhagen or one of the country's smaller airports. There's a good range of scheduled and budget flights, and even the lowest scheduled fares are often a lot cheaper than the long and arduous journey by train, ferry or coach. From North America, a handful of airlines operate direct scheduled flights to Copenhagen, though it may be cheaper to fly to London and pick up an onward flight from there with a budget carrier, also the only option if you're travelling from Australia, New Zealand and South Africa, from where there are no direct flights.

Airfares depend on the **season**, with the highest between early June to mid-September; prices are reduced during the low season, November through to April (excluding Christmas, New Year and Easter, when prices are hiked up and seats are at a premium). Ticket prices from the UK don't vary seasonally as much as those from North America; note also that flying on weekends is generally more expensive; price ranges quoted below assume midweek travel.

Flights from the UK and Ireland

Direct services **from London** to Copenhagen are operated by SAS, British Airways, easyJet and Sterling. There are also numerous direct services to Copenhagen from the UK's **regional airports**, including Aberdeen (SAS), Birmingham (SAS), Edinburgh (Sterling, BMI, BMIbaby and SAS), Glasgow (BMI and BMIbaby), Manchester (SAS) and Newcastle (SAS and BA). A cheaper alternative is to take a budget flight to neighbouring Sweden; Sturup airport in Malmö is a short bus journey from the centre of Copenhagen via the Øresunds Bridge (see p.64).

There are also direct services from the UK to regional airports in Jutland. **Billund** is served by flights from London with Sterling, and from Birmingham and Manchester with BA, while **Esbjerg** has Ryanair services from London and BMIbaby and BMI have flights from Aberdeen. From London, Sterling also fly to **Aalborg**, and Ryanair to **Århus**.

Airfares from the UK continue to drop as new operators join the fray, and aren't particularly affected by seasonal variation, though you'll pay slightly more at the weekend and if you book late. The prices quoted here are based on the average price of a mid-week flight booked a month in advance. At the time of writing, the lowest fares to Copenhagen from London are offered by easyJet and Sterling, both at around £80 return (with limited numbers of discounted seats at around £60). Ryanair often has special offers for around £50 or less for its flights to Esbjerg, Århus and Malmö (Sturup) in Sweden. Special offers and discounted tickets apart, the **scheduled fares** of the major airlines are pretty well matched; the cheaper seats tend to be found on smaller carriers such as Sterling and BMI. Expect to pay around £125 for a return ticket from Britain to Denmark with BA or SAS.

From Ireland, the most straightforward option is a direct flight to Copenhagen from Dublin with SAS; Ryanair also fly to Billund and Malmö (Sturup) from Dublin, while Aer Lingus fly from Dublin, Cork and Shannon to Copenhagen via London Heathrow. Scheduled **midweek fares** to Copenhagen are around €174 year-round; flights with Ryanair from Dublin to Billund or Malmö (Sturup) are around €85. If you're flying from one of Ireland's regional airports, it tends to be cheaper to find one of the numerous special deals to London, and then take advantage of the more competitive airfares available from there.

There are no direct flights to Denmark **from Belfast**, so your best bet is probably to fly via London, Glasgow or Edinburgh with British Midland or SAS, and get a budget flight from there.

Flights from the US and Canada

From the US and Canada, the majority of flights to Denmark involve changing planes at a European hub; you make save money by taking a cheap flight to **London** and travelling on to Denmark with a budget airline from there (see p.27). In terms of direct flights to Copenhagen, SAS and Continental have services from **Newark** ($950–1300 high season, $550–950 low season); and SAS also fly direct from **Chicago** and **Washington** (both $1200–1300 high, $600–850 low), as well as **Seattle** ($1650–1750 high, $650–950 low). Delta also fly direct from Atlanta ($1100–1200 high, $600–700 low).

There are no direct flights from Canada, so the best plan is to fly to the UK, and take a cheap flight from there, or travel from a US hub.

Flights from Australia, New Zealand and South Africa

As there are **no direct services** to Denmark from Australia, New Zealand or South Africa, you'll need to change planes at a European or Asian gateway city. Fares are pretty steep, so if you're on a tight budget it's worth flying to London, Amsterdam or Frankfurt, and picking up a cheap flight from there.

The most direct routes from Australia and New Zealand involve a minimum of two stops en route, one Asian – Singapore, Kuala Lumpur, Hong Kong or Bangkok – and one European – Amsterdam, Vienna or London. Expect to pay AUS$2450–2750/NZ$2900–3300 high season and AUS$1700–2000/NZ$2100–2400 low season for return tickets to Copenhagen from **Sydney** with Austrian Airlines and Qantas, from **Melbourne** with Qantas and British Airways, from **Perth** with Air France and Qantas or from **Auckland** with Qantas and Air New Zealand. Flights from **Christchurch** and **Wellington** tend to go via Sydney or Auckland and cost around NZ$150–300 more.

From Johannesburg in **South Africa** to Copenhagen, KLM fly via Amsterdam (R7500–8500 high season, R6500–7500 low season), BA via London (R8000–9000 high, R7000–8000 low), and Lufthansa via Frankfurt (R10,000–11,000 high, R8000–9000 low).

Trains

Taking a **train** can be a relaxed way of getting to Denmark from the UK, though it's likely to work out considerably more expensive than flying, especially if you're over 26.

You can either cross over to mainland Europe by boat and pick up a train from there, or go via Eurostar through the **Channel Tunnel** from Waterloo International in London. Almost all ticketing for train travel within Europe is handled by **Rail Europe** (see p.32), who provides the fastest and most convenient routings via the Eurostar to Brussels, and then on to Denmark on an overnight train via Hamburg or Cologne. Rail Europe can sell you through-tickets from most UK starting points; through-tickets for the train/cross-channel ferry option are only available from a few agents (detailed on p.32) and larger train stations. You could, with careful planning, organize your own train and ferry tickets – a less expensive if more complicated process.

To get the **cheapest fares** with Rail Europe, you'll need to book a round-trip between twenty-one days and four months in advance with one Saturday night away. With this type of ticket, the fare to Denmark is currently £250–350 one way and £350–550 return. The journey takes around 20 hours, via Brussels and Hamburg or Cologne. As always, check for special offers.

Rail passes

Rail passes can reduce the cost of train travel significantly, especially if you plan to travel extensively around Denmark or visit as part of a wider tour of Scandinavia or Europe. There's a huge array of passes available, covering regions as well as individual countries, and offering discounts on private rail, ferry and bus services in Denmark (we've detailed these at relevant points in the Guide). Some have to be bought before

Fly less – stay longer! Travel and climate change

Climate change is the single biggest issue facing our planet. It is caused by a build-up in the atmosphere of carbon dioxide and other greenhouse gases, which are emitted by many sources – including planes. Already, flights account for around 3–4% of human-induced global warming: that figure may sound small, but it is rising year on year and threatens to counteract the progress made by reducing greenhouse emissions in other areas.

Rough Guides regard travel, overall, as a global benefit, and feel strongly that the advantages to developing economies are important, as are the opportunities for greater contact and awareness among peoples. But we all have a responsibility to limit our personal "carbon footprint". That means giving thought to how often we fly and what we can do to redress the harm that our trips create.

Flying and climate change

Pretty much every form of motorized travel generates CO_2, but planes are particularly bad offenders, releasing large volumes of greenhouse gases at altitudes where their impact is far more harmful. Flying also allows us to travel much further than we would contemplate doing by road or rail, so the emissions attributable to each passenger become truly shocking. For example, one person taking a return flight between Europe and California produces the equivalent impact of 2.5 tonnes of CO_2 – similar to the yearly output of the average UK car.

Less harmful planes may evolve but it will be decades before they replace the current fleet – which could be too late for avoiding climate chaos. In the meantime, there are limited options for concerned travellers: to reduce the amount we travel by air (take fewer trips, stay longer!), to avoid night flights (when plane contrails trap heat from Earth but can't reflect sunlight back to space), and to make the trips we do take "climate neutral" via a carbon offset scheme.

Carbon offset schemes

Offset schemes run by **climatecare.org**, **carbonneutral.com** and others allow you to "neutralize" the greenhouse gases that you are responsible for releasing. Their websites have simple calculators that let you work out the impact of any flight. Once that's done, you can pay to fund projects that will reduce future carbon emissions by an equivalent amount (such the distribution of low-energy lightbulbs and cooking stoves in developing countries). Please take the time to visit our website and make your trip climate neutral.

Ⓦ**www.roughguides.com/climatechange**

leaving home, while others can only be purchased in the country itself. **Rail Europe** is the umbrella company for all national and international rail tickets, and its comprehensive website (see p.32) is a useful starting point for information on available passes.

ScanRail pass

If you're planning to visit Denmark as part of a larger tour of Scandinavia and want to travel around by train, it's well worth considering a **ScanRail pass** (Ⓦwww.scanrail .com), which covers Sweden, Norway and Finland as well as Denmark. It's available to all, although you do have to buy it in your home country before you travel (for details of outlets, see p.32). The ScanRail pass is available for travel on any five days in a two-month period (adult £174/US\$297); any eight days in a two-month period (adult £210/US\$343); any ten days in two months (adult £234/US\$399) and 21 consecutive days (adult £270/US\$461). Over-60s get a discount of about twelve percent, children fifty percent and people under 26 and over 12 thirty percent. There's also an eight-day **ScanRail Drive Pass**, which allows five days of train travel and two days of car rental, with the option of adding additional car days. Passes start at £216/US\$410 for an economy car and £32/US$59 for additional car days.

Inter-Rail pass

If you have no clear itinerary, the **Inter-Rail pass** (ⓦwww.interrail.com) might be your best bet. These are only available to European residents, and you will be asked to provide proof of residency before being allowed to purchase one. They come in over-26 and (cheaper) under-26 versions, and cover 29 European countries grouped together in **zones**. These zones include **A** (UK and the Republic of Ireland); **B** (Norway, Sweden and Finland); **C** (Germany, Austria, Switzerland and Denmark); and **E** (France, Belgium, the Netherlands and Luxembourg). The passes are available for 16 days (one zone only; £206), 22 days (two zones only; £285), and one month (all zones; £393); those aged 12 to 26 get a thirty percent discount on the above prices. Inter-Rail passes do not include travel between Britain and the continent, although holders are eligible for discounts on cross-Channel ferries and Eurostar trains.

Eurail passes

Allowing unlimited free first-class train travel in eighteen European countries, including Denmark, the **Eurailpass** (ⓦwww.eurail .com) is only available to non-Europeans, and must be purchased before arrival. It comes in a number of different versions, but none are likely to pay for themselves if you're only planning to travel within Denmark, for which you'd be better off buying a Eurail Denmark pass (see p.34). The standard Eurailpass is available in increments of 15 days (US$605), 21 days (US$785), one month (US$975), two months (US$1378) and three months (US$1703). If you're under 26, you can save money with a **Eurailpass Youth**, which is valid for second-class travel in increments of 15 days (US$394), 21 days (US$510), one month (US$634), two months (US$896) and three months (US$1108). The same applies if you're travelling with between one and four companions on a joint **Eurailpass Saver**, available in increments of 15 days (US$512), 21 days (US$668), one month (US$828), two months (US$1172) and three months (US$1450). You stand an even better chance of getting your money's worth out of a **Eurail pass Flexi**, which is good for ten or fifteen days' first-class travel within a two-month period (at US$715 and US$940 respectively). This, too, comes in under-26/second-class (**Eurail pass Youth Flexi;** US$465/611) and group (**Eurail pass Saver Flexi;** US$608/800) versions.

Buses

Taking the **coach** to Denmark can be a bit of an endurance test, and with airfares falling it can actually prove more expensive than flying. It's only worth taking the bus if time is no object and price all-important, or if you specifically do not want to fly.

The major UK operator is **Eurolines** (see p.32), which offers coaches to **Copenhagen** either via Brussels (20hr) or Amsterdam (25hr). **Fares** to Copenhagen start at £102 return, though the Euro-Apex fare (must be booked thirty days in advance; return within one month) reduces this to £92. There's a ten percent discount if you're under-26. Note that in the peak summer months, all fares increase slightly. Another option is the **Euroline Pass**, which offers unlimited coach travel in much of Europe, including Denmark. The pass is valid either for 15 days (£135 Nov–March excluding Christmas; £159 April to mid-June & mid-Sept to Oct; £225 mid-June to mid–Sept & over Christmas) or 20 days (same seasons: £205/£219/£299). Once again, seniors and the under–26s are entitled to discounts of around ten percent. Euroline tickets and passes are bookable online via the company website (see p.32) and through most major travel agents (see opposite).

There are no through-services from anywhere in the UK outside London, though **National Express** coaches from all over the British Isles connect with Eurolines services in London.

By ferry from Britain

There's just one direct **ferry** service between Britain and Denmark, run by **DFDS Seaways** (☎0870/252 0524, ⓦwww .dfdsseaways.co.uk) between Harwich and Esbjerg. Journey time is 20 hours and **fares** vary enormously according to the season, number of passengers and type of cabin accommodation, but discounts and special deals, such as DFDS Seaways' discounted midweek returns, can reduce costs greatly. Unsurprisingly, fares are usually at their lowest during the winter months. DFDS Seaways start at £34 per person for a low-season midweek return, plus £50 each way for a car; in summer, per-person return fares begin at £49, plus £57 for the car; these fares include a berth in standard communal two- to six-berth cabin with en-suite shower.

Airlines, agents and operators

Online booking

ⓦ www.expedia.co.uk (in UK)
ⓦ www.expedia.com (in US)
ⓦ www.expedia.ca (in Canada)
ⓦ www.lastminute.com (in UK)
ⓦ www.opodo.co.uk (in UK)
ⓦ www.orbitz.com (in US)
ⓦ www.travelocity.co.uk (in UK)
ⓦ www.travelocity.com (in US)
ⓦ www.travelocity.ca (in Canada)
ⓦ www.zuji.com.au (in Australia)
ⓦ www.zuji.co.nz (in New Zealand)

Airlines

Aer Lingus Ireland ☎ 0818/365 000, ⓦ www .aerlingus.com.
Air New Zealand Australia ☎ 13 24 76, New Zealand ☎ 0800/737 000, ⓦ www.airnz.co.nz.
Austrian Airlines Australia ☎ 1800/642 438 or 02/9251 6155, ⓦ www.aua.com.
bmi UK ☎ 0870/607 0555 or ☎ 0870/607 0222, Ireland ☎ 01/407-3036, ⓦ www.flybmi.com.
bmibaby UK ☎ 0871/224 0224, Republic of Ireland ☎ 1890/340 122, ⓦ www.bmibaby.com.
British Airways UK ☎ 0870/850 9850, US and Canada ☎ 1-800/AIRWAYS, Australia ☎ 1300/767 177, New Zealand ☎ 09/966 9777, ⓦ www.ba.com.
Continental Airlines US and Canada ☎ 1-800/523-3273, ⓦ www.continental.com.
Delta US and Canada ☎ 1-800/221-1212, ⓦ www .delta.com.
easyJet UK ☎ 0905/821 0905, ⓦ www.easyjet.com.
KLM (Royal Dutch Airlines) Australia ☎ 1300/303 747, New Zealand ☎ 09/921 6040, South Africa ☎ 11/961 6767, ⓦ www.klm.com.
Lufthansa South Africa ☎ 0861/842 538, ⓦ www .lufthansa.com.
Qantas UK ☎ 0845/774 7767, Ireland ☎ 01/407 3278, US and Canada ☎ 1-800/227-4500, Australia

☎ 13 13 13, New Zealand ☎ 0800/808 767 or 09/357 8900, SA ☎ 11/441 8550, ⓦ www .qantas.com.
Ryanair UK ☎ 0871/246 0000, Ireland ☎ 0818/303 030, ⓦ www.ryanair.com.
SAS (Scandinavian Airlines) UK ☎ 0870/607 2772, Ireland ☎ 01/844 5440, US & Canada ☎ 1-800/221-2350, South Africa ☎ 011/484 4711, [ⓦ www.scandinavian.net.
Sterling UK ☎ 0870/787 8038, ⓦ www .sterling.dk.
South African Airways South Africa ☎ 0861/359722, ⓦ www.flysaa.com.

Agents and operators

Backroads US ☎ 1-800/462-2848, ⓦ www .backroads.com. Six-day summer cycling tours around Funen.
Bentours Australia ☎ 02/9241 1353, ⓦ www .bentours.com.au. Ferry, rail, bus and hotel passes, plus a host of tours throughout Scandinavia.
ebookers UK ☎ 0800/082 3000, Ireland ☎ 01/488 3507, ⓦ www.ebookers.com. Low fares on an extensive selection of scheduled flights and package deals.
Euro-Bike & Walking Tours US ☎ 1-800/321-6060, ⓦ www.eurobike.com. Well-organized one-week summer cycling tours around Funen and Zealand.
Nordic Saga Tours US ☎ 1-800/848-6449, ⓦ www.nordicsaga.com. Package holidays, transportation and accommodation throughout Denmark and Scandinavia.
North South Travel UK ☎ 01245/608 291, ⓦ www.northsouthtravel.co.uk. Friendly, competitive travel agency offering discounted fares worldwide. Profits are used to support projects in the developing world, especially the promotion of sustainable tourism.
Scanam World Tours US ☎ 1-800/5452204, ⓦ www.scanamtours.com. A wide selection of package deals, including cycling tours, plus rail passes and tailor-made trips.
Scanmeridian UK ☎ 020/7431 5322, ⓦ www .scanmeridian.co.uk. Scandinavia specialist offering tailor-made trips, city breaks and holiday cottage rentals.
Scantours UK ☎ 020/7839 2927, ⓦ www .scantoursuk.com, US ☎ 1-800/223-7226, ⓦ www .scantours.com. Huge range of package deals, plus hotel booking, rail passes, customized itineraries and city sightseeing tours.
STA Travel UK ☎ 0870/163 0026, US ☎ 1-800/781-4040, Canada ☎ 1-888/427-5639, Australia ☎ 1300/733 035, New Zealand ☎ 0508/782 872, ⓦ www.statravel.com.

Worldwide specialists in independent travel; also student IDs, travel insurance, car rental, rail passes, and more. Good discounts for students and under-26s.
Trailfinders UK ☎ 0845/058 5858, Ireland ☎ 01/677 7888, Australia ☎ 1300/780 212, Ⓦ www.trailfinders.com. One of the best-informed and most efficient agents for independent travellers.

Rail contacts

European Rail UK ☎ 020/7387 0444, Ⓦ www.europeanrail.com. Pre-booked European rail tickets, which are subject to an annoying £5 quotation fee.
Europrail International Canada ☎ 1-888/667-9734, Ⓦ www.europrail.net. Rail passes and pre-booked tickets.

Eurostar UK ☎ 0870/518 6186, Ⓦ www.eurostar.com. Pre-booked cross-channel Eurostar rail tickets.
Eurotunnel UK ☎ 0870/535 3535, Ⓦ www.eurotunnel.com. Pre-booked rail tickets through the Eurotunnel for motorists.
Rail Europe UK ☎ 0870/837 1371, US ☎ 1-877/257-2887, Canada ☎ 1-800/361-RAIL, Ⓦ www.raileurope.co.uk. Pre-booked European rail tickets and passes.
Rail Pass Express US ☎ 0877-RAILPASS Ⓦ www.railpass.com. Rail passes galore, including Scanrail, Eurail and InterRail.

Coach and bus contacts

Eurolines and **National Express** UK ☎ 0870/580 8080, Ireland ☎ 01/836 6111, Ⓦ www.nationalexpress.com/eurolines.

Getting around

Although Denmark is largely made up of islands, travelling around the country is swift and straightforward. Public transport – trains, buses and the essential ferries – is punctual and efficient, and where you need to switch from one type to another, you'll find the timetables impressively well integrated.

And with Denmark being such a small country, you can get from one end to the other in half a day. Domestic airports are evenly spaced out, though given the ease of land transport, in-country flights are only really worth considering if you're really pushed for time or to catch connecting flights out of the country. Besides being small, Denmark is also very flat, with scores of villages linked by country roads that are ideal for effortless cycling.

By rail

With an exhaustive and reliable network run by the Danish state railway Danske Statsbaner (DSB; ☎ 70 13 14 15, Ⓦ www.dsb.dk), **trains** are easily the most efficient and convenient way to travel in Denmark. InterRail, Eurail and ScanRail **passes** are valid on all routes except the few private lines that operate in some rural areas, on which they tend to afford substantial discounts

(we've detailed these at relevant points in the Guide). There are just a few out-of-the-way regions that trains fail to penetrate, though these can be easily navigated by buses, which often run in conjunction with local train connections. Train passes are valid on bus services operated by DSB (for more on buses, see p.34).

Trains range from **inter-city express** services (**IC Lyn**), with a buffet car, to smaller **local trains** (**regionaltog**). Departure times are listed on notices both on station concourses and the platforms (departures in yellow, arrivals in white), and announced over loudspeakers. On the train, each station is usually called a few minutes before you arrive. Watch out for *stillekupé* – special quiet compartments where children, pets and mobile phones are prohibited.

Tickets should be bought in advance from train stations, either from ticket booths or

Mileage Chart (distances in kilometres)

	Esbjerg	Frederikshavn	Helsingør	Holstebro	Copenhagen	Nyborg	Odense	Randers	Silkeborg	Skagen	Svendborg	Viborg	Aalborg	Århus
Esbjerg	X	279	337	105	302	167	140	196	123	319	179	140	215	167
Frederikshavn	279	X	515	190	480	345	318	144	177	38	357	140	64	181
Helsingør	337	515	X	376	45	171	293	173	337	555	203	364	451	134
Holstebro	105	190	376	X	341	205	179	93	74	230	217	51	126	118
Copenhagen	302	480	45	341	X	136	168	154	302	520	168	329	416	115
Nyborg	167	345	171	205	136	X	33	202	167	384	33	193	280	172
Odense	140	318	293	179	168	33	X	175	140	358	45	167	254	146
Randers	196	144	173	93	154	202	175	X	51	183	214	41	79	39
Silkeborg	123	177	337	74	302	167	140	51	X	217	179	37	113	44
Skagen	319	38	555	230	520	384	358	183	217	X	396	180	103	221
Svendborg	179	357	203	217	168	33	45	214	179	396	X	205	292	184
Viborg	140	140	364	51	329	193	167	41	37	180	205	X	76	66
Aalborg	215	64	451	126	416	280	254	79	113	103	292	76	X	117
Århus	167	181	134	118	115	172	146	39	44	221	184	66	117	X

automated machines; the latter take all major credit cards but no cash. Note that there's an extra charge of 40kr if you buy tickets on board. Trains don't require advance seat reservations (20kr), but there's no guarantee that you'll get a seat if you don't make one. All trains have an inspector who checks tickets: he/she is almost certain to speak English and will normally be able to answer questions about routes and times. **Fares** are calculated on a zonal system. As a guide, one way fares between Copenhagen and Odense cost 234kr; Copenhagen–Århus is 317kr. Both of these fares include the cost of a seat reservation, and your train ticket will also get you around on the local buses (and S-trains in Copenhagen) in the departure and arrival town of your journey on the day the ticket is valid. The price of a return ticket is no cheaper than two one-ways. If you're between 16 and 25 and plan to do lots of train travel, it may be worthwhile buying a **DSB Wildcard** (175kr and valid for one year), which gives you a 50 percent discount on normal cross-regional tickets (from Copenhagen to Lolland, for instance). There are no other student discounts, but people over 65 qualify for the same discounts as Wildcard holders. Travelling in a group of eight or more also entitles you to a 25–30 percent discount – get details from any Danish tourist office. There are also great savings to be had when crossing the Storebælt with a so-called *Orange* ticket. These must be booked seven to twenty-eight days in advance, and cost 150kr for one journey (135kr if you buy online at ⓦwww.dsb.dk) for all destinations that involve crossing the Storebælt – though as there are a limited number of Orange seats on each train, you'll need to be flexible with your travel times.

Another option for non-Europeans is the new **Eurail Denmark Pass** (ⓦwww.eurail .com), which must be purchased before arrival. It allows free unlimited first- or second-class train travel for either 3 days (US$111/74) or 7 days (US$174/111) within a one-month period.

A final possibility is the **EuroDomino Pass**, though it's only available to those who have been resident in Europe for six months, and you must purchase it before you leave home. Valid for between three and eight days, it offers unlimited standard (or second) class train travel within any one of 28 European countries – including Denmark – over a one month period. Three days' travel within a month costs £79, and eight days £154. There are discounts of around 25 percent for those aged 12–26, and 15 percent for the over–60s.

As for **timings**, DSB's *Køreplan* (30kr from any newsagent) details all DSB train, bus and ferry services in the country, including the local Copenhagen S-train system, all private services and some international routes, and is a sound investment if you're planning to do a lot of travelling. If you're not, smaller **timetables** detailing specific routes can be picked up for free at tourist offices and station ticket offices.

By bus

There are only a handful of **long-distance bus** services in Denmark, though there are plenty of local buses that connect the regional centres with the surrounding countryside; all routes are detailed in the relevant Travel Details sections within the guide. Of the long-distance routes **Abildskous Rutebiler** (ⓣ70 21 08 88, ⓦwww .abildskou.dk) runs buses from Copenhagen to Århus (some via Ebeltoft), Aalborg, Thisted (via Viborg and Nykøbing Mors) and Silkeborg. As a guide to prices, a one-way ticket to Ebeltoft, Arhus and Silkeborg costs 230kr. **Søndergaards Busser** (ⓣ70 10 00 33, ⓦwww.sondergaards-busser .dk) operates a Fjerritslev–Copenhagen bus, with stops in Løgstør, Hobro, Randers and Grenå; one-way tickets range from 240kr to 280kr. **Bornholmerbussen** (ⓣ44 68 44 00, ⓦwww.graahundbus.dk) runs a service between Copenhagen and **Bornholm** via the Øresunds Link and Ystad in Sweden (200kr one way). All of the above offer discounts to students on less busy services. Fares represent quite a saving over full-price train tickets but, while just as efficient, long-distance buses are much less comfortable than trains.

Local buses really come into their own in the few areas where trains are scarce or connections complicated – much of Funen and northwest Jutland, for example. In Jutland, the excellent government-run

X-busser (☎98 90 09 00, ⓦwww.xbus
.dk) is especially useful, with a fast, efficient
network that crisscrosses the peninsula.

By car

Given the excellent public transport system,
the diminutive size of the country and the
comparatively high price of petrol (around
9.20kr per litre at the time of writing), **driving** isn't really economical unless you're in a
group. **Car rental** is expensive, though it's
worth checking the cut-price deals offered
by some airlines in conjunction with tickets.
You'll need an international driving licence
and must be aged at least 20 to take to the
roads, although many firms won't rent to
anyone under 25 – and some require you to
be over 28. Costs start at around 2800kr a
week for a small hatchback with unlimited
mileage; Rent a Wreck (see below) offers the
best deals for limited mileage (100km per
day) at 1750kr for a week – the cars aren't
really wrecks, they're just not new.

As for **rules of the road**, Danes drive
on the right, and there's a speed limit of
50kph in towns, 80kph in open country
and 110kph or 130kph on motorways.
Dipped headlights need to be used at all
times. There are random breath tests for
suspected drunken drivers, and the penal-
ties are severe. Note that in towns, a park-
ing-time disc must be displayed if you
park anywhere that isn't metered; you can
get the discs from petrol stations, police
stations, and at banks, where they have
advertising on the back and are free; otherwise they cost around 20kr. You set the
time when you've parked on the hands of
the clock, then return before your allotted
time (indicated by signs) is up.

The national motoring organization,
Forenede Danske Motorejere, operates a 24-
hour **breakdown service** (☎45 88 00 25) for
AA members; if you're not an AA member,
Dansk Autohjælp (☎70 10 80 90) and Falck
(☎70 10 20 30) can be summoned from
callboxes by the road. A standard call-out
fee will be charged – Dansk Autohjælp is the
cheapest at 547kr per hour.

Hitching is illegal on motorways, but
otherwise it's a fairly easy and reasonably
safe way to get around, though thumbing a
lift isn't very common these days.

Car rental companies

Alamo US ☎1-800/462-5266, ⓦwww.alamo.com.
Auto Europe US and Canada ☎1-888/223-5555,
ⓦwww.autoeurope.com.
Avis UK ☎0870/606 0100, Ireland ☎021/428
1111, US ☎1-800/230-4898, Canada ☎1-
800/272-5871, Australia ☎13 63 33 or 02/9353
9000, New Zealand ☎09/526 2847 or 0800/655
111, Denmark ☎70 24 77 07 or ☎32 51 22 99
(Copenhagen Airport), ⓦwww.avis.com.
Budget UK ☎0870/156 5656, Ireland ☎09/0662
7711, US ☎1-800/527-0700, Canada ☎1-
800/268-8900, Australia ☎1300/362 848, New
Zealand ☎0800/283-438, Denmark ☎33 55 05 00
or ☎32 52 39 00 (Copenhagen Airport), ⓦwww
.budget.com.
Europcar UK ☎0870/607 5000, Ireland ☎01/614
2800, US & Canada ☎1-877/940-6900, Australia
☎393/306 160, Denmark ☎33 55 99 00 or ☎32 50
30 90 (Copenhagen Airport), ⓦwww.europcar.com.
Europe by Car US ☎1-800/223-1516, ⓦwww
.europebycar.com.
Hertz UK ☎020/7026 0077, Ireland ☎01/870-
5777, US & Canada ☎1-800/654 3131, New
Zealand ☎0800/654 321, Denmark ☎33 17 90 20
or ☎32 50 93 00 (Copenhagen Airport), ⓦwww
.hertz.com.
Holiday Autos UK ☎0871/400 4461, Ireland
☎01/872 9366, Australia ☎299/394 433, ⓦwww
.holidayautos.co.uk.
National UK ☎0870/400 4581, US ☎1-800/CAR-
RENT, Australia ☎02/13 10 45, New Zealand
☎03/366 5574, Denmark ☎39 63 23 75, ⓦwww
.nationalcar.com.
Rent-A-Wreck Denmark ☎70 25 26 70, ⓦwww
.rent-a-wreck.dk.
SIXT Ireland ☎1850/206 088, UK ☎0870/156
7567, US ☎1-877/347 3227, Denmark ☎32 48 11
00, ⓦwww.e-sixt.co.uk.
Suncars UK ☎0870/500 5566, Ireland
☎1850/201-416, ⓦwww.suncars.com.

Cycling

If the weather is good, the best way to
explore Denmark is to follow the locals and
hop on a **bicycle**. The mostly flat, pastoral
landscape lends itself beautifully to leisurely
cycling, and a bike is also an easy and cheap
way of getting around the towns. Traffic is
sparse on most country roads, and all large
towns have cycle tracks – though watch out
for sometimes less-than-careful drivers on
main roads. Remember also that lights are a
legal requirement at night – you'll be stopped

and fined if the police catch you without them. Bikes can be **rented** at nearly all youth hostels, campsites and tourist offices, at most bike shops and at some train stations for 50–75kr per day or 300kr per week; there's often a 200kr–500kr refundable deposit, too. If you want to do some long-distance cycling (see p.45 for national cycle routes), take the frequent westerly winds into account when **planning your route** – pedalling is easier facing east than west. The Danish cycling organization Dansk Cyklistforbund (☏33 32 31 21, ⓦwww.dcf.dk) offers cycling advice and sells good informative maps of local and national cycling routes.

You can take bikes on all types of public transport except city buses. On trains, you'll have to pay according to the zonal system used to calculate passenger tickets – for example, 50kr to take your bike from Copenhagen to Århus, with 20kr on top if you reserve a place in advance, which you need to do at least two hours before departure; reserving is obligatory between May and August, and recommended all other times. The *Cykler i Tog* brochure (free from train stations) lists rates and rules in full. For a similar fee, long-distance buses have limited cycle space, while ferries let bikes on free or for a few kroner. Domestic flights charge around 200kr for carrying cycles.

Ferries

Ferries connect all the Danish islands, and vary from the state-of-the-art catamaran linking Zealand and Jutland to raft-like affairs serving tiny, isolated settlements a few minutes off the (so-called) mainland. Where applicable, train and bus fares include the cost of ferry crossings (although you can also pay at the terminal and walk on), while the smaller ferries charge 25–75kr for foot passengers. We've detailed routes, fares and timings at the relevant places throughout the Guide.

Planes

Domestic flights are hardly essential in somewhere of Denmark's size, but can be handy if you're in a rush – it's less than an hour's flying time from Copenhagen to anywhere in the country. There are domestic airports at Aalborg, Århus, Billund, Esbjerg, Thisted, Sønderborg and Rønne, all of which are served by flights to and from Copenhagen. Roskilde Airport also runs seasonal flights to the small island of Anholt, while Billund has scheduled flights to Bornholm. **Airlines** operating domestic flights are SAS (☏60 72 77 27, ⓦwww.scandinavian .net), Cimber Air (☏74 42 22 23, ⓦwww .cimber.dk) and **Sterling** (ⓦwww.sterling .dk). **Fares** vary only slightly between the companies, although it can be worthwhile to look for special offers. The longer in advance you book, the cheaper the flight, and you can get good deals, such as 326kr one-way from Copenhagen to Rønne on Bornholm. Weekend flights are generally cheaper than during the week.

Accommodation

Accommodation is going to be your major daily expense while in Denmark, and you should plan where you'll be staying carefully. Even if you're on a budget, hotels are by no means off-limits if you seek out the better offers, while hostels, sleep-ins and campsites are plentiful and of a uniformly high standard.

Rates at some **inns** (called *kro*) in rural areas are less than those for a basic hotel room, and standards are often better. Note also that staying in a hotel or inn means there won't be a curfew (common in hostels in big cities), and that an all-you-can-eat breakfast – so large you won't need to buy lunch – is normally included in the rates.

Accommodation price codes

The accommodation listed in this Guide has been graded according to the following price bands, based on the cost of the **least expensive double room in summer**. Where weekend and holiday rates are discounted, we've given two grades: the first relates to weekdays, the second to weekends and holiday periods (ie ❸/❷).

❶ Under 200kr
❷ 201–300kr
❸ 301–400kr

❹ 401–500kr
❺ 501–600kr
❻ 601–850kr

❼ 851–1100kr
❽ 1101–1300kr
❾ Over 1301kr

Wherever you stay (and especially in peak season), it's a good idea to **book in advance**, which is most easily done via the Danish tourist board website (see p.55); booking directly on the net yourself can result in discounts of up to 35 percent.

Hotels

Visiting Denmark by way of a standard package trip, which includes accommodation as well as flights (see p.31 for operators) is one way to stay in a **hotel** without spending a fortune. Another is simply to be selective. Most Danish hotel rooms include phone, TV and bathroom, for which you'll pay from around 700kr for a double (singles from around 450kr); going without the luxuries can result in big savings: in most towns you'll find hotels offering rooms with access to a shared bathroom for as little as 400kr for a double (250kr a single). You'll find that rates may vary according to the season or day of the week, especially in the so-called "conference towns" where, outside the summer season (roughly mid-June to mid-Aug), hotels are packed with business travellers during the week (Mon–Thurs). In these towns, rates are reduced significantly during summer and on weekends, and we've given two rates where this is the case (see box, above). In the rest of the country, room rates tend to be some 50 percent higher during the summer season and over holidays.

Hostels and sleep-ins

Hostels (vandrerhjem) are Denmark's cheapest accommodation option bar camping. Almost every town has one, they're much less pricey than hotels, and they have a high degree of comfort. Most offer a choice of various sizes of private room, generally from two single beds to three bunk-beds;

and often with private toilet and shower too; we've given price codes for these double rooms within the Guide, but expect to pay 300–500kr. All hostels also have shared dormitory-type accommodation with up to six beds in a room, for which you'll pay around 110kr per bed; dorms are only available during the summer season in some hostels. Nearly all hostels also have shared cooking facilities. Other than in major towns or ferry ports, it's rare for hostels to be full, but during the summer (ie it's always wise to phone ahead to make a reservation, and to check on location – some hostels are several kilometres outside the town centre.

As at all Scandinavian hostels, sleeping bags are not allowed, so you'll need to bring either a sheet sleeping-bag or rent hostel linen (40–50kr), which can become expensive over a long stay. It's a good idea, too, to get an **HI card**, since without one you'll be hit with the cost of either an overnight card (35kr) or a year-long Danish membership card (160kr); these are available on the Hostelling International website (𝕎www.hihostels.com). If you're planning on doing a lot of hostelling, it's worth contacting Danhostel Danmarks Vandrerhjem, Vesterbrogade 39, DK-1620 Copenhagen V (☏33 31 36 12, 𝕎www.danhostel.dk) to get a copy of their free guide to Danish hostels, *Danmarks Vandrerhjem*, which is published in several languages including English; their informative free hostel/campsite map of Denmark is also useful.

Sleep-ins are a similarly cheap option if you're on a budget but don't want to camp. Originally run by the local authorities, sleep-ins are now just a more backpacker-oriented version of a hostel – privately run and generally packed with young people. Some open between May and August only, but most now open year-round. For bed and (shared) shower facilities, expect to pay around 100kr; bear in mind that you'll need your own sleeping bag, that only one night's stay is permitted in a few cases, and that there may be an age restriction (typically 16- to 24-year-olds only, although this may not be strictly enforced).

Private rooms and B&Bs

Tourist offices can supply lists of **private rooms** for rent in the homes of locals. Vaguely akin to British-style bed and breakfasts, these vary greatly in standard, but can be an easy way of getting to know the locals – whether you want to or not. The main thing to look out for is the distance to the town centre; some are far from the action, linked only by infrequent public transport options. Reckon on paying 400–500kr for a double. Throughout the country, you'll come across places that call themselves **B&Bs** but are actually no different to private rooms; many of these are detailed online at ⓦwww .net-bb.dk, and there's also a separate B&B network on Funen. Note that despite the name, breakfast isn't included in any B&B or private room rates, and is only sometimes offered for an additional cost; there's often access to a kitchen, however.

Camping

Camping is by far the cheapest accommodation option in Denmark, and if the weather is good, it can really enhance the outdoor experience, as most sites are located near beaches or other beautiful natural landscapes. If you don't already have an International Camping Card from an organization in your own country, you'll need a Camping Card Scandinavia to camp in Denmark, which costs 80kr for both individuals and families, can be bought from any campsite and is valid on all official sites in Scandinavia until the end of the year in which it was bought. A Transit Pass can be used for a single night's camping and costs 20kr per person. **Camping rough** without the landowner's permission is

illegal and an on-the-spot fine may well be imposed. However, the Danish Forest and Nature Agency is running a two-year trial (ending in 2008) which allows free low-impact camping in some 200 designated woodland areas. The rules are strict: only one night at each site, only two tents per site, no open fires or camping stoves are allowed, and the site has to be left as you found it. Check ⓦwww.skovognatur.dk for information and a list of designated areas; local tourist offices should be able to advise if there are any sites nearby.

Campsites (*campingplads*) can be found virtually everywhere. Most are open from April through to September, and a few all year round – we've indicated months of opening throughout the Guide. There's a rigid **grading system**: one-star sites have toilets and at least one shower; two-stars also have basic cooking facilities and a food shop within 2km; three-stars include a laundry and a TV room; four-stars also have a shop; while five-stars include a cafeteria and other facilities such as a swimming pool. **Prices** vary from 55 to 65kr per person, though you may pay more at city sites or those in other particularly popular locations. Many campsites also have **cabin accommodation**, usually basic huts without bedding but with cooking facilities; they're pleasant enough, and at 2000–4000kr for a six-berth affair for a week, they may represent a saving for several people sharing, although on busy sites cabins are often booked up a year in advance. Most campsites also have full hook-ups for **trailers** and **camper vans**.

We've listed the best of the sites in the Guide, but any Danish tourist office can give you a free leaflet listing all the region's sites; there's also an official guide, *Camping Danmark*, available from kiosks, bookshops and tourist offices (95kr). For further information on camping, contact the national camping association, Campingrådet, Hesseløgade 16, DK-2100 Copenhagen Ø (☎39 27 88 44, ⓦwww.campingraadet.dk).

Food and drink

Although good food can be pretty pricey in Denmark, there are plenty of ways to eat affordably and healthily, and with plenty of variety, too. Much the same applies to drink: the only Scandinavian country free of social drinking taboos, Denmark is an imbiber's delight – both for its huge choice of tipples, and for the number of places where they can be sampled.

Traditional **Danish cooked food** is centred on meat and fish: beef, veal, chicken and pork are frequent menu items – though rarely bacon, which is mainly exported – along with various forms of salmon, herring, eel, plaice and cod. Combinations of these are served with potatoes and another (usually boiled) vegetable, or salad. However it's the traditional **cold dishes** that make the Danish cuisine so unique. **Smørrebrød** – slices of rye bread heavily laden with layers of meat or fish – dominates daytime menus at home, school, work and at traditional lunchtime restaurants. **Restaurant** meals can be expensive, especially in the evening, but there are other ways to eat Danish food that won't ruin your budget or your diet. For more on eating and drinking, see the *Danish Food and Drink* colour section.

Breakfast and brunch

Breakfast (*morgenmad*) can be the tastiest Danish meal – and the least meaty one, too. Almost all hotels offer a sumptuous breakfast as a matter of course – as do youth hostels, though the latter don't include breakfast in their rates, where you can often attack a buffet table laden with cereals, bread, cheese, boiled eggs, fruit juice, milk, coffee and tea for around 45kr. Breakfast elsewhere will be far less substantial: many cafés offer a very basic set meal for around 30kr, but you're better advised to go for **brunch** instead. Served from around 10am until mid-afternoon, brunch is a delicious and filling option consisting of variations of international-style breakfasts (American, English etc), with plenty of fresh fruit and home-made bread – you'll pay 60–140kr, depending on your choices.

Lunch

You have two main choices when it comes to **lunch** (*frokost*) – hot or cold. In towns, the best way to find an inexpensive cooked lunch is simply to walk around and read the signs chalked up outside any café, restaurant or bar. These notices, put out between 11.30am and 2.30pm, detail the **tilbud** or **dagens ret** – essentially the dish of the day – a plate of chilli con carne or lasagne for around 50kr, or a three-course set lunch for 80–120kr. Some restaurants offer a fixed-price (80–100kr) open buffet, where you can help yourself to as much as you like.

The cold alternative is the delicious and quintessentially Danish **smørrebrød**, or open sandwich: slices of rye bread heaped with meat (commonly sliced ham, beef or chicken), fish (salmon, eel, caviar, cod roe, shrimp or herring) or cheese, and generously piled with assorted trimmings (tomatoes, mushrooms, cucumber, pickles, slices of lemon etc). It's best sampled in one of the many traditional smørrebrød restaurants, often open at lunchtime only. A selection of three or four slices – known as pieces – starts at about 100kr. A much less expensive alternative are the dedicated shops that sell readymade smørrebrød to take away (10–25kr a piece); many open until 10pm on weekdays. At cafés, you'll also be able to find a filling sandwich (30–50kr) or salad with fresh bread for 50–70kr, and in the winter there always a daily soup on the menu (50–70kr).

Dinner

Dinner (*aftensmad*) can present a wide choice of cuisines, but the costs tend to be a lot higher than at lunch – although pizzerias and similar places charge the same in the evenings as during the day, and many youth hostels serve simple but filling meals for 50–75kr, though you have to order in advance. The most cost-effective dinner option (70–90kr), however, is usually an **ethnic restaurant** (most commonly Chinese or Middle Eastern, with a smaller number of Indian, Indonesian and Thai); as well as à la carte dishes, these often have a buffet table – ideal for gluttonous over-indulgence, and you usually get soup and a dessert thrown in as well. **Danish restaurants** that are promising for lunch often turn into expense-account affairs at night, offering an atmospheric, candle-lit setting for the slow devouring of immaculately prepared meat or fish; you'll be hard-pushed to spend less than 200kr per person.

Fast food

Open throughout the day, American **burger** franchises are as commonplace and as popular as you'd expect, as are **pizzerias**, which are dependable and affordable at any time of day, with many offering special deals such as all-you-can-eat-salad with a basic pizza for about 50kr, or a more exotic dish or pizza topping for 50–70kr. **Shawarmas** (kebabs) and **China boxes** (your selection of Chinese dishes from a buffet, served in a takeaway box) are also easy to find in most larger towns; both cost around 30kr. You can also get a very ordinary self-service meat, fish or omelette lunch in a **supermarket cafeteria** for 50–90kr.

There's also the very popular sausage stands (*pølsevogn*) found on all main streets and at train stations. These serve various types of **sausage** (*pølser*) for 16–24kr: hotdogs with trimmings such as roasted onion, remoulade and pickled cucumber; long, thin *wieners*; fatter *frankfurters*; or the dressing-soaked *franske hotdog*. Alternatives include a **toasted ham and cheese sandwich** (*parisertoast*) for 12–15kr (vegetarians can ask for the ham to be left out) and **chips** (*pommes frites*), which come in big (*store*) and small (*lille*) forms and cost 10–15kr.

Danish pastries

One local speciality not to be missed is a **Danish pastry** (*wienerbrød*), tastier and much less sweet than the imitations sold abroad. Most cafés will serve reasonable versions, though they're best bought straight from the excellent and plentiful **konditorier** (patisseries) and eaten on the move or in the *konditori*'s coffee bar. **Coffee** (all Italian or French versions are widely available, as is freshly made filter coffee) or **tea** (including fruit and herbal brews) will cost 12–35kr.

Alcohol

If you've arrived in Denmark from near-teetotal Norway or Sweden, you're in for a shock. Not only is drinking **alcohol** entirely acceptable in Denmark, it's quite common to see people strolling along the pedestrianized streets swigging from a bottle of beer. Although extreme drunkenness is frowned upon, alcohol is widely consumed – albeit in moderation – throughout the day by all sections of society.

Although you can buy booze inexpensively at supermarkets, the most sociable **places to drink** are bars, cafés and British-style pubs, where the emphasis is on beer – although you can also get spirits and wine (or tea and coffee).

Bottled beer generally costs 20–30kr for a third of a litre, though the stronger **gold beer** (*guldøl*) costs 20–30kr per bottle. **Draught beer** (*fadøl*) is more expensive, with a quarter of a litre costing 18–40kr, half a litre up to 80kr. It can be touch weaker than both types of bottled beer, but tastes fresher and is more popular. Most Danish beer is lager-style, the most common brands being Carlsberg and Tuborg, although a number of towns have their own locally brewed rivals. You'll also see special Christmas and Easter beers – stronger than normal to enhance the festive feel. The two days when they are released – "J-Day" and "P-Day" ("J" for "*Jul*" and "P" for "*Påske*" – Christmas and Easter respectively) see beer enthusiasts all around the country venturing out to taste the new offerings. If you prefer something weaker, there's also always a Lys Pilsner on offer, a very low-alcohol lager.

In recent years, an astounding number of **microbreweries** have popped up around the country, and produce a wide range of more adventurous ales, including some very similar to British-style bitter. Some of the best offerings are from Fur Brewery, Thisted Bryghus and GourmetBryggeriet in Roskilde.

However, if you're after Guinness and genuine British draught beers, you'll find there's at least one themed Brit or Irish pub in most larger towns.

Wines and spirits

Most international **wines and spirits** are widely available in bars, a shot of the hard stuff costing 15–35kr, a glass of wine upwards of 25kr; but note that as most Danes drink wine with meals rather than socially, bars won't have the same range as restaurants. While in the country, you should also investigate the many varieties of **snaps**, a barley-based spirit that comes in various flavours, and is drunk ice-cold from a shot glass. Danes consume snaps eagerly, especially with smørrebrød, but more than two or three are likely to turn you pale if you're not used to it. A tasty relative is the gloriously spicy and strong Gammel Dansk Bitter Dram – snaps-based, but made with bitters, and drunk at breakfast time or as a pick-me-up during the day. In the winter, warm **gløgg** is also available in most bars. A spicy mulled wine prepared with snaps soaked raisins and nuts, it's enjoyed with æbleskiver, deep-fried dough-balls with a slice of apple in the centre.

The media

Denmark's 35 national newspapers tend to offer predominantly serious and in-depth coverage of worthy issues, and can't help but seem a little anachronistic when compared to the tabloid dominance elsewhere in Europe. Danish TV is dominated by subtitled imports, but the country's radio stations do offer the chance to take in plenty of Danish music.

Newspapers and magazines

For a country of its size, Denmark has an impressive number of **newspapers**. There's an **English-language** newspaper, *Copenhagen Post* (ⓦ www.copenhagenpost.dk), which covers domestic issues and has an in-depth listings section covering events of interest to non-Danish speakers; it comes out every Friday and costs 15kr. The main Danish-language dailies (each costing 15–22kr) are *Politiken*, a reasonably impartial broadsheet with strong arts features; the moderate/centrist *Berlingske Tidende*; the tabloid-ish *Ekstra Blade*; *Jyllands-Posten*, a well-respected right-wing paper, at times somewhat provocative; and *Information*, left-wing, intellectual and rich in cultural and social debate. The weekly *Weekendavisen*, published on Thursdays, has excellent background features. The best sports coverage can be found in the two daily tabloids: *BT*, which has a conservative bias, and *Ekstra Bladet*. Of the many free weekday newspapers doled out in the cities, you'll find excellent entertainment **listings** in *Politiken* and the Thursday edition of *Information*. The free **music** magazine *Gaffa* (monthly) lists most of the bigger concerts; you can find it in cafés, record shops and the like.

In Copenhagen, **overseas newspapers** are sold at the Magasin du Nord department store, Illum department store, the stall on the eastern side of Rådhuspladsen, and newsagents along Strøget and in newsagents at Central Station, which also stock foreign magazines. Most UK and US weekday titles cost 25–40kr and are available the day after publication.

Radio and TV

The national broadcasting corporation Danmarks Radio (DR) is the oldest and largest media enterprise in the country, funded by a levied television licence tax. As well as its TV stations, it operates four national FM stations, thirteen digital audio stations and eleven web-based stations (at Ⓦ www.dr.dk). On the whole, Danish radio is very supportive of the local arts scene, with plenty of local music on the airwaves. There's a very short *News In English* programme on weekdays at 10.30am, 5.05pm and 10pm on Radio Denmark International (1062MHz). The BBC World Service can be picked up on short wave 6195KHz, 9410KHz and 12,095KHz; you may also be able to pick up BBC Radio 4 on long wave 198Mhz.

Though **Danish television** has expanded significantly over the past decades – from one national station to four land and four cable channels – Danish-language programming still lags behind the diversity of offerings found on radio, though this is in part due to the amount of television programs licensed and imported from abroad and subtitled in Danish. The four national television stations are the non-commercial DR1 and DR2, and the commercial TV2 and TV2 Zulu – though, apart from the advertising, you'll probably struggle to spot the difference between them. The cable channels, some of which are shared with Sweden and Norway, are all commercial and prolific in the latest American dramas, sitcoms and soaps (almost always with Danish subtitles). If you're staying in a hotel, or a youth hostel with a TV room, you may also have the option of German and Swedish channels – plus several dozen international cable and satellite stations.

Festivals

Denmark's cities, villages and seaside towns come alive in the warmer months, when dozens of outdoor festivals and events are staged to take advantage of Scandinavia's extended daylight hours – and even the chillier months are made warmer with film, music and other cultural festivals to help get people out of their houses. Music-wise, jazz is king, and the Danes' taste for all styles of jazz, from bebop to fusion, is explored through festivals all across the country. The largest of these – two of the biggest in Europe, in fact – are the Copenhagen Jazz Festival and the Roskilde Festival, held in late June/early July. Equally, film festivals screening the latest arthouse movies alongside documentaries and features have become immensely popular over the last decade.

Festivals Diary

January

Odense Winter Jazz Festival Ⓦ www.vinterjazz .dk. Late Jan to early Feb. With over 200 concerts in some fifty venues, this ten-day winter festival attracts some of the biggest names in Danish and Scandinavian jazz.

March

Ålborg Opera Festival Ⓦ www .aalborgoperafestival.dk. First two weeks of March. The only opera festival in Denmark, with performances in concert halls, churches and cafés all over the city.

Copenhagen NatFilm Festival Ⓦ www.natfilm .dk. Late March to early April. This two-and-a-half-week festival featuring movies of all genres is the largest film event in Denmark, involving every single cinema in Copenhagen. Part of the program is also screened in Odense, Aalborg and Århus.

April

Birthday of Queen Margrethe II, Copenhagen April 16. The queen's birthday is celebrated every year outside the Amalienborg Palace. Following the changing of the guard at noon, the royal family steps out onto the palace balcony to be greeted by thousands of flag-waving Danes repeatedly shouting "Margrethe, Margrethe, kom nu frem, ellers går vi aldrig hjem" ("Margrethe, Margrethe, come on out, or we will never go home").

May

Architecture and Design Days ⓦ www.cphadd .com. Early May. For three days, dozens of cultural institutions and architecture firms lead tours of Copenhagen's best buildings and pieces of fine design.

Ålborg Carnival ⓦ www.karnevaliaalborg .dk. Late May. 100,000 onlookers come for this lively collection of parades and parties, during which the city's canals are filled with groups of decorated boats, and music and dancing continues all day long and well into the night in the central Kildeparken.

Copenhagen Carnival ⓦ www.karneval.dk. Late May. Samba and capoeira shows, saisa stages and kitschy, garish float parades, all held in the central Fælledparken park – Rio in Denmark.

June

Spot Festival, Århus ⓦ www.spotfestival .dk. Early June. Staged at a dozen or so venues across central Århus and intended to promote pan-Scandinavian and Danish music, with concerts from around 100 groups over two days.

July

Århus International Jazz Fest ⓦ www.jazzfest .dk. Mid-July. A small community feel pervades at this ten-day festival, with concerts held in small venues like cafés, tents, bars and art centre lobbies. Many of the musicians arrive straight from their shows at the larger Copenhagen Jazz Festival.

Copenhagen Jazz Festival ⓦ www.festival .jazz.dk. Early July. The capital's largest festival, in which streets, outdoor spaces, bars and concert halls are used as venues for everything from live bebop to post-industrial fusion, with spoken-word poetry and world music thrown in for good measure too.

Langelandsfestival ⓦ www.langelandsfestival .dk. Late July. A coterie of mostly Danish rock bands play to an audience of around 25,000 on one of Denmark's most verdant islands.

Roskilde Festival ⓦ www.roskilde-festival.dk. Late June/early July. One of the largest music festivals in the world, Roskilde is a massive party

and loads of fun. The lineup regularly features show-stopping names such as Pink Floyd or The Strokes, plus hundreds of smaller groups spread across six sound stages over four days. See p.148.

Skagen Festival ⓦ www.skagenfestival.dk. Early July. A lively festival featuring the latest in international folk music, with dozens of groups playing Celtic, bluegrass, zydeco and Scandinavian fiddle music. Recent acts have included Runrig and Jim McCann.

August

Copenhagen Fashion Week ⓦ www .denmarkfashion.com. Early Aug. The annual show for more than 2000 fashion designers and clothing brands is the largest of its kind in the Nordic countries. While the exclusive runway shows are off-limits to the general public, the week is full of other associated events, talks and showings, as well as sales at many of the city's clothing shops and boutiques.

Cultural Harbour ⓦ www.kulturhavn.dk. Early Aug. Four days of dancing, music, theatre and artistry aboard boats moored in Copenhagen's harbour and on the quay.

Odense International Film Festival ⓦ www .filmfestival.dk. Mid-Aug. One of Denmark's main cinematic showcases, screening over 200 Danish and foreign feature films, shorts and documentaries.

Malmö Festival ⓦ www.malmofestivalen.se. Mid-Aug. Attracting well over a million and a half visitors during its eight days, this lively event includes over 250 free concerts, cultural events, a food festival (crayfish being a speciality) and handicrafts exhibits.

Skanderborg Festival ⓦ www.smukfest.dk. Mid-Aug. Music fest held in a gorgeous beech forest, and attended by some 50,000 people who come to hear everything from folk to heavy metal and hip hop. See p.315.

Tønder Festival ⓦ www.tf.dk. Late Aug. A superb folk music festival held in Tønder on the banks of the Vidå River, showcasing artists such as Steve Earle and Arlo Guthrie.

September

Århus Festival ⓦ www.aarhusfestuge.dk. Early Sept. One of Denmark's largest cultural events sees dance, theatre, opera and art exhibitions take over the city for ten days.

Copenhagen Film Festival ⓦ www .copenhagenfilmfestival.dk. Late Sept. Well over 100 international movies, with many filmmakers on hand to talk about their work.

Copenhagen Golden Days ⓦ www.goldendays .dk. First three weeks of Sept. A unique three-week festival that celebrates the influential rule of Christian IV, and includes musical events, theatre performances, exhibitions and city walking tours.

October

Copenhagen Cultural Night ⓦ www .kulturnatten.dk. Second Fri in Oct. Some 300 venues all over the capital – churches, libraries, schools and exhibition halls – open their doors and put on musical shows, poetry readings, art exhibitions and a number of other cultural events. **Copenhagen Gay and Lesbian Film Festival** ⓦ www.cglff.dk. Late Oct. Copenhagen's oldest film festival, this very popular event attracts a diverse audience with its large number of dramas, documentaries and animated shorts, to say nothing of the legendary post-screening parties.

November

Copenhagen Irish Festival ⓦ www.irishfestival .dk. Early Nov. A small festival that nonetheless attracts some of the larger names in Irish and Celtic folk music.
Copenhagen International Documentary Festival ⓦ www.cphdox.dk. Mid-Nov. Denmark's oldest documentary festival screens over 150 international films each year, and has established itself as one of Europe's premier platforms for socially conscious documentaries, many of which you'll be hard-pressed to see anywhere else.

December

Copenhagen Christmas Fairs Nov–Dec. Not a festival so much as a magical ethos that takes over the entire city, with a prolific number of Christmas markets and events, and the fairy-tale Tivoli Gardens dressed in Christmas lights.

Sports and outdoor activities

Though it's connected to mainland Europe via a 68km border with Germany, Denmark is primarily made up of islands – over five hundred of them in total, a quarter of which are inhabited – which, combined with scores of inland waterways, make for some excellent watery activities, from swimming, canoeing and kayaking to windsurfing and sailing. Denmark's interior consists of long stretches of undulating and varied terrain, with hedges, small trees and other flora providing shelter from the wind that blows in off the coast, allowing for invigorating coastal journeys by bike or on foot.

Cycling

Given its superb, rolling landscape of moors, hills and heaths, Denmark is easily the most enjoyable country in Europe for cycling, and riding has become something of a national pastime here. You can find both leisurely and challenging riding on the network of eleven **national cycle routes**, which cover a total of 4000km. These lengthy, well-signed paths run along or near the country's major roadways and pass through some of its most important and interesting attractions, following lesser-trafficked tarmac, special cycle lanes or defunct rail lines. All are marked on the maps at the start of each chapter in this Guide. The most enjoyable places for biking include the southern Funen coast and its surrounding archipelago, as well as Bornholm, criss-crossed with the best-maintained and least-trafficked paths in the country.

A few **general rules** to keep in mind: lock up your bike even if you'll be away from it for a few minutes, as bicycle theft is not uncommon, especially in the larger cities; cycle racks are common outside most commercial establishments in Denmark. Note also that cycling with a rucksack is very dangerous – instead, divide your luggage between

Denmark's 11 National Cycle Routes

No. 1 The West Coast Route (550km; see maps on p.250, p.282 & p.350)

No. 2 Hanstholm to Copenhagen (420km; see maps on pp.132 & p.350)

No. 3 Hærvejen (450km; see maps on p.305 & p.350)

No. 4 Søndervig to Copenhagen (310km; see maps on p.132, p.282, p.305)

No. 5 The East Coast Route, Skagen to Sønderborg (650km; see map on p.250, p.305, p.350)

No. 6 Esbjerg to Copenhagen (325km; see maps on p.132, p.282, p.305)

No. 7 Sjællands Odde to Gedser (230km; see map on p.132)

No. 8 Rudbøl to Møn (360km; see maps on p.132, p.202, p.250)

No. 9 Elsinore to Rødby (250km; see map on p.132)

No. 10 Touring Bornholm (105km; see map on p.178)

No. 11 The Limfjord Route (610km; see map on p.282)

side panniers (line them with plastic bags to avoid condensation). If you're cycling for long distances, remember to pack a pump, patches, a tyre lever, an extra tube, lights, a lock, sun cream, water bottles and of course a helmet. The churches found along the national routes always have toilets and water. The Danish Cyclists' Association (ⓦwww.dcf.dk) has brochures and route maps on all aspects of cycling.

Hiking

At the moment Denmark maintains only one national park, the Rebild Bakker in Jutland (see p.353), but there are numerous protected and state-owned conservation areas and natural forests which are criss-crossed by bark- or gravel-covered **walking** or cycling paths. One of the most enjoyable long-distance rides is the Jutland-based Mols route, which extends 80km from Grenå to Århus, passing by manor houses, abandoned railway lines, an old watermill and the ruins of Kalø Slot. When in forests, be sure to keep to the signposted paths. For more information, visit the Danish Ramblers' Association (ⓦwww.dvl.dk).

Swimming and beaches

Over 7000km of coastline – an amazing amount considering Denmark's relatively small landmass – allows for excellent **swimming** opportunities. Nearly all beaches are spotlessly clean, with wide stretches of silky sand and negligible undertow (except on Jutland's west coast). It's virtually impossible to single out the country's best swathes of beach, as all have their pluses and minuses, but the two busiest are Gilleleje and Tisvildeleje in north Zealand (see pp.140 & 000), where wealthy Copenhageners hang out most weekends. Balka is the most attractive beach on Bornholm, while Grenå Strand (see p.337) in east Jutland and Gudmindrup Strand (see p.153) on Zealand's Odsherred peninsula both enjoy the warm waters of the protected Kattegat. Hesslebjerg on Langeland (see p.238) is also outstanding, as are the wild and windy west coast beaches in Jutland, Højer, Blokhus and Blåvand (see p.301), as well as Lakolk on Rømø island (see p.270). The warm months of July and August are probably the most pleasant for swimming, though the water doesn't reach its peak temperature until September. Winter bathing is something of an institution among Danes, who hack through the ice, jump in, and then rush into hot saunas run by the local winter bathing club afterwards. There are clubs in Copenhagen (by Amager Strandpark), Århus (near the harbour) and most other large coastal towns. Ask at the local tourist office for information about nearby clubs. Note that **nude bathing** is fairly common, and that nudist beach areas are not always separate from standard ones, though most of them are signed in some way.

Canoeing and kayaking

Kayaking and canoeing along Denmark's many rivers and waterways is a popular summertime activity, and there are numerous outlets from where you can hire equipment.

Canoeing is best along the placid Suså river (see p.164), which wends its way through Zealand's central and southern heartland, and the Gudenåen (see p.320), Denmark's longest river. **Kayakers** are better off in inshore waters like the Helnæs Bay, though if you're experienced you might want to try out a trip across the Svendborg sound (see p.226) to one of the southern Funen isles. A more laid-back option is a canal kayak tour of Copenhagen (see p.65).

Windsurfing and paragliding

As suggested by the thousands of modern turbine windmills you'll see here, Denmark is a windy place, and boasts some of the best conditions for **windsurfing** on the continent. Beginners will want to head to the protected shores and inlets, while those with more experience will find more enjoyment on the open coast. Not all of the major beaches have places that hire out equipment, however, so it's best to head to Klitmøller (or the Vandet Sø sea, just east; see p.286) or the northern edge of Hvide Sande (see p.296), both with established windsurfing scenes and places where you can have a lesson (around 500kr for four hours, including gear hire) or will rent you gear to head out on your own (300kr per day). There are also good spots in Skagen (see p.376), Fyns Hoved (see p.223), southern Langeland (see p.238) and Århus bay (see p.329). For more information on windsurfing, contact the Danish Sailboard Association (Ⓦwww.dbo .dk). Given all the extra wind blowing around, **hang-gliding** and **paragliding** have become popular activities among Danes, as has **kite surfing**, the latter of which is best at either Klitmøller or Hvide Sande, both of which have outlets where you can rent gear (750kr per half-day); lessons are also available. For up-to-date information, contact the Danish Hang-gliding and Paragliding Union (Ⓦwww .danskdrageflyverunion.dk).

Fishing

With some of the best fishing in Europe, Denmark is a great place to go angling. To **fish** in Denmark's coastal waters, fjords and national rivers, you must first apply for a licence, available at most local tourist offices.

These are valid for one year and cost 125kr, though you can also buy one-day (30kr) or one-week (90kr) licences. Natural lakes and streams are usually privately owned, but local angling societies will issue temporary angling passes for a nominal fee (40kr–150kr per day or 100kr–300kr per week). Note that you can fish from anywhere along the Danish coast as long as there is a public road which leads to the shore and a legitimate beach between the water and any farmland.

Several companies organise **sea-fishing** tours from Copenhagen, Helsingør, Korsør and Frederikshavn; for more on these, and general fishing information, enquire at tourist offices. Mackerel, cod and sea trout are the most common open-sea fish, though you will also find eel, turbot, plaice and flounder. Jutland's west coast is good for cod, flatfish, garfish and mackerel, and its east coast and Lake District are known for salmon, pike and bass; Limfjorden in the north tends to have more variety. Funen has sea trout and fat-bellied cod, best in the Langeland belt, and you can find herring in the Lillebælt, Store-bælt and Langelandbælt. Zealand has larger varieties of cod, plus carp, whitefish pike and zander. Bornholm's various fjords, bays, inlets and open coastline are perfect habitats for silver sea trout.

For **freshwater** varieties, Denmark's many lakes and rivers are filled with pike, perch, zander and trout, most abundantly in the waterways of Jutland. For **fly fishing**, try the Gudenåen, Karup and Storå rivers in Jutland. The best resource on fishing is Ⓦwww.sportsfiskeren.dk, the website of the Danish Angling Society.

Horse riding

Horseback riding in Denmark can be a lovely way of seeing the country's spectacular scenery; head for the grasslands that front the north Jutland coast at Hirtshals, the trails along the island of Rømø or the multitude of paths in Zealand's deciduous Gribskov forest. Horse riding outfits are fairly common (we've listed them in relevant places in the Guide), with most charging around 80kr per hour for a ride on an Icelandic horse – the most common breed in Denmark and great for first-timers as they tend to be rather stocky and quite amicable.

Golf

Denmark's rippling landscape is perfectly suited to **golfing**, though you may find the greens on the country's seventeen courses far flatter than those elsewhere. Courses generally charge around 200kr for 18 holes, though this may be a bit higher on weekends when the greens are at their busiest. You're likely to be asked for some documentation of your handicap or membership in a club at home, though such procedures are often done away with for tourists. Be prepared to walk, as electric golf carts are rare. Of the country's best courses, there's the Copenhagen Golf Club, adjacent to lush woodlands just outside the city centre. The course in Odense is particularly large, and those at Harre Vig and on Bornholm are the most picturesque. For more on golfing in Denmark, as well as details of the country's courses, get in touch with the Danish Golf Union (⊛www.dgu.org).

Culture and etiquette

Like its Scandinavian neighbours, Denmark is a modern European nation whose history has nevertheless brought about a number of subtle social and cultural differences that can throw off even the most anthropologically-aware of travellers.

Much social interaction among Danes is governed, at least to some extent, by the doctrine of **Janteloven** ("The Law of Jante"), a sort of unwritten code of behaviour coined by Dano-Norwegian author Aksel Sandemose in the 1930s, and based on his observations of Danish society. In general, Janteloven describes the sort of egalitarian comportment visible in Norway, Denmark and to some extent, Sweden, in which hubris, bragging and personal celebration are frowned upon, and sometimes even a difference of opinion will go unvoiced. The sentiment is that placing oneself higher than another member of society is a conceit that works against the values of the egalitarianism held to be so foundational to Scandinavian societies, but many self-critical Danes – especially those who've made the choice to settle abroad – would argue that instead of encouraging egalitarian values, such conduct breeds mediocrity and stifles entrepreneurial thought, out-of-the-box thinking and creativity. Such behaviour should, however, be understood in its historical context: there's a long tradition of social equality here, which equates in fellow citizens treating each other as equals and which has helped maintain a sense of solidarity in this territorially fractured country. But all this talk of adherence to strict social mores shouldn't suggest that Danes are in any way unfriendly or antisocial. In fact, among the Nordic countries, they are probably the most welcoming and friendly to foreigners, a hospitality best described by the Danish precept of **hygge** (the oft-given English translation of "cosiness" doesn't quite do it justice), which sort of suggests a mixture of conviviality and intimacy. You'll sense *hygge* when you sit sipping hot *gløgg* in a toasty warm candlelit café while snow is falling outside, or around a midsummer's eve bonfire with people chit-chatting around you and the odd traditional folksong being sung.

Danes often greet each other with a simple, informal "hej", a **standard greeting** that is a mite less colloquial than the English "hi". There is no single word in the Danish language for "please" – so when a Dane doesn't use it when speaking to you in English, it's not because they're rude – the word just doesn't come naturally. Danes are also renowned for being direct and to the point, which can sometimes be interpreted as impolite – if they want something, they'll say "giv mig…" ("give me…") – but they can also be extremely easy-going, seldom taking themselves too seriously.

Drinking and smoking

Though Danes enjoy a drink – **alcohol** is available more readily than in other Scandinavian countries, and is sold everywhere, from department stores and gas stations to vending machines and supermarkets – you're unlikely to have many encounters with truly boisterous public drunkenness, and such behaviour is definitely frowned upon. While Danes have made themselves known as some of Europe's staunchest opponents to **smoking** restrictions, the country has progressed more or less along with other European countries in public smoking reform, and you'll find fewer smokers than in, say, France or Italy. Cigarettes (around 35kr per packet) are sold at kiosks, grocers' shops and petrol stations.. All trains and buses in Denmark are non-smoking, and more and more smoke-free places are popping up everywhere as the country catches up with social health concerns. In January 2007, smoking was banned in all government ministries, shopping centres, cultural centres and many larger cafés, bars and restaurants, though the latter are allowed to set up special sections for smoking patrons.

Shopping

Shopping is undoubtedly one of the highlights of a visit to Denmark, with many well known and up-and-coming Danish designers selling their wares in raft of eclectic and original shops which offer a refreshing alternative to the usual selection of bland chain stores.

Exclusive handmade and luxury goods abound, often bearing witness to Denmark's fine traditions of innovative design, something that can be seen in products as diverse as clothing (look out for designer names such as Stig P and Munthe plus Simonsen), furniture (Arne Jackobsen), lighting (Poul Henningsen), glassware (Holmegaard), porcelain (Kongelig Dansk), jewellery and silverware (George Jensen), stereo equipment (Bang & Olufsen), and handmade bicycles (the Christiania bike) to mention but a few. Quality is very high – as are, unfortunately, the prices.

Most designer shops are found in town and city centres rather than the large scale shopping malls that have made an appearance in many town and city outskirts, and tend to attract more run-of-the-mill international chain stores.

Most towns also have Saturday morning fruit and veg **markets** on the main square. These tend to include stalls selling cheese from the local dairies and a fishmonger selling fresh, smoked and marinated fish.

Travelling with children

Denmark is a child-friendly country, and places without facilities for children are few and far between – even the more exclusive cafés and restaurants have high-chairs, changing facilities and a children's menu. The low level of traffic and many pedestrianized streets also mean Denmark is an easy country to explore with kids both on foot and, given the dedicated cycle lanes in most town and city centres and designated cycle routes throughout the country, by bike. Danish beaches are also, on the whole, child-safe. The water tends to be shallow, and the waters at all (bar those on the west coast) are generally very calm.

Most of the country's museums cater for children in some way, many have dedicated children's sections, others are specifically geared towards children, so travelling with kids doesn't mean that you'll miss out on the country's cultural side.

Top attractions for kids

Tivoli (p.92)
Legoland (p.312)
Den Fynske Landsby (p.212)
Bakken (p.125)
Experimentarium (p.125)
Zoos in Copenhagen (p.100) Aalborg (p.361) and Odense (p.211)

Travel essentials

Costs

There's no getting away from the fact that Denmark is an **expensive** country, although you can cut costs substantially if you spend wisely. If you stay in youth hostels or camp-sites and don't eat out, it's possible to get by on £25/US$45/€37 per day. Otherwise, staying in inexpensive hotels, moving around the country visiting museums, eating in a restaurant each day and buying a few snacks and going for a drink in the evening, you can expect to spend a minimum of £40–50/US$70–90/€60–75 per day. Going up a notch, staying in a mid-range hotel, eating lunch and dinner at restaurants and/or cafés, doing a couple of museums during the day, and maybe catching a club at night

will set you back substantially more – expect to spend a minimum of £80–100/US$140–180/€120–150 per day.

Crime and personal safety

Denmark is one of the most peaceful coun-tries in Europe. Most public places are well lit and secure, the majority of people genuinely friendly and helpful, and street crime and hassle relatively rare.

It would be foolish, however, to assume that problems don't exist. Like any capital city, Copenhagen has its fair share of **petty crime**, fuelled by a growing number of drug addicts and alcoholics after easy money. Keep an eye on your cash and passport, employ your common sense and you should have little reason to visit the **police**. If you do, you'll find them courteous, concerned and usually able to speak English. If you have something stolen, make sure you get a **police report** – essential if you are to make an insurance claim. Should you need them, **foreign embassies** in Copenhagen (see box on p.50) are usually pretty helpful.

As for **offences** you might commit, **nude sunbathing** is universally accepted in all the major resorts (elsewhere, there'll be nobody around to care). Being **drunk** on the streets can get you arrested, and **drinking and driving** is treated especially rigorously. **Drug** offences, too, meet with the same strict attitude that prevails throughout the rest of Europe.

Disabled travellers

In many ways, Denmark is a model destination for disabled travellers: wheelchair access is generally available at hotels, hostels, museums and public places, and Danes are usually happy to assist in other ways.

There are many **organized tours and holidays** specifically for people with disabilities – the contacts listed below will be able to put you in touch with specialists offering trips to Denmark. The Danish tourist board (see p.55) publishes the comprehensive, free *Access in Denmark – a Travel Guide for the Disabled*, which covers everything from airports to zoos, while their website, ⊛www .visitdenmark.com, has specific information about disabled access to hotels, museums and public transport under the Inspiration tab.

The Association of Accessibility Denmark (☎36 35 96 98, ⊛www.godadgang.dk) is the certifying body for places with good access for disabled people (look for the blue "A" in a blue circle on a white background). They judge places on their suitability for wheelchair users, people with reduced mobility, sight and hearing impaired people, people suffering from asthma and/ or allergies, people with mental disabilities, and finally people with reading disabilities; contact them for more information on accessibility in the country.

Electricity

The Danish electricity supply runs at 220–240V, 50Hz AC; sockets generally require a two-pin plug. Visitors from the UK will need an adaptor; visitors from outside the EU may need a transformer.

Entry requirements

Citizens of the European Union, US, Canada, Australia and New Zealand need only a valid **passport** to enter Denmark for up to three months. South African citizens must obtain **visas** from the embassy in Pretoria (see p.52) before travelling. Visas cost about R260, depending on the exchange rate, are valid for a maximum of ninety days and require proof of travel and health insurance. All other nationals should consult the relevant embassy about visa requirements.

For **longer stays**, EU nationals can apply for a residence permit while in the country which, if it's granted, is usually valid for up to five years. Non-EU nationals can only apply for residence permits before leaving home, and must be able to prove they can support themselves without working.

In spite of the lack of restrictions, **checks** are frequently made on travellers at the major points of entry. If you're young and are carrying a rucksack, be prepared to prove that you have enough money to support yourself during your stay. You may also be asked how long you intend to stay and why.

Danish embassies and consulates abroad

Australia Sydney: Gold Fields House, 21st floor, 1 Alfred St, Circular Quay, Sydney, NSW 2000, ☎+61(2)9247 2224; Ground Floor, 492 St Kilda Rd, Melbourne 3004, Victoria ☎+61(3)9866 1242; ⊛www.gksydney.um.dk.
Canada 47 Clarence St, Suite 450, Ottawa, Ontario K1N 9K1 ☎613/562-1811, ⊛www.ambottawa .um.dk.
Ireland 121–122 St Stephen's Green, Dublin 2 ☎01/475 6404, ⊛www.ambdublin.um.dk.
New Zealand Level 7, Forsyth Barr House, 45 Johnston St, Wellington 6001 ☎04/471 0520, ⊛www.danishconsulatesnz.org.nz.
South Africa Parioli Office Park, Block B2, Ground Floor, 1166 Park St, Pretoria ☎012/430 9340, ⊛www.ambpretoria.um.dk.
UK 55 Sloane St, London SW1X 9SR ☎020/7333 0200, ⊛www.amblondon.um.dk.
US 3200 Whitehaven St NW, Washington DC 20008 ☎202/234-4300, ⊛www .ambwashington.um.dk.

Gay and lesbian travellers

Denmark legalised **homosexuality** in 1930 and it was the first country in the world to legalise same-sex partnerships (in 1989). Danish society is accordingly very tolerant of homosexuality – many Danes pride themselves on their liberal attitudes, and heads won't generally turn if a gay or lesbian couple are seen kissing or holding hands. This liberal attitude has led to Copenhagen becoming one of the world's **premier gay cities** – its emancipated attitude is best illustrated by the way the main cruising spot, H.C. Ørstedsparken, has been equipped with "birdboxes" containing condoms and lubricating gel, while police patrols here are instructed not to chase out cottaging men, but to protect them from the homophobic violence that sporadically occurs.

Paradoxically, Denmark's liberal traditions mean that there are fewer specifically gay and lesbian venues than in less tolerant cities, and that everything tends to be more mixed. For general **information**, the national organization for gays and lesbians, the Landsforeningen for Bøsser og Lesbiske (LBL), close to H.C. Ørstedsparken at Teglgårdsstræde 13 in Copenhagen (☏33 13 19 48, 🖳www .lbl.dk), provides a very well-run advice service (Mon–Fri 11am–3pm) and is an excellent place to pick up news of any gay- or lesbian-oriented events in the country. Their first-floor library and reading room (Mon–Thurs 5–7pm) is packed with gay literature and magazines, but you have to be a member to take anything out. They also run a youth hotline (Tues 7–9pm; ☏33 36 00 80). LBL run a very useful listings website (🖳www .gayguide.dk) and publish a free monthly Danish-language paper, *PAN Bladet*, with dozens of handy listings – fairly easy to decipher even if you don't speak Danish – that you can pick up at all major gay hangouts.

The hugely popular annual **Copenhagen Pride** takes place in August. After parading through the street, the event ends with an all-night party.

Health

Should you require medical attention, then you can rest assured that health care in Denmark is superb. There are **emergency departments** at most hospitals, although in Copenhagen, as a number of specialist hospitals don't deal with emergencies, see p.122 for details of those that do. Emergency departments provide free treatment for EU and Scandinavian nationals, though citizens of other countries are unlikely to have to pay. For **medical emergencies**, call ☏112.

If you need a **doctor or dentist**, the local tourist office will give you details of doctors and dentists on call, and local practitioners are listed in the area's tourist office brochure. Outside tourist office opening hours, or if you don't have the brochure, call ☏112. Doctors' fees start at 400kr, to be paid in cash; dentist fees start at 200kr and can be paid with cash or cards. If you're an EU citizen and you have a European Health Insurance Card (EHIC) – available from post offices in your home country – you can claim back doctors' fees and charges for medicine from the local health department. You'll need to produce the relevant receipts and card.

Most larger towns and all cities have 24-hour **pharmacies**, which we've detailed throughout the Guide.

Insurance

Most people will want to take out some kind of **travel insurance** for their trip. A typical policy usually provides cover for the loss of baggage, tickets and – up to a certain limit – cash or cheques, as well as cancellation or curtailment of your journey.

Before paying for a new policy, however, it's worth checking whether you are already covered. Some all-risks home insurance policies may cover your possessions when overseas, and many private medical schemes include cover when abroad. In Canada, provincial health plans usually provide partial cover for medical mishaps overseas, while holders of official student/teacher/youth cards in Canada and the US are entitled to meagre accident coverage and hospital in-patient benefits. Students will often find that their student health coverage extends during the vacations and for one term beyond the date of last enrolment.

Rough Guides has teamed up with Columbus Direct to offer you **travel insur-**

ance that can be tailored to suit your needs. Products include a low-cost **back-packer** option for long stays; a **short-break** option for city getaways; a typical **holiday package** option; and others. There are also annual **multi-trip** policies for those who travel regularly. Different sports and activities (trekking, skiing, etc) can be usually be covered if required.

See our website (Ⓦwww.roughguides insurance.com) for eligibility and purchasing options. Alternatively, UK residents should call ☏0870/033 9988; Australians should call ☏1300/669 999 and New Zealanders should call ☏0800/55 9911. All other nationalities should call ☏+44 870/890 2843.

Internet

Finding somewhere to access the **Internet** will seldom be a problem in Denmark. Access is free at most libraries (though you may have to book a one-hour slot in advance), while internet cafés – these days primarily geared towards gaming – can be found in almost all towns, and charge 20–30kr/hr. Larger airports (only Copenhagen and Billund at the time of writing), train stations and shopping malls also have self-service Internet cafés where you enter money into a machine that provides you with a log-in name and password, which you can use to access the Net in any branch within the same café chain throughout the country. Most tourist-oriented hotels, hostels and campsites tend to have a dedicated room with a couple of broadband-connected computers, while business-class places will have wireless internet access, as do an ever-growing number of cafés and restaurants – the early-opening, countrywide *Baresso Coffee* chain is making a name for itself as the prime spot for wi-fi access.

Laundry

Most hotels in Denmark provide a pricey laundry service; you'll save lots of money by going to one of the many local laundromats (signed *møntvask* or *vasketeria*) found in the residential areas of most towns. Prices per load (including detergent and softener) range between 30kr and 40kr.

Mail

Like most other public bodies in the country, the Danish **post office** runs an exceedingly tight ship – within Denmark, anything you post is almost certain to arrive the next day. You can buy stamps from most newsagents, and from post offices. Mail under 50g costs 7kr to other parts of Europe, and 8kr to the rest of the world. Poste restante is available at any post office, and many hotels, youth hostels and campsites will hold mail ahead of your arrival.

Maps

The **maps** in this book should be adequate for most purposes, but drivers, cyclists and hikers will require something more detailed. Local tourist offices give out free reasonable city and regional maps, but for anything better you'll have to pay.

The best city maps are produced by Kraks, either in booklet or folding form and at various scales. Country maps are produced by Kümmerley & Frey (1:300,000), Ravenstein (1:500,000), and Baedeker (1:400,000). The Danish Youth Hostel Association also produces a very informative country map (including all hostels, campsites, ferry links and cycle routes), which you can order free of charge from Ⓦwww .danhostel.dk. Detailed maps of all the **regions** are covered by the 1:200,000 Kort og Matrikelstyren map published by Aschehoug. The Danish Cyclist Organization *Dansk Cyklist Forbund* (see details p.45) also sells good regional maps and booklets of recommended cycle routes.

Money

The Danish currency is the **krone** (plural kroner). It's made up of 100 øre, and comes in notes of 1000kr, 500kr, 200kr, 100kr and 50kr, and coins of 20kr, 10kr, 5kr, 2kr, 1kr, 50øre and 25øre. At the time of writing, the exchange rate was approximately 11.14kr to the pound, 7.46kr to the euro and 5.92kr to the US dollar. For the latest rates, go to Ⓦwww.xe.com

Banks are plentiful, and the easiest place to change travellers' cheques and foreign cash; there's a uniform commission of 30kr per transaction, so change as much as is feasible in one go. Banking hours are Mon–

Public holidays

New Year's Day; Maundy Thursday; Good Friday; Easter Sunday; Easter Monday; Common Prayer Day (fourth Friday after Easter); Ascension Day (fifth Thursday after Easter); Whit Sunday and Whit Monday (seven weeks after Easter); Constitution Day (June 5); Christmas (December 24–26).

Wed & Fri 10am–4pm, Thurs 10am–6pm. Copenhagen's airport and Central Station have late-opening exchange facilities, which charge a similar amount of commission.

Forex exchange bureaux charge only 20kr to exchange cash and 10kr to exchange travellers' cheques, but are much rarer. There are three in Copenhagen, one in Helsingør, Odense, Aalborg and Århus; see the relevant accounts in the Guide for details.

Alternatively, the red Kontanten high-street cash machines (**ATMs**) give cash advances on credit cards and, if you've a Link, Cirrus or Maestro symbol on your ATM card, will allow you to withdraw funds from your own account in local currency (check with your home bank), which can work out cheaper than changing cash or travellers' cheques.

Opening hours and public holidays

Shop **opening hours** are Mon–Thurs 10am–5.30pm, Fri 10am–6/7pm and Sat 9am–1/2pm; shops are closed on Sundays. Supermarkets stay open a bit later. On the first Saturday of the month, shops stay open until 5pm.

Most shops and businesses are closed on **public holidays** (see box above), when public transport services are also reduced.

Phones

Public telephones come in two forms. Coin-operated ones are white and require a minimum of 3kr for a local call (the machines irritatingly swallow one of the coins if the number is engaged), and 5kr to go international; cards for the blue cardphones come in denominations of 30kr, 50kr and 100kr and work out a little cheaper – they're sold in newsagents and post offices. Most hotel rooms have a phone, but it's much cheaper to make calls from the public phone at reception. Youth hostels and campsites generally have public phones; if not, the warden will probably let you use the house one for a payphone fee.

You should be able to use your **mobile phone** in Denmark if it's been connected via the GSM system common to the rest of Europe, Australia, New Zealand and South Africa. This means that the vast majority of mobile phones from these countries will work here, though if you haven't used your mobile abroad before, check with your phone company. The North American mobile network is not compatible with the GSM system, so you'll need a tri-band phone that will be able to switch from one band to the other. If you plan to make a lot of mobile calls while in Denmark, you could also invest in a Danish SIM card for use in your phone; these are available in all mobile phone shops. For 99kr, you'll get a Danish number plus about forty minutes of domestic calling time. The most commonly used network is TDC (the national landline network), but coverage with Orange, Telia and others is just as good. Top-up cards can be bought in supermarkets, kiosks, and phone shops.

Calling Denmark from abroad, the **international code** is +45; codes for international calls from Denmark are given opposite. To make a **collect international call**, dial the operator on ☎80 30 40 00 and ask to be connected to the operator in your own country, who will then put through the collect call – full instructions for this "Country Direct" system are displayed in phone booths (in English), and you can dial ☎80 60 40 50 for free assistance. Be warned that **directory enquiries** (international ☎113, domestic ☎118) are expensive – the initial charge of 8kr per minute climbs ridiculously high whilst the operator puzzles out your request. Almost all operators speak English. To save money, use the phone books in all public phone booths, the national phone company's website (☻www.tdc.dk), or the online

Calling home from abroad

Note that the initial zero is omitted from the area code when dialling the UK, Ireland, Australia and New Zealand from abroad.

US and Canada international access code + 1 + area code.
Australia international access code + 61 + city code.
New Zealand international access code + 64 + city code.
UK international access code + 44 + city code.
Republic of Ireland international access code + 353 + city code.
South Africa international access code + 27 + city code.

(Danish-language) yellow pages (ⓦwww.degulesider.dk).

Time

Denmark is one hour ahead of GMT, six hours ahead of US Eastern Standard Time, and nine ahead of US Pacific Standard Time.

Taxes

A sales tax (MOMS) of 25 percent is added to almost everything you buy – but it's always included in the price. Non-EU citizens can claim a refund at the airport, provided you fill out a Global Refund Cheque at the point of purchase.

Tipping

Service is included on all restaurant, hotel and taxi bills, so unless you feel you've been given an exceptionally good service, adding anything on is not necessary – though a tip will obviously be appreciated.

Toilets

Clean **public toilets** in the cities and towns are numerous and easy to find, and are either snazzy, pod-like structures, or larger, permanent constructions with an attendant on hand. You usually have to pay around 2kr..

Tourist information

Denmark's tourist offices at home and abroad have heaps of free information leaflets and magazines. They can also point you in the right direction should you have any special travel requirements, or need information about special events. We've detailed local offices throughout the Guide.

Danish tourist board offices abroad

Australia Level 4, 81 York Street, Sydney, New South Wales 2000 ☎02/9262 5832, ⓦwww.scandinavia.com.au.
Canada Box 115, Station N, Toronto, ON M8V 3S4 ☎416/823-9620.
Ireland No tourist-board office, but the embassy (see p.50) handles tourist information.
New Zealand No tourist-board office but the embassy (see p.50) supplies tourist information.
South Africa No tourist-board office, but the embassy (see p.50) handles tourist information.
UK 55 Sloane St, London SW1X 9SY ☎020/7259 5959, ⓦwww.visitdenmark.com.
US Scandinavian Tourist Board, 655 3rd Ave, 18th floor, New York, NY 10017 ☎212/885-9700, ⓦwww.visitdenmark.com.

Tourist offices and government sites

Australian Department of Foreign Affairs ⓦwww.dfat.gov.au, ⓦwww.smartraveller.gov.au.
British Foreign & Commonwealth Office ⓦwww.fco.gov.uk.
Canadian Department of Foreign Affairs ⓦwww.dfait-maeci.gc.ca.
Irish Department of Foreign Affairs ⓦwww.foreignaffairs.gov.ie.
New Zealand Ministry of Foreign Affairs ⓦwww.mft.govt.nz.
US State Department ⓦwww.travel.state.gov.

Guide

Guide

Copenhagen and around

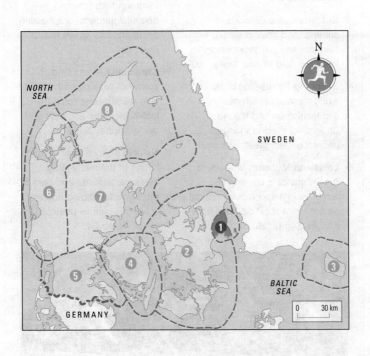

CHAPTER 1 # Highlights

✳ **The National Museum** From Viking treasure to Ancient Egyptian statues, Inuit harpoons to Chinese tea-sets, the fascinating and diverse exhibits here are a must-see. See p.94

✳ **Rosenborg Slot** Check out the rich royal history and dazzling crown jewels at this fairytale castle. See p.86

✳ **Outdoor cafés** Glorious in summer and cosy in winter, with blankets and outdoor heaters to keep the cold at bay. See p.109

✳ **Shopping** Browse the latest in world-famous Danish design and fashion on and around Strøget – the world's longest pedestrianized street. See p.80

✳ **Louisiana Museum of Modern Art** Outstanding painting and sculpture in a spectacular coastal setting just a short distance from the city. See p.126

✳ **Ny Carlsberg Glyptotek** Rodin sculptures, Roman and Etruscan treasures and French Impressionist paintings as well as a stunning, palm-filled café. See p.93

✳ **Tivoli** The city's beloved pleasure park has the perfect mix of traditional and modern fairground attractions, beautiful gardens, great eating spots and lots of live music. See p.92

✳ **Christiania** A beguiling sprawl of twisting paths lined with mural-bedecked houses, laid-back cafés and bars and quirky shops. See p.85

✳ **Nyhavn** Enjoy a beer or lunch in one of the many lively cafés, restaurants and bars in the colourful gabled houses lining this picture-postcard canal. See p.84

△ Café culture, Nyhavn

Copenhagen and around

Situated halfway down the eastern side of Zealand and just 11km from Kastrup International Airport, on the adjacent island of Amager, Denmark's small yet outward looking and vibrant capital **Copenhagen** (København) is the arrival point for most visitors to Denmark and, with its excellent transport connections, the natural starting point for onward travel to the rest of the country. Even though it only has a population of around one million, it's Denmark's one truly large city and a stark contrast to the sleepy provincialism of the rest of the country. That said, it's a remarkably easy and relaxing place to spend time in – unlike most European capitals, walking between all of the major sights is a viable option due to its compact size, and large sections of the city centre are pedestrianized – and should you need it, there's a reliable and efficient public transport system. What's more, you're just a short ride away from some beautiful sandy beaches and open green country-side, while the city's proximity to the sea, its lovely harbourfront and numerous canals and lakes offer plenty of options for waterside relaxation when you've had enough of pounding the streets.

Historically, the city owes its existence to its position on the narrow Øresund strait, which separates Denmark from Sweden – one of the great trading routes of medieval Europe and now the site of the region's grandest engineering feat, the massive **Øresund bridge**, which connects the city by road and rail to the Swed-ish town of Malmö. It's this location, poised between Scandinavia and the rest of Europe, that continues to give Copenhagen its distinctive character. Compared to the relatively staid capitals further north, Copenhagen has a more laid-back, European flavour; the freedom with which its most famous export, Carlsberg, flows in the city's hundreds of bars is in stark contrast to the puritanical licensing laws found elsewhere in Scandinavia. Yet Copenhagen is also a flagship example of the Scandinavian commitment to liberal social values – exemplified by its laid-back attitudes to everything from gay marriage to pornography – and its continued (if precarious) respect for the unique "free city" of Christiania.

However, like most European cities, Copenhagen is facing modern changes and challenges. On the one hand, the Øresund bridge has given the city the infrastructure to become the western Baltic's leading urban centre, and there are many who would like to see it take full advantage of this and develop into a truly internationalist, forward-looking metropolis. On the other hand, there are some who regard the bridge as an irrelevance at best and, at worst, a symbol of all those foreign influences that threaten to undermine traditional Danish values. Above all, these influences are typified by Copenhagen's burgeoning immigrant community and simmering racial tensions – and the resulting rise of right-wing politicians – which pose increasing challenges to the city's tolerant image. For all that, it's worth remembering that the city's occasional smugness and resistance to change is the result of its citizens' pride in their capital – as a visitor, you'll be made to feel welcome wherever you go, especially since absolutely everybody speaks English.

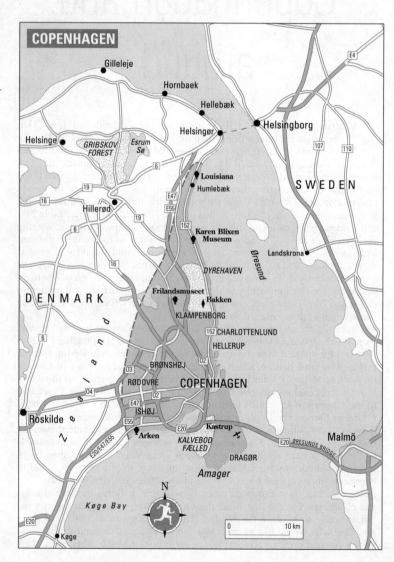

The area **around Copenhagen** – either in its outlying suburbs or slightly further afield – offers some easily accessible sights that are well worth seeing on day-trips. Just to the north, along the Øresund coast, stretch a series of well-heeled suburbs: a visit to their attractions – the Danish Aquarium, Experimentarium and Bakken amusement park among them – can be followed up by lazing on the adjacent beaches. Further north up the coast is the stunning modern art museum of Louisiana, while to the south of the city, another bastion of contemporary art, Arken, occupies an equally fabulous seafront location. All of this offers a taster for the rest of Zealand, covered in Chapter Two.

Copenhagen

Denmark's political, financial and artistic centre, **COPENHAGEN** is one of Europe's most user-friendly cities, a small and welcoming place where people rather than cars set the pace – and as most of the attractions, hotels, restaurants and nightlife are within the same square mile or so of the city centre, you'll quickly get your bearings. Copenhagen also offers a range of entertainment that belies its relatively modest size: by day, there's a cornucopia of historic royal palaces, national museums, art galleries and excellent shops; by night there are plenty of cosy bars, an intimate club and a live music network that could hardly be bettered, and exciting and ambitious arts venues like the new Operæn opera house and Playhouse theatre (the latter currently under construction). It's a city that comes into its own in summer – cafés spill out onto the streets, live music (especially jazz) is around every corner and the harbour comes to life with plentiful tour boats and busy open-air swimming pools. That's not to say you shouldn't come in winter: temperatures may hover around freezing but the cafés and bars provide warming *glögg*, Tivoli gets even more festive around Christmas, and temporary ice-skating rinks pop up around the city.

Much of Copenhagen dates from the seventeenth and eighteenth centuries, a cultured ensemble of handsome Renaissance palaces, parks and merchants' houses laid out around the waterways and canals that give the city, in places, a pronounced Dutch flavour. Successive Danish monarchs left their mark here, in particular Christian IV, creator of many of the most striking landmarks including Rosenborg Slot and the district of Christianshavn; and Frederik V, who graced the capital with the palaces of Amalienborg and the grandiose Marmorkirke. These landmarks remain the highest points in a refreshingly low and undeveloped skyline.

Arrival and information

However you **arrive** in Copenhagen, you'll find yourself within easy reach of the city centre. Copenhagen airport is just a few kilometres to the southeast on the edge of the island of Amager, while almost all trains and buses deposit you near the city's main transport hub, Central Station, right in the heart of the city.

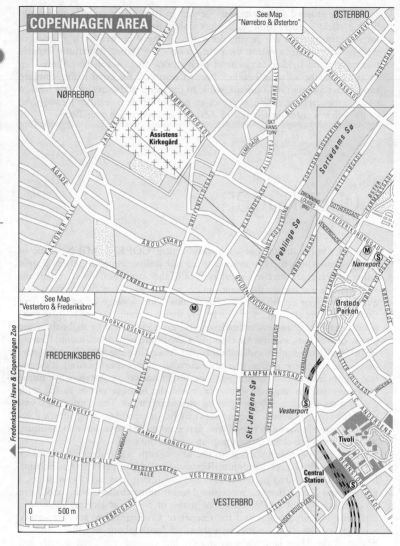

COPENHAGEN AREA

ØSTERBRO

See Map
"Nørrebro & Østerbro"

NØRREBRO

Assistens
Kirkegård

See Map
"Vesterbro & Frederiksbro"

FREDERIKSBERG

Fredenksborg Have & Copenhagen Zoo

Peblinge Sø

Sortedams Sø

Nørreport

Ørsteds
Parken

Vesterport

Tivoli

Central
Station

VESTERBRO

0   500 m

By air

Getting into the city from Copenhagen **airport** (Ⓦwww.cph.dk), 11km southeast
of the city in the suburb of Kastrup, couldn't be easier. A rail line runs regularly and
directly to Central Station (10–13min; 27kr), and there's also a much slower city
bus (#250S; 27kr, and #96N nightbus; 54kr) to Central Station and Rådhuspladsen, only really convenient if you want to get off on the way. A taxi to the centre
will cost about 180kr – there's a rank outside the arrivals hall. Inside arrivals, the
helpful **information desk** (daily 6am–midnight) has free maps of the city and

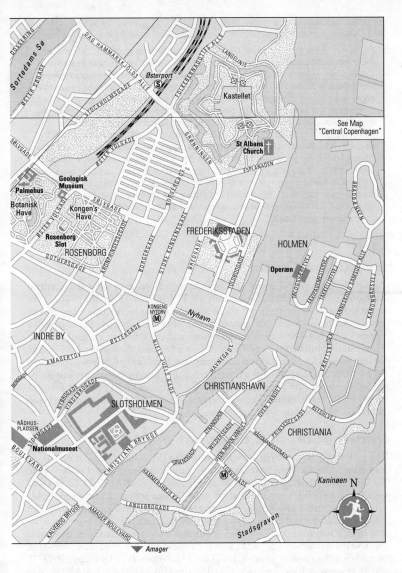

Amager

runs an efficient **hotel booking service** (daily 6am–11pm; 100kr per reservation) with some very good last-minute deals. The airport also has two late-opening
banks (daily 6am–10pm), car rental agencies (see p.121) and a post office. If you've
flown with Ryanair, you'll arrive at **Malmö**'s Sturup airport across the bridge in
Sweden (see box, p.64); the *Flybuss 737* awaits every Ryanair arrival and crosses
the Øresund bridge to Central Station (50min; 100kr). Alternatively, take the local
airport bus *Flybuss* to Malmö Central Station (45min; 95Skr) and catch the train
to Copenhagen from there.

Copenhagen and Malmö

For centuries, the Swedish city of **Malmö** (in Danish, Malmø) across the Øresund, and the surrounding province of Skåne, were part of a Danish empire with its capital in Copenhagen. With the Swedish capture of Skåne in the seventeenth century, however, Malmö was reduced from the second city of a major northern European power to a neglected outpost of a greater Sweden, in which power rested firmly with distant Stockholm. The sense of rejection persists – Malmö's residents derisively call people from Stockholm *null åttas*, "zero-eights", after the telephone code for Stockholm.

In July 2000, Malmö's historical ties with the Danish capital were renewed with the opening of the **Øresund Bridge**, Scandinavia's biggest-ever engineering project. The "bridge" (actually a road and rail link made up of a four-kilometre tunnel, a four-kilometre artificial island and an eight-kilometre cable bridge) has brought the two cities within a 35-minute train ride of one another, effectively transforming Malmö into a satellite-cum-suburb of Copenhagen and placing the Danish capital at the heart of a new region, the so-called **Øresund**, which looks set to dominate the western Baltic for the foreseeable future.

By bus and train

All coaches, buses and trains to Copenhagen arrive at or near the **Central Station** (signed as Hovedbanegården or København H in the S-tog train network), from where there are excellent connections to virtually every part of the city via bus or local train, although there is no stop here on the new metro system (see p.66). The station also has shops and cafés, foreign exchange bureau (daily 8am–9pm), bicycle rental service (see p.68), and, downstairs, left-luggage lockers (see p.122). The national train company, DSB (daily 6.30am–11pm; ☎70 13 14 15, ⓦwww.dsb.dk), has a travel agency and information centre just inside the main entrance off Vesterbrogade. Eurolines coaches (☎70 10 00 30, ⓦwww. eurolines.dk) from around Europe and buses from Malmö Sturup airport stop behind Central Station on Ingerslevgade.

Information and discount cards

The new Copenhagen Right Now **tourist office** (May–June Mon–Sat 9am–6pm; July–Aug Mon–Sat 9am–8pm, Sun 10am–6pm; Sept–April Mon–Fri 9am–4pm, Sat 9am–2pm; telephone enquiries Mon–Fri 10am–4pm ☎70 22 24 42; ⓦwww. visitcopenhagen.dk), across the road from the Central Station at Vesterbrogade 4A, offers maps, general information and accommodation reservations (see p.69). The office also distributes the free *Copenhagen This Week*, an up-to-date monthly news and listings magazine. Far better for youth and budget-oriented help, though, is the **UseIt** information centre (mid-June to mid-Sept daily 9am–7pm; mid-Sept to mid-June Mon–Wed 11am–4pm, Thurs 11am–6pm, Fri 11am–2pm; ☎33 73 06 20, ⓦwww.useit.dk), centrally placed in the Huset complex at Rådhusstræde 13, about a kilometre northeast of the station in the shopping area of Indre By. A wide range of help for travellers is available, including poste restante and free email services, accommodation and entertainment information, luggage storage facilities and an extremely useful free magazine called *Playtime*.

If you plan to visit many museums, either in Copenhagen or in nearby towns like Helsingør and Roskilde, you might want to buy a **Copenhagen Card**, which come in versions valid for either 24hr (199kr) or 72hr (429kr) and are available from tourist offices, hotels and travel agents and train stations. The card covers transport on the entire metropolitan system and gives entry to most museums in the area, as well as twenty to fifty percent discounts on some car hire, ferry rides and theatre tickets.

City transport

The best way to explore Copenhagen is either to **walk** or **cycle**: the inner city is compact, much of the central area of Indre By is pedestrianized and there's

Guided tours

If you've limited time to see Copenhagen, a **guided tour** can be a good option. There's something to suit everyone, with a wide variety of combinations of sights and means of transport available, be it bus, boat, bicycle, kayak or on foot.

Copenhagen Sightseeing Tours ☎32 66 00 00, ⊛www.sightseeing.dk. Eight bus tours (with multilingual headphone commentary) departing several times daily from Rådhuspladsen, by the Lure Players statue adjacent to the town hall. Options include the "City Tour", which passes all the major sights (130kr; 1hr 30min), the "Open Top Tours", which runs a hop-on/hop-off system (120kr to 220kr per day), the "Grand Tour", which includes the Royal palaces and the parliament (195kr; 2hr 30min), and a "City and Harbour" tour, by coach and boat (175kr; 2hr 30min). There's a ten percent discount if you book online.

City Safari Dansk Arkitektur Center, Gl. Dok, Strandgade 27B, Christianshavn ☎33 23 94 90, ⊛www.citysafari.dk. Guided bike tours starting from the Architecture Centre (see p.84) on Strandgade. "Historical Copenhagen" tours depart daily in summer (1.30pm; 250kr including bike; 3hr) and according to demand during the rest of the year – book in advance at all times. "Copenhagen by Night" tours depart daily in the summer (8pm; 250kr including bike; 3hr), and include a drink in one of the city's trendy cafés. There's a 30kr reduction if you bring your own bike.

Copenhagen Adventure Tours ☎40 50 40 06, ⊛www.kajakole.dk. These original innovative and challenging tours aboard well-designed, safe and easy-to-handle kayaks give a unique view of the city. Leaving from Christianshavns Kanal, Strandgade 49 in front of *Restaurant Kanalen*, the standard ninety-minute tours (May–Sept; 165kr), take in the central city canals and Christianshavn; longer trips include the Little Mermaid and Holmen. The price includes a drink in a canalside floating bar.

DFDS Canal Tours ☎32 96 30 00, ⊛www.canaltours.dk. Two one-hour options, starting from Nyhavn or Gammel Strand and taking in various city sights; however, at 60kr, you'll get more for your money with Netto-Bådene (see below). DFDS also run three hop-on/hop-off waterbus routes; a two-day unlimited-use ticket which includes the Copenhagen Sightseeing (see above) costs 220kr, a one-day ticket 50kr, and a single trip 30kr. Bring a raincoat and warm clothing if the weather is bad, as the boats are quite exposed.

Netto-Bådene ☎32 54 41 02, ⊛www.havnerundfart.dk. Offering a combination of the two DFDS boat tours listed above, Netto-Bådene's one-hour tour for only 30kr is a lot better value. Tours start and finish at Holmens Kirke, and depart daily from April to mid-Oct between 10am and 5pm (July & Aug 10am–7pm) two to five times an hour.

Walking Tours A number of English-language guided tours are available from various points throughout the city; the tourist office has a list of tours taking in most of the city-centre highlights and lasting up to two hours. If you're after something different try the Watchman's Round (mid-July to mid-Sept daily 9pm; rest of year Fri & Sat 7pm; 50kr), which leaves from outside Peder Oxe on Gråbrødretorv. The tour takes just over an hour and follows an eighteenth-century watchman on his round while he tells tales (in English) of the old city. Check ⊛www.nattevaegterne.dk for more info.

a comprehensive network of excellent bike paths – you'll often find it's just as quick to walk or cycle as to wait for a bus. For travelling further afield, there's an integrated network of **buses**, **metro lines** and **S-Tog** and local **trains**.

Tickets

All city transport operates on an integrated **zonal system** extending far beyond the suburbs and encompassing S-Tog trains, the metro system, regional trains and buses. There are an astounding 95 zones (pick up a free leaflet from any S-Tog station); you may find it easiest at first simply to state your destination and you'll be sold the appropriate ticket. The city centre and immediate area, as you'd expect, are in zones 1 and 2. **Fares** are based on a combination of zones and time: the cheapest ticket – *billet* – costs 18kr and is valid for one hour's travel within any two zones, with unlimited transfers between buses and trains. Another option is the **klippekort** ticket, a discount card containing ten stamps which you cancel individually according to the length of your journey and the value of the *klippekort*. The cheapest *klippekort* costs 115kr, with each stamp being valid for an hour's travel within any two zones; each stamp in a 155kr *klippekort* is valid for one hour within any three zones – good value if you plan to travel outside the city centre – and is also valid to and from the airport. Unlimited transfers are allowed within the time period of the ticket, and two or more people can use the same *klippekort* simultaneously, provided you clip the required number of stamps per person. There's also an excellent-value **24-hour ticket** (105kr) which is valid on all transport in zones as far away as Helsingør and Roskilde, as well as night buses. Finally, a new option is the *Flexicard 7 days* giving unlimited travel for seven days; it costs 190kr for two zones and 220kr for three. *Billets* can be bought on board buses or at train stations, while *klippekort*, 24hr tickets and *Flexicard - 7 days* are only available at bus or train stations and HT Kortsalg kiosks; *klippekort* should be stamped when boarding the bus or via machines on train station platforms. Except on buses, it's rare to be asked to show your ticket, but if you don't have one you face an instant fine of 500kr. Route maps can be picked up free at stations, and most free maps of the city include bus lines and a diagram of the S-Tog and metro network.

Rail and metro

The **S-Tog** train service (W www.s-tog.dk) is a metropolitan network laid out in a huge "U" shape covering Copenhagen and the surrounding areas. Ten of its twelve lines stop at Central Station (in Danish, Hovedbanegården or København H), while the two remaining lines run a circular route around the centre. Each line has a letter and is also colour-coded on route maps. Lines running similar routes, but stopping at fewer stations, have a + symbol after the letter, so check carefully or you could whizz straight past your destination. Services run about every ten to fifteen minutes between 5am and 12.30am, and stations are marked by red hexagonal signs with a yellow "S" inside them. Maps of the network are freely available from all stations; the maps in this Guide mark S-Tog stops with "S" and metro stops with "M".

The new underground **metro system** (W www.m.dk) is fast and efficient (departures every couple of minutes). It circumvents Central Station in a "U" shape, connecting the island of Amager with northwest Copenhagen via two brand-new stations conveniently located at Christianshavn and Kongens Nytorv. The metro's two lines – M1 and M2 – cross the S-Tog and regional trains at Nørreport. A final section of the metro is due to open in 2007, linking the city with Copenhagen airport.

Useful bus routes

#5A Assistens Kirkegård, Nørrebrogade (near Skt Hans Torv and Blågårdsgade), Nørreport Station, Nørre Voldgade, Rådhuspladsen, Central Station.

#6A Sortedams Dosseringen (the lakes), Statens Museum for Kunst, Nørreport Station, Gammel torv-Nytorv, Rådhusstræde, Vester Voldgade, Rådhuspladsen, Vesterport Station, Roskildevej, Frederiksberg Slot, City Zoo.

#26 Valby Langgade, Carlsberg Brewery, Pile Allé, Frederiksberg Allé, Vesterbrogade, Central Station, Rådhuspladsen, Vester Voldgade, Kongens Nytorv, Dronnings Tværgade, Øster Voldgade, Østerport Station, Indiakaj, Langeliniekaj and the Little Mermaid.

#66 Åboulevard, Vesterport Station, Tivoli and Central Station, Christians Brygge on Slotsholmen, City Hostel, Christianshavns Torv, Christiania, Operæn.

By bus

The city's **bus** network (@www.hur.dk) is much more comprehensive than the S-Tog system, and can be a more convenient way to get around once you get the hang of finding the stops – marked by yellow placards on signposts – and if you avoid travelling during the rush hour (7–9am and 5–6pm). The excellent **free city map** produced by the tourist office (see p.64) includes a list of all bus routes in the centre. The city's bus terminal is a slick black building on Rådhuspladsen; you can pick up bus-route maps here, and get general information about the metropolitan transport system. Other useful buses leave from Central Station's Tivoli side entrance, and the bridge at the end of the tracks. Buses with an "S" suffix only make limited stops, offering a faster service – check they make the stop you require before you get on – while an "A" suffix indicates that service runs frequently. All buses have a small electronic board above the driver's seat displaying both the zone you're currently in and the correct time – so there's no excuse for not having a valid ticket. There's a skeletal **night bus** service (running once or twice an hour) though fares are double daytime rates. Night bus numbers always end with "N"; stops are well marked by yellow signs on major routes into and out of the city.

Harbour buses

Another option for getting around are the city-run yellow **harbour buses**, which sail along the harbour between Nordre Toldbod (near the Little Mermaid) and the Royal Library, and stop five times on the way (twice on the Christianshavn side). Services leave daily every twenty minutes from about 6.30am to 7pm (unless the harbour area is frozen) and cost 36kr (*klippekort* – see opposite – can also be used). Tickets are valid for one hour and are transferable to the rest of the transport network; bikes cost an extra 17kr. Compared to the city's canal tours (see p.65), harbour buses are a cheap way to experience Copenhagen from the waterfront.

Taxis

Taxis are plentiful; there's a flat starting **fare** of 19kr, plus 11kr per kilometre travelled (14kr after 4pm and at weekends). There's a handy taxi rank outside Central Station, or phone Taxamotor (℡38 10 10 10 for a cab, ℡35 39 35 35 for a minibus). Alternatively, just hail one in the street – if it's showing a green

"*Fri*" sign on top, it's available. A fun new addition to the scene are rickshaw-styled **cycle taxis** (April–Oct only); the flat starting fare is 35kr, plus a 3kr per-minute charge.

Cycling

If the weather's good, the best way to see Copenhagen is to follow the locals and hop on a **bicycle**. Cycling is also an excellent means of exploring the immediate countryside, as a 10kr charge allows you to take bikes onto S-Tog trains for two hours through any number of zones; you can also buy a special bicycle *klippekort*, valid for ten journeys and costing 95kr. The superb city-wide cycle lanes make biking very safe here, though remember that lights are a legal requirement at night (you'll be stopped and fined if the police catch you riding without them).

Of the city's numerous **bike rental** outlets, the most central are Københavns Cyklebørs, at Gothersgade 157 in Indre By (Mon–Fri 8.30am–5.30pm, Sat 10am–1.30pm; ☎33 14 07 17, ⓦwww.cykelboersen.dk; 60kr/day, 270kr/week, 200kr deposit), and Københavns Cykelcenter, along the side of Central Station at Reventlowsgade 11 (Mon–Fri 8am–5.30pm, Sat 9am–1pm; ☎33 33 86 13, ⓦwww.copenhagen-bikes.dk; 75kr/day, 340kr/week, 500kr deposit). From April to September, you can also take advantage of the free **City Bike scheme** (ⓦwww.bycyklen.dk), when two thousand bikes (easily recognized by the advertisements painted onto their solid wheels) are scattered about the city at S-Tog stations and other busy locations; a refundable 20kr deposit unlocks one. You deposit the bike in the racks found at main stations when you've finished with it (and get your coin back automatically as you relock it), or just leave it out on a sidewalk, in which case someone else will happily return it and pocket the coin. Don't secure a City Bike with your own lock, and don't take one outside the city limits (the old rampart lakes mark the border) or you risk a fine.

Driving and parking

Given the excellent public transport system, the size of the city, and the comparatively high price of petrol and parking, renting a **car** just for use in Copenhagen isn't really economical unless you're in a group. If you decide to bite the bullet, you'll need to familiarize yourself with the city's **parking** rules. A pay-and-display system operates (Mon–Fri 8am–10pm, Sat 8am–5pm) on the inner city's streets (the area inside the lakes), with rates varying depending on which colour-coded zone you are in. Stretching out from the centre, the zones are red (25kr per hour), green (15kr), and blue (9kr). Each pay-and-display meter has a map on it detailing the extent of each zone. Outside the centre, there's two hours' free parking Mon–Fri 8am–7pm, but you have to set a P-disc (see Basics, p.35). "STOPFORBUD" means no stopping, whilst "PAKERING FORBUDT" means no parking unless a time limit is displayed, in which case you must use a P-disc. It's usually not too difficult to find a street parking space, but note that your car will be towed away if you overstay or park where you shouldn't. Downtown car parks are thin on the ground: there's a handy one at Israel Plads by Nørreport Station, one at Vesterbrogade 23 near Tivoli and the Central Station, and another attached to the Q8 station near Vesterport Station at Nyropsgade 42 (all 20kr per hour, 200kr per day).

Accommodation

Accommodation in Copenhagen is plentiful but relatively expensive, with prices on a par with other Western European capitals, and in high season (July, August & Christmas) you'll need to book ahead. The tourist office has a website (Ⓦ www.bookcopenhagen.dk) and phone line (Ⓣ 70 22 24 42) for you to pre-book accommodation (50kr booking fee). If you're willing to take a chance, however, you can make great savings if you book on the day of your arrival via the **hotel booking service** at the tourist office (see p.64). They'll find you a room, although queues for this service can be lengthy during high season, and there's a 100kr charge. The office also has several terminals with free Internet access, enabling you to book for yourself via their website.

Room rates are generally at their highest in summer, though in the majority of big hotels prices rise and fall on a daily basis according to demand, and you can get excellent weekend rates in business hotels. It's always worth checking hotel websites for **special rates** and packages; if you book online in advance you can often get discounts of up to 35 percent.

A more affordable **guesthouse** sector is slowly starting to develop, which offers a more homely and personalized alternative to hotels, but rooms fill quickly in the summer months; check out Ⓦ www.bedandbreakfast.dk. Another inexpensive option is to contact the tourist office (see p.64) or Use It (see p.64) and ask about private rooms in local homes. Some of these are in as good a location as the best hotels, and prices are very reasonable, at 350–400kr per double. There are a number of good **hostels** scattered around the city centre and suburbs, while **campsites** provide an alternative if you're really watching the pennies.

The codes given at the end of each listing are for a **standard double room** mid-week in high season, followed by the cost of the same room at the discounted weekend rate. Unless stated, **breakfast** is included in the price. Note that we list a few gay and lesbian-friendly accommodation options on p.120.

Hotels

Copenhagen has experienced a **hotel** boom in recent years. New places – particularly at the high end – pop up constantly in all corners of the city, and include several exciting designer hotels in great, central locations, which offer an interesting, more stylish, alternative to the bland chains. Most of the budget and mid-range options are just west of Central Station, in Vesterbro, with the majority of the inexpensive ones clustered along the slightly seedy streets of Helgolandsgade, Colbjørnsensgade and Istedgade. Further mid-price options can be found around Nyhavn canal and out towards the suburb of Frederiksberg.

Indre By

The following hotels are shown on the map on p.76.

Copenhagen Strand Havnegade 37 Ⓣ 33 48 99 00, Ⓦ www.copenhagenstrand.dk. Bus #29. Long and narrow converted red-brick warehouse on the waterfront behind the Royal Theatre, though very few rooms have a view. They're a bit on the small side, but all are comfortable and neat, with parquet flooring and heavy dark-mahogany furniture. Rates are reduced substantially during weekends. ❾/❽

Ibsens Vendersgade 23 Ⓣ 33 13 19 13, Ⓦ www .ibsenshotel.dk. Bus #5A, #40 or #350S. Set between Nørreport station and the lakes, this cosy and welcoming three-star has comfortable and attractively outfitted rooms – all dark wood and navy blue and gold fabrics. Each floor is themed – the fourth is "romantic", the fifth "bohemian", and there's an Italian restaurant and a small Italian garden on the ground floor. ❻

Jørgensen Rømersgade 11 Ⓣ 33 13 81 86, Ⓦ www.hoteljoergensen.dk. Bus #5A, #14, #40,

#42, #43 or #350S, or Nørreport S-Tog/metro. Friendly and relaxed place within easy walking distance of the city centre, offering a good range of good-value rooms with a mixture of en-suite and shared facilities, as well as three dorm-style rooms (140kr) with TV, sleeping 6–12. The double rooms are all comfortable, decent-sized and well furnished, and there's a good buffet breakfast. The clientele is a happy mix of young travellers and families; note that there's an age limit of 35. ⑤–⑥

Opera Tordenskjoldsgade 7 ⊤ 33 47 83 00, ⓦ www.hotelopera.dk. Bus #29, or Kongens Nytorv metro. Slightly worn at the edges, with a restaurant reminiscent of Agatha Christie's *Murder on the Orient Express*, this classy old hotel is full of character and appeal. Rooms come with heavy drapes and carpeting, and have an altogether very theatrical feel. Major reductions during weekends and summer. ⑨/⑦

Skt Petri Krystalgade 22 ⊤ 33 45 91 00, ⓦ www.hotelsktpetri.com. Bus #6A. Though it's located in a former discount department store slap bang in the centre, there's certainly nothing downmarket about this super-trendy designer hotel. As reflected by the price, rooms are lush to the extreme, with massive fluffy duvets and swanky colour-conscious decor. There's a posh café/restaurant next to the lobby and if you're lucky you might get access to the *Bar Rouge* downstairs bar/nightclub, although there's a strict dress code and entry tends to be by invite only. 1995kr.

Sømandshjemmet "Bethel" Nyhavn 22 ⊤ 33 13 03 70, ⓦ www.hotel-bethel.dk. Bus #29, or Kongens Nytorv metro. You don't need to be a sailor to stay at this seamen's hostel (although you get a 10 percent discount if you are), which boasts a fantastic location on Nyhavn and rates that don't see you paying over the odds for the privilege. The self-contained rooms are perfectly adequate, and the corner ones with fantastic views are worth paying a bit more for. There's a small breakfast area which serves cakes and coffee throughout the day. ⑥

Frederiksstaden

The following hotels are shown on the map on p.76, and are reachable by buses #1A, #15, #26 and #29.

Copenhagen Admiral Toldbodgade 24–28 ⊤ 33 74 14 14, ⓦ www.admiralhotel.dk. A great location right by the waterfront next to Nyhavn and the new Playhouse, and set in a 200-year-old, six-storey former granary which has kept its rustic maritime interior, with vaulted ceilings and wooden beams throughout. Rooms are comfortable, and half of them have great views of Inderhavnen and cost

a bit more. Although the Admiral is geared mainly towards business travellers, rates don't tend to go down during weekends. There's a classy restaurant, *Salt*, on the ground floor; note that the breakfast buffet (115kr) isn't included. ⑨

Comfort Hotel Esplanaden Bredgade 78 ⊤ 33 48 10 00, ⓦ www.choicehotels.dk. Set in a pleasant location near Churchillparken and Kastellet, this pleasant hotel has decent en-suite rooms, with the choice of bathtub or shower. Breakfast (95kr) is not included. There's a good restaurant – *Sankt Petersborg* – next door, and parking in the back yard (95kr) that must be booked in advance. ⑨/⑧

Front Skt Annæ Plads 21 ⊤ 33 13 34 00, ⓦ www .front.dk. One of the classier hotels in town, with a range of shower-only en-suite rooms each with a different colour scheme (orange, beige, maroon, light grey or rose-pink), and thick fluffy carpets giving it something of a retro-glam Seventies feel.. Breakfast (145kr) is not included, but there's free access to the hotel's fully equipped gym. Prices go up 300kr for sea view. ⑨

Rådhuspladsen and around

The following hotels are shown on the map on p.76.

Hotel Fox Jarmers Plads 3 ⊤ 33 95 77 55, ⓦ www.hotelfox.dk. Central Station S-Tog or bus #5A, #6A or #250S. Great-value, exciting new hotel with 61 rooms designed along individual themes (psychedelic movies, Manga cartoons); all use their space creatively and with a flair that makes even the small singles stylish and inviting. Doubles come in medium, large and extra large; some have showers, others baths – state your preference when booking. There's a good restaurant, and breakfast is served on airplane-style compartmentalized trays in the bright and funky lobby, which doubles as a cocktail bar Thursday to Saturday evenings. Bikes and rollerblades for hire. ⑧

Marriott Kalvebod Brygge 5 ⊤ 88 33 99 00, ⓦ www.marriott.com/cphdk. Bus #8. In a great harbourfront spot at the end of Bernstorffsgade, the high-rise *Marriott* offers all the American-style swagger and amenities you could want – large, plush, well-equipped rooms (many with views over the harbour or city), restaurant, terrace café (summer only), bar, fitness room, sauna and solarium, and pricey shops. Breakfast not included. ⑧/⑦

Radisson SAS Royal Hotel Hammerichsgade 1 ⊤ 33 42 60 00, ⓦ www.radissonsas.com. Central Station S-Tog or bus #6A or #28. Built in 1960, this five-star tower is the work of Danish architect/

designer Arne Jacobsen, from the high-rise building itself to the door handles. Several renovations later, it remains faithful to its original style and decor, a time capsule back to the jet-set glamour of the 1960s – the huge lobby has a glamorous sweeping staircase and a classy bar perfect for that pre-dinner drink. The rooms aren't that big but they are a model of tasteful, minimalist Danish design with AJ furniture, pastel fabrics, maple-wood panelling and stylish lighting. For effortless style, slick service and sheer Scandinavian cool this is still the one to beat. Rates significantly reduced at weekends. Breakfast not included. ⑨

The Square Rådhuspladsen 14 ☏ 33 38 12 00, ⓦ www.thesquare.dk. Central Station S-tog. Great new addition to Copenhagen's hotels, slap-bang in the centre (hence no parking). Spacious, stylish modern lobby scattered with lovely red Arne Jacobsen swan chairs; the minimalist look is carried through into the smartly decorated rooms. Those overlooking the square experience some traffic noise, so you might want to request a room further back. Breakfast (there's no restaurant) is served on the sixth-floor dining room, which affords views over the city. 1635kr.

Vesterbro

The following hotels are shown on the map on p.96.

Absalon Helgolandsgade 15 ☏ 33 24 22 11, ⓦ www.absalon-hotel.dk. Bus #10, or Central Station. On the corner of Istedgade, this large but friendly family hotel, with a cheaper annexe, offers a wide choice of rooms (some en suite), plus a number of deluxe doubles and suites. It's nothing special and the decor is rather dated, but it's reasonably priced, convenient and clean, and sound-proofing keeps things nice and quiet. There's free Internet access in the lobby. ⑥

Ansgar Colbjørnsensgade 29 ☏ 33 21 21 96, ⓦ www.ansgar-hotel.dk. Bus #10, or Central Station. Former Danish Mission hotel close to Central Station, with small en-suite rooms kitted out in light Scandinavian style. There's a pleasant courtyard (summer only), and Internet access in the lobby. ⑥

Bertrams Hotel Guldsmeden Vesterbrogade 107 ☏ 33 25 04 05, ⓦ www.hotelguldsmeden .dk. Bus #6A. The newest branch of the Danish Guldsmeden chain, exquisitely done up in French colonial style with dark wooden interiors and fake furs lying around. Rooms are fairly large, bright and breezy, and come with the choice of shower or bath. Breakfast is sourced from *Emmery's* bakery next door. ⑨

Centrum Helgolandsgade 14 ☏ 33 31 31 11, ⓦ www.dgi-byen.dk. Bus #10, or Central Station. One of the trendier options in this area of town, and recently given a cool, modern revamp: black leather sofas and cosy lighting in the lobby, and tasteful whites, creams and pale wooden furniture in the modestly sized en-suite rooms. Guests get free access to the DGI-byen sports centre. ⑧

Guldsmeden Vesterbrogade 66 ☏ 33 22 15 00, ⓦ www.hotelguldsmeden.dk. Bus #6A or #26. Small and charming hotel occupying a nineteenth-century building almost opposite the City Museum. The en-suite rooms are done out in French colonial style, with a laudable attention to detail, and some have small balconies, though the view isn't that enticing. Parking 50kr. ⑨

Løven Vesterbrogade 30 ☏ 33 79 67 20, ⓦ www .loeven.dk. Bus #6A or #26. There's no sign and the heavy steel door and scruffy entrance is a tad off-putting (ring the bell marked 1st floor *Løven*), but this is one of central Copenhagen's real bargains, offering affordable, no-frills accommodation in plain but pleasantly decorated rooms (mostly en suite) sleeping up to four. Breakfast isn't included, but there's a large and well-equipped communal kitchen, and a great bakery next door for fresh bread and pastries. The major drawback is the noise from the road – rooms facing the courtyard are quieter. ⑨

Missionshotellet Nebo Istedgade 6 ☏ 33 21 12 17, ⓦ www.nebo.dk. Central Station. Next door to Central Station (take the back exit) this well-run, recently renovated Danish Mission hotel is one of the best deals this close to the centre. Rooms – some en suite, others with shared facilities – are simple but adequate and clean, and staff are friendly and relaxed. ⑥

Tiffany Colbjørnsensgade 28 ☏ 33 21 80 50, ⓦ www.hoteltiffany.dk. Bus #10, or Central Station. Small, charming and welcoming hotel, a cut above most in the area and specially suited to those who want a more independent stay – the large, well-furnished double or family rooms all come equipped with mini-kitchens comprising a micro-wave, fridge and toaster, and continental breakfast is left in the fridge (with freshly baked rolls left at your door each morning). ⑧

Frederiksberg

The following hotels are shown on the map on p.96.

Avenue Åboulevard 29 ☏ 35 37 31 11, ⓦ www.avenuehotel.dk. Bus #67, #68, #250S, or Forum metro. Comfortable and welcoming place between Frederiksberg and Nørrebro, a ten-minute bus ride from the centre. Having recently undergone a thorough refurbishment, the spacious rooms are stunning, with simple and stylish yet cosy interiors. There's a breakfast buffet (served outdoors in the summer) and free parking. ⑦

Euroglobe Niels Ebbesens Vej 20 ☎ 33 79 79 54, ⓦ www.hoteleuroglobe.dk. Bus #3A or #29. Basic but exceptionally good-value place, a 15min walk from the city centre on one of Frederiksberg's elegant and peaceful streets. Rooms (all with shared bathrooms) are a touch monastic – white walls, minimal furniture and a sink – but they're clean and bright; those up in the eaves have a bit more character. There's also a kitchen for guests' use. No credit cards. ⑤

Memory Søndre Fasanvej 4 ☎ 38 87 13 42, ⓦ www.hotel-memory.dk. Bus #4A, #14 or #15. Small, reasonably priced hotel on the main road running along the western edge of Frederiksberg

Have (about 15min by bus to the town centre), occupying a quaint old ochre villa with white shutters. The nine en-suite rooms are cosy and well furnished, so book well ahead. Breakfast is served in your room. Cash or Visa cards only. ⑥

Sct Thomas Frederiksberg Allé 7 ☎ 33 21 64 64, ⓦ www.hotelsctthomas.dk. Bus #26. In a great location just past lively Vesterbrogade, this place is close to the delis and food shops on Værnedamsvej and a 10min walk from Frederiksberg Have. The friendly owners, pleasantly decorated rooms (some cheaper with shared facilities) and easy-going atmosphere have made it a runaway success, so be sure to book ahead (a couple of months in high season). Internet access, tea and coffee and buffet breakfast are included in the price, and there's bike rental (100kr/day) in summer. Parking 50kr per day. Cash and Visa cards only. ⑥

Hostels and sleep-ins

Copenhagen has a great selection of **hostels** and **sleep-ins**, which are ideal for those on a budget, though they're often a little way away from the centre. They're mostly aimed at school groups and the hordes of young Swedes who descend on the city during the summer months looking for cheap alcohol and thrills (and hence may have age restrictions), but some are more relaxed and quieter, and have private rooms. **Space** is only likely to be an issue in the peak summer months (June–August), when you should call ahead or turn up as early as possible on the day you want to stay to be sure of a bed. For the most up-to-date information on hostels, head for Use-It (see p.64).

Rådhuspladsen and around

The following place is shown on the map on p.76.
Danhostel Copenhagen City H.C. Andersen's Boulevard 50, Indre By ☎ 33 11 85 85, ⓦ www.danhostel.dk. Bus #5A, or a short walk from Central Station. Brand new trendy and bright HI "design" youth hostel with funky interiors and designer furniture, located in a multistorey building overlooking the harbour and the green copper spires of the city. With 1020 beds (120kr) in four-to-six person rooms (all with en suite bathrooms), it's the largest city hostel in Europe. No curfew.

Vesterbro

The following places are shown on the map on p.96.
City Public Hostel Absalonsgade 8, Vesterbro ☎ 33 31 20 70, ⓦ www.city-public-hostel.dk. Bus #6A or #26. Easy-going and handily placed hostel, ten minutes' walk from Central Station next to the City Museum. There's a large and noisy 68-bed dormitory (110kr) on the lower floor, and less

crowded 6- to 32-bed dorms (some single-sex) on other levels (140k), plus a kitchen and a barbecue out back. 24hr check-in and no curfew. Breakfast is 30kr. Open May–Aug.
Sleep-in-Fact Valdemarsgade 14 ☎ 33 79 67 79, ⓦ www.sleep-in-fact.dk. Bus #6A or #26. In the heart of Vesterbro, this is a sports centre out of season and guests get access to the facilities. The eighty beds (120kr) are divided between two large hall-type rooms, which can get very noisy at times. Reception is open 7am–noon & 3pm–3am. Sheets 30kr, and a small breakfast is included in the price. Open July & Aug only.

Nørrebro

The following places are shown on the map on p.101.
Sleep-In Green Ravnsborggade 18 ☎ 35 37 77 77, ⓦ www.sleep-in-green.dk. Bus #5A or #350S. In the centre of hip Nørrebro, this place has bright 8-, 20- and 38-bed dorms (100k), good all-volunteer staff, and organic snacks sold at the reception/chill-out room. Alcohol is not permitted on the premises.

Extra charge for bedding (30kr) and organic break-fast (40kr). Max age 35. Open June–Oct.

Sleep-In Heaven Struenseegade 7 ☏ 35 35 46 48, ⓦ www.sleepinheaven.com. Bus #250S. Popular hostel next to Assistens Kirkegaard, with two large dorms (130kr), subdivided into four- and eight-bed sections, plus two tiny self-contained "bridal suites" (④), though you still have to share a bathroom. Also has lockers, free Internet access, and takes credit cards. Sheets 30kr, breakfast 40kr. Max age 35. Open all year.

Around Copenhagen

For the locations of the following see the map on p.62.

Ajax Copenhagen Bavnehøj Alle 30, Sydhavnen ☏ 33 21 24 56, Ⓕ 33 25 24 56. Bus #1A, #3A, #10, or Enghave or Sydhavnen S-Tog stations. Set in the clubhouse of Copenhagen's top handball club, in the twilight zone between Vesterbro and Sydhavnen, and offering four basic dorms, from 3-bed (110kr) to 16-bed (80kr), as well as access to a cooking area and outdoor grill. You can also rent tents here (70kr), and camping is possible in the garden. Breakfast costs 30kr, and HI card is required. Open as the Roskilde Festival finishes (see p.146) until mid-Aug.

Danhostel Copenhagen Amager Vejlandsallé 200, Amager ☏ 32 52 27 08, ⓦ www .copenhagenyouthhostel.com. Bus #4A, #30, or Bellacenter metro and a 500m walk. Cheap but basic two-bed (③) and five-bed rooms (110kr), plus a laundry and kitchen. It tends to be crowded and noisy, though there's no curfew. Reception is open 24hr, check-in daily 1–5pm. Closed Dec. Breakfast 45kr, sheets 40kr.

Danhostel Copenhagen Bellahøj Herbergvejen 8, Brønshøj ☏ 38 28 97 15, ⓦ www.youth-hostel .dk. Bus #2A. More homely than its rivals, situated in a residential part of the city (15min by bus from the centre), with two-, four-, six- and fourteen-bed rooms (doubles ③, dorms 110kr). There's a fully equipped kitchen and cheap laundry facili-ties, too. Reception is open 7am–8pm, check-in daily until 5pm, and there's no curfew, although there's a dormitory lockout from 10am–1pm. Breakfast 48kr, sheets 40kr. Closed Jan.

Danhostel Ishøj Strand Ishøj Strandvej 13, Ishøj ☏ 43 53 50 15, ⓦ www.vandrerhjemmet.dk. Ishøj S-tog station, then bus #300S. Five-star HI hostel out near Arken (see p.128) and some beautiful beaches, with spacious four-person rooms and dorms (130kr), plus a decent restaurant, *Noah*. No curfew. Check-in daily 2–6pm.

Campsites

Some of the campsites near Copenhagen are in peerless locations by beaches or in woods, and all are easily accessible by public transport. Some also have **cabins** – usually basic huts without bedding, though pleasant enough – but they're generally fully booked a year in advance. There's little difference in price among them (60–80kr per person per night, plus up to 40kr per tent), nor in facilities: all have laundries, kitchen areas with cookers, also TV rooms, playgrounds and the like.

Absalon Korsdalsvej 132, Rødovre ☏ 36 41 06 00, ⓦ www.camping-absalon.dk. Bus #1A to Avedøre Havnevej, then a 10min walk. Friendly campsite about 9km to the west of the city (exit 24 on E47), with good facilities for campers or those with caravans, and pleasant cabins (❷ for two people) for rent.

Charlottenlund Fort Strandvejen 144, Charlotten-lund ☏ 39 62 36 88, ⓦ www.campingcopenhagen .dk. Bus #14. Situated in the old fort at beautiful Charlottenlund beach, this excellent campsite is the best within striking distance of the city centre (the bus stops right outside), and has sites for camper vans and trailers as well as tents. If you're camping, try to get a pitch around the back, where there's greater protection from the elements. Open mid-May to mid-Sept.

Nærum Ravnebakken, Nærum ☏ 45 80 19 57, ⓦ www.camping-naerum.dk. Jægersborg S-Tog station, then private train to Nærum. Fifteen kilome-tres north of the city centre, in a pleasant setting beside some woods, this site is very family-oriented, with great play areas for kids. Cabins are also availa-ble (390kr for up to 4 people). Open April to mid-Sept.

Tangloppen Ishøj Havn, Ishøj ☏ 43 54 07 67, ⓦ www.fdmcamping.dk/tangloppen. Ishøj S-Tog station, then bus #128. Right next door to Arken (see p.128), and facing onto a lagoon, this is a wonderful option if you want a beach, modern art and not much else – shelter is minimal, and tents take a battering here in bad weather. There's also a cheap café selling grilled food, and a number of cabins and hook-up points for trailers and camper vans. Open April to mid-Oct.

The city

Copenhagen is a very manageable city, and you can walk right across the compact centre in half an hour. The historic core of the city is **Slotsholmen**, originally the site of the twelfth-century castle and now home to the huge royal and governmental complex of Christiansborg. Facing Slotsholmen over the Slotsholmen Kanal is the medieval maze of **Indre By**, the bustling heart of the city, traversed by **Strøget**, the world's longest pedestrianized street, and packed with an abundance of shops, cafés and bars, as well as an eclectic clutch of museums and churches. On the opposite side of Slotsholmen from Indre By, the island of **Christianshavn** is one of the inner city's most relaxed and bohemian areas, and home to the "free city" of Christiania, Copenhagen's famous alternative – lifestyle community. Northeast of Indre By, the fairy-tale palace of **Rosenborg**, one of several royal residences in the city, sits at the heart of the inner city's greenest area – Kongens Have and the lush Botanical Gardens – and within striking distance of two excellent art museums. Abutting Kongens Have, **Frederiksstaden**, Frederik V's royal quarter, is dominated by the huge dome of the Marmorkirke church and centred on the royal palaces of Amalienborg. South of Indre By, close to the town hall and main square, Rådhuspladsen, you'll find the more earthy pleasures of the delightful **Tivoli** pleasure gardens, as well as the excellent **National Museum** and **Glyptoteket** art and sculpture gallery.

If you're willing to venture a little out of the centre, you'll discover distinctive and contrasting districts. To the west, multicultural **Vesterbro**, with its ethnic eateries and trendy nightlife, rubs shoulders with the genteel, villa-lined streets of **Frederiksberg**, where you'll find the tranquil Frederiksberg Have, the city's zoo, and the delights of the Carlsberg brewery visitor centre. To the north of the centre lies the formerly working class but increasingly gentrified district of **Nørrebro**, centred on the trendy bars and restaurants of Sankt Hans Torv and Blågårdsgade; to its east snooty **Østerbro** is home to Copenhagen's old money, as well as the city centre's largest open space, Fælled Park.

Slotsholmen

The small island of **Slotsholmen** is the historical and geographical heart of Copenhagen. It was here, in 1167, that Bishop Absalon founded the castle that became the nucleus of the future city, and it's been the seat of Danish rule ever since. A hotchpotch of sights are crammed into the area, from ruins to state and royal buildings, as well as a bunch of diverse museums. Dominating the island is the austere grey bulk of **Christiansborg Slot**, home to the Danish parliament and the dazzling Royal Reception Rooms. On the northern side of Christiansborg are the delightful **Slotskirke**, and **Thorvaldsens Museum**, a charming collection of the work of the nineteenth-century Danish sculptor. To the south you'll find the **Tøjhusmuseet**, with its world-class collection of guns and cannons, the **Det Kongelige Bibliotek** and its sleek modern extension, the Black Diamond, as well as the newest – and arguably best – of the area's museums, the **Dansk Jødisk**.

Christiansborg Slot and the Royal Riding Ground

The history of Christiansborg (see the box on p.78 for a full account) is inseparably linked to that of Copenhagen. Since 1167, there has been a castle of some sort on this site: the current **Christiansborg Slot** (Ⓦ www.ses.dk /christiansborg), a hefty granite-faced neo-Baroque building, was constructed

The Danish monarchy

Denmark's **monarchy** is one of the oldest in the world, but the royal line of the current monarchs, the **House of Glücksborg**, dates back only to 1853 and the reign of Christian IX, who was nicknamed the "father-in-law of Europe" through having married off his female progeny to various European royals (including Alexandra, who wed Edward VII of England). Denmark's rulers were always men until the country's first and current queen, **Margrethe II** (1940–), came to the throne in 1972. Highly educated and independent, with her own interests and work (as a stage designer and translator), Margrethe – together with her French husband, the **Prince Consort Henrik II** – has done much to make the monarchy more approachable and human, although one aspect of her relaxed public demeanour – her chain-smoking – has come under criticism from some quarters. Prince Henrik, however, was never as popular a figure, and has also come under public scrutiny for his penchant for eating dog-meat, a habit picked up during his childhood in Vietnam, and one which he maintains despite being such an avowed dog-lover that he has published a book of poems eulogising his pet dachshunds. The heir to the throne, **Crown Prince Frederik**, is currently riding a wave of popularity; the eternal bachelor, and once a regular face in the trendy bar scene around Sankt Hans Torv, he married his Tasmanian wife, Crown Princess Mary, in 2005, and they now have a young son, Christian. His younger brother, **Prince Joachim**, divorced his Hong-Kong born wife Princess Alexandra in 2003 – they have two young sons, Nikolai and Felix.

Like their British counterparts, the Danish monarchy have been pretty much stripped of any real power, but are for the most part respected by ordinary Danes – a proudly patriotic lot who, on the whole, see their royal family as a living manifestation of the country's history and tradition. You'll encounter little cynicism towards the monarchy and their burden to the taxpayer, not least because Denmark's royals have reduced the pomp to a minimum. Not that they live the simple life – in addition to the largely ceremonial splendour of the **Royal Reception Rooms** (see p.78), they have several palaces, including their principal home, **Amalienborg** (see p.89), a summer residence at **Fredensborg** (see p.143) and, for visits to Jutland, **Marselisborg** and **Gråsten** palaces.

between 1907 and 1928 around what little that remained of the previous palace, destroyed by fire in 1884. Its illustrious occupants include the Supreme Court, prime minister's office, the Royal Reception Rooms and the **Folketinget** (Ⓦ www.folketinget.dk), home to the Danish Parliament, located in Christiansborg Slot's south wing – to the left as you face the building. If you want to see Danish democracy at work, you can visit the main parliamentary chamber, the Folketingssal, and watch from the public galleries at any time during the surprisingly informal parliamentary sittings (usually from 1pm on Tues & Wed, and from 10am Thurs & Fri; no sessions June–Sept), but you'll get a much better impression of it all by taking one of the free guided tours in English (July to mid-Aug Mon–Fri & Sun 2pm; Oct–May Sun 2pm).

Heading back round to the main entrance and the north wing, look to the right as you go through the passageway for the inconspicuous entrance to the **Ruinerne under Christiansborg** (Ruins under Christiansborg; May–Sept daily 9.30am–3.30pm; Oct–April Tues, Thurs, Sat & Sun 9.30am–3.30pm; 35kr); the foundations from previous castles – Absalon's castle and Københavns Slot – preserved in two massive subterranean rooms. Diagrams and explanations help you decipher the stone and brick jumble of ring walls, foundations, drains and wells, and though it's still fairly easy to lose the plot, it's all surprisingly absorbing, the mood enhanced by the subdued lighting and eerie silence.

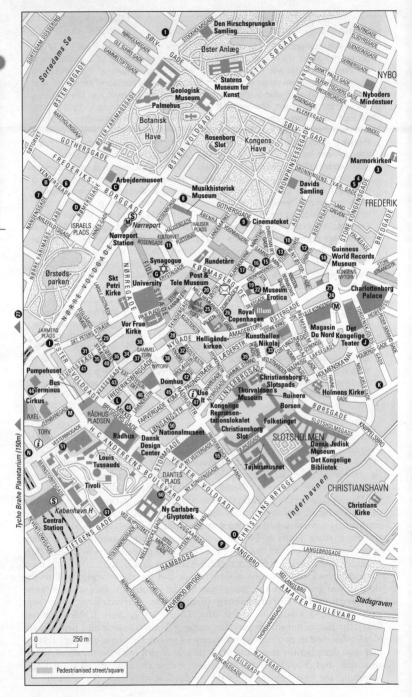

Tycho Brahe Planetarium (150m)

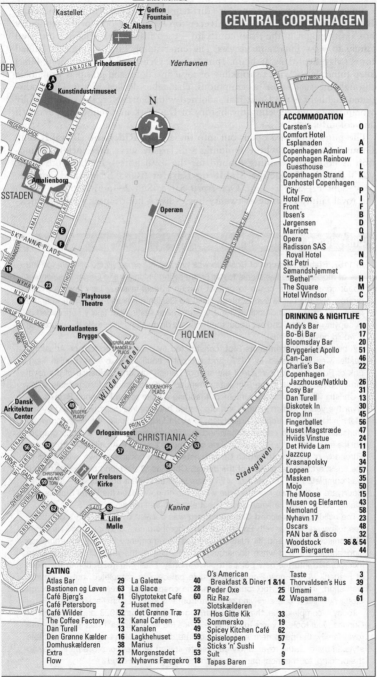

CENTRAL COPENHAGEN

Little Mermaid
Kastellet
Gefion Fountain
St. Albans
ESPLANADEN Frihedsmuseet
Yderhavnen
NYHOLM
Kunstindustrimuseet
N
Amalienborg
Operæn
Playhouse Theatre
Nordatlantens Brygge
HOLMEN
Dansk Arkitektur Center
Orlogsmuseet
CHRISTIANIA
PUSHERSTREET
Vor Frelsers Kirke
Stadsgraven
Kaninø
Lille Mølle

ACCOMMODATION

Carsten's	O
Comfort Hotel Esplanaden	A
Copenhagen Admiral	E
Copenhagen Rainbow Guesthouse	L
Copenhagen Strand	K
Danhostel Copenhagen City	P
Hotel Fox	I
Front	F
Ibsen's	B
Jørgensen	D
Marriott	Q
Opera	J
Radisson SAS Royal Hotel	N
Skt Petri	G
Sømandshjemmet "Bethel"	H
The Square	M
Hotel Windsor	C

DRINKING & NIGHTLIFE

Andy's Bar	10
Bo-Bi Bar	17
Bloomsday Bar	20
Bryggeriet Apollo	51
Can-Can	46
Charlie's Bar	22
Copenhagen Jazzhouse/Natklub	26
Cosy Bar	31
Dan Turell	13
Diskotek In	30
Drop Inn	45
Fingerbøllet	56
Huset Magstræde	47
Hviids Vinstue	24
Det Hvide Lam	11
Jazzcup	8
Krasnapolsky	34
Loppen	57
Masken	35
Mojo	50
The Moose	15
Musen og Elefanten	43
Nemoland	58
Nyhavn 17	23
Oscars	48
PAN bar & disco	32
Woodstock	36 & 54
Zum Biergarten	44

EATING

Atlas Bar	29	La Galette	40	O's American Breakfast & Diner	1 &14
Bastionen og Løven	63	La Glace	28	Peder Oxe	25
Café Bjørg's	41	Glyptoteket Café	60	Riz Raz	42
Café Petersborg	2	Huset med det Grønne Træ	37	Slotskælderen Hos Gitte Kik	33
Café Wilder	52	Kanal Cafeen	55	Sommersko	19
The Coffee Factory	12	Kanalen	49	Spicey Kitchen Café	62
Dan Turell	13	Lagkhuset	59	Spiseloppen	57
Den Grønne Kælder	16	Marius	6	Sticks 'n' Sushi	7
Domhuskælderen	38	Morgenstedet	53	Sult	9
Extra	21	Nyhavns Færgekro	18	Tapas Baren	5
Flow	27				

Taste	3
Thorvaldsen's Hus	39
Umami	4
Wagamama	61

Nowadays, the royal presence at Christiansborg is limited to the **Kongelige Repræsentationslokaler** (Royal Reception Rooms) – look for the red sentry box on the right in the main courtyard – used mainly as a place for the royal family to wow important visitors. The entertaining English-language guided tours (May–Sept daily at 11am, 1pm & 3pm; Oct–April Tues–Sun 3pm; 60kr) keep things lively with a sprinkling of royal anecdotes and gossip as you amble through the succession of sumptuous, chandelier-decked rooms. The undisputed highlight is the Great Hall, adorned with Bjørn Nørgaard's wonderfully vibrant tapestries depicting the history of Denmark in a refreshingly modern and colourful way.

The inner courtyard opens out into the elegant **Ridebane** (Royal Riding Ground Complex), whose buildings still largely serve their original function as home and training ground for the royal horses. In the south wing, you'll find the **Kongelige Stalde og Kareter** (Royal Stables and Coaches; May–Sept Fri–Sun 2–4pm; Oct–April Sat & Sun 2–4pm; 20kr), in which the royal family's retinue of twenty horses live a life of luxury within unex-

Christiansborg through the ages

In 1167, **Bishop Absalon** of Roskilde was granted the small village of Havn (on the site of modern Indre By) by his foster brother King Valdemar the Great. Absalon set about constructing a castle to protect herring traders in the village from Wendish pirates, and the castle subsequently ensured Danish domination of Øresund and a large part of the Baltic until, in 1369, a strong Hanseatic fleet finally succeeded in occupying the town and set about methodically dismantling the castle to ensure that it would never be rebuilt.

A new castle, **Københavns Slot**, constructed by the church to replace Absalon's castle, was completed in 1417, and promptly confiscated by the Danish king, Erik of Pomerania, who made it the seat of Danish rule and residence of the royal family. Over the years, the Slot was extended and modernized innumerable times – Christian IV completely refurbished it, adding a spire to the infamous Blue Tower. Over the years, foreign visitors and dignitaries became increasingly amused by the Slot's mishmash of architectural styles; to avoid further ridicule, the newly crowned Christian VI had the castle demolished in 1730, replacing it with a much grander palace inspired by the Rococo palaces of France's Louis XIV. Architects from all over Europe were called in to furnish **Christiansborg**, as it became known, with some of the finest art and decoration of the period. Christian VI died long before the palace was completed in 1766, and only 28 years later, in 1794, it burnt down – the Outer Courtyard with its two low, Baroque wings (which now house the Royal Stables, the Riding School and the small Court Theatre) are all that remain.

The building of a **second Christiansborg** was delayed by the country's dire position following the war with England and the bombardment of Copenhagen in 1807. The palace square and its ruins were used as emergency housing for homeless Copenhageners, and when construction finally began, the walls of the ruins were incorporated into the new palace to save money. Finally, in 1828, during the reign of Frederik VI, the new Romanesque-style palace was completed, but its lifetime was short: in 1884 it, too, burnt down. The chapel – the present Christiansborgs Slotskirke– is the only surviving structure from this second Christiansborg.

Today's complex, the **third Christiansborg**, dates from 1928 and the reign of Christian X; it took 21 years to complete, since the three parties it was to house – the royal family, the parliament and the supreme court – couldn't agree on a suitable style. In the end, the royal family decided to stay at Amalienborg (see p.89), leaving the building, for the most part, to parliament and supreme court.

pectedly lavish quarters decorated with pillars, vaulted ceilings, and walls and cribs of Tuscan marble – apparently not even the king's own chambers were this extravagant. The Harness Room contains a motley collection of old riding uniforms, harnesses and horse portraits. Beyond the stables is the royal family's collection of coaches, carriages and cars. Incongruously situated above the Royal Stables, the **Teatermuseet I Hofteatret** (Theatre Museum; Tues & Thurs 11am–3pm, Wed 11am–5pm, Sat & Sun 1–4pm; 30kr; Ⓦ www.teatermuseet.dk) occupies the charming former Court Theatre of 1767. Each room explores a particular theme of Danish theatrical history – opera, pantomime, ballet and drama – and though the exhibitions aren't particularly captivating (with few labels in English), the **auditorium** itself is an unexpected gem, its deep, sloping stage, plush velvet upholstery, elegant royal boxes and beautifully decorated oriental ceiling evoking an atmosphere of theatrical excitement.

Around Christiansborgs Slotsplads

Back on Christiansborg Slotsplads, the graceful domed building tacked on the northwest end of the palace is **Christiansborgs Slotskirke** (Sun noon–4pm, and daily noon–4pm during Easter, July and third week of Oct; free; Ⓦ www.ses.dk/christiansborg), all that remains of the second Christiansborg, which burnt down in 1884. Designed by C.F. Hansen, one of the most important Danish Golden Age architects, it's a beautiful example of the simple Neoclassical architecture typical of the period. The lavish custard-and-cream-coloured marble stucco interior is topped off by Thorvaldsen's (see below) magnificent angel frieze, which encircles the dome. At the southern end of Christiansborg Slotsplads, the flamboyant red-brick building with the distinctive gabled green copper roof and fanciful spire formed out of four entwined dragons' tails is the seventeenth-century **Børsen** (Stock Exchange) – centrepiece of Christian IV's plan to make Copenhagen the centre of trade in the Baltic region. It's now owned by the Chamber of Commerce and is not open to the public.

Tucked behind Christiansborg's Slotskirke, **Thorvaldsen's Museum** (Tues–Sun 10am–5pm; July & Aug guided tours in English Sun 3pm; 20kr, free on Wed; Ⓦ www.thorvaldsensmuseum.dk) is a refreshing antidote to the pomp of Slotsholmen's historical heavyweights. The Neoclassical building, with its striking ochre-coloured facade, was built in 1839 to house the enormous collection of works and personal possessions (and the body) of Denmark's only sculptor of note, Bertel Thorvaldsen (1770–1844), who actually spent much of his life in Rome. While none of the pieces is famous in its own right, the collection makes for an enjoyable wander amid the roll call of gods and mortals – Byron, Christian IV and Napoleon among others – set off beautifully by the richly coloured walls, mosaic floors and finely painted ceilings. The excellent free audioguides bring it all to life. The hall to the left of the entrance is stuffed with the plaster models of some of Thorvaldsen's most important commissions – hulking homages to the likes of Pius VII and Maximilian I – but the succession of small rooms surrounding the inner courtyard where the sculptor is buried are far more rewarding. Highlights include the enchanting *Cupid and Psyche* (room 2) and **Jason with the Golden Fleece** (room 5) – the piece that made his name. The rest of the museum is largely taken up with Thorvaldsen's considerable, but unexceptional, collection of antiquities – ancient Egyptian artefacts, Greek coins and pottery and Etruscan gold jewellery – as well as some of his possessions; there's also a short film about his life screened on the lower ground floor.

South of Christiansborg

Walking from Christiansborg Slotsplads past the main entrance to the Folketing and along Tøjhusgade you come to the exhaustive **Tøjhusmuseet** (Royal Danish Arsenal Museum; Tues–Sun noon–4pm; 40kr; free Wed; ⓦ www.thm .dk), appropriately housed in Christian IV's old Tøjhus (Arms House). Though unlikely to excite unless you're a fan of military hardware, the sheer scope of the paraphernalia on display is undeniably impressive – it's reputedly the world's finest collection of eighteenth- and nineteenth-century armaments. Cannons (some dating back to the fifteenth century), tanks and artillery line both sides of the enormous **Cannon Hall** – a handsome sight in itself, with its succession of whitewashed arches and expanse of cobbled floor. On the first floor, the even longer **Armoury Hall** displays endless rows of swords and firearms, with just the odd suit of armour for relief.

Adjacent to the Tøjhusmuseet, the **Bibliotekshaven** (Royal Library Garden; entrance on Tøjhusgade) is a peaceful haven and a great spot for a picnic. At its far end stands the red-brick, Venetian-inspired **Det Kongelige Bibliotek** (Royal Library; entrance from the Black Diamond extension on the waterfront); the left side of the building is home to the excellent new **Dansk Jødisk Museum** (Danish Jewish Museum; June–Aug Tues–Sun 10am–5pm; Sept–May Tues–Fri 1pm–4pm, Sat & Sun noon–5pm; 40kr). With an exhibition space designed by Daniel Libeskind, it recounts the largely peaceful co-existence of Jews and Danes in Denmark for over four centuries, and takes as its inspiration the concept of *Mitzvah* or "good deed", as seen in one of the few Jewish success stories of World War II: the escape from imminent deportation to concentration camps of seven thousand Jews, helped across the Øresund to safety in neutral Sweden by the Danish Resistance, the Danish people and, reputedly, several German officers who turned a blind eye. It's a fitting and, at times, moving memorial to this proud period in Denmark's history, moving deftly from the events of 1943 to broader themes such as the history of Jewish immigration to Denmark and the concept of "homeland", all amply illuminated by personal histories, possessions and a beautiful array of paraphernalia used in Jewish rituals.

From here, walking around the right side of the building takes you to the waterfront and the library's stunning black-granite and glass extension, known as **Den Sorte Diamant** (Black Diamond: building Mon–Sat 8am–7pm, free; library & exhibitions Mon–Fri 10am–7pm, Sat 10am–5pm 30kr; ⓦ www .kb.dk). The collections are for members only, but the wonderful glass-walled foyer with harbour views and soaring, light-filled atrium is open to all and includes a concert hall, bookshop, restaurant, café and exhibition space – head up the escalator for the best views.

Indre By

The heart of both medieval and modern Copenhagen, **Indre By** ("inner city") is where the city began, as the former site of the small, marshy fishing village of Havn, whose fortunes were transformed by the arrival of Bishop Absalon in 1167. Although it was subsequently ravaged by a series of fires and bombarded by first the Swedish and then the British, the medieval town's tangle of tiny streets, squares and ancient churches survived and is still very much in evidence today. Indre By is the hub of the city's day-to-day activity and its main shopping district – a maze of lively, attractive streets and squares, made all the more enjoyable for the fact that its two main thoroughfares are pedestrianized and wide enough to accommodate the inevitable hordes of shoppers. The first is **Strøget**, the colloquial name (it's not on any street signs) given to the series of connecting streets that run across Indre By from Rådhuspladsen in the west to Kongens Nytorv in the east. The other main street, **Købmagergade**, leaves Strøget at Højbro Plads, heading north towards Nørreport Station via Kultorvet square.

Indre By also has its fair share of historic buildings, churches and museums. Foremost among these is the wonderfully quirky **Rundetårn**, while, close by, the eclectic collections of the **Musikhistorisk Museum**, **Arbejdermuseet** (Workers' Museum), **Post and Tele Museum** and **Erotica Museum** make for enlightening diversions from shopping. At some point or another, most visitors also make it to **Nyhavn**, a bevy of colourful restaurants and bars in a picture-postcard canalside setting that draws tourists by the boatload.

Along Frederiksberggade to the Latin Quarter

Heading east from Rådhuspladsen, **Frederiksberggade** is the first – and tacki-est – of the series of streets that make up Strøget, but you soon reach Kattesun-det on the left, which leads to the altogether trendier area centred on **Larsb-jørnstræde**, one of the liveliest streets in the city, overflowing with hip new and used clothes shops, independent music stores, secondhand bookshops and chic cafés. Shopping done, it's a few minutes' walk along Studiestræde or Skt Peders Stræde to the more rarefied atmosphere of the **Latin Quarter**, home to **Copenhagen University**, founded in 1475 to train Catholic priests. The impressive neo-Gothic main building, dating from 1836, is now used mainly for administration – statues of the university's most distinguished professors, includ-ing Nobel prizewinner Niels Bohr, who discovered the structure of the atom, stand in front. Immediately south of the university on the peaceful, cobbled Frue Plads, the dusky pink **Vor Frue Kirke** (daily 8am–5pm) is surprisingly modest, given its status as Copenhagen's cathedral. Built in 1829 to a design by the ubiquitous C.F. Hansen, town planner and architect, it's largely unremark-able, though you might want to pop inside to see the weighty figure of Christ and the apostles – some crafted by Bertel Thorvaldsen (see p.79), others by his pupils.

Across from the university on the other side of Nørregade, **Skt Petri Kirke** (May–Nov Tues–Fri 11am–3pm, Sat noon–3pm; ⓦ www.sankt-petri.dk) is one of the city's best-preserved medieval buildings, dating from the mid-fifteenth century. The church's most interesting feature is the atmospheric Italian-style sepulchral chapel from 1683 (25kr); its numerous tombs and crypts are the rest-ing place of many prominent Danish members of the court and political figures from the period of absolute monarchy, including the architect Neils Eigtved.

East to Højbro Plads

Back on Strøget, the next section, heading northeast as far as the bustling square of Højbro Plads, comprises the busy shopping stretches of **Nygade**, **Vimmel-skaftet** and **Amagertorv**. At the junction with Nørregade, Strøget is flanked by the busy squares of **Gammeltorv** and **Nytorv** ("old" and "new" squares), two large, ancient spaces that mark the site of the first marketplace in Havn, when it was still a fishing village. The wide, gently sloping expanse and presence of the city's C.F. Hansen-designed **Domhus** (Law Courts), with its suitably forbid-ding row of Neoclassical columns, lend a faintly Roman whiff to Nytorv, while Gammeltorv's most striking feature is the **Caritas Fountain**, dating from 1608. Ten years older than the similarly risqué – but much more famous – Manneken Pis in Brussels, the fountain's water flows from Caritas's breasts and from the little boy at her feet taking a leak. Continue east down Nygade, then left just

△ Street performers on Amagertorv

before reaching Helligåndskirken down cobbled Valkendorfsgade and through Kringlegangen to reach **Gråbrødretorv**, a charming, café-lined cobbled square that's a favourite spot with locals. Back on Strøget, **Helligåndskirken** (Church of the Holy Ghost; Mon–Fri noon–4pm), founded in 1296 as part of a Catholic monastery of the same name, is one of the oldest churches in the city, though largely rebuilt after the Great Fire of 1728. Entrance is through a beautifully carved sandstone portal dating back to 1620; inside, look out for an impressive altarpiece donated by Christian VI depicting the ascension of Christ. Past the church, at the busy junction with Købmagergade, **Højbro Plads** is always lively, with its two perennially popular cafés and abundance of street entertainers and buskers. To the right of the statue of Absalon is the delightful canalside stretch of **Gammel Strand** ("Old Beach"), its row of cafés and restaurants with outside tables and views over the canal are a great spot for lunch.

Along Købmagergade to Kultorvet

From Højbro Plads you can either continue east along the Østergade section of Strøget to Kongens Nytorv – a route described opposite – or head north up Indre By's other main shopping street, **Købmagergade**. At no. 24, a red-carpeted, peepshow-style entrance announces the **Museum Erotica** (May–Sept daily 10am–11pm; Oct–April Mon–Thurs & Sun 11am–8pm, Fri & Sat 10am–10pm; 89kr; Ⓦ www.museumerotica.dk), part shrine to all things erotic, part historical romp through sexual history – everything from Indian miniature paintings of the Kama Sutra to *Playboy* pin-ups. Towards the end, the erotic is pretty much replaced by the pornographic, with a selection of 1970s blue movies providing a hardcore finale. More prosaic exhibits can be found nearby at Købmagergade 37, in the **Post & Tele Museum** (Tues & Thurs–Sat 10am–5pm, Wed 10am–8pm, Sun noon–4pm; 40kr, free on Wed; Ⓦ www .ptt-museum.dk), which charts the history of communication in Denmark, from Christian IV's 1624 decree establishing the Danish Royal Post Office to modern-day mobile phones. On the whole, it does a good job of bringing its rather dry subject matter to life with a well-displayed collection of old telephones, radio equipment, mock-ups of old post offices, philatelic displays and historical artefacts; you can pick up a free English translation of the display boards from the desk on the second floor. The museum has a lovely, rooftop café.

One of the city's most intriguing landmarks, the 42-metre-high **Rundetårn** (Round Tower; June–Aug Mon–Sat 10am–8pm, Sun noon–8pm; Sept–May Mon–Sat 10am–5pm, Sun noon–5pm; 25kr; ⓦwww.rundetaarn.dk) looms two-thirds of the way up Købmagergade. It was built by Christian IV as part of the **Trinitatis** complex, which combined three important facilities for seventeenth-century scholars and students: an astronomical observatory, a church and a university library – the tower functioned both as observatory lookout and as the Trinitatis church tower. It's still a functioning observatory, and the public can view the night sky through the astronomical telescope in the winter period (mid-Oct to mid–March Tues & Wed 7–10pm). Inside, a wide cobbled ramp spirals its way to the top for a wonderful view of the hive of medieval streets below and the city beyond.

The short stretch of Købmagergade from Rundetårn to Kultorvet is unremarkable; just north of Kultorvet, at Åbenrå 30, the thoroughly entertaining **Musikhistorisk Museum** (Musical History Museum; May–Sept Mon–Wed & Fri–Sun 1–3.30pm; Oct–April Mon, Wed, Sat & Sun 1–3.30pm; free; ⓦwww .musikhistoriskmuseum.dk) has an impressive quantity of musical instruments and sound-producing devices spanning the globe and the last thousand years. There are recordings of most of the instruments to listen to (helpful with some of the odder ones, where it's a mystery even which end the sound comes out) and two rooms where children can play with sounds.

If you've made it this far, you might want to press on a little further, across traffic-heavy Nørre Voldgade, to Rømersgade 22, where the **Arbejdermuseet** (Workers' Museum; daily 10am–4pm, Nov–June closed Mon; 50kr; ⓦwww .arbejdermuseet.dk), housed in the former Worker's Hall, provides an engrossing guide to working-class life in Copenhagen from the 1870s onwards. The exhibition relies heavily on reconstructed scenes chronicling the workers' living and working conditions – a 1930s Depression-era apartment (complete with suitably wretched looking mannequins), shops selling consumer durables of the day and so on; the 1950s apartment with family photos, newspapers and TVs showing newsreels of the time is a far brighter affair, its occupants clearly benefiting from the influx of Marshall Plan American funding to a battered postwar Europe. The ground floor and basement are given over to the shop and temporary exhibitions on topics ranging from Nelson Mandela to the Paris Commune.

East to Kongens Nytorv and Nyhavn

Back at Højbro Plads, head east off the square along the alley named Lille Kirkestræde and then left to reach the grandiose **Skt Nikolaj Kirke**, now deconsecrated and functioning as **Kunsthallen Nikolaj** (daily noon–5pm; 20kr, Wed free), a gallery given over to temporary exhibitions of contemporary multimedia art. The final section of Strøget – **Østergade** – is the most exclusive section of the entire thoroughfare; off to the left, look out for the quaint alleyway and courtyard of **Pistolstræde**, with its crooked and colourful medieval timber buildings housing a couple of tiny boutiques. Østergade soon opens out onto the spacious grandeur of **Kongens Nytorv**, which has an equestrian statue of its creator, Christian V, at its centre; in summer weary shoppers head for the outdoor seats of the square's high-ceilinged, glass-fronted cafés; in winter, for the cosy dens selling *gløgg* mulled wine and *æble-skiver* (see p.41). The southern end of the square is dominated by the grand late-nineteenth-century **Det Kongelige Teater** (Royal Theatre; ⓦwww.kgl-teater.dk; see p.111). Next door, **Charlottenborg Palace** (daily 10am–5pm, plus Wed until 7pm; ⓦwww.charlottenborg-art.dk) is home to the Royal Academy – the spacious, light rooms of the exhibition hall (30kr) at the back display eclectic displays of contemporary art, architecture and decorative art.

Heading off the northeast side of Kongens Nytorv, picture-postcard **Nyhavn** ("new harbour") – created in 1671 as a canal leading from the city's main port to Kongens Nytorv – is mostly known for its sunny northern side, with a long row of bars, cafés and restaurants set in brightly coloured and picturesque gabled houses, some dating back as far as 1681 – Hans Christian Andersen lived at varying times in nos. 18, 20 & 67.

Christianshavn

Facing Indre By and Slotsholmen across the waters of Inderhavnen, and linked to them by Knippelsbro bridge, is the charming island of **Christianshavn**. Nicknamed "Little Amsterdam" on account of its pretty canals, cobbled streets and old Dutch-style houses with brightly painted facades, it's a laid-back area with a cosy, neighbourhood feel, and is a pleasant spot to hang out and watch the boats meander up and down the canals. Built on land reclaimed by Christian IV in the early 1600s, the area served two purposes: to protect the city from attack (hence the line of defensive fortifications) and to provide housing for Dutch merchants and local shipbuilding workers. The island's sights are, for the most part, low-key, but you won't want to miss **Vor Frelsers Kirke**, with its magnificent spire, the "free city" of **Christiania**, or a peep at the new **Operæn** opera house. The central Christianshavns Torv is the district's hub and a natural starting point – the metro station is here, as are stops for all buses crossing Christianshavn.

Strandgade and the Wilders Canal

From Christianshavns Torv, crossing the Wilders Canal and walking up Torvegade takes you to **Strandgade**, whose eastern side is home to some of the island's oldest houses. On the waterfront side at Gammel dock is the **Dansk Arkitektur Center** (Danish Architecture Centre; daily 10am–5pm; free; ⓦwww.dac.dk). The temporary exhibitions here tend to the very special-ized, but the excellent bookshop stocks Denmark's largest selection of titles on architecture and design (most in English) – the place to get your glossy coffee-table book on the likes of Arne Jacobsen or Verner Panton (see box on p.117). From here, head east along Bådsmandsstræde to the delightful **Wilders Canal** – Christianshavn at its most Dutch – bristling and tinkling with the bobbing masts and halyards of its many sailing boats. The only sight here is the **Orlogsmuseet** (Royal Danish Naval Museum; Tues–Sun noon–4pm; 40kr, free on Weds; ⓦwww.orlogsmuseet.dk), on the corner of Bådsmandsstræde ("Boatswain's Alley") and Overgaden Oven Vandet. It's devoted to the illustri-ous history of the Danish Navy and boasts a collection of four hundred **ship models** – some dating back to the sixteenth century – as well as an assortment of uniforms, weapons, nautical instruments, maritime art and detailed models of sea battles.

Just south of the Royal Naval Museum, soaring skywards through the trees on Skt Annæ Gade, is the unmistakable copper-and-gold spire of Christianshavn's famous landmark, **Vor Frelsers Kirke** (April–Aug Mon–Sat

11am–4.30pm, Sun noon–4.30pm; Sept–March Mon–Sat 11am–3.30pm, Sun noon–4.30pm; tower closed Nov–March and on wet and windy days; @www .vorfrelserskirke.dk). It was completed in 1696, though the lavish **spire**, with its helter-skelter exterior staircase and large golden globe carrying a three-metre Jesus waving a flag, was added to the otherwise plain exterior in the mid-eighteenth century. If you've a head for heights, you might want to climb it (20kr), an adrenalin-rushing spiral of four hundred slanted steps (slippery after rain) gradually becoming smaller and smaller; the reward is a great view of Copenhagen and beyond. Inside, the Baroque extravagance reaches its peak in the showy altar; look out too for the two stucco elephants appearing to hold up the gigantic organ – the animal became the symbol of the nation's highest order, the Order of the Elephant.

Christiania

Stretching for almost a kilometre along either side of the moat and old ramparts that flank the eastern side of the island, the remarkable "Free City" of **Christiania** (@www.christiania.org) is living proof of Copenhagen's liberal social traditions. Ever since a group of young and homeless people colonized the complex of disused military barracks here in the spring of 1971, the area has excited controversy, sympathy and admiration in equal amounts. Declared a "free city" by its residents later that year with the aim of operating autonomously from Copenhagen proper, it inevitably became best known outside Denmark for its open selling of hash on "Pusherstreet", while its continued existence on some of Copenhagen's finest real estate has fuelled one of the longest-running debates in Danish society. Christiania has had a rollercoaster ride at the hands of successive governments, who either largely left it alone or tried to bring this city within a city under the municipal machinery. Its **future** remains in the balance under the current right-wing government despite the community's radical scaling-down of its hash booths on Pusherstreet in 2004. The latest threat comes from proposed new property laws that would render its policy of collective use (no one owns their own home) illegal, so opening the door for property developers and what residents see as inevitable gentrification.

It's best to head for the **main entrance** on Prinsessegade (the others are on the corner of Prinsessegade and Bådsmandsstræde and at Bådsmandsstræde 43), which leads straight into the heart of the area; at the small shack on the right, 50m or so in, you can pick up the excellent *Christiania Guide* (5kr). Don't be intimidated by the idea of wandering around by yourself: naturally, the area has a grungy, offbeat feel and you'll get more than the odd whiff of dope, but the atmosphere is welcoming and relaxed (cars aren't allowed). It's worth joining one of the **guided tours** (July & Aug daily 3pm; Sept–June Sat & Sun 3pm; 90mins; 30kr; booking advisable in summer ☎32 57 96 70) that leave from the main entrance. Conducted by residents, they're a good introduction to the nooks, crannies and workings of this rather complex community. Covering about 85 acres, Christiania spreads out in a loose network of unpaved paths and small green open spaces on both sides of Christian IV's old moat between Christianshavn and Amager (a bridge, Dyssebroen, connects the two sides), many of its ramshackle homes hugging the reedy water's edge in a picture of rural charm. It's a peculiar mix of huge old barracks and warehouses – livened up with vivid murals and now housing community projects like work-shops, art centres and crèches – and small, colourful homes. The best place to start your wanderings is in the large converted warehouse to the right of the main entrance – the **Loppe building** – whose music venue, *Loppen* (see p.113), and highly-rated *Spiseloppen* restaurant (see p.106) have ensured its fame beyond the free city's walls. It also houses Gallopperiet, Christiania's art gallery and information centre (Tues–Sun noon–5pm), and the *Info* café and craft shop. Continuing straight ahead, you soon come to the closest Christiania gets to a commercial centre – **Carl Madsen Plads** – a small square lined with stalls selling snacks, cheap clothing, CDs, jewellery, incense and the like. The square marks the start of the once infamous **Pusherstreet**, now only really noteworthy for the *Sunshine Bakery*, a good spot to pick up a picnic lunch. Push on instead to the small square on the right, crowded in summer with the chilled-out clientele of *Nemoland* (see p.110), Christiania's most popular bar.

Holmen and Operæn

Continuing north from Christiania along Prinsessegade brings you to the area of **Holmen** – five reclaimed islands, formerly home to the old naval station founded by Frederik III, and now housing several prestigious art and film schools. Occupying a prime waterfront spot at the northern end of Philip de Langes Allé, Copenhagen's new **Operæn** (opera house), opened in 2005 was designed by Henning Larsen and funded by Denmark's richest man, the shipping magnate Maersk Mc-Kinney Møller. It's an undeniably striking – if not immediately appealing – building, completely dominated by the immense slab of the 158-metre-long **"floating" roof**, which extends 32m beyond the orb-like foyer and stepped entrance plaza out to the water's edge like a giant diving board. You're free to wander round the plaza and foyer (daily 10am–9pm, closes to non-ticket holders 4hrs before performances), but to fully appreciate the building's unique architecture, including the lavish auditorium with its gold-leaf ceiling, you'll have to get tickets for a performance (see p.111) or join a **guided tour** (Sat & Sun 9.30am & 4.30pm; 100kr).

Rosenborg, Frederiksstaden and Kastellet

There's quite a contrast between the narrow, tangled streets of Indre By and the open parks and boulevards of the more modern areas on the northeastern side of the city centre, which owe their character to two royal builders. The first, Christian IV, built the fanciful **Rosenborg Slot**, once protected to the west by the old city ramparts which are now converted into parks housing the glorious cornucopia of the **Botanisk Have** (Botanical Gardens), and the fortress of **Kastellet** to the north. The second, Frederik V, gave his name to the district he created, **Frederiksstaden** – a sumptuous royal quarter boasting proud aristocratic monuments such as the **Marmorkirken** and the palaces of **Amalienborg**. Some of the city's main art museums are also found here. The huge **Statens Museum for Kunst** (Royal Museum of Fine Art) and the fine **Hirschsprungske Samling** (Hirschsprung Collection) are major draws for art lovers, while the **Kunstindustrimuseet** (Danish Museum for Decorative Art) is a must-see if you're interested in Danish design.

Rosenborg Slot and around

Rising enchantingly from the carefully manicured lawns of Kongens Have, the Dutch-Renaissance palace of **Rosenborg Slot** (May & Sept–Oct daily 10am–4pm; June–Aug daily 10am–5pm; Nov–April Tues–Sun 11am–2pm; 65kr, joint ticket with Amalienborg 80kr; ⓦwww.rosenborg-slot.dk) looks like a setting for one of Hans Christian Andersen's more romantic tales. Surrounded by a moat and decorated with spires and towers, this playful, red-brick palace was built by Christian IV in 1606 as a summer residence, and was where he drew his final breath more than forty years later. Over the centuries it has become a storehouse for various royal collections of furniture, jewels, regalia, armoury, paintings and porcelain. Devoted to Christian IV, the first section of the **ground floor** is a relatively dark affair – oak-panelled rooms, royal busts and grand paintings of sea battles abound. Further along, the heavy panelling gives way to stuccoed nymphs and marble, and the atmosphere is lightened by some bizarre oddities that tickled the fancies of various monarchs – the highlight is a seventeenth-century armchair with hidden tentacles in the armrests that would grab the wrists of anyone unlucky enough to sit in it. The victim would then be doused in water before being released to the sound of a small trumpet. The **first floor**, covering Frederiks IV to VII, is a labyrinth of rooms stuffed with largely uninspiring pieces of furniture or artwork, while the **second floor** is dominated by the Long Hall, its walls covered with enormous tapestries from 1690 showing Christian V's victories in the Scanian War of 1675–79. In the **basement**, the Green Cabinet is home to a sumptuous collection of regalia and jewellery, while a further flight of stairs leads down through massive steel doors into the **Treasury**, containing hundreds of gold items and the fabulous silver Oldenborg Horn, allegedly dating from 989 AD, as well as the crown jewels.

Adjacent to the slot lies central Copenhagen's oldest and prettiest park, **Kongens Have** (Royal Gardens; daily 6am–sunset; free), known also as Rosenborgs Slotshave. From the palace, it's a short stroll down to the park's southern entrance on Gothersgade. On the eastern edge of Kongens Have, on Kronprinsessegade, the exquisite **Davids Samling** Islamic collection (Tues & Thurs–Sun 1–4pm, Wed 10am–4pm; free; ⓦwww.davidmus.dk) is an Aladdin's cave of Persian, Arabian and Indian antiques, some dating back to the sixth century, with everything from delicate embroidered silks and savage-looking daggers to illuminated manuscripts and Korans. The museum is closed for refurbishment until June 2008.

Botanisk Have and the Geologisk Museum
Across Øster Voldgade from Kongens Have, the glorious **Botanisk Have** (Botanical Gardens; summer daily 8.30am–6pm; winter Tues–Sun 8.30am–4pm; free; ⓦwww.botanic-garden.ku.dk) make for a lovely wander around the small coniferous forest, rock gardens and waterfalls populated by herons, ducks and freshwater terrapins, with further botanic thrills provided by the circular **palmehus** (palm house; daily 10am–3pm), **kaktushus** (cactus house; Wed, Sat & Sun 1–2pm) and the **orkidehuset** (orchid house; Wed, Sat & Sun 2–3pm). At the northeastern corner of Botanisk Have, by the junction of Sølvgade and Øster Voldgade, the **Geologisk Museum** (Geological Museum; Tues–Sun 1–4pm; 25kr, free Wed; ⓦwww.geological-museum.dk) is really only of interest to mineral enthusiasts; apart from its collection of **meteorites** hailing from a major fall thousands of years ago in Greenland, the collection is unexceptional.

Statens Museum for Kunst and Den Hirschsprungske Samling
Across Sølvgade from the Geologisk Museum, in the southeastern corner of Østre Anlæg park, the **Statens Museum for Kunst** (Royal Museum of Fine Arts; Tues & Thurs–Sun 10am–5pm, Wed 10am–8pm; free; 70kr for special exhibitions; ⓦwww.smk.dk) is a huge, sprawling affair housed in two contrasting wings: the older Dahlerup Building and the bright new wing. The stairs in the entrance hall of the **Dahlerup Building** lead to an enormous collection of European works from the fourteenth to nineteenth centuries, including rooms devoted variously to the almost photographic images of the Dutch and

Flemish masters, Italian religious paintings (including a number by Tintoretto), and a smattering of lesser-known Brueghels, Rembrandts and Van Dycks. The **new wing** is spread over five floors, its light and spacious design an excellent backdrop for an extensive, if rather lightweight, collection of contemporary art. Highlights include the colourful post-surrealist abstractions of the CoBrA movement (made up of mid-twentieth-century artists from *CO*penhagen, *BR*ussels and *A*msterdam – hence the name), an enormous, quirky photographic self-portrait by Gilbert & George and, in an adjacent room, Dane Øyvid Nygaard's impressive *The Light Conductor* sculpture, reminiscent of the Silver Surfer superhero. There's also an important collection of modernist works, including a small selection of the Danish artist Asger Jorn's dramatic canvases, examples of works from twentieth-century movements such as Surrealism and Expressionism, and works by Picasso and Matisse.

Crossing Østre Anlæg park from the Fine Arts museum brings you to the back of the Neoclassical pavilion housing the **Den Hirschsprungske Samling** (Hirschsprung Collection; Mon & Wed–Sun 11am–4pm; 35kr, Wed free; Ⓦwww.hirschsprung.dk), the best collection of nineteenth-century Danish art in the city. The works were donated to the state in 1902 by second-generation German-Jewish immigrant, tobacco magnate and patron of struggling Danish artists, Heinrich Hirschsprung – a large portrait of him smoking a cigar hangs in the entrance hall. Following the collection clockwise takes you through all the major periods of nineteenth-century Danish art. The **Golden Age** (roughly 1810–40) is initially reflected through a collection of pieces by C.W. Eckersberg, one of Denmark's first professional artists, whose work was rooted firmly in romantic and idealistic traditions (*Woman Before a Mirror* is typical, with a poetic picture of a flesh-and-blood Venus de Milo); there are also some gentle Danish landscapes by his students, such as Christen Købke and William Bendz. Room 15 contains one of the gallery's most popular paintings, Harold Slott-Møller's *Spring*, a simple but engaging painting of a young girl, her hair garlanded with yellow flowers. The haunting symbolism of the almost pre-Raphaelite paintings of Ejnar Nielsen and Vilhelm Hammershøi takes centre stage in room 19 – Nielsen's *The Blind Girl* is particularly melancholy. Room 20 contains a large collection of works by painters from Skagen – a town on the northernmost tip of the country renowned for its bewitching light – some of whom Hirschsprung personally supported.

Frederiksstaden and around

Bordered by the harbourfront to the east and cut in two by the broad sweep of Bredgade, the **Frederiksstaden** district to the east of Rosenborg was commissioned by Frederik V and designed by Danish architect Nicolai Eigtved as a royal quarter fit for a noble elite. Rising majestically on the western side of Bredgade is the large green dome – modelled on and intended to rival that of St Peter's in Rome – of the grandiose **Marmorkirken** (Marble Church; Mon–Thurs 10am–5pm, Fri–Sun noon–5pm; free; Ⓦwww.marmorkirken.dk). Frederik V himself laid the church's first stone in a grand ceremony in 1749, but the building took 145 years to complete, largely due to the expense of the original Norwegian marble – eventually, N.F.S. Grundtvig (see p.123) finished the job using cheaper Danish marble. The **interior** of the church is grandly proportioned, if a bit drab – you can see the change from Norwegian to Danish marble about a quarter of the way up the walls. The real reason to visit, though, is to climb the 260 steep, twisting steps to the top of the **bell tower** (mid-June to Aug daily 1 & 3pm, Sept to mid-June Sat & Sun 1 & 3pm; 25kr). A guide will take you through the passages and staircases that lead to the summit where the grand vista of Copenhagen is laid before you; on a clear day you can see as far as Malmö, Helsingør and across the city to Roskilde.

Heading across Bredgade from Marmorkirken and along Frederiksgade, you reach Amalienborg Slotsplads. The square is surrounded by the four palaces of **Amalienborg**, centrepiece of Frederik V's Louis XV-inspired model town, and the home of the Danish royal family since 1794 when their former home, Christiansborg, burnt down (see p.78). The four almost identical palaces are functional rather than sumptuous – you're free to wander around the Slotsplads, though you'll be challenged by the bearskin-hatted **Livgarden** (Life Guards) if you get too close. You might want to time your visit with the **changing of the guard** (daily at noon), during which they march back to their barracks beside Rosenborg Slot.

The first palace on the left from Frederiksgade – Christian VIII's Palace – is home to **De Danske Kongers Kronologiske Samling** (Royal Danish Collection; May–Oct daily 10am–4pm; Nov–April Tues–Sun 11am–4pm; 50kr, joint ticket with Rosenborg Slot 80kr; ⓦ www.amalienborgmuseet.dk), de facto shrine to the monarchy. It's a mishmash of family mementoes, garish military pictures and carefully preserved living quarters, the latter shielded behind glass screens yet still managing to transmit something of the character of the monarchs who inhabited them. Some are filled with assorted regalia and military tackle, while others are more homely affairs, with family portraits, pipes and slippers. Look out also for the absorbing Europe-wide royal family tree revealing the generations of inbreeding that have gone into producing the monarchs of today. Diagonally across the Slotsplads, past the enormous **equestrian statue** of Frederik V, is the Queen's current residence in Christian IX's (her father's) palace. To the right, Frederik VIII's Palace (also called Brockdorff's Palace) is home to the crown prince and his young family.

Kunstindustrimuseet

Just north of Amalienborg and a must for anyone with an interest in design, the **Kunstindustrimuseet** (Danish Museum of Decorative Art: permanent exhibition June–Aug Tues–Sun noon–4pm; Sept–May Tues & Thurs–Sun noon–4pm, Weds noon–6pm; temporary exhibits and post-1900 collection June–Aug Tues–Fri 10am–4pm, Sat & Sun noon–4pm; Sept–May Tues & Thurs–Fri 10am–4pm, Weds 10am–6pm, Sat & Sun noon–4pm; 40kr; ⓦ www .kunstindustrimuseet.dk), at Bredgade 68, traces the development of European (particularly Danish) design, as well as examining the influence of Eastern styles on Western design through a notable collection of Oriental artefacts – Japanese porcelain and sword-hilt decorations, Chinese Ming vases and the like. Most of the museum is used for displaying items from the permanent collection, which covers the period from the Middle Ages to 1900, though the wing on the right as you enter is kept for later pieces, and for temporary exhibits focusing on Danish design. Of particular interest is the collection dedicated to twentieth-century Danish designers, featuring the simplistic forms of Kaare Klint, intricate Poul Henningsen lamps, and chairs by Wegner and Arne Jacobsen.

Nyboder

At some point during your exploration of the area, it's worth taking a detour a little to the west of Frederiksstaden, across Borgergade to the cobbled streets and ochre terraces of the **Nyboder** district, built by Christian IV to provide free housing for his sailors, though all but one of the rows of buildings here are nineteenth-century reconstructions. The solitary original row runs along

Sankt Pauls Gade, where you can also gain a bit more insight into the history of the area in the **Nyboders Mindestuer** museum (Wed 11am–2pm, Sun 11am–4pm; 10kr), a collection of furniture and domestic objects reflecting life at Nyboder in the 1880s.

Kastellet and around

At the far end of Bredgade, the straight streets of Eigtved's Frederiksstaden are replaced by the green open spaces of Kastellet (see opposite) and Churchillparken, named after the British wartime leader. Within Churchillparken, the moving **Frihedsmuseet** (Resistance Museum; May–Sept Tues–Sat 10am–4pm, Sun 10am–5pm; Oct–April Tues–Sat 10am–3pm, Sun 10am–4pm; free; ⓦ www.natmus.dk) offers a comprehensive account of Denmark's role in World War II, grasping the thorny issue of the Danish government's collusion with German rule. Exhibits take you through the slow build-up of resistance, beginning with the first acts of sabotage carried out in 1942 by a remarkable group of teenage boys from Århus called the **Churchill Gang**, whose courage and spirit spurred on other groups (mostly made up of Danish communists). The covert 1943 mass evacuation of Denmark's **Jewish population** (see p.80), who faced imminent deportation to concentration camps, is also documented. Just past the museum stands the incongruous British St Alban's Church, beside which is the dramatic **Gefion Fountain**, created in 1908 by Anders Bundgaard and based on the story of the goddess Gefion

△ Little Mermaid

who, according to legend, was promised as much land as she could plough in a single night. She promptly turned her four sons into oxen and ploughed out a chunk of Sweden (creating Lake Vänern), then picked it up and tossed it into the sea – where it became the Danish island of Zealand.

Just past Churchillparken, the unmistakable star-shaped fortress of **Kastellet** (daily 6am–10pm; free) was conceived by Christian IV as the key element in the city's defences – occupied by troops since 1660, it remains the only part of the city's ancient defence system still in use. The fortress is formed by five grass-covered bastions surrounded by a series of moats; you enter via one of two gates – Kongensporten, near Churchillparken to the south, and Norgesporten, at the opposite end near the Little Mermaid. Kastellet's principal attraction has for generations been the chance for a leisurely stroll around its grassy bastions and ramparts – the odd sheep munching away on its slanted slopes. This is still a working military complex – though these days mainly with administrative duties – so some areas are off-limits: keep an eye out for the *Adgang Forbudt* ("No Entry") signs.

A stone's throw from Kastellet (take Norgesporten gate) on the stretch of coastline called Langelinie, and poised on a pile of carefully positioned rocks by the harbour's edge, is the statue of the **Den Lille Havfrue**, better known as the **Little Mermaid**. Created in 1913 by Edvard Eriksen, this rather plain bronze figure has become the city's most enduring symbol despite its modest dimensions, and continues to exert an inexplicable magnetism on Danes and visitors alike. Inspired by the 1837 Hans Christian Andersen story of the same name, the statue was commissioned by Carlsberg brewery boss and art lover Carl Jacobsen after he had seen a performance of a ballet based on the story at the Royal Theatre; the face is that of the prima ballerina, Ellen Price, the body that of Eriksen's wife (Price wouldn't pose nude). As de facto city emblem, the statue has been the victim of several subversive pranks over the years including decapitations, amputations and various daubings.

Rådhuspladsen and around

Sandwiched between Indre By and Vesterbro, the area around the buzzing **Rådhuspladsen** town hall square is Copenhagen at its most frivolous, touristy and sometimes downright tacky. Top of the bill are the wonderful pleasure gardens of **Tivoli** – tagging along for the ride are plenty of other mass-appeal family amusements of varying quality. That said, the area is far more than an enormous fairground. Just south of the Rådhuspladsen lurk a few of the city's cultural heavyweights: the **Ny Carlsberg Glyptotek**, with its soothing collections of sculptures and paintings; the unmissable **Nationalmuseet**, home to many of Denmark's historic treasures; and the slick **Danish Design Centre**.

Rådhuspladsen

Flanked by two busy roads, the pedestrianized expanse of **Rådhuspladsen** is Copenhagen's principal square, though you're more likely to come across it by accident than design, en route to Tivoli or the shops of Indre By. The enormous Italianate red-brick **Rådhus** (City Hall; Mon–Fri 10am–4pm, free; English-language guided tours Mon–Fri 3pm, Sat 10am & 11am, 30kr; ⓦwww.copenhagencity.dk), designed by Martin Nyrop and completed in 1905, is worth a little exploration, though given the building's size, you're better off joining a guided tour, which takes you behind locked doors to a series of impressive wood-panelled rooms such as the Banqueting Hall, lined with the coats of arms of Denmark's merchant towns. At 106 metres, the Rådhus's **tower** (tours June–Sept Mon–Fri 10am, noon & 2pm, Sat noon; Oct–May Mon–Sat noon; 20kr) is Denmark's highest. It's about three hundred steps up to the balcony, and a further fifty through a narrow passage-way to the spire (there is a lift too), but you'll be rewarded with a view along the length of Strøget to Kongens Nytorv. In a side room close to the entrance, what looks like a mass of inscrutable dials is in fact the astronomical timepiece of **Jens Olsen's Verdensur** (Jens Olsen's World Clock; Mon–Fri 8.30am–4.30pm, Sat 10am–1pm; 10kr). Set in motion in 1955, the clock features a 570,000-year calendar plotting eclipses of the moon and sun, solar time, local time and various planetary orbits – all with incredible accuracy. It's fascinating to watch, too, as hundreds of ticking dials track the movements of the planets.

A few overpriced family attractions vie for attention on either side of the town hall. To the south, at Hans Christian Andersens Blvd 22, is the predictable **Louis Tussauds** (daily 10am–11pm; 80kr; ⓦwww.tussaud.dk), the Danish version of London's Madame Tussauds; while on the northern side of the Rådhuspladsen, at no. 57, the new **Hans Christian Andersen's Wonderful World** exhibi-tion (mid-June to Aug daily 9.30am–10.30pm; Sept to mid-June Mon–Thurs & Sun 10am–6pm, Fri & Sat 10am–8pm; 83kr; ⓦwww.topattractions.dk) is a lighthearted jaunt through the life and works of the celebrated fairy-tale author, aimed squarely at the kids, with mock-ups of his childhood home, study and so on, as well as animated tableaux of his ever-popular stories.

A few minutes' walk southeast of the Rådhus, at Hans Christian Andersen Blvd 27, is the Henning Larsen designed, glass-fronted **Danish Design Centre** (Mon–Fri 10am–5pm, Weds open till 9pm & free from 5pm; Sat & Sun 11am–4pm; 40kr; ⓦwww.ddc.dk). It's largely given over to temporary exhibitions; the tiny permanent display in the basement won't keep you more than the minute or so it takes to peruse the small selection of design icons such as Wonderbras, Zippo lighters, jeans, computers and coffee pots. It's the **shop** that makes it worth the effort, with an excellent range of books on design and architecture, plus drawers full of dinky designer gadgets.

Tivoli

Across Hans Christian Andersen's Boulevard from the Rådhus, with entrances at the junction with Tietgensgade and a little west at Vesterbrogade 3, is Denmark's most popular tourist attraction. Ninety percent of all foreign visitors to the city flood through the gates of **Tivoli** (mid-April to mid-June & mid-Aug to late Sept Mon, Tues, Weds, Thurs & Sun 11am–11pm, Fri 11am–12.30am, Sat 11am–midnight, mid-June to mid-Aug closes at midnight Mon, Tues, Weds, Thurs & Sun, & 12.30am Fri & Sa; mid-Nov–Dec 23 daily 10am–11pm; adults 75kr, children 35kr; ⓦwww.tivoli.dk), and though the relatively small number of **rides** here can't compete with the stomach-flipping thrills of modern theme parks, its popularity shows no signs of dimming – and to the Danes, Tivoli is nothing short of a national treasure. Since the gardens opened in 1843, the number of rides has grown over the years from two to around twenty-five, but Tivoli has stayed faithful to its pleasure garden image – the delightful landscaped **gardens**, fairground stalls, plentiful restaurants, bandstands, theatres and concert halls as much a part of the experience as the rides. All in all, it's an expensive day out, with rides costing 15–60kr (multi-ride ticket 200kr for adults, 150kr for children), prices for food around twenty percent higher than the outside world and those for alcoholic drinks a white-knuckle ride in themselves, but a few hours spent wandering among revellers of all ages indulging in the mass consumption of ice cream, with the squeals from the rides echoing round the park, is an experience well worth having, while on a fine summer's night, with the twinkling illuminations and fireworks exploding overhead (every Wed & Sat at 11.45pm), it's almost magical. As one of the few still-functioning nineteenth-century pleasure gardens, Tivoli has its historical aspect too, with a number of playful and well-maintained period buildings, notably the Chinese-style, open-air **Pantomime Theatre**, built in 1874. **Music**, some of it free with the admission price, plays a large part in Tivoli; check the posters for details of that day's events. In addition to the recently revamped **Concert Hall**, which features a stunning saltwater aquarium in its basement, there are also several smaller venues and bandstands playing jazz and blues, while the open-air "Plænen" stage, given over most of the time to displays of acrobatics and dance, hosts Danish rock bands (and the occasional international rock and pop act) free every Friday at 10pm (see p.113).

Tycho Brahe Planetarium

At Gammel Kongevej 10, a ten-minute walk west from Tivoli and pleasantly situated at the southeastern corner of Skt Jørgens Sø (the southernmost of the lakes that enclose central Copenhagen), is the **Tycho Brahe Planetarium** (Mon–Fri 9.30am–9pm, Sat & Sun 10.30am–9pm; 25kr exhibition only, 95kr including IMAX film; Ⓦwww.tycho.dk). Named after the famous sixteenth-century Danish astronomer, this distinctive cylindrical, sand-coloured brick affair is home to a rather pedestrian exhibition on the stars, planets and space travel, with the obligatory lump of moon rock. The only real reason to come here is the **IMAX cinema**, which shows hourly films (you'll need to hire headphones with English translations; 15kr), though they're more likely to be about ancient Egypt, deep-sea exploration or dolphins than anything astronomical.

Ny Carlsberg Glyptotek

Back on Hans Christian Andersen's Boulevard, at Dantes Plads 7, is the newly renovated **Ny Carlsberg Glyptotek** (Tues–Sun 10am–4pm; 40kr, Wed & Sun free; Ⓦwww.glyptoteket.dk), Copenhagen's finest art gallery, opened in 1897 by the philanthropic Carlsberg brewing magnate Carl Jacobsen as a venue for ordinary people to see the collection of classical and modern art that he had generously donated to the state. Its focal point is the delightful glass-domed **Winter Garden** (*vinterhave*), filled with soaring palm trees, a fountain and statues, and with the added highlight of a superb **café** (see p.107) – the perfect spot for lunch or a morning coffee and pastry.

The Glyptotek was undergoing extensive refurbishment and reorganization at the time of writing; for specific locations consult the new floor plan. The entrance hall leads you into the oldest section of the gallery, the Dahlerup building where, spread over two floors, you'll find the collections of **French and Danish sculpture**, with a bit of Danish painting thrown in. The French sculpture collection is dominated by a particularly fine haul of **Rodins** – the largest outside France, including a version of *The Kiss*. The Danish sculpture and painting is, unsurprisingly, rather less stimulating, though it does provide a good reflection of Golden Age painting, with some idealized landscapes by C.W. Eckersberg and more realistic paintings depicting the travails of Danish peasants by Wilhelm Marstrand.

Head through the enticing Winter Garden into the Kampmann Building for the antiquities collection, now reorganized and renamed **The Mediterranean Horizon**. It's a worthy attempt to go beyond merely labelling the treasures from Ancient Greece, Rome, Egypt, Etruria and the Near East by providing background on the geographical, cultural and artistic links between the various cultures, and using selected pieces from the collections to high-light artistic concepts and themes of the time. Worth particular mention are the **Greek and Roman** portrait sculpture and statues; an amusing mix of the greats – the portrait of Caligula, which still retains some of its original paint, and large Alexander the Great are particularly striking – and some surprisingly warts-and-all private portraits of rich commoners. There's a small but excellent collection of **Egyptian** artefacts – statuary, stelae, tomb models, reliefs and the obligatory handful of mummies – but it's the large and diverse haul of **Etrus-can** works that really stands out, reputedly the largest (and best) outside Italy.

Occupying the modern, purpose-built Henning Larsen-designed French Wing (rooms 56–66; access from the Winter Garden), the museum's excellent collec-tion of nineteenth- and twentieth-century **French painting** from Jacques-Louis David to Gauguin shouldn't be missed. The lower ground floor (rooms 56–60) displays works by the precursors of the Impressionists, with artists from the Barbi-zon school well represented via works by Corot, Delacroix, Courbet and Manet, including a version of the latter's well-known *Execution of Emperor Maximilian* and *The Absinthe Drinker*. The ground floor is given over to the **Impression-ists** (rooms 61 & 62), with some exquisite Monets – notably *The Lemon Grove*, a wonderful play of colour and technique – a few lesser-known Renoirs and a complete set of charming Degas bronze figurines. The exhibition continues upstairs with the **Post Impressionists** (rooms 63–66), including works by Toulouse-Lautrec, Pissarro, Bonnard and Van Gogh. **Gauguin** is particularly well represented (he was married to a Dane) with over thirty paintings.

Nationalmuseet

To the east of Rådhuspladsen, on Ny Vestergade, the excellent **National-museet** (Tues–Sun 10am–5pm; free; ⓦ www.natmus.dk) is home to the country's finest collection of Danish artefacts, from the Ice Age to the present day, as well as fascinating ethnographic collections from around the world. The **Prehistoric Denmark** galleries, covering 14,000 years of prehistory and featuring the Viking collections, were undergoing extensive **renovations** at the time of writing, and were closed to the public until 2008. The new galleries here will continue to display the remarkable number of intact finds excavated from the country's peat bogs, which acted as a preservative on anything buried in them, often precious objects deliberately thrown in to curry favour with the marsh gods. Highlights to look out for include the 3500-year-old oak coffin and body of **Egtved Girl**, whose clothes, comb, bracelets and blonde hair have all survived eerily intact, and the beautifully crafted **Trundholm Sun Chariot** (1400 BC), an enchanting model made by sun-worshippers that depicts a magi-cal horse-drawn chariot pulling a gold-leaf sun disc across the heavens. The **Viking collection** makes for a dazzling finish to the period, with everyday tools and artefacts, clothes and weapons as well as plentiful examples of shim-mering filigree silver jewellery, coins and ingots, many of them from private stashes buried by the wealthy in times of unrest.

Upstairs on the first floor, the story continues with an extensive display of religious and royal paraphernalia, weapons, furniture and household objects spanning the Middle Ages and Renaissance. The collection is particularly strong on the relics of **Danish Christianity** – stern-looking late-Viking crucifixes give way to more naturalistic representations, while the Latin alphabet arrives to replace the runes – with rooms full of the elaborate gold altars, ceremonial robes and grails used to glorify Christ (and the Church). If you've not yet had enough, head up to the second floor, where the exhaustive "**Stories of**

Denmark" picks up the story from 1660 to the present day, with an enormous array of objects ranging from royal garments to pop posters and plastic bowls, all spotlighting key historical and cultural events in the country's history.

The bulk of the rest of the museum is taken up by the huge and exceptionally diverse **ethnographic collection** – a captivating journey through non-European art and culture with Africa, China, India and Japan particularly well represented. Given the extent of the displays, it's wise to focus on particular areas of geographical interest, though the section on **Inuit culture**, spread over the first and second floors and featuring exhibits from northern Canada, Alaska and Greenland, shouldn't be missed: check out the exhaustive array of whale-bone carvings, harpoons, sealskin kayaks, furry boots and clothing, and spooky looking sealskin whaling costumes.

Vesterbro and Frederiksberg

The two districts immediately west of the city centre, Vesterbro and Frederiksberg, couldn't be more different. **Vesterbro** has always been determinedly working class, and also has the city's most diverse racial mix, yet despite encroaching gentrification, it still contains the city's red-light district and is one of the most colourful areas of Copenhagen, with the broadest selection of affordable ethnic restaurants and shops and a vibrant street life. In stark contrast, **Frederiksberg**'s wealthy residents tend to stay behind the doors of their grand villas, and the spacious and leafy roads here are relatively lifeless.

Vesterbro

Vesterbro is centred around the roughly parallel streets of **Vesterbrogade**, **Istedgade** and **Sønder Boulevard**, which run from Central Station at the eastern end of the district to the Carlsberg Brewery and Frederiksberg Have in the west. Vesterbrogade is the district's major artery and one of the city's main shopping streets – more affordable than Strøget and with good restaurants and

△ Elephant Gate

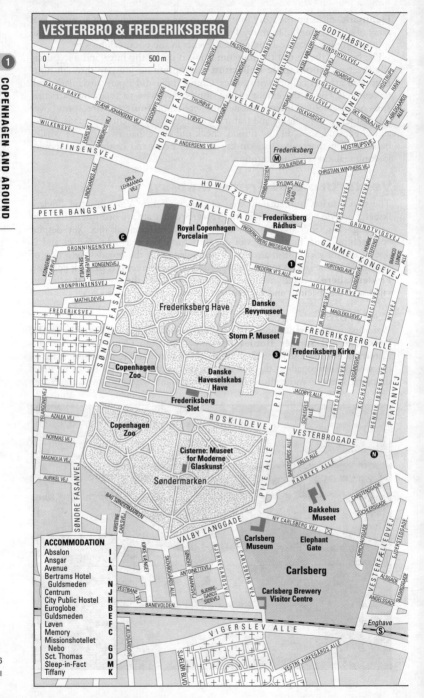

VESTERBRO & FREDERIKSBERG

0 — 500 m

GODTHÅBSVEJ
FALSTERSVEJ
GULDBORGVEJ
AKSEL MØLLERS HAVE
SINDSHVILEVEJ
LANGELANDSVEJ
BENTZONSVEJ
ADILSVEJ
ROARSVEJ
HELGESVEJ
HOSTRUPS HAVE

DALGAS HAVE
STÆHR JOHANSENS VEJ
SEEDORFFS VÆNGE
THURØVEJ
LYØVEJ
SPØRGSMÅLSVEJ
NORDRE FASANVEJ
NYELANDSVEJ
ROLFSVEJ
FOLKVARSVEJ
SKT. NIKOLAJ VEJ
FALKONER ALLE
DR. ABILDGAARDS HAVE

WILKENSVEJ
EVERSVEJ
RAMSBORGS VEJ
FINSENSVEJ
ORLA LEHMANNS VEJ
P. ANDERSENS VEJ
HERMANSSTIEN
Frederiksberg (M)
SOLBJERGVEJ
HOSTRUPSVEJ
CHRISTIAN WINTHERS VEJ

LINDEVANGS ALLE
KONGENS TVÆRVEJ
ARVEPRINS SENSNESVEJ
KONGENSVEJ
HOWITZVEJ
HERMANSSTIEN
SYLOWS ALLE
SYLOWS PLADS

PETER BANGS VEJ
SMALLEGADE
Frederiksberg Rådhus
GRUNDTVIGSVEJ
RATHSACKSVEJ
CERESVEJ

DRONNINGENSVEJ (C)
Royal Copenhagen Porcelain
FREDERIKSBERG BREDEGADE
GAMMEL KONGEVEJ
HENRIK STEFFENS VEJ
BIANCO LUNOS ALLE

ARVEPRINSENSVEJ
KRONPRINSENSVEJ
FREDERIK VI'S ALLE (1)
HORTENSIAVEJ
EDISONSVEJ

MATHILDEVEJ
FREDERIKSVEJ
SØNDRE FASANVEJ
Frederiksberg Have
Danske Revymuseet
HOLLÆNDERVEJ
DR. PRIEMES VEJ
AMICISVEJ
NYVEJ

ALLÉGADE
MAGLEKILDEVEJ
FREDERIKSBERG ALLE

Storm P. Museet
Frederiksberg Kirke (3)
FRYDENDALSVEJ
KOCHSVEJ
HENRIK IBSENS VEJ
PLATANVEJ

Copenhagen Zoo
Danske Haveselskabs Have
JACOBYS ALLE
SCHLEGELS ALLE
ASGÅRDSVEJ

PELARGONIEVEJ
AZALEA VEJ
Frederiksberg Slot
ROSKILDEVEJ
PILE ALLE
VESTERBROGADE

NORMAS VEJ
Copenhagen Zoo
BAKKEGÅRDS ALLE
HALLS ALLE
RAHBEKS ALLE
(N)

MAGNOLIA VEJ
AURIKEL VEJ
SØNDRE FASANVEJ
Cisterne: Museet for Moderne Glaskunst
Søndermarken
CARSTENSGADE
KÜCHLERSGADE

BAG SØNDERMARKEN
KRISTINE CARLSENS VEJ
Bakkehus Museet
JERICHAUSGADE
EJDERSTEDGADE

NY CARLSBERG VEJ
VESTERFÆLLEDVEJ
ALSGADE

VALBY LANGGADE
Carlsberg Museum
Elephant Gate
ANGELSGADE
SLESVIGSGADE

KIRKE VÆNGET
SKOVRIDDERGS ALLE
ANTOINETTEVEJ
SØNDER MARKSVEJ
GL. CARLSBERG VEJ
Carlsberg

VESTBANE VEJ
BJERGGÅRDS SIDEVEJ
BJERREGÅRDS ALLE
Carlsberg Brewery Visitor Centre

BANEVOLDEN
KJELDGÅRDSVEJ
Enghave (S)

VIGERSLEV ALLE
SJÆLØR BLVD
VESTRE KIRKEGÅRDS ALLE

ACCOMMODATION

Absalon	I
Ansgar	L
Avenue	A
Bertrams Hotel Guldsmeden	N
Centrum	J
City Public Hostel	H
Euroglobe	B
Guldsmeden	E
Løven	F
Memory	C
Missionshotellet Nebo	G
Sct. Thomas	D
Sleep-in-Fact	M
Tiffany	K

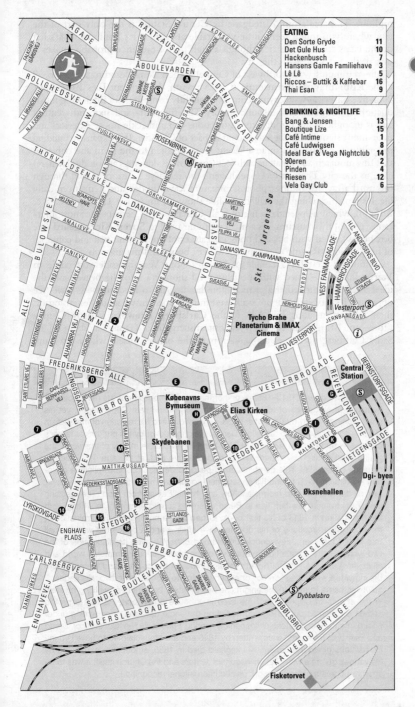

EATING

Den Sorte Gryde	11
Det Gule Hus	10
Hackenbusch	7
Hansens Gamle Familiehave	3
Lê Lê	5
Riccos – Buttik & Kaffebar	16
Thai Esan	9

DRINKING & NIGHTLIFE

Bang & Jensen	13
Boutique Lize	15
Café Intime	1
Café Ludwigsen	8
Ideal Bar & Vega Nightclub	14
90eren	2
Pinden	4
Riesen	12
Vela Gay Club	6

nightlife. The area around Istedgade by Central Station is the only part of the city where you might feel a little vulnerable at night – it's home to what's left of the city's red-light district, though a high police presence probably makes it one of the safest areas in the city.

Fifteen minutes' walk northwest of Central Station along Vesterbrogade at no. 59 is the **Københavns Bymuseum** (City Museum; daily except Tues 10am–4pm; 20kr, free on Fri; @ www.bymuseum.dk), a slightly confusing but interesting introduction to Copenhagen's chaotic history. The fifteenth- and sixteenth-century city is brought to life through reconstructions of ramshackle house exteriors and tradesmen's signs, while the subsequent impact of Christian IV's expansive building programmes can be seen in an adjacent room devoted to the form and cohesion that this monarch and amateur architect (some of his drawings are on display here) gave to the city. The rest of Copenhagen's thousand-year history is told through the usual array of paintings, photos, miniature town models and items from daily life. It's worth catching the half-hour slide show (in English at 11.15am, 12.45 & 2.15pm), which helps make sense of it all. Upstairs – and perhaps the most interesting part of the museum – is a small room devoted to **Søren Kierkegaard** (see box below), filled with bits and bobs: caricatures of the man himself and paintings of his girlfriend Regine Olsen, plus jewellery, books and manuscripts.

Continuing west for a couple of minutes along Vesterbrogade you come to **Værnedamsvej** – lined with speciality food shops, it's a foodie heaven and the ideal place to put together a picnic before heading up to Frederiksberg Have (see opposite). It's a twenty-minute walk west from Værnedamsvej along Vesterbrogade, then a left turn along Pile Allé, to the **Carlsberg Brewery Visitor Centre** (Tues–Sun 10am–4pm; 40kr; @ www.visitcarlsberg.dk) at Gamle Carlsberg Vej 11. Sadly, Carlsberg no longer admit visitors to the brewery itself, whose low hum

Søren Kierkegaard

Søren Kierkegaard (1813–1855) – one of the most famous, if not the most comprehensible, philosophers of all time – is inextricably linked with Copenhagen, yet his championing of individual will over social conventions and his rejection of materialism did little to endear him to his fellow Danes. Weighed down by his puritanical father's endless lectures on the suffering of Christ and the inevitable misery of the world, the young Kierkegaard developed a morbid, depressive and, at the age of 25, deeply religious personality. This combination of periodic depressions and religious devotion led him, in 1841, to end his engagement to the love of his life, Regine Olsen, for fear of drawing her into his melancholy and himself away from God. The resulting emotional trauma saw him flee to Berlin where he turned feverishly to writing, with the publication in 1843 of his first book, **Either/Or** – a philosophical examination of the conflicting emotions of his doomed love affair – and a concerted writing spell that lasted ten years. Few people understood *Either/Or*, with its discussion of the two worlds – the "aesthetic" (man's love of the bodily, sensory, material world and all its sins) and the "ethical" (man's relationship with the spiritual and eternal) – and the individual's resulting "dread" or angst at trying to reconcile the two. Kierkegaard, however, came to revel in the enigma he had created, becoming a "walking mystery in the streets of Copenhagen" (he lived in a house on Nytorv). He was a prolific author, sometimes publishing two books on the same day, and often writing under pseudonyms. His greatest philosophical works, *Either/Or*, *The Concept of Dread* and *Fear and Trembling*, were written by 1846 and are often claimed to have laid the foundations of **existentialism**. Kierkegaard died in 1855, emotionally exhausted by his various quarrels with rival philosophers, writers and the Church itself; it was to be another 60 years before his work gained international recognition.

①

Carlsberg: The quest for the perfect pint

Danes have been knocking back **Carlsberg beer** since the mid-nineteenth century when J.C. Jacobsen, a young Copenhagen brewer, established a brewery on a hill at Valby, calling it Carlsberg ("Carl's hill") after his son. With its Bavarian-style brewing techniques, it was a runaway success – J.C. was way ahead of his time and set great store by scientific research as the basis for improving production, setting up a research laboratory and expressing his overall aims for the company in a mission statement entitled "The Golden Words", which went so far as to make profit a secondary consideration to the pursuit of the perfect pint. In 1871, young Carl set up his own brewery, "New Carlsberg" and, as the two breweries prospered and the money flowed in, both father and son sought to use their wealth for the greater good: J.C. through the Carlsberg Foundation, which funded and supported Danish scientific research; Carl, with his more artistic leanings, through the **New Carlsberg Foundation**, among whose achievements was the establishment, in 1897, of the Ny Carlsberg Glyptotek sculpture and art museum (see p.93), which the foundation still runs today. This munificence wasn't just a glorified PR exercise, since the Carlsbergs extended their social principles to their workforce: in a time when there was no social security, Carlsberg employees received medical aid and pensions, as well as additional perks like annual balls and picnics and, of course, a daily beer ration. Carlsberg merged with the other Danish beer giant Tuborg in 1970, becoming Carlsberg A/S; their brands are now drunk all over the world, although only seven percent of Tuborg's sales are in Denmark.

and pungent whiffs pervade the air, and have replaced the brewery tours with a rather less intoxicating centre covering the history of beer brewing and consumption in Denmark, starting with Egtved Girl (see p.94), who had a small pot at her feet containing the first known Danish beer, and with plenty on the story of the company and its founder (see box above), complete with models of old workers' quarters and old brewing machinery. Thankfully, Carlsberg have retained the tradition of handing out a free beer in the bar at the end of your visit, and you can sample your brew overlooking the new fully operational Jacobsen Microbrewery. While you're in the vicinity, take a look at the wonderful **Elephant Gate**, around the corner from the visitor centre on Ny Carlsberg Vej: four elephants carved in granite supporting the building that spans the road.

Frederiksberg

"A city within the city" is how Frederiksbergers like to describe their independent district. Positioned between Vesterbro and Norrebro (see p.100), it covers a large area – almost twice the size of Indre By – and, with its own council and city hall, tries to be completely self-contained. Away from the main roads, you'll find street after street of distinctively grand villas, quite unlike the apartment blocks characteristic of other residential areas of the city.

Just beyond the City Museum (see opposite), the wide, tree-lined Frederiksberg Allé branches off Vesterbrogade and slopes gently up to the expansive English-style gardens of **Frederiksberg Have** (daily 6am–sunset; free), which stretch out in a network of pathways, lakes and canals that criss-cross beautiful lime-tree groves. Throughout the eighteenth century, the city's top brass came here to mess about in boats, though nowadays you'll have to settle for one of the tours in the large, manned rowing boats which depart regularly from in front of Frederiksberg Slot. The grassy slopes, ponds and fountains attract hordes of picnicking locals in summer and intriguing follies, temples and grottoes abound. At their southern end, the gardens take on a distinctly more ordered, French-inspired look as they slope up to the pale yellow **Frederiksberg Slot**, the royal family's summer residence until the mid-1800s, when it was taken over by the Danish Officers' Academy.

Next to Frederiksberg Slot, **Zoologisk Have** (Copenhagen Zoo; April, May & Sept Mon–Fri 9am–5pm; early to mid-June & mid- to end Aug daily 9am–6pm, Sat & Sun 9am–6pm; mid-June to mid-Aug daily 9am–10pm; Oct daily 9am–5pm; March Mon–Fri 9am–4pm, Sat & Sun 9am–5pm; Nov–Feb daily 9am–4pm; 100kr; ⓦwww.zoo.dk) is one of the largest zoos in Europe. It tries to keep its animals in enclosures that reproduce their natural environments as closely as possible – a policy that has led, in many cases, to contented animals and therefore successful breeding results. But as with all zoos, it can still be a rather depressing affair watching the huge bears and big cats pacing around their compounds, though the African savannah area in the section south of Roskildevej is a more uplifting open-plan affair, with giraffes, impala and okapi looking a little more at home, and there's a wonderful primate house here too, which provides welcome warmth in winter.

The only attraction on the northern side of the park is the **Royal Copenhagen Porcelain Visitor Centre** at Søndre Fasanvej 5 (Mon–Fri 9am–4pm; 40kr; ⓦwww.royalcopenhagen.com); two short films recount the history and production processes of the world famous porcelain – "Flora Danica", a multi-coloured wildflower pattern and "Musselmalet", with blue decorations based on Meissen models are the best-known designs – while a bevy of factory workers are on hand to demonstrate it all. The **factory shop** (Mon–Fri 9am–5.30pm, Sat 9am–2pm) sells the wares at reduced prices, though you may still find 1000kr for a cup and saucer beyond the bounds of reason.

Nørrebro and Østerbro

To the north and east of the city centre, the districts of Nørrebro and Østerbro both developed mainly during the mid-nineteenth century, but have deeply contrasting histories. **Nørrebro's** roots are staunchly working class, and its residents have a reputation for political activism and rebellion. In the 1980s, immigrants started to arrive here, bringing much-needed cultural diversity to the city; they now rub shoulders with Danish yuppies lured by the low property prices. Though rather short on specific sights, Nørrebro is one of the most exciting, up-and-coming parts of the city – a great mix of markets, ethnic food stores and restaurants, designer and secondhand shops and hyper-trendy cafés, bars and clubs. At the heart of Nørrebro, the small square of **Sankt Hans Torv** is a hub of Parisian-style cafés and bars catering to the city's bright young things, while two streets close by are well worth a wander. **Ravnsborggade**, just to the east, is lined with secondhand furniture and knick-knack shops interspersed with Danish designer clothes shops; while **Elmegade**, leading south off the square, has a mass of small, quirky deli-bars, selling all sorts of food from eastern European to Japanese sushi. Southeast across busy Norrebrogade, you come to the large intersection with **Blågårdsgade**, a pleasant, pedestrianized street and the heart of Copenhagen's immigrant and alternative communities – there's an intriguing mix of inexpensive restaurants and bars along here, and a pleasant tree-fringed square, Blågårds Plads.

Northwest of Blågårdsgade, heading along Nørrebrogade for around half a kilometre takes you to the unmistakable, graffiti-covered yellow walls of Copenhagen's most famous cemetery, **Assistens Kirkegård** (dawn to dusk; free); built to cope with the dead from the 1711–12 plague outbreak, it had become the eternal resting place of choice for Copenhagen's wealthier gentlefolk by around the end of the eighteenth century. The Kapelvej entrance, where you'll find an

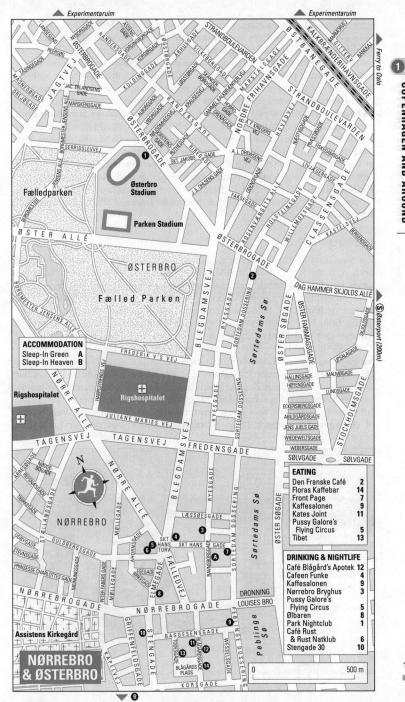

Experimentaruim

Experimentaruim

Ferry to Oslo

Østerport (200m)

Østerbro Stadium

Parken Stadium

Fælledparken

ØSTERBRO

Fælled Parken

ACCOMMODATION
Sleep-In Green   A
Sleep-In Heaven   B

Rigshospitalet

Rigshospitalet

NØRREBRO

Assistens Kirkegård

NØRREBRO & ØSTERBRO

EATING
Den Franske Café   2
Floras Kaffebar   14
Front Page   7
Kaffesalonen   9
Kates Joint   11
Pussy Galore's
  Flying Circus   5
Tibet   13

DRINKING & NIGHTLIFE
Café Blågård's Apotek   12
Cafeen Funke   4
Kaffesalonen   9
Nørrebro Bryghus   3
Pussy Galore's
  Flying Circus   5
Ølbaren   8
Park Nightclub   1
Café Rust
  & Rust Natklub   6
Stengade 30   10

0   500 m

information office with maps, is the best place to start. Close to here (and well signposted) are the cemetery's two most famous graves, those of **Hans Christian Andersen** and **Søren Kierkegaard**, but don't expect anything grand. Rather more imposing is the owl-topped tomb of the Bohr family, where Nobel Prize-winning Danish physicist Niels Bohr is interred; you might also want to keep an eye out for the "Jazz Corner", where the American musician Ben Webster is buried alongside several lesser-known Danish jazz players.

Østerbro's history is one of traditional wealth and privilege. Stretching from the fringes of Fælledparken in the west through to the commercial docks, warehouses and wealthy residences along the Øresund coast to the east, this salubrious suburb is home to Copenhagen's moneyed classes, who luxuriate in the expensive houses along the coastal fringes. Østerbro's highlight for the visitor are the enormously popular green expanses and tree-lined avenues of **Fælledparken** (Community Park), with acres of lawn, a scent garden, playgrounds, skateboarding rink, and, at weekends, informal football matches (all are welcome to join in).

Amager

Just southeast of the city centre, and connected to it by a series of lifting bridges, is the large island of **AMAGER** (pronounced *Ama*), home to some lovely beaches and stretches of park and currently undergoing gradual renovation and gentrification from a staunchly working-class neighbourhood of huge apartment blocks to an up-and-coming yuppie quarter. Crossing Langebro bridge from H.C. Andersens Boulevard and Rådhuspladsen takes you onto the harbour strip of **Islands Brygge**; a working industrial harbour until the mid 1980s, it's since had a complete facelift and is now one of the city's most popular hangouts on hot summer days, with a harbour pool (see p.122) and the adjacent Havneparken, a 400-metre long grassy strip edging the northwestern side of the island where the Islands Brygge Kulturhus (see p.113) hosts bands and entertainment year-round and has a laid-back waterfront café/restaurant.

Across the island on its eastern coastline, the newly developed **beach** area of **Amager Strandpark** (ⓦwww.amager-strand.dk; bus #12 or Lerparken

△ Amager Strandpark

metro) is another big attraction, a two-kilometre-long artificial island boasting beautiful – and extremely popular – soft sandy beaches, and kayaking and other watersports in the shallow lagoon between the island and Amager "mainland". Once you've had your fill of the beach, head to the southern end of Amager Strandpark and **Kastrup Fort**, a remnant of the city's fortification from 1886. It's open to the public, though not much of its past is evident, apart from the casemate and some old cannons. There's a good kids' playground, however and, during summer months, a restaurant, *Krunch* (see p.109), plus fantastic views of the Swedish coast.

At the southeastern corner of Amager, beyond Kastrup airport, itself at the centre of a rapidly developing area of new housing and business, the atmospheric fishing village of **Dragør** (bus #30 from Rådhuspladsen, #350S from Nørreport station) makes for a pleasant stroll, with quaint cobblestoned streets and couple of low-key sights. Down by the pretty harbour, bristling with fishing boats, the **Dragør Museum** (May–Sept Tues–Sun noon–4pm; 20kr) is devoted to the maritime history of the village from the thirteenth-century herring trade to the arrival of the Dutch in the early sixteenth century, with displays of model ships, navigation instruments and curios collected by sailors during their travels. Once you've had your fill of seafaring paraphernalia, head for the real highlight of the village – the museum-run warehouse café *Pakhuset* (daily 10am–4pm), which specializes in sandwiches made with herring from the traditional **smoke house** just around the corner. Finally, it's worth taking a quick peep into the **Mølsteds Museum** (May–Aug Sat & Sun noon–4pm; free), in the centre of the old village on Dr Dichs Plads, which displays works by local celebrity Christian Mølsted (1862–1930), known for his atmospheric and colourful paintings of the land- and seascapes around Dragør.

Eating

Copenhagen's **restaurant** scene has seen a dramatic improvement in the quantity and variety of establishments over recent years, with options covering the whole range from cheap ethnic eateries to Michelin-starred expense-account affairs. As soon as summer arrives, the city is transformed as those cafés and

Brunch

Copenhageners have taken to the concept of **brunch** with alacrity, and most cafés now offer a range of options from a restrained yoghurt, muesli and fruit combo to American-style blowouts. All are usually very good value, at 45–100kr, and are available until at least 2pm (sometimes all day), either plated up or as an all-you-can-eat buffet – so if you're on a budget brunch is a good way to fill up. The following are some of the best brunch spots in the city:

Bastionen og Løven (p.106)
Dan Turèll (p.104)
Den Franske Café (p.109)
Det Gule Hus (p.107)
Marius (p.105)
Pussy Galore's Flying Circus (p.108)
Sommersko (p.105)
Thorvaldsens hus (p.105)

restaurants that can, spill out onto the pavements – and for less than balmy nights, most will turn on gas heaters or provide you with blankets to help along that *hygge* (cosy) feeling. Copenhagen's abundant **cafés** are extremely versatile, serving coffee and cake, and **brunch** (see box on p.103) and lunch for most of the day; many also double as bars after dark, and serve a (generally more expensive) evening menu. Though Copenhagen is a long way behind London or Paris in terms of quality and diversity of **ethnic restaurants**, the immigrant community's impact is increasingly being felt, particularly in the Vesterbro and Nørrebro areas, where there's a large array of Turkish and Indian places, along with a good selection of (slightly pricier) Thai restaurants and Japanese sushi joints.

Eating out in the capital's restaurants can be very expensive, especially if you throw in a bottle of wine, for which you'll pay upwards of 175kr for something decent; that said, it's worth bearing in mind that some of the more pricey restaurants listed below are open for lunch, too, with daytime set menus offering a considerably more affordable way of sampling some of the city's finer, more adventurous cuisine.

It's advisable to book ahead for dinner at upmarket restaurants and for lunch at traditional smørrebrød places. Note that the **opening hours** given for each listing are for the venue's actual closing time; the kitchen often closes one or, in the case of café/bars, often two hours earlier. For a glossary of food terms, see Language p.429.

Details of some gay-friendly restaurants and cafés are given in "Gay Copenhagen" on p.120.

Indre By

The following places are shown on the map on p.76.

Atlas Bar Larsbjørnstræde 18 ☎33 15 03 52. On trendy Larsbjørnstræde, the *Atlas Bar* features a globetrotting range of dishes (lunch 80kr plus, dinner 100kr plus) of an exotic – and generally spicy – nature, like Mexican chilli or Bali chicken. Portions are large and the changing menu is chalked up on a bar blackboard daily – one side meat, the other fish and vegetarian. Always packed at lunchtime, when it's a good idea to book in advance. Mon–Sat noon–midnight.

Dan Turèll Store Regnegade 3 ☎33 14 10 47. This busy French-style place devoted to the memory of author Dan Turèll is renowned as one of the city's best café-bars. Packed with delicious home-made delicacies, brunch (weekdays 95kr, weekends 132kr) is served until 1pm, and is a lot more extensive at weekends. Otherwise, sandwiches, pies and salads make up the lunchtime menu, while dinner features well-prepared fish and meat dishes (no veggie options) starting at 160kr; big and tasty DT burgers are available throughout the day. Booking essential Fri & Sat evening. Kitchen open Mon–Thurs 9.30am–10pm, Fri & Sat 9.30am–11pm, Sun 10am–8.30pm.

Domhuskælderen Nytorv 5 ☎33 14 84 55. This very popular traditional basement joint with a large outdoor seating area on Nytorv attracts a mix of tourists, shoppers and locals. The lunch menu is extensive, with a full range of generous smørrebrød (from 50kr a piece) and a filling smørrebrød platter for 138kr. Things get more expensive in the evening, with a hearty meat and veg menu including the likes of pork, guinea fowl and venison in the 150kr price range. Daily 11am–10pm.

Extra Østergade 13 ☎35 26 09 52. Large, trendy new restaurant at the exclusive end of Strøget, run by one of the city's top chefs and offering tapas and Spanish cuisine. Main courses start at 169kr and tapas between 16kr (oysters) and 395kr (caviar); there's also a three-course lunch menu for 298kr. Mon–Sat noon–11pm.

Den Grønne Kælder Pilestræde 48 ☎33 93 01 40. This busy but relaxed vegetarian eatery offers a good selection of scrumptious seasonal dishes – wild mushroom lasagne is one of the few constants on the ever-changing menu – as well as organic wine, beer and home-made bread. Dinner here is relatively cheap compared to other city centre restaurants, starting at 95kr for generous portions. Mon–Sat 11am–10pm.

Huset Med Det Grønne Træ Gammeltorv 20 ☎33 12 87 86. Frequented mostly by lawyers and solicitors from the nearby law courts, this old-fashioned, wood-panelled and extremely cosy spot is one of the best places in the downtown area for Danish food, with a sumptuous *smørrebrød* spread and 14 different types of snaps. April–Aug

Mon–Fri 11.30am–3.30pm; Sept–March Mon–Sat 11.30am–3.30pm.

La Galette Larsbjørnstræde 9. Tucked away at the end of a small alley off Larsbjørnstræde and with outdoor seating in summer, this cosy, authentically Breton pancake joint is excellent value. Made with flour imported from Brittany, the sweet and savoury and sweet buckwheat galettes come with a range of fillings, and you can wash them down with a jug of equally authentic cider. Prices range from 25kr for a plain galette to 80kr for one with caviar and smoked salmon. Mon–Sat noon–11pm, Sun 4–10pm.

La Glace Skoubogade 20. Unmissable patisserie where time seems to have stood still, with primly dressed waitresses ministering to a genteel clientele who come for the beautifully sculpted, cream-heavy cakes and pots of real hot chocolate (48kr a pot). If that sounds too much you could just settle for a coffee and a Danish. Mon–Thurs 8.30am–5.30pm, Sat 9am–5pm, Sun 11am–5pm.

Marius Nørre Farimagsgade 55 ☏ 33 11 83 83. On the sunny side of Nørre Farimagsgade, this corner café prides itself on serving the best brunch in town at the weekends (11am–3/4pm, book ahead), offering two types of American brunch – one including chorizo and potato pancakes (99kr), the other with bacon, hash browns and buttermilk pancakes (95kr) – and an array of side orders that set you up perfectly for the day. The rest of the week, freshly made bagels, wraps, burgers and home-made pasta set the tone for lunch and dinner. Tues & Wed noon–11pm, Thurs noon–1am, Fri noon–2am, Sat 11am–2am, Sun 11am–4pm.

Nyhavns Færgekro Nyhavn 5 ☏ 33 15 15 88. A good lunchtime option along the sunny side of this restaurant-heavy stretch, serving an amazing lunchtime buffet with ten different types of herring for 98kr. There's also the filling "Nyhavns platter" of five heavily laden pieces of smørrebrød for 159kr; individual pieces starting at 49kr a piece. In the evening, the à la carte restaurant upstairs does a two-course menu – typically traditional meat or fish dishes – for 195kr. Daily 9am–1am.

Peder Oxe Gråbrødretorv 11 ☏ 33 11 00 77. This popular French-inspired steakhouse, with outdoor seating in fine weather, is busy for both lunch and dinner and serves up a small menu of meat and fish mains alongside rich desserts. The main attraction is the juicy organic burger made with finest beef (115kr), and for an extra 35kr you can help yourself to the salad buffet The only drawback is tight squeeze indoors. Daily 11.30am–1am.

Riz Raz Kompagnistræde 20 and Store Kannikestræde 19. The hot and cold Mediterranean veggie buffet here is one of the city's best (and healthiest) budget options: all the fresh salads, pasta, falafel, rice and feta you can eat for 59kr (69kr in the evening). There's also a more carnivorous menu of kebabs, steaks and the like. As you'd expect, it's usually packed, but turnover is high and there's outdoor seating available. Daily 11.30am–midnight.

Slotskælderen Hos Gitte Kik Fortunstræde 4. It may not look much from the outside, but this is one of the best places in town to sample smørrebrød. There's no menu – just walk up to the table, presided over by Gitte herself, pick your toppings from the heaped plates of delicacies, and the made-up smørrebrød will be brought over to you. Prices start at 37kr for a slice with herring. Tues–Sat 11am–5pm.

Sommersko Kronprinsensgade 6. Excellent Parisian-style brasserie on "boutique street", attracting a young and trendy clientele and popular meeting spot at weekends. Breakfast options include freshly made bread and a soft boiled egg (45kr); there's then a delectable brunch (10am–3pm) in three sizes (85kr–115kr), and a fabulous array of sandwiches, burgers, soups and salad. Evenings see innovative pasta dishes, fish and meat mains. Mon–Wed 8am–midnight, Thurs 8am–1am, Fri 8am–4am, Sat 9am–4am, Sun 10am–midnight.

Sticks 'n' Sushi Nansensgade 59 ☏ 33 11 14 07. This classy but pricey sushi bar on fashionable Nansensgade is among one of the city's oldest and best Japanese eateries. The menu changes according to season and there's an adventurous note to the sushi – duck breast in orange-teriyaki and goat's cheese in pata negra ham make an appearance – and you can choose from several different set menus. There's a *Sticks 'n' Sushi Takeaway* (seating also available) further down Nansensgade at no. 47, which is also open during the day and offers a similar menu. Mon–Thurs 6–10pm, Fri & Sat 6–11pm.

Thorvaldsens Hus Gammel Strand 34 ☏ 33 32 04 00. Bustling canalside café/restaurant, popular with business lunchers and serving up a daytime menu of mostly Danish fare, ranging from hearty brunch (daily 11am–3pm; 98kr) and herring smørrebrød (from 65kr) to burgers, steaks and fish dishes for 135kr upwards. It's all a bit more upmarket and á la carte in the evening – foie gras, saddle of wild boar and the like – with main courses from 200kr. There's a great view of the colourful frescoes of Thorvaldsen's Museum from the seats outside. Mon–Thurs & Sun 10am–midnight, Fri & Sat 10am–2am.

Christianshavn

The following places are shown on the map on p.76.

Bastionen og Løven Voldgade 50 ☎ 32 95 09 40, ⓦ www.bastionen-loven.dk. Set in the old miller's house (with outside seating) next to Lille Mølle up on the ramparts, this is a charming, relaxed spot for a bite of traditional Danish food. The lunchtime menu offers delicious soups, salads or smørrebrod from 60kr – try the delectable kalveleverpostej (calf's liver paté). The evening menu changes monthly but features tasty soups and meat and fish mains from 175kr. The large and very popular weekend brunch buffet (10am–2pm; 150kr; book ahead) is an unbeatable way to start your tour of Christianshavn. Summer: daily 10am–midnight; winter Mon–Fri noon–midnight, Sat & Sun 10am–midnight.

Café Wilder Wildersgade 56. Popular and relaxed locals' café, great for coffee and a croissant, pasta or salads, and usually packed on Sundays with brunch junkies tucking into the "Wilders Brunch" (90kr) – a generous helping of egg, bacon, sausage, yoghurt, cheese and fruit. Daily 9am–2am.

Kanalen Wilders Plads 2 ☎ 32 95 13 30, ⓦ www .restaurant-kanalen.dk. Intimate, romantic canalside restaurant in a pink eighteenth-century building. The lunchtime menu consists of traditional Danish fare like fried herring with beetroot and potatoes; the evening set menu is mostly French, changes frequently and costs from 340kr for three courses. Mon–Sat 11.30am–midnight.

Lagkagehuset Torvegade 45 This fantastic bakery/café is laden with a mouthwatering array of Danish pastries, fruity muffins and cakes. A great place to pick up a sandwich, cake and coffee to eat by the canal – there's also some counter seating. Daily 6am–7pm.

Morgenstedet Langgaden, Christiania. Small and cosy Christiania favourite serving great-value vegetarian and vegan food from an organic kitchen – there are usually five dishes, such as salads, stews, curry and ratatouille. Turn left at the end of Pusherstreet and walk for about 5mins. No alcohol is served, but you can bring your own. Tues–Fri noon–9pm.

Spicey Kitchen Café Torvegade 56 ☎ 32 95 28 29. Good, cheap curries – mostly chicken or lamb – for around 65kr are the order of the day here, though you may have to wait for a table in the rather cramped interior. They also do kebabs and a range of veggie dishes. Takeaway is available; credit cards are not accepted. Mon–Wed 2pm–midnight, Thurs–Sun noon–midnight.

Spiseloppen The Loppe Building, Båds-mandsstraede 43, Christiania ☎ 32 57 95 58, ⓦ www.spiseloppen.dk. Upstairs from the music venue *Musikloppen*, this excellent restaurant has a reputation far beyond Christiania borders for serving superb food from a changing but always imaginative international menu. Meat and fish mains start at 155kr; also has a good variety of vegetarian options. Very popular, so book ahead. Tues–Sun 5–10pm.

Rosenborg and Frederiksstaden

The following places are shown on the map on p.76.

Café Petersborg Bredgade 76 ☎ 33 12 60 16. Served up in a small unpretentious basement restaurant popular with business lunchers in the know, the Danish food here includes an extensive smørrebrød list and a large selection of traditional à la carte meals, including a daily special from 80kr upwards. The building used to house the Russian consulate, hence the name, and the old atmosphere still lingers. Mon–Fri 11.45am–10pm

The Coffee Factory Gothersgade 21. Coffee for the *feinschmecker* (ie, someone who can taste which estate a coffee comes from), with an extensive selection of the finest blends from around the world – though they're no purists and are just as happy to whip you up a *tofficino* (espresso topped with milk, toffee, cream and hazelnuts). There's also a delicious array of brownies, muffins, cookies, pastries and cakes on offer; as well as sandwiches. Mon–Fri 7.30am–7pm, Sat 9am–6pm.

O's American Breakfast & Diner Gothersgade 15 ☎ 33 12 96 12, and Øster Farimagsgade 27 ☎ 35 43 99 91. Full-on American diner-cum-steakhouse, with a vast assortment of fry-ups that could take care of your calorie count for an entire week. Especially recommended are the filling breakfast/ brunches (from 69kr) that come with pancakes, hash browns, sausages and eggs, and – at the Gothersgade branch – can be enjoyed as early as 3am during weekends. Dinner (only at Gothersgade branch) is New Orleans-style soul food: Jambalaya chicken and chicken gumbo are among the two favourites. Gothersgade Mon–Thurs 9.30am–10pm Fri–Sun 3am–10pm; Øster Farimagsgade daily 9am–3pm.

Sult Vognmagergade 8B ☎ 33 74 34 17. Situated inside Cinemateket, the global cuisine here cannot be faulted, and neither can the friendly service. Well-prepared, beautifully presented dishes leave the open kitchen throughout the day, from the all-you-can-eat brunch buffet (Sat & Sun 10am–3pm; 150kr including coffee/tea and juice) and classic Danish lunch dishes (starting at 65kr for herring) to scrumptious evening meals such as halibut with gnocchi for 175kr. The obligatory coffee, burgers and salads are also available at any time. Tues–Sun 10am–10pm.

Tapas Baren Dronningens Tværgade 22 ⓣ33 36 07 70. Wonderful northern Spanish restaurant with menu dominated by tapas; try the delicious *Espárragos rellenos con caviar oricios* – pickled white asparagus stuffed with sea urchin caviar (105kr). For afters, there's a choice between Spanish cheeses and sweets, and there's a wide selection of Spanish wines. Mon–Wed 5–11pm, Thurs 5–11.30pm Fri–Sat noon–11.30pm.

Taste Store Kongensgade 80-82. Exquisite little deli near the Marmorkirken producing largely organic veg and meat salads, sandwiches (from 48kr), soups and cakes that cannot be bettered. The daily hot special (95kr, 60kr to go) is a bargain. You can eat in at a small, stylish seating area with Arne Jacobsen chairs – or, on a sunny day, take your food to a bench in Amalieparken. Mon–Thurs 11am–4pm, Fri 11am–5.30pm.

Umami Store Kongensgade 59 ⓣ33 38 75 00 Ⓦwww.restaurantumami.dk. Currently *the* place to eat out in the city, this large and super-cool French-Japanese restaurant, with its fabulous food, minimalist décor and fashionable crowd is Copenhagen's answer to London's *Nobu*. Sip on a martini of lemongrass-infused sake in the lounge bar, before heading up to the delights of the sushi bar or the restaurant, where you'll find dishes ranging from relatively inexpensive tempura (75kr upwards), oxtail soba noodle soup (105kr) or noodles (110kr) to more expensive mains like grilled veal tenderloin with wasabi (210kr) or guinea-fowl breast teriyaki (175kr). Mon–Thurs noon–3pm & 6–10pm, Fri noon–3pm & 6–11pm, Sat 6–11pm, Sun 6–10pm.

Rådhuspladsen and around

The following places are shown on the map on p.76.

Café Bjørg's Vestervoldgade 19 ⓣ33 14 53 20. This busy, trendy café/bar on the edge of Indre By serves up good-value sandwiches, salads, burgers and brunch (daily 10am–1pm, till 2pm on weekends; 89kr) by day, and a more expensive menu – steak, chicken and fish dishes from 100kr – by night. Mon–Thurs & Sun 10am–midnight, Fri & Sat 10am–2am.

Flow Gyldenløvesgade 10 ⓣ33 14 43 43. Organic vegetarian restaurant (with a takeaway next door) serving Ayurveda-inspired meals that should make you feel energetic, balanced and cheerful. The menu changes each evening but might include

dishes such as beetroot pie or cream-baked fennel with home-made spelt bread. No alcohol or smoking. Daily 5–8pm.

Glyptoteket Ny Carlsberg Glyptotek, Dantes Plads. The gallery's incomparable glass-domed, palm-filled Winter Gardens is one of the best lunchtime settings in town, and the food is excellent, too. There's open sandwiches, salads, great home-made cakes and wonderful coffee, as well as a 145kr brunch. Come on a Wednesday or Sunday and you won't have to pay the gallery entrance fee to eat here. Tues–Sun 10am–4pm.

Kanal Cafeen Frederiksholm Kanal 18 ⓣ33 11 57 70. Dating back to 1852 and close enough to Parliament to be a popular lunch spot for politicians, this rather cramped but cosy *smørrebrød* place offers 36 toppings (English list available; from 35kr per topping) including all the standards; for the more adventurous there's pigs' head pâté (winter only) or pressed belly of lamb. Booking essential. Mon–Fri 11.30am–4pm.

Wagamama Tietgensgade 20 ⓣ33 75 06 58. Large, bright new branch of the fast-growing London-based chain, dishing up unfailingly delicious bowls of steaming Asian soups, curries or noodles at very reasonable prices, all in the 70-90kr price bracket and ranging from chilli chicken ramen to mandarin and sesame beef salad, with several good veggie options on offer too. Mon–Thurs & Sun noon–11pm, Fri & Sat noon–midnight.

Vesterbro

The following places are shown on the map on p.96.

Det Gule Hus Istedgade 48 ⓣ33 25 90 71. Unmissable yellow villa offering great breakfasts; options include pancakes (21kr), three types of brunch (one vegetarian, one decidedly carnivorous, one French, all 69kr) or standard continental with freshly baked bread (49kr). Lunch – soup, burgers, club sandwiches, nachos and salads – and evening meals like grilled tuna or warm goat's cheese salad (always with at least one veggie option) are also available, and start at 118kr. Mon–Thurs 10am–midnight, Fri & Sat 10am–2am, Sun 10am–11pm.

Hackenbusch Vesterbrogade 124 ⓣ33 21 74 74. Laid-back dive, with a café/bar at the front serving three types of brunch (from 75kr; Mon–Fri 11am–2pm, Sat 11am– 3pm), including a veggie option, as well as burgers and sandwiches heaped with salad. Try the spicy and delicious "frog burger" (65kr); the ingredients are a well-kept secret, though it's based on beef. The excellent evening-only Mediterranean-style restaurant at the back has steak, fish and veggie mains such as braised shank of lamb for around 120kr, plus a daily special for 88kr. Mon–Sat 11am–10pm, Sun 11am–9pm.

Lê Lê Vesterbrogade 56 ⓣ 33 22 71 35. Busy new Vietnamese restaurant opposite the City Museum, with French-colonial style decor and simple but elegant and tasty food. Fixed-price lunches (75kr) consist of five choices, from pho rice-noodle soup or cold rice-noodle salad to stir-fried vegetables in curry and coconut sauce. At dinner the choices are more varied and main course prices max out at 135kr. As the place is packed at dinner, and they don't take bookings, it's a good idea to arrive early or prepare for a long wait at the bar (which serves Vietnamese beer, of course). Mon & Weds–Sun 11.30am–11pm.

Riccos – Butik & Kaffebar Istedgade 119. One of the best coffee joints in town, with a small seating area in the back room. The owner describes himself as a coffee nerd, and if he's not working behind the counter, he's travelling the globe in search of the finest beans. Apart from coffee in various forms – hot as well as cold – there's also cakes and Italian ice cream. Daily 9am–11pm.

Den Sorte Gryde Istedgade 108. Meat, meat and more meat in this tiny takeaway joint (a few seats available), be it roast chicken, BBQ steak, beef stew, juicy burgers dripping with cheese and bacon or *flæskesteg* – fat slices of pork with crackling, served in a sandwich or with potatoes, red cabbage and pickles. Fortifying, filling and delicious. Mon–Sat 4pm–midnight, Sun 2pm–midnight.

Thai Esan Lille Istedgade 7 ⓣ 33 24 98 54. Taking advantage of fresh ingredients from the numerous Thai food shops in the area, this very popular place serves a wide range of cheap, hot food in a fairly authentic Thai atmosphere. The chicken in oyster sauce (85kr) or the Tom Yom shrimp soup for only 65kr are both good choices. Mon–Thurs & Sun noon–11pm, Fri & Sat noon–midnight.

Fredriksberg

The following place is shown on the map on p.96.

Hansens Gamle Familiehave Pile Allé 10–12 ⓣ 36 30 92 57. This historic outdoor restaurant (there's a sliding roof in use during winter) dishes up some of the city's most delectable open sandwiches, with a fantastic spread of herrings, cold meats and cheeses, all lavishly decorated with fresh salad, pickles, fried onions and other smørrebrød essentials. Beautifully prepared traditional hot meals, such as *biksemad* (80kr) and *flæskesteg* (142kr) are also on offer. Daily 11am–midnight.

Nørrebro

The following places are shown on the map on p.101.

Floras Kaffebar Blågårdsgade 27. This glitzy café on Blågårds Plads is known predominantly as a coffee place, with many exotic blends on offer, but also does an array of daily specials like warm salads or pasta for 90kr upwards, plus soups, sandwiches and home-made cakes. Brunch is served daily (10am–3pm; 89kr). Mon–Wed 10am–midnight, Thurs–Sat 10am–1am, Sun 10am–11pm.

Front Page Sortedam Dossering 21 ⓣ 35 37 38 29. Corner café (not to be confused with the restaurant next door) with outdoor lakeside seating. As well as the usual array of sandwiches (59kr) and salads (69kr), there's also superb tapas – a 95kr plate is enough for two. Also recommended is the daily brunch (from opening time till 3pm); for 79kr you get a plateful of bacon and eggs, chorizo, yoghurt, fruit, cheese and fresh bread. Mon–Wed 11am–1am, Thurs 11am–2am, Fri–Sat 10am–2am, Sun 10am–1am.

Kaffesalonen Peblinge Dossering 6. Friendly neighbourhood coffee-house which also offers main meals such as lightly grilled tuna steak and vegetarian pasta (89kr). The excellent breakfast of a bagel, cheese, ham and yoghurt (until 11am; 49kr) and brunch (10am–2pm; 85kr) draws in the crowds too, and the superb lakeside location makes it a great spot to enjoy a quiet couple of cool draught beers. Mon–Fri 8am–midnight, Sat & Sun 10am–midnight.

Kates Joint Blågårdsgade 12 ⓣ 35 37 44 96. Small, intimate and somewhat bohemian place, where you can find dishes from most corners of the world (the blackboard menu changes daily). Amongst the tasty offerings is the perennial favourite, Jamaican jerk chicken. Cheapest is Tandoori chicken and rice for 62kr. Daily 5.30–10.30pm.

Pussy Galore's Flying Circus Sankt Hans Torv 30 ⓣ 35 24 53 00. Modern café/bar on trendy Sankt Hans Torv, where the young and famous hang out. Food here is great throughout the day: the infamous brunch (daily 9am–4pm; 80kr) pulls in a large crowd, while the breakfast plate is good value at a mere 25kr. From 11am onwards, you can choose from club/tuna/grilled chicken sandwiches, tasty burgers, soups and salads (all from 70kr) or more full-on meals like steak or grilled fish (from 79kr). Mon–Fri 8am–2am, Sat & Sun 9am–2pm.

Tibet Blågårds Plads 10 ⓣ 35 36 85 05. Very popular and unique Tibetan restaurant, with unusual dishes such as the traditional *momo* starter – steamed veg or meat dumplings (35kr), or *thantuk*, thin rice-noodle soup with beef or vegetables (60kr), making up the menu at both lunch and dinner. Tues–Sun 1–11pm.

Østerbro

The following place is shown on the map on p.101.

Den Franske Café Sortedam Dossering 101. Despite its name, nothing here comes across as particularly French, but its tranquil lakeside setting makes it a popular choice – especially with families, and it's a good place to try out standard Danish fare such as *frikadeller* at very reasonable prices. Brunch (10am–2pm; 83kr, weekends 105kr) is also popular. Daily 10am–11pm.

Amager

Krunch Øresundsvej 14 ☎32 84 50 50. Organic restaurant near the Amager Bio concert venue, with a delightful selection of seasonal buffet dishes (129kr all-you-can-eat) and daily specials like steak with chilli-baked beetroot and new potatoes (95kr). The weekend brunch (10am–4pm, 98kr) is very popular – fill up on eggs, bacon, pancakes, cheese and fruit. *Krunch* also operates a popular beach tavern at Kastrup Fort (see p.103), Amagerstrandvej 246 (open May–Sept), selling fantastic sandwiches and cold and hot drinks, as well as food from a barbecue out front in the evening. Tues–Fri 5–10pm, Sat & Sun 10am–10pm. Bus #2A and #12.

Drinking

Copenhagen's drinking holes run the whole gamut from rather dingy *kaffebars* to ultra-hip cocktail places. Most serve some kind of light food, and it's worth bearing in mind that the distinction between bars and cafés is often blurred, with cafés that primarily serve meals during the day morphing into bars by night. **Opening hours** vary significantly from venue to venue, though you'll be able to find somewhere to drink at any time of the day or night.

Indre By

The following places are shown on the map on p.76.

Bo-Bi Bar Klareboderne 14. Rumour has it that this bar was opened in 1917 by a sailor who'd just returned from New York, and styled it on the bars he'd frequented there – the cosy red decor has stayed pretty much the same ever since, though the clientele in this small, atmospheric drinking hole is now inner-city professional types, artists and writers. Daily 10am–2am.

Bloomsday Bar Niels Hemmingsens Gade 32. Irish bar named after the day in James Joyce's *Ulysses* when his "stream of consciousness" takes place. Especially popular with Copenhagen's large Irish population for not being a themed pub and the good selection of draught beers and cider. Other attractions are a big-screen TV showing football, and pool tables and darts in a large room at the back. Sunday afternoons are known for their Irish music sessions. Daily noon–2am.

Charlie's Bar Pilestræde 33. *Charlie's* is the only bar in Denmark to be awarded the prestigious Cask Marque for its vast selection of high-quality real ales. If you want a seat in this cosy and popular hangout, you'll need to arrive early. Mon–Weds 2pm–2am, Thurs–Sat noon to 2am, Sun 2–11pm.

Dan Turèll Store Regnegade 3–5. Named after the popular Danish author, this swanky café-bar, covered in steel and mirrors, sports Turèll book covers on the wall and an arty but sociable student crowd. During summer, the large front opens out onto the street. Mon–Thurs 9.30am–midnight, Fri & Sat 9.30am–2am, Sun 10am–10pm.

Hviids Vinstue Kongens Nytorv 19. Old-fashioned place dating back to 1723 – Hans Christian Andersen was a regular – whose many crowded rooms are patrolled by courteous uniformed waiters. There's a wide selection of Danish beers (27 at last count) and a great lunch deal – three pieces of *smørrebrød* and a Tuborg – for 55kr. Outdoor seating on Kongens Nytorv square in summer and popular place for *gløgg* in winter. Mon–Thurs & Sun 10am–1am, Fri & Sat 10am–2am.

Krasnapolsky Vestergade 10. This once hip and trendsetting establishment has mellowed out somewhat and now attracts a more mixed crowd of shoppers, tourists and serious party-goers. Friday and Saturday a visiting DJ delivers mainstream R&B, funk and disco-hits in the back-room dancing area. The bartenders can be difficult, but don't let this put you off. Mon–Thurs 11am to midnight, Fri & Sat 10am–5am.

The Moose Sværtegade 5. This deceptively large bar in a long, narrow listed building is one of the cheapest places to get tanked up before hitting the clubs, especially on Tues, Thurs and Sat, when it's happy hour from 9pm onwards. Mon & Sun 1pm–3am, Tues & Wed 1pm–6am, Thurs–Sat 1pm–7am.

Musen og Elefanten Vestergade 21. Personable bar set up in homage to its owner's twin obsessions: Carlsberg Elephant Beer – one of the strongest in Denmark – and traditional rock music. Draught Elephant flows from a carved trunk at the first-floor bar, while rock fiends sit around discussing the trade and tapping their toes to the loud music. Mon & Sun 1pm–3am, Tues & Wed 1pm–6am, Thurs–Sat 1pm–7am.

Rådhuspladsen and around

The following places are shown on the map on p.76.

Bryggeriet Apollo Vesterbrogade 3. Slap bang in the middle of the entertainment zone and offering Bryggeriet's organic beer, freshly brewed on the premises and served up amidst gleaming vats, copper kettles and heavy wooden tables. If you want, you can have your beer served in a Belgian "Kwak", similar to a short yard-glass – be careful not to pour it all over yourself. Not surprisingly, it's a tad pricey, but fun. Mon & Sun 1pm–3am, Tues & Wed 1pm–6am, Thurs–Sat 1pm–7am.

Zum Biergarten Axeltorv 12. Heaving new Bavarian-style beer hall housed in the old waterworks building, offering plenty of Oktoberfest-ish atmosphere with long rickety wooden tables and huge litre-mugs of German microbrewery beer. When the weather allows, there's outdoor service, including food prepared on an open grill. Tues & Wed 4pm–11pm, Thurs 4pm–2am, Fri 2pm–3am, Sat 4pm–3am.

Frederiksstaden and around

The following places are shown on the map on p.76.

Andy's Bar Gothersgade 33B. A so-called morning-pub, where the city's party-goers head when they can dance no more. Always crowded and noisy with an exuberant booze-fuelled clientele, so not the best option if you're stone-cold sober. That said, the easy atmosphere will soon have you believing that the person on your left is your best friend in the whole wide world. Daily 11pm–6am.

Nyhavn 17 Nyhavn 17. Located on fashionable Nyhavn, this is a cross between a British pub and a maritime museum, with old iron diving helmets, ships' figureheads, anchors and rudders scattered around the dimly lit interior – the gleaming brass bar fittings are the only bright feature. Popular among tourists and Danes alike, with moderately priced draught beers and ciders. Mon–Thurs & Sun 10am–2am, Fri & Sat 10am–3am.

Christianshavn

The following places are shown on the map on p.76.

Fingerbøllet Wildersgade 39. "The Thimble" is a real locals' hangout, where people of all ages come to drink beer and play billiards – old jeans and faded T-shirts seem to be the appropriate dress code. Mon–Sat 11am–2am, Sun noon–2am.

Nemoland Pusherstreet, Christiania. One of Christiania's two main watering holes, and among Copenhagen's most popular open-air bars, with occasional live gigs during summer, when it's often packed with tourists and shoppers enjoying their purchases from nearby Pusherstreet. It's quieter during the winter, with regulars playing backgammon or billiards. Mon–Thurs & Sun 10am–2am, Fri & Sat 10am–3.30am.

Woodstock Pusherstreet, Christiania. Housed in a former military barracks full of 1960s spirit, this is a chilled-out place to enjoy a drink (and perhaps a smoke) in the ramshackle bar kitted out with old garden furniture. Mon–Thurs & Sun 10am–2am, Fri & Sat 10am–3.30am.

Vesterbro & Frederiksberg

The following places are shown on the map on p.96.

Bang & Jensen Istedgade 130, Vesterbro. High stucco ceilings and a mahogany counter left over from its former incarnation as a pharmacy add to the character of this place, which is the priciest in Vesterbro. It's usually packed before concerts at Vega (see p.113), and on Saturday nights when *Ingeborgs Cocktail Saloon* takes over, and the in-house DJ sets the mood with electronic jazz grooves. Mon–Fri 8am–2am, Sat 10am–2am, Sun 10am–midnight.

Boutique Lize Enghave Plads 6, Vesterbro. Hugely popular cocktail bar across the square from Vega (see p.113) and another good option for a pre-concert drink. In addition to the dazzling range of cocktails, there's a good selection of local and imported microbrewery draught beers. Wed 8pm–midnight, Thurs 8pm–2am, Sat & Sun 8pm–4pm.

Café Ludwigsen Sundesvedsgade 2, Vesterbro. Outrageously popular late-night bar (despite the "café" in the name, there's no food) where the young, free and on-the-pull congregate en masse after hours. Mon–Wed noon–2am, Thurs noon–5am, Fri & Sat noon–6am, Sun 3pm–2am.

Ideal Bar Enghavevej 40, Vesterbro. Housed in the Vega music complex (see p.113), this stylish bar is known for its laid-back attitude and excellent cocktails. Post-gig, the atmosphere is relaxed, with patrons sinking into the large leather sofas; things get going after midnight, when the dance tunes start playing. Wed 7pm–4am, Thurs–Sat 7pm–5am.

90eren Gammel Kongevej 90, Frederiksberg. Famous for its painstakingly pulled draught beer, an operation which can take up to twelve minutes, this is the only bar in Copenhagen serving uncarbonated Carlsberg beer (it's brewed at the nearby brewery). The strong hoppy flavour is reminiscent of English real ale and – supposedly – very similar to the original Carlsberg beer produced in the mid-nineteenth century. Mon–Wed 11am–1am, Thurs–Sat 11am–2am, Sun 1pm–1am.

Pinden Reventlowsgade 4, Vesterbro. Traditional, smoky drinking den where local old-timers hang out on worn-out furniture playing the odd game of dice. Mon–Sat 2pm–2am, Sun 4pm–2am.

Riesen Oehlenschlægersgade 36, Vesterbro. Basic, no-frills student hangout with indie music playing in the background and an affordable selection of imported beer, as well as the obligatory cocktail menu. Wed & Thurs 8am–2.30am, Fri & Sat 8pm–3.30am.

Nørrebro

The following places are shown on the map on p.101.

Café Blågård's Apotek Blågårds Plads 20. Homely bar that's still patronized by some of the left-wing activists who used to clash on this square with the police during the 1970s. They're now joined by a less committed crowd who come to sample the bar's many wines and Urquell draught beer. Gets packed at weekends, when there's also live jazz, blues or rock. Winter daily 3pm–2am; summer noon–2am.

Caféen Funke Blegdamsvej 2. Despite the location on hip Sankt Hans Torv, this unpretentious, laid-back place has nothing to do with the hype across the square. Cheap beer, a Tuesday night backgammon tournament and live music or stand-up comedy a couple of nights a week. Mon–Wed & Sun 2pm–2am, Thurs–Sat 2pm–5am.

Kaffesalonen Peblinge Dossering 6. Popular lakeside café, worth seeking out in the summer when tables are moved out onto a floating dock and the draught beer pumps flow. Mon–Fri 8am–midnight, Sat & Sun 10am–midnight.

Nørrebro Bryghus Ryesgade 2. Immensely popular brewery pub housed in an old factory, with a range of homebrews that sell out quicker than they can be bottled. Mon–Wed 11am–midnight, Thurs–Sat 11am–2am, Sun 11am–10pm.

Pussy Galore's Flying Circus Skt Hans Torv 30. Named after the nubile heroine of the James Bond movie *Goldfinger* – you'll be stirred, if not shaken, by delicious cocktails, an extensive list of snaps, tasty sandwiches and outdoor seating on one of Nørrebro's hippest squares – definitely a place to be seen. Mon–Fri 8am–2am, Sat & Sun 9am–2am.

Ølbaren Elmegade 2. A small, crowded place frequented by beer enthusiasts (or nerds, depending on your perspective), with an incredibly wide range of beer from all over Europe. Service can be slow. Winter Mon 9pm–1am, Tues–Thurs & Sat 4pm–1am, Fri 3pm–1am; summer Mon 9pm–1am, Tues–Thurs & Sat 8pm–1am, Fri 3pm–1am.

Nightlife and entertainment

Copenhagen is Scandinavia's party town, with a wide range of **clubs** catering to all ages and tastes and a great array of **live music**. Of the latter, the **jazz** scene has traditionally been the city's liveliest – a legacy of the number of respected American jazz musicians such as Dexter Gordon and Ben Webster who lived here during the 1960s and 1970s – while the annual jazz festival is world-renowned. There's also a healthy local **rock** scene; many big-name international acts include Copenhagen on their tours, while many more turn up for the huge annual Roskilde Festival (see p.146). A number of the smaller venues double as cafés or restaurants during the day and bars in the evening, before becoming live music venues or nightclubs after midnight.

As far as the high arts go, Copenhagen is currently undergoing something of a renaissance. For decades, the grandiose **Det Kongelige Teater** on Kongens Nytorv was the one-stop venue for productions by the various royal companies of opera, ballet and theatre. Opera has now moved to its own venue, the new Operæn (see p.86), while the Det Kongelige Teater is set to move to new premises in 2007/8. The city puts on a wide range of **classical music** and is home to a number of top-class ensembles, including the Zealand Symphony Orchestra and the excellent Danish National Symphony Orchestra/DR (@www.dr.dk/dnso), also set to move to new purpose-built premises in Amager in 2008. Look out, too, for classical music concerts in many of Copenhagen's grandest churches and larger museums – check with the tourist office. For **ballet** lovers, there's the fairly traditional repertoire of the Royal Ballet, staged at Det Kongelige Teater and occasionally at Operæn, as well as at Tivoli during the summer and at Christmas, while modern dance, though still limited to a handful of venues, has developed a stronger presence in recent years. Copenhagen has a diverse **theatre** scene, though as most productions are in Danish they're unlikely to be of interest to most visitors. You could see whether there's anything being staged by the **London Toast Theatre** (ⓦwww.londontoast.dk), a well-established English theatre company which performs in the city's mainstream theatres.

Danes are keen **cinema**-goers, and in addition to the usual Hollywood flicks there's usually at least one Danish move being shown, while foreign-language films get good representation too – most films are screened in their original language, with Danish subtitles. The city's **arthouse** cinemas, particularly Cinemateket at the Filmhuset, home to the Danish Film Institute (see p.116), always have a good selection of more offbeat offerings. At weekends, it's definitely worth booking ahead for all films, particularly for new releases. In March/April, the city takes part in the **Night Film Festival** (ⓦwww.natfilm.dk) with screenings of more esoteric foreign films (with English subtitles) into the wee hours. In addition, the **Copenhagen International Film Festival** is held during the autumn (see p.44).

For **listings** information on all entertainment and nightlife, pick up a copy of the English-language *Copenhagen Post* (ⓦwww.cphpost.dk; 20kr) from the tourist office or bookshops, or check out their website, ⓦwww.cphpost.dk; alternatively there's English-language listings at ⓦwww.aok.dk and ⓦwww.kulturnaut.dk. There's also a few free Danish-language listings pamphlets: for film, check out the weekly *Film Kalenderen* (in English at ⓦwww.aok.dk), available from the tourist office and cinemas, or the film calendar in the free city paper *metroXpress*, available from train stations. For theatre and modern dance, there's the monthly *Teater Kalenderen*, available from the tourist office and performance venues. In addition, Det Kongelige Teater produces the *Kalendar* leaflet, detailing all of the season's productions – opera, theatre, concerts and ballet – across its various venues, including Operæn. Alternatively, check out their website, ⓦwww.kglteater.dk.

Tickets to most venues listed below can be bought through **Billetnet** (credit card booking line ☎70 15 65 65, 10am–9pm; ⓦwww.billetnet.dk), at Vesterbrogade 3 beside Tivoli's main entrance, and in all post offices (☎33 15 10 12; 10kr booking fee). You can also **book online** at many of the venues – we've given websites where they exist. Det Kongelige Teater holds back around 25 tickets for that evening's performance at the old theatre and Operaen, but you have to go in person to the box office at August Bournonvilles Passage 1, just off Kongens Nytorv, to buy them. You might want to chance it and wait till 4pm when any unsold tickets for that night's performances are sold off at a fifty percent discount.

For more details of festivals and annual events in Copenhagen see Basics, pp.42–44.

Live music venues

The places listed below are shown on the maps on p.76, p.96 and p.101.

Amager Bio Øresundsvej 6, Amager ☎32 86 02 00, ⓦwww.amagerbio.dk. Converted cinema that's now one of the city's largest and most popular live music venues, hosting big names from the local and international music scene. Tickets start at 185kr.

Café Blågård's Apotek Blågårds Plads 20, Nørrebro ☎ 35 37 24 42, ⓦ www.kroteket.dk.. Homely venue with packed live jazz, blues, rock or world music every Monday, Friday and Saturday. Monday is jazz jam and free, Friday and Saturday 20kr. Daily 3pm–2am (in summer from noon).

Café Rust Guldbergsgade 8, Nørrebro ☎ 35 24 52 00, ⓦ www.rust.dk. One of the best-known venues in town, this multifaceted place on busy Skt Hans Torv hosts up-and-coming live indie rock, hip-hop and electronic acts on its main stage. Downstairs is the very hip *Rust Natklub* (see p.114). Tickets are 50–130kr. Wed–Sat 9pm–5am.

Copenhagen Jazzhouse/Natklub Niels Hemmingsensgade 10, Indre By ☎ 33 15 26 00, ⓦ www.jazzhouse.dk. Copenhagen's premier jazz venue, this large, smart two-level club is frequented by aficionados of all ages. Gigs start at 8.30pm weekdays and 9.30pm Fri and Sat, with music ranging from traditional jazz and jazz-funk, fusion and neobop to world music at its best. Thursdays to Saturdays the *Natklub* nightclub (see p.114) takes over at midnight (or whenever the gigs finish) and continues until the early hours of the morning. 120kr. Mon–Wed & Sun 6pm–midnight, Thurs–Sat 6pm–5am.

Drop Inn Kompagnistræde 34, Indre By ☎ 33 11 24 04. A cosy café-cum-jazz bar that has (often free) live jazz, blues or folk every night (from 10pm). In the summer there's both indoor and outdoor seating, and sandwiches and light meals are available throughout the day. Mon–Thurs 11am–4am, Fri 11am–5am, Sat noon–5am, Sun 2pm–5am.

Huset Magstræde Rådhusstræde 13, Indre By ☎ 33 69 32 00, ⓦ www.husetmagstraede.dk. Located in the same complex as Uselt, on the first floor of the building across the courtyard, jazz flows from *Jazzscenen* most nights from around 9pm, while *Musikcafeen* on the third floor, is a platform for up-and-coming bands. Entry starts at 40kr with big reductions for students. Mon & Tues 10am–11pm, Wed–Sat 10am–midnight, Sun 10am–5pm.

Det Hvide Lam Kultorvet 5, Indre By ☎ 33 32 07 38. Mon 10am to midnight, Tues–Wed 10am–1am, Thurs–Sat 10am–2am, Sun noon to 1am. Traditional jazz gigs Tues–Sun 8.30pm to midnight. Small, dark basement bar with no stage but loads of atmosphere, and musicians giving it all they've got on the New Orleans jazz front most nights.

Islands Bryggos Kulturhus Islands Brygge 18, Amager. Popular new cultural centre next to the harbour pool on the banks of Inner Havnen, with live gigs (starting at 9pm) four or five times a week ranging from jazz, blues and world music

to full-blown classical concerts. Tickets start at 40kr. Mon–Weds 11am–11pm, Thurs & Fri 11am–midnight, Sat 10am–midnight, Sun 10am–11pm.

Jazzcup Gothersgade 107, Indre By ☎ 33 33 87 40. An exciting arrival on the Copenhagen jazz scene, this innovative café, CD shop and music venue has live jazz every Fri and Sat afternoon. Some of the best Danish and international musicians play here, including names from the world music circuit. Tickets 40–60kr. Mon–Thurs 11.30am–5.30pm, Fri 11am–6.30pm, Sat 10am–5.30pm.

Loppen Christiania, Christianshavn ☎ 32 57 84 22, ⓦ www.loppen.dk. This cool converted warehouse on the edge of Christiania hosts (from 11pm) both established and experimental Danish rock, jazz and performance artists, and quite a few visiting British and American ones too. Some gigs are free, others 60–200kr. Tues–Sun 9pm–2am.

Mojo Løngangsstræde 21C, Indre By ☎ 33 11 64 53, ⓦ www.mojo.dk. Small blues venue with plenty of down-at-heel ambience, popular with aficionados of all ages. The nightly live music starts around 10pm and is followed at weekends with a DJ. Less established local acts get things going before the big names come on stage. There's a daily happy hour (8–10pm); entrance is either free or 60/120kr, depending on what's on. Daily 8pm–5am.

Pumpehuset Studiestræde 52, Indre By ☎ 33 93 19 09, ⓦ www.pumpehuset.dk. This spacious former pumphouse is one of the city's best concert venues, with capacity for 600 punters. A broad sweep of up-and-coming or fading international rock acts and big Danish names perform about eight times a month. Tickets 60–250kr.

Stengade 30 Stengade 18, Nørrebro ☎ 35 36 09 36, ⓦ www.stengade30.dk. Housed in a 1970s squat, this is the city's prime punk rock, indie and metal venue. Every Tuesday, the Play It jam session is open for everyone, and the live acts are often followed by all-night dance parties with a mix of techno, indie and rock depending on the DJ. 50kr. Tues & Wed 9pm–2am, Thurs 9pm–5am, Fri–Sat 10pm–5am.

Tivoli Vesterbrogade 3, Indre By ☎ 33 15 10 01, ⓦ www.tivoli.dk. Surprisingly good outdoor rock-pop concerts every Friday night at 10pm from April to September – with a good crowd and decent weather, they can be great fun. Entry is free with general Tivoli admittance.

Vega Enghavevej 40, Vesterbro ☎ 33 25 70 11, ⓦ www.vega.dk. Located in a former union hall, this top music venue retains its 1950s and 1960s decor while showcasing plenty of modern alternative rock. With a capacity of 1500, the Store Vega stage is used for big international names, while the smaller Lille Vega hosts smaller bands or more intimate big-name shows. Tickets 150–400kr. **Femøren** Amager Strandpark, Amager. Huge, inexpensive open-air rock concerts by top local bands and international acts from June to August on a temporary stage, a stone's throw from Amager beach. For details of upcoming events, ask at Uselt or the tourist office (see p.64).

Clubs

The places listed below are shown on the maps on p.76, p.96 and p.101.

Diskotek In Nørregade 1, Indre By ☎ 33 11 74 78, ⓦ www.discotekin.dk. Two nightclubs under one roof: the Spanish-inspired *La Hacienda*, with cushy sofas and soul and R&B tunes, and the more electronic *Dance Floor*. You can move freely between the two, and both are pretty mainstream, catering for a young audience. You pay a fixed bar-fee when you arrive (women half-price) and fill yourself up on beer, wine or champagne all night. Entry 500kr, bar fees 25–100kr. Fri 11pm–8am, Sat 11pm–10am.

Natklub Niels Hemmingsensgade 10, Indre By ☎ 33 15 26 00, ⓦ www.jazzhouse.dk. When the live gigs are over at *Copenhagen Jazzhouse* (see p.113), *Natklub* takes over, with in-house DJs serving up a mix of Latin, house, acid jazz, bossa nova and old-school disco tunes to dance the night away. Entry 60kr. Fri & Sat midnight–5am.

Park Nightclub Østerbrogade 79, Østerbro ☎ 35 42 62 48, ⓦ www.park.dk. Housed in the ground floor of popular *Park Café*, with an open-air deck during summer, this packed, retro-style club offers R&B, soul, disco and house music at its most smooth, and caters to a fun, diverse crowd. Entry 50kr. Thurs 11pm–5am, Fri & Sat 11am–6pm.

Rust Natklub Guldbergsgade 8, Nørrebro ☎ 35 24 52 00, ⓦ www.rust.dk. Crowded, multi-level dive named after Mathias Rust, who famously landed his small plane on Moscow's Red Square in 1987; his adventure resulted in the pan-Scandinavian peace initiative, the Next Stop Sovjet, which was based in this building. Today, it hosts a small basement nightclub which focuses on underground electronic dance music and another larger dancefloor which hosts guest DJs playing hip-hop, house and cool, funky grooves. There's also a laid-back, minimalist cocktail bar for chilling out. Over-21s only. Entry 50kr, Thurs free. Wed–Sat 11pm–5am.

Vega Natklub Vega, Enghavevej 40, Vesterbro ☎ 33 25 70 11, ⓦ www.vega.dk. One of the top clubs in the city, based in the *Lille Vega* section of this top music venue (see p.113) and offering all you could possibly ask of a fantastic night out. Resident and internationally renowned guest DJs raise the roof with funky beats and soulful sounds. There's also an upstairs chill-out lounge with soothing tunes and fancy cocktails. Gets very busy after 1am. Free until 1am, then 60kr. Fri & Sat 11pm–5am.

Woodstock Vestergade 12, Indre By ☎ 33 11 20 71, ⓦ www.woodstock.dk. Basically a large dancefloor and not much else, *Woodstock* pulls in a large, fun-loving older crowd willing to bop to anything with a beat, though the music is predominantly retro, going all the way back to Elvis. Entry 30kr on Thurs (plus 100kr for an open bar), 50kr Fri & Sat. Thurs–Sat 10pm–5am.

Classical music, theatre, opera and dance venues

Den Anden Opera Kronprinsensgade 7, Indre By ☎ 33 32 55 56 (Mon–Fri 11am–3pm), ⓦ www.denandenopera.dk. An offbeat alternative to Det Kongelige Teater, "The Other Opera" stages small-scale new works by contemporary Danish composers.

Black Diamond Concert Hall Christians Brygge 9, Slotsholmen ☎ 33 47 47 47, ⓦ www.kb.dk. This stunning waterfront venue has quickly become a stalwart of the classical music scene and even has its own resident string quartet, which puts on regular performances.

CaféTeatret Skindergade 3, Indre By ☎ 33 12 58 14, ⓦ www.cafeteatret.dk. Part theatre, part trendy café (featuring its own programme of events) frequented by actors and arty types, *CaféTeatret* puts on a range of innovative performances – theatre, dance, cabaret – mostly in Danish. Mon–Fri 3–6.30pm, Sat 1–3pm.

Dansescenen Øster Fælled Torv 34, Østerbro ☎ 35 43 20 21 (Mon–Fri 2–6pm), ⓦ www.dansescenen.dk. The only place in Copenhagen with regular performances of modern dance, showcasing top Scandinavian ensembles as well as the work of the current choreographer in residence. The Dansescenen programme (available from the Tivoli ticket office) has a section in English.

△ Operæn

Folketeatret Nørregade 39, Indre By ☏ 33 12 18 45 (Mon–Fri 4.30–7pm, Sat & Sun 2–7pm), ⓦ www.folketeatret.dk. One of the oldest theatres in town. The main stage (Store Scene) tends to show musicals and family-oriented stuff; the smaller Hippodromen shows more experimental work as does the tiny stage, Boxen; Snoreloftet shows cabaret.

Kanonhallen Øster Fælled Torv 37, Østerbro ☏ 35 43 20 21 (Mon–Fri 2–6pm), ⓦ www.kanonhallen. net. One of the best venues in the city for contemporary Danish theatre and dance, with an excellent reputation for cutting-edge productions and as a venue for several annual festivals.

Det Kongelige Teater Kongens Nytorv, Indre By ☏ 33 69 69 69 (Mon–Sat noon–6pm), ⓦ www. kglteater.dk. Copenhagen's grandest and oldest theatre with all the gilt and velvet pomp you could ask for. The permanent troupe performs a variety of mainstream contemporary and older plays, though most drama is now staged in the two more modern venues – the adjacent 1930s extension, Stærekassen, and TurbineHallerne, a former Turbine Hall, at Adelgade 10. Despite the arrival of the new Operæn, the old theatre still stages some opera, as well as the fairly conservative productions of the Royal Ballet and some classical concerts. Prices rise according to the scale of the production (100–1200kr), and tickets for popular works sell out very fast. Tickets bought from the box office

after 4pm on the day of performance are reduced by 50 percent.

Operæn Holmen ☏ 33 69 69 69, ⓦ www.operaen. dk. The city's spanking new opera house has two stages, the opulent, maple-encased, gilt-ceilinged Store Scene main stage, with seating for up to 1700, and the much more intimate Takkelloftet, used for more experimental productions. The Royal Ballet also uses the main stage for occasional performances.

Radiohusets Koncertsal (Studio 1) Julius Thomsens gade 1, Frederiksberg ☏ 35 20 62 62 (Mon–Fri 10am–6pm, Sat 10am–1pm). A classic of twentieth-century Danish architecture, but also something of a white elephant, having been built ten metres shorter than originally planned due to lack of funds, a shortcut which drastically affected the acoustics. The home of DR (Danish Radio), the Danish National Symphony Orchestra and Radio Choir, it's set to move to swanky new purpose-built premises in Amager in 2008, but for now it hosts regular classical music performances (Sept–May) by its celebrated orchestra. Tickets start at around 60kr; unsold tickets are sold on the door from 90 minutes before the performance.

Tivoli Koncertsal Tietgensgade 20, Indre By ☏ 33 15 10 12, ⓦ www.tivoli.dk. Tivoli's recently revamped concert hall stages a variety of classical performances and some opera, often featuring the major national orchestras.

Cinemas

Cinemateket at Filmhuset Gothersgade 55, Indre By ☏ 33 74 34 12, ⓦ www.dfi.dk. Home of the Danish Film Institute, this three-screen,

state-of-the-art complex shows the best of local and international arthouse film – the more eagerly anticipated films sell out quickly, so bookings are advisable. The Benjamin theatre shows children's films and free documentaries. Closed Mon.

Empire Bio Guldbergsgade 29F, Nørrebro ☏ 35 36 00 36, ⓦ www.empirebio.dk. Very popular cinema with huge, comfy seats and a good selection of both Danish and international movies.

Gloria Biografen Rådhuspladsen 59, Indre By ☏ 33 12 42 92, ⓦ www.gloria.dk. Small cinema located right in the centre of the city, with an eclectic programme of mainstream, some foreign-language and arthouse favourites. It also sells a range of arthouse films through its own video distribution arm, some of which can be hard to find elsewhere. A cine buff's delight.

Grand Teatret Mikkel Bryggers Gade 8, Indre By ☏ 33 15 16 11. Very central cinema, in the heart of Indre By, and showing the best of mainstream international films.

Husets Biograf Magstræde 14, Indre By ☏ 33 32 40 77. Located on the second floor of the Huset building, this small cinema shows esoteric, arthouse fare.

Danish film: Dogme95

The Danes' love affair with celluloid stretches back to the 1920s, when the country's thriving film studios looked as though they might become Europe's answer to Hollywood. The success was spearheaded by internationally renowned director **Carl Theodor Dreyer** (see p.412), with his series of dark, dramatic pieces like *The Master of the House* (1925) and the French-produced *Passion of Joan of Arc* (1928); he continued to make films until his death in the 1960s. Nowadays, the Danish film industry is booming again with a new set of filmmakers achieving international critical acclaim, in particular the group originally associated with **Dogme95**. Established in 1995 by Lars von Trier, the golden boy of Danish film, Dogme95 (ⓦ www. dogme95.dk) is perhaps the most distinctive European film movement of recent years. Founded in reaction to the domination of Hollywood, with its reliance on special effects and massive budgets, Dogme 95 is basically a set of rules drawn up by von Trier and Thomas Vinterberg and dubbed the **Vow of Chastity**, which aim to enhance cinematic realism by a series of rules: the film must be in colour, only hand-held cameras and natural lighting are allowed, shooting must be done on location with no props and sets, and no special costumes, special effects or extraneous soundtracks are permitted. Although the four main exponents of the movement – von Trier, Thomas Vinterberg, Søren Kragh Jacobsen and Kristian Levring – are all Danish, anyone can make a Dogme film if it follows the manifesto, and over thirty accredited movies have been made, including ones from as far afield as Korea and Argentina. That said, the best-known Dogme films are Danish: *Idiots* (1998), by von Trier himself, *Festen* (1998) by Thomas Vinterberg and *Mifune's Last Song* (1999) by Søren Kragh Jacobsen. More recent successes have included the Copenhagen-set *Italian for Beginners* (2002) by Lone Scherfig.

Some commentators derided Dogme95 as a cheap gimmick, but although it was largely ignored outside the European arthouse scene initially, it soon gained international recognition. Ironically, the Dogme Secretariat (responsible for accrediting films made in the Dogme mould) disbanded in 2002 for fear that Dogme was becoming too much of a genre in itself (one of the rules of the Vow of Chastity was no genre films), and claiming that it and the original founders had "moved on". Although the movement still exists, Dogme productions no longer have to receive official accreditation – they simply have to follow the manifesto.

The most famous member of the Dogme group, **Lars von Trier** (see p.414), is now an internationally acclaimed director, with several Cannes prizes under his belt and big Hollywood names like Nicole Kidman and Danny Glover headlining his projects. He continues to reject the technical artifices of film-making, filming his most recent productions – *Dogville* and *Mandalay* – on sound stages with no set, and encouraging more intense "method" performances from his actors. Ever controversial, von Trier's current project is the *USA – Land of Opportunities* trilogy, of which *Dogville* and *Mandalay* are the first two instalments; the third, *Wasington* [sic], due out in 2008, is a gritty, uncompromisingly cynical look at what von Trier sees as "America's sins and hypocrisy".

Imperial Ved Vesterport 4, Vesterbro ☎ 70 13 12 11, ✆ www.biobooking.dk. Copenhagen's largest cinema, and the usual venue for gala openings and premieres. The enormous single screen shows mainly middle-of-the-road Hollywood blockbusters, and has reclining seats and a stunning sound system.

Vester Vov Vov Absalonsgade 5, Vesterbro ☎ 33 24 42 00, ✆ www.vestervovvov.dk. Three-screen arthouse cinema, with a decent bar and café for pre-screen nibbles. Also has a large and fairly comprehensive collection of film posters, some of them for sale.

Shopping

Shopping is one of the highlights of a visit to Copenhagen, with Denmark's fine tradition of innovative design (see contexts pp.409–411) evident in products as diverse as furniture, clothing, glassware and stereo equipment. Most of the city's top shops are in Indre By: for clothes shopping, **Strøget** and **Købmagergade** are mostly lined with international chains. **Kronsprinsensgade** (off Købmagergade) is home to many of the best and most internationally recognized modern **Danish designer clothes** shops, though the streets stretching further east towards Gothersgade are also rich hunting grounds for up-and-coming labels. If your taste is for vintage, Larsbjørnstræde, Studiestræde and Skt Peders Stræde, all adjacent to the Latin Quarter, have the broadest selection of cheap **secondhand** and **ethnic clothes** shops. Good **design** is important to the Danes and you'll find a range of shops selling imaginative and

Danish design

The Danes' love affair with **design** has been going strong for a century, and its guiding principle – the successful merging of form, function and aesthetic appeal – is seen in everything from furniture and Bang & Olufsen electronics to Copenhagen's new metro system, and has been copied the world over. Danish designers have always been driven by a democratic, social ideal that good design is the right of all, as essential in the home as in public arenas – after all, it's a country where the climate means a lot of time is spent indoors. Pioneers of the 1920s such as **Poul Henningsen** and **Kaare Klint** got the ball rolling with their classic designs; the former with his stunning lighting, the latter taking classics of furniture design and reworking them for modern needs. But it wasn't until the 1940s and 1950s that Danish design became an international phenomenon via interiors and furniture designer **Finn Juhl**, who furnished parts of the UN building in New York; as well as the work of creative visionaries such as **Hans J. Wegner**, who took chair design to new heights with such classics as the Round Chair (1949). The torch was carried from thereon by the likes of **Vernor Panton**, with his more futuristic moulded plastic chairs in bright, bold colours, and **Poul Kjærholm**, whose steel-framed chairs have also become timeless classics.

But for many, it's the prolific architect/designer **Arne Jacobsen** (1902–71) who symbolizes Danish design at its best, and whose legacy is the most enduring. Still revered, copied, exhibited and coveted, classic "AJ" designs pervade the city – in its shops, cafés, restaurants and hotels, and the skyline itself. He turned his hand to everything from furniture to cutlery to coffee pots to buildings, a vision at its most ideologically complete in the swish **Radisson SAS Royal Hotel** (see p.70), for which he designed everything from the door handles to the high-rise building itself. However, he's probably most famous for his iconic chairs, the "Number 7", the "Ant", the "Swan" and the "Egg" – the latter two designed specifically for the *SAS Royal Hotel* and notable for their natural, curvy shapes intended to suggest the presence of the human form even in its absence. For more on Danish design, see Contexts, pp.409–11.

stylish furniture, glassware, kitchenware, crockery and table decorations – for an all-under-one-roof style taster, you can't do better than the outstanding **Illums Bolighus** (see opposite).

Copenhagen has no shortage of delis and excellent bakeries where you can get the vital ingredients for a picnic, or pick up something special to take home. There's also a good selection of centrally located **supermarkets** – opening hours are usually Monday to Friday 8 or 9am–7pm, Saturday 8 or 9am–4pm. Netto, the cheapest chain, has central branches at Nørre Voldgade 94, Fiolstræde 9 and Landemærket 11. In the Tivoli area, there's the more upmarket Irma, in Rådhusarkaden, Vesterbrogade 1 and Iso at Vesterbrogade 23.

Finally, if you prefer everything under one roof, head for Fisketorvet shopping centre, just south of Central Station at Kalvebod Brygge. We've detailed Denmark's retail **opening hours** in Basics (p.53), but for food and basic supplies you'll find that a few of the capital's central supermarkets are open later than normal and on Sundays. Failing that, the supermarket in Central Station is open every day 8am–midnight.

Clothes and accessories

Bruuns Bazaar Kronprinsensgade 8–9, Indre By ⓦ www.bruunsbazaar.com. Catering for both men and women, Bruuns is one of Europe's most fashionable labels, and the clothes are as expensive and exclusive as you'd expect.

Georg Jensen Amagertorv 4. Flagship store of the renowned silversmiths, selling a sophisticated mix of classics and more modern designs, from beautifully worked brooches and solid rings to elegant watches.

København K Studiestræde 32B, Indre By. Down a small passage off Studiestræde, this is *the* place for secondhand leather, velvet, suede, corduroy, denim and lace; the men's section is especially good. Opens 11am.

Kønrøg Teglgårdstræde 4, Indre By. Eyecatching one-off designs for men and women from this collective of ten young Danish designers.

Munthe plus Simonsen Grønnegade 10, Indre By ⓦ www.muntheplussimonsen.com. Hot fashion to burn a hole in your pocket; the Danish designers Naja Munthe and Karen Simonsen have established an international reputation with garments that blend Far Eastern influences with Scandinavian simplicity.

Nørgaard på Strøget, Mads Nørgaard & Englebørn Amagertorv, Indre By. A family business with two generations of designers, each catering for a different group. Nørgaard på Strøget – the oldest shop – houses women's and teenage wear in all price brackets. Mads Nørgaard is geared towards the trendy man, whereas Englebørn is an exclusive kidswear shop with equally exclusive prices.

Noa Noa Købmagergade 5, Østergade 16, Larsbjørnstræde 16, Indre By ⓦ www.noanoa.com. Popular Danish chain stores with a wide range of cotton and linen womenswear separates in pastel and natural shades.

Pede & Stoffer Klosterstræde 15 & 19, Indre By. Casual, trendy gear for men (no. 15) and women (no. 19), from a range of up-and-coming designer labels.

Sanita Langelinie Promenaden Langelinie Allé 28, Østerbro ⓦ www.sanita.dk. Danish clogs in many colours and patterns from basic black to furry animal-print and pink plastic.

Stig P Kronprinsensgade 14, Indre By; and Ravnsborggade 18, Nørrebro. The first designer shop to find its way to Kronprinsensgade and still going strong, with a broad selection of designer labels as well as Stig P's own leatherwear. The Indre By branch is womenswear only, but Ravnsborggade has a large men's section.

Design and interiors

Bang & Olufsen 26, Kongens Nytorv, Indre By ⓦ www.bang-olufsen.com. Check out the latest in hi-fi equipment at the city's flagship store.

Bodum Home Store Østergade 10, Indre By. ⓦ www.bodum.dk. Four floors of wares from the makers of the cafetiere, par excellence.

Casa Shop Store Regnegade 2, Indre By ⓦ www.casashop.dk. Classic and modern Danish and international design, from furniture to watches. Arne Jacobsen icons are well represented, holding their own against the latest in spindly chairs, stylish sofas and funky lighting.

Georg Jensen Amagertorv 4, Indre By. The emporium of the renowned Danish silversmith features works by the great man himself as well as other craftsmen, and has been turning out simple yet stylish silverware, from jewellery and cutlery to candlesticks and tableware, for over 100 years.
Illums Bolighus Amagertorv 10, Indre By. Four cool, elegant and very Scandinavian floors overflowing with an eyecatching assortment of Danish and international design, from fabulous kitchenware and glassware to slimline Poul Henningsen lamps and Arne Jacobsen furniture classics – though such quality and refinement doesn't come cheap.
Paustian Kalkbrænderløbskaj 2, Østerbro ⓦwww .paustian.dk. Stylish furniture shop designed

by Danish architect Jørn Utzon (famous for the Sydney Opera House), and beautifully situated on the Østerbro harbourfront. Expensive furniture and smaller must-have bits for your home, by local and internationally renowned designers, and a good in-house café.
Royal Copenhagen Porcelain Amagertorv 6, Indre By. Even if you're not excited by the idea of china, it's worth a quick peep at one of Denmark's most famous exports, still being produced to centuries-old designs. Each piece is handmade and handpainted, with the painter's signature as verification on the bottom – hence the extortionate prices (you can get it all considerably cheaper at the factory outlet in Frederiksberg; see p.100).

Book and music shops

Arnold Busck Købmagergade 49, Indre By ⓦwww.arnoldbusck.dk. Huge, central chain bookstore on three floors, selling new titles and a good selection of English-language fiction.
Jazzcup Gothersgade 107, Indre By. New jazz CD store with a massive selection of both local and international music, as well as an in-house bar and frequent live gigs (see p.113). Closed Mon.

Nordisk Korthandel Studiestræde 26–30, Indre By ⓦwww.scanmaps.dk. Great guidebook and map store with friendly staff and an extensive range of walking, cycling and driving maps of Denmark.
Politikens Boghandel Radhuspladsen 37, Indre By. Large, mainstream bookstore with possibly the best range of English-language fiction and nonfiction in the city.

Food and drink

A.C. Perch's Thehandel Kronprinsensgade 5, Indre By. One of Europe's oldest tea shops, founded in 1835 and retaining much of its delightful original wooden interior, around which wafts the wonderful aroma of teas from around the globe.
Czar Købmagergade 32, Indre By. Follow the pungent pong to discover Copenhagen's finest selection of cheeses, from all over Europe; you're welcome to sample them – just take a ticket and wait to be served. There's also a good charcuterie and wine section at the back.
Emmerys Nørrebrogade 8, Nørrebro ⓦwww .emmerys.dk. Trendy bakery where the young, rich and health conscious queue up every weekend for their organic non-dyed, non-yeast bread; plenty

of scrumptious cakes on offer too. Also outlets on Østerbrogade 51, Vesterbrogade 34, Vesterbro, and Store Standstræde 21, Frederiksstaden.
Reinh van Hauen Mikkels Bryggers Gade 2–4 and Østergade 22, Indre By. The king of Danish bakeries (with over 27 years of organic baking to its credit) serves up mouthwatering *rundstykker* (crispy bread rolls) and pastries.
Sømods Bolcher Nørregade 24 & 36, Indre By. Bus #16. A tasty range of boiled sweets, made without chemical additives according to ageold recipes; you can also watch the elaborate sweet-making process, during which millimetrethin strands of multicoloured mixture are coiled together.

Markets

Det Blå Pakhus Holmbladsgade 113, Amager. Lergravsparken or Amagerbro metro. A year-round weekend fixture, Copenhagen's largest indoor flea market boasts 4500 square metres of uninhibited clutter, featuring objects of every conceivable size,

shape, form and value. Entrance 15kr. Sat & Sun 10am–5pm.
Frederiksberg Rådhus Gammel Kongevej, Frederiksberg. Popular trading place for locals of all ages – and thanks to this prosperous neighbourhood's

wealthy residents, you might turn up a few quality wares. Sat & Sun 10am–5pm.

Gammel Strand Flea Market Gammel Strand, Indre By. The city's most central flea market, situated by the canal on Gammel Strand and selling the usual range of old china, bric-à-brac, paintings and glassware. May–Sept Fri & Sat 8am–5pm.

Israels Plads Israels Plads, Indre By. On the children's playground behind the fruit and veg market just off Frederiksborggade, this Saturday flea market is rumoured to be the place where Copenhagen's

high-street shops get rid of stuff they can't sell, and is a good spot to hunt out unused clothes and jewellery. May–Oct Sat 9am–3pm.

Kongens Nytorv Kongens Nytorv, Indre By. Hunt for a bargain in this central flea market, then head across to Nyhavn for a herring lunch. Sat 9am–3pm May–Oct.

Nørrebro market Along the wall of Assistens Kirkegården, Nørrebro. If you search patiently, you may unearth some real bargains at this central flea market. May–Sept Sat 7am–2pm.

Gay Copenhagen

Given that homosexuality has long been legal in Denmark and gay and lesbian couples are allowed to marry, it's not surprising that Copenhagen is one of the world's **premier gay cities**. Heads don't generally turn if a gay or lesbian couple are seen kissing or holding hands, and many Copenhageners pride themselves on their liberal attitudes. Paradoxically, though, Copenhagen's liberal traditions mean that there are relatively fewer specifically gay and lesbian venues. For general **information**, the national organization for gays and lesbians, the Landforeningen for Bøsser og Lesbiske (LBL), at Teglgårdsstræde 13 (☎33 13 19 48, ⓦwww.lbl.dk), provides a very well-run advice service (Mon–Fri 11am–3pm) and is an excellent place to pick up news of gay- or lesbian-oriented events in the city. LBL also run a very useful listings website ⓦwww.gayguide.dk and publish a free monthly Danish-language newsletter *PAN Bladet*, with dozens of useful listings – it's fairly easy to decipher even if you don't speak Danish, and you can pick it up at all major gay hangouts. Also readily available is the monthly *Out and About*, mostly in Danish and published by Copenhagen Gay Life (ⓦwww.copenhagen-gay-life.dk), a network of gay and gay-friendly businesses and organizations that also publishes a very useful *Gay map of Copenhagen*, available in gay-friendly hotels, bars and cafés.

The city's hugely popular annual gay pride march, **Copenhagen Pride**, takes place in August, with a suitably flamboyant street parade followed by an all-night party; check out ⓦwww.copenhagenpride.dk.

Accommodation

In addition to the places listed below, you can find gay or gay-friendly private accommodation by contacting Enjoy Bed & Breakfast (☎70 22 02 25, ⓦwww. ebab.dk).

Carsten's Guest House 5th floor, Christians Brygge 28 (ring the bell marked "Carsten Appel"), Indre By ☎33 14 91 07, ⓦwww .carstensguesthouse.dk. Bus #5A, #66, or ten minutes' walk from Central Station or Rådhuspladsen. Run by a gay couple, Carsten's has a very friendly and international atmosphere. A few individual rooms are on offer, though they're on the small side and walls are thin, and there's also some dorm accommodation (165kr). Breakfast (not included, 65kr) can be served to your room

or on the lovely roof terrace, and there's also a comfortable and attractive TV lounge, and a kitchen for guests' use. They also have a couple of apartments and studio flats in the city centre available for rental. ⑤

Copenhagen Rainbow Guesthouse Frederiksberggade 25, Indre By ☎33 14 10 20, ⓦwww .copenhagen-rainbow.dk. Bus #2A, #5A, #6A, #10, #12, #14, #26, #29, #33, #66–69, #250S. Gay-only guesthouse in an excellent position just off Rådhuspladsen on Strøget. There's five different rooms, some en suite, and all with TV and tea- and coffee-making facilities, and free Internet access in reception. ⑥

Hotel Windsor Frederiksborggade 30, Indre By ☏ 33 11 08 30, ⓦ www.hotelwindsor.dk. Bus #5A, or Nørreport station. On the second and third floor of a residential apartment block, this long-established and unpretentious gay hotel has newly refurbished rooms, some en-suite and some sharing shower and toilets. ⑥

Bars and clubs

Can Can Mikkel Bryggers Gade 11, Indre By. Small and friendly bar during the day which gets livelier at night, when it's mostly frequented by gay men. Cheap booze throughout the day. Mon–Thurs & Sun 2pm–2am, Fri & Sat 2pm–5am.

Cosy Bar Studiestræde 24, Indre By ⓦ www .cosybar.dk. Popular, late-night/early-morning cruise and dance venue (mostly gay men, but a lot of straight people as well) for the partygoer with stamina. DJ Tues & Thurs–Sat. Mon–Thurs & Sun 10pm–6am, Fri & Sat 10pm–8am.

Café Intime Allégade 25, Frederiksberg ⓦ www .cafeintime.dk. Small, cosy, candlelit piano bar frequented by a good mix of gay and straight people who have a thing about musicals. The floor is open for wannabe performers on Mon and Tues. Loads of fun. Daily 6pm–2am.

Masken Studiestræde 33, Indre By ⓦ www .maskenbar.dk. Nearly every segment of the city's gay and lesbian population makes it to this raucous bar at some point during the week, possibly because of the cheap beer. There's supposedly a "girls' night" in the basement section on Thursdays from 8pm which seldom attracts the crowds, whilst Fridays are for young gays and lesbians and can be very cruisy. Mon–Thurs 4pm–2am, Fri & Sat 4pm–5am, Sun 3pm–2am.

Oscars Rådhuspladsen 77, Indre By ⓦ www .oscarbarcafe.dk. A traditional first port of call on a night out, the very popular *Oscars* serves good, traditional Danish food as well as every kind of soft and alcoholic drink imaginable. Gets cruisy late in the evening. Daily noon–2am.

PAN Bar & Disco Knabrostræde 3, Indre By ⓦ www.pan-cph.dk. Vibrant, loud, raunchy and cruisy, this is Copenhagen's only permanent gay nightclub, though it attracts a straight crowd too. It offers a variety of groovy beats for disco divas, and also has a popular karaoke bar. 60kr. Fri & Sat 11pm–5am.

Vela Gay Club Viktoriagade 2–4, Vesterbro ⓦ www.velagayclub.dk. Predominantly lesbian venue with daily happy hour (8–9pm); gets busy during weekends when the party continues into the wee hours. Wed & Thurs 8pm to midnight, Fri & Sat 8pm–5am.

Listings

Airport information ☏ 32 31 32 31; for online information on arrivals and departures visit ⓦ www.cph.dk.

Banks and exchange Banks and exchange bureaux are plentiful, and the easiest place to change travellers' cheques and foreign cash; there's a uniform commission of 30kr per transaction, so change as much as is feasible in one go. The airport and Central Station have late-opening exchange facilities which charge a similar amount of commission. Forex exchange bureaux charge only 20kr to exchange cash and 10kr to exchange travellers' cheques but are much rarer; branches are at Central Station (daily 8am–9pm), Nørre Voldgade 90, near Nørreport Station (Mon–Fri 9am–7pm, Sat 10am–4pm), and Gothersgade 8, near Kongens Nytorv (Mon–Fri 9am–7pm, Sat 10am–4pm). There are ATMs throughout the city.

Car Rental Agencies Avis, airport ☏ 32 51 22 99, ⓦ www.avis.dk; Budget, Vester Farigmagsgade 7 ☏ 33 55 05 00, airport ☏ 32 52 39 00, ⓦ www .budget.dk; Europcar/Interrent, Gammel Kongevej 13 ☏ 33 55 99 00, airport ☏ 32 50 30 90, ⓦ www .europcar.dk; Hertz, Ved Vesterport 3 ☏ 33 17 90 20, airport ☏ 32 50 93 00, ⓦ www.hertzdk.dk; Rent-A-Wreck, Amager Strandvej 100 ☏ 70 25 26 70 ⓦ www.rent-a-wreck.dk.

Dentists For emergencies contact Tandlæ-gevagten, Oslo Plads 14 ☏ 35 38 02 51 (Mon–Fri 8am–9.30pm, Sat & Sun 10am–noon). Be prepared to pay at least 200kr on the spot.

Fitness centres Scandinavia's leading health-club chain, SATS (ⓦ www.sats.com), has several branches in the city – a day's membership costs 150kr and entitles you to use the full range of facilities. The most central branch is on the fifth floor of the Scala centre, just opposite Tivoli at Vesterbrogade 2E (☏ 33 32 10 02); other branches include Vesterbrogade 97, Vesterbro (☏ 33 25 13 10), Gothersgade 8F, Indre By (☏ 33

93 33 95) and Bragesgade 8, Nørrebro (ⓣ35 81 27 81).

Internet Internet access is available free of charge at Uselt, Rådhusstræde 13, Indre By, and at the city's libraries (though not the Royal Library), but you may have to wait. Of Internet cafés, the *Sidewalk Express* chain has branches all over the city, including Central Station; other options include the huge *Boomtown*, Axeltorv 1–3, opposite the Tivoli main entrance (daily 24hr); *B1*, Bragesgade 1, Nørrebro (Mon–Thurs & Sun 11am–1am, Fri & Sat 11am–4am); *Faraos Cigarer*, Skindergade 27 (Mon–Sat 10am–midnight, Sun noon–midnight); and *Nethulen*, Istedgade 114, Vesterbro (Mon–Fri 9.30am–11pm, Sat–Sun 4–11pm). You'll pay 15–25kr/hour at all of the above.

Laundry Central coin-operated laundries include: Istedgades Møntvask, Istedgade 45; Quickvask, Rosenørns Allé 37; Møntvask, Fælledvej 23; and Vasketeria, Dronningensgade 42. An average load costs about 30kr. Alternatively head for the new Laundromat Café, Elmegade 15, where you can have a bite to eat while your laundry gets done for 32kr per load.

Left luggage The DSB Garderobe office, downstairs in Central Station, stores luggage for 30kr per item per day and has lockers for 30kr and 40kr per day. Uselt, Rådhusstræde 13, has free lockers for one-day storage. Copenhagen Airport's left-luggage facility is in the walkway between terminals 2 and 3, and charges 30kr per day (maximum one month), and has small and large lockers for 20kr and 50kr per day (maximum 3 days).

Libraries Hovedbiblioteket at Krystalgade 15–17 in Indre By (Mon–Fri 10am–7pm, Sat 10am–2pm) is the main library with some English-language books, magazines and newspapers.

Lost property The police department's lost property office is at Slotsherrensvej 113, Vanløse ⓣ38 74 88 22. For items lost on a bus, call ⓣ36 13 14 15; on a train or S-tog, call the central train information office on ⓣ70 13 14 15; for the metro, call ⓣ70 15 16 15; for items lost on a plane, contact the airline or Copenhagen Airport on ⓣ32 47 47 25.

Mail The main post office is at Købmagergade 1, Indre By (Mon–Fri 10am–5pm, Sat 10am–2pm) and there's a late-opening one inside the

Central Station (Mon–Fri 8am–9pm, Sat & Sun 10am–4pm).

Medical treatment For medical emergencies call ⓣ122. There are emergency departments at Amager Hospital, Italiensvej 1, Amager (ⓣ32 34 32 34); Bispebjerg Hospital, Bispebjerg Bakke 23, Emdrup (ⓣ35 31 35 31) and Frederiksberg Hospital, Nordre Fasanvej 57, Frederiksberg (ⓣ38 16 38 16). If you need a doctor, call ⓣ33 15 46 00 (Mon–Fri 8am–4pm) and you'll be given the name of one in your area; outside these hours, call ⓣ70 13 00 41.

Newspapers and magazines Overseas newspapers are sold at Magasin du Nord and Illum department stores (see p.119), the stall on the eastern side of Rådhuspladsen, and some newsagents along Strøget; the newsagents in Central Station stock a large range of foreign newspapers and magazines. The English-language *Copenhagen Post* newspaper (ⓦwww .copenhagenpost.dk) covers city issues and has an in-depth listings section; it comes out every Friday and costs 15kr.

Pharmacies Copenhagen's two main 24-hour pharmacies are Steno Apotek, Vesterbrogade 6C in front of Central Station (ⓣ33 14 82 66) and Sønderbro Apotek, Amagerbrogade 158, Amager (ⓣ32 58 01 40).

Swimming pools The most central (and best) indoor pool is the one in the DGI Byen sports centre (June–Aug Mon, Tues, Thurs & Fri 6.30am–7pm, Wed 6.30am–9pm, Sat & Sun 9am–5pm; Sept–May Mon–Thurs 6.30am–midnight, Fri 6.30am–7pm, Sat & Sun 9am–5pm), featuring a gorgeous elliptical pool, children's pool and diving area. Entry is 52kr; swimsuit hire costs 25kr with a deposit of 150kr or photo ID. It also has a spa where 245kr buys you access to a sauna, steam rooms, plunge pools and the swim centre (call ⓣ33 29 81 00 to book). The city also has two wonderful, free open-air harbour pools, at Islands Brygge, Amager (June–Aug Mon–Fri 7am–7pm, Sat & Sun 11am–7pm; Islands Brygge metro), which offers an adult pool, children's pool and diving pool; and one at Havneholmen, next to Fisketorvet shopping centre (June–Aug daily 11am–7pm; bus #1A, #30, #65E or Dybbølsbro S-Tog), which also has the mocked-up sandy "Copencabana" beach, complete with volleyball and other sports.

Around Copenhagen

Copenhagen's suburbs are relatively characterless, though there are a few attractions dotted about here and there, along with a number of surprisingly good beaches and refreshing tracts of open park and woodland, all within easy reach of the city centre by bus or train from Central Station. Just to **the north of the city, in** the inland suburb of Bispebjerg, there's the intriguing **Grundtvigs Kirke**, while the string of well-heeled areas that hug the coastline here hold a few places of interest. Weather permitting, a day-trip to the attractions in and around Hellerup and Charlottenlund, notably the **Experimentarium** and **Danish Aquarium**, or Klampenborg, home to the amusement park **Bakken** and the **Ordrupgaard** art museum, can be combined with a lounge around on the adjacent sandy beaches. There's more pastoral detours inland to the peaceful **Frilandsmuseet** open-air museum at Sorgenfri. A full day's jaunt further north up the Øresund Coast will allow you to take in the charming **Karen Blixen Museum** and the wonderful **Louisiana** museum of modern art, with its superb coastal setting, while to the south of the city, there's more contemporary art at the controversial **Arken**, again enjoying a prime seafront location.

Grundtvigs Kirke

Five kilometres northwest of the city centre, and fifteen minutes by bus #6A, #66 or #69, is the astonishing yellow-brick creation of **Grundtvigs Kirke** (Mon–Sat 9am–4pm, Thurs until 6pm, Sun noon–4pm or noon–1pm in winter), overlooking the city from the top of Bispebjerg hill. It was designed in 1913 by Peder Vilhelm Jensen-Klint – father of the designer Kaare Klint – as a monument to the Danish theologian and pedagogue N.F.S. Grundtvig (see box below). Resembling a kind of enormous church organ, with parallel

N.F.S. Grundtvig and the Folkehøjskole

Although less internationally renowned than contemporaries Søren Kierkegaard and Hans Christian Andersen, it was **N.F.S. Grundtvig** (1783–1827) who left the most indelible mark on Danish history and culture. A man given to manic bouts of frenzied activity – he's still the most prolific Danish author ever – Grundtvig forged a career as a priest and scholar, developing the grand humanist vision that would go on to shape almost every aspect of Danish cultural and social life. To many, his most enduring legacy was the establishment of the uniquely Danish **Folkehøjskole** ("People's High School") system: residential colleges for adults offering courses in arts, crafts and, more recently, computers and the media, in which Grundtvig's philosophy of equality, democracy, participation and the pursuit of knowledge were put into practice. The first opened in 1844, and Folkehøjskoles soon spread throughout the country and abroad – there are now schools as far afield as the US, India and Nigeria.

One of the main principles of the Folkehøjskole is to provide an education which eschews the usual authoritarian teacher–pupil relationship in favour of shared experience and knowledge. Schools also avoid competitiveness (there are no exams) and vocational training – the aim is to produce rounded human beings rather than good little workers.

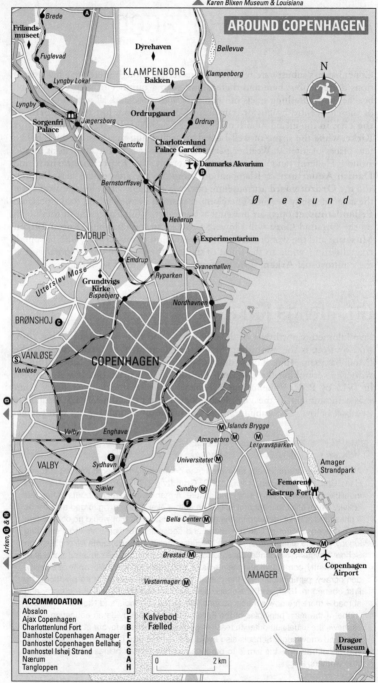

▲ Karen Blixen Museum & Louisiana

AROUND COPENHAGEN

N

Øresund

Dyrehaven

Bellevue

KLAMPENBORG
Bakken

Klampenborg

Brede

Frilands-
museet

Fuglevad

Lyngby Lokal

Lyngby

**Sorgenfri
Palace**

Jægersborg

Ordrupgaard

Ordrup

Gentofte

**Charlottenlund
Palace Gardens**

Danmarks Akvarium
B

Bernstorffsvej

Hellerup

Experimentarium

EMDRUP

Emdrup

Svanemøllen

Ryparken

Utterslev Mose

**Grundtvigs
Kirke**
Bispebjerg

Nordhavnen

BRØNSHØJ C

VANLØSE S

Vanløse

COPENHAGEN

D

Valby

Enghave

Ⓜ *Islands Brygge*

Amagerbro Ⓜ

Ⓜ *Lergravsparken*

**Amager
Strandpark**

VALBY

E
Sydhavn

Universitetet Ⓜ

Sjælør

Sundby Ⓜ

Femøren
Kastrup Fort

Arken, G & H

F

Bella Center Ⓜ

Ørestad Ⓜ

Ⓜ

(Due to open 2007)
**Copenhagen
Airport**

Vestermager Ⓜ

AMAGER

ACCOMMODATION

Absalon	D
Ajax Copenhagen	E
Charlottenlund Fort	B
Danhostel Copenhagen Amager	F
Danhostel Copenhagen Bellahøj	C
Danhostel Ishøj Strand	G
Nærum	A
Tangloppen	H

Kalvebod
Fælled

**Dragør
Museum**

0   2 km

yellow-brick buttresses running upwards, the church dwarfs the neighbouring housing, built using similar motifs. Inside, the cavernous, unadorned space and large, high windows provide a suitably reverential atmosphere, with wonderful acoustics and beautiful natural lighting.

The Experimentarium, Charlottenlund and the Danish Aquarium

Five kilometres north of the city centre, and a short S-tog ride (Line C) or twenty-minute bus trip (#1, #14 or #21; get off at Tuborgvej), the snooty suburb of **HELLERUP** holds the **Experimentarium** (Mon & Wed–Fri 9.30am–5pm, Tues 9.30am–9pm, Sat & Sun 11am–5pm; 120kr; ⓦwww .experimentarium.dk), sited in the old Tuborg brewery bottling hall at Tuborg Havnevej 7. The exhibition aims to make science more understandable and accessible to the masses, and makes for an educational and entertaining few hours, particularly if you've got children, with plenty of fun, hands-on exhibits. There are also occasional lectures giving simple explanations of scientific topics illustrated by down-to-earth experiments using things like bubbles and prisms, as well as demonstrations by guides (called "pilots"), on processes ranging from cheese-making to dissection.

A couple of kilometres further north and a twenty-minute S-tog ride from Central Station or a forty-minute bus ride (#14) and you're in the equally snooty suburb of **CHARLOTTENLUND**. From the train station – walk up the station concourse and turn right – it's a ten-minute stroll through some woods to the immaculate lawns and beautiful tree-lined avenues of **Charlottenlund Slot** (closed to the public) and its gorgeous gardens (24hr; free), which make an excellent spot for a picnic. The bus drops you off on the other side of the park, on Kystvejen, in front of the aquarium; from here head west through the park to reach the slot. The **Danish Aquarium**, in the white building on the eastern edge of the park (Feb–April & Sept–Oct 10am–5pm; May–Aug 10am–6pm; Nov–Jan 10am–4pm; 85kr; ⓦwww.danmarks-akvarium.dk), is home to thrree hundred species of fish, plus crocodiles, turtles, sharks, frogs and a tank of half-fish, half-reptile mudskipper, remarkable creatures which hop between land and water. In a designated children's area (weekends and holidays 11am–4pm), there are three touch pools where you're allowed to handle native marine animals such as hermit crabs and sea anemones. Heading towards the sea from the Aquarium, past the popular *Jorden Rundt Café* (a great spot for a brunch or light lunch), you arrive at a stretch of lawn leading to a small sandy **beach**, ever popular with cityfolk – on hot days you can hardly move here for exposed flesh. A small private bathing pier, Søbadet (June–Aug 9am–7pm; 20kr) occupies the left side of the beach, with showers, toilets and a café, as well as an enclosed section divided into male and female nudist bathing areas.

Klampenborg, Bakken and Ordrupgaard

Past Charlottenburg and the Aquarium, bus #14 and the C-line S-tog continue northwards to the wealthy suburb of **KLAMPENBORG**. Turning right out of the train station brings you to the attractive and very popular **Bellevue Beach**, with a nudist area to the left as you face the sea. Turning left out of the station, a ten-minute signposted walk through woodlands takes you to the **Bakken** amusement park (April–June & mid-Aug to mid-Sept Mon–Fri 2pm–midnight, Sat 1pm–midnight, Sun noon–midnight; July to mid-Aug daily noon–midnight; pass for all 34 rides 199kr; Ⓦ www.bakken.dk), a noisier, brasher version of Tivoli with beer halls, cheap restaurants and gaudy fairground rides. When it all gets a bit too frenetic, you can head off northward into the enormous **Dyrehaven** (Deer Park), a former royal hunting ground which almost entirely surrounds Bakken. Populated by an abundant deer population, its ancient oak and beech woods are wonderful for walking and picnicking.

If you head south, out of the park, following the edge of Dyrehaven west on Klampenborgvej for a kilometre or so, or alternatively take bus #388 towards Lyngby, you reach **Ordrupgaard** (Tues–Sun 1–5pm, Weds until 8pm; 65kr; Ⓦ www.ordrupgaard.dk), a manor house dating to 1918, set in lovely grounds and home to the outstanding collection of French and Danish Impressionist art assembled by insurance magnate and banker Wilhelm Hansen and his wife. It's said to be the finest collection of Impressionist French art in northern Europe, with pieces by Manet, Degas, Monet, Renoir and many more.

The Karen Blixen Museum and Louisiana

Further north along the coast lie a couple of captivating attractions well worth the train ride. Roughly ten kilometres from Klampenborg, in the quiet village of **RUNGSTED**, is the charming **Karen Blixen Museum** (May–Sept Tues–Sun 10am–5pm; Oct–April Wed–Fri 1–4pm, Sat & Sun 11am–4pm; 40kr; Ⓦ www.karen-blixen.dk), Rungsted Strandvej 111. The museum is housed in the family home of the writer who, while long a household name in Denmark for her short stories (often written under the pen name of Isak Dinesen) and outspoken opinions, enjoyed a resurgence of international popularity during the mid-1980s when the film *Out of Africa* – based on her 1937 autobiographical account of running a coffee plantation in Kenya and her love affair with the dashing English hunter Denys Finch-Hatton – won seven Oscars. Blixen lived in the house after her return from Africa in 1931 until her death in 1962, and much of it is maintained as it was during her final years. The **living quarters** (timed admission) feature a short film of her life and work and several rooms with furniture, personal effects and photographs left as they were when she died. The light-filled study at the end is where she wrote most of her books, surrounded by mementoes of her time in Kenya and with lovely views out to sea. The house is backed by delightful woodlands (the ticket office can provide a map), established as a **bird sanctuary** by Blixen, and is also her final resting place – her simple **grave** lies beneath a huge beech tree.

The closest station to the museum is Rungsted Kyst, on the regionaltog line, from where it's a fifteen-minute walk – turn left out of the station, right onto Rungstedvej, then right at the harbour, from where the house is signposted – or a short ride on bus #388. Bus #388 also makes the journey from Klampenborg S-Tog station. On your return, you can follow the path from the museum through the woods back on to Rungstedvej, from where it's just five minutes' walk back to Rungsted Kyst station.

In **HUMLEBÆK**, a sizeable coastal village 10km further north up the coast from Rungsted, and on the same train line, you'll find **Louisiana** (daily 10am–5pm, Wed until 10pm; 72kr; Ⓦ www.louisiana.dk), one of Europe's most intriguing modern art museums. Situated right on the Øresund coast, at the northern edge of the village on Gammel Strandvej 13, it's a short signposted walk from Humlebæk train station; bus #388 stops right outside. With its compelling mixture of unusual architecture and outstanding modern art in a memorable natural setting, Louisiana is worth at least half a day, though be prepared for huge crowds on summer weekends. The gallery's layout and frequent rearrangement to accommodate temporary exhibitions can make for some confusion, but the collection – divided between the museum buildings and the sculpture garden outside – reflects most of the important art movements of the twentieth century.

The entrance is through a nineteenth-century villa (built by a man whose three wives were all called Louise, hence the museum's name), beyond which stretches a twisting array of modern glass corridors, laid out in a roughly circular shape and offering stunning views out over the gardens and sculptures. Start walking clockwise around the gallery to reach the purpose-built gallery housing **Giacometti**'s gangly, gaunt bronze figures. From here, corridors connect to a collection of work by artists of the **CoBrA** movement (named after the cities of Copenhagen, Brussels and Amsterdam), a left-wing collective of artists whose work is characterized by distinctive and colourful abstracts. Here you'll find Henry Heerup's odd wood sculptures, including the bizarre *Ironing Board Madonna*, and some large and characteristically tortured abstracts by Asger Jorn, former CoBrA member and one of the country's most renowned artists. You'll also find small rooms dedicated to the bright, Constructivist works of Rodchenko and Delaunay, with their straight lines and simple colours, and large spaces filled with German Anselm Kiefer's energetic canvases. There's also a fine collection of **Pop Art**, with works by Warhol, Robert Ryman and Lichtenstein providing the backdrop to Claes Oldenburg's models of oversized cigarette butts and a lunch box, and Jim Dine's stark *White Bathroom*. The grounds **outside** are dotted with small copses and carefully tended lawns scattered with world-class sculpture – the strange, flat, abstract sculptures of Alexander Calder rub shoulders with Max Ernst's surreal creations and Henry Moore's dramatic *Bronze Woman*.

The Frilandsmuseet and around

For a dose of fresh air and rural charm, you might want to take a day-trip out to the **Frilandsmuseet** (mid-April to mid-Sept Tues–Sun 10am–5pm; free; Ⓦ www.natmus.dk) – a wonderful mixture of heritage park, city farm and woodland retreat just half an hour north of the city (bus #184 from Nørreport drops you at the entrance, or take B or B+ S-tog lines to Sorgenfri station, from where it's a 15-minute walk past Sorgenfri Palace). Established on its present site in 1901 as part of the National Museum, it displays over a hundred buildings dating back to the seventeenth century from across Denmark and its former territories. The office at the entrance provides a map of the lopsided cottages and farmsteads, which are grouped together according to region and furnished according to various trades – bakers, potters, blacksmiths and so on – and offer a vivid picture of how rural communities lived in northern Europe. A few hundred metres to the north, **Brede Værk** preserves parts of the industrial community – factory workers' cottages, children's nursery and vegetable allotments – that grew up around the large cloth mill that existed here from 1831 to 1956. While you're here it's worth going on a tour (June–Aug Sun noon and 1.30pm; 50kr) of the mill owner's grand **summer residence**; the free exhibition (mid-April to mid-Sept Tues–Sun 10am–5pm) in the main factory building reveals the other side of the story, focussing on the impact of the industrial revolution on common folk. Brede train station is by the entrance to Brede Værk; to get back to Copenhagen you can either catch a private train to

Jægersborg, from where B and B+ S-tog trains continue on, or you can make an interesting diversion past the Frilandsmuseet and south through the park to the splendid **Sorgenfri Palace**, one-time home of Frederik V (now home to Count Christian of Rosenborg and closed to the public). Cross Kongevejen in front of the palace to take S-tog B or B+ back from Sorgenfri station.

Arken

Situated 20km southwest of the city centre, on a beautiful windswept beach near the working-class suburb of Ishøj, is the eye-catching **Arken** museum of modern art (Tues & Thurs–Sun 10am–5pm, Wed 10am–9pm; 40kr; ⓦwww .arken.dk). The obscure location – take S-tog line A, A+, E or EX to Ishøj, and then bus #128 or a 25-minute signposted walk – seems almost wilfully perverse for a museum that aspires to be an internationally recognized showcase for contemporary art, but it is worth the trouble of getting there, and you'll also find a fantastic beach right on the museum's doorstep. Be warned, though, that due to construction work on a new extension, there is some disruption to the galleries and exhibitions until January 2008. The building resembles a beached sailing ship – a striking sight when seen from across the dunes, with its large, white, angled expanses and steel wings. The interior is slightly bewildering, and the unusual character of the building and its location can tend to overwhelm the exhibits themselves. As well as temporary exhibitions devoted to contemporary art, there's a constantly expanding permanent collection of around four hundred pieces centred around Danish, Nordic and International art post 1990, among them pieces by stellar names such as Jeff Koons and Damien Hirst as well as some pre-1990 works, including several massive abstracts by Danish painter Asger Jorn, one of the driving forces behind the CoBrA movement. On the first floor there's an excellent restaurant with great views over the bay.

Travel details

Trains

Copenhagen to: Aalborg (29 daily; 4hr 43min); Århus (38 daily; 3hr 15min); Esbjerg (9 daily; 3hr); Frederikshavn (11 daily; 5hr 20min); Helsingør (every 20min; 45min); Hillerød (every 10min; 40min); Holbæk (2–3 hourly; 1hr 10min); (Kalund-borg 2–3 hourly; 1hr 46min); Køge (every 10min; 42min); Næstved (2–3 hourly; 1hr); Malmö (3 hourly; 35min); Nykøbing F (hourly; 1hr 40min); Odense (every 30min; 1hr 30min); Ringsted (3–4 hourly; 40min); Rønne (3–5 daily; via ferry from Ystad; 3hr); Roskilde (every 5–10min; 25min); Slagelse (2–3 hourly; 1hr 15min).

Buses

Copenhagen to: Aalborg (3–5 daily; 4hr 45min); Århus (4–7 daily; 3hr 5min); Ebeltoft (2–3 daily; 3hr); Esbjerg (9 daily; 3hr); Fjerritslev via Grenå, Randers, Hobro and Løgstør (4–6 daily; 5hr 55min); Malmö (hourly; 55min); Thisted via Viborg and Nykøbing Mors (1–2 daily; 6hr 10min); Rønne via Ystad (3–5 daily; 3hr); Silkeborg (2 daily; 4hr).

Ferries

Copenhagen to: Rønne (1 daily; 6hr).

Flights

Copenhagen to: Århus (SAS: 3 daily; 35min); Aalborg (Cimber Air, Sterling Air & SAS: 10–16 daily; 50min); Billund (Cimber Air: 5 daily; 45min); Karup (Cimber Air: 12 daily; 50min); Rønne (Cimber Air: 6 daily; 35min); Sønderborg (Cimber Air: 6 daily; 45min).

2

Zealand

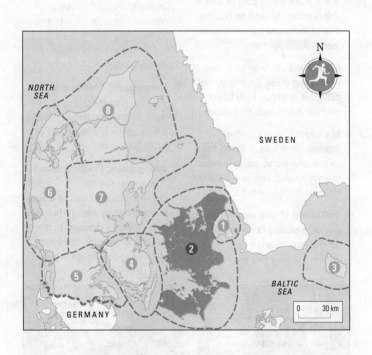

CHAPTER 2 # Highlights

* **Gilleleje and Tisvildeleje**
These twin north-coast beach towns are some of Denmark's swankiest places to swim and sunbathe, with great dining options, too. See p.140

* **Roskilde** A mere half-hour from Copenhagen, this medieval town offers a striking Gothic cathedral and a superb museum of Viking shipbuilding, as well as hosting one of the world's largest music festivals. See p.145

* **Møns Klint** Have an invigorating walk along these gleaming chalk cliffs, set between lush forest and the Baltic Sea. See p.166

* **Marielyst** Every summer thousands of beach bums flock to this one-horse seaside resort town for sand, sea and a dab of hedonism. See p.169

* **Trelleborg Viking ring fortress** Set on a grassy knoll at the confluence of two rivers, this concentric ring-fortress ruin offers a fascinating insight into the complexities of Viking society. See p.159

* **Storebælt bridge** Head to Korsør for some superb vistas of this astonishing engineering triumph connecting Zealand and Funen. See p.160

* **Kronborg Slot** Best known as the home of Shakespeare's *Hamlet*, this pearl of a Gothic fortress sits on a grassy promontory overlooking the Baltic. See p.135

* **Holmegaard Glassworks** Try your hand at making your own work of glass sculpture or take a look at the professionals at work. See p.164

* **Viking plays, Frederikssund** These over-the-top dramatizations of Viking folklore and mythology feature hundreds of performers dressed to the nines and wielding medieval-style weaponry to great effect. See p.152

△ Viking play, Frederikssund

Zealand

As the largest of Denmark's islands and the home of its capital (covered in Chapter 1), **Zealand** (*Sjælland*) is the country's most important – and most visited – region. But while almost everyone who visits Zealand spends some time in Copenhagen, it's well worth venturing on from here to explore the rest of the island – some lively, others more rural, still others positive backwaters – in order to get a glimpse of how different, and how enjoyable, the rest of Denmark can be. Past Copenhagen's dormitory suburbs and beaches, things slide into the happily provincial, with woods and expansive parklands appearing almost as soon as you leave the city. And given the swiftness of the metropolitan transport network, which covers almost half the island, and the fact that nowhere on Zealand is more than ninety minutes away from Copenhagen, you can head out on day-trips and be back in the capital in easy time for an evening drink.

North of Copenhagen's suburban sprawl, the city's arterial ring road branches off to edge up along the 60km-long Kattegat coast, a dramatic landscape of verdant forests that's peppered with castles and royal palaces, not to mention a string of lovely beaches – some low-key, others decidedly more à la mode – where Copenhageners have long been coming to swim, sunbathe and eat out at the excellent selection of restaurants. Other highlights of **northern Zealand** include **Helsingør**, site of the renowned **Kronborg Slot**, better known as the Elsinore Castle of Shakespeare's *Hamlet* and an impressive fortification that nevertheless quite unfairly steals the spotlight from the more eyecatching **Frederiksborg Slot** in nearby **Hillerød**. With its fertile grasslands, fjorded peninsulas and medieval towns, **central** and **western Zealand** has a more rural feel. West of Copenhagen on the Roskilde Fjord, **Roskilde** is Denmark's former capital and boasts an extravagant cathedral that's still the last resting place for the country's monarchs, as well as an engaging museum displaying five of the fourteen Viking ships salvaged from the fjord. The town is also within easy distance of the **Hornsherred** and **Odsherred** peninsulas, ideal for cycling or days on the beach. South of Roskilde, the E20 motorway cuts straight through central Zealand, from the sandy Baltic beaches and well-preserved medieval centre of **Køge** on the east coast to the quaint town of **Korsør**, best known for its multi-billion-kroner **Storebælt bridge**, Zealand's link to the island of Funen. The countryside of **southern Zealand** is even more pastoral, with its vast swathes of farmland and sloping hillsides prettied up by a handful of towns that hold some appealing accommodation and eating options. Just off Zealand, south coast and connected to the mainland by road bridge, the islands of **Møn**, **Lolland** and **Falster** are wonderfully bucolic, with first-class summer beach towns, medieval churches and plenty of opportunities for walking and cycling.

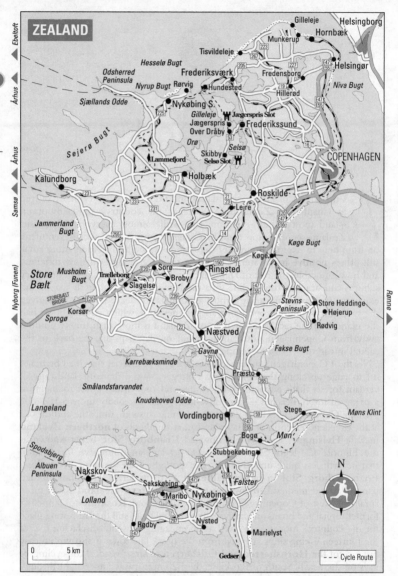

Ebeltoft ◀

Århus ◀

Århus ◀

Samsø ◀

Nyborg (Funen) ◀

Rønne ▶

Northern Zealand

The coast north of Copenhagen as far as Helsingør rejoices under the tag of the "Danish Riviera", a label that aptly describes its line of tiny one-time fishing hamlets now inhabited almost exclusively by wealthy Danes. With its magnificent castle and pretty medieval streets, **Helsingør** is the perfect spot from which to start your exploration of the **north coast**, with its pretty villages and fantastic dune- and forest-backed sandy beaches at **Hellebæk**, **Gilleleje** and **Tisvildeleje**. Heading inland, **Hillerød** is home to the stunning Frederiksborg Slot and Museum of National History, precariously positioned across three small islands on an artificial lake. All of these places are easily seen in a day-trip from the capital, and the best means of getting to them is the #388 bus, which runs north to Helsingør from Klampenborg, itself the last stop on line C or F of the S-Tog system; you could also take one of the frequent trains between Copenhagen and Helsingør, but the views are obscured by trees for much of the journey. Transport to Hillerød from Helsingør and the north coast is limited to slow regional trains, with one line heading south from Gilleleje and one southwest from Helsingør.

Helsingør

Some 45km north of Copenhagen (and just 45 minutes away by *regionaltog*), **Helsingør** is strategically positioned at the narrowest point of the Øresund, with the Swedish town of Helsingborg just 4km away on the opposite coast. Helsingør's wealth was founded on the Sound Toll of 1429, which was levied on ships passing through this narrow strait between the Baltic and the North Sea. With the toll long abolished, it's the ferries crossing to and from Sweden that now serve as the town's livelihood, with boatloads of Swedes taking ample advantage of Denmark's easily accessible (and relatively cheap) alcohol. Boozecruising apart, Helsingør's main draw is the mighty and ever-popular Kronborg Slot.

Arrival, information and accommodation

The **train station** is on Jernbanevej, just a couple of minutes' walk from the town centre and ten minutes' walk from Kronborg Slot. Buses stop outside the train station. The **tourist office** (third week of June to third week of Aug Mon–Thurs 9am–5pm, Fri 9am–6pm, Sat 10am–3pm; rest of year Mon–Fri 10am–4pm, Sat 10am–1pm; ☎49 21 13 33, ⊛www.visithelsingor.dk) is just across from the train station at Havnepladsen 3. As well as information on the town itself, they have ferry timetables for all of the companies.

Despite catering to so many ferry passengers and visitors to the castle, Helsingør is pretty low on **accommodation** options, so if you want to stay during the busy summer season, it's wise to book ahead.

Accommodation

Danhostel Helsingør Vandrerhjem Nordre Strandvej 24 ☎49 21 16 40, ⊛www .helsingorhostel.dk. Occupying a lovely restored villa and with lawns sweeping down to a beach, this is one of the best youth hostels in Denmark. There are double rooms (❹) within chalet-type enclosures and a few large dorms (150kr), as well as free wireless Internet. It's a couple of kilometres out of town, either via a twenty-minute walk north along the coastal road (Nordre Strandvej), or via bus #340 from the station; get off just after the sports stadium.
Hamlet Bramstræde 5 ☎49 21 05 91, ⊛www. hotelhamlet.dk. Friendly and comfortable hotel with decent-sized rooms and a couple of roomy suites, though the decor – dark wooden furniture and dark green walls – is in need of a lift. There's a restaurant on site. ❼
Helsingør Camping Strandalleen 2 ☎49 28 12 12, ⊛www.helsingorcamping.dk. Lovely little campsite between the main road Lappen (which begins where Skt Annagade ends) and the sea, so close to town and to the beach. There's a shop (May–Sept), bike rental and playground, as well as some cabins (from 268kr per night).
Marienlyst Nordre Strandvej 2 ☎49 21 40 00, ⊛www.marienlyst.dk. The top choice in town, this modern hotel has a lovely seafront location,

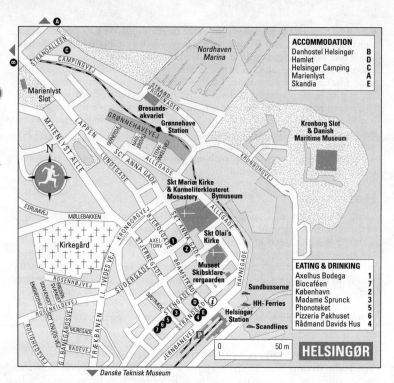

ACCOMMODATION

Danhostel Helsingør	B
Hamlet	D
Helsingør Camping	C
Marienlyst	A
Skandia	E

EATING & DRINKING

Axelhus Bodega	1
Biocaféen	7
København	2
Madame Sprunck	3
Phonoteket	5
Pizzeria Pakhuset	6
Rådmand Davids Hus	4

HELSINGØR

0   50 m

Danske Teknisk Museum

lavishly-decorated rooms and resort-style amenities: restaurants, beach park, spa and pool. ⑧–⑨

Skandia Bramstræde 1 ℡49 21 09 02, ⓦwww .hotelskandia.dk. Basic but comfortable rooms

(some with harbour views, others with shared bathrooms), a central location (two minutes' walk from the train station and main street) and the cheapest prices in town make this a very popular option year-round. ⑥

The town

Helsingør is a lively and likeable town and, away from the hustle of the ferry terminals and tourist hordes at Kronborg, a quiet and relaxing place with a well-preserved **medieval quarter** and ample cafés and restaurants. The bustling pedestrianized main street, **Stengade**, is lined with shops and eateries and linked by pretty, narrow alleyways of rickety half-timbered houses to **Axeltorv**, the town's small market square (markets on Wed, Fri & Sat mornings) and a good spot to linger over a beer. Toward the corner of Stengade and Skt Anna Gade is the town's cathedral, the red-brick, copper-spired **Skt Olai's Kirke** (daily: May–Aug 10am–4pm; Sept–April 10am–2pm), extensively remodelled and expanded over the centuries from its humble origins as a Romanesque church founded in 1200. Inside, the white walls en route to the fussily ornate altar set off the run of dark portraits of past rectors. Look out too for the font, to the left of the entrance, its balusters endowed by wealthy citizens and engraved with their children's names. Just beyond is the fifteenth-century **Sct Mariæ Kirke** (Mon–Sat 9am–noon, plus Thurs 4–6pm) with its pretty red-brick cloister, and the adjacent **Karmeliterklosteret Monastery** (guided tours only: summer

Mon–Fri at 2pm; 20kr), the best-preserved medieval monastery in Scandinavia. Erik of Pomerania gave the site to Carmelite monks in 1430; following the Reformation, in 1541, the monastery was turned into a hospital for the old and poor, during which time it gained some pre-eminence (and notoriety) for its innovative brain operations. The unnerving tools of this profession are still on show next door, at Skt Anna Gade 36, in the **Bymuseum** (daily noon–4pm; 20kr), an otherwise rather dry trawl through the town's history, with no English labelling. You'll get a better sense of what Helsingør was all about at the **Museet Skibsklarerergaarden** (Shipping Agent's House; Mon–Fri noon–4pm, Sat 10am–1pm; free), Strandgade 91, a lovely eighteenth-century building once occupied by agents responsible for collecting the Sound Toll. The rooms have been reconstructed much as they were during the last days of the toll (it was abolished in 1857) and there's also a souvenir shop done out in period style, complete with a blackboard chalked-up with the names of ships once present in the Sound and their captain's names. You enter the museum through the shop at the same address.

Other than the castle (see below), there's little else to keep you in town; those with kids might want to make the ten-minute walk north of the centre to the harbour at Strandpromenaden 5, where the **Øresundsakvariet** (Øresund Aquarium; June–Aug daily 10am–5pm; Sept–May Mon–Fri 10am–4pm, Sat & Sun 10am–5pm; 50kr; ⓦwww.oresundsakvariet.ku.dk) is home to a collection of local sea creatures, some of which inhabit the "touch basin". A further fifteen minutes' walk out of town to the northwest via Skt Anna Gade and Loppen, the stately Neoclassical pile of **Marienlyst Slot** (daily noon–4pm; 30kr) was built in the eighteenth century as a royal summer residence, and is situated to make the most of the cooling sea breezes and stunning views. There's not much to see in the Louis XVI-style interior; the rooms are largely devoid of furniture, with just the odd gilt mirror and chandelier to set the tone, but the collection of paintings, mostly of local seascapes and the brooding Kronborg over the centuries, are wonderfully atmospheric and include a few by Golden Age painter C.W. Eckersberg. You can walk up behind the palace into the hilly gardens and forest (maps are available from the ticket desk), where you'll find a shady glade and a statue marking the supposed site of *Hamlet's* grave, placed here in 1858 as a means of perpetuating the area's *Hamlet* associations; the views over the Øresund and Kronborg from the glade are stunning.

Kronborg Slot and the Maritime Museum

Tactically placed on a sandy curl of land extending seawards into the Øresund and a fifteen-minute walk from the train station, the spectacular castle of **Kronborg** (April & Oct Tues–Sun 11am–4pm; May–Sept daily 10.30am–5pm; Nov–March Tues–Sun 11am–3pm; ⓦwww.kronborg.dk; 60kr, joint ticket with Maritime Museum 75kr) dominates Helsingør and is the town's main draw. It's famous principally as the setting – under the name of Elsinore Castle – for Shakespeare's *Hamlet*, though it's still uncertain whether the playwright actually ever visited Helsingør at all (see box p.136). Nonetheless, the association endures in Kronborg's thriving trade in *Hamlet* souvenirs and the annual staging of the play in the castle grounds, a tradition begun in 1816. In 2000, the castle was awarded UNESCO World Heritage Site status and a ten-year restoration project began; be prepared for a little disruption in some rooms. **Guided tours** of the royal chambers take place in English daily at 2pm, and well-informed attendants also hover in every room ready to answer questions.

Originally constructed in the fifteenth century by Erik of Pomerania, the fortress of Krogen was the key to control of the Øresund for hundreds of years. As Helsingborg on the other side of the strait was also under Danish rule, Denmark's monarchs were able to extract a toll from every ship that passed through it. During the sixteenth century, Frederik II rebuilt (and renamed) the castle as a splendid Renaissance palace with sumptuous interiors, commissioning Dutch architect Antonius Van Opbergen, who took his ideas from the Dutch Renaissance buildings of Antwerp. Upon completion in 1585, Kronborg was the largest castle in northern Europe, and its international reputation soon caught Shakespeare's ear. However in 1629, during the reign of Frederik's son, Christian IV, the castle was largely destroyed by a massive **fire** – only the royal chapel survived – and the cost of rebuilding it would have bankrupted the struggling Danish state had Christian IV not doubled the Sound Toll to pay for it. Christian's castle sported lavish baroque interiors – liberally sprinkled with his distinctive monogram – though he opted to rebuild the exterior to the same Renaissance style. His enjoyment of the castle (supposedly his favourite) was short-lived, however; only twenty years after the fire, it was bombarded and overrun by the Swedes, who carted off most of Kronborg's treasures. Over the next three centuries, it was largely given over to military use, being deemed too uncomfortable for the royals, but in 1924 the military moved out and a major restoration programme began.

Even now, as you enter the castle via a series of gates, bridges, moats, earthen ramparts and brick defences, you get a sense of the fortress's former power and invincibility, with antique cannons pointing menacingly out across the narrow sound. Crossing over the final bridge, you go through the forbidding Dark Gate, to the small forecourt and castle courtyard. The main keep is rather ornate, with plenty of Renaissance features, two spindly towers roofed with green copper jutting out into the usually blustery sky, and another tower providing a fully functioning lighthouse. The interior isn't as grand as you might expect: white walls and wood floors long ago replaced the more lavish gilt-leather wall cladding and black-and-white floor tiles, and the furniture, though beautiful, is rather sparse. That said, the rooms are still impressive: of private apartments on the **second floor**, the King's Chamber and Queen's Chamber are adorned with magnificent fireplaces and fine circular ceiling paintings. On the **third floor**, the 62-metre-long ballroom is a stunning space, though sadly lacking

Kronborg and Hamlet

The origins of the story of a tragic Danish prince stretch back far beyond Shakespearean times. The earliest mention of a character called **Amled** can be found in a story, derived from Icelandic and Celtic sagas, written around 1200 by one of Bishop Absalon's scribes, a certain Saxo Grammaticus. An earlier, Elizabethan version of the *Hamlet* story, thought to have been written by **Thomas Kyd**, had already appeared on the London stage twenty years before Shakespeare's **Hamlet** was produced in 1602. Quite how the semi-mythical Danish prince and the very real Danish castle became connected isn't entirely clear, though it's probable that Elizabethan England got wind of Kronborg from sailors who had passed through the Øresund, returning with stories of the mist-shrouded fortress that subsequently metamorphosed into Shakespeare's Elsinore. Another vague theory has it that Shakespeare spent part of his so-called lost years (1585–1592) in Kronborg, rather than in Spain as was previously believed. That there are still conflicting stories has done nothing to diminish Kronborg's thriving trade in *Hamlet* souvenirs, nor the hundreds of requests for the whereabouts of "Hamlet's bedroom".

most of its original features. The paintings hanging along its length are from a series commissioned by Christian IV for Rosenborg Slot (see p.86), and there's more to look at on the walls of the Little Hall, which has seven of the fourteen splendid tapestries woven in 1590 as part of a series depicting Danish kings, and which once decorated the ballroom during festivities. In the Corner room, part of a guest suite designed for James VI of Scotland (later James I of England) and his wife, who was Christian IV's sister, you can see the original black-and-white flooring that Christian had laid throughout the castle.

Be sure to see the beautiful **Chapel**, directly across the courtyard from the ticket office: the only part of the castle to survive the fire of 1629, its elaborate and colourful carving, at its zenith in the royal pew opposite the pulpit, gives an idea of the richness of the castle's original Renaissance interiors. An altogether gloomier atmosphere pervades the dark, labyrinthine **casemates** (cellars; guided tours noon & 1.30pm), where the body of Holger Danske, a mythical hero from the legends of Charlemagne, is said to lie in wait, ready to wake again when Denmark needs him – although the Viking-style statue depicting the legend detracts somewhat from the cellars' authentic aura of decay. The castle also houses the national **Handels og Søfartsmuseet** (Maritime Museum; same hours; ⓦ www.maritime-museum.dk; 40kr), a well-organized jaunt through the history of Danish seafaring up to the modern-day domination by the Maersk shipping dynasty; alongside the usual nautical trinkets and paintings, exhibits include the world's oldest ship's biscuit, figureheads of busty Viking maidens; look out also for the display on the valuable work done by the *SS Storebjørn* icebreaker, whose lovely 1920s wood-panelled officers' saloon, complete with table laid for dinner, is a sight to behold. From the museum, you can walk along the fortress wall to the **coastal batteries** (daily sunrise–sunset), which afford some lovely views over the Sound.

Eating and drinking

You'll find plentiful **eating** options along the main drag, Stengade, which offers the full range of fast-food, cafés and restaurants, a couple of which are located in preserved historic buildings. Wherever you eat, you might want to consider skipping dessert in favour of one of the immense home-made **ice creams** from *Brostræde Is* at Brostræde 2.

Given the proximity of the capital, **nightlife** is a rare commodity hereabouts, but for a relatively sedate evening drink, there are several decent bars along Stengade (rowdier boozing goes on at the top end of Axeltorv, popular with well-oiled Swedes living it up). Possibilities include the tame *Biocaféen* (daily 10am–6pm, weekends until 10pm), Stengade 26, with live music in the evenings, while just off Axeltorv at Sudergade 27, *Axelhus Bodega* (daily 8am–2am, weekends until 5am) is a friendly, cheap local bar. *Hotel København*, Skt Anna Gade 17, has a lively atmosphere, good music and a pool table; look for the window stuffed full of beer steins.

Cafés and restaurants

Kronværket Café & Restaurant Kronborg Slot ☎ 44 47 73 02. Superbly situated on the castle approaches, this is an excellent spot for coffee or lunch. Create your own sandwiches for 55kr or go for the delicious "Kronborg Platte" of herrings, beef, fish and cheeses for 139kr. Or take the romantic option for a special evening meal – two courses for 249kr or three for 289kr (book ahead). Closed Mon.

Madame Sprunck Stengade 48 ☎ 49 26 48 49. Atmospheric old timbered building in a tiny courtyard; the cosy café serves up good pasta, burgers and salads, while upstairs is a more formal

Ferries to Sweden

Two ferry companies operate regular boats between **Helsingør** and **Helsingborg in Sweden**. The trip takes approximately twenty minutes and as tickets are rarely sold out, it's easiest just to buy at the terminal when you want to travel. HH Ferries (☏49 26 01 55, ⦿www.hhferries.dk) has half-hourly return trips running virtually round-the-clock and costing 46kr, with open return car prices starting at 466kr and including up to nine passengers. The ships operated by Scandlines (☏33 15 15 15, ⦿www.scandlines.dk) run slightly more frequently, and cost 40kr return, or 508kr for a car plus up to nine passengers. Both advertise frequent special day-return deals (*dagsbillet*) on their websites.

restaurant (evenings only) with meat and fish mains from 192kr. Outside seating in summer. Daily 11.30am–5pm, 6–9.30pm.

Phonoteket Music & Café Stengade 36 ⦿www.phonoteket.dk. Sitting at the small tables in this modern café, you can listen to any one of the 15,000 CDs sold in the adjacent music store whilst you munch on cakes from an excellent local *konditori*; try the divine *fragilité* nut cake. Their coffee is also especially good.

Pizzeria Pakhuset Stengade 26 ☏49 21 10 50. Excellent, cheap, authentic pizza and pasta in this friendly, unpretentious trattoria-style place – think red-and-white check tablecloths and Chianti bottles suspended from the rafters. Family-friendly and great value. Daily Mon–Sat noon–10pm, Sun 1–10pm.

Rådmand Davids Hus Strandgade 70, ☏49 26 10 43. This charming building dating from 1694 was once the residence of one of the king's councillors. During the daytime, this café serves tapas-sized Scandinavian lunches like meatballs on rye bread (45kr) and by night it's a cosy, candlelit bar. Limited space so book ahead for lunch in busy times. Mon–Thurs 10am–6pm, Fri & Sat 10am–3am.

The north Zealand coast

Helsingør is the gateway to the **north Zealand coast**, whose succession of fine sandy beaches and cute fishing villages has long made it a favoured spot for summer homes, and it's still a popular destination for weekending Copenhageners searching for sun, sand and sea. Driving along the lovely coastline provides pre-eminent glimpses of the shallow green waters and golden sand; the road is never more than a few blocks away from the beach, and if you're driving and fancy a dip, it's quite easy to park on the side of the road and walk to the dunes. A private railway operates from a small terminal adjacent to the main station in Helsingor and runs as far as the former fishing town and latter-day tourist hub of Gilleleje, stopping frequently along the coast. Alternatively, bus #340 from Helsingor covers the same stretch, as does cycle route No.47.

Hellebæk, Hornbæk and around

From Helsingør, the coast road (Nordre Strandvej) runs west past a string of fine beaches towards the sleepy village of **HELLEBÆK**, some 5km north, where there's a well-known (if unofficial) stretch of shoreline dedicated to nude bathing – and very little else. Trains from Helsingør stop at Hellebæk and then continue for 7km to the moderately larger **HORNBÆK**, a tiny fishing hamlet until the late nineteenth century, when the capital's middle classes discovered its beautiful sandy beaches, sand dunes and fabulous sea views, and set about building their holiday villas along its coastal paths. For a time, Hornbæk was also a favourite summer haunt of various Golden Age artists, who came to capture its ever-changing light, salty fishing scenes and seascapes. The small harbour and beaches aside, there's not much to see in Hornbæk itself, though the tiny white church on Kirkevej is worth a peep for its C.W. Eckersberg altar and the four finely detailed model ships suspended from the ceiling. To the east of town, the lovely **Hornbæk Plantage** pine forest is a great spot for walking or cycling; maps of the forest trails and information on bike hire are available from the tourist office (see below).

There are a couple of worthy distractions around Hornbæk. Some three kilometres further west along the coast, just beyond the small village of **Dronningmølle** (bus #340; tell the driver you want to stop at Munkeruphus), the hamlet of Munkerup holds the **Munkeruphus** art gallery (mid-March to mid-June & Sept–Dec Fri, Sat & Sun noon–5pm; mid-June to Aug Tues–Sun noon–5pm; 40kr; ⓦwww.munkeruphus.dk), Munkerup Strandvej 78, situated in a lovely colonial-style country house surrounded by beautiful landscaped grounds that afford lovely views out to the sea. The exhibitions focus on twentieth-century and contemporary Danish art and change frequently; there's a lovely café serving cakes and light lunches.

Just west of Munkerup, and signposted off to the right along Fyrvejen, a non-operational restored lighthouse built in 1771 houses the **Fyrhistorisk Museum på Nakkehoved** (Nakkehoved Lighthouse Museum; mid-May to mid-Oct Mon & Wed–Sun 1–4pm; 25kr), an exhibition on navigation and seafaring in the area – though the collection is of less interest than the stunning views over the Øresund and Kattegat, which you can enjoy with a drink from the little café here. If you're going further west, note that a coastal path runs the 2km from the eastern edge of town to the lighthouse at the outskirts of Gilleleje – heading along Hovedgade, the path starts just beyond the church at the junction with Klokkervang.

Practicalities

Hornbæk's **tourist office** (mid-June to Aug Mon 1–7pm, Tues & Thurs 1–5pm, Wed & Fri 10am–5pm, Sat 10am–2pm; rest of the year same hours but closed Tues; ⓣ49 70 47 47, ⓦwww.hornbaek.dk) is in the library just off the main street. The town itself is a lovely, relaxed spot to **stay overnight**. Staff at the tourist office can find you private rooms (from 420kr) or summer cottages (both for a 20kr booking fee). Otherwise, there's the homely *Ewaldsgården* (ⓣ49 70 00 82, ⓦwww.ewaldsgaarden.dk; mid-June to Aug; ⓞ), Johannes Ewalds Vej 5, a farmhouse pension close by the train station and ten minutes' walk from the beach, which has single, double and family rooms. Alternatively, around the corner at Sauntevej 18, *Hotel Bretagne* (ⓣ49 70 16 66, ⓦwww.hotelbretagne.dk; ⓞ) offers a lovely location on Hornbæk's lake, and charming rooms (some with shared bathroom) with a seaside feel. Hornbæk's **campsite** (ⓣ49 70 02 23, ⓦwww.camping-hornbaek.dk) is beautifully situated on the edge of Hornbæk Plantage, just ten minutes' walk from the beach.

For **food**, there are a few cafés on the main street, Nordre Strandvej, including the popular *Café Dig & Mig* at no. 340, which has a garden. However nothing beats the delicious – if pricey – fresh fish and seafood from *Fiskehuset* (Mon–Fri 9am–5.30pm, Sat & Sun 9am–2pm) on the harbour; there are a few tables outside, but their takeaway menu means you can eat gourmet food anywhere along the beach. If you'd rather something more formal, head for *Restaurant Hansen's Café* (Mon–Sat 4–9pm, Sun noon–9pm; ⓣ49 70 04 79, ⓦwww.hansenscafe.dk), Havnevej 9; it's set in one of the oldest houses in the town, and has bags of olde-worlde charm, great Danish-French cooking and outside seating in summer.

Gilleleje

From Hornbæk, trains continue 9km along the coast to **GILLELEJE**, another appealing fishing and tourism centre. The town's beaches aren't the best along the north Zealand coast, but there's a lovely working **harbour** cluttered with trawlers, dinghies, tour boats, ferries and a few old wooden ships, and surrounded by a half dozen restaurants, fish shops and smokehouses serving the local catch. The shop-lined main street, Vesterbrogade, runs parallel to the beach; at its western end, about ten minutes' walk from the centre, is the **Gilleleje Museum** (June–Aug Mon & Wed–Sun 1pm–4pm, Sep–May Mon & Fri 1–4pm, Thurs 1–6pm, Sat 10am–2pm; ⊛ www.holbo.dk; 25kr), housed on the first floor of the public library at Vesterbrogade 56; it's notable really only for a small section on Gilleleje's role in the evacuation of eighteen hundred Danish Jews in 1943 (see p.402).

Before you reach the museum, at the intersection with Nordre Strandvej, a path heads off along the coast along the top of the dunes. Follow it and you'll be walking in the footsteps of the famed Danish writer and philosopher **Søren Kierkegaard** (see p.98) who, as a young man, took lengthy soul-searching walks here, mulling over the meaning of life and later recalling: "I often stood there and reflected over my past life. The force of the sea and the struggle of the elements made me realize how unimportant I was." A monument to him now stands a little way along the path bearing his maxim: "Truth in life is to live for an idea". The **tourist office**, Gilleleje Hovedgade 6F (June–Aug Mon–Sat 10am–6pm; Sep–May Mon–Fri 10am–4pm, Sat 10am–noon; ☏ 48 30 01 74, ⊛ www.gilleleje-turistbureau.dk) has a useful town map as well as maps of the different routes Kierkegaard used to walk. A little further east along Gilleleje Hovedgade is the pretty **Seamen's Church**, in whose attic many Jews were concealed in 1943 (see above); adjacent to it, at no.49, the **Skibshallerne & Fiskerhuset** (June–Aug Mon & Wed–Sun 1–4pm; 25kr) explores the town's fishing heritage – there's a reconstructed fisherman's home of the 1850s and exhibits on the history of North Zealand fishermen from the Middle Ages.

There's no real reason to stay in Gilleleje, but if you do want to linger, best option is the lovely *Gilleleje Badehotel* (☏ 48 30 13 47, ⊛ www.gillelejebadehotel .dk; ❼), a grand but homely old beach hotel, recently renovated in true Scandinavian style with white walls, wood floors, wicker sofas and open fires. It's right on the beach (though it's a rocky bit) and away from the main town bustle, tucked away down a quiet residential road a kilometre west at Hulsøvej 15. Alternatively, the tourist office has a list of private rooms from 350kr (25kr booking fee) or there's a **campsite**, just southeast of town at Bregnerødvej 21 (☏ 49 71 97 55). The **restaurants** around Gilleleje harbour range from an exorbitantly overpriced sushi bar to a bare-bones seafood kiosk. Best bet is the *Gilleleje Havn* (☏ 48 30 30 39, ⊛ www.gillelejehavn.dk), Havnevej 14, a classy place with a smart beige interior, tables overlooking the harbour and traditional Danish dishes from 148kr. Much more economical is the nearby *Røgeriet* (smokehouse), Havnen 1, selling seasoned fillets of mackerel, halibut, herring, eel and salmon which you can pick up for a song and eat on the picnic tables just out front.

Tisvildeleje

From Gilleleje, bus #363 largely follows the coast to the windswept village of **TISVILDELEJE**, its expanse of sandy beaches backed by **Tisvilde Hegn** (locally called simply "Hegn"), a forest of wind-tormented beech trees planted here during the eighteenth century to try to anchor the drifting sands. You can wander up through the extensive forest – populated by foxes, deer and hares – on various trails (the tourist office can provide a map) leading off from the beach car park; one of these emerges, after four kilometres, at a peaceful clearing

△ Red deer stag, Tisvildeleje

containing the **Asserbo Slotsruin** – a jumble of stone walls surrounded by a little moat which comprise all that remains of a small castle built on the site of a twelfth-century Carthusian monastery. But the real reason to come to Tisvildeleje is for its **beaches** – the main one is wide, duned and loaded with facilities, and smaller beaches are easily reached by walking along paths leading east and west – or to visit its many good restaurants and soak up the charming, upmarket atmosphere.

There's a summer-only **tourist office** (mid-June–Aug Mon–Fri noon–5pm, Sat 10am–3pm) in the central train station at Banevej (the town is the terminus of the Hillerød line so there is no coastal service from Gilleleje). For **accommodation**, central options include the charming, beautifully furnished *Strand Hotel* (T48 70 71 19, Wwww.strand-hotel.dk; ●), bang in the centre of the village at Hovedgaden 75, which offers a spot of luxury and a fine terrace restaurant. Alternatively, there's the more homely, family-run *Kildegaard* boarding house (T48 70 71 53, Wwww.kildegaard-tisvildeleje.dk; ●), just a few minutes from the beach at Hovedgaden 52, which prides itself on its *hygge*-heavy friendly atmosphere. The **youth hostel** at Bygmarken 30 (T48 70 98 50, Wwww.danhostel.dk/tisvildeleje), 1km east of the village and 500m from a beach, is part of the *Sankt Helene Centeret* holiday and conference complex, and has dorm beds (150kr) as well as family rooms; the centre also has a small campsite (Wwww.helene.dk) and an onsite restaurant, and is very busy in summer.

Several upscale **eateries** along the main street, Hovedgade, make Tisvildeleje an excellent option for summer dining; reservations are highly recommended during peak season. Just to the west on the road into town, ⚞ *Bio & Bistro* (daily 6–10pm; T48 70 41 91, Wwww.tisvildebistro.dk), Hovedgaden 38, has perfected the classic French bistro feel, with exposed beams, rustic-chic table settings and a Gallic-style menu. There are often live bands on Friday and Saturday evenings (a separate cover usually applies), and you can even catch a movie after dinner in the small attached cinema (50kr); they also serve the delicious

Ølfabrikken Porter stout, made by the local microbrewery, Ølfabrikken. Just across the road at no.55, *Tisvildeleje Caféen* (daily 2–4pm & 6–9.30pm; ☎48 70 88 86) is a tad less formal, and with an all-you-can-eat grilled buffet of steaks and fish (225kr), it's a better deal, too; they also have an inexpensive à la carte lunch menu.

Hundested and around

The marina town of **HUNDESTED** is best known as the former home of famed Danish polar explorer Knud Rasmussen, and the **Knud Rasmussens Hus** (April–Oct Tues–Sun 11am–4pm; 25kr; ⓦwww.knudrasmussenshus.dk), Knud Rasmussens Vej 9, has been turned into a museum dedicated to his life and work. Rasmussen – Scandinavia's most famous explorer after Thor Heyerdahl and Erik the Red – spent the first twelve years of his life in Greenland, and once his family moved to Denmark he never stopped trying to get back, leading numerous expeditions across Greenland and Arctic Canada, mapping the coastline and interior, writing ethnographic tomes about Eskimo society and translating volumes of indigenous folktales into Danish. In 1918, he built this thatched Arts and Crafts-styled cottage on a promontory 30m above the beach in Hundested, a setting which reminded him of the stark Greenland landscape, and spent his later years here penning books and planning journeys; the house has changed little since Rasmussen died in 1933. Hundested is also the departure point for **ferries** across the Isefjord to Rørvig (see p.154). Just south of here in Lynæs, an old fishing village that's one of the best locations for windsurfing in Denmark, is a small **campsite**, *Lynæs Camping*, Søndergade 57 (☎47 93 73 22, ⓦlynaes.dk-camp.dk).

Hillerød and around

Smack in the middle of northern Zealand, and reachable by S-Tog from Helsingør and Copenhagen, **HILLERØD** is best known as the location of the glorious **Frederiksborg Slot** (daily: April–Oct 10am–5pm; Nov–March 11am–3pm; 60kr; ⓦwww.frederiksborgmuseet.dk). Laid out across three small islands within an artificial lake and set within magnificent baroque gardens, its fairytale grandeur, opulence and romance outstrip the more famous Kronborg. The castle was originally the home of Frederik II and birthplace of his son Christian IV who, at the start of the seventeenth century, began rebuilding the castle in an unorthodox Dutch Renaissance style. It's the unusual aspects of the design – a prolific use of towers and spires, Gothic arches and flowery window ornamentation – that still stands out, despite the changes wrought by a serious fire in 1859 and subsequent restoration.

You can see the exterior of the castle for free simply by walking through the main gates, across the seventeenth-century S-shaped bridge and into the central courtyard. Since 1882, the interior has functioned as a **Museum of National History**, largely funded by the Carlsberg brewery and intended to heighten the nation's sense of history and cultural development. It's a good idea to get an audioguide (20kr) to get the most out of the sixty-odd rooms charting Danish history since 1500. Many are surprisingly free of furniture and household objects, and attention is drawn to the ranks of portraits along the walls – a motley crew of flat-faced kings and thin consorts who between them ruled and misruled Denmark for centuries. A few rooms deserve special mention. **The Rose** (room 19; to the left of the ticket office) has been reconstructed to look as it did in the time of Christian IV when it served as a dining room, its low vaulted ceiling and imitation gilt leather creating a lavish yet intimate space. On the first floor, the **chapel**, where Denmark's monarchs were crowned between 1671 and 1840, is exquisite, its vaults, pillars and arches gilded and embellished, and the contrasting black marble of the gallery riddled with gold lettering. The shields, in tiered rows around the chapel, are those of the knights of the Order of the Elephant – an honour begun by the king in the late seventeenth century that continues to the present day (Churchill and Montgomery were recipients, but it's now limited to Danish royalty and foreign heads of state). From the chapel, head through room 23 along the Privy Passage to Christian V's **Audience Chamber** (room 24) – the only living quarters from the seventeenth century to have been preserved, and a baroque triumph of stucco and marble flourishes. The **Great Hall**, above the chapel, is a reconstruction, but this doesn't detract from its beauty. It's bare but for the staggering wall and ceiling decorations: tapestries, wall reliefs, portraits and a glistening black marble fireplace. In Christian IV's day the hall was a ballroom, and the polished floor still tempts you to some fancy footwork as you slide up and down its length. It's worth setting aside some time for the **Modern Collection** on the third floor – effectively Denmark's national portrait gallery, with paintings, busts and photos of more recent royals, politicians, scientists, writers and artists, including Karen Blixen, Niels Bohr, and a rather camp and gory self-portrait by Lars Von Trier (on the balcony section). Room 82 is devoted to the current royal family – look out for the portrait of Margrethe II by Andy Warhol.

Away from the often crowded interior, the **baroque gardens**, on the far side of the lake, are astonishingly intricate in their landscaping, with a cascade of canals and fountains (summer only) and some excellent photogenic views of the castle from their stepped terraces. The quickest way to them is through the narrow Mint Gate to the left of the main castle building, which adjoins a roofed-in bridge leading to the King's Wing. In summer you can also do a thirty-minute **boat trip** on the lake aboard the *M/F Frederiksborg*, which leaves every half-hour from outside the castle (mid-May to mid-Sept Mon–Sat 11am–5pm, Sun 1–5pm; 20kr).

From central Hillerød, you can get to Frederiksborg via a **footpath** that runs from Torvet, the town's main square, and skirts the lake toward the castle – it's a pretty ten-minute walk; alternatively, buses #701 and #702 run from the train station, or you can follow the signs (*Slottet*) from the town centre.

Fredensborg

While you're in Hillerød, it's worth hopping on the train to the small town of **FREDENSBORG** to see a current royal residence, the picturesque **Fredensborg Slot** (July daily 1–4.30pm; guided tours 40kr; joint ticket with the Reserved Garden 60kr), home to Queen Margrethe II for most of the year. Built by Frederik IV to commemorate the 1720 Peace Treaty with Sweden (the name means "fortress of peace"), this Italian Baroque palace is opened up to the public in July when the queen decamps to her summer home, Marselisborg (see p.329). The lavish interior is filled with baroque furnishings and features gorgeous stucco work and ceiling paintings, but unless you're a die-hard fan of Queen Margrethe, as are most of the visitors, you'd do better just to have a stroll around the lovely **grounds**. The guided tours of the adjacent Reserved Garden take in the Queen's veggie patch and herb garden, and a grand orangery stuffed with citrus trees, olive trees and the like. The rest of the extensive gardens are open year-round (daily dawn–dusk; free): grand, seemingly endless tree-lined avenues radiate out from the palace to the waters of the beautiful bird haven of **Esrum Sø**, Denmark's second largest lake, where you can swim and hire boats. The gardens also hold **Normandsalen**, seventy life-sized sandstone statues of Norwegian and Faroese eighteenth-century peasant folk arranged in a grassy amphitheatre; the statues on display are replicas of disintegrating originals carved in 1773 and intended as an ethnographical record of the various folk costumes of the region.

Fredensborg station is a ten-minute walk from the town centre. The friendly **tourist office** (April Mon–Fri noon–4pm; May & Sept Mon–Fri noon–4pm, Sun noon–3pm; June–Aug daily 11am–5pm; Oct to mid-Nov Mon–Fri noon–4pm; ☎48 48 21 00, ⓦwww.visitfredensborg.dk), at the entrance to the Slot, has plenty of information on the town and environs. For **food**, the lakeside *Restaurant Skipperhuset* (May–Sept Tues–Sun noon–6pm; book ahead ☎48 48 17 17, ⓦwww.skipperhuset.dk), Skipperallé 6, offers beautifully presented traditional Danish lunches.

Practicalities

From Hillerød's train and bus station, it's a ten-minute signposted walk to the town centre. The **tourist office** is at Møllestræde 9 (mid-June to Aug Mon–Fri 10am–6pm, Sat 10am–3pm; rest of the year daily 10am–5pm; ☎48 24 26 26, ⓦwww .hillerodturist.dk), off the western end of Slotsgade, the main pedestrianized shopping street. There's no real reason to stay in Hillerød, and for good **food**, you needn't even leave the castle confines. Set in one of the gatehouses, *Spisestedet Leonora* (daily 11am–4pm) serves fantastic smørrebrød, starting at 44kr a piece – one should suffice unless you're really hungry. In the town itself, *Encore Café & Brasserie* on Torvet has relatively inexpensive burgers, salads, sandwiches and delicious cakes, while *Engelhardt's Café*, in the Slotsarkaderne shopping arcade, does good-value sandwiches and light snacks.

Central and western Zealand

Still within easy day-trip range of the capital, **central** and **western Zealand** hold some interesting possibilities, most notably the former Danish capital of **Roskilde**, home to a spectacular Viking ship museum and one of the most impressive cathedrals in Denmark. Beyond Roskilde, the towns around the waters of the **Roskilde Fjord** and **Isefjord** hold a number of churches, castles and duned beachfronts that more than justify a diversion from the beaten path. The hilly **Hornsherred peninsula** offers **Skibby Kirke** and its stark medieval-era frescoes, while the nearby **Selsø Slot** preserves much of its pre-nineteenth-century charm. There are more frescoes further north within **Over Dråby**'s medieval church and **Jægerspris Slot**, former home of Frederik VII and filled with many of the idiosyncratic monarch's personal belongings, while just across the Roskilde fjord, **Frederikssund** is best known for the popular Viking plays staged outdoors in the summer. Due west of Roskilde at the southern tip of the Isefjord, **Holbæk** is a popular midway stopping point for tourists visiting the fjordlands and Hornsherred and Odsherred peninsulas, with an interesting open-air museum and a lovely youth hostel. Continue northwest to reach the **Odsherred peninsula**, where **Nykøbing** is a lively summer residence for vacationing Danes and a perfect place to set down your bags and head out to the beaches on the peninsula's north and west coasts. South of here, the E20 motorway runs from **Køge** on the east coast, with its busy beaches and characterful medieval centre, to sleepy **Korsør** in the west, which holds a pair of engaging museums and the remains of a coastal fortress. On the way, the road passes through appealing **Ringsted** and the smaller **Sorø**, from where you can take boat trips or indulge in a bit of river kayaking; it's also well worth taking time to visit **Trelleborg**, site of one of the Viking age's most impressive administrative settlements.

Roskilde and around

Less than an hour by train from Copenhagen and some 35km to the west, **ROSKILDE** has been the site of a settlement since prehistoric times, and was later inhabited by the Vikings, who exploited the Roskilde fjord (which extends nearly 40km north towards Frederiksværk) as a quick route to the

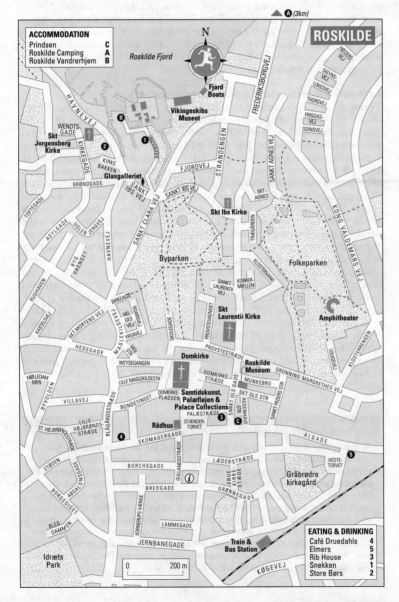

ACCOMMODATION

Prindsen	C
Roskilde Camping	A
Roskilde Vandrerhjem	B

EATING & DRINKING

Café Druedahls	4
Elmers	5
Rib House	3
Snekken	1
Store Børs	2

open sea. But it was the arrival of Bishop Absalon in the twelfth century that made the place the base of the Danish church – and, as a consequence, the national capital for a while. Roskilde's importance waned after the Reformation, and it came to function mainly as a market for the neighbouring rural communities – much as it does today, as well as serving as dormitory territory for Copenhagen commuters. In high season especially, it can be crammed with day-trippers seeking the dual blasts from the past supplied by its royal tombs and Viking boats, while the first week of each July sees a massive influx of visitors when it hosts the brilliant **Roskilde Festival**, Europe's biggest open-air rock event. Yet at any other time the ancient centre and town museums make Roskilde one of Denmark's most appealing towns, and the surrounding countryside is quiet and unspoilt, and holds the absorbing Lejre Forsøgscenter, a reconstructed Iron Age village.

Arrival, information and accommodation

Trains from Copenhagen arrive at the train station at the southern edge of the city centre on Jernbanegade; the bus terminal is within the same complex. Roskilde's **tourist office**, Gullandstræde 15 (April–June Mon–Fri 9am–5pm, Sat 10am–1pm; July & Aug Mon–Fri 9am–6pm, Sat 10am–2pm; Sept–March Mon–Thurs 9am–5pm, Fri 9am–4pm, Sat 10am–1pm; ☎46 31 65 65, ⓦwww.visitroskilde.com), sells the Copenhagen card (see p.64), which offers free or discounted entry to most of Roskilde's museums.

Copenhagen is less than an hour's drive northeast of Roskilde, so many people visit as a day-trip from the capital, but if you're heading towards Funen or further south in Zealand you could **stay** here for the night at the sleekly designed, wooden **youth hostel**, *Roskilde Vandrerhjem* (☎46 35 21 84, ⓦwww.rova.dk; dorms 150kr, doubles ❺/❹), ideally located on the harbour at Vindeboder 7. If that's full, *Roskilde Camping* (☎46 75 79 96, ⓦwww .roskildecamping.dk; mid-March to mid-Sept), on the forested edge of the fjord about 4km north of town, has small, clean cabins (❺) with furnished terraces, though with such a nice setting it too can get very crowded at peak times. It's linked to the town centre by bus #603 towards Veddelev. Roskilde itself has a paltry selection of **hotel** options: best is the pricey but central *Prindsen*, Algade 13 (☎46 30 91 00, ⓦwww.prindsen.dk; ❾/❼), whose elegant lobby leads to quiet rooms that range from the austere to the ostentatious. A more comfortable and central option would be to organise a stay in a **private home** through the tourist office (225kr per person; 25kr booking charge; breakfast extra).

The Roskilde Festival

Held over four days and nights at the end of June, the **Roskilde Festival** (ⓦwww .roskilde-festival.dk) is the largest outdoor music event in Europe, regularly attracting crowds of 100,000 strong. Over **150** rock, electronica, hip-hop and world music **bands** perform on six stages; recent guests have included Pink Floyd, Bob Dylan, Sígur Ros and The Strokes. Most festival-goers pitch their tents in the free camping grounds conveniently located nearby the stages, where the festivities continue long after the bands stop playing at 2am, and it's all remarkably peaceful, with hard drugs little used – or at least little seen – due in part to the extensive security measures taken by the festival organisers. **Ticket prices** are high – upwards of 1400kr for a four-day pass – but sell out several weeks in advance, so contact the tourist office or buy online early if you want to be assured entry.

The town and around

Roskilde is laid out around its central square, **Stændertorvet**, from which the pedestrianized Skomagergade and Algade extend west and east, lined with busy cafés and boutiques. On the north flank of the square lies the major pointer to the town's former status – its fabulous **Domkirke** (April–Sept Mon–Sat 9am–4.45pm, Sun 12.30–4.45pm; Oct–March Tues–Sat 10am–3.45pm, Sun 12.30–3.45pm; 25kr), founded by Bishop Absalon in 1170 on the site of a

△ Roskilde Domkirke

tenth-century church erected by Harald Bluetooth, and finished during the fourteenth century – although portions were added right up to the twentieth. The result is a mishmash of architectural styles, though one that hangs together with surprising neatness. Every square inch seems adorned by some curious mark or etching – the facade itself, with its slender Gothic spires and sunken Romanesque porticos, is a beauty to behold – but it's the claustrophobic collection of coffins containing the regal remains of twenty-one kings and eighteen queens in four large **royal chapels** that really catches the eye. The most richly endowed chapel is that of Christian IV, a previously austere resting place jazzed-up – in typical early nineteenth-century Romantic style – with bronze statues, wall-length frescoes and vast paintings of scenes from his reign. A striking contrast is provided by the simple red-brick chapel just outside the cathedral, where Frederik IX was laid to rest in 1972. Try to get to the Domkirke just before the hour to see and hear the animated medieval **clock** above the main entrance: a model of St Jørgen gallops forward on his horse to wallop the dragon, and the hour is marked by the creature's squeal of death. Upstairs in the Great Hall, a small **Cathedral Museum** (April to mid-June Mon–Fri 11am, 1pm & 2pm, Sat 10am, Sun 1pm & 2pm; mid-June to Sept Mon–Fri every 30min between 11.05am and 2.35pm, Sat every 30min between 9.05am and 11.35am, Sun every 30min between 1.05pm and 3.35pm; Oct–March Tues–Fri noon & 1pm, Sat noon, Sun 1pm & 2pm) provides an engrossing introduction to the Cathedral's colourful history. Ask one of the staff to open up the museum for you.

From one end of the cathedral, a roofed passageway, the **Arch of Absalon** (off-limits to anyone not currently a member of the Danish clergy), feeds into the yellow **Bishop's Palace**. The incumbent bishop nowadays confines himself to one wing, while the others have been turned into showplaces for (predominantly) Danish art. The main building houses the **Museet for Samtidskunst** (Museum of Contemporary Art; Tues–Fri 11am–5pm, Sat & Sun noon–4pm; 30kr, Wed free), whose diverse temporary exhibitions reflect current trends. The theme continues in the west wing, where the **Palæfløjen** gallery (Tues–Sun noon–4pm; free), run by the local arts society, extends outdoors, turning up a striking collection of sculpture beneath the fruit trees of the bishop's garden. The less compelling **Palace Collections** (mid-May to mid-Sept daily 11am–4pm; rest of the year Sat noon–4pm; 25kr) are made up of paintings, furniture and other artefacts belonging to the wealthiest Roskilde families of the eighteenth and nineteenth centuries.

From the cathedral, head east along Domkirkestræde to arrive at the tartan-painted doors of the **Roskilde Museum** (daily 11am–4pm; 25kr), Sankt Ols Gade 18, which open to reveal a mildly enticing array of anthropological and archaeological goodies, with strong sections on medieval pottery, toys and textiles. The well-displayed collection includes the skeletal remains of a giant prehistoric ox found at the bottom of a nearby lake, where it drowned after jumping in to avoid the arrowheads of approaching hunters sometime around 8600 BC Look out also for the strange photos that satirist Gustav Wied (who lived in Roskilde for many years and whose rooms are reconstructed here) took of his family.

Heading north from the cathedral, past the green lawns of the **Byparken** city park, is the **Glasgalleriet** (Mon–Fri 10am–5.30pm, Sat & Sun noon–4.30pm; free; ⓦ www.glasgalleriet.dk), Vindeboder 1, a good little glass gallery in the old Roskilde Gasworks building. However, the main draw hereabouts is the **Vikingeskibs Museet** (Viking Ship Museum; daily 9am–5pm; May–Sept 80kr, rest of the year 45kr; ⓦ www.vikingeskibsmuseet.dk), one of the most enthralling and best-known attractions in Denmark. Set in the green surrounds

Take my boats, please!

In 1997, while the Roskilde harbour was being dredged and ground broken for the Vikingeskibs Museet, archaeologists and museum curators around Scandinavia were astounded when building crews happened upon the intact remains of **nine Viking ships** just above the bedrock. Dating from the late Viking Age to the early Middle Ages (1025 to 1336), the vessels include the largest Viking ship found to date – 36m long, with plank seating for 72 oarsmen. Nearly all of the ships recovered were fully intact – the moisture and chemical properties of the soil had served to preserve them – and they are now being held in on-site conservation chambers. Budgetary concerns notwithstanding, the museum has tentative plans to include the boats in the main museum collection over the next decade, but there is pervading speculation among some that once new buildings are dug to house them, further fleets of subterranean ships will be hit upon, ultimately with no place to store them, and the perpetual scenario – itself worthy of a Borges novella – will begin yet again.

of Strandengen on the banks of the fjord, fifteen minutes' walk north of the centre, the museum is centred around the reconstructed remains of five excellent specimens of Viking shipbuilding: a deep-sea trader, merchant ship, man-of-war, a ferry and a longship. Each was retrieved in 1962 from the fjord a few kilometres north of town at Skuldelev, where they had been sunk to the bottom of the narrow channel to block against invading forces. The vessels give an impressive indication of the Vikings' nautical versatility, their skills in boat-building and their far-ranging travels to places as various as Paris, Hamburg and North America. Downstairs, a **film** detailing the discovery is shown on request. The museum's core documentation – along with changing exhibitions on subjects like the Franks and the Viking experience in Ireland – does a good job of portraying a balanced view of Viking history, which reflects the fact that they sailed abroad not merely to rape and pillage, but also to find quiet landscapes where they could settle down, farm and live more or less untroubled pastoral lives (for more on the Vikings, see Contexts, p.389). Boat-building and sail-making **demonstrations** also take place outdoors all year – the Vikings' sails were spun from a special wool produced from wild Norwegian sheep – and in the summer, you can also experience the seaworthiness of the reconstructed ships moored on the fjord by way of a boat jaunt: you'll be handed an oar when you board, and will be expected to pull your weight as a crew member (50min; 50kr on top of the museum ticket). There's also a decent gift shop, selling a host of Viking-related books in English and more helmeted knick-knacks than you'll know what to do with.

From the adjacent docks, the **cruise boat** *M/F Harald Blåtand* (☎47 38 87 50; twice daily; 80kr one way, 120kr return) sails up the pretty fjord to Frederikssund and back, a journey of a little less than two hours each way. You can also do either the outbound or return leg of the trip on the Frederikssund bus, which takes the same amount of time but costs about half as much.

Around Roskilde: the Lejre Forsøgscenter

If the Vikingeskibs Museet has put you in the mood for a bit of history, you might want to head 8km west of Roskilde to the village of Lejre, where Iron Age Denmark is kept alive and kicking at the **Lejre Forsøgscenter** (Lejre Experimental Centre; May, June & mid-Aug to mid-Sept Tues–Fri 10am–4pm, Sat & Sun 11am–5pm; July to mid-Aug daily 10am–5pm; 75kr; ⓦwww.lejrecenter.dk), a vast open space where volunteer families spend the summer living in a reconstructed Iron Age settlement, farming and carrying out domestic chores using implements – and wearing clothing – copied from those of the period. Modern-day visitors are welcome, and you can try your hand at grinding corn or paddling a dugout canoe. The serious social scientific purpose is to gain an understanding of family life in Denmark 2500 years ago, but the centre can be a lot of fun to visit as a day-trip, especially if you're travelling with kids. To get here, take a local train from Roskilde to the village of Lejre; from Lejre station, bus #233 covers the 4km to the historical centre's entrance.

If you have time to spare on your way back, get off the bus a few stops before Roskilde train station at **Ledreborg Slot** (June & Sept Sun 11am–5pm; July & Aug daily 11am–5pm; 75kr; Ⓦwww.ledreborgslot.dk), a palatial eighteenth-century mansion whose imaginative French-style landscaped gardens, complete with a maze, are often filled with Copenhageners soaking up the weekend sun. The Holstein-Ledreborg family still live in the Baroque manor house, but in the summer, you can go in and check out the paintings, tapestries and furniture, including some ornate candelabra, all left more or less as they were 250 years ago.

Eating and drinking

Eating well isn't a problem in Roskilde, with plenty of options to serve most budgets in the maze of streets around the Domkirke and on Skomagergade and Algade. For more bucolic eating, stock up at the Irma supermarket, 21 Skomagergade, and have a picnic in the pleasant little park at the top of the steps behind the harbour, from where there are good views of the town. In the evenings, serious party animals head to Copenhagen to let down their hair, but a few spots in the town centre and by the railway station offer less frenetic **entertainment**.

Cafés, restaurants and bars

Café Druedahls Skomagergade 40 Ⓦwww.drue dahls.dk. A modern café on the pedestrianized strip offering salads, sandwiches and menu full of exotically flavoured teas (from 35kr), as well as some large brunch plates. Daily 10am–9pm.

Elmers Hestetorvet 1. Set in a historic building just opposite the train station, with heaps of bevelled wood panels and brass trimmings, this student pub is one of the few places which stays open late during the week, and serves over sixty beers, many of them Danish. Mon–Wed 11am–midnight, Thurs 11am–2am, Fri & Sat 11am–dawn.

Rib House Djalma Lunds Gård 8 ☏46 36 36 46, Ⓦwww.ribhouse-roskilde.dk. This spacious, multi-levelled restaurant is among the city's best deals, offering a carnivorous lunch menu of juicy spare ribs, steaks, burgers and club sandwiches (65kr)

and reasonably priced meaty dinners (from 109kr). Daily noon–10pm.

🏃 **Snekken** Vindeboder 16 ☏46 35 98 16, Ⓦwww.snekken.dk. Capacious, ultra-modern café-lounge with black leather couches, abstract art and views onto the harbour. Main courses are few and pricey (around 200kr), so it's best to opt for the much cheaper sandwiches or salads. Their huge brunch spread (Sat & Sun 11.30am–4.30pm; 98kr), with sausages, scrambled eggs, Parma ham, muesli, gravadlax and a virgin bloody mary, should keep you full for most of the day. Daily 11.30am–11pm.

Store Børs Havnevej 43 ☏46 32 50 54. Located on the waterfront and across the docks from the Viking Ship Museum, this fish restaurant does great smørrebrød and home-smoked salmon specials from 78kr, and more substantial fish dishes for 178kr. Mon–Sat noon–11pm, Sun 11am–10pm.

The Hornsherred Peninsula and Frederikssund

West of Roskilde, the hilly **Hornsherred Peninsula** divides the thin, sheltered Roskilde fjord from the larger Isefjord. It holds a series of perfectly preserved, idyllic little villages ranged around central commons and ponds and, along the western coast, to long, quiet beaches and hidden coves. The lack of a railway and the paucity of local buses mean the region is best toured by bike – the Roskilde tourist office (see p.146) has maps of suggested routes.

Skibby and Selsø Slot

About halfway up the peninsula some 25km from Roskilde in the village of Skibby, **Skibby Kirke** (Mon–Sat 8am–4pm) is Hornsherred's largest church, with original foundations that date back to 1100. It's worth visiting to take a look at its well-maintained frieze of medieval murals depicting wealthy princes enjoying leisurely rides atop spotted horses, the message being that decadence and secularism on earth will be punished accordingly in the afterworld. Just behind the altar, a small hole in the wall marks the spot where, in 1650, humanist monk Poul Helgesen deposited his Skibby Chronicle, a history of Denmark in Latin that's now held in the National Museum in Copenhagen.

Five kilometres east of Skibby, on shore of the pristine Selsø Lake, the stately **Selsø Slot** (May to mid-June Sat & Sun 1–4pm; mid-June to mid-Aug daily 11am–4pm; mid-Aug to Oct Sat & Sun 1–4pm; 40kr; ⓦ www.selsoe.dk) hasn't been renovated or modernized since the early 1800s – there is still no electricity, plumbing or heating – and its unrestored interior, packed with original marble and wood detailing, provides an authentic picture of early Danish aristocratic living. Built in 1576, the opulent Renaissance manor house has been unoccupied since 1829, when its last hereditary owner died; most of its effects were auctioned off to pay land debts, the knights' banquet hall became a granary and an adjacent room was turned into an apiary. Today, the restored stucco-ceilinged **banquet hall** is adorned with four-metre-high marble panels, several large restored murals of battle scenes by Danish court artist Hendrick Krock and, most striking of all, two large gilded mirrors from 1733 – the only items not despatched in the auction. The banquet hall is known for its fine acoustics, and between June and August classical music **concerts** (90kr) are staged here, spectacular events illuminated by candlelight. Selsø is adjacent to a 1500-acre bird sanctuary, and a viewing tower in the castle garden allows you good views of the grounds.

Over Dråby and Jægerspris Slot

Some 9km north of Skibby, the peninsula's main road passes through tiny **Over Dråby**, whose eleventh-century **Dråby Kirke** (Mon–Fri 8am–4pm), Kirkevej 3, has vaults and walls adorned with mint-condition medieval chalk paintings that represent some of the best-preserved ecclesiastical frescoes in Denmark, painted in the mid-1400s by the so-called Isefjordsmester, one of Denmark's many anonymous fresco painters. Painted in a naïve style and depicting various biblical scenes, the most appealing frescoes are set along the chancel arches and the nave's central arch. From here, continue 1km northwards to arrive at **Jægerspris Slot** (50min guided tours only: mid-March to Oct Tues–Sun at 11am, noon, 1pm, 2pm and 3pm; 45kr; ⓦ www.kongfrederik.dk), established during the fifteenth century as a royal hunting seat and last used by the eccentric Frederik VII, who lived here during the mid-1800s with his third wife, Grevinde Danner. The castle rooms retain many of their original furnishings, including the King's impressive weapons collection and his beloved pipe, an item he almost certainly puffed on as he signed the Danish constitution on June 5, 1849, thereby ending absolutism in Denmark. Most Danes didn't care much for Countess Danner, who was notorious for her repeated infidelities

– a reputation she tried to redress when she inherited the castle after the king's death and turned it into an institution for orphaned girls. Her modest tomb is located in the castle grounds.

Frederikssund

Southeast of Jægerpris, where the east and west banks of the Roskilde Fjord close in to a distance of a few hundred metres, a small bridge – the only place to cross over from Hornsherred to northern Zealand – leads to the sizeable town of **FREDERIKSSUND**, founded and named by narcissistic monarch Frederik III. A ferry crossing that doubled as a tax collection facility was in service over the fjord during the Middle Ages, after which a semi-permanent "bridge" of adjacent ships was used to cross the waters; the modern bascule drawbridge provides a decidedly less romantic crossing, and is much derided by locals for the regular traffic problems it causes. Frederikssund itself is best known for its extravagant summer **Viking plays** (Tues–Sat 8pm, Sun 4pm; 125kr; ☎47 31 06 85, ⓦ www.vikingespil.dk), staged for the last fifty years or so on the grassy Kalvøen lawns just south of the centre. Something of a cultural institution in Denmark, these elaborate dramas based on Viking mythology are well worth attending even if you don't speak Danish: the cast consists of several hundred amateur actors resplendent in medieval-style costumes, and performances feature burning longboats and lots of smoke bombs; written summaries of the plays are available in English. If you book in advance, you can get in the mood by reserving a place on a post-performance tour (190kr) to a nearby recreated Viking settlement to join in a communal feast – think steins of foaming beer and beef cooked on an open spit.

The only other point of interest in town, just east of the bridge at Jenriksvej 4, is the **J.F. Willumsens Museum** (Tues–Sun 10am–5pm; 40kr; ⓦ www.jfwillumsensmuseum.dk), a newly renovated exhibition space showing hundreds of works by Danish artist Jens Ferdinand Willumsen, best known for his mixed-media creations employing engraving, sculpture, ceramics, architecture and even photography. Pay special attention to *Jotunheim*, a wintry Norwegian landscape of wood, zinc and copper, and the radiant and explosive *Fear of Nature After the Storm, No.2*. Willumsen's own private art collection is also displayed on the premises and includes an El Greco, an artist with whom he shared an interest in dramatic use of light and expressive human figures.

Practicalities

Frederikssund is a mere 35 minutes on the S-train from Copenhagen; the train station, which also receives buses, is right in the town centre. The **tourist office** (Mon–Fri 10am–5pm, Sat 10am–1pm, until 2pm in summer; ☎47 31 06 85, ⓦ www.frederikssund-tourist.dk), Havnegade 5A, has information on the entire Hornsherred peninsula, and can help with finding (commission-free) a place to stay at nearby inns and B&Bs. One of the nicest places to **stay** is the *Villa Bakkely* (☎30 63 45 10, ⓦ www.villabakkely.dk; ❸), eight blocks south of the station at Roskildevej 109, which has seven rooms with flat-screen TVs and shared bathrooms. Hotels are limited to the central *Rådhuskroen* (☎47 31 44 66, ⓦ www.hotel-raadhuskroen.dk; ❻), Østergade 1, which has a good restaurant (daily noon–9pm) serving sizeable Danish, Continental and Italian dishes from 150kr. Of other places to **eat**, the best option is *Toldboden* (daily noon–10pm; ☎47 36 17 77), Færgevej 1 in the harbour's old customs house, with lovely views all around and very good Dano-French fusion cuisine; mains are around 200kr, and there's a three-course menu for 325kr.

Odsherred Peninsula

Until the middle of the 1800s, Zealand's craggy northwestern corner was very nearly a separate island; only after a fifty-year project to reclaim the fjordland west of Holbæk did the land take its current shape. Nowadays, the farmland of the **Odsherred Peninsula** stretches from the Lammefjord in the south to Sjællands Odde in the northwestern corner of Zealand, and holds a variety of landscapes, from stretches of sandy beach to grassy, rolling hillocks, with train service running the length of the peninsula, as well as a few gentle attractions and appealing beaches.

Holbæk

Sitting pretty on the southern bank of the Holbæk Fjord (an inlet of the larger Isefjord), **HOLBÆK** is a veritable metropolis compared to anywhere else on the peninsula, and makes a good base for trips to the surrounding fjords. The only point of interest in the town itself is the well-organized **Holbæk Museum** (Tues–Fri 10am–4pm, Sat & Sun noon–4pm; 30kr; ⓦ www.holbmus. dk), Klosterstræde 18, a collection of thirteen seventeenth-, eighteenth- and nineteenth-century houses ranged around a courtyard whose various rooms contain recreations of everything from a nineteenth-century general store (where you can purchase food) to a large town hall.

The **train station**, with services to and from Roskilde, is a few blocks south of the centre on Jernbaneplads, and is also home to the small **tourist office** (ⓣ 59 43 11 31, ⓦ www.holbaek-info.dk); staff can book rooms in local hotels or B&Bs for a 20kr charge, though there's little reason to look any further than the town's outstanding, newly renovated **youth hostel**, ⚐ *Holbæk Vandrerhjem* (ⓣ 59 44 29 19, ⓦ www.holbaekvandrerhjem.dk; dorms 150kr, doubles ❹), one block from the water at Ahlgade 1B. With a spacious lobby decked out in Persian carpets and two dozen bright and sparkling-clean rooms, it has enough character to make you forget you're staying in a hostel; several of the rooms also have superb views across the fjord, and its lively **restaurant** serves juicy steaks and fish dishes in several fjordside dining rooms. In the town centre, *Café Millers* (Mon–Sat 10am–10pm, Sun 11am–10pm; ⓣ 59 44 53 68), Ahlgade 59, is decked out in 1950s Americana and serves inexpensive fare such as buffalo wings, burgers and pizza. Nearby at Nygade 5, ⚐ *Bryghuset No.5* (Mon–Thurs 11am–11pm, Fri & Sat 11am–4am; ⓣ 59 44 25 11, ⓦ www.bryghusetno5.dk) serves local specialities like salmon steak with rocket and a divine aubergine lasagne. Later in the evening, it becomes one of the town's most popular bars; try a pint of the tasty No. 5 ale, brewed downstairs in Denmark's smallest microbrewery.

Nykøbing Sjælland and surrounding beaches

Peppered with holiday homes, Holbæk's northern surrounds are a popular summer destination for vacationing Danish families who come to laze on the beaches or amble around the cosy, café-filled pedestrianized streets of **NYKØBING** (sometimes called Nykøbing S, for Sjælland, or Zealand). Though the numerous craft workshops, exhibition spaces and galleries here make for a pleasant wander, Nykøbing is primarily a handy place to base yourself for trips to the **beaches** north and west of town, the closest of which are 4km north at Nordstrand and Skærby (reachable via bus #601) which front the Nyrup Bay. The beaches are somewhat sandier, and the water shallower, on the western side of the peninsula at **Gudmindrup Lyng Strand** (bus #56), and were recently voted the best in Denmark by one of the national newspapers, and are a great place to catch the sunset to boot. All have refreshment kiosks and basic facilities. The small harbour of Rørvig, 7km north, is the departure point for **ferries** (25 minutes; 38kr, 116kr for car) across the Isefjord to Hundested and the Knud Rasmussens museum (see p.142). Odsherred is also known for its excellent **nature walks**, the most enjoyable being the Isefordsstien path, which begins from Rørvig and ends in Kongsøre, and takes you through the wetlands where there's a raised hide from which you can indulge in a bit of birdwatching. Ask at the tourist office for specific details and hiking maps.

The friendly Nykøbing **tourist office** (T 59 91 08 88, W www.odsherred .com), Svanestræde 9, has information on the entire Odsherred region, and has a useful and detailed bike trail map (50kr) of the peninsula. The local **youth hostel**, *Anneberg Vandrerhjem* (T 59 93 00 62, W www .odsherred-naturskole.dk; closed Dec & Jan; dorms 110kr, doubles ❷), Egeb-jergvej 162, is set in a mid-nineteenth-century schoolhouse and offers clean rooms with hardwood floors and a bit more personality than at most Danish hostels. In terms of **eating** options, the most enjoyable place is *Madkunsten* (daily 11.30am–3.30pm & 6–9pm; T 59 93 17 27), whose delicious menu includes steamed mussels in red wine sauce (138kr) and an inventive chilli, shrimp and guacamole sandwich (88kr).

West along the E20

Linking Copenhagen and the rest of Zealand to Funen and Jutland, the E20 motorway cuts clear across Denmark's heartland. Outside of the capital, the road passes through **Køge**, a thirty-minute S-tog ride from the capital and a popular place from which to explore Zealand's beaches and cliffs. Travelling west, **Ringsted** was once one of Denmark's most important settlements, and its massive twelfth-century church is the final resting place of numerous Danish kings and queens. Beyond Ringsted, the road and rail network out of Copenhagen splits into two: one line heads further south to the islands of Falster, Lolland and Møn (see p.166) via Næstved, while the other heads westwards across the plains of central Zealand towards the diverting small harbour town of **Korsør** and, eventually, the multimillion-kroner **bridge and tunnel** that has carried road and rail traffic across the 18km-wide Store Bælt since it opened in 1998 (see p.160). The E20 also passes through **Sorø**, a good base for exploring Zealand's rural centre; and **Trelleborg**, site of a Viking ring fortress.

Køge and around

Not too long ago, **KØGE** was best known for the pollution caused by the rubber factory and chemical works on its outskirts, and few ventured here to sample the sandy beaches of Køge Bay. Its more distant past is equally unpalat-able, having been a centre for witch-burning in medieval Europe, and the spot where over three thousand Swedish soldiers lost their lives during the 1677 Battle of Køge Bay (see box opposite). The witches and warring are long gone today, and although the rubber plant does still dominate the massive harbour, the evocatively preserved medieval centre and the beaches have been cleaned up in recent years – and an extension of the S-train network means that it's all within easy reach of the capital. It's also a good base for touring the **Stevns Peninsula**, which bulges into the sea just south of the town, and for a quick jaunt to admire the majestic **Vallø Slot** from its pleasant gardens.

Trains and buses arrive at the central **train station**, a short walk from the centre, first along Jernbanegade and then Nørregade, which takes you to the hub of the action, Torvet. Saturday is the best day to visit Køge, with free entertainment in the streets keeping things lively, and plenty of action in the

The Battle of Køge Bay

The site of many naval skirmishes, **Køge Bay**'s most famous battle took place on July 1, 1677, when 48-year-old **Admiral Niels Juel** won a decisive victory against the militarily superior Swedish fleet. Juel's victory was secured when he surprised the Swedes by cutting through the dispersed configuration of Swedish battleships, preventing communication between the Swedish commanders and providing the Danish fleet with clear and direct longitudinal shots of the port and starboard flanks of the enemy ships. Danish firepower accounted for much of the damage inflicted, but a third of the Swedish fleet was maimed by friendly fire from their own battleships, which were maintaining their positions just opposite. After ten hours of fighting, the Swedes were forced to pull back and concede defeat, having lost 25 of their 36 vessels and a third of their regiment – nearly four thousand men; Denmark had limited its losses to zero ships and a few hundred sailors. It was the most decisive unassisted naval victory in the country's history, making Juel the most famous European admiral of his time. His prize money was ten percent of the value of the captured Swedish ships; when the king could not meet this amount in cash, he made up the difference in kind by granting him ownership of all the crown's land on Tåsinge, including the opulent Valdemars Slot (see p.232).

harbourside bars as the day wears on. From the square, head for the cobbled streets and courtyards that lead off Brogade, which hold numerous old buildings as well as craft shops and cafés to while away the day in. Nearby, at Nørregade 4, the **Køge Museum** (June–Aug Tues–Sun 11am–5pm; Sept–May Mon–Fri 1–5pm, Sat 11am–3pm, Sun 1–5pm; 30kr joint ticket with the Kunstmuseum) contains remnants from Køge's bloody past, not least the local executioner's sword, said to have been wielded frequently on Torvet, a place which, perhaps not surprisingly, is also said to harbour various ghostly presences, including sightings of the Devil, who's said to have appeared as a clergyman, a frog, a dog and a pig.

Once its market stalls are cleared away, a suitably spooky stillness falls over Torvet and the narrow cobbled streets that run off it. One of these, Kirkestræde, is lined with sixteenth-century half-timbered houses and leads to **Skt Nikolai Kirke** (mid-June to Aug Mon–Fri 10am–4pm, Sun noon–4pm; Sept to mid-June Mon–Fri 10am–noon), where pirates captured in Køge Bay were hung from the **tower** (July to mid-Aug Mon–Fri 10am–1.30pm; 5kr), which is opened up every half an hour to allow visitors to climb to the top and admire the lovely views of town. Along the nave, look for the somewhat defaced faces of angels carved into the pew-ends; their noses were sliced off by drunken Swedish soldiers during the seventeenth century. The unattractive black-marble and pine font, meanwhile, replaces an earlier one defiled by a woman who performed "an unspeakable act" in it. On a more aesthetic level, the intriguing **Kunstmuseum Køge Skitsesamling**, Nørregade 29 (Køge Museum of Sketches; Tues–Sun 10am–5pm; 30kr joint ticket with Køge Museum; Ⓦ www.skitsesamlingen.dk) holds a motley grouping of drawings, sculptures and models made by important Danish artists of the twentieth century, plus temporary exhibitions of works in progress by both local and international artists. The pièce de résistance, on the third floor, is Bjørn Nørregård's colourful preparatory work for the Queen's tapestries, which are displayed at the Royal Reception Rooms in Copenhagen (see p.78). Free guided tours take place every Sunday at 2pm.

The town's **beaches**, which draw many a Copenhagener on weekends, stretch along the bay to the north and south of town and are easily reached from the centre. Søndre Strand is few minutes' walk from the train station (head south on

Østre Banevej), while the more expansive Solrød and Greve are larger and have watersports outlets, and are just a few minutes' ride north on the S-train.

Practicalities

The **tourist office** (June–Aug Mon–Fri 9am–5pm, Sat 9am–2pm; Sept–May Mon–Fri 9am–5pm, Sat 10am–1pm; ☎56 67 60 01, ⓦwww.visitkoege.com) is on the Torvet. To take full advantage of the local sands, stay at one of the two **campsites** beside Søndre Strand: *Køge Sydstrand* (☎56 65 07 69, ⓦwww.publiccamp.dk/koge; April–Sept) is virtually on the sand, while *Vallø* (☎56 65 28 51, ⓦwww.valloecamping.dk) is across Strandvejen, close to a pine wood. Further away, 3km west of the town centre along Vamdrupvej, is Køge's **youth hostel** (☎56 65 14 74, ⓦwww.danhostelkoege.dk; April to mid-Dec), with bunks (140kr) and some double rooms (❹). To get here, take bus #210 from the train station and get off when the bus turns into Agerskovvej, from where it's a ten-minute walk. Hotel-wise, best option is the *Hvide Hus* (☎56 65 36 90, ⓦwww.hotelhvidehus.dk; ❼), Strandvejen 111, a luxury design resort hotel just 100m from the beach.

In terms of **eating** options, cheapest is *Milas Pizza* (☎56 16 80 42; daily noon–9.30pm), Strandvejen 35, with good pizzas from 65kr, though butcher-cum-brasserie ✻ *Slagter Stig & Co* (Mon–Thurs noon–10pm, Fri & Sat noon–11pm, Sun 1–10pm; ☎56 65 48 09, ⓦwww.slagterstigogco.dk), Carlsenvej 8, is a more enjoyable choice with a buffet (noon–11pm; lunch 54kr, dinner 64kr), and tasty plates of charcuterie from 23kr. For a filling meal in an atmospheric timbered setting, *Christiansminde* (daily 11.30am–10pm ☎56 63 68 56, ⓦwww.chrs-minde.dk), Brogade 7, serves novel specialities (from 138kr) like ostrich with chanterelles, or lobster with a cognac-mushroom sauce. Just across at no.19, *Hugos Vinkælder* offers drinks in a cosy medieval cellar, with dozens of international stouts and bitters on tap and warm *gløg* served in winter.

Valløby

Some 7km south of Køge, the settlement of **Valløby** is a bucolic hamlet unremarkable save for its lovely ochre-coloured Renaissance castle, **Vallø Slot**, which originally served in the 1580s as a noble (and later, royal) residence. The castle has been owned or occupied almost exclusively by women since 1738, when Queen Sofie Magdalene, wife to Christian VI, established the premises as the Vallø Adelige Frøkenkloster ("Vallø Noble Home for Unmarried Ladies of Rank"), a residence intended primarily to assist aristocratic spinsters who weren't quite rich enough to own their own castles; these days, while "official" nobility is no longer a prerequisite for residence, high net worth generally is. The castle itself is closed to visitors, but the surrounding park grounds (8am–sunset) comprise some of the most beautifully tended land in this part of Zealand, spanning English-style gardens, pastures and farmlands noted for their magnolias, walnut and maidenhair trees. **Trains** from Køge stop at Vallø station, about a ten-minute walk to the castle.

The Stevns Peninsula

Easily reached from Køge, the **Stevns Peninsula** is somewhat neglected in terms of tourism largely on account of its rugged coastline, less suited to traditional beachlife than the sandier spots north of Køge. It's worth a visit, however, the dramatic 18km-long stretch of white chalk and limestone cliffs, best seen from the coastal settlement of **Højerup**, whose pretty cliffside church lost its eastern half in 1928 when a landslide saw a good half of the building cascading into the sea, sending choir, altar, coffins and preserved skeletons crashing onto the beach below. Now safe to visit, the church sits on a promontory that affords spectacular views down to the water. You can reach many towns in Stevns, including the main settlement of **Store Heddinge** and the fishing harbour of **Rødvig** – a good place from which to embark on a coastal hike – on the private train line from Køge (InterRail, ScanRail and Eurail passes not valid). Bus #253 runs between all main peninsula towns from Køge. Rødvig has a small **tourist information** centre at Havenvej 21 (Mon–Fri 9am–4pm, hours vary in summer; ☎56 50 64 64, ⓦwww.stevnsinfo.dk); staff will hire out **bicycles** or arrange stays at local B&Bs.

Ringsted

Though little more than a small rural town today, **RINGSTED**'s central location made it one of the most important settlements in Zealand from the end of the Viking era until the Reformation. It was the burial place of medieval Danish monarchs as well as the site of a regional *ting*, the open-air court where prominent merchants and nobles made the administrative decisions for the province. There's not much to see or do here, but if you're en route to other parts of Zealand, it's worth stopping for an hour or two to take a quick peek at its church. The three *ting* stones around which the nobles gathered – and upon which the elders sat – remain in Ringsted's market square, Torvet, but they're often concealed by the market itself, or the backsides of weary shoppers. Instead, it's the sturdy brick **Skt Bendts Kirke** (May to mid-Sept Mon–Fri 10am–noon & 1–5pm; mid-Sept to April Mon–Fri 1–3pm) that dominates the Torvet, just as it has done for over eight hundred years. It's the only structure remaining of the Ringsted monastery, a Benedictine cloister levelled by fire in

△ Skt Bendts Kirke

the eighteenth century, and is the oldest brick church in Scandinavia. Erected in 1170 under the direction of Valdemar I (Valdemar the Great), the church was the final resting place for all Danish monarchs until 1341 – there are at least a dozen royal tombs marked by tablets in the floor – and many affluent Zealanders also had themselves buried here, presumably so that their souls could spend eternity in the very best company. During the seventeenth century, a number of the coffins were opened to dig more space for future coffins; the finds are collected in the **Museum Chapel** within the church. Besides the lead slab found inside Valdemar I's coffin, there's a decorative silk brocade found in that of his son, Valdemar the Victorious, plaster casts of the skulls of Queen Bengård and Queen Sofia, and a replica of the Dagmar Cross, discovered when Queen Dagmar's tomb was opened in 1697 – the original is in the National Museum in Copenhagen.

Practicalities

Trains arrive at the local station, a fifteen-minute walk from the centre; the **tourist office** (mid-June to Aug Mon–Fri 10am–5pm, Sat 9am–2pm; Sept to mid-June Mon–Fri 10am–5pm, Sat 10am–1pm; ☎57 62 66 00, ⓦwww.met-2000.dk), is near to the Torvet at Sct Bendtsgade 6. There's no real reason to stay here, but if you do have the urge, best option is the superb local **youth hostel**, *Amtsruegården* (☎57 61 15 26, ⓦwww.amtstuegaarden.dk; May to mid-Dec), set on a wooded cul-de-sac just alongside the church – clean, efficient and one of the more competently run hostels in the country, offering doubles (❸) and dorms (118kr). As a convenient place for a bite to eat en route through Zealand, Ringsted is packed with places to **eat** and **drink**, most of which are set around the Torvet and just north on Nørregade.

Cafés, restaurants and bars

Café Aspendos Møllegade 11 ☎57 67 05 09. This cosy corner café is a good spot for brunch (11am–3pm; 58kr), and also serves burgers, nachos and pricier pasta dishes starting at 100kr. Mon–Sat 11am–10pm, Sun noon–10pm.

Italy & Italy Torvet 1C ☎57 61 53 53, ⓦwww.italy-italy.dk. The pick of restaurants in town, with country-style decor and a terrace looking right onto the church lawn. Pizza and pasta dishes are affordable at 65kr, while the larger main courses like the king prawn scampi in padella start at around 140kr. There's also a great ice-cream parlour just next door. Mon–Wed & Sun noon–10pm, Thurs–Sat noon–11pm.

Løve Pub Nørregade 12 ⓦwww.lovepub.dk. Set in an old apothecary, this pub features dark pine tables and glass-cased bookshelves of ancient editions and pulls a respectable crowd, though you'll sometimes find after-hours dancing on weekends. Thurs 7pm–dawn, Fri 1pm–dawn, Sat 6pm–dawn.

Rådhuskroen Sct Bendtsgade 8 ☎57 61 68 97, ⓦwww.raadhuskro.dk. Just next to the tourist office, this immensely popular, upscale restaurant-pub offers a menu of steaks, schnitzels and mountainous salads written up on a chalk board, most at around 150kr. Mon–Wed 11am–9pm, Thurs–Sat 11am–10pm, Sun 4–9pm.

Vallentin's Café & Bar Pileborggade 11 ⓦwww.spiced.dk. Located a few blocks east of the Torvet, this simple bar is popular with younger locals, especially for its regular summer events like beer tastings or barbecue dinners held on the leafy terrace out back. Wed 6–11pm, Thurs 6pm–2am, Fri & Sat 6pm–4am.

Sorø and around

A small provincial town of about seven thousand inhabitants, **SORØ**'s primary claim to fame is that it's home to the **Sorø Akademi**, the oldest grammar school in Scandinavia and Denmark's equivalent of Eton. You can potter around the grounds to take in the school's venerable old buildings, which include an **abbey church**, Sorø Klosterkirke (May–Aug Mon–Fri 9am–4pm; Sept–April first Sunday of each month noon–4pm); look out for the painstakingly restored murals on the left wall, about halfway down the aisle. Otherwise there's little of interest in Sorø save for the **Vestsjællands Kunstmuseum** (mid-May to mid-Aug Tues–Sun 10am–4pm, mid-Aug to mid-May Tues–Sun 1–4pm; 20kr; Ⓦwww.vestkunst.dk), Storgade 9, which has a small collection of works spanning several centuries of Danish painting and sculpture, including several brilliant busts by Thorvaldsen. The surrounding area, however, with its lakes and pockets of forest, makes for some excellent biking, hiking or canoeing. The town sits on the shores of **Lake Sorø**, which has landings from which to swim and a diving basin about 500m north of the end of central Søgade. You can also take in an afternoon **boat tour** around the lake with Sorø Bådfart (mid-May to Aug Sat & Sun, plus Wed mid-June to Aug; Ⓦwww.baadfart.dk; 50kr); board at any of the four landings around the lake. Alternatively, hiring a **canoe** and paddling along the calm, narrow Suså river is one of the best ways to explore central Zealand, with the river winding through forest and bog to empty into the northern end of Lake Tystrup; rough camping is allowed at a number of spots along the banks. Contact Broby Kanoudlejning (Ⓣ57 64 81 50, Ⓦwww.brobykanoudlejning.dk; 200kr for three hours, 360kr per day; take bus #27, direction Næstved), Næstvedvej 79 in the nearby town of Broby.

Practicalities

Getting to Sorø is simple, since all **buses** traversing central Zealand pass through the town centre. Sorø doesn't have a **train station** of its own, but the station at Frederiksberg is just 1km south, from which it's a quick walk to the town centre; you can also take bus #806/807. Your first stop in town should be the helpful local **tourist office** (mid-June to mid-Aug Mon–Fri 10am–5pm, Sat 9.30am–2pm, Sun 1–4pm; mid-Aug to mid-June Mon–Fri 10am–5pm, Sat 9.30am–noon; Ⓣ57 82 10 12, Ⓦwww.soroeturisme.dk), Storgade 15. **Bikes** can be hired just nearby at Cykelhuset (Ⓣ57 82 01 21), Rolighed 11A. The town's **youth hostel**, *Kongskilde Friluftsgård* (Ⓣ57 84 92 00, Ⓦwww.kongskildefriluftsgaard.dk; dorms 120kr, doubles 495kr), is located a few kilometres south of town. *Sorø Camping* (Ⓣ57 83 02 02, Ⓦwww.soroecamping.dk; March–Oct), just west of the town centre at Udbyhøjvej 10, is set back just a few metres from Lake Pedersborg and rents out several dirt-cheap but clean cabins (❶) with kitchenettes. In the town centre, the most picturesque place to stay is the 335-year-old *Hotel Postgården* (Ⓣ57 83 22 22, Ⓦwww.hotelpostgaarden.dk; ❼), Storgade 25, with lovely rooms in florals and pastels; all but four have private baths. The somewhat upscale **restaurant** here is very popular, with a terrace set in the courtyard out back. For a more picturesque setting, walk fifteen minutes northwest of the centre to the town bridge, at the foot of which sits ⚡ *Støvlet Katrines Hus* (daily 11.30am–4pm, 5.30–9pm; Ⓣ57 83 50 80, Ⓦwww.stovletkatrineshus.dk), Slagelsevej 63, a thatched and timbered old red building looking onto Lake Sorø that serves an upscale menu of tasty dishes such as foie gras and broiled mullet with purée of celery; three courses will cost you 315kr.

Trelleborg Viking fortress

Some 12km west of Sorø, the Viking ruins at **Trelleborg** (April–Oct Mon–Thurs and Sat & Sun 10am–5pm; 50kr) represent one of Scandinavia's most important historical sites. Located between two rivers on a hilly headland, the circular complex dates from 980 and, though the eight thousand oak trees used for the original stocky constructions and tall fortress walls have long since rotted away, it still comprises the best-preserved of Denmark's four Viking ring fortresses. The original complex had a main stronghold and an outer ring wall with four gates, and was intended as much for defence purposes as it was a centre of administration and trade. On the walk to the site from the car park, a large reconstructed **longhouse** sporting bulky wooden doors and internal staved timber supports offers a vague sense of what things might have looked like back then. The sixteen longhouses built here by the Vikings would have housed four hundred or so people, the bodies of whom rest in the nearby burial grounds (alongside a mass grave containing the remains of some of their would-be attackers). The excellent on-site **museum**, with full documentation in English, has a scale model of the fortress alongside some of the findings from the site – swords, buckles and a sacrificial burial hole with the elfin skeletons of two children and a goat. During July, would-be Vikings from all over the country show up in full regalia to take part in lively **markets**, jousting matches and even a full-on dramatization of a historic Viking battle.

To get to Trelleborg, take the train to Slagelse, 5km east, then transfer to bus #312 (free with train ticket), which leaves hourly for the ten-minute ride to Trelleborg.

Korsør

Separated from Funen by the Store Bælt, just 18km wide at this point, **KORSØR** has long served as western Zealand's connection to the rest of Denmark, though the ferries that once plied these waters have now been replaced by the impressive **Storebælt bridge and tunnel**, some 3km north of town, which has been carrying all road and rail traffic west to Funen since it opened in 1998. Korsør isn't a hotbed of activity these days, but it's worth a quick diversion when travelling to or from Funen, with a couple of mildly diverting museums and a seventeenth-century fortress tower. Trains now stop at the station close to the Storebælt bridge, from where buses into town terminate at Caspar Brands Plads, right in the centre next to the town hall. Before you head into town, continue a few hundred metres past the train station (if you're arriving via the bridge, take exit 43 at the toll station) to the **Storebælt Udstillingscenter** (Great Belt Bridge Centre; Wed–Sun 11am–4pm; free), Storebæltsvej 88, which will tell you everything you could possibly want to know about the engineering expertise behind the magnificent Storebælt link. Of particular note is a scale replica of the boring machine used to drill out the 8km-long railway tunnels that run 75m below the water's surface. Just on from the centre, take a quick look at the small **Iceboat Museum** (May–Sept daily 11am–4pm; free), which holds one of the seventeenth-century iceboats used to traverse the Store Bælt in the days when steamships were too weak to plow through the thick ice. During the winter, it took eight hours to haul the laden craft across the frozen waters, and the exhibition displays photos from some of the more bitter crossings. Once you've had your fill, head to the tiny headland behind the museum to take in the jaw-dropping views of the modern Storebælt bridge.

Buses drop passengers both at Korsør's train station in the town's centre, where two main intersecting pedestrianized streets, Algade and Nygade, hold most of

The Storebælt bridge to Funen

Suggestions for a fixed connection across the Store Bælt were made as early as 1855, but ground wasn't broken for such a project until 1986. The multi-billion kronor **Storebælts-forbindelsen** or "Great Belt fixed link" (Ⓦwww.storebaelt.dk) took twelve years to build and, at 13km in length, is Europe's second longest road and rail bridge after the Øresund link (see p.64). One-way tickets are 200kr per car, though there are discounts if you travel on weekends.

the action. Just around the corner is the town's best-preserved building, the rococo-style merchant's home of **Konggården** (daily 10am–4pm, Wed until 8pm; Ⓦ www.kongegaarden.dk; free), Algade 25, now a gallery of sculptures and drawings by Jewish artist Harald Isenstein. A kilometre or so west of here, adjacent to the fishing harbour, is the **Korsør Søbatteri** (Korsør coastal battery; Tues–Sun 11am–4pm; free), locally known as the *Fæstningen* ("fortress"), a small grassy plot containing a handful of old buildings, the largest of which is now a **museum** (same hours as fortress; free), with displays on life in Korsør over the years, as well as models of the luxurious ships and ferries that once made the crossing over to Funen. It's also worth climbing to the top of the **tower** (ask at the museum for the key) to take in the view down to the harbour.

Practicalities

Korsør's **tourist office** (June–Aug Mon–Fri 9am–5pm, Sat 10am–2pm, Sun 11am–2pm; Sept–May Mon–Fri 10am–4pm, Sat 10am–1pm; ☏ 58 35 02 11, Ⓦ www.visitkorsoer.dk) is centrally placed at Nygade 7. If you're on your way to Funen, you're much better off looking for **accommodation** over the bridge in Nyborg or, better still, Odense, but best option in Korsør is the *Svenstrupgaard* youth hostel (☏ 58 38 15 19, Ⓦ www.svenstrupgaard.dk; dorms 150kr, doubles ④), Svenstrup Strandvej 3, with sleek and spacious rooms, some with inlaid vaulted brick ceilings and exposed timbers. In terms of **food**, *Havfruen* (daily 8am–10pm; ☏ 58 37 61 65, Ⓦ www.hav-fruen.dk), Algade 24, is one of the more atmospheric spots, with burgers (from 28kr) and steaks (from 89kr) served up in an appealing modern setting. There's also an excellent bakery at the intersection of Nygade and Algade.

Southern Zealand and the islands

Made up almost entirely of rolling farmlands, **southern Zealand** is seriously rural, though its prosperity and power during the Middle Ages is still evident in the imposing buildings of towns like **Næstved**, while **Vordingborg** castle and

△ Zealand coastline

its attached museum offer more chances to get a handle on Danish medieval history. Of the three sizeable islands off the southern Zealand coast, **Falster** has some of the most prized (and touristed) beachfront in the country, while **Lolland** is a bit more rural, with several quaint inland towns. The smallest of the three, and with gleaming white cliffs, quaint harbour villages and medieval churches, **Møn** is by far the most popular with visitors, though it never feels overrun with tourists. All of the islands are connected to mainland Zealand by road, and Falster and Lolland have rail links, too. Most of Southern Zealand is served by buses, though as services are infrequent outside of the main settlements, it's wise to rent a bike or car if you want to explore the far reaches of the islands.

Næstved and around

Some 25km south of Ringsted, **NÆSTVED** is easily the largest town in southern Zealand. Aside from a smartly restored medieval centre and a minor museum, there's little to keep you here, though it is a good jumping-off point for canoe trips down the peaceful, little-visited **River Suså**, as well as a visit to the agreeable **Gavnø slot**. Næstved's many brick buildings – a defining feature of many once-important cities along the Baltic coast – mark it out as one of the more powerful towns of the Hanseatic League, the trading alliance that dominated European commerce during the Middle Ages. The town is centred around the large, colourless Axeltorv square, lined with late-1960s office buildings and chain boutiques broken only by the Løve Apoteket, built in the 1640s and still in business today. Just south of Axeltorv is the fourteenth-century **Sct Peders Kirke**, whose chancel bears an elaborate fresco of King Valdemar IV

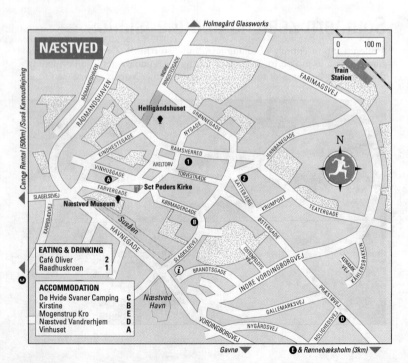

and Queen Helvig, both on bended knees before God, perhaps in thanks for the king's successful sale of Estonia to Germany in 1346. Across the church square is Denmark's oldest town hall, dating from the 1400s, as well as the *boderne* – medieval craftsmen's stalls – that now make up part of the **Næstved Museum** (Tues–Fri & Sun 10am–4pm, Sat 11am–2pm; 15kr, 20kr for joint ticket with Helligåndhuset; ⓦwww.naestved-museum.dk), where there's a small collection of locally made, mostly modern Danish arts and crafts – primarily ceramics, glass and silverwork. A few minutes' walk north at Ringstedgade 4, the museum's main exhibition space, **Helligåndshuset** (same hours and ticket as the Næstved Museum), is dominated by medieval artefacts squirreled away from the region's many churches – altarpieces, crucifixes and statues of saints.

Practicalities

Transportation links to Næstved are very good, with regular trains and buses from the north and south arriving at the **train station**, five minutes' walk east of the town centre along Ramsherred and Jernbanegade. Free parking is available at the harbour, in the southwest of town on Havnegade, where the **tourist office** (June & Aug Mon–Fri 9am–5pm, Sat 9am–2pm; July Mon–Fri 9am–6pm, Sat 9am–2pm; Sept–May Mon–Fri 9am–4pm, Sat 9am–noon; ☎55 72 11 22, ⓦwww.visitnaestved.com) is housed in the yellow Det Gule Pakhus, Havnen 1. Regardless of how you arrive, you'd do well to rent a **bicycle** if you're planning on getting out of town to explore southern Zealand's unbeaten paths; try Brotovets Cykler, Brotorvet 3 (Mon–Thurs 7am–5.30pm, Fri 7am–7pm, Sat 9am–2pm; 50kr per day).

There's a decent selection of places to **stay** in the town centre, including several old inns and hotels, but the **eating** options are somewhat spartan; all the hotels have good restaurants, however. The modern *Café Oliver* (☎55 77 88 81, ⓦwww .cafeoliver.dk; daily 11am–10pm, plus Fri & Sat until midnight), Jernbanegade 2, is a pleasant spot for a sandwich or salad (around 70kr), and has a terrace. A more enjoyable option is the *Raadhuskroen* (Mon–Thurs 11am–11pm, Fri 11am–midnight, Sat 10am–midnight; ☎55 72 01 56, ⓦwww.raadhuskroen.com), Skomagerrækken 8, whose lunch menu features a dozen variations of smørrebrød, including a tasty one with chilli-lime gravadlax, with pricier fish and steak dinner dishes starting at 189kr. You can eat in the stately, wooded interior rooms or the covered terrace out back, there's live jazz Saturday afternoons in the summer, and the bar is a good spot for an evening drink.

Accommodation

De Hvide Svaner Camping Karrebækvej 741 ☎55 44 24 29, ⓦwww.dehvidesvaner.dk. The closest campsite to town, located on the coast by Karrebæksminde, 3km from a popular beach. Facilities include a large swimming pool, and it's very popular with families. Mid-June to mid-Oct.

Hotel Kirstine Købmagergade 20 ☎55 77 47 00, ⓦwww.hotelkirstine.dk. This gorgeous 250-year-old former mayoral home boasts charming, well-sized rooms that still retain lots of old-world class. Six smaller-sized rooms are priced 200kr cheaper, though you have to ask specifically for these if you want them. ❼

Mogenstrup Kro Præstø Landevej 23 ☎55 76 11 30, ⓦwww.firsthotels.com. Some 9km southeast of town in the village of Mogenstrup, this elegant old inn has plenty of atmosphere, and gorgeous rooms decked out with hardwood floors, Oriental carpets and four-poster beds. Booking online will often get special rates. Take bus #76. ❼

Næstved Vandrerhjem Præstøvej 65 ☎55 72 20 91, ⓦwww.danhostelnaestved.dk. The town's only affordable option, set in a modern building just outside the centre and with predictable dorms (120kr; 150kr en-suite) and doubles (❹), but friendly staff. From the train station, turn left into Farimagsvej and left again along Præstøvej.

Vinhuset Skt Peders Kirkeplads ☎55 72 08 07, ⓦwww.hotel-vinhuset.dk. Set on the church square, this recently renovated hotel has small but bright and delightfully dainty rooms with flat-screen TVs. Its medieval-style cellar restaurant, *Le Boeuf*, is one of the town's better eating options. ❼/❻

Around Næstved

Næstved's surrounds hold several good possibilities for side-trips, most popular of which is a day or two spent paddling a **canoe** through the placid waters of the Suså river, a great way to get out into the dramatic landscape in this part of Denmark, from pasturelands to old water mills and chalk-white churches. The negligible current in this part of the river allows for leisurely progress – you could easily get to Bavelse Sø, 18km away, in well under a day – and there are basic camping places and a few bed and breakfasts along the way for **overnighting**. Canoes are available from Suså Kanoudlejning (☎57 64 61 44, ⓦwww.kanoudlejning.dk; May–Sept; 350kr per day, 660kr for two days), whose launching spot is Slusehuset, a ten-minute walk northwest of Axeltorvet at Åstien 8; you can also reserve online, though you should always book at least a day in advance.

The high-tech **Holmegaard Glassworks** (June & mid-Aug to Dec Mon–Fri 10am–4pm, Sat & Sun 10am–5pm; July to mid-Aug daily 10am–6pm; 79kr; ⓦwww.holmegaard.com) are also worth a visit, and are reachable via a fifteen-minute bus journey (#75) northwest of town to Fensmark. The professional glassblowers here have been producing household and decorative objects for nearly two hundred years, and tours allow you into their studios to watch them create. For an extra 99kr, you can also test your own wind-power by blowing the molten glass to create your own unique piece of sculpture. A museum showcases thousands of glass products, and there's also a shop selling glass sculpture, dishware and everything else produced here.

A few miles southwest of Næstved at the mouth of the River Suså, the island of **GAVNØ** is home to the eighteenth-century rococo **Gavnø Slot** (daily: May 10am–5pm; June–Aug 10am–4pm; 65kr; ⓦwww.gavnoe .dk), an imposing structure whose strategic location at the mouth of the Suså river made it important for regulating shipping in and out of Næstved during the Middle Ages. You're given free reign to explore various corridors and staircases plastered with **portraits** depicting a motley and cluttered grouping of subjects, from Sir Isaac Newton to Queen Margrethe I. You can also peek into a number of rooms containing assorted displays of antiquities, costumes and embroidery. Most noteworthy is the Red Damask Room, whose assemblage of French and Danish Louis XVI furniture includes a four-poster bed whose wooden canopy is adorned with carved-out stars – evidently an early Danish alternative to counting sheep. The palace grounds (included in the ticket price) are enhanced by a delightful **tulip garden** and an exotic **butterfly preserve**, both of which attract hordes of visitors in the summertime. A pretty arched bridge connects the island to Næstved, though the *Friheden* ferry (☎55 77 38 36, ⓦwww.rundfart.dk; round-trip 75kr) also runs about three times a day during the summer between Næstved, the palace, and the small, touristy harbour town of **Karrebæksminde**, the latter known for its excellent **beaches**. The most popular beaches of the swimming spots are on Enø island, just south of town, and accessible via a small bridge. Karrebæksminde is 12km southwest of Næstved; you can get here on bus #80 from the train station, or cycle along the banks of a canal which links the two towns.

Vordingborg

South of Næstved, the 22 motorway skirts the Dybsø Fjord on its way to **VORDINGBORG**, a compact place whose protected harbour made it an ideal base for twelfth-century military raids into the Baltic to fight off the Wends. For several hundred years, the town was a popular royal residence, and as the spot where the Jutlandic Code and the Danish constitution were both ratified, it continues to maintain immense historical resonance for modern Denmark. Skulking behind dilapidated encircling walls at the easternmost end of the pedestrianized Algade, the town's one real draw is twelfth-century **Vordingborg castle** (June–Aug daily 10am–5pm; rest of the year Tues–Sun 10am–4pm; 30kr), looming over which – and dominating the entire town – is the 36-metre-high **Gåsetårnet** ("Goose Tower"), one of nine such towers built hereabouts to serve as lookouts. This one was constructed in 1365 by King Valdemar IV, and its spire is crowned with a shiny gold-plated goose, said to have been placed there by the king as a slight on the Hanseatic League, with whom Denmark was fighting at the time: with its beak pointing towards the League's headquarters at Lübeck, the subtle implication was that the Hanseatic states were as threatening to Denmark as a flock of cackling wild geese. You can enter the tower's cellar, used as a prison in the nineteenth century, or climb up four floors to the top and sneak a panoramic peek through the small embrasured openings. In its heyday, the fortress was surrounded by a massive brick and stone **ring wall**, some 8m high and 800m long, as well as a complex arrangement of individual moats that encircled the wall from the outside. Only the foundations are still visible, but a rich array of archeological items found on the site are on display at the **Sydsjællands Museum** (South Zealand Museum; June–Aug 10am–5pm; Sept–May Tues–Fri 10am–4pm, Sat & Sun 1–4pm; ☏55 37 25 54; 30kr; ⓦwww.sydmus.dk), housed in the seventeenth-century former barracks. Each June, museum archeologists set **digs** around, which usually turn up old bits of the fortress and various household items from the Middle Ages. If you're interested in helping out digging, even for a few hours, contact the museum for specific information. The only other thing to see in Vordingborg is the fifteenth-century **Vor Frue Kirke** (10am–2pm), Kirketorvet 14A, whose facade sports a fetching patchwork of red and yellow brick; inside highlights are the Renaissance pulpit from 1601 and a very ornate Baroque altarpiece from 1642, monogrammed with Christian IV's initials. Standing at the nave, crank your head back to spot the faint chalk **frescos** that cover the triumphal arch, where several nativity scenes are overshadowed by a caricature painting of local bricklayer Jeppe Murer, wearing a dunce's cap and imbibing from a chalice.

Trains, which arrive from central Zealand as well as from Falster, disembark at the town's station, a few minutes' walk west of Algade. There's a small, helpful **tourist office** at Algade 96 (Mon–Fri 9am–5pm, Sat 9am–noon; June–Aug Sat until 2pm; ☏55 34 11 11, ⓦwww.visitvordingborg.dk); staff can suggest local bicycle tours in the area – the Knudghoved Odde peninsula is especially nice – and will rent out bikes (50kr per day). Though **accommodation** choices are better on Møn or in Næstved, Vordingborg does have an acceptable **youth hostel** at Præstegårdsvej 18 (☏55 36 08 00, ⓦwww.danhostel.dk/vordingborg; dorms 150kr, doubles ❸), while just opposite the tower at Slotstorvet, there's the pricey but drab *Hotel Kong Valdemar* (☏55 34 30 95, ⓦwww.hotelkongvaldemar.dk; ❻). In terms of **eating**, *Snekken* (April–Sept Tues–Sun noon–10pm; Oct–March Tues–Thurs 5–10pm, Fri–Sun 1–10pm; ☏55 37 05 74) is an inexpensive Chinese restaurant offering nice views of the boatyard. Most of Vordingbord's restaurants, however, are overshadowed by a distinguished five-star establishment just north of town. ⌘ *Babette* (Tues–Fri noon–midnight, Sat 6pm–midnight; ☏55 34 30 30, ⓦwww.babette.dk), Kildemarksvej 5, is a snazzy, professionally run Franco-Danish fusion place that serves innovative fish, meat and vegetable dishes, and its sleek, modern interior is a perfect setting in which to enjoy the changing three-course menu (405kr). Reservations are required.

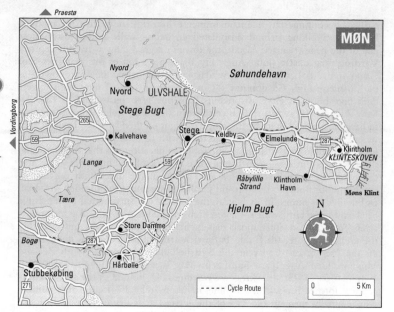

Møn

Connected to Zealand (and Falster) by the Queen Alexandrine bridge, the oblong island of **MØN** is one of the most popular destinations in southern Zealand, with sandy beaches that make for some great walking and a handful of inviting bed and breakfasts, and it's well worth making the effort to visit. Its main town, **Stege**, is a good place to start exploring, with a helpful tourist office and the lion's share of the island's restaurants. Over on the east coast, you're sure to want to spend a few hours at the famed **Møns Klint** cliffs, strolling through the clifftop forest or along the beaches that run below. Elsewhere on the island, highlights include the fourteenth-century frescoes within the **medieval churches** at Fanefjord, Keldby and Elmelund, as well as a visit to the tiny, car-free islet of **Nyord**.

There's no train service to Møn, so if you're travelling by public transport, take bus #62 or #64 from Vordingborg.

Stege

If you don't have your own transport, **STEGE** is the best base from which to explore Møn, since it's the hub of the island's minimal bus service. Buses drop you next to the tourist office, on the north side of the drawbridge which leads to the town centre. From here, Stege is bisected by its long, pedestrianized main street, Storegade, which runs from up the harbour past the looming burnt-umber Gothic roof of the town church, and terminates at the **Mølleporten** medieval gates – Stege's name is derived from *stike*, wooden poles rammed into the sea inlet as a further defence against intruders. Connected to the Mølleporten is **Empiregården** (May–Oct daily 10am–4pm; Nov–April Tues–Sun 10am–4pm; 30kr; Ⓦ www.moensmuseum. dk), Storegade 75, a town museum within a former merchant's house dating back to the 1780s. The collection here includes archaeological and ethnographic exhibits covering everything from fossilized fauna to fresco-filled churches.

Once you've had your fill of Stege, it's a good idea to prime yourself for exploring Møn by stopping off at the superb **tourist office** (late June to late July Mon–Fri 9.30am–5pm, Sat 9am–6pm; Sept to mid-June Mon–Fri 9.30am–4.30pm, Sat 9am–noon; ℡55 86 04 00, Ⓦwww.visitmoen.com), Storegade 2, where knowledgeable staff hand out a dozen excellent English-language brochures and cycling maps of the island, and can help with B&B **accommodation** across the island. The only hotel option in town is the *Ellens Cabaret* (℡55 81 54 54; Ⓞ), at Langelinie 48 near the centre, a ratchety modernist building with boring, pastel-flavoured rooms, some of which have balconies overlooking the water. Otherwise, there's an inexpensive **campsite** on Falckvej 5 (℡55 81 84 04; May to mid-Sept). In contrast to its poor choice of places to stay, Stege does offer the best **places to eat** on Møn, most of them lining Storegade and catering to a diverse range of tastes.

Cafés, restaurants and bars

Café Anden Møllebrøndstræde 2. Set just at the medieval gates in the north of town, this is as good a spot as any for a drink, with bottled beers for 18kr and draught for 22kr. Mon–Thurs 3pm–2am, Fri & Sat 3pm–5am, Sun 2pm–midnight.

Café Laika Havnen 1 ℡55 81 46 07, Ⓦwww.cafe-laika.dk. Set across from the tourist office, this quaint dockside restaurant-bar offers picnic tables and a sizeable menu of things like wine-steamed mussels (62kr) and chicken fajitas (78kr), as well as pricier steak and fish plates. April–Oct daily 11am–midnight (kitchen closes at 9pm).

David's Storegade 11 Ⓦwww.davids.nu. A slick modern café with juices, cakes and very good coffee. The large glass windows are great for people-watching, and there's a terrace out back. Mon–Fri 10am–5pm, Sat 10am–4pm.

Færgen Møn Storegade 2 ℡20 94 40 48, Ⓦwww.faergenmon.dk. While the selection of fish and meat offerings at the buffet is smaller than at other town retaurants, this weathered ferry, moored just alongside the tourist office, has heaps of atmosphere, and is bedecked with memorabilia from the era when it served as the main link between Møn and Zealand. July & Aug only; noon–4pm lunch buffet (119kr), 6–9pm dinner buffet (139kr).

Støberiet Storegade 59 ℡55 81 42 67, Ⓦwww.slagterstig.dk. Delicatessen-cum-restaurant that's the pick of the options in town. You select meat, fish or salad ingredients and have them prepared right in front of you – try the *inbagte rejer*, deep-fried baby prawns. You can eat in the spacious, airy atrium or out back in the quiet, tree-lined garden. Mon–Sat 8am–10pm, Sun 1–10pm.

Ulvshale and Nyord island

To the northwest of Stege, the **Ulvshale** ("wolf's tail") peninsula is a dense, lush forest of beech, ash, lime, rowan and hornbeam that provides a suitable habitat for the venomous – and rare – black adder. The forest has a handful of pleasant, signposted paths, ideal for leisurely walks; one path ends a few hundred metres east of the bridge to **Nyord island**, a landscape of grazing pastures, agricultural fields and salt meadows whose main draw is the tiny village (also called **NYORD**) in its the southwestern corner. In 1769, Christian VII sold Nyord to the island's twenty tenant farmers in exchange for their adept piloting services, and for the next two hundred years or so they lived completely self-sufficient lives here, more or less in isolation from the rest of Denmark. As a result, Nyord retains a uniquely rural charm, and it's well worth spending an hour or so walking among the sickle-shaped cottages and farmhouses down to the rustic harbour. A few streets up from here, you can have a meal at the island's central meeting point, *Lolles Gård* (℡55 81 86 81), Hyldevej 1, which serves a few simple Danish dishes from around 115kr. You can also camp on Nyord at *Ulvshale Camping* (℡55 81 53 25, Ⓦwww.ulvscamp.dk; April–Oct), just on the Nyord side of the bridge and right on a wide, duned beach – a superb spot for **swimming**.

Møns Klint

Backed by the dense Store Klinteskov woodlands, the **Møns Klint** chalk cliffs stretch for about eight kilometres along Møn's eastern coast, and offer some extremely scenic walking. The forest along the top is home to some twenty species of orchid as well as peregrine falcons, while the sparkling white cliffs provide a gorgeous contrast to the turquoise waters below and the sea breeze keeps things cool. The paths that thread through the trees have plenty of look-out points that afford some dazzling coastal views; there are also steps leading down to the stony beach below. Due to open in 2007 right at the entrance to the cliffs walk, the **GeoCenter Møns Klint** (ⓦ www.moensklint.dk) nature centre will give the lowdown on the cliffs and the forest, and guided nature walks are planned, too. Opening hours and details of the walks were unavailable at the time of writing; check the website or contact the tourist office in Stege for up-to-date information.

Bus #52 runs between Stege and the nature centre four to five times a day depending on the season. If you want to stay and soak up the atmosphere, you could try the excellent, spacious *Møns Klint* **youth hostel** (ⓣ55 81 20 30, ⓦ www.danhostel.dk/moen; May to Oct; dorms 150kr June–Aug only, doubles ❷), fifteen minutes' walk from the cliffs at Langebjergvej 1. The management are very friendly and the dorm rooms have no more than four beds each; many of them overlook the placid Hunosø lake (no swimming), where there are picnic tables right by the water. A few hundred metres south of the hostel at Klintvej 544, *Camping Møns Klint* (ⓣ55 81 20 25, ⓦ www.campingmoensklint.dk; April–Oct) is the best campsite on the island, in an enclosed, hedged area just by the roadside. The *Bakkegården* B&B (ⓣ55 81 93 01, ⓦ www.bakkegaarden64. dk; ❹), at Busenevej 64 at the southernmost edge of the Store Klintskov forest, has twelve simple rooms and picture-perfect views over the fields to the sea, while just north of Møns Klint is the *Liselund Slot* (ⓣ55 81 20 81, ⓦ www. liselundslot.dk; ❽), Langebjergvej 6, a late eighteenth-century estate hotel with a dozen stylish rooms, many of which overlook a lush lawn. In terms of **eating** options, head 6km southwest of the cliffs to **KLINTHOLM HAVN** (bus #52 from Stege); though this unkempt harbour village, with its rusting dry dock and fish packery, offers zero charm, you will find good Italian meals at *Porto Fino* (ⓣ55 85 51 81), Thyravej 4A – the crispy meat lasagne is especially tasty (78kr). There's also pricier Danish food next door at *Hyttefadet* (March to mid-Oct daily noon–10pm; ⓣ55 81 92 36), where the speciality is the scrumptious fried flounder (89kr).

Keldby, Elmelund and Fanefjord

Møn's many well-preserved medieval churches are notable mostly for their vibrant **frescoes**, painted by an anonymous fifteenth-century artist known simply as *Elmelundmesteren* ("Elmelund master"). They depict the objects of everyday medieval life in sometimes humorous scenes, and were painted in a naïve, unprepossessing style for the benefit of rural peasants, whom it was thought would have little appreciation for more ornate, representational work. The paintings are characterized by human figures with triangular faces and sleepy eyes amidst magical environments of stars, flowers and miniature trees. Just east of Stege, the church at **Keldby** (daily: April–Sept 7am–4pm; Oct–March 8am–4pm) has several notable frescoes, include one showing Joseph making porridge for the baby Jesus, though the best of the paintings are a few kilometres further on at **Elmelunde** (same hours); here, inside Møn's oldest church, the frescoes include some handsome scenes of Adam tilling his field with a horse-drawn plough – many of the motifs were taken from pictorial bibles of the late Middle Ages. Southwest of Stege, the large church at **Fanef-jord** sports fresco-covered arches in its western vault depicting the sacrifice of Isaac and the Archangel Michael counting souls and, more intriguingly, a scene of several local women being warned against the devilish nature of town gossip; on the south side are images of a rich and poor man together in prayer, similarly intended to remind locals to keep their minds towards religious matters. The church (same hours as Elmelunde) is reachable via bus #62 (get off at Store Damme, then walk). Elmelunde and Keldby are connected to Stege via bus #52. If you want to stay here, the only option is *Pension Elmehøj*, Kirkebakken 39 (℡55 81 35 35, ⓦwww.elmehoj.dk; ❹), a friendly **B&B** in an ivy-covered manor house just opposite the church.

Falster

In 1914, Franz Kafka visited the eastern coast of Falster, describing the area as having "a really awful beach with some terribly peculiar Danes". To be fair to Kafka's aesthetic sensibilities, **FALSTER** isn't the most interesting place to visit in southern Zealand, but there are still some pleasant woods on the western side and some excellent, clean (if very crowded) beaches on the lengthy Baltic (eastern) coast. The island's main town, **NYKØBING** – usually written Nykøbing F (for Falster) – has a quaint medieval centre, a few places to stay and eat, and a couple of attractions of moderate interest: the **Medieval Centre** (May–Sept daily 10am–4pm; 80kr; ⓦwww.middelaldercentret.dk), an experimental open-air museum set in a recreated village, which aims to provide an insight into the hardship of medieval life; and the **Folkepark Zoo** (daily: May–Sept 9am–6pm; Oct–April 10am–4pm; 40kr), which offers the chance to come face to face with a llama as well as some native Danish creatures.

From Nykøbing's central **train** and **bus** station, bus #800 runs (via ferry) to Langeland, and continues on to Svendborg and eventually Odense in Funen (see p.202). The town's **tourist office** (Mon–Thurs 10am–5pm, Fri 10am–6pm, Sat 10am–1pm; ℡54 85 13 03, ⓦwww.tinf.dk), set right near the Torvet at Østergågade 7, can help with private accommodation around the island (around 200kr per person per night, plus a steep 60kr booking fee); there's no real reason to stay in Nykøbing – the beach resorts to the south make better bases – but the island's one **youth hostel** (℡54 85 66 99, ⓦwww.danhostel.dk/nykoebingfalster; closed mid-Dec to mid-Jan) is about 2km from the Nykøbing train station at Østre Allé 110, and offers dorms (120kr) and doubles (❻), and an adjoining **campsite** (℡54 85 45 45, ⓦwww.fc-camp.dk). In terms of food, *Czarens Hus*, Langgade 2 (℡54 85 28 29), is an old-fashioned place with gilded wallpaper and low doors that serves pricey Danish mains, most of which are some variation on steak (from 135kr).

South to the beaches

One of the few towns in Denmark that manages to justify its reputation as a fully-fledged seaside resort, **MARIELYST** is home to the best beaches in the country – some 28 kilometres of them – which, as you'd expect, are hugely popular during the summer, when the island's population more than doubles and the local nightlife gets pretty lively. Although the sands are packed to the gills in season (Easter to August), finding a secluded spot is fairly easy, especially if you have a bike, since a path runs parallel to the shore for the entire stretch.

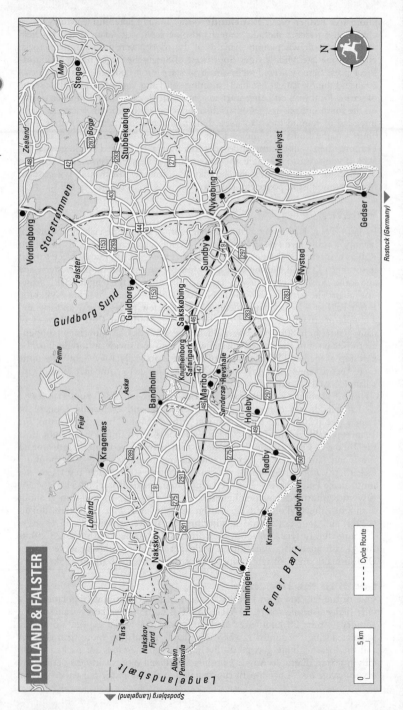

LOLLAND & FALSTER

Southern Zealand and the islands

N

Rostock (Germany) ▶

Spodsbjerg (Langeland) ▶

--- Cycle Route

0   5 km

Stege
Møn
Zealand
48
287
Bøgø
Stubbekøbing
293
271
Marielyst
Vordingborg
Storstrømmen
42
43
44
Nykøbing F
Falster
153
293
9
297
Sundby
Nysted
Guldborg Sund
153
Guldborg
Saksøbing
46
283
283
Femø
Knuthenborg
Safaripark
47
Bandholm
Maribo
48
Søndersø
Revshale
Askø
Holeby
297
Fejø
Kragenæs
289
49
Lolland
9
275
Rødby
50
291
275
Rødbyhavn
Nakskov
291
Kramnitse
9
Hummingen
Tårs
Femer Bælt
Nakskov
Fjord
Albuen
Peninsula
Langelandsbælt

Bathing spots are sandy and clean for most of the shoreline, with sandbars extending several metres out in many places; the best ones are a few minutes' walk east of the town centre, or south towards the forested nature reserve of Bøtø. At the very southern end of the strip, 4.5km south of the town centre, the Fribadestrand stretch is a designated nude area.

The helpful **tourist office** (mid-June to Aug Mon–Sat 9am–4pm, Sun 10am–2pm; Sept to mid-June Mon–Fri 9am–4pm, Sat 10am–2pm; ℡54 13 62 98, Ⓦwww.marielyst.dk), Marielyst Strandpark 3, is just off Skovby Ringvej as you enter Marielyst from Nykøbing; staff hand out detailed beach maps, provide a list of private rooms and hire out bicycles (40kr per day). While most **accommodation** is comprised of holiday cottages with a minimum rental period of one week, there a few good options for shorter stays. The best hotel is the ⚑ *Nørrevang* (℡54 13 62 62, Ⓦwww.norrevang.dk; ❼), Marielyst Strandvej 32, whose eighty A-frame bungalows, studios and double rooms are the most comfortable places to stay in town. They also have a popular, decently priced restaurant in a modernized thatch-roofed, half-timbered building. A cheaper alternative is one of several B&Bs in town; best of all are the two bright and spacious rooms rented out by Lizzi Jensen (℡54 13 61 27; ❸, breakfast 50kr per person), a few blocks north of the town centre at Tranevej 9, which look onto a garden terrace. Of the five **campsites** in the area, the most central is *Marielyst Camping* (℡54 13 53 07, Ⓦwww.marielyst-camping.dk; early April to mid-Sept), Marielyst Strandvej 36, offering pitches and simple wooden cabins (❷) 400m metres from the beach.

You'll have no trouble finding somewhere to **eat** or **drink**. The most popular option is *Larsens Plads* (Mon–Fri noon–10pm, Sat & Sun 11am–10pm; ℡54 13 21 70), Marielyst Strandvej 57, a massive establishment with seating for seven hundred that focuses around its large buffet of grilled steak, ham and salads. Though the meat sits for a while under the heat-lamps and isn't always full of flavour, the 119kr all-you-can-eat lunch or dinner buffet is still a very good deal, as is the 199kr all-you-can-eat-and-drink dinner special (6–9pm). It's a great place to come after the beach, as you can catch the sunset from the tables out front. Just south, *Tannhäuser* (11am–10pm), Bøtøvej 1, has simple pizzas and burgers from 35kr. **Bars** and **clubs** are plentiful, with several places within a few hundred feet of each other along Marielyst Strandvej. The bar at *Larsens Plads* (daily 10pm–4am) is where the fun starts for younger Danes, especially if the karaoke machine is switched on. Across the street, *Klein* (daily 8pm–late), is the best-run bar and disco in town, with two rooms of music.

Lolland

Larger and less crowded than Falster, **LOLLAND** is otherwise much the same: wooded, with good beaches and lots of quiet, explorable corners. Unlike Falster, it does have a few social problems, however: holding the dubious honour of the country's highest unemployment rate (seven percent), due largely to the recent closure of the Nakskov shipyards, it's latterly been tagged as the "social disaster of Denmark". It's a lovely place to visit, however, and feels the least overrun of the southern islands. A private railway (InterRail, ScanRail and Eurail passes not valid) runs to Lolland from Nykøbing on Falster, taking in lakeside **Maribo** and seaside **Nakskov**, where ferries leave for Langeland.

Maribo and around

Delectably positioned on the Søndersø lake, the sleepy town of **MARIBO** provides Lolland's most scenic setting for a short stay. The town centres around the Torvet, mostly modern and characterless save for a few Norwegian maple trees and the white stone town hall which houses the island's largest **tourist office** (Mon–Fri 10am–5pm, Sat 10am–1pm; ☎54 78 04 96, ⓦwww.turistlolland.dk), a good place to pick up brochures detailing cycling tours around Lolland. **Trains** and **buses** arrive at the Jernbanepladsen square, several blocks north, where you'll also find two of Lolland's finest museums: the **Storstrøms Kunstmuseum** (Art Museum; Tues–Sun noon–4pm; 30kr joint ticket with Stiftsmuseum; ⓦwww.storstroems-kunstmuseum.dk), with paintings, sketches and sculptures representing artistic trends from Denmark's Golden Age through to the present day, with plenty of works from Funen and Skagen artists like Kristian Zahrtmann and Johan Rohde. Upstairs in the same building, the **Lolland-Falsters Stiftsmuseum** (same hours and ticket; ⓦwww.aabne-samlinger.dk/maribo) displays local archeological finds and costumes, and has several rooms covering the experience of Polish immigrants who settled here in the late eighteenth century to work in the cane fields and the sugar processing plants. Otherwise, there's little to do but have a wander; you could focus your exploration on the spectacularly located **Maribo Domkirke**, back in the centre of Maribo, just east of the Torvet and reachable via the picturesque Kirkestræde or Smedestræde; originally a Bridgettine abbey founded in 1418, it's on a lovely site overlooking the lake. Several excavated foundation walls to the north and south of the church mark the site of two large cloisters; the stones from the original structure were used for the foundations of the town's oldest homes. From here, a sand-sprinkled path runs the circumference of Søndersø Lake and offers some lovely walking or cycling; a dock halfway around offers good **bathing** opportunities.

The best place to **stay** in Maribo is the lakefront *Hotel Maribo Søpark* (☎54 78 10 11, ⓦwww.maribo-soepark.dk; ❼),Vestergade 29, with spacious rooms (some with balconies) that look out onto the lake as well as an outdoor swimming pool and a very good restaurant. The town's lakeside **youth hostel** (☎54 78 33 14, ⓦwww.danhostel.dk/maribo), with dorms (110kr) and doubles (❷) is at Sdr Boulevard 82B. *Maribo Sø Camping*, Bangshavevej 25 (☎54 78 00 71, ⓦwww.maribo-camping.dk; early April to late Oct), boats one of the best locations in Zealand, on a grassy knoll on the west bank of the lake a few minutes' walk from the town centre. In terms of **food**, you need head no further than *Bangs Have* (☎54 78 19 11, ⓦwww.bangshave.dk;Tues–Sun 11am–3pm & 5–10pm), Bangshavevej 23; in addition to a variety of fish dishes, they serve a massive Sunday brunch plate (135kr) that includes chorizo, pesto chicken and artichoke hearts.

Nakskov and the western beaches

The harbour town of **NAKSKOV** is dominated by the towering Danisco sugar refinery that is seen (and heard) from many parts of the centre. Most of Denmark's sugar beet is grown on Lolland – something you'll quickly notice when looking over the fields – and the refining process takes place in Nakskov between September and January, when the noisy facility operates 24 hours a day, 7 days a week. In the town centre, a block south of the tourist office, the **Maritime Museum** (Feb–March Sat 10am–1pm; April–Oct Mon–Wed 1–4pm, Sat 10am–1pm; 20kr; ⓦwww.skibsmuseum-nakskov.dk), Havnegade 2, has some thoughtfully curated displays on local shipbuilding and a 1953 Russian submarine which played a minor role in the Cuban missile crisis. All parts of the sub – from command centre to torpedo room to the tiny living quarters – are open to visitors.

Beaches in the area vary from stony to super-silky sand. The closest to the centre is 3km west of town in Hestehoved, a small strip of sand with little in the way of facilities or amenities but a good, clean spot for bathing nonetheless; the beach at Langø, half an hour south of the centre by bus #18, is similar but generally less crowded. A more rewarding option involves hopping on the *m/s Vesta* (℡54 92 54 51; 75kr), which sails several times a day from Nakskov harbour to the secluded, sandy beachfront on the uninhabited **Albuen peninsula**, where you can have a dip and then return by boat, bus or foot (it's a 7km walk). East of Albuen, the beachfront extends 38km east along Lolland's southwestern coast all the way to Hyllekrog. A bike path runs along for the entire stretch, so finding a beach to your liking is quite simple; the best spot is at Hummingen.

The central **Nakskov Turistbureau**, Axeltorv 3 (Mon–Thurs 9am–5pm, Fri 9am–6pm, Sat 9am–12.30pm, opens at 10am in winter; ℡54 92 21 72) has dozens of brochures and maps covering activities in town and around, and also rents out 3-speed bicycles for 50kr per day. The pick of places to **stay** is the *Hotel Harmonien* (℡54 95 91 90, ⓦwww.hotel-harmonien.dk; ◑), Nybrogade 2, with luxuriously styled rooms done in lavender tones, with leather seats and incredibly comfortable beds. Rooms come cheaper at the gorgeous nineteenth-century *Store Riddersborg* farmhouse (℡54 94 81 39, ⓦwww.storeriddersborg.dk; ◍), located on the road to Langø a few hundred metres from the water at Bogøvej 8–10. The most picturesque **camping** is at *Albuen Strand Camping* (℡54 94 87 62, ⓦwww.albuen.dk), set at the base of the peninsula at Vesternæsvej 70, which has a large swimming pool and rents out bicycles and plain cabins (◐). *Lido Steakhouse* (Mon–Fri 11.30am–9pm, Sat 11am–1pm, 5.30–9pm; ℡54 92 23 13), Søndergade 8–10, is the most characterful **restaurant** in town: worn velour seating, early twentieth-century wallpaper and Danish music provides a great setting for the well-priced traditional dishes such as plaice béarnaise with shrimp sauce (72kr).

The *Bodega Guldhornet*, Nybrogade 2, has a pool table, a few tattered old benches and cheap beer.

Travel details

Trains

Frederikssund to: Copenhagen (every 10 min; 50min).

Helsingør to: Copenhagen (every 20min; 20min); Gilleleje (every 20min; 40min–1hr).

Hillerød to: Helsingør (every 30min; 15min); Hundested (every 30min; 50min).

Holbæk to: Nykøbing Sjælland (every 30min; 1hr).

Korsør to: Ringsted (every 30min; 25min); Roskilde (every 30min; 40min).

Nykøbing Falster to: Gedser (every 30min; 55min); Nakskov (every 30min; 45min); Rødbyhavn (every 30min; 1hr 10min).

Nykøbing Sjælland to: Holbæk (every 30min; 1hr).

Næstved to: Køge (1–2 hourly; 40min–1hr 10min); Vordingborg (every 20min; 15–20min).

Roskilde to: Copenhagen (every 30min; 20–30min); Korsør (every 30min; 40min); Køge (every 30min; 25–45min); Nykøbing Falster (every 30min; 1hr 40min).

Sorø to: Slagelse (every 15min; 10min).

Vordingborg to: Nykøbing Falster (every 30min; 25min); Næstved (every 20min; 15–20min).

Buses

Holbæk to: Nykøbing Sjælland (1–2 hourly; 1hr); Ringsted (Mon–Fri 10 daily, Sat & Sun 4–5 daily; 1hr); Sjællands Odde (2–3 daily; 1hr 50min).

Klintholm Havn to: Stege via Keldby and Elmelunde (hourly; 30min).

Køge to: Store Heddinge (7 daily; 40min).

Maribo to: Nakskov (7 daily; 55min); Rødby (5 daily; 45min); Vordingborg (14 daily; 1hr).

Nakskov to: Maribo (7 daily; 55min); Rødby (hourly; 50min).

Nykøbing Falster to: Gedser (10 daily; 1hr 10min); Marielyst (8 daily, summer only; 30min); Odense via Rudkøbing, Langeland (Mon–Fri hourly, Sat & Sun 6 daily; 3hr 30min); Stege (7 daily; 55min).

Nykøbing Sjælland to: Holbæk (1–2 hourly; 1hr); Rørvig (8–11 daily; 15min).

2

Næstved to: Køge (hourly; 40min); Ringsted (hourly; 40min); Slagelse (hourly; 50min); Vordingborg (hourly; 35min).

Ringsted to: Køge (Mon–Sat hourly, Sun 6 daily; 30min); Næstved (hourly; 40min).

Rørvig to: Nykøbing Sjælland (8–11 daily; 15min).

Slagelse to: Næstved (hourly; 50min); Roskilde (Mon–Fri hourly, Sat & Sun 7–8 daily; 50min).

Stege to: Klintholm Havn via Keldby and Elmelunde (hourly; 30min); Nykøbing Falster (7 daily; 55min).

Store Heddinge to: Køge (7 daily; 40min).

Vordingborg to: Næstved (hourly; 35min); Stege (hourly; 40min).

Ferries

Gedser to: Rostock, Germany (6–7 daily; 50min).

Helsingør to: Helsingborg, Sweden (frequent; 20min).

Hundested to: Rørvig (6–7 daily; 50min).

Køge to: Bornholm (6–7 daily; 50min).

Sjællands Odde to: Århus (Mon–Fri 6–9 daily, Sat & Sun 5–6 daily; 1hr); Ebeltoft (6–7 daily; 50min).

Tårs to: Spodsbjerg (6–7 daily; 50min).

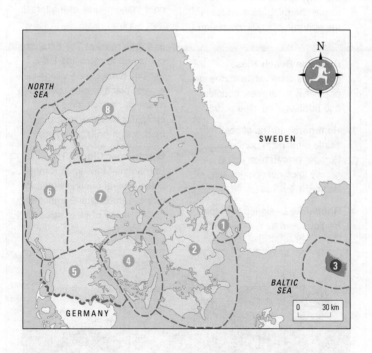

3

Bornholm

CHAPTER 3 # Highlights

✳ **Bornholms Kunstmuseum**
This superb museum boasts a stunning clifftop location and some breathtaking paintings by Denmark's foremost modern artists. See p.187

✳ **Christiansø** Once a tactical stronghold of the Danish navy, this tiny, sparse island with its single charming guesthouse is the epitome of idyllic seclusion. See p.192

✳ **Dueodde Beach** These gorgeous chalk-white dunes are popular with families, couples and nudists alike. See p.196

✳ **Hammershus** The largest castle remains in northern Europe, placed high up on a grassy knoll overlooking the Baltic. See p.185

✳ **Rundkirke** Designed to inspire religious awe as well as fend off marauding pirates, these fortified medieval churches are some of Bornholm's most distinctive buildings. See p.191

✳ **Almindingen woodlands** Take a walk through this gorgeous forest, criss-crossed with trails, then cool off with a pint at the *Christianshøj Kroen* restaurant, right in the middle of the forest. See p.195

✳ **Svaneke market** The Saturday crafts and farmers' market at this tiny harbourside village is a great place to pick up hand-made glass sculptures and sample *æbleskive*, delicious fried dough-balls. See p.191

✳ **Bornholmer Clocks** The Bornholms Museum in Rønne holds several pristine examples of these traditional Bornholm clocks, many of them still ticking away. See p.182

△ Hammershus castle

Bornholm

S urrounded by the Baltic Sea and closer to Sweden than it is to Denmark, some 200km away across the water, **Bornholm** is said to have been formed when God cobbled together the most beautiful parts of Scandinavia and flung them into the middle of the ocean, and this landscape of stark granite cliffs, flowing wheat fields, bucolic harbourside towns and long dune-lined beaches is known to Danes as *solskinsøen*, the "island of shining sun". With a near-Mediterranean climate that provides more hours of sunlight than anywhere else in Denmark, a string of gorgeous beaches and an unspoiled interior criss-crossed by several hundred kilometres of well-marked cycling and hiking trails, Bornholm has become a haven for lovers of the outdoors. These natural attributes, combined with a tasty regional cuisine, a handful of pristine medieval churches and attractions such as an excellent modern art museum ensure that the island is well worth a detour from the mainland.

All but one of Bornholm's major towns are situated along the coast, which is soft and sandy in the south, jagged and rocky to the north. At the southwestern tip, the capital town of **Rønne** is a busy transportation hub with limited charm but all the major facilities and amenities of a proper centre. From here, it's an easy bus ride up the coast to the northwest corner, where the ruins of **Hammershus** offer some captivating insights into a thousand years of military history. Continuing clockwise around the coast, the appealing seaside towns of **Sandvig**, **Allinge** and **Gudhjem** are home to several excellent hotels and restaurants, and are well placed for a visit to one of Scandinavia's best art museums as well as the tiny and remote island of **Christiansø**, some 20km distant and a haven for eider ducks and day-tripping tourists. Back on Bornholm itself, the unspoilt harbour town of **Svaneke** has a charming weekend market and a convivial microbrewery. Bornholm's interior offers some diverting attractions, from the fortified **rundkirke** churches to the fascinating natural history centre at **Åkirkeby**, as well as endless opportunities for walking, cycling and picnicking in the huge **Almindingen woodlands**. In the southeast, the beaches at **Dueodde**, **Snogebæk** and **Balka** represent some of Europe's finest swathes of white sand and are justifiably popular during the summer, while the nearby harbour town of **Nexø** is a good place to have a meal before hitting the beach.

Summer in Bornholm lasts longer than anywhere else in Denmark, and is by far the **best time to come** – if you can, try and time your visit for mid-May or late September, when the weather is still superb but the bulk of the crowds are gone. The Baltic waters are usually warm enough for a quick dip

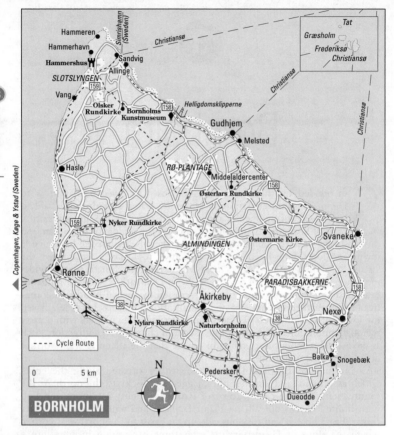

as late as October, but winter is very cold and well near untenable for most visitors, with many of the towns pretty much shutting down. Spring is chilly but gorgeous, with cherry blossoms blooming throughout the countryside and contrasting beautifully with patches of late snow on the hillsides.

Some history

Bornholm has been inhabited since as early as 5500 BC, though its strategic location in the Baltic has ensured a fairly turbulent history, characterized by repeated attacks by Viking pirates, Hanseatic despots and by neighbouring Scandinavian countries. In the sixteenth century, it was established as a **fiefdom** under the Danish crown, with small outposts of royal control set up across the island. Following the Swedish–Polish war, in which the Polish-aligned Danes lost dearly to Sweden, the 1658 **Treaty of Roskilde** awarded sovereignty to the Swedish king – but Bornholmers, by then fiercely Danish at heart, soon rebelled against their occupiers, killing the Swedish commandant, disarming his soldiers and swiftly winning back their Danish nationality. The island remained fairly peaceful until **World War II**, when its strategic position saw it occupied by German forces and used as a lookout post and a base from which to prevent

Allied warships and submarines from entering Nazi-occupied waters. During an extended Soviet occupation at the end of the war, hundreds of buildings in Rønne and Nexø were destroyed, requiring extensive postwar periods of reconstruction, which was swiftly followed by the arrival of **tourism**, today central to the island's economy. These days, Bornholm receives more than 600,000 visitors annually – well over ten times its native population – but manages to absorb its tourists quite well, and rarely feels overcrowded, even in high season.

Arrival, getting around and accommodation

Nearly all visitors to Bornholm arrive by **ferry**; these dock at the main harbour town of Rønne, just steps from the main bus station and a five-minute walk from the town centre. The **airport** is 5km east of Rønne, and connected to it by bus #7. From Rønne's bus station, Bornholm Amts Transport (BAT; ☏56 95 21 21, ⓦwww.bat.dk), operate nine **bus** routes around the island, which depart roughly

---

Getting to and from Bornholm

Bornholm's main – but still tiny – port at **Rønne** is busy throughout the year, with daily **ferry** services to Copenhagen and Køge, as well as cities in Sweden, Germany and Poland. Most of the Denmark-bound ferry routes time well with **bus** and **train** connections to destinations further on. If you want to take your car to Bornholm, the best option is to drive to Køge and take the ferry from there.

From Copenhagen

The best and quickest way to travel overland from the Danish mainland to Bornholm is by the **DSB train-ferry** combo journeys that run to Rønne via Ystad, Sweden. Trains depart Copenhagen's Central Station several times daily, the first departing at 6.39am and the last at 9.39pm. The schedule occasionally changes, so you'd do well to check with either the Bornholm or Copenhagen tourist offices (see p.183 & 64) or DSB (☏70 13 14 15; ⓦwww.dsb.dk/bornholm) for up-to-date details. Tickets start at 240kr, the journey takes about three hours including the ferry and, during the week, seat reservations are obligatory. **Buses** run by **Gråhundbus** (☏44 68 44 00, ⓦwww.graahundbus. dk; 2.5hr; 220kr) represent a slightly less comfortable option, with daily services to Rønne from Central Station which also make use of the ferry. Another alternative is a flight with **Cimber Air** (☏70 10 13 18, ⓦwww.cimber.dk), which runs regular daily flights (40min) from Copenhagen to Rønne; buy tickets at least two weeks in advance to take advantage of discounted *eventyr* fares of as little as 326kr return – normal one-way tickets generally start at 700kr.

From Køge

Bornholms Trafikken (☏56 95 18 66; ⓦwww.bornholmstrafikken.dk) operates regular ferries to Rønne from Køge, 30km south of Copenhagen and easily accessible by S-Tog (see p.154). The trip takes six hours and one-way tickets cost 240kr, but buying at least a week in advance gets you a return for 360kr (238kr from mid-Aug to late June). In peak season, there are two ferries daily, one early in the morning and one around midnight; off-season, there is only one late-evening boat. Though it's less direct and can be a bit pricier than some of the other options, taking the overnight ferry will save you on a night's hotel. Bringing along a bike will cost an extra 20kr or so, while prices for a car and up to five passengers start at 1280kr. Booking online gets you a 75kr discount.

hourly and pass through Rønne's centre en route to destinations across the island, the longest of which – Rønne to Svaneke – takes just under an hour. Fares are priced per zone, with the furthest possible travel distance being five zones; tickets cost 10kr per zone, and are valid for unlimited rides within one zone for thirty minutes; fifteen minutes are added on to the ticket's validity for each additional zone. You can save money by purchasing a *RaBATkørt* multi-ride ticket, which gives a 10–30 percent discount on fares and can be used by more than one person. There are also one-day (65kr) and week (440kr) passes; all tickets are available on board the bus. If you're here for only a short time, or just want to get a sense of the island, hop on bus #7, which makes a four-hour counter-clockwise circumnavigation of Bornholm, stopping at all the major settlements. This daily route departs Rønne harbour every two hours from 8.05am and costs 50kr. **Bicycles** are the most popular and efficient way to get around the island, which is criss-crossed by some 235km of bikeable roads and paths (see below); we've detailed rental outlets throughout the chapter. Finally, the short **sightseeing flights** operated by Klippefly, located at the airport (☎56 95 35 73, ⓦwww.klippefly.dk), are a novel way to see the island, and start at 175kr per person.

Accommodation is plentiful but pricey (and often booked up throughout the season), but a handful of youth hostels and good camping facilities can help to cut costs, and you can also camp out at Bornholm's half-dozen *lejrpladser* open camping areas for 15kr a night. Note that many of Bornholm's smaller hotels and pensions open from May to September only and do not include breakfast in their rates; we've highlighted exceptions to this in our reviews.

Cycling around Bornholm

Bornholm's extensive network of **cycle routes** was established in the early 1980s, and today the island boasts over 235 kilometres of coastal roads, bark-covered paths and gravelled forest roads that wend their way through the island's fields, moors, woods and sandy coastline. All routes are clearly marked with green and white signs that indicate directions and distances, and with bikes given right of way in nearly all situations, they're all very safe for riders. Seven-speed cycles can be hired in most towns for around 70kr per day, 300kr per week, and bikes can be taken on local buses for a 25kr fee. We've listed the major rental outlets below, most of which are open year-round Monday to Friday from 9am to either 5pm or 5.30pm, and Saturday from 9am to noon – the outlet in Rønne has extended hours.

For more on biking on the island, visit ⓦwww.cykel.bornholm.info, a superb source of information on all aspects of cycling, including detailed pages on what to pack, how to ride and where to put the kids, in addition to plenty of interactive 3-D maps of dozens of suggested cycling routes.

Bike rental outlets

Åkirkeby Åkirkeby Cykler, Storegade 21 ☎56 97 00 47, ⓦwww.aakirkeby-cykler.dk.
Allinge Nordbornholms Cykelforretning, Pilegade 1 ☎56 48 02 91.
Balka Boss Cykler, Kænnikegårdsvej 1 ☎56 49 44 74, ⓦwww.bosscykler.dk.
Dueodde *Bornholms Familiecamping*, Krogegårdsvej 1 ☎56 48 81 50, ⓦwww .bornholms-familiecamping.dk.
Gudhjem Sct Jørgens Gård, Ejnar Mikkelsensvej 14 ☎56 48 50 35. May–Sept only.
Rønne Bornholms Cykeludlejning, Nordre Kystvej 5 ☎56 95 13 59, ⓦwww .bornholms-cykeludlejning.dk. Daily 8am–4pm & 8.30pm–9pm.
Svaneke Boss Cykler, Søndergade 14 ☎56 49 75 74, ⓦwww.bosscykler.dk. May–Sept only.

Rønne and around

Though it does hold the lion's share of the island's accommodation and restaurants **RØNNE** is not what draws visitors to Bornholm, and few locals consider it to be truly *bornholmsk*. But with its quiet cobbled streets and pretty old houses, the town does merit a little more time than just a quick glance through the bus window as you arrive or depart the island. Founded in 1327, Rønne functioned mostly as a small port town until the seventeenth century, when the island's administrative centre was moved here from Åkirkeby on account of the growing importance of the harbour. Today, it's Bornholm's largest settlement and the centre of most of the island's commercial activity.

As Rønne is small and compact, finding your way around is relatively uncomplicated. From the harbour, Snellemark cuts through the town centre, passing along the southern end of **Store Torv**, originally a training ground for the Danish military and today the town's market square; main market days are Wednesday and Saturday, and the stalls sell a good range of picnic fare – fresh breads, cheeses, fruit etc. Between here and the smaller Lille Torv, a block east, lie most of the town's shops, restaurants and conveniences. Rønne is characterized by its colourful and well preserved half-timbered, brick-tiled buildings, which comprise Denmark's largest collection of eighteenth- and nineteenth-century **wood-framed houses**. The most picturesque of these quaint, bright two-storey structures line the crooked, cobbled streets that branch off Store Torv

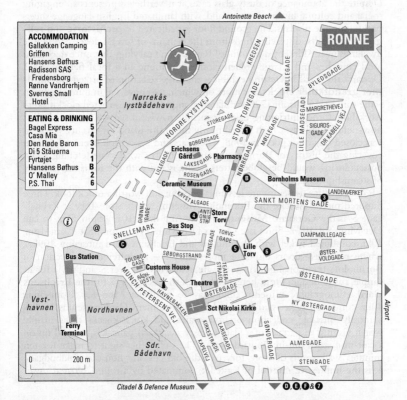

The Bornholmer clock

Grandfather clocks have been associated with Bornholm since 1744, when a Dutch ship containing five specimens from England ran aground off the Rønne coast and the salvaged pieces were repaired and restored by local craftsmen. They learned enough about the construction of the longcase enclosures, cast-iron weights and internal mechanisms to begin making their own – by the turn of the century, Bornholm had developed its own rich tradition of handcrafted clockmaking. Each component of a **Bornholmer clock** – from the pendulum to the glass face and the pastel-painted or gilded wooden body – was meticulously crafted by hand, and the finished pieces were exported to the rest of Europe and beyond. Today, original Bornholmer clocks are proudly displayed in local homes, and if in good condition, older models can fetch upwards of 60,000kr.

to the west. In the bombardment of 1945, ten percent of all Rønne's buildings were levelled, but the so-called *bombehuse* ("bomb houses"), red- and yellow-brick replacement homes built around the ones which survived, manage to blend in quite well with the original buildings. Once you've had your fill of the architecture, head to the **Bornholms Museum** (July & Aug daily 10am–5pm; Sept to late Oct Mon–Sat 10am–5pm; late Oct to Dec Mon–Sat 1–6pm; 40kr, combined ticket with Ceramic and Erichsens Gård museums 109kr; Ⓦ www.bornholmsmuseum.dk), set in a former hospital at Sankt Mortensgade 29. Despite the abundance of dusty glass cases, it nevertheless presents an engaging social and cultural history of the island, with laminated English-language sheets backing up the displays. The ground floor is dedicated to **prehistoric** and **religious artefacts**, displaying finds from the remains of several dozen Stone Age dwellings near Åkirkeby, a handful of Runic stone carvings that once decorated local churches and a large golden clothes pin found in a local field in 2002. Upstairs, the most interesting exhibit is the large selection of prized **Bornholmer grandfather clocks** (for more on which, see above), all in mint condition – the earliest dates from 1770 and stands alongside a reconstructed clockmaker's workshop. Other intriguing exhibits include a wistful section on Bornholm's now-defunct railway, which served nearly the entire island for seventy years – it was closed down for good in 1968, when cars and buses took over; and a room covering the history of Bornholm's tourist industry, with some fetching 1930s posters luring would-be globetrotters to the island with the romantic imagery of steamship travel.

Rønne's other museums are less engaging, but still worth a quick look. Three hundred metres west of the Bornholm Museum, across Store Torv at Krystalgade 5, is the **Ceramic Museum** (July & Aug daily 10am–5pm; Sept to late Oct Mon–Sat 10am–5pm; late Oct to Dec Mon–Fri 1–5pm, Sat 10am–1pm; 40kr, combined ticket with Bornholms and Erichsens Gård museums 109kr), where two busy floors display a representative – if cluttered – collection of Bornholm's traditional brown stoneware, renowned all over Scandinavia for its simple, rustic design. From here, head north to Laksegade 7 for the **Erichsens Gård** ethnographic museum (mid-May to mid-Oct Mon–Sat 10am–5pm; 40kr, combined ticket with Bornholms and Erichsens Gård museums 109kr), a mostly missable collection of housewares and knick-knacks that's mainly worth visiting to partake of a plate of tasty *stønnkager* pancakes, cooked up on a cast-iron stove out in the garden area. The only other sight to make for, ten minutes' walk south of Store Torv past the old customs house at Toldbodgade 1, is the impressive **citadel** of Kastellet, dominated by a round, bloated tower that vaguely recalls Bornholm's *rundkirke*. Construction on the fortress began in 1687 at the behest of Frederik V, but the project was abandoned mid-build, leaving only the turrets and storehouses completed. Today, it houses the **Forsvarsmuseet** (Defence Museum; May–Oct Tues–Sat 11am–5pm; 35kr), whose motley assortment of military gear and armaments includes an interesting exhibit on Bornholm's role in World War II.

Though **swimming** is best on the eastern side of the island, Bornholm's southern coast holds plenty of good, sandy tracts, the nearest of which is at Galokken, 2km south of town. From here, the coast stretches another 30km east, offering hundreds of secluded spots for bathing, easily accessed from the main road. Bus #7 follows this route, but it's much more convenient to take a bike.

Nylars Rundkirke

Some ten kilometres southeast of Rønne, the **Nylars Rundkirke** (early May to late Oct Mon–Sat 9am–5pm, plus Sun 9am–5pm late June to early Aug) is the best-preserved of Bornholm's four medieval *rundkirke* (for more on which, see box, p.191). Built in 1165 to honour St Nicholas (from which Nylars is derived), it has changed little since the sixteenth century, when it underwent a major restoration, and sports the typical tri-level *rundkirke* construction that allowed it to be used for both defensive and religious purposes. Look out for the two runic stones at the south entrance and, inside, several elegant frescoes depicting the Garden of Eden on the nave's column, which date back to 1250. The church is reachable via bus #6 from Rønne – tell the driver to show you where to get off, then walk several hundred metres north along Kirkevej. If you're on a bike, you can get to the church from Rønne via the Rønne–Åkirkeby path in half an hour or so.

Practicalities

Rønne's spacious and helpful **tourist office**, the Bornholms Velkomstcenter, is just opposite the ferry terminal at Nordre Kystvej 3 (April to mid-June & early Aug to Oct Mon–Fri 9am–4pm, Sat 9am–noon; mid-June to early Aug daily 9am–5pm; Nov–March Mon–Fri 9am–4pm; ℡56 95 95 00, ⊛www .bornholm.info), which sells a great selection of booklets and maps of hiking and cycling routes around Bornholm (for details of bike rental outlets, see the box on p.180. **Internet** access is available across Nordre Kystvej inside the Snellemark Sentret (Mon–Fri 9.30am–9pm, Sat 9am–6pm, Sun 11am–6pm). It's hardly necessary to rent a car, but a **scooter** might be good if biking isn't an option for you: Avis, Snellemark 19 (℡56 95 22 08), hires them at 250kr per day.

There are plenty of places to **stay** in and around the centre, but many are booked up from May to September, thanks in part to the hordes of Danish youth groups that descend en-masse during the summer vacation. Consequently, planning ahead is highly recommended, but if phoning round doesn't turn any leads, ask for help at the tourist office, which has details of a few inexpensive rooms in private houses; alternatively, Bornholms Booking Centre, Kirkegade 4 in Allinge (June–Aug 10am–5pm, Sat 10am–3pm; April–May & Sept–Dec Mon–Fri 11am–4pm; ℡56 48 00 01, ⊛www .bornholmsbookingcenter.dk) can help locate vacancies all over the island for an 85kr fee. Rønne has a number of very good places to **eat**, from picturesque waterside restaurant dining to takeaways. Most can be found along Store Torvegade towards the north of town. Bornholm's limited **nightlife** scene is also centred in Rønne, the picks being the Irish pub *O'Malley*, Store Torvegade 2, the trendier *Palæ Caféen*, Store Torvegade 20, and *Den Røde Baron*, Sankt Mortens Gåde 48, a disco popular amongst the younger set.

Accommodation

Galløkken Camping Strandvejen 4 ☎ 56 95 23 20, ⓦ www.gallokken.dk. About 1km from Rønne, this great campsite is at the edge of a patch of lushly forested coastal land and is just a few minutes' walk from the beach. Facilities are great and there's a handful of new four-person wooden cabins (495kr, 375kr outside of July and early Aug). Open May to Aug.

Griffen Ndr Kystvej 34 ☎ 56 90 44 45, ⓦ www .hotelgriffen.dk. Only a half kilometre from downtown Rønne, this spacious seaside hotel offers 140 rooms, many with a balcony or terrace and all with the expected mod cons, including use of the sauna and pool. Open May–Sept. ❼

Hansens Bøfhus Nørregade 2 ☎ 56 95 00 69, ⓦ www.hansens-beufhus.dk. The cheapest hotel rooms in town – bare-bones but clean, and located in an annexe behind the *Hansens Bøfhus* restaurant just across the main square. ❷

Radisson SAS Fredensborg Strandvejen 116 ☎ 56 95 44 44, ⓦ www.radissonsas.com. Located a few kilometres south of the town centre, this mid-level chain hotel is a bit off the beaten path, but it's very comfortable and offers Ikea-esque furniture and balconies overlooking the Baltic. The attached restaurant, while rather expensive, is superb. Bus #7. ❽

Rønne Vandrerhjem ☎ 56 95 13 40, ⓦ www .danhostel-roenne.dk. This well-run hostel is located 1km southeast of town on Arsenalvej 12 and offers both dorms (115kr) and private rooms (ⓢ). Open April–Oct.

Sverres Small Hotel Snellemark 2 ☎ 56 95 03 03, ⓦ www.sverres-hotel.dk. Just around the corner from the tourist office, the pricey rooms (some with shared bathrooms) at this pension that fancies itself a hotel are light and airy, with little in the way of furniture or amenities, but breakfast is included. ❹–❻

Cafés and restaurants

Bagel Express Lille Torv 10. Simple, airy café selling fresh bagels spread with any number of toppings, from cream cheese to hummous. Mon–Sat 10am–6pm.

Casa Mia Antoniestræde 3 ☎ 56 95 95 73. Very good pizzas and inexpensive pasta dishes served in a homely Mediterranean-style setting and presided over by a friendly Italian-born Bornholmer. Tues–Sun 5–10pm.

Di 5 Stâuerna Strandvejen 113 ☎ 56 90 44 44. Though this sophisticated restaurant is a bit out of the centre, its fine continental food is some of the best on the island. Beautifully presented dishes like mushroom steak with chilli sauce or gorgonzola filet of veal with garlic start at around 200kr, and there's also plenty of fish options. Daily 11am–9pm.

Fyrtøjet Store Torvegade 22 ⓦ www.fyrtoejet.dk. Large, bright and done out in classy wood accents, this rustic-style restaurant serves tasty lunch dishes from 42kr – try the beef hash or the open shrimp sandwich. The dinner buffet (6–9pm; 149kr) includes steamed fresh vegetables, cuts of roast beef and various rice and pasta dishes. April to mid-Sept daily noon–9pm.

Hansens Bøfhus Nørregade 2 ☎ 56 95 00 69, ⓦ www.hansens-beufhus.dk. Traditional place serving excellent lunch plates of *æggekage, Sol over Gudhjem* and pan-fried plaice. It's more popular at dinnertime, when they haul out their menu of fourteen different steak and beef dishes that includes their yummy speciality, a porterhouse steak with horseradish sauce and redcurrants. Mon–Sat noon–9pm, Sun 5–9pm.

P.S. Thai Lille Torv 13 ☎ 56 96 25 01. Located just opposite the post office, this small Thai place has a selection of curries, pad Thai and assorted meat and veggie dishes from 38kr. You can take-away, or eat at the stools out front. Daily 5–8pm.

The north: Hammershus to Svaneke

Bornholm's north coast is astoundingly rocky, the jagged, exposed bedrock and snaggled cliffs barbed with grottoes and ravines at water level, and with a series of cliffs that reach nearly a hundred metres high in some places. A century ago, all this igneous rock made the island the hub of Denmark's once-raging granite industry, a fact made dramatically clear in the barren, bored-out landscape of inland quarries and a handful of deep, artificial lakes. At the northeastern tip of the island, the evocative remains of the **Hammershus** castle, the largest fortress complex in northern Europe, are well worth a visit, while the nearby **Hammerknuden** cliffs and **Slotslyngen** forest provide for hours of invigorating walking. Working east along the coast, past the thriving neighbouring towns of **Allinge** and **Sandvig**, **Gudhjem** is a perfect base for explorations around the island, with a good choice of places to stay and eat. The town also receives a breathtaking light off the sea, which has made it a haven for Bornholm's great landscape artists, many of whose works are on display at the nearby **Bornholm Art Museum**. East of here, the land softens somewhat, with a few paths along the pebbled and rough-sand beaches, while at the far eastern tip, **Svaneke** is perhaps the most picturesque and alluring town on Bornholm, best known for its delightful weekend market and thriving craft galleries.

The northwest tip: Hammershus and around

Sitting pretty atop a beautiful coastal hillock nearly one hundred metres above the sea, the craggy ruins of the once-majestic **Hammershus castle** (unrestricted access; free) are Bornholm's biggest tourist attraction. Built around 1260 by Jakob Erlandsen, archbishop of Lund, the stronghold has served as a citadel, barracks, prison and a convent, and was the home of the island's various rulers until 1658, when a number of Bornholmers armed themselves and overtook it, thereby returning rule of the island back to Denmark. The castle was abandoned in 1743 and partially dismantled, after which islanders hauled away its stone to build homes across Bornholm. There was a partial restoration in 1900, though you'd never know it, as much of the original structure is largely in rubble, but the craggy outlines of the tower, armoury, chapel and stables still give a sense of Hammershus in its heyday.

You enter the castle grounds from the bus and car park to the northeast, where a **visitor centre** (May to late Oct daily 10am–6pm) doles out information on the history and layout of Hammershus and runs English-language guided tours on demand; considering the paltry documentation around the ruins, it's well worth going along on one of these if you can. From here, a path leads across a dual-arched Gothic brick bridge – the only intact medieval bridge still standing in Denmark – over what was once the outer moat, and continues up past a weapons and goods store to the **fæstningsporten**, the main gatetower. From here, you pass a storehouse which contains the buttery cellar – minions were often paid in provisions like butter and corn – and, past a stables and granary, arrive at the heart of the castle, dominated by the massive square **manteltårnet** tower, which served as the entrance to the inner hold, the commandant's studio and, at the very top, one of Denmark's most notorious prison cells. It was here that Christian IV's illegitimate daughter Leonora Christina and her husband Corfitz Ulfeldt were imprisoned after being convicted of treason; at one point they managed to escape by climbing down the outside walls via knotted bedsheets, but were recaptured soon after. While the tower itself stands largely intact, much of the rest of the brickwork in and around here has crumbled away; you can see out to the surrounding headland, encircled by the ruins of a 1km-long perimeter wall that once protected the entire fortress grounds.

Exiting the fortress grounds to the south takes you along any of three 2km paths that wind through the **Slotslyngen forest** down to the fishing village of Vang, where there's a good restaurant (see p.187) and a stop for bus #1 south to Rønne or north to Allinge. The hike closest to the coast offers the best views out to the sea. On the opposite (northern) side of the fortress, an equally narrow path heads north for 1.5km to the enclosed harbour of **Hammerhavn**, from where you can hop on a motorboat for a 40-minute trip along the coast (☎56 48 04 55, ⓦwww.hammerhavnensbaadfart.dk; 50kr), which gives a good perspective on how intimidating Bornholm must have looked to would-be attackers, whose cliffs must have seemed a formidable obstacle to soldiers weighed down by their chain-mail armour and heavy weaponry. The boats only seat a dozen passengers, and so are small enough to enter some of the narrow gorges creviced into the cliffs.

Allinge and Sandvig

The largest settlements along Bornholm's northwestern coast, Allinge and Sandvig were established as fishing villages in the medieval era, and later served as centres for Bornholm's thriving quarrying industry. There's little to do or see in either town, but both offer a pleasant stopoff on the way to or from Hammershus. **ALLINGE** is the larger of the two, its harbour (the departure point for boats to Christiansø; see p.192) dominated by a slew of restaurants and cafés; smack in the town centre, look out for the sizeable runic stone out in the churchyard of the sixteenth-century Gothic church. Just outside town, the tall, brick-red *tårnhuset* tower is topped by a small glass observation room that affords great views of the town and sea. From here, a small path follows the old railway line west for several hundred metres to the rocky mound of **Madsebakke**, where a sloping ridge overlooking the sea holds Denmark's largest extant display of *helleristinger* (rock engravings), medium-sized boulders covered with simple carved figures of ships, animals, footprints and crosses which date back to the early Bronze Age. From here, continue another kilometre or so north along the path to reach the small cove of **SANDVIG**, slightly more charming to look at than Allinge and with a fine sandy shallow beach that's good for a dip. From Sandvig, it's a fifteen-minute walk northwest along Bredgade out to the escarpment of **Hammerknuden**, a grassed-over mass of rounded rock topped with heathy vegetation that complements the stark views out to the sea. Several paths lead to the edge of the cliffs here, dominated by the now-disused Hammer Fyr lighthouse; one of the tracks leads down to the craggy coast.

Buses #1 and 7 run to Hammershus, while both Allinge and Sandvig are served by routes #1, 2, 7 and 9. **Tourist information** can be found at Nordbornholms Turistbureau, Kirkegade 4 in Allinge (Mon–Fri 10am–5pm, plus June–Aug Sat 10am–5pm; ☎56 48 00 01, ⓦwww.bbc.dk), which also books hotel rooms for an 85kr fee. The good selection of **accommodation** options hereabouts are a good bet to use as a base for exploring the north-west. In Allinge, *Danchels Huse* (☎56 48 22 18, ⓦwww.danchelshus.dk; ⓪), set in pretty gardens at Havnegade 38, offers inexpensive rooms with modern furnishings; rates include breakfast, and home-cooked dinners are available in the summer. In Sandvig, there's the aptly-named *Hotel Romantik*, Strand-vejen 68 (☎56 48 03 44, ⓦwww.hotel-romantik.dk; ⓪), right on the water and with sea-view rooms that include breakfast. About 1.5km southwest of Sandvig, just across from the Hammer Sø lake and a few hundred metres from Hammershus, the *Sjøljan* **youth hostel**, Hammershusvej 94 (☎56 48 03 62, ⓦwww.danhostel.dk/sandvig; May–Aug), has dorms (150kr) as well as a few private rooms (❷), and decent shared facilities. Nearby lies one of the island's best campsites, *Lyngholt Familie Camping* (☎56 48 05 74, ⓦwww.lyngholt.dk/camping), set in the Slotslyngen forest a few minutes' walk south of Hammershus at Borrelyndvej 43, a luxurious site in which you can smoke your own fish, bake yourself in a sauna, cool down in a pool and then retire to any number of cabins of varying sizes and comfort (from ❹).

In terms of **eating**, Sandvig is home to one of the island's best restaurants, *Gastronomen*, at Hammershusvej 9 (June–Sept daily 6–10pm; ☎56 48 07 87, ⓦwww.gastronomen.dk). Based on available ingredients and suggestions of diners, the tasty, experimental menu changes daily; reservations recommended. In Allinge, *Toldkammeret*, Havnegade 19 (June–Sept daily 11.30am–10pm; ☎56 48 48 49, ⓦwww.restaurant-toldkammeret.dk), set in a harbourside former customs house, offers excellent Danish lunches and dinners (from 185kr) like crisp Baltic cod with creamy potatoes, mushrooms and bacon. Just south of Hammershus, the harbourside settlement of Vang holds ✴ *Le Port*, Vang 81 (daily 11am–10pm; ☎56 96 92 01, ⓦwww.leport.dk), a upmarket place that's a great option for a romantic dinner, with delicious French cuisine, appropriately blasé service and sunset views towards the water from tables on the terrace; the garlic-fried prawns are especially tasty. Count on 800kr for dinner for two with wine, or arrive before 4pm to order off the 90kr lunch menu. Bus #1A stops just below the restaurant at Vang's harbour.

Bornholms Kunstmuseum and Helligdomsklipperne

Nine kilometres east along the coast from Allinge, the outstanding **Bornholms Kunstmuseum** (Bornholm Art Museum; April–May & Sept–Oct Tues–Sun 10am–5pm; June–Aug daily 10am–5pm; Nov–March Tues & Thurs 1–5pm, Sun 10am–5pm; 50kr; ⓦwww.bornholms-kunstmuseum.dk), Søndre Strandvej 95, is one of the most impressive art museums in Denmark. Opened in the 1990s and extensively renovated in 2003, the streamlined stone and glass structure is appealingly placed just inland from the Helligdomsklipperne cliffs (see p.188), and maintains some interesting architectural features, including a small observation tower and a stream trickling through the main gallery, fed by water from nearby springs. The **galleries** hold a grouping of early- to mid-twentieth-century paintings by artists from both Bornholm and mainland Denmark, with particular focus given to the **Bornholm School** (see box, below), of which Karl Isakson, Kræsten Iversen, Olaf Rude, Edvard Weie and Oluf Høst are the most famous and best represented. The colours and forms in works like Rude's *Still Life* and Kristian Zahrtmann's *Leonora Christina Receives her Oldest Daughter Anna Cathrina at Maribo Cloister* paint a clear picture of the strong current of modernism which defined Danish painting in the early twentieth century. Look out also for three of Høst's best-known works, stark

The Bornholm School

With its remote location, unique landscape and resplendent light that lasts well into the evening, Bornholm has been attracting artists for hundreds of years. Around the beginning of the twentieth century, a definitive style of visual arts began to emerge from the artists who congregated here, one which helped forge the way for classic modernism to take over European painting. Known collectively as the **Bornholm School**, painters such as Karl Isakson and Edvard Weie drew inspiration from the island's ever-changing landscape and made inventive use of pure, muted colour to produce work that explored new aesthetic directions. Other Danish artists such as Niels Lergaard, Kraesten Iversen and Oluf Høst soon followed, settling in towns like **Gudhjem** and **Svaneke** and later decamping to **Christiansø** in search of further seclusion and inspiration. Even today, Bornholm has the highest per-capita concentration of artists and artisans in Europe, a group whose work extends to glass blowing, goldsmithing, sculpture and textile and jewellery design.

and ghostly sketch-like portraits of life at his Bognemark farmhouse, just east of the museum grounds. More modern trends in local painting, sculpture and graphic arts are also represented, and the museum houses the largest collection of Danish handicrafts outside of Copenhagen, though these are still much less interesting than the paintings. Just behind the museum, there's a good spot from which to take a look at the 22-metre-high **Helligdomsklipperne** ("Sanctuary Cliffs") that characterize Bornholm's northern coast, and which sheltered ships during stormy weather for centuries (hence the name). Steps lead down from the clifftop to the water, from where you can gaze up at the imposing granite faces etched with dozens of jagged grottoes and caves, several of which are large enough to enter.

To get to the museum, you can take bus #7 from Rønne, Allinge and Gudhjem via the coastal Helligdomsvej; be careful along this busy stretch of road if you're walking or cycling. Ambitious hikers might opt for the rough 6km path from Gudhjem, a knobbly, rutted route that nevertheless offers some scenic views, following the cliffs along the Salene bay to end up right at the museum; allow at least ninety minutes. Another option is the regular boats which ferry passengers between Gudhjem harbour and the base of the Helligdomsklipperne, from where steps lead up to the museum.

Gudhjem

For hundreds of years, Danish artists have been attracted to the gorgeous light that falls on the diminutive fishing village of **GUDHJEM** ("God's Home"). With its steep streets lined by brightly coloured, red-roofed houses scenically spread between two harbours, Gudhjem is one of Bornholm's more picturesque villages, and its central position along the north coast makes it a great base for seeing the rest of the island. The town is centred around the assortment of boutiques, cafés, restaurants and galleries that line the lively Brøddegade, a street so steep that cycling on it is banned. Once you've had a wander along here, head west to the **Oluf Høst Museum**, Løkkegade 35 (Mon–Sat 10am–5pm, Sun 2–5pm; 45kr; @www.ohmus.dk), which pays homage to the island's best-known artist, famous for his colourful explorations of local life, from sunsets to summer bathers and wintry sea views. Høst lived and painted here until his death in 1966, and the studio has been converted to display a collection of his lesser-known works (the more famous ones can be seen at the Bornholms Kunstmuseum; see p.187). From the museum, Nørresand takes you around to the small harbour, where the waterside smokehouse is a great place to try the local speciality, a **Sol Over Gudhjem** sandwich (see p.190). From the dock here (the departure point for summer ferries to Christiansø; see p.192), the *M/S Chimera* (mid-June to mid-Aug Tues–Thurs 6pm; ✆56 48 51 76; 3hr; 160kr, equipment rental 50kr) heads out on **fishing trips** in the waters around Gudhjem, a great opportunity to see the Helligdomsklipperne cliffs and coastal rock formations hereabouts as well as to catch your dinner.

Practicalities

Gudhjem's good range of places to **stay** makes it pretty popular with visitors, so it's always worth reserving rooms in advance. If you're stuck for a bed, the small **tourist office** (Mon–Fri 11am–4pm; ✆56 48 52 10), Åbogade 9, can locate rooms in private homes. Another option is to take a week-long rental of a section of *Gadegård*, Gudhjemvej 52 (✆56 48 52 85, @www.pfunch.dk; 3500kr per week), a picturesque farmhouse to the south of town owned by a gregari-

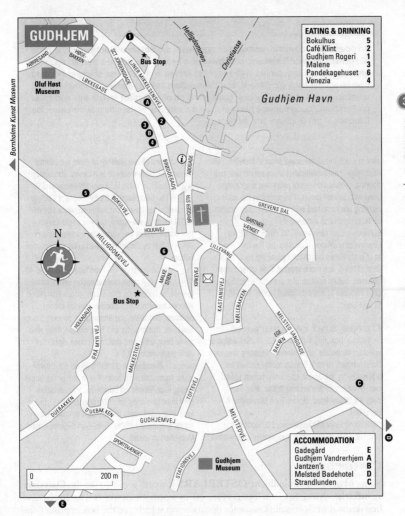

GUDHJEM

EATING & DRINKING	
Bokulhus	5
Café Klint	2
Gudhjem Rogeri	1
Malene	3
Pandekagehuset	6
Venezia	4

Gudhjem Havn

Bornholms Kunst Museum

Oluf Høst Museum

Bus Stop

N

Bus Stop

Gudhjem Museum

ACCOMMODATION	
Gadegård	E
Gudhjem Vandrerhjem	A
Jantzen's	B
Melsted Badehotel	D
Strandlunden	C

0   200 m

ous and charming couple; the rental part sleeps up to four. Gudhjem also has several excellent **restaurants** and **cafés**, from top-notch options to more casual spots overlooking the harbour. For dessert, try *Karamel Kompagniet* (Ⓦwww .karamelkompagniet.dk), Holkavej 2, which sells delicious homemade toffee.

Accommodation

Gudhjem Vandrerhjem Ejnar Mikkelsensvej 14 ☎56 48 50 35, Ⓦwww.danhostel-gudhjem.dk. This year-round youth hostel, with dorms (150kr) and doubles (③) has a prize location right at the harbour and enviable views onto the sea from most of the rooms. They also have laundry facilities and hire out bicycles (70kr per day) and fishing gear..

Jantzen's Hotel Brøddegade 33 ☎56 48 50 17, Ⓦwww.jantzenshotel.dk. The classiest hotel hereabouts, with sixteen smallish but charming rooms in a creaky fin-de-siècle building; some have sea views and cast-iron balconies. The breakfasts are divine, and are included in the rates. ⑥
Melsted Badehotel Melstedvej 27, Melsted ☎56 48 51 00, Ⓦwww.melsted-badehotel.dk. Just

Sol over Gudhjem

An open smoked herring sandwich on rye bread, the **Sol Over Gudhjem** is the pride of kitchens all over Bornholm, consisting of a herring fillet topped with an egg yolk and onion ring, and served with radishes, chives and salt. The smoking helps to counteract the herring's oiliness, and the resultant taste is somewhat reminiscent of a delicious steak tartare. *Sol over Gudhjem* is on offer at most restaurants and cafés on Bornholm, but is perhaps best eaten on a sunny day whilst sitting at the shoreside benches of the Gudhjem smokehouse.

east of Gudhjem in the small town of Melsted, this Gustavian-meets-minimalist place sports pale oak flooring, terraces off every room and a sprawling lawn with lounge chairs. The rooms in the main building are furnished with extremely comfortable beds. Breakfast is included. ⑦
Strandlunden Melstedvej 33 ⑦ 56 48 52 45, Ⓦ www.strandlundencamping.dk. The facilities at this sheltered beachfront camping spot, 1km east of town, are more spartan than other camp-grounds, but its spectacular waterside location offers access to a sandy small beach. Mid-May to mid-Sept.

Cafés and restaurants

Bokulhus Bokulvej 4 ⑦ 56 48 52 97. Set within a spectacular estate, and offering elegantly prepared Danish meals (with a French touch) served on a terrace; try the house speciality, bacon baked cod. Most mains are around 200kr. May–Oct daily 11.30am–9pm, closed Tues May–June & Sept–Oct.
Café Klint Ejnar Mikkelsensvej 20. Right at the harbour, offering tasty and inexpensive sandwiches

and burgers, plus a number of more substantial continental dishes served in a casual atmosphere.
Gudhjem Røgeri Ejnar Mikkelsensvej 9. The best place to try the *Sol over Gudhjem* sandwich, the town's smokehouse has a sizeable buffet lunch (noon–4pm), but you could save a few dozen kroner by buying the same shrimp or smoked fish by the kilo and eating on the benches outside.
Pandekagehuset Brøddegade 15 ⑦ 56 48 55 17. A great budget option with a small terrace, serving tasty thin crêpes (from 20kr) filled with an assortment of goodies like ice cream, peaches, chocolate and almonds, or savoury fillings like ham, mushrooms and blue cheese. They also serve beer, wine and delicious coffee. April–Oct daily 8am–midnight.
Venezia Brøddegade 33 ⑦ 56 48 53 53. Down-stairs from *Jantzen's* hotel, this is one of the better dining experiences on Bornholm, with an Italian chef here preparing fresh Mediterranean-style food. Pizza and pasta dishes start at 80kr, larger mains are around 150kr. Tues–Sun 5–9pm, closed Mon–Wed in winter.

Østerlars

Some 6km south of Gudhjem, **ØSTERLARS** is worth a visit to see the **Østerlars rundkirke** (Mon–Sat 9am–5pm; 10kr) on its northern outskirts. The largest and best-known of Bornholm's *rundkirke* (for more on which, see the box opposite), the building features the distinctive conical roof as well as slanting external buttresses tacked on in the Middle Ages to support the walls. Inside, the elegant restored pulpit and altarpiece both date from the seventeenth century, while twelve lovely fourteenth-century frescoes, fully restored in 2006, are worth a peep. The church is located immediately east of Gudhjemvej, halfway between Østerlars town and the **Bornholms Middelaldercenter** (Medieval Centre; May–late Oct Mon–Fri 10am–4pm; 95kr, 65kr after mid-Aug; Ⓦ www.bornholmsmiddelaldercenter.dk), a reconstructed fourteenth-century Scandinavian village where various re-enactments of period life are staged in the summer. Buses #3 and #9 stop just outside.

Svaneke

With a picturesque market square lined with cafés, tiny boutiques and craft galleries and spectacular scenery of steep cliffs, **SVANEKE** places high in the list of Born-

Bornholm's rundkirke

Considered to be the country's best examples of medieval Scandinavian architecture. Bornholm's whitewashed **rundkirke** ("round churches") are iconic structures. Built in the Middle Ages, when Bornholm was plagued by attacks from marauding Gothic, Wendish and Slavic pirates from across the Baltic, these stocky three-level constructions were as much storehouses and fortresses as they were places of worship. Grain and weapons would be amassed inside, while the roofs (which were originally flat) were used as platforms from which to launch mortar attacks against assailants. Today, the island's *rundkirke* are still used for mass on Sundays, as well as serving as concert venues throughout the year; check what's on at the tourist offices.

holm's most charming towns. Since the island's now-defunct railway never reached this far east, the town remained relatively isolated from modern development, and today's residents look with some scorn towards over-developed eyesores like Nexø, championing Svaneke's rich past with strict laws prohibiting any building taller than three storeys. Until a few years ago, the town was a favourite haunt of Danish retirees, but recent years have seen a massive influx of **craftsmen** – mostly potters and glass-blowers – whose workshops now dominate the town.

Start by exploring the large Torvet which, on Saturday mornings, hosts one of the most atmospheric (and eccentric) **markets** in Scandinavia, with crowds of locals and visitors perusing the stalls selling knitwear, jewellery, knick-knacks, and *æbleskive* – scrumptious fried balls of dough dabbed with jam and powdered sugar – while enjoying accordion players and mime acts. From here, head east along Brænderiegænget to visit some of Svaneke's craft workshops, many of which are opened up to visitors so that you can watch the craftsmen as they work. At the **Pernille Bülow glassworks** (June–Aug Mon–Fri 9am–9pm, Sat & Sun 9am–6pm, Sept–May Mon–Fri 9am–6.30pm, Sat 9am–5pm, Sun 9am–4pm; Ⓦwww.pernillebulow.dk), no.8, you can try your hand at making your own glass vase or purchase a professionally-blown one fashioned by Pernille herself. For ceramics, try the studios a block north of here at Nansensgade 4 and 8.

Practicalities

Svaneke's **tourist office**, which also covers Nexø and the beach towns of Dueodde and Snogebæk, is 100m northwest of the Torvet at Storegade 24 (Mon–Fri 10am–5pm, plus Sat 9am–2pm May–Aug; ☎56 49 70 79, Ⓦwww.nexoe-dueodde.dk) It's quite close to the harbour, from where daily boats sail to Christiansø during the summer (see p.193). Though there isn't much in the way of **accommodation** in Svaneke, one sure bet is ⚓ *Siemsens Gård*, Havnebryggen 9 (☎56 49 61 49, Ⓦwww.siemsens.dk; April–Oct; ❼), a former merchant's home across the harbour that's now a well-run hotel offering antique-furnished rooms, some with a terrace looking onto the leafy yard out back, others with views across a large courtyard straight out to sea. Just next door at Havnebryggen 5, the *Hotel Østersøen* (☎56 49 60 20, Ⓦwww.ostersoen.dk; 700kr), is a converted old farmstead with two dozen spacious flats done up in rustic, olde-worlde style with large kitchens and one to three bedrooms. Between June and August these can only be rented by the week (from 4000kr), but during the rest of the year there are some excellent bargains to be had on single-night stays, with the cheapest flats going for 675kr. Other options include a **youth hostel**, half a kilometre south of town at Reberbanevej 9 (☎56 49 62 42, Ⓦwww.danhostel-svaneke.dk; 150kr;

April–Oct), and a **campsite**, *Svaneke Familiecamping*, Møllebakken 8 (☎56 49 64 62, ⓦwww.svaneke-camping.dk; mid-May to mid-Sept), set on a quiet bit of land 500m north of town, with a few small wooden cabins (from 250kr).

In terms of **eating** and **drinking**, the cosy bar and restaurant inside the 🍴 *Bryghuset* brewery, Torvet 5 (ⓦwww.bryghuset-svaneke.dk), is a worthy choice, both to try the draught beers – best are the hoppy, golden ale and fresh-tasting, unfiltered pilsner – or for a **meal**, with solid mains like local oven-baked salmon and marinated spare-ribs (119kr). Across the square at Brænderigænget 3, *Pakhuset* (daily noon–9.30pm; ⓦwww.restaurantpakhuset .dk) has an upscale menu with juicy steaks (from 125kr) served with a dozen or so sauces, from garlic to blue cheese, as well as cheaper (69kr) burgers. For lighter fare, the popular restaurant at the *Siemsens Gård* hotel serves a dozen or so novel takes on *smørrebrød*.

Christiansø and Frederiksø

Rugged, grassed-over specks in the middle of the Baltic, some 18km northeast of Bornholm, Christiansø, Frederiksø and Græsholm are the largest islands of the remote Ertholmene ("Green Pea") archipelago, and make a lovely day-trip from Bornholm spent walking the abandoned battlements and having a meal at the lone – and lovely – inn. Characterized by its enclosing fortress wall and fortified stone tower, **CHRISTIANSØ** is the largest of the islands at just 710 metres across, and has a population of around a hundred as well as supporting a seabird breeding colony, while the even smaller **FREDERIKSØ**, accessed via a steel footbridge from Christiansø, holds little more than its museum of local history.

With a view to keeping a close watch on the militarily superior Swedes, Christian V established a **naval base** on Christiansø in 1684, erecting two blocky stone towers surrounded by bastions and enclosing walls abutting the rough sea. The island served as a resting point for Denmark's navy during its eighteenth-century military incursions in and around the Baltic, but in 1855, when relations with Sweden had improved, the base was decommissioned, and many of the soldiers who had come to call the island home chose to stay

△ Christiansø harbour

on as fishermen. Today, the island and its buildings are still owned and run by Denmark's **Ministry of Defence**, which funds (at great expense) a school, church, doctor, library and full-time sheriff-cum-mayor. Residents pay no local taxes, a fringe benefit which no doubt encourages many of them to stay on, though now that cheap imports have made it virtually untenable to make a living as an independent trawler fisherman, many have turned to tourism as their main source of income.

The Danish government, ever proud of its military past, has kept the island's grounds and fortress buildings in rather good nick, and the manicured paths which lead around the island can make for a very pleasant afternoon stroll. At the top of the steps that lead up from Christiansø's boat dock is the island's combined inn, restaurant and provisions shop (see p.194), though the best way to start exploring is to head straight over the bridge to Frederiksø, where the **Lille Tårn** stone tower holds a ragtag **museum** (May–Sept Mon–Sat 11.30am–4pm; 10kr) ranged around the islands' naval past – including a scale model of the fortifications as they looked in 1855 – as well as some information on the bird species that inhabit the area (mostly auks, guillemot and eider ducks). Once you've had your fill, cross back over to Christiansø, where you can climb up the craggy stairs of the larger **Store Tårn** (Mon–Sat 11.30am–4pm, Sun 11am–2pm; 10kr) and take in a lovely panorama of the archipelago from the lighthouse at the top. The only other thing to do here is take a leisurely stroll along the island's fortifying perimeter wall, taking time to admire the mighty black **cannon** that man the southwestern edge of the parapet and the well-tended gardens and pretty half-timbered or stone cottages in which the islanders live. On the eastern side of the island, there's a small inlet and a **bathing jetty** from where you can wade into the cool Baltic. If you want to take back a bit of Christiansø, look out for the locally-made *slåensnaps*, a tasty, tart *snaps* made from sloe berries that grow here – you can pick up a bottle at the small grocery adjacent to the inn.

Practicalities

Between May and September, regular Christiansøfarten **boats** (☎56 48 51 76, ⓦ www.christiansoefarten.dk) ply the choppy waters between Christiansø and Bornholm, leaving from Gudhjem, Allinge and Svaneke; journey time varies from sixty to ninety minutes (see the box below). Out of season, a postal boat makes the trip once per day. Round-trip tickets cost 170kr between May and September, and are slightly cheaper off-season.

Christiansøfarten ferries

Note that the timings below apply between May and September only.

	To Christiansø	From Christiansø
Gudhjem (daily)	10am 12.30pm	2pm 4.30pm
Allinge (Mon–Fri only)	– 12.30pm	11am 4.15pm
Svaneke (Mon–Fri only)	10am	2.30pm

Since Christiansø is so small, you only need a few hours (at most) to fully explore it, but if you're in the mood for some real seclusion, the island makes for a peaceful place to **stay**. The wonderful ⚓ *Christiansø Gæstgiveri* (☎56 46 20 15, ⊛www.christiansoekro.dk; ❼; closed Jan) has six rustic-style rooms, each with private bath, and its outstanding **restaurant** serves scrumptious seafood dinners and lunches, and is very popular with day-trippers. The owners also run a small **campsite** (☎56 48 51 76) on the eastern side of the island. During the summer, you'll need to book well in advance for both options.

Åkirkeby and the interior

Bornholm's **interior** is characterized by undulating heathery hills and agricultural fields, and is cut through by roads that give access to a handful of diverting small-scale sights. The main inland settlement is **Åkirkeby**, a relatively unattractive, modern place which nevertheless holds an absorbing natural history museum covering Bornholm's unique geological history. To the north, the dense **Almindingen forest** is perfect for a day spent hiking among the trees, with castle ruins and canyons to explore.

Åkirkeby

The oldest merchant settlement on the island, **ÅKIRKEBY** was founded in 1346 as a trading centre for local farmers, and served as the island's administrative and religious centre until the honour was passed to Rønne in 1660. Today, it offers little of interest besides **Natur-Bornholm** (daily April–Oct 10am–5pm, last entry 4pm; 85kr; ⊛www .naturbornholm.dk), a few minutes' walk from the town centre at Grønningen 30. It's well worth setting aside an afternoon to fully explore this museum, designed by Danish architect Henning Larsen and filled with fascinating environmental and geological exhibits that take you through billions of years of Bornholm's history – there's everything from dinosaur fossils to a sample of the oldest rock in the world, forged an unimaginable 3.85 billion years ago in Greenland. By no coincidence, the museum is located on the Klintebakken hills atop the faultline where the island's granite and gneiss northern half is fused with the soft and supple sandstone of the south; just out behind the building, you can visit the remarkable quarry where the two separate seismic plates meet.

Unless you're headed to the island's woodlands for some hiking, you'll have little use for the town's **tourist office**, Hans Romersvej 1 (Mon–Fri 10am–4pm; ☎56 97 45 20, ⊛www.bfb.dk), and with ample coastal inns and hotels splayed out from Åkirkeby in all directions, there is little real reason to stay here. If you do want a bed for the night, best option is *Ny Søborg Spise-og sovehus*, Lykkesvej 20 (☎56 97 50 50, ⊛www.ny-soeborg.dk; ❺), a family-run pension with thirty or so smallish rooms, lush garden views and ample breakfasts included; it's a ten minute walk north of the town's church. Otherwise, *Åkirkeby Camping* (☎56 97 55 51, ⊛www.aakirkebycamping.dk; mid-April to Sept), Haregade 23, has a few cabins (❺; ❷ out of season) with small kitchenettes. **Food-wise**, your best bet is *Gåsen*, Jernbanegade 1, which serves tasty Danish meals in a 200-year-old former school. It's open for lunch year-round, and dinner too during the summer.

Almindingen forest

The third largest woodlands in Denmark and occupying most of Bornholm's central highlands, **Almindingen forest**'s 2400 hectares are peppered with lakes, ponds and bogs that help support a rich array of plants and animals. The forest is dense in some parts, less so in others, and latticed by a dozen or so trails that are perfect for an afternoon of leisurely, sheltered walking. Several of Bornholm's arterial roads pass through Almindingen, so getting to and around it by bike, bus or car is easy, and there are numerous car parks at the various forest entrances. The eastern and western portions of forest offer the best **hiking**; you can pick up detailed free trail maps at the Åkirkeby tourist office (see opposite). At the eastern edge, easily accessible from Nexø (take bus #7 or #61 north to Oksemyrevej, then walk 1km west), a trio of paths in the **Paradisbakkerne** hills follow a long, lush valley replete with trickling streams and small lakes, and home to families of wild deer. For slightly more vigorous walking and some interesting sights, head to the Almindingen's hilly western quarter, where there are several signposted 4km-long trails. The northernmost one begins at the 14km marker on the Rønne–Svaneke road, where the small ⚔ *Cristianshøj Kroen* (Thurs–Sat noon–8pm, Sun noon–5pm, ☎56 97 40 13) **restaurant-café** serves good Danish food, from salads to more substantial main meals. From here, the trail continues past the ruins of the medieval Gammelborg and Lilleborg castles and a small woodland lake, then heads up to the **Rokkestenen**, a large boulder which can be rocked back and forth on its fulcrum. Another option here leads from the car park on the Vestermarie road through to **Ekkodalen** ("echo valley"), a fifty-metre rift well-known as the only place in Denmark where you can speak your name and hear it said back several times over. From here, the path runs northwest to the mound of Rytterknægten, Bornholm's highest point – not exactly a Guinness Book entry at 162 metres, but a superb vantage point all the same. Almindingen is also an excellent place to see some of the remains of Bornholm's prehistory – **burial sites**, **passage graves** and **barrows** that date back to the Bronze and Neolithic ages, though as these are spread out in different parts all across the forest, it's best to pick up the detailed map from the tourist office.

Dueodde and the southern beaches

Bornholm's southeastern tip, known as the "golden seaside" for its wide, clean stretches of sand, is the island's **beach** country, comprising several kilometres of sandy strand that run from Dueodde on the south coast to Nexø, halfway up the island's eastern shore. The beaches are busiest in July and August, but you should easily be able to find a quiet spot. Beachbum-types head straight for **Dueodde**, the most popular beach on the island, with high dunes, a lighthouse and a spot for nude sunbathers, while families usually descend on **Balka**, due to the child-friendly sandbars on its kilometre-long beach. In between the two is **Snogebæk**, a thin trip of near-private beachfront that has the area's best dining options. Further north is **Nexø**, a town proper rather than a beach resort and home to an interesting butterfly park. Note that most facilities in the beach towns are open from May to September only.

Dueodde

Some nine kilometers southeast of Åkirkeby on Bornholm's southeastern tip, the twelve kilometres of sandy coastline that fronts **DUEODDE** (pronounced "doo-oh-uh") comprises one of the best-known **beaches** in Denmark. The powdery sand here is some of the finest in Europe and was long used in the production of hourglasses, while the shoreline encompasses a variety of terrain, from towering sand dunes and extensive coastal sandbars to places where the dense forest reaches all the way to the water's edge. The kilometre-long strip of beach running just north of what passes for Dueodde town is sheltered by trees, while to the south, the broader Østersøstranden beach has shallow water and sandbars; note that the point from which the beach narrows has been designated Bornholm's only (semi-) official **nudist beach**, Jomfrugård. Looming over the coastline is the 47m-high Dueodde Fyr **lighthouse** (May–Oct dawn to dusk; 5kr), which you can climb to get some breathtaking views, especially beautiful when the sun is setting over the plains just west.

The beaches' popularity means that there's plenty of **accommodation** around Dueodde, though this is dominated by long-stay, apartment-style places. For shorter sojourns, best bet is *Dueodde Badehotel*, Sirenevej 2 (①56 48 86 49, ⓦwww.dueodde-badehotel.dk; May to late Oct), just minutes from the beach, with sparkling white apartment-style rooms with kitchenettes (⓻), and a few cheaper ones without (⓹). Breakfast is 65kr extra unless you book a week ahead, when it's included in the price. The rustic apartments at the *Hotel Bornholm* (①56 48 83 83; ⓦwww.hotelbornholm.dk; May–Sept; ⓼), just 300m from the beach, have full kitchens and terraces and offer access to a pool; you pick up keys to the apartments at the office in Nexø, at Pilegaardsvejen 1. Prices drop by several hundred kroner outside of July and there are further discounts if you stay for a few days. Elsewhere, beds in four-person rooms with shared bath at the *Dueodde Vandrerhjem og Camping*, Skrokkegårdsvejen 17 (①56 48 81 19, ⓦwww.dueodde.dk; April–Nov) are absurdly high in July and early August (360kr) but drop to a much more acceptable 160kr other months. **Camping** is best at *Møllers Dueodde Camping*, Duegårdsvej 2 (①56 48 81 49, ⓦwww.dueodde-camp.dk), whose prize location is set right in the pines just beside the beach and excellent facilities, including a large pool, bike rental, cafeteria, laundry and **two-person** cabins (⓶). For **food**, you're best-off heading over to Snogebæk (see below), though the restaurant at the *Dueodde Badehotel* serves decent grilled meat and fish and has a 59kr breakfast buffet. For something simpler, *Granpavillonen*, Fyrvej 5, has good and affordable pizza.

Snogebæk, Balka and Nexø

Just north of Dueodde, the small hamlet of **SNOGEBÆK** is mostly dominated by newer homes and summer cottages, but as there's little of interest save for a few restaurants (reviewed opposite), it's best to continue just north to **BALKA**. The extensive sandbar here means you have to walk out very far before the water gets deep, meaning that it's great for young children but it makes swimming a bit of a chore. There's **windsurfing** and **kayak rental** available right on the beach from Windsurfing Bornholm (ⓦwww.windsurfing-bornholm.dk; 100kr for one hour); if you're here with kids, you might also want to check out the island's **zoo**, Sdr Landevej 32 (June–Aug Tues–Sun 10am–4pm; 45kr; ⓦwww.balka-dyrepark.dk), a home-grown place that's pleasant enough, with kangaroos, prairie dogs, a large selection of birds and a Shetland pony available for rides.

Several kilometres north of Balka is the harbour town of **NEXØ**, a soulless centre of fishery processing plants that was heavily bombed during the Second World War and now offers zero interest aside from the **Bornholm Butterfly and Tropical Park**, Gammelrønnevej 14B (early May to late Oct daily 10am–5pm; 50kr; Ⓦsommerfugleparken.dk), where you can observe over a thousand radiantly-coloured butterflies living in a self-contained ecosystem within a steamy greenhouse. The town also has a **tourist office**, Sdr Hammer 2A (Mon–Fri 10am–5pm, plus May–Aug Sat 9am–2pm; Ⓣ56 49 70 79, Ⓦwww.nexoe-dueodde.dk), which doles out information and maps on all the beach towns.

Balka offers two expensive places to **stay**: the *Hotel Balka Søbad*, Vestre Strandvej 25 (Ⓣ56 49 22 25, Ⓦwww.hotel-balkasoebad.dk; ❸), a modern hotel complex located right on the sand offering well-sized rooms, a sauna, a large swimming pool and a private beach; and the *Hotel Balka Strand*, Boulevarden 9A (Ⓣ56 49 49 49, Ⓦwww.hotelbalkastrand.dk; ❼), a similar place with less exciting rooms set two hundred metres from the beach. For **food**, Snogebæk has the best options hereabouts: *Æblehaven*, Hovedgaden 15 (Ⓣ56 48 88 85, Ⓦwww.aeblehaven.com), serves traditional Scandinavian meals and good wines on a pebbled terrace, while the smokehouse at the harbour (May–Oct 10am–6pm, until 8pm June–Aug) is a great place to have a drink and try out the fresh catch of the day. For dessert, you could snack on the delicious and expensive chocs available at *Kjærstrup Chocolate by Hand*, Hovegaden 4 (daily: July to mid-Aug 11am–sunset; June & late Aug to Sept 11am–5pm; Ⓦwww.kjaerstrup.dk), which also sells organic ice cream.

Travel details

Trains

Rønne to: Copenhagen (3–5 daily; 2hr 50min inc. ferry).

Buses

The frequencies below relate to the peak summer season (late June to mid-Aug); outside of that time, services are reduced during the weekend.

Allinge/Sandvig to: Hammershus (every 30min; 15min), Rønne (every 30min; 45min–1hr), Vang (7 daily; 20min).

Dueodde to: Rønne (hourly; 45min).

Gudhjem to: Allinge/Sandvig (hourly; 20min); Rønne (12 daily; 35min).

Hammershus to: Allinge/Sandvig (every 30min; 15min); Rønne (every 30min; 55min).

Nexo to: Svaneke (hourly; 15min); Rønne (every 20 min, 50min-1hr 10min).

Rønne to: Allinge/Sandvig (every 30min; 45min–1hr); Åkirkeby (hourly; 30min); Dueodde (hourly, 45min); Hammershus (every 30min; 55min); Gudhjem (12

daily; 35min); Nexo (every 20min, 50min–1hr 10min); Svaneke (hourly; 55min); Vang (hourly; 35min).

Svaneke to: Dueodde (hourly; 45min); Rønne (hourly; 55min); Allinge/Sandvig (hourly; 25min).

Vang to: Allinge/Sandvig (7 daily; 20min); Rønne (hourly; 35min).

Ferries

Allinge to: Christiansø (1–2 daily; 1hr 10min).

Christiansø to: Allinge (1–2 daily; 1hr 10min); Gudhjem (1 daily; 55min), Svaneke (mid-May to mid-Sept 1 daily; 1hr 25min).

Gudhjem to: Christiansø (1 daily; 55min).

Rønne to: Køge (2 daily; 6hr); Ystad (3–6 daily; 1hr 15min–2hr 30min).

Svaneke to: Christiansø (mid-May to mid-Sept 1 daily; 1hr 25min).

Flights

Rønne to: Copenhagen (3–6 daily; 35min).

4

Funen

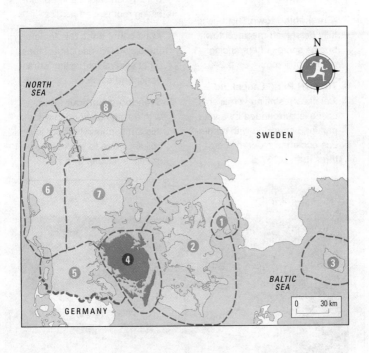

CHAPTER 4 # Highlights

✳ **Egeskov Slot** Built on a bed of thousands of oak timbers, this fifteenth-century fairytale castle is surrounded by dazzling gardens. See p.227

✳ **Ladby Boat** The burial vessel of a Viking chieftain, preserved *in situ* in a subterranean museum, is well worth seeing. See p.222

✳ **Ærøskøbing town** This beautifully preserved medieval town boasts scores of entrancing gabled buildings. See p.240

✳ **TICKON Park, Langeland** Tranekær's striking vermilion castle is surrounded by a vast parkland speckled with numerous eccentric modern sculptures. See p.237

✳ **Odense nightlife** This lively city of students and young professionals is one of Funen's most happening spots for getting out, socializing and partying. See p.214

✳ **Valdemars Slot** Soak up a bit of sumptuous noble ambience via a stroll around the gilded corridors, plush salons and opulent sitting rooms. See p.232

✳ **Åfart canal boat** This trip along the placid Odense canal stops off at several interesting attractions. See p.211

✳ **Svendborg Harbour** Filled with dozens of wooden ships, this atmospheric harbour is a brilliant place to soak up some maritime flavour. See p.223

△ Tall ship, Svendborg

4

Funen

C hristened "the garden of Denmark" by locally-born Hans Christian Andersen for the lawn-like neatness of its fields and the abundance of produce harvested from them, **Funen** (*Fyn*) is the smaller of the two main Danish islands, and one which is attracting more and more visitors; many are drawn by the mythology of Andersen himself, while others come to enjoy the island's bucolic feel and gorgeous coastline. Unlike Zealand and Jutland, attractions here are mainly low-profile, consisting of a myriad remote **castles** and **manor houses** – 124 to be precise – many of which maintain tree-lined avenues, landscaped gardens and fertile agricultural fields that are often as enjoyable to visit as the buildings themselves. Towns and villages are also small-scale, their thatched, half-timbered buildings fronted by hollyhocks and orchards. Funen has a well-developed **bus** network (though less in the way of **trains**) that facilitates access to most of the major sites, plus a few of the minor ones, though given their diminutive size, "mainland" Funen and its southern archipelago are best explored by **bicycle**, with well-marked paths that circumnavigate much of the coastline and pass through the major urban areas, all of which are detailed in cycling maps available from local tourist offices.

Arriving from Zealand across the massive Storebælt bridge, the isolated **Hindsholm Peninsula** has several good beaches, while nearby **Odense** is Denmark's third-largest city and an obvious base if you'd like to explore villages by day but want some urban zip by night. Indeed, Funen is small enough (and Odense central enough) that you could hole up here for a few days and easily venture out during the day to see the rest of the island. South of here, past the dazzling **Egeskov castle**, coastal Funen is dominated by two towns: maritime **Svendborg** is the top scenic draw, with its good beaches, great restaurants and handful of interesting museums, while further west is the more rustic **Fåborg**, with its pretty pastel-painted houses and superb art museum. The fragmented archipelago of pretty **islands** off Funen's south coast is summer vacation territory for many Danes. The largest, **Tåsinge** and **Langeland**, are both accessible via road bridge and offer plenty of opportunities for walking and swimming, as well as a couple of grand old buildings. The smaller **Ærø** holds a delectably preserved medieval town and a slew of atmospheric inns and hotels, while the tiny spits of land that make up the rest of the archipelago are beautifully unspoilt and preserve a uniquely remote charm that's best appreciated on foot or by bike.

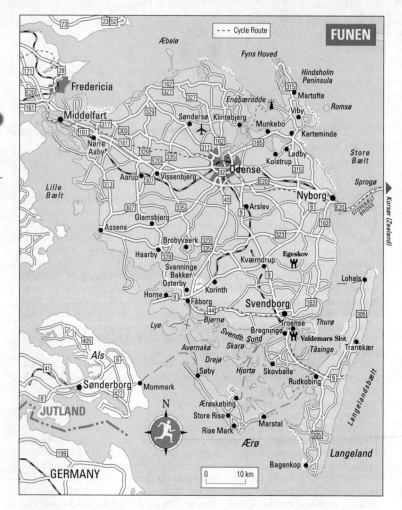

Odense and around

Funen's sole industrial centre, and one of the oldest settlements in the country, **ODENSE** – named after Odin, chief of the Norse gods, and pronounced
"OWN-suh" – gained prominence in the early nineteenth century when
the opening of the Odense canal linked the city to the sea and made it the
major transit point for produce of the island's farms. Nowadays, Denmark's
third-largest city feels much less industrial, a pleasant provincial university
centre with interesting museums and excellent shopping, its large manufacturing sector hugging the northern bank of the canal well out of sight
of the compact old centre. The **old town** itself houses some fine museums
and – thanks to the resident students – a surprisingly vigorous nightlife, and

is great for a spot of aimless wandering. Odense is also known, throughout Denmark at least, as the birthplace of Hans Christian Andersen, and although it's all done quite discreetly, this fact is celebrated with souvenir shops and hotels catering for travellers lured by the prospect of a romantic Andersen experience – something they (almost inevitably) won't find. Elsewhere in town, it's worth making the effort to take in one of several absorbing **art collections** and check out the morbid contents of the crypt that lies beneath the city's **Gothic cathedral**. Odense, like Funen itself, is occasionally known as the "green garden of Denmark", and has an accordingly large number of **public gardens** – most notably in the southern part, where the lush Munke Mose meadow follows the narrow Odense canal. To the **north** and **south of town** lie a few attractions of a rather different nature, from the reconstructed nineteenth-century buildings of Funen Village to the novel approach to the prehistoric era at the Iron Age Village.

Some history

Most archeological records show Odense to have been a centre for pre-Christian worship of the Norse god **Odin**, though once organized religion came to Scandinavia, the city quickly asserted itself as one of the nuclei for cultural and social activity in Denmark. During the first hundred years after the Reformation, Odense, already at the geographical centre of Funen, also established itself as the economic and trading hub, the profits from which enabled the building of some of the more elaborate timber-framed merchants' buildings in town; and when the **Odense canal** was constructed in 1803, the city was opened up to the northern fjord waterways, paving an easier road to industrialization. Odense has always been something of a cultural mecca, and in the early 1800s it became known as "Little Copenhagen" due to the royal governors, noblemen and upper class families who came to enjoy the thriving theatre and music scenes and join in the other pursuits of Danish high society. It was also known as the "City of Beggars" however, due to the fact that half of its populace – soldiers, day labourers and vagrants – lived in squalid conditions in the western section of town. Today, the population is mostly made up of middle-class Danes, though the western suburbs are home to one of Denmark's larger immigrant communities.

Arrival and information

Odense's **train station** is part of the large Odense Banegård complex, at the northern edge of the town centre along Østre Stationsvej. From here, it's a ten-minute walk to most city sights, as well as several hotels and one of the hostels. **Long-distance buses** terminate behind here at the bus station on the northern side of the train tracks, while **city buses** depart just east of here on Dannebroggade. Odense **airport** (Ⓦ www.odense-lufthavn.dk) is 10km north of town; it's not reachable by public transport, however. Odense's centre is 5km north of the E20 motorway, though bear in mind that much of it is pedestrianized and so off-limits to vehicular traffic. Moreover as the jumble of one-way streets that are actually driveable can confuse and irritate even the most patient of drivers, you're best off leaving your car in one of the numerous, well-signposted metred city **car parks**. The largest concentration is around Vindegade and Slotsgade, just south of the train station, though at 8kr per hour, parking gets expensive very quickly; cheaper rates (4kr) are charged for the lots located outside Odense's inner ring road. You can leave your car in most central car parks and on many city streets for no charge between 6pm and 8am

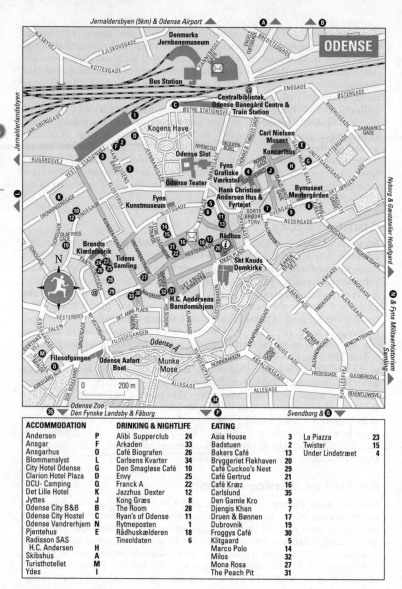

Jernaldersbyen (5km) & Odense Airport   **A**   **B**

ODENSE

Nyborg & Gæsteatelier Hollufgård ▶

Ⓝ & Fyns Militærhistorism Samling ▶

Svendborg & **Q** ▼

ACCOMMODATION		DRINKING & NIGHTLIFE		EATING			
Andersen	P	Alibi Supperclub	24	Asia House	3	La Piazza	23
Ansgar	F	Arkaden	33	Badstuen	2	Twister	15
Ansgarhus	O	Café Biografen	26	Bakers Café	13	Under Lindetræet	4
Blommenslyst	L	Carlsens Kvarter	34	Bryggeriet Flakhaven	20		
City Hotel Odense	G	Den Smagløse Café	10	Café Cuckoo's Nest	29		
Clarion Hotel Plaza	D	Envy	25	Café Gertrud	21		
DCU- Camping	Q	Franck A	22	Café Kræz	16		
Det Lille Hotel	K	Jazzhus Dexter	12	Carlslund	35		
Jyttes	J	Kong Græs	8	Den Gamle Kro	9		
Odense City B&B	B	The Room	28	Djengis Khan	7		
Odense City Hostel	C	Ryan's of Odense	11	Druen & Bønnen	17		
Odense Vandrerhjem	N	Rytmeposten	1	Dubrovnik	19		
Pjentehus	E	Rådhuskælderen	18	Froggys Café	30		
Radisson SAS		Tinsoldaten	6	Klitgaard	5		
H.C. Andersen	H			Marco Polo	14		
Skibshus	A			Milos	32		
Turisthotellet	M			Mona Rosa	27		
Ydes	I			The Peach Pit	31		

(after 2pm on Saturday and all day Sunday), but you'll quickly be slapped with a 510kr fine if you don't feed the meters outside those times.

Information

The **tourist office** (mid-June to Aug Mon–Fri 9.30am–6pm, Sat & Sun 10am–3pm; rest of the year Mon–Fri 9.30am–4.30pm, Sat 10am–1pm; ☎66 12 75 20, ⓦwww.visitodense.com) is centrally located within the Rådhus complex on Vestergade. In addition to booking accommodation (35kr charge), they offer English-language walking tours of Odense (July & Aug Tues–Thurs 11am; 50kr) and hand out the helpful, free *What's On* guide, which has comprehensive listings of city happenings, with summaries in English. They also sell three brochures that are useful if you're planning on cycling anywhere in Funen: *Twelve Biking Tours in Southern Funen* (35kr), *Bike Map Funen* (75kr) and *Cycle Routes in Odense* (free). You can also buy the **Odense Eventyrpas** (120kr for one day, 160kr for two days), which covers admission to all but one of the city museums and allows unlimited travel on local buses; it's also available at the city's train station, youth hostels, campsites and many hotels.

City transport

Nearly all of Odense's key attractions are in the compact city centre, which is best explored **on foot**. For some of the outlying sights and accommodation, however, you'll need to take a city **bus**. Flat-fare tickets for travel within the city limits cost 16kr (pay as you board): if you have to use more than one bus, ask the driver for an *omstigning* ("transfer ticket"). Be sure you have exact change, as drivers won't, and if you plan on using buses a lot, consider buying the Odense Eventyrpas (see above). If you can't face the buses, you can **rent a bike** from City Cykler, Vesterbro 21 (Mon–Fri 10am–5.30pm, Sat 10am–1pm; ☎66 12 97 93, ⊛www.citycykler.dk; from 99kr per day, 500kr per week). Make sure to pick up the free brochure/map *Cycle Routes in Odense* from the tourist office, which lists comprehensive suggestions for touring in and around the centre and up the Odense canal – the city and environs hold over 350km of bikeable paths. An English-language website (⊛www.cykelby.dk) provides additional information about biking around Odense.

Accommodation

Thanks to the Hans Christian Andersen connection, Odense has no shortage of pricey **accommodation**. There are several affordable alternatives, though, including two hostels just outside the city centre, a number of central and affordable B&Bs and a couple of campsites in and around town. All of them fill up during the summer, so it's a good idea to book ahead.

Hotels

Ansgar Østre Stationsvej 32 ☎66 11 96 93, ⊛www.hotel-ansgar.dk. A short walk from the train station, this beautifully renovated hotel offers spacious, colourful rooms with all mod cons, and a good restaurant. ❼/❻

Ansgarhus Kirkegård Allé 19 ☎66 12 88 00, ⊛www.ansgarhus.dk. One of Odense's inexpensive options, conveniently located just outside the city centre – it's a fifteen-minute walk from the station via Jernbanegade, turning right down Vindersgade. Rooms are modern, airy and comfy, if spartanly furnished. ❺

City Hotel Odense Hans Mules Gade 5 ☎66 12 12 58, ⊛www.city-hotel-odense.dk. Bright and sparkling new upmarket option with a prominent yellow façade, just three minutes' walk from the train station: continue straight along Østre Stationsvej. Though lacking any real character, the rooms are cosy with en-suite bathrooms. ❻

Clarion Hotel Plaza Østre Stationsvej 24 ☎66 11 77 45, ⊛www.choicehotels.dk. Located 100m from the train station, this stately place looks and feels a bit like a castle – uncommon, given that it's a chain hotel – and has 66 rooms rather nicely done up in old English style. Breakfast is served in a bright covered terrace. ❼

Det Lille Hotel Dronningensgade 5 ☎66 12 28 21, ⊛www.lillehotel.dk. Small hotel run by a friendly proprietor; the pleasant rooms all have shared bathrooms. ❸

Radisson SAS H.C. Andersen Claus Bergs Gade 7 ☎66 14 78 00, ⊛www.radissonsas.dk. Ideally placed on the quiet cobblestone streets in the east part of town, and just 100m from H.C. Andersen's museum, this old-style chain hotel feels a bit worn at times, but the rooms are spacious and have all necessary mod cons. Service is first-rate, there's a sauna in the basement and the buffet breakfasts are memorably lavish. ❼/❾

Turisthotellet Gerthasminde 64 ☎66 11 26 92, Ⓦwww.turist-hotellet.dk. Cosy, Gothic-looking hotel with one room in the small tower, and the others below, though none are in any way spacious. Rates are fairly reasonable, though it's a tad less central than most of the city's other hotels. ❺

Ydes Hans Tausens Gade 11 ☎66 12 11 31, Ⓦwww.ydes.dk. Inexpensive, basic place with smallish rooms, comfortable beds and very friendly staff. Reception is located at its slightly more upscale sister hotel, *Domir*, just down the street at no.19. ❺

Bed and breakfasts

Andersen Lahnsgade 74 ☎66 12 52 56, Ⓦwww .andersenbb.dk. Bright, well-maintained B&B located across the central Munke Mose park. All the rooms have hardwood floors, and one has French doors that lead right outside. ❸

Jyttes Ramsherred 17 ☎66 13 89 36, Ⓦwww .jyttes-bb.dk. A few steps from the Andersen museums in a lovely restored building, this is the best placed B&B in town. The rooms feel a bit lived in, but this adds to the charm of the place. Breakfast is 40kr per person extra. Book ahead during summer. ❸

Odense City B&B Billesgade 9 ☎66 13 00 74, Ⓦwww.odensecity-bedandbreakfast.dk. A few minutes north of the train station, this modern, industrial-looking building has a few compact rooms, all of which share a bathroom. ❸

Pjentehus Pjentedamsgade 14 ☎66 12 15 55, Ⓦwww.pjentehus.dk. Beautifully renovated old house in the heart of Odense's cobbled section, with a garden that guests can use. Rooms are adequate, if on the small side, with shared bathrooms. Breakfast costs 40kr extra. ❸

Skibshus Skibshusvej 152 ☎66 13 72 88, Ⓦwww .bedandbreakfastodense.com. This pretty red building is a little out of the centre, ten minutes' walk north

of the train station. Rooms (both en suite and with shared facilities) are quiet, warmly furnished and look onto a garden courtyard with a picnic table. ❸

Hostels

Odense City Hostel Østre Stationsvej 31 ☎63 11 04 25, Ⓦwww.cityhostel.dk. Just next door to the train station, this is an efficient, brightly-decorated hostel with somewhat anti-septic dorms (200kr) and doubles (❻) spread out over several floors.

Odense Vandrerhjem Kragsbjergvej 121 ☎66 13 04 25, Ⓦwww.odense-danhostel.dk. Much quieter than its urban counterpart, offering dorms (200kr) and slightly cheaper doubles (❹/❺) than its urban counterpart. The bland interiors are offset by the great setting in a wood-beamed farmhouse placed around a cobbled and grassy courtyard, some 2km southeast of the town centre; take bus #61 or #62 from the train station or cathedral south towards Tornbjerg or Fraugde and get out along Munkeb-jergvej at the junction with Vissenbjergvej. Open March–Dec.

Campsites

Blommenslyst Middelfartvej 494 ☎65 96 76 41, Ⓦwww.blommenslyst-camping.dk. Facilities are pretty basic here, but the location, just next to a picturesque lake, is perfectly lovely. There are some extremely small cabins (370kr) that sleep four and have basic kitchenettes. The site is about 10km from Odense; half-hourly buses #830, #831, #832 or #833 from the train station make the journey in twenty minutes.

DCU-Camping Odensevej 102 ☎66 11 47 02, Ⓦwww.camping-odense.dk. Near Funen Village, this is the only campsite actually in Odense. It's fully equipped, with excellent cooking facilities and a few cabins (❸). Take bus #21, #22 or #23 from the Rådhus or train station towards Højby, or take the Odense Åfart boat and it's a kilometre from the Funen Village stop.

The City

Since most of Odense is very easily explored on foot, you'll want to familiarize yourself with the half a dozen pedestrianized streets which wend their way through the centre, among them the central **Vestergade** and a number of smaller streets which branch off of it, such as the cobbled passageways of the upscale Brandts Passage or the more down-to-earth Vintapperstræde; both of these narrow walkways have some of the city's best shops as well as many of its most popular bars and cafés.

Around the station

The first museum you're likely to see when you arrive to Odense – at least if you're coming by train – is quite a bit more interesting than you might initially think. **Danmarks Jernbanemuseum** (Danish Railway Museum; daily 10am–4pm; 48kr; Ⓦwww.railmuseum.dk), immediately behind the station, houses some of the state railways' most treasured artefacts, from aged train carriages to a recreation of an early twentieth-century station, all with excellent descriptions in English. The most notable of the carriages are those which belonged to Danish royalty: Frederick VII's 1854 personal saloon, an old wooden jalopy found abandoned in a Jutland meadow. In much better condition are two sumptuous royal saloon cars from the 1870s, upholstered in thick silk brocade and furnished with plush velvet chaise lounges and recliners.

On the other side of Østre Stationsvej, just south across the manicured Kongens Have park, is the city's palace, **Odense Slot**, currently in use as a municipal office building but worth a quick glance. The adobe-roofed Italian Baroque structure was built in 1720 by Frederik IV just before he embarked on the much grander Fredensborg Slot (see p.143), a structure with which it shares some similarities – most notably in the symmetrical layout, bevelled windows and colour scheme of its facade. During the early 1800s, when the slot was the royal residence of prince governor Christian VIII, H.C. Andersen's mother was employed here as a washerwoman and often brought young Hans to work with her so the shy youngster could play with other children – the future Danish king Frederik VII among them – in the front yard. The adult Andersen's maladroit likeness is prominently visible in the bronze statue of him out front.

Around the corner from the slot, there's a celebration of Odense's second most famous son in the shape of the **Carl Nielsen Museet** (June–Aug Thurs & Fri 2–6pm, Sun noon–4pm; rest of the year Thurs & Fri 4–8pm, Sun noon–4pm; 25kr), set inside the concert hall at Claus Bergs Gade 11 and an enjoyable hodgepodge of a museum which celebrates the acclaimed composer. The **exhibits** detail Nielsen's life and achievements, with mimeographed scores, photos, letters and even a crochet set he used to while the time away after a serious heart attack late in his life confined him to a bed. Nielsen's personal items are arranged in recreations of the rooms he used to compose his music, and you can listen to some of his works on headphones, including excerpts from his major pieces and the polka he wrote when still a child.

Carl Nielsen

Born just outside Odense in 1865, **Carl Nielsen** displayed prodigious musical gifts from an early age, and went on to gain (posthumous) worldwide acclaim as a composer, particularly for his lush, sweeping symphonies; the musical cognoscenti in his own country later regarded him as having salvaged Danish music from a period of decline. Although Nielsen's work was performed outside of Denmark, he failed to reach any significant international recognition during his lifetime – a point which continually nagged at his ego. Despite his travels, and long period of residence in Copenhagen, Nielsen championed the inspirational qualities of Funen's environment and the island's tuneful dialect, even writing a now-beloved essay romanticizing the landscape in which "even trees dream and talk in their sleep with a Funen lilt". If you've never heard of Nielsen, be assured that his music is nowhere near as half-baked as his prose: one of his greatest works was the cantata, *Springtime in Funen*, which he wrote in 1921 for the thousand singers of the Danish National Choral Society, and it's since become a key work in the repertoire of Danish national heritage. In addition to his symphonic and operatic works, Nielsen was also well-loved for his popular songs based on Danish folk poetry. An English translation of his well-written autobiography, *My Childhood on Fyn* is on sale at the museum shop.

The Hans Christian Andersen and around

Odense's showpiece museum is the **Hans Christian Andersens Hus** (June–Aug daily 9am–6pm; Sept–May Tues–Sun 10am–4pm; 50kr; Ⓦmuseum .odense.dk), at Bangs Boder 29 in the house where the writer was born and which he described in *The Fairy Tale of My Life*. Oddly enough, Andersen

Hans Christian Andersen

Few storytellers are as well-known for their poignant observations on the frailty of humanity as **Hans Christian Andersen**, the grandfather of the modern fairy tale and author of 156 stories, 800 poems, 43 plays and 11 novels. Born on April 2, 1805, Andersen grew up very poor, and spent his first years in what was then one of Odense's slum quarters, living in a single room that doubled as a workshop for his father, a cobbler by trade. It was a rough upbringing: Hans's ill-tempered mother was fifteen years older than his father, whom she married when seven months pregnant with Hans (she also had an illegitimate daughter by another man), while descriptions of his grandmother, often given charge of the young Hans, range from "mildly eccentric" to "pathological liar". Despite – or perhaps because of – such domestic hardship, Hans clung to the belief that his future lay in more artistic endeavours than the unglamorous factory jobs that otherwise awaited him. Bright and ambitious, he read Shakespeare and Grimm at an early age, and began acting, singing and writing his own poetry and drama while still in primary school. The young Hans was a highly emotional child, however, and he regularly suffered humiliation at school because of his awkwardly gangly figure and "effeminate" interests.

At the age of 24, Andersen published his first stories in Danish journals, popular tales which he considered a mere diversion on his path to becoming a successful novelist; nonetheless, this was the kind of writing that would eventually bring him unprecedented fame and cement his place in the canon of great European literature. The first collection of his stories, **Tales, Told for Children**, appeared in 1835 as a small, inexpensive booklet, and was followed two years later by a larger volume containing classics such as **The Little Mermaid**, **The Emperor's New Clothes** and **The Princess and the Pea**. Andersen's style was initially criticised for being too vulgar and grotesque, but by the time he reached his early thirties, he had written his way from destitute child to wealthy adopted son of the upper classes, heralded across Europe as a literary sensation.

Andersen's ability to identify and empathise with the outcast, the unfortunate and the hopeless undoubtedly helped to make his stories so compelling. The painful feeling of "being different" is a recurrent motif in his work, most notably in *The Little Mermaid*, whose central character takes her own life because she cannot be loved by a beautiful prince. In terms of Andersen's own love life, his latent bisexuality has been the subject of much academic speculation – he frequently maintained close friendships with younger male contemporaries, perhaps most notably Edvard Collin, son of one of Andersen's benefactors, to whom he once wrote, "I languish for you as for a pretty Calabrian wench ... my sentiments for you are those of a woman". Andersen's relationships with women, meanwhile, were perpetually tragic: his innumerable crushes were almost never reciprocated, something which drove him further into his shell of self-pity: he never married and, as far as anyone can tell, died a virgin, described by one of his biographers as a "self-pitying and desperate man". Tall and lanky, with gaunt features highlighted by a long nose, closely-set eyes and a well-receded hairline, Andersen perhaps knew he wasn't going to be anyone's prince charming, and fame and critical acclaim thus became something of a narcotic for him – although despite all the admiration bestowed on him throughout his life, his abject loneliness persisted. He died at the age of 71, and was buried in a modest plot at Assistens Kirkegård, Copenhagen (see p.100).

was only really accepted in his own country towards the end of his life; his real admirers were abroad, which perhaps explains why he left Odense at the first opportunity and travelled so widely. Though he wrote novels and a few (best-forgotten) plays, it's his **fairy tales** that have gained most renown, partly autobiographical stories (not least *The Ugly Duckling*) that were influenced by *The Arabian Nights*, German folk stories and the traditional Danish folk tales passed on by inmates of the Odense workhouse where his grandmother tended the garden.

Few of the less-than-fairytale aspects of Andersen's life are touched upon in the museum, and there's a nagging falseness about some aspects of the collection, especially if you know anything about the life of the man himself. Still, as Andersen was a first-rate hoarder, it's stuffed with intriguing items: bits of school reports, his certificate from Copenhagen University, early notes and manuscripts of his books, chunks of furniture and his umbrella as well as paraphernalia from his travels, including the piece of rope he carried to facilitate escape from hotel rooms in the event of fire. A separate gallery contains a library of Andersen's works in seventy languages, and headphones for **listening** to some of his best-known tales as read by the likes of Sir Laurence Olivier. Nearby is a very mixed collection of illustrations and other art inspired by his writing, including Andersen's own meticulous papercuttings and drawings, many of which were used to illustrate his books.

The Andersen theme is continued just next to the Hus at **Fyrtøjet** (Tinderbox; late June to early Aug daily 10am–5pm; early Aug to late June Tues–Sun 11am–4pm; 70kr; ⓦwww.fyrtoejet.com), Hans Jensens Stræde 21, a sort of indoor cultural playground for kids based on Andersen's stories. Upon entrance, visitors are presented with a suitcase containing things they will need on their journey, during which they dress up in costumes and explore the fairytale worlds that Andersen created. There are also frequent storytelling events and other organized group activities, though none of these are offered in English.

The streets around the Andersen museums – primarily Overgade and Nedergade – are characterized by picture-perfect half-timbered houses on spotlessly clean cobbled avenues, rather lacking in character and resembling more a theme-park "Scandinavian village" than anything authentically Danish. Indeed, if Andersen himself were around he'd hardly recognize the neighbourhood, which is now one of Odense's most gentrified and expensive. To get a flavour of the city's history, head to the **Bymuseet Møntergården** (Møntergården City Museum; Tues–Sun 10am–4pm; free; ⓦmuseum.odense.dk), a few streets away at Overgade 48–50, where there's a large assemblage of important archeological finds found on Funen. The main permanent exhibit consists of a few rather hastily put-together walls that offer a cursory overview of human toolmaking; the upper floor is more engaging, displaying hundreds of prehistoric items, including tools, pottery, weaponry and other implements.

Sankt Knuds Domkirke and around

Ten minutes' walk southwest of the Bymuseet, the thirteenth-century **Skt Knud's Domkirke** (April–Oct Mon–Sat 9am–5pm, Sun noon–5pm; Nov–March Mon–Sat 10am–4pm, Sun noon–5pm; ⓦwww.odense-domkirke. dk) is one of the finest Gothic churches in Denmark. The exterior is a riot of profiled bricks and layered silled windows, while inside, the main draw is the finely detailed sixteenth-century wooden altarpiece, rightly regarded as one of the greatest works of the German-born master craftsman, Claus Berg. Commissioned in 1521 by Queen Christine, the massive altar is swathed in 23-carat gold, its central carvings depicting characters and scenes from the Old

Testament; the outer sixteen panels show (horizontally, from left to right) the Passion and the events from Easter to the Pentecost. At the base of the altar, supporting the panels, rests a portrait of the royal family, kings Hans and Christian II on the left, their queens to the right, and a resurrected Christ in the centre to emphasize the role of religion in holy matrimony.

You might also want to visit the crypt to see one of the most unusual and ancient finds Denmark has to offer: the **skeleton of Knud II** (aka Canute), who was slain in 1086 by Jutish farmers angry at the taxes he'd imposed on them. The murder took place in the original wooden church that stood here, Skt Albani Kirke, in which the king was laid to rest in 1101, but the miraculous events of the following years (see "Contexts", p.390) resulted in his canonization as Knud the Holy, Denmark's first saint; his remains were subsequently moved to the present Domkirke. If you look closely at the skeleton, which rests on ninth-century silk pillows, you can observe some bone fragmentation in the pelvic region – it's believed that Knud was bludgeoned to death while genuflecting at the altar. Close to Knud's is another coffin thought to hold the remains of his brother Benedict (though some claim them to be St Alban, whose body was brought to Denmark by Knud), while displayed alongside is the fading but impressive Byzantine-style silk tapestry sent as a shroud by Knud's widow, Edele.

There's more (but not much more) about Andersen a few minutes northwest of the church at the tiny **H. C. Andersens Barndomshjem** (H.C. Andersen's Childhood Home; June–Aug daily 10am–4pm; Sept–May Tues–Sun 11am–3pm; 10kr), Munkemøllestræde 3–5, set in the house where Andersen lived from 1807 to 1819 before moving to Copenhagen, where he spent most of the rest of his life. Andersen was memorably not terribly fond of Odense, perhaps because of the destitute conditions in which he grew up, and the few austere rooms here, which hold little in the way of furniture or accoutrements, serve as a reminder of the poverty in which Andersen grew up.

Odense's art museums

Although most visitors come to Odense on the H.C. Andersen trail, the city also offers a couple of excellent art museums. Best of these is the **Fyns Kunstmuseum** (Funen Art Museum; Tues–Sun 10am–4pm; 30kr; ⓦ www.museum .odense.dk/kunst), a few minutes' walk from the cathedral at Jernbanegade 13. The collection here gives a good sense of the region's importance to Danish art during the late nineteenth century, when a number of Funen-based painters gave up creating portraits of the rich in favour of impressionistic landscapes and studies of the lives of the peasantry. The first floor documents this chronological transition quite well, beginning with a number of mid-eighteenth–century Rococo portraits by islanders such as Jens Juel, and moving on to representatives of the Funen and Skagen schools like Johannes Larsen and Peter Hansen. Of these, the most striking is Hans Brendekilde's enormously emotive and tragic 1889 *Udslidt* ("Exhaustion"), a tragic study of the lot of a peasant farmer. From the ground floor, head upstairs via the central stairway, where you'll pass Svend Wiig Hansen's radiant frieze *Den dræbte sol* ("Murdered sun"), part of a work originally painted in the Skt Nikolai church in Copenhagen. The work on the first floor is decidedly more modern, with installations and graphic art pieces from Asger Jorn, Richard Mortensen and Egill Jacobsen drawn from the museum's large collection of contemporary Danish works; look out for Helge Holmskov's larger-than-life, bespectacled iron bust of sculptor Adam Fisher from 1968. Although the museum's collection is usually rotated once a year, the seminal Danish works are always kept on display, among them stirring pieces by Nordic greats like Vilhelm Hammershøi, Michael and Anne Ancher and P.S. Krøyer.

If you're in the mood for some more modern art, head along Vestergade, then Jernbanegade, and turn down Brandts Passage to reach the **Brandts Klædefabrik** (ⓦwww.brandts.dk), an expansive former textile factory that's now given over to a number of cultural endeavours: three museums, a gallery, an art school, a music library and a cinema, along with trendy cafés and classy restaurants. The various **galleries** here occupy more than five thousand square metres of gorgeous oak floors and 8m-high lofted walls, while retaining the grittiness of the original factory building, and together put on more annual art exhibitions than anywhere else in the country – approximately 25 annually. The **Kunsthallen** gallery (July & Aug daily 10am–5pm; Sept–June Tues–Sun 10am–5pm; 30kr, combined ticket with the Photographic Art Museum and Danmarks Mediemuseum 50kr) is an increasingly prestigious spot for exhibitions of high-flying new talent in art and design; close by are the varied displays of the large **Museet for Fotokunst** (Museum of Photographic Art; same hours; 25kr, combined ticket 50kr), taken from the cream of modern art photography and almost always worth a look. There's also the more down-to-earth **Danmarks Mediemuseum** (Danish Media Museum; same hours; 25kr, combined ticket 50kr; ⓦwww. mediemuseum.dk), with its bulky machines and devices chronicling the development of printing, bookbinding and illustration from the middle ages to the present. Further down Brandts Passage on the second floor of no. 29, the **Tidens Samling** (Old-Time Museum; daily 10am–5pm; 30kr; ⓦwww.tidenssamling. dk) furnishes visitors with intimate insight into changing trends in interiors and fashion and home interiors since the beginning of the last century.

A ten-minute walk south of Brandts at Filosogangen 30, the folksy, six-roomed **Filosofgangen Art Gallery** (Tues–Sun 11am-5pm; free) is of much less note than the other ones in the city, but it's worth a quick peek if you're waiting to board the Åfart boat down the canal, with a mishmash of modern Danish engravings, collages, driftwood sculptures and the like. Almost all the works are for sale, and the artists themselves are occasionally on hand.

Out from the centre

While Odense's most famous sights are conveniently contained within walking distance of the city centre, the northern and southern outskirts hold a couple of worthwhile attractions. Boat and bus transportation to most sights is quite good, though you can get to all of them fairly easily. In the summertime, one of Odense's most enjoyable activities is an afternoon jaunt aboard the **Odense Åfart** (ⓦ www.aafart.dk; 35kr single, 55kr return), a small passenger vessel which sails daily along the Odense canal from Munke Mose park in the city centre, stopping at the Odense Zoo and ending up at Fruens Bøge, a short walk from Den Fynske Landsby. Bus #42 follows more or less the same route, but as services are infrequent, the boat is actually the most efficient way to travel. It departs on the hour from May to mid-August (10am–5pm), and at 11am, noon, 2pm and 5pm from mid-August to mid-September. On Saturday afternoons from late June to August, when passengers are serenaded by a jazz band, the fares go up a bit (50kr single, 100kr return), and it's best to book tickets in advance on ⓉⓉ66 10 70 80.

The boat's first stop is at the **Odense Zoo** (April & Sept–Oct Mon–Fri 9am–5pm, Sat & Sun 9am–6pm; May–June & Aug Mon–Fri 9am–6pm, Sat & Sun 9am–7pm; July daily 9am–7pm; Nov–March daily 9am–4pm; 100kr; ⓦwww .odensezoo.dk), quite enjoyable as far as zoos go, with the usual lions, tigers and giraffes. More interesting is the new tropical building, home to several manatees from French Guiana, a couple of giant 150-kilo tortoises and, appropriately housed in the chilly basement, a family of penguins. A few minutes further on along the canal, the next stop is the **Den Fynske Landsby** open-air museum (April–May & Sept–Oct Tues–Sun 10am–5pm; Nov–March Sun 11am–3pm; 40kr; June–Aug daily 10am–7pm; 55kr; Ⓦmuseum.odense.dk), a reconstructed nineteenth-century country village that's lent an air of authenticity by its period gardens and wandering geese. From the farmhouse to the poorhouse, all the buildings are originals from other parts of Funen, their exteriors painstakingly reassembled and interiors carefully refurbished. In summer, traditional trades such as blacksmithing are revived in the former workshops, and there are free shows at the open-air theatre. Though often crowded, the village is well worth a visit, and there's the added lure of a free glass of the village-brewed beer, which is handed out on special occasions. An English-language film shown in the main building gives some good historical context on the social and political changes that were going on in the eighteenth and nineteenth centuries. The village is located several kilometres south of the city centre on Sejerskovvej, and bus #42 runs to the village from the city centre (get out at the Den Fynske Landsby sign).

Another worthy option south of the centre is **Gæstatelier Hollufgård**, where the landscaped **gardens** (daily dawn–dusk; free) of a sixteenth-century manor house are decorated with large, innovative sculptures by up-and-coming and established Danish and international artists. Although the works are frequently rotated, there's always a selection of interesting and challenging pieces representing contemporary trends. The gardens are reachable via a twenty-minute ride on bus #82 towards Neder Hollu.

Jernalderlandsbyen

Some 5km northwest of Odense at Store Klaus 40, and easily reachable from the town centre (take bus #91 north towards Allesø), the **Jernalderlands-byen** (Iron Age Village; July to mid-Aug Mon–Fri & Sun 10am–4pm; mid-Aug to June Mon–Thurs 8.30am–3.30pm, Fri 8.30am–2pm; 25kr; Ⓦwww .jernalderlandsbyen.dk) is one of many prehistoric collections in Denmark based on archeological findings from all over the country, but this one at least makes an effort to be a bit different. The recreated prehistoric dwellings are in active use as workshops where you can see such ancient trades such as shoe-making and metalwork. There's also an interesting simulated TV news broadcast covering events in Bronze Age Denmark, alongside displays describing how ancient symbols are used in modern times. Fans of jousting, chain mail and smithery all across Funen count down the days to the village's hugely popular Iron Age market, held every year on the third weekend in May.

Eating

Most of Odense's **restaurants** and **cafés** are squeezed into the central part of the city, which means there's a lot of competition and, potentially, some very good bargains to be had during the day – and many of the places listed here are also good for a **drink** in the evenings. And thanks to the city's immigrant population, there are also plenty of great ethnic restaurants alongside the Danish places. Lazy, late-morning **brunch** is a well-established tradition here, with many cafés offering weekend (if not daily) brunch menus or buffets; the greatest concentration of these places is around Gråbrødretorv and along Brandts Passage, and we've noted the best spreads in our reviews.

Danish and Scandinavian

Badstuen Østre Stationsvej 26 www.badstuen.dk. Inexpensive café on the upper floor of the Badstuen cultural centre that offers the best meal deals in town. Served promptly between 5.30pm and 6.30pm, the meat- or fish-based dish of the day is just 35kr, while salads, open sandwiches and burgers go for around 15kr throughout the day. Mon–Thurs 11am–10pm.

Baker's Café Fisketorvet 2. Excellent sandwiches and freshly baked pastries; if the weather is right, you can get a takeaway and eat right on the square.

Bryggeriet Flakhaven 2 66 12 02 22, www.bryggeriet.dk. This brewery-cum-restaurant is a great place to ponder your day over a home-brewed pilsner, lager, ale or wheat beer, while meals range from light sandwiches – try the herring smørrebrød platter for 78kr – or pasta and meat dishes such as spare ribs from 129kr. The shiny copper fermenting casks make the chartreuse-green walls a little easier to handle, though there are also tables out front. Mon–Thurs 11am–11pm. Fri 11am–1am, Sat 11am–midnight, Sun 3pm–10pm.

Café Cuckoo's Nest Vestergade 73 65 91 57 87, www.cuckoos.dk. One of the few spots with any life early in the week, and one of the best places for Sunday brunch buffet (10am–2pm; 99kr). Lots of seating options, from settees to massive rattan divans, are set across two courtyards and smaller dining rooms inside. Evenings and weekends in summer they often have live jazz music out front.

Café Gertrud Jernbanegade 8 65 91 33 02, www.gertrud.dk. Adorned with brass trimmings, dark wood and movie memorabilia, this Scandinavian bistro offers a great daily brunch (9am–4pm; Sun from 10am; 84kr) which includes ham, homemade muesli, fruit and local cheese, and you can people-watch from the tables out front while you eat. Mon–Sat 9am–10pm, Sun 10am–10pm.

Café Kræz Gråbrødre Plads 6 66 11 38 11, www.kraez.dk. Tasty salads, sandwiches and soups, as well as pancakes with a beef or chicken filling (112kr). There's brunch (from 80kr; 10am–3pm) at weekends, outdoor seating and occasional live bands. Mon–Sat 10am–10pm, Sun 10am–9pm.

Carlslund Fruens Bøge Skov 7 65 91 11 25, www.restaurant-carlslund.dk. Typical Danish restaurant which does delicious smørrebrød and is famous for its æggekage (110kr). There's live jazz on summer Saturdays, and reservations recommended. You can get here on the *Odense Åfart* (see p.211), but if you're here past 4pm or so, you'll need to either walk the 3km back to town or take the train from Fruens Bøge. Mon–Sat noon–9pm.

Den Gamle Kro Overgade 23 66 12 14 33, www.den-gamle-kro.dk. Four dining rooms are packed into this creaky old 1683 inn, festooned with old-world stained glass, cast iron stoves and etched ceramic tiling. Meals are traditional Scandinavian and continental dishes like flambéed pepper steak run from 160kr to 260kr. If you can, try to get a seat in the covered, leafy courtyard or the vaulted cellar. Reservations recommended. Mon–Sat 10am–10.30pm, Sun 10am–9.30pm.

Druen & Bønnen Vestergade 15 66 11 18 13, www.druenogboennen.dk. Odense's newest café-cum-wine bar, with curious furry rawhide seats and chess and backgammon tables, offers very good coffee and Scando-Mediterranean breakfast plates – paté, salmon and charcuterie – in the morning, and freshly made brie, salmon and tomato sandwiches in the afternoons and evenings. Mon–Sat 10am–10pm.

Froggys Café Vestergade 68 65 90 74 47. A pleasant spot for a quick daytime bite, or for more substantial evening meals such as butterfish in white wine sauce or hazelnut chicken; the Sunday brunch buffet (10.30am–3pm; 89kr) is popular with those nursing hangovers, and there's either a DJ or live music on weekend evenings until 5am. Decor is classic-meets-modern, with 1950s Hollywood posters, chandeliers and trendy leather benches. Mon–Wed 9am–midnight, Thurs 9am–3am, Fri & Sat 10am–5am, Sun 10am–midnight.

Klitgaard Gravene 4 66 13 14 55, www.restaurantklitgaard.dk. Upscale place awash with earthen tones, while designer crockery and smallish portions perpetuate the minimalist aesthetic. The seafood is some of the best you'll find on Funen, and draws a full house most nights. The *rødfisk* and Norwegian lobster (255kr) is especially good. Tues–Sat 6pm–midnight.

Under Lindetraeet Ramsherred 2 66 12 92 86, www.underlindetraet.dk. Set in a picture-perfect restored inn dating back to 1771, this is easily the most atmospheric and lavish Danish restaurant in town, but considering the superb setting and the excellent gourmet food, the three- and four-course menus (395kr) of traditional Danish dishes might actually be considered a bargain. Mon–Fri noon–2.30pm & 6–9.30pm, Sat for 6–9.30pm.

Ethnic and international

Asia House Østre Stationsvej 40 66 12 19 24. Friendly, atmospheric and very popular Thai place, with tatami walls and a thatched ceiling that make it a bit easier to swallow the pricey fish and meat mains (from 140kr). The all-you-can-eat buffet on Fridays and Saturdays (148kr) is a great bargain. Tues–Sun 5pm–10pm.

Djengis Khan Overgade 26 ☎ 66 12 88 38, ⓦ www.djengis-khan.dk. The 115kr all-you-can-eat Mongolian barbecue dinner here is quite a good deal, assuming you can stand the over-the-top decor, crammed with chintz and chinoiserie. Sun–Thurs 4.30–11pm, Fri & Sat 4.30pm–midnight.

Dubrovnik Vindegade 93 ☎ 66 13 65 82. Cosy, popular Croatian place offering tasty and very reasonable food; try the creamy goulash soup or the *palacinkesa sladokedom*, blini-like crepes with clotted cream. A three-course menu will set you back just 119kr (139kr on weekends). Tues–Sat 5–9pm.

Marco Polo Jernbanegade 14 ☎ 66 14 27 60, ⓦ www.rest-marcopolo.dk. Very popular Italian restaurant, with mains at 99–149kr. In addition to the usual pasta dishes, more innovative options include Tournedos à la Marco Polo (*oksemørbrad* with ratatouille) and Soufflé de Tacchine, a chicken and spinach soufflé. Daily 5–10pm.

Milos Mageløs 7 ☎ 66 11 28 66, ⓦ www .restaurant-milos.dk. Set just off the main drag, this Greek restaurant offers some of the best deals in town, with ample portions of classic dishes such as moussaka and kleftiko. Mon–Sat noon–10pm, Sun 5–10pm.

Mona Rosa Vintapperstræde 4 ☎ 65 91 49 13, ⓦ www.monarosa.dk. Summer evenings see this reasonably priced Mexican restaurant packed with families and couples, spread across two terraces that give onto the cobbles of Vintapperstræde. The lunch set menu is 69kr, while à la carte starts at around 100kr. Mon–Thurs & Sun noon–10pm, Fri & Sat noon–10.30pm.

The Peach Pit Mageløs 1 ☎ 65 90 75 00. Pizza parlour offering huge and very tasty slices (15kr) as well as kebabs and burgers. Mon–Thurs & Sun 10am–midnight, Fri & Sat 10am–6am.

La Piazza Brandts Passage 33–35 ☎ 66 14 60 70, ⓦ www.la-piazza.dk. Beautifully prepared pasta dishes (from 100kr) and more than 100 wines (159kr–2500kr) make this Italian café a great lunch option; it gets packed with local families in the evenings. Mon–Thurs 5–9.30pm, Fri & Sat 11.30am–3.30pm & 5.30–10pm, Sun 5–9.30pm.

Twister Jernbanegade 16 ☎ 66 13 17 22. One of the town's more popular kebab places, with a falafel and hummous fast-food joint at the front, and a sheesha room at the back that's very popular with a younger set, who puff away at the 40kr hubbly-bubblies. Mon–Wed 11am–11pm, Thurs–Sat 11am–2am, Sun 3–11pm.

Drinking, nightlife and live music

After the sun sets, the pedestrianized streets come alive as everyone heads out to take advantage of Odense's superb nightlife. The city has a surfeit of **late-opening cafés** that have usurped the role of nightclubs as evening hangouts, many of them sleek, fashionable places that attract their share of scantily clad Danish demoiselles and their hangers-on. Most of these establishments also function as restaurants in their own right, though the ones listed below are generally more known for their non-culinary goings-on.

Many bars put on **live music** on weekends, and several city music halls and concert spaces also host regular performances by bands from the Nordic countries – and occasionally further afield. On Thursdays in July between 7pm and 10pm there are live free rock concerts at Kongens Have, the public garden across from the train station, while the **Odense Symphony Orchestra** (☎ 66 12 00 57, ⓦ www.odensesymfoni.dk) puts on over one hundred classical music concerts each year at the Koncerthus, Claus Bergs Gade 9. The season stretches from September until April and tickets run between 65kr and 175kr, though if you have student ID you can get them on the day of the concert for 20kr. The box office is open on concert days from 4pm onwards, plus Mondays and Tuesdays from 2pm to 5pm. Additionally, on Saturday mornings in July, orchestra members perform their much-beloved "**Vegetable Concerts**" alongside the market stalls at Sorte Brødre Torv. For details of upcoming events, pick up the leaflets available at most cafés, music shops and the tourist office, check out Rytmeposten (ⓦ www.rytmeposten.dk) or grab a copy of the free *Odense Sommer Jazz* from the tourist office, which lists all of the city's summer jazz events.

For details on Odense's **gay and lesbian** scene, get in touch with the local organisation Lambda (☎ 40 89 62 49, ⓦ www.lambda.dk).

Bars, clubs and live music venues

AliBi Supperclub Brandts Passage 37 @www .supperclub.dk. A sleek bar that just manages to meld brick classicism with a high modernist aesthetic. There are frequent (loud) bands and stand-up comedians, while the weekend DJs fuel a hot club scene. Served until 10pm, the pasta dishes and spicy burgers are not bad at all. Mon–Wed 10am–10pm, Thurs 10am–2am, Fri & Sat 10am–5am, Sun 11am–10pm.

Arkaden Vestergade 68 @www.cityarkaden.dk. If spring break ever took place in Odense, it would happen here. With six separate bars set in a mall-like arcade, this collection of loud and libidinous places to drink and dance is popular with both younger and older locals. Fri & Sat 10pm–late.

Café Biografen Brandts Passage 39–41 ☎66 13 16 16, @www.cafebio.dk. Enduringly fashionable Odense institution, decorated with a dazzling display of classic film posters. While the restaurant – serving sandwiches, salads and great weekend brunches – is quite popular, it's the bar that really gets going at night, mostly for a late-twenties to early forties semi-professional crowd.

Carlsens Kvarter Hunderupvej 19 @www .carlsens.dk. Inexpensive, unpretentious pub serving fruity Belgian beers, English ales and a couple of Funen microbrews. Danish folk music occasionally accompanies. Mon–Sat 11am–1am, Sun 1–7pm.

Den Smagløse Café Vindegade 57 @www .densmagloesecafe.dk. Divey, smoky and unpretentious rock pub that gets packed with local students on account of the beer prices – pints are 25kr before 9pm, 30kr after. Couches, table football and a pool table in back. Mon 1pm–2am, Tues–Sat until 3am, Sun 1pm–midnight.

Envy Brandts Passage 31 @www.envy-lounge .com. With tweed-covered seats, modern "art" and mood lighting on the terrace, this is one of the city's trendiest night spots, where the media hopefuls and tragically hip come to soak up the glam amidst Brazilian lounge and drum 'n' bass music. The expensive cocktails make the clientele here a bit more select than other places. Brunch (daily 10am–4pm, Sun from 11am; 85kr) is popular, as are tapas and omelettes (65kr). Mon–Wed 9.30am–midnight, Thurs–Sat 9.30am–2am, Sun 10.30am–11pm.

Franck A Jernbanegade 4 ☎66 12 27 57, @www.francka.dk. Modern café serving decent food and a good brunch (daily 10am–4pm; 89kr), though it's best known for its after-dinner boozing, when the DJs get out their top-40 Euro hits and the dance floor rumbles with the heels of the over-30 crowd. Cocktails start at 65kr. Mon–Wed 10am–1am, Thurs–Sat 10am–3am, Sun 11am–11pm.

Jazzhus Dexter Vindegade 65 ☎63 11 27 28, @www.dexter.dk. This expansive bar is a great place to hear some of the finest jazz in Denmark, from swing to fusion, four or five times a week until early morning. There is a cover (usually 50kr) all nights except Mondays, when students show off their licks at the open-mike jam sessions.

Kong Græs Asylgade 7. Odense's oldest disco, popular with twentysomethings and still *the* place to go after-hours, with live music, stand-up comedy and lots of dancing. Cover around 50kr. Friday 10pm–5am, Saturday 10pm–5.30am.

The Room Brandts Passage 6–8 @www .the-room.dk. While the crowd at this new bar-cum-lounge-cum-club is sometimes a bit cheesy, the dance music is loud and full of energy, and it's one of the better places to let your hair down. An evening menu has a few spartan tapas dishes and some more substantial build-your-own burgers. Mon–Wed & Sun 10am–midnight, Thurs–Sat 10am–3am.

Ryan's of Odense Fisketorvet 12. Odense's resident Irish drinking establishment is the closest you'll come to a spit-and-sawdust pub, with faux whiskey casks and live music on weekends. Mon–Wed 11am–2am, Thurs 11am–3am, Fri & Sat 11am–5am, Sun 4pm–midnight.

Rytmeposten Østre Stationsvej 35 ☎66 13 60 20, @www.rytmeposten.dk. Funen's prime live music venue, this converted post office hosts a lot of heavy rock bands. Tickets generally start at 100kr.

Rådhuskælderen Vestergade 15–17. Basement bar which vies with *Tinsoldaten* as a late-night place to go on the pull, with bands playing light rock two or three times a week. Minimum age 25. Thurs midnight–6am, Fri & Sat 10pm–8am.

Tinsoldaten Frue Kirkestræde 3. This smoky dive-bar attracts early morning stragglers and is well-known as Odense's last-ditch pick-up joint; the fun doesn't usually begin until well after 3am, when other places let out. Wed 10pm–8am, Thurs 10am–9am, Fri 10pm–noon, Sat midnight–1pm.

Listings

Banks and exchange There's a Den Danske Bank at Flakhaven 1, and a Nordea Bank at Vestergade 6; Forex is at the train station (Mon–Fri 9am-6pm, Sat 10am–3pm). There are ATMs all around town.

Bookshops Arnold Busck, Vestergade 54; and B.O. Bøger, Vestergade 59–61 both sell maps, guidebooks and some English-language titles.

Car rental Avis, Østre Stationsvej 37 ☎ 66 14 39 99; Europcar/Østergaard, Vestre Stationsvej 13 ☎ 66 14 15 44, PS Biludlejning, Middelfartvej 1 ☎ 66 14 00 00.

Embassies Netherlands, Christiansgade 70 ☎ 66 11 27 77; UK, Albani Torv 4 ☎ 66 14 47 14.

Emergencies ☎ 112 for police or ambulance.

Hospitals There is an emergency department at Odense University Hospital, J.B. Winsløws Vej (☎ 66 11 33 33).

Internet access Free access is available at the city's library (Mon–Thurs 10am–7pm, Fri 10am–4pm, Sat 10am–2pm, plus Sun Oct–March 10am–2pm) in the train station complex, for which you must book in advance on ☎ 65 51 43 01. Internet cafés include Boomtown Netcafé Pantheonsgade 4 (Mon–Fri 9.30am–11pm, Sat–Sun 4–11pm; 20kr/hr); Galaxy Netcafe, Train station (Mon–Fri 7.30am–1am; Sun 9am–1am; 17kr/hour). There's also a single terminal at the tourist office which you can use for free.

Laundry Møntvask, at Vesterbro 44 (Sun–Fri 7am-8pm, Sat 7am–7pm) charges 30kr per wash including soap.

Left luggage The train station has both large (20kr) and small (10kr) lockers for luggage storage. You can also store bags in the building next to the tourist office for a pricey 10kr per hour per item.

Markets There are fruit and vegetable markets at Rosenbæk Torv (Fri & Sat 7am–1pm) and H.C. Andersens Torv (Wed & Sat 7am–1pm).

Newspapers Overseas newspapers (and a few magazines) are sold at the kiosk in the train station, and at Politikens Kiosk, Skt Knuds Kirkestræde 15.

Pharmacy Apoteket Ørnen (☎ 66 12 29 70), Vestergade 80, is open 24-hours.

Post offices The main office is in the train station at Dannebrogsgade 2 (Mon–Fri 8am–9pm, Sat & Sun 10am–4pm), and offers poste restante.

Swimming pools There is a centrally located indoor public pool at Klosterbakken 5 (Mon–Fri 6.30am–7.30pm, Sat 7am–1pm; 26kr; ☎ 65 51 53 30), and an outdoor one 6km west of the city centre at Elsesmindevej 50 (May–Aug daily 10.30am–7pm, 26kr; ☎ 65 51 53 60).

Taxis Taxis can be hailed at the train station, or call Odense Taxa on ☎ 66 15 44 15. Initial price is 24kr, with 12.56kr added on for each kilometre driven. There is an extra 9kr tacked on between 8pm and 6am weekdays and all day Saturday and Sunday.

Travel agents Kilroy Travels, Vestergade 100 (Mon–Fri 10am–5.30pm ; ☎ 70 15 40 15, Ⓦ www.kilroytravels.com).

The northeast coast

Funen's easternmost town, **Nyborg** is connected to Zealand by the 18-kilometre **Store Bælt** ("Great Belt") road and rail link (see p.160). Most visitors see little more of Nyborg than its train station, but unless you're in a great rush to press southwards to Funen's islands or to reach Odense, it's worth sparing a few hours to take a stroll around the old town and Nyborg's thirteenth-century **castle**, the seat of Danish political power for two hundred years. North of here, **Kerteminde** is the home of one of Funen's most beloved painters of wildlife as well as an aquarium that runs under the fjord, and is within easy distance of the meadows and forests of the **Hindsholm peninsula**, just north.

Nyborg

Due to its location at the centre of the Store Bælt, **NYBORG** was strategically important to pre-modern Denmark. At one point, it was Funen's only fortified town, and since medieval times has been characterized by the large stockades and sinuous moats which wended their way around the town to protect it against invaders approaching from both the Storebælt coast and from Funen's interior.

Small and easily navigated, Nyborg is a mostly modern town today, though a number of dark red-brick buildings and the remains of the Nyborg slot fortification on its western periphery stand as reminders to a rich past. The central, pedestrianized Nørregade is home to most of the town's commercial action, with half a dozen cafes and boutiques that terminate at the town's main church,

For most Danes, eating is inextricably linked with the sense of social occasion and cosy bonhomie known as "hygge" – good food and beautiful presentation are hugely important here, and great pride is taken in preparing delicious meals. The modern Danish cuisine that you'll find in the restaurants is of an equally high standard, renowned for its use of super-fresh seasonal produce, from vegetables to meat, fish and seafood. In terms of drinking, you'll find a very relaxed attitude to alcohol here, and plenty of appealing bars in which to try marvellous locally produced beers.

Danish
food and
drink

Danish cuisine

Caught, salted, dried and smoked here for centuries, herring is central to Danish cuisine. The most popular preparation, and a fixture of the smørrebrøds table, is **marinated herring** – raw herring left in a salt solution for several years (the longer it's left, the softer it becomes), and then marinated in sweet white vinegar flavoured with anything from onion and black pepper to cloves, sherry, dill or a hot tomato mixture. **Smoked herring** is also very popular, and is a regional speciality of places such as Bornholm and Dragør, where it's prepared in coastal smokehouses (*røgeri*). In fact, the huge variety of locally caught fish and seafood is one of Danish cuisine's strongest suits, and classic fish dishes such as fresh fried plaice served with new potatoes and a buttery parsley sauce are always surefire winners. There are 12.6 million pigs in Denmark, more than double the number of people, an indication of why you'll also see a lot of pork on traditional menus. Though Denmark is known abroad for its bacon, the locals regard this bland but salty export with disdain, instead reserving their favour for the more sophisticated concoctions – flavour-packed salamis and cold cuts – laid out on smørrebrød tables. Among hot pork dishes, you'll find a host of hearty choices on offer in the restaurants, from *medister pølse* (a thick, spiced pork sausage eaten with sweet and sour pickled red cabbage) to the festive *flæskesteg*, roast pork with crackling.

▼ Smørrebrød selection

Smørrebrød

The quintessentially Danish open sandwich, quite different in style and flavour to the Swedish *smörgåsbord*, **smørrebrød** is delicious and utterly addictive, and you'll find no shortage of restaurants dedicated to this culinary phenomenon. It consists, simply enough, of a thin slice of dark, dense rye bread (*rugbrød*), loaded up with delectable combinations of hot or cold meat or fish and garnished with dollops of sauce and thin slices of fresh or pickled vegetables. A smørrebrød meal is usually served into three courses – a herring starter, a hot and cold meat option, and a cheese board at the end – and traditionally, each course is washed down with a shot of ice-cold **snaps**, a strong, clear spirit typically flavoured with caraway or aniseed and intended to cleanse the palate.

Classic smørrebrød

Dyrlægens natmad Liver paté (*leverpostej*) with a thin slices of salted beef and squares of meat aspic, garnished with raw onion rings and cress.

Stjerneskud Fried plaice and shrimp topped with a dollop of mayonnaise, red caviar, a sprig of dill and a slice of lemon.

Rullepølsemad Thin slices of *rullepølse* (rolled pork belly seasoned with herbs), topped with horseradish and cress.

Ribbensteg Slices of cold roast pork with sweet-and-sour pickled red cabbage (*rødkål*), garnished with a slice of orange.

Røget ål Fillets of smoked eel topped with scrambled egg and thin slices of radish.

Spegepølsemad Slices of salami topped with rémoulade (mayonnaise laced with pickles and capers) and crispy roasted onions (*ristede løg*).

Sol over Gudhjem Smoked herring with chopped raw onions and capers, topped with a raw egg yolk.

Smørrebrød is generally eaten at lunchtime, and there's a certain etiquette to be followed when ordering. In specialized smørrebrød restaurants, the traditional way is to tick off your choice of pre-set pieces (*stykke*) from a long **smørrebrøds list** (*smørrebrøds seddel*). Two or three pieces will usually fill you up, but you can always order more if necessary, and we've listed the most common combinations above. In less traditional restaurants, you can usually get a **smørrebrøds platter** consisting of a selection of four to five pre-combined pieces; other places just lay out the three courses of toppings **buffet-style** (*det kolde bord*), so you can get creative and make up your own (though don't be tempted to mix meat and fish on the same piece – it'll look and taste awful).

Danish pastries

Light, flaky and best bought straight from a bakery in the morning, a real **Danish pastry** melts in the mouth and makes the perfect accompaniment to a cup of coffee and a shot of herby, spicy Gammel Dansk bitters – a combination traditionally enjoyed by office workers during their Friday morning break. Danish pastries are known here as Viennese bread (**wienerbrød**) – the recipe was introduced by a Viennese baker in the mid-nineteenth century – but the Danish version has long since taken on a life of its own. *Wienerbrød* come in all shapes and sizes, and are flavoured with a variety of spices and fillings – and each has its own nickname. Look out for **hanekam** ("rooster's comb"), comb-shaped, with almonds and icing, and **bagerens dårlige øje** ("the baker's infected eye"), a decidedly unappetizing name for this delicious buttery confection with a dollop of jam or custard at its centre.

Skål!

Danes have always been big **beer** drinkers, and the arrival of many small independent breweries, including a number of microbreweries, means that there's never been a better time to sample the country's locally made brews. The list below details some of the best beers, and where to try them.

Denmark's best beers

Jacobsen Dark Lager, Carlsberg's Jacobsen microbrewery, Copenhagen. A dark, Bavarian-style lager brewed using the original Carlsberg recipe from 1847, this is the inspiration for all Danish beers. See p.99

Hancock Dark Gambrinus, Hancock Bryggerierne, Skive. A heavy, inky lager that in spite of its strength (9.5 percent) doesn't taste overly alcoholic. See p.289

Nørrebro Northbridge Extreme, Nørrebro Bryghus, Copenhagen. US-inspired ale from Copenhagen's most popular brewery-restaurant. See p.111

Ølfabrikken Porter, Ølfabrikken, Tisvildeleje. A traditional stout brewed with a modern twist that makes it lighter and very moreish. See p.141

Fur Ale, Fur Bryghus, Fur. Brewed with water filtered through the cliffs of north Fur, this delightful lager's only problem is that there isn't enough of it. See p.290

Brøckhouse IPA, Brøckhouse, Hillerød. From one of Denmark's oldest modern microbreweries, this is an award-winning pale ale with a strong, hoppy flavour, best sampled at Copenhagen beer parlours such as *90eren*. See p.111

Thy Pilsner, Thisted Bryghus, Thisted. Among the best of the classic Danish pilsners brewed using techniques borrowed from the Czechs. See p.284.

Vor Frue Kirke (June–Aug 9am–6pm, Sept–May 9am–4pm), Gammel Torv 1, dating from the late fourteenth century. It's been reconstructed, remodelled, renovated and added to countless times over the years, and although most of what you see today is from a late nineteenth-century rebuild, the current structure still holds a few old fittings that merit a look inside: a fourteenth-century crucifix at the chancel arch; the marble, neo-Gothic main font from 1876 and, just south of the chancel, a post-Reformation wooden font from 1585; as well as an exquisite Baroque pulpit from 1653.

Head west from here on Nørregade to reach the **Torvet**, flanked to the north and east by several stately-looking municipal buildings, including Nyborg's original 1803 red-brick Gothic town hall and clocktower. After a fire in 1797 razed many of the town's buildings, the new constructions, built with limestone quarried from the Stevns cliffs of eastern Zealand, were designed by Johan Jakob Encke, whose German background accounts for the Neoclassical feel of much of what's visible here today. One exception, dominating the west side of the square, is the **Nyborg Slot** (daily: April–May & Sept–Oct 10am–3pm; July 10am–5pm; June & Aug 10am–4pm; 30kr, joint ticket with Mads Lerches Gård 45kr; ⓦ www .museer-nyborg.dk), Denmark's oldest intact castle, built around 1200 by Valdemar the Great as part of a chain of coastal fortresses to guard against piracy. For more than two hundred years, the Danehof – a summertime national assembly comprised of king, clergy and nobility – met here (most notably in 1282 to draw up Denmark's first constitution), which effectively made Nyborg the Danish capital until 1443, when power moved to Copenhagen. The castle bears little evidence of those years, however, since the three main fortified buildings fell into disrepair after the Prussian War of 1864; much of the castle's land was sold off to townspeople and the surrounding buildings partitioned and turned into residential properties. All that remains on view today is a chunk of the front portal and a stubby, elongated building, its distinctive harlequin brickwork the result of a 1920s restoration. Inside here the rooms themselves are much more evocative of the past than the odd table, chest, or suit of armour with which they're decorated. The first floor is by far the most impressive: check out the **Banquet Hall**, hung with a series of illuminated historical paintings and two massive genealogies of Christian III. To the south is the **Danehof Hall**, where the assembly met and discussed the constitution; the unusual geometrical wall pattern was added in 1520. The three upstairs floors hold a dozen chambers and rooms, some of them decorated and furnished, others bare, still others closed off, though you could safely give them all a miss and head out behind the castle, where you can climb up to the **ramparts**, now decked with replicas of the original cannon, to imagine what the Nyborg infantry might have seen as they scanned the woods for approaching Swedish troops. Just below here, two posterns – brick, tunnelled passages that run under the ramparts – allowed soldiers easy access between the lookout area and the stronghold, and allow you easy access to a pleasant **pond**, once a moat, with a pebbly walking path around it. There is good documentation out here explaining the ruins, but you might want to time your visit to coincide with one of the English-language **tours** (June–Aug Wed & Sat 2pm; rest of the year Sat 2pm; free) which take you through the castle's nooks and crannies, and allow you to explore the grounds with a more informed idea of what the place was like during its military heyday. Between late June and August, the castle also hosts Danish and international musicians who come to perform choral, piano chamber and opera **concerts** in the Banquet Hall. Tickets can be purchased from the tourist office or by visiting ⓦ www.nyborgslotskoncerter.dk.

For the more impressive exemplars of the buildings that survived the fire, head a block south of Torvet along Skippergade, which follows the course of the medieval moat; the appropriately beige-and-brown Garvergården building at no.26 was the town's tannery. Just around the corner from the Torvet at Slotsgade 11, it's also worth taking a look at **Mads Lerches Gård** (daily: April–May & Sept–Oct 10am–3pm; July 10am–5pm; June & Aug 10am–4pm; 30kr, joint ticket with Nyborg Slot 45kr). Built in 1601, this exquisite oxblood-red house belonged to one Mads Lerche, an active local merchant and mayor of Nyborg in the late 1500s. With two storeys and three wings, it's quite typical of many of the older structures you'll see in other Funen towns, with plenty of front windows, distinctive triangular half-timbering and a corbelled second floor that hangs over the first, a very common building style in the 1500s and 1600s. It now houses the small town museum displaying ethnographic odds and ends like flat-irons, toys, a rusty horse-drawn carriage and various domestic appliances assembled in a pantry though it's best enjoyed from the outside. Once you've had your fill of the old town, several nearby **beaches** offer adequate swimming and awesome views of the mammoth Storebælt bridge, though it can get a bit windy this close to the *bælt*. The favourite bathing spot is the sand at Fynsbadestrand, located on Hjejlevej immediately south of *Nyborg Strandcamping* (see opposite).

Practicalities

Nyborg sits at the base of the Nyborg Fjord, dominated to the east by the mammoth Storebælt bridge linking Funen to Zealand; thanks to this bridge, the **train station** is now placed one kilometre outside of town. From here both trains and buses depart for destinations all across Funen. From the station, it's an easy walk to the town centre where the **tourist office** is centrally located just opposite the castle at Torvet 9 (mid-June to mid-Aug Mon–Fri 9am–5pm, Sat 9.30am–2pm; rest of the year Mon–Fri 9am–4pm, Sat 9.30am–12.30pm; ☎65 31 02 80, @www.nyborgturist.dk). Although the bright lights of Odense are just 25km west, Nyborg isn't a bad place to hole up for a night, with a few inexpensive **accommodation** options in the centre and several pricier ones on the coast. In terms of **food**, *Alanya* (☎65 31 13 23; Mon–Sat 12.30–10pm), Torvet 3, is a Turkish restaurant set in a somewhat dark basement, but has a courtyard terrace out back and a delicious 59kr lunch buffet (daily 11.30am–4.30pm); dinners are a bit more pricey. Otherwise, a block away on Nørregade, *Central Caféen* (☎65 31 01 83; daily 11.30am–9pm) is a tad fusty on the inside, and much better at the back on the pleasant covered terrace, where you can enjoy traditional Danish dishes from 140kr. If you have your own transport, though, you'd do better to head to the atmospheric *Teglværksskoven* (☎65 31 41 40, @www.teglvaerksskoven .dk; April–Sept daily noon–9pm, Oct–March Thurs–Sat noon–9pm & Sun noon–5pm), 3km northeast of town at Strandalleen 92, right in the forest and one of the better places to eat in eastern Funen, with well-prepared traditional dishes like the juicy "Forest steak" (148kr). They also rent out several new and tidy double rooms in a building alongside (❹). For evening revelry, *Slotscafeen*, just opposite the castle at Slotsgade 5, is as smoky and ratty a bar as you'll ever find, but a fine place to soak up some local colour.

features like granite bathroom floors and immaculate period furniture, along with views out either to the Storebælt bridge or to the forest in back. They occasionally offer some enticing summer deals and prices at weekends are always a bit lower. ⑨ **Nyborg Strandcamping** Hjejlevej 99 ☏65 31 02 56, ⓦwww.strandcamping.dk. Lovely campsite with forested grounds just in front of a small beach. Open April–Sept.

Villa Gulle Østervoldgade 44 ☏65 30 11 88, ⓦwww.villa-gulle.dk. This B&B is a step up from the norm, though the rooms here, some en suite, some with shared bathrooms, are a mite stodgy. They also rent out rowing boats (80kr per hour). ④, en suite ⑤

Kerteminde and around

Kerteminde is surely the prettiest little town in the whole world, positioned as it is deep in the bay, by the mouth of the fjord, facing the Great Belt and the sunrise.

Johannes Larsen.

Some 20km north of Nyborg, past the huge cranes and construction platforms at Munkebo – until recently a tiny fishing hamlet, but now the home of Denmark's biggest shipyard – lies **KERTEMINDE**, itself a place with firm maritime links, originally in fishing and now increasingly in tourism. During the sixteenth and seventeenth centuries, all of Odense's exports were shipped from here, and the doorframes of many older residences still bear the imprints of early Odense warehouses used to store merchandise. These days, though, the town is a centre for sailing and beach holidays, and can get oppressively busy during the peak summer weeks. At any other time of year, though, it makes for a well-spent day, split between the town itself, the Viking-era Ladby Boat just outside, and the verdant Hindsholm Peninsula just to the north.

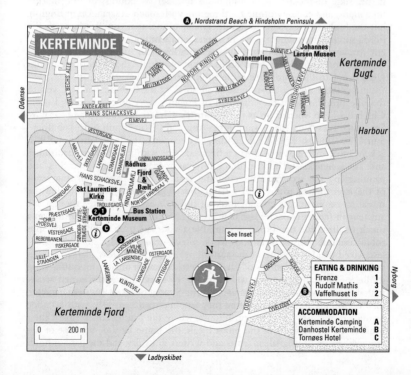

Ⓐ, Nordstrand Beach & Hindsholm Peninsula ▲

KERTEMINDE

Odense ◀

Johannes Larsen Museet

Svanemøllen

Kerteminde Bugt

Harbour

Rådhus

Fjord & Bælt

Skt Laurentius Kirke

Bus Station

Kerteminde Museum

See Inset

N

Nyborg ▶

Kerteminde Fjord

0   200 m

EATING & DRINKING
Firenze	1
Rudolf Mathis	3
Vaffelhuset Is	2

ACCOMMODATION
Kerteminde Camping	A
Danhostel Kerteminde	B
Tornøes Hotel	C

▼ Ladbyskibet

Kerteminde straddles the mouth of the Kerteminde Fjord, its harbour – home to Funen's largest fishing fleet – sheltered by two large escarpments to the north and south. The town's centre is ranged around the worn, fifteenth-century **Skt Laurentius Kirke** on Strandgade, whose broad tower and brick nave date to 1350. Inside are a number of Baroque artefacts, namely the front pews, whose monogrammed entrances illustrate the pre-twentieth century gender and class divisions that existed among parishioners: men sat on the south side and women on the north, with the wealthier members of the congregation placed closest to the altar. Walk up to the chancel and squint upwards, where high up in one of the vaulted wings hangs a pair of boots and rapier sword belonging to a local soldier who died fighting off the Swedes in the 1659 Battle of Nyborg. The streets just around the church are the town's oldest: Chr. Jydesvej and Reberbanen, built to avoid transport of night-soil past the homes of the wealthy on Vestergade; the three compact, quiet lanes which connect Fiskergade with Lillestranden; and a neat and prettily preserved nucleus of shops and houses along Strandgade and Langegade.

At Langegade 8, in an old trading post dating from 1630, the town **museum** (March–Oct Tues–Sun 10am–4pm; 25kr) sports ten or so rooms that recreate the living and working conditions of townspeople over the years: a middle-class salon, a peasant's living room and a child's playroom, though the only exhibit of real interest centres on the tools of corporal punishment. From here, head south towards the harbour, across the road from the bus station on Margrethes Plads 1, to arrive at the **Fjord&Bælt** (mid-Feb to late June & mid-Aug to Nov Mon–Fri 10am–4pm, Sat & Sun 10am–5pm; late June to mid-Aug daily 10am–6pm; 90kr; Ⓦ www.fjord-baelt.dk). This new (but hardly state-of-the-art) aquarium has a number of exhibits on the marine inhabitants and ecology of the fjord region, with much description in English, but the highlight is a 50m-long underwater tunnel that runs 4m beneath the fjord's surface from where you can observe seals and porpoises in their natural environment, though visibility is sometimes less than superb. The centre also organizes one-hour boat trips (100kr) and two-hour snorkelling excursions (200kr) out to the fjord during the summertime.

On a grander note, a ten-minute stroll north of the harbour will take you to the one-time house of the "birdman of Funen", the painter Johannes Larsen, which has been opened up as the **Johannes Larsen Museet** (March–May & Sept–Oct Tues–Sun 10am–4pm; June–Aug daily 10am–5pm; Nov–Feb Tues–Sun 11am–4pm; 60kr). The delightful, airy residence, built by Larsen in 1901, is kept more or less as it was when he lived here, with many of his furnishings and knick-knacks still extant, the walls crammed with studies, sketches and paintings by the artist and his contemporaries. Larsen painted all four walls of the front dining room with a naturalistic winter motif – he intended the mural to be viewed as though looking through bay windows – though the amateurish figures make it clear that his talent lay in his sketches, working on a much smaller scale (see box opposite). Next door is Larsen's studio, a spacious room containing his most famous work, *Morning Sun* (1936), a study of a faceless, naked maiden wading in the sun-drenched sea. Out back, a large modern building showcases hundreds of Larsen's sketches – most notably his outstanding studies of birds in flight – as well as works by some fifty other Funen artists, including several haunting portraits by Fritz Syberg of his in-laws. After taking in the grounds and all the artistry they inspired, you can relax with a coffee or juice in the café set in the washhouse, where the painters once rinsed their brushes. To the chagrin of the pious locals, the home became a haunt of the country's more bacchanalian artists and writers in its day, and the garden holds

Johannes Larsen

A born and bred Kerteminder, **Johannes Larsen** (1867–1961) is one of the best-known painters of the Funen school (see p.210), and is remembered for his detailed depictions of wildlife – especially birds – and rural landscapes. Larsen studied in Copenhagen under Kristian Zahrtmann, aligning himself closely with several contemporaries – most notably Peter Hansen, Fritz Syberg and Poul Christiansen, all of whom were often chidingly described as the "peasant painters" because of their modest, rural motifs. Larsen was interested in landscape too, but it was his fascination with wildlife that came to dominate his work throughout the latter part of his life, with many of his days spent at his home at Møllebakken taking in the seascape and making notes and sketches of the numerous birds which call these shores home. Admiring the work at his museum in Kerteminde, you quickly become aware of the amazing detail of his technique: many of his pencil sketches are virtual anatomical studies of the wings, legs and joints of gulls and other sea birds, often in full flight. In part, Larsen's intricate knowledge of such **anatomy** came about with the help of local townsfolk, who would regularly bring him the carcasses of birds found dead in town. In 1921, Larsen set sail with explorer and sketch artist **Achton Friis** aboard the *M/S Rylen*, a small wooden sailboat, for a four-year expedition around 132 of Denmark's small islands, during which he observed, recorded and sketched the island's landscapes; both he and Friis were convinced that the islands would soon be overcome by summer homes and plantations – a prediction which has pretty much come true. The trip culminated in the book *De Danskes Øer* (Islands of the Danes), a beautiful collection of these sketches and paintings; you can purchase a copy in the Larsen museum shop.

a detailed sculpted female figure by frequent visitor Kai Nielsen. A story goes that during one particularly drunken party, the piece was dropped and the legs broke off. Someone called the local *falck* (emergency services), but despite much inebriated pleading, the (sober) officer who rushed to the scene refused to take the sculpture to hospital.

If you're tired of museums and fancy a swim, continue north along Hindsholmvej to reach Nordstrand, the town's **beach**, a clean and quiet patch of fine sand. Bus #481 runs there five times a day, with the last return at 5.45pm.

Practicalities

Buses from Nyborg (#890, #891, 37kr) and Odense (#880, #890, 51kr) arrive at a tiny station across from the Fjord&Bælt centre on Hans Schacksvej. Kerteminde's **tourist office**, around the corner at Hans Schacksvej 5 (mid-June to Aug Mon–Sat 9am–5pm; Sept to mid-June Mon–Fri 9am–4pm, Sat 9.30am–12.30pm; ☎65 32 11 21, ⓦwww.kerteminde-turist.dk), has details of local accommodation bargains, which include over a dozen private rooms and B&Bs. A five-minute walk north of here on Hindsholmvej, you can **rent bicycles** (100kr per day) at the Statoil petrol station. Aside from B&Bs, the only truly low-cost **accommodation** option, a ten-minute walk from the town centre at Skovvej 46, is the *Danhostel Kerteminde* **youth hostel** (☎65 32 39 29, ⓦwww.dkhostel.dk), which has dorms (150kr) in simple, chalet-like rooms with four beds, and similarly sized doubles (❸). To get there, cross the Kerteminde fjord via the Langesbro road bridge, take the first major road left and then turn almost immediately right. There's also a **campsite**, *Kerteminde Camping* (☎65 32 19 71, ⓦkertemindecamping.dk-camp.dk; May to mid-Aug); it's not far from the Larsen museum at Hindsholmvej 80, the main road running along the seafront – a twenty-minute walk from the centre. If you want something more upmarket, try the central three-star *Tornøes Hotel* (☎65 32 16 05, Ⓦwww.tornoeshotel.dk; Ⓞ), Strandgade 2, right on the water and offering thirty bright rooms with all mod cons. Ask for one of the lovely sea-view ones, as they only cost a few kroner more.

Inexpensive **eating** in Kerteminde isn't hard to come by, but a meal at *Rudolf Mathis* (☎65 32 32 33, Ⓦwww.rudolf-mathis.dk), Dosseringen 13, is well worth a few extra kroner. Set just on the harbour across the Langesbro bridge in an old smokehouse – look for the traditional twin white chimneys – it's famous all across Funen for its haute cuisine steak and seafood dishes, like grilled ocean mullet with kidney bean and ginger sauce (495kr for a three-course meal). In the town centre, *Firenze*, Trollegade 2F, is a small family-run Italian restaurant with sizeable pizzas for 72kr and specials like grilled scampi (125kr), while immediately next door, *Vaffelhuset Is* is the town's favourite ice-cream joint – there's often a queue outside for the delicious homemade flavours scooped into large waffle cones.

Around Kerteminde: Ladby

An easy trip from Kerteminde is to head 4km southwest of town to the village of **LADBY** where, along the banks of the fjord at Vikingvej 123, you'll find the **Ladbyskibet** (Ladby Boat; March–May & Sept–Oct Tues–Sun 10am–4pm; June–Aug daily 10am–5pm; Nov Wed–Sun 11am–3pm; 25kr; Ⓦwww .kert-mus.dk), a chieftain's burial vessel that offers a fascinating glimpse into Viking history. The 22-metre boat was buried, as per Viking tradition, with its owner and all his possessions, and rested peacefully underground for close to a thousand years; it was discovered in 1935 and remains in the original spot where it was buried. Though the wood from the boat has mostly rotted away, its weight over so many centuries has left a perfect impression into the land here – preserved in the tiny purpose-built subterranean museum – though the chieftain himself, along with any riches and valuables he was buried with, were removed by grave robbers not long after his burial. He was interred along with weapons, eleven horses and a pack of hunting dogs, whose skeletal remains are still visible, as is what's left of the ship's prow, originally a carved dragon's head, now just the beast's coiled mane, forged from iron. It's a fasci-nating find, and the high-tech air-cooled chamber lends a Star Trek feel, but even the closest of inspections won't require more than half an hour. A new museum will open here in 2007 to display the full range of effects found along with the ship, formerly held in the National Museum in Copenhagen. From the museum's parking lot, it's a short walk along a grassy path to the buried boat. From Kerteminde, bus #482 runs regularly to the museum between Monday and Friday, dropping you off 1km away – the route to the museum is well signposted. At weekends, bus travel is more complicated – you have to ring ☎65 32 51 43 to order the *telekørsel* bus, which only runs on demand. In any event, it's much more pleasant to cycle there.

The Hindsholm Peninsula

North of Kerteminde is the small and verdant **Hindsholm Peninsula**, nota-ble for its picturesque farmsteads and rolling hillocks and especially good for camping and bike rides (see opposite for rental information; bus #483 also runs to its far north 3–4 times daily). The first place of interest, 4km north of Kerteminde, is the small village of **VIBY**, whose whitewashed Gothic church has a few beautiful frescoes dating to the late 1500s. If you fancy a **boat trip** around the fjord, head west of here to Lodshuse, where the *M/S Svanen* (☎65 97 70 61, Ⓦwww.svanen-munkebo.dk; mid-June to Sept; 30–120kr) picks up passengers several times a day to sail around the Odense fjord, stopping at the small, scenic islands of Viggelsø and Enebærodde, juniper-covered conservation areas for migratory birds and dotted with old lighthouses. Both of these islands offer some lovely hiking in unspoilt, wild terrain, too. Another worthwhile target hereabouts is the ancient **underground burial chamber** of Mårhøj Jættestue (unrestricted access), 10km north of Kerteminde near Martofte; the bodies, of course, are long gone, and you'll need a torch to explore properly as it's very dark inside. With few trees, shrubbery or dunes to offer coastal protection, much of the land here is virtually untouched, a completely unspoilt landscape that didn't go unnoticed by Funen school painters Larsen and Syberg, who discovered the area early on in their careers and made much of the special light here. Reachable via a tiny road bridge, the **beaches** around the **Fyns Hoved** promontory are some of Funen's best, and by far the least populated. The 25m cliffs at the northern end of the peninsula afford some excellent views out to the island of **Samsø**.

The peninsula is a great place to pitch a tent and revel in quiet seclusion; there are two good **campsites**: *Bøgebjerg Strand* (T65 34 10 52, Wwww .bogebjerg.dk; April to mid-Sept), Blæsenborgvej 200, on the eastern shore just opposite the island of Romsø, has a pristine campsite with a pool and private beach. They also rent bikes (50kr per day) and motorboats (400kr per day) and have a few pricey four-person cabins (355kr plus 200kr surcharge if staying for one night only), though you can only rent these by the day outside the high season. Simpler, much more remote and open year-round is *Fyns Hoved Camping* (T65 34 10 14, Wfynshoved.dk-camp.dk), Fynshovedvej 748 at the peninsula's northernmost tip, which has basic two-person wooden cabins (❷) and a gorgeous little beach that looks north towards the island of Samsø off the eastern Jutland coast.

Southern Funen

With its acres of agricultural land interspersed with thick forests, and salt-marshes, reedbeds and gorgeous beaches along the coast, southern Funen is the ideal place to get out and explore Denmark's quiet pleasures. Most of the towns are lined up along the Baltic coast; the largest of these, **Svendborg**, holds a few interesting sights and a bevy of excellent restaurants that can easily occupy you for a day or two, while southwest along the coast, the attractive marina town of **Fåborg** is home to one of Funen's most prized art galleries. Both towns offer easy road and ferry access to the islands of the South Funen Archipelago (see p.232).

Svendborg

A favourite stop for the Danish yachting fraternity, whose marinas clog the coastline from here to Fåborg, 24km west, **SVENDBORG** exudes a certain gritty charm, with colourful houses lining the cobbled lanes that dip down to the water. The town's relatively sizeable population gives it a decidedly urban feel – but don't let this put you off. As well as boasting some of the best nightlife in an otherwise very quiet region, Svendborg is a great place to spend an hour or two meandering around narrow backstreets, spattered with beautiful bronzes by one of Denmark's best-known sculptors, locally born Kai Nielsen, or heading down to the harbourfront to take in the bustling shipyard, packed with beautiful old wooden boats from all over Scandinavia and the Baltic.

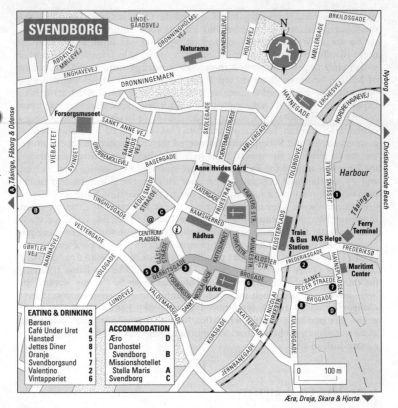

Ærø, Drejø, Skarø & Hjortø ▼

During the nineteenth century, nearly half of all Danish wooden-hulled ships were built in Svendborg, and the boatbuilding yards here still launch dozens of new vessels each year.

Arrival, information and accommodation

Svendborg sits at the mouth of the Svendborg Sound, 44km south of Odense, to which it is linked by frequent **trains**. Regular **buses** also run from Odense (#970 or #801), Nyborg (#910) and Fåborg (#930). The #800 long-distance bus originating in Odense also stops at the A9 entrance to town (though not the town centre) before continuing on through to Rudkøbing on Langeland, lumbering onto the ferry to Tårs on Lolland and finally terminating in Nykøbing on Falster. Buses arrive at the train station, a quick walk from the ferry terminal at the southern edge of town, where there are luggage **lockers** (10kr per day).

The eager-to-please **tourist office** (mid-June to Aug Mon–Fri 9.30am–6pm, Sat 9.30am–3pm; Sept to mid-June Mon–Fri 9.30am–5pm, Sat 9.30am–12.30pm; ☎62 21 09 80, ⓦwww.visitsydfyn.dk), Centrumpladsen 4, covers the entire southern Funen area and can provide details of private accommodation, up-to-date ferry timetables and free copies of the *South Funen Hikers Guide*, which offers good suggestions for walking tours in and around Svendborg. The office also has a single **Internet** terminal (free), though there are many more at Zero (daily 10am–2am; 24kr per hour), located inside the Bycenter shopping mall just across the roundabout. In terms of **accommodation**, Svendborg's large and very modern *Danhostel Svendborg* (☎62 21 66 99, ⓦwww.danhostel-svendborg.dk; dorms 150kr, doubles ❹), ten minutes' walk from the town centre at Vestergade 45, occupies the Lange company's former foundry and feels more like a simple, mid-range hotel than a hostel. Hotels include the excellent *Ærø* (☎62 21 07 60, ⓦwww.hotel-aeroe.dk; ❼), Brogade 1, whose modernish rooms retain a classy, antique feel, and with a downstairs restaurant that's regularly packed out in the summer. With much higher prices and slightly higher standards, *Hotel Svendborg*, Centrumpladsen 1 (☎62 21 17 00, ⓦwww.hotel-svendborg.dk; ❼), is smack in the town centre with spacious rooms that offer all the modern conveniences – and predictability – of a mid-grade business hotel. If you don't mind staying outside of town, the reasonably priced *Missionshotellet Stella Maris* (☎62 21 38 91, ⓦwww.stellamaris.dk; ❻), a ten-minute bus ride (#202) along the coast, is a grand white estate overlooking the Svendborg Sound, with a range of different rooms and a subtle ecumenical bent. Although none of the area's **campsites** are located particularly close to Svendborg centre, Tåsinge, a few kilometres south, has two good choices (see p.234).

The town and around

Svendborg has a few museums whose historical collections could occupy the better part of a day, perhaps before boarding the last evening ferry to one of the islands. All are operated centrally and share the same phone number and website (☎62 21 02 61, ⓦwww.svendborgmuseum.dk). The most interesting of these is the **Forsorgsmuseet** (Social Welfare Museum; May–Sept Tues–Sun 10am–4pm, Oct–April Tues–Sun 1–4pm; 40kr), Grubbemøllevej 13, a captivating place housed in a former poorhouse with displays detailing how the Danish state has cared for (or ignored) its citizens over the years. The extensive collection includes exhibits on the national health service, with nostalgic recreations of 1950s doctors' and dentists' offices, and a moving section on the experience of orphaned and fostered children in twentieth-century Denmark, including heart-wrenching accounts and letters told by the orphans themselves about their parents and the treatment they received from their caregivers. From here, head east to the beautiful, half-timbered **Anne Hvides Gård** (May–Aug Tues–Sun 10am–4pm; 25kr), Fruenstræde 3. Dating from 1560, this is Svendborg's oldest secular building, and has served variously as an aristocratic estate, manor house, theatre, inn and municipal office complex over the years. The building now holds the city museum, with displays of local archeological artefacts as well as changing cultural exhibits on things like aristocratic dress and jewellery. The more macabre highlights include a group of skulls from a cadre of medieval thirtysomethings and a glass jar containing the 250-year-old brain of a local woman. If preserved animal life is more your thing, it's worth checking out the virtual Noah's Ark of stuffed Danish fauna at the superb **Naturama** (Tues–Wed & Fri–Sun 10am–5pm, Thurs 10am–8pm, also mid-June to mid-Aug Mon 10am–5pm; 70kr; ⓦwww.naturama.dk), Dronningemaen 30, whose innovative displays offer some novel insights into the animal world. Spread over three floors of a round building, each level is divided into sections on marine, terrestrial and airborne creatures, and makes sophisticated use of lighting, sound, film and photography to follow the habitats of northern European wildlife through a 24-hour day, with scenes that often make the animals look rather eerily lifelike; the five hundred woodland birds suspended in mid-air on the top floor are especially impressive.

Svendborg's past as a centre for shipbuilding means there's lots on offer for anyone interested in maritime history, and the harbour, a few minutes south of the centre at the end of Havenpladsen, is as good a place as any to get a feel of Funen's erstwhile naval importance. The quay is home to several beautifully preserved wooden ships, a handful of which you can board to check out galley riggings and instruments. To gain access, ask at the **Maritimt Center** (Mon–Fri 8am–5pm, weekends variable hours; ☎62 80 02 14; ⓦwww.maritimt-center.dk), Havnepladsen 2, which also organizes summer afternoon and evening schooner tours (125–200kr, depending on route and time of day) in a dual-masted wooden ship that plies the waters of the Svendborg Sound. Another well-advised option, and one in which you can stop off at some of the sights around the outskirts of Svendborg, is a ride on the **Helge steamer**, which departs from the harbour three to five times daily for the island of Tåsinge (see p.232), calling at Vindebyøre (Svendborg's extension just across the Svendborg Sound), zigzagging back to Christiansminde, a beach resort next to Svendborg's exclusive marina, and then on to the thatched village of Troense, criss-crossed by quiet streets of carefully preserved houses. From here, it heads to Grasten on the small island of Thurø and a few minutes' walk from a beachside campsite; and finally onto the region's must-see, the seventeenth-century Valdemars Slot (see p.232). The return sailing time is two hours, and **tickets** (early May to mid-September; 80kr round-trip from the harbour; information on ☎33 15 15 15) are good for one stop-off along the way, and are purchased on board.

Though this part of Funen is not exactly a haven for beach-bums, a few **beaches** around town do draw their share of locals and visitors. The sand at Christiansminde, 1km east of the centre and accessible via a marked path from the harbour, is popular with a younger, partying set, while Smøremosen beach on nearby Thurø island is better for families; Thurø also has a few worthwhile sights, including a lovely seventeenth-century church and some pleasant forested walks. The Helge ferry runs to both of these beaches, or you can take bus #201. Another excellent way to see the Sound is by paddling around it: several kilometres south of the centre in Skovballe, Sea Kayaking Centre Svendborg (☎62 54 19 20, ⓦwww.havkajakcenter.dk), Skaregårdsvej 9, rents out one- and two-person **sea kayaks** for the day (300kr); they also operate a simple campsite and hire out large felt tents (300kr). To get there, take the bus #901 to Lundby, from there it's a 6km walk – if you ring ahead, someone can usually come to pick you up at the bus stop.

Eating and drinking

Svendborg has one of Funen's best selection of **restaurants**, mostly located between the town centre and the ferry terminal along Brogade, and drawing in crowds of locals from all over the island. Accordingly, it's also an excellent place to try some of Funen's culinary specialities, but it's advisable to book ahead in the summer to be sure of a table. Similarly, there's no shortage of things to do after-hours.

Cafés, restaurants and bars

Børsen Gerritsgade 31 ⓦwww.borsenbar.dk. This very popular wooden-beamed café-bar is adorned with large exposed copper pipes that deliver fresh draught beer to the bar. Snacks and drinks are served inside or at the tables on the pedestrian walk out front. Along with its adjoined pub, The

Face Inn, things really get going here at weekends, which see all-night dancing.

Café Under Uret Gerritsgade 50 ⓦwww.under-uret .com. Youthful café-bar whose weekend live music and all-night dancing rakes in large numbers of Funenites who probably shouldn't be out past curfew. Mon–Thurs 9.30am–midnight, Fri & Sat 9.30am–1am, Sun 10.30am–11pm.

Hansted Vestergade 2A. A basement music bar with over fifty Danish, Belgian and English beers. On Tuesday evenings, there's live Scandinavian or Celtic folk music, while on the weekends bands play everything from jazz to pop. Hookah pipes (60kr) lend a bit of edge to the otherwise predictable pubby scene. Open until midnight weekdays, 3am weekends. Sun–Thurs 2pm–midnight weekdays, Fri & Sat 2pm–3am.

Jettes Diner Kullinggade 1 ☎62 22 17 48, ⓦwww.jettesdiner.dk. Period diner offering a variety of scrumptious continental meals, including big salads and over twenty juicy burgers (from 42kr) as well as pricier chilli and steak dishes and large, creamy milkshakes (35kr). April–Sept daily noon–10pm, Oct–March closed Mon.

Oranje Jessens Mole ☎62 22 82 9, ⓦwww.oranjen.dk. Set in a ship moored at the harbour, with a yummy catch of the day and unbeatable views out to the Sound. Mains run from 158kr. May to mid-Sept daily 11am–3pm & 5.30–9.30pm.

Restaurant Svendborgsund Havnepladsen 5 ☎62 21 07 19, ⓦwww.restaurantsvendborgsund.dk. Harbourside restaurant with a small covered terrace out front, offering traditional Danish sailors' fare, from the basic *æggekage* (118kr) to sizeable T-bone steaks (198kr); the *stegt flæsk* is especially good. Daily 11am–10pm (until 9pm off-season).

Valentino Frederiksgade 9 ☎62 22 21 61, ⓦwww.restaurant-valentino.dk. This homey Mediterranean-styled place has great pizzas to go at just 40kr. Its proximity to the train station makes it perfect for getting some food for the journey, and its late hours make it *the* destination for exhausted clubbers with the munchies. Sun–Thurs 4pm–midnight, Fri & Sat 4pm–6am.

Vintapperiet Brogade 37 ⓦwww.vintapperierne.dk. A cosy, friendly wine bar, set in a courtyard and offering nibbles as well as around a hundred different wines; it's also the only place in town to get that much-needed midday shot of absinthe. Mon–Fri 11am–5.30pm, Sat 10am–3pm.

Egeskov Slot

"There are as many windows as there are days in a year, as many doors as weeks, as many chimneys as months and as many corners as seasons. The gardens are among the largest and finest in Funen".

H.C. Andersen on Egeskov

Some 12km north of Svendborg, the Renaissance castle of **Egeskov Slot** (daily: July 10am–7pm; May–June & Aug–Sept 10am–5pm; 150kr, grounds only 95kr; ⓦwww.egeskov.dk) is easily one of the best-preserved in Denmark, with a facade of perfectly preserved embrasures, pointy turrets and concealed machicolations (openings in the parapet from which stones or burning objects could be dropped on attackers) plus a 5m-deep moat, all of which poignantly evoke its importance as a defensive fortification during its heyday. Egeskov was built in 1554 in the middle of a lake by one Frands Brockenhuus, who felled an entire forest (hence the name, "Oak Forest Castle") to underlay its foundations, and its double walls are thick enough to hold hidden staircases and deep wells that ensured ample water supply in event of a siege. The imposing entrance doors lead to an array of rooms displaying a frightening armoury of daggers and swords, some of which probably felled the myriad lions, tigers and cheetahs whose hides and heads now hang on the walls; other rooms hold pristine examples of Louis XVI chests and secretary desks, while upstairs, there's a music room, assorted galleries with more examples of over-the-top aristocratic wealth, and a lavish guestroom containing two Sumatran busts of slaves brought back from the field as trophies. Less spectacular is the array of smaller museums in other buildings, which include displays on agriculture, horse-drawn vehicles and motorbikes, a grocers' museum and, best of all, the **Egeskov Veteranmuseum**, which has some three hundred antique cars and aircraft.

The castle's grandeur is better appreciated, however, from the beautifully manicured **grounds**, which boast an intricate bamboo maze designed by Danish philosopher-poet Peit Hein as well as award-winning rose and fuchsia

△ Egeskov Slot

gardens, an aviary and a romantic water garden surrounded by azaleas and rhododendrons. It'd be no big chore to spend an entire day lounging around here, but bear in mind that the grounds are packed with visitors during high season. On Wednesdays in July the castle and gardens remain open until 11pm, when the grounds come alive with cannons, open-fire barbecues and fireworks. If you want to stay overnight, there's a free campsite (no facilities) next to the car park. The castle is just twenty minutes from Fåborg by bus #920, or ten minutes by train from Svendborg, then a short walk or ride on bus #920.

Fåborg and around

An alternative base for exploring the south Funen coast, **FÅBORG** is likeably small and sedate, rarely as overwhelmed by holidaymakers as Svendborg and with equally good connections to the archipelago (ferries sail to Søby on Ærø, and to Bjørnø, Lyø and Avernakø; see p.244). The town was established in 1229 as a gift from King Valdemar to his daughter-in-law, Eleonore of Portugal, but was later levelled by a succession of fires, in 1672, 1715 and 1728, during which hundreds of the original wooden houses were destroyed. Fortunately, many of them were rebuilt in the same style, accounting for the lovely half-timbered homes which still grace the town's narrow, cobbled roads; of these, the buildings on Grønnegade, itself once *grønne* ("green") with trees, are in the best condition. Industry thrived around Fåborg in the 1960s, with an active mill and ironworks, but these days the main source of income is the large number of Danish tourists who come here to experience a bit of coastal village life. As such, Fåborg is worth a visit on the merit of its aesthetic charm alone, though it also holds an engaging museum of twentieth-century Danish art – and on a clear summer evening, the atmospheric marina is a great place from which to watch the (often breathtaking) sunset over the southwestern edge of the Fåborg fjord.

The best place to start exploring is the pedestrianized shopping street of Østergade, which threads west all the way to the Torvet, Fåborg's main square, at the centre of which is a bronze reproduction of Kai Nielsen's *Ymerbrønd* **statue** – the sandstone original is housed in the Fåborg Museum. From here, it's a few metres east to the numerous picturesque rows of houses along Adelgade and Tårngade, both of which branch just off the Torvet; those at Tårngade 6 and 8 have remained virtually untouched since the 1715 fire, while on Adelgade, nos.19 and 21 are part-built with stones from the church of Skt Nicolai, which was partially dismantled in 1600. At the eastern end of this block, the chunky yellow **Klokketårnet** (mid-June to Aug Mon–Fri 11am–4.15pm, Sat & Sun 10am–1pm; 10kr) is all that remains of Skt Nicolai – you can climb the spire for some good views around the town and harbour. Immediately west of the Torvet, **Holkegade** once fed the town from its *holk* ("well"), and the building at no.3 functioned as the local distillery until an explosion in 1728 reduced it to mere cinders, along with nineteen other homes on the block. The building at no.1 has served variously as a trading post, butcher and a telephone exchange, and now holds **Den Gamle Gård** (April to mid-May Sat & Sun 11am–3pm; mid-May to Oct daily 10.30am–4.30pm; 30kr), a largely missable collection of porcelain dishes and nineteenth-century furniture that's notable only for the dainty photo of H.C. Andersen's would-be girlfriend Riborg Voigt.

Folksy housewares aside, the town's main attraction is east of here in the shape of the **Fåborg Museum** (April–Oct daily 10am–4pm; Nov–March Tues–Sun 11am–3pm; 40kr; ⑩www.faaborgmuseum.dk), Grønnegade 75, which showcases an impressive collection of richly coloured landscapes by most of the

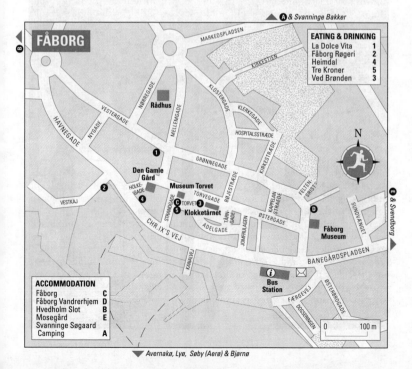

better-known artists of the Funen School (see p.210). The collection is well laid out in small, themed rooms – landscapes, portraits, animals, flowers and so on. From the foyer, which holds Kai Nielsen's larger-than-lifesize marble statue of local patron and museum founder Mads Rasmussen, the first gallery contains nearly all of the School's showcase works: Johannes Larsen's *April Shower* (1907), Peter Hansen's *Ploughman Turns* (1902), and Fritz Syberg's romantic *Evening Games in Svanninge Hills* (1900), the latter a brash and stunning depiction of fin-de-siècle social interaction. All three artists were closely mentored by their teacher, Kristian Zahrtmann, whose vaguely impressionistic *Adam and Eve in the Garden of Eden* (in the same room) is a good example of his characteristically vibrant use of colour juxtaposed with muted fore- and backgrounds, a style which clearly inspired many of his disciples. The rest of the museum is a similar – if less distinguished – collection of landscapes and portraits, sculptures and sketches, but it's worth heading to the back room to see the original of Kai Nielsen's *Ymerbrønd*, a sandstone likeness of Norse giant Ymer suckling from the udder of a cow, with both animal and human anatomy in full view – legend has it that the milk gave Ymer enough strength to create the world and all of mankind. Though it seems fairly tame these days, the statue caused uproar when it was first unveiled at the Torvet in 1913.

The waters around Fåborg offer a few decent **beaches**, though the sand isn't nearly as alluring as on some of the islands off the coast here. Nearest is the

△ Thatched house, Fåborg

deep-watered Klinten Strand, not terribly big but only 1.5km from the town centre; to get here, follow Langelinie along the coast from the harbour or take bus #930 or #962 towards Svendborg and get out at the *Danland Hotel*, from which it's a short walk. North of town, the lovely hilly area of **Svanninge Bakker** offers some of south Funen's best opportunities to get close to nature, with well-marked bicycle and walking paths threading past meadows, streams and lakes. The hills begin just 3km north of Fåborg: take bus #360 or #961, or just walk 3km north along Odensevej, the main road towards Odense.

Practicalities

Buses from Nyborg, Odense and Svendborg arrive at the bus station on Banegårdspladsen, where there's also a friendly and helpful **tourist office** (☎62 61 07 07, ⊛www.visitfaaborg.dk; May–Sept Mon–Sat 9am–5pm, plus June & July Sun 10am–3pm; Oct–April Mon–Fri 10am–4.30pm, Sat 10am–2pm); staff can help with a list of inexpensive private rooms (❸, plus 25kr booking fee), and sell DSB train and bus tickets. **Ferries** to Søby (Ærø), Bjørnø, Lyø and Avernakø leave from a small quay between the tourist office and the central marina.

Accommodation options in and around town run the gamut from austere to extravagant, while Fåborg's coastal location means there's a good selection of fish **restaurants**, as well as a few places offering solid Italian and continental fare, and a handful of cheaper cafés and late-night kebab and pizza joints. If you're saving your kroner, you can stock up on provisions at the Super Brugsen or Føtex markets, which are next to each other on Mellemgade, near the bus station.

Accommodation

Fåborg Vandrerhjem Grønnegade 71–73 ☎62 61 12 03, ⊛www.danhostel.dk/faaborg. Right next to the town museum, this is one of the country's most picturesque youth hostels. The simple, modern dorms (150kr) and doubles with shared bath (❷) occupy two old-fashioned wooden buildings that date back to the late nineteenth century, but feel much older. April–Oct.

Hotel Fåborg Torvet 13–15 ☎62 61 02 45, ⊛www.hotelfaaborg.dk. This lovely old brick building has been open as a hotel for nearly a century, and has loads of fin-de-siècle class to prove it. Rooms are classy and have firm, comfy beds. ❻

Hotel Mosegård Nabgyden 31 ☎62 61 56 91, ⊛www.hotelmosegaard.dk. Around 6km southeast of town and 200m from the water, this country-styled mid-range hotel offers simple, bright rooms hung with pretty landscape paintings; the shared-bath singles (❸) make it a great bargain if you're on your own. To get here, take bus #930 towards Svendborg, get off at Nabgyden, then walk 2km towards the water. ❺

Hvedholm Slot ☎63 60 10 20, ⊛www .royalclassic.dk. This eighteenth-century estate, 5km outside of town in Horne, offers some lavish, castle-style opulence. Each of the rooms will blow your socks off, boasting over-the-top furnishings that include four-poster beds, crystal chandeliers and red silk-upholstered settees. ❼

Svanninge Søgaard Camping ☎62 61 77 94, ⊛www.svanningecamping.dk. This medium-sized site is splayed out on a verdant nineteenth-century farming estate a half mile north of town and offers small cabins (❸).

Restaurants and bars

La Dolce Vita Mellemgade 11A ☎62 61 13 99. The laid-back, rustic feel in this inexpensive, Italian-run place makes it an enjoyable departure from the sometimes cloying nature of traditional Danish restaurants. Selections from the sizeable pizza and pasta menu cost around 85kr. Daily 1–3pm & 5–9.30pm.

Fåborg Røgeri Vestkaj 3 ☎62 61 42 32. Great for summer lunches, this harbourside smokehouse serves several dozen inexpensive smoked-fish dishes, which you can enjoy either on wooden picnic tables out front or take with you on the road in vacuum-packed bags. July–Aug daily 10am–9pm, April–June & Sept Thurs–Sun.

Heimdal Havnegade 12. A charming bar with lots of interior wood in an excellent setting looking out over the harbour. Mon–Fri 10am–2am, Sat & Sun 10am–3am.

Tre Kroner Strandgade 1 ☎62 61 01 50, ⊛www.tre-kroner.dk. This corner restaurant has been serving patrons since 1821, and today its lively owner and musically themed interior ensure it retains a very rustic atmosphere. There are good Danish smørrebrød plates, but you're better off ordering the excellent house speciality, *æggekage* (75kr). Summer daily 11am–10pm; winter Mon–Wed 11am–6pm, Thurs & Fri 11am–10pm, Sat & Sun 11am–4pm.

Ved Brønden Torvet 5 ⓣ 62 61 11 35, ⓦ www .ved-bronden.dk. This refined restaurant features meticulous wooden furnishings and specialises in fairly priced seafood plates like baked salmon with lobster sauce (140kr). Daily 11am–10pm.

The South Funen archipelago

With quaint fishing villages, rolling hills and fine sandy beaches (and their bridge and ferry links to the mainland), the dozen-odd islands that lie off Funen's craggy southern coastline have long been popular destinations for day- or weekend trips spent walking or cycling through beautiful and unspoilt countryside. Closest to Svendborg is **Tåsinge**: peaceful, grassy and largely undeveloped except for the wonderful old estate of Valdemars Slot. It's connected by road bridge to **Langeland**, greener and with a lot more opportunity for good hiking or biking the rolling hills. Reachable via ferries from Langeland, Svendborg and Fåborg, **Ærø** is the prettiest of the southern islands and well worth the effort for its ancient burial sites, abundant stretches of sandy beach, traditional farms and, in the principal town of **Ærøskøbing**, a peach of a medieval merchants' town. Off the north coast of Ærø are the six small islands of **Bjørnø**, **Lyø**, **Avernakø**, **Drejø**, **Skarø** and **Hjortø** – flat, grassy places, each with fewer than a hundred inhabitants and all with plenty of idyllic peace and quiet. There are very basic camping facilities on each of the islands, though if you want proper **accommodation**, contact the tourist office in Fåborg (see p.231), which can arrange stays with local families for around 150kr per person per night.

Tåsinge

Connected to mainland Funen by a bridge over to Svendborg, **TÅSINGE** is peaceful, grassy and largely undeveloped. Aside from walking or biking around the pleasant countryside however, the only draw is located just outside the island's main town of **TROENSE**, clustered around a short stretch of road that runs between the seafront and a series of austere but lovable half-timbered thatched houses. Apart from the small and eminently missable art gallery and the equally unenthralling **Søfartssamlingerne** (Maritime Museum; May–Sept Tues–Sun 10am–5pm, Oct–April Tues–Fri 3–5pm; 25kr; ⓦ www.soefartsmuseum.dk), there's not much going on here, and you'd be well advised to head along the road for a kilometre or so to **Valdemars Slot** (April & Oct Sat & Sun 10am–5pm; May–June & Aug daily 10am–5pm; July daily 10am–6pm; Sept Tues–Sun 10am–5pm; 65kr slot, 100kr for all museums; ⓦ www.valdemarsslot.dk), one of the crown jewels of Denmark's aristocratic landed estates and manor houses. With twenty-one opulently furnished rooms, it's the largest private home in Denmark and a must-see on any trip to southern Funen. Built by master architect Hans van Stenwinkel, the castle was commissioned in 1644 by King Christian IV – renowned for his palatial constructions all over Denmark – as a residential estate for his son, Christian Valdemar, but these paternal hopes were dashed when Valdemar died in battle in Poland in 1656. In 1678, the castle and surrounding land were bestowed upon Admiral Niels Juel in payment for his miraculous victory over Sweden in the battle of Køge Bay (see p.155). Valdemars is still owned by his descendants, and uniquely, it never quite feels

Denmark's Romeo and Juliet

Residents of southern Funen (and Tåsinge in particular) are especially proud of the story behind Denmark's own Romeo and Juliet, circus-hand **Elvira Madigan** and Swedish army officer **Sixten Sparre**. A tightrope walker in her father's travelling circus, Danish-born Madigan caught the eye of Sixten Sparre, a young officer in the Swedish cavalry, as he watched one of her shows. The two fell deeply in love and, despite Madigan's overprotective family (who weren't very keen on her marrying a Swede), succeeded in exchanging several love letters in which they planned their mutual escape, with Sparre planning to go AWOL from his regiment and Madigan severing ties with her family. During a performance on June 20, 1889, they made their escape, travelling through Sweden to Copenhagen and boarding a train for the Funen coast. A month later, after a romantic eight-day sojourn at the *Hotel Svendborg*, the couple fled, hotel bill unpaid, to say their last words at the Bregninge church, then marched off to the nearby Nørreskoven forest with a bottle of wine, a picnic basket and Sparre's revolver. Their bodies were found in the woods four days later, a bullet wound to each of their temples, the gun still in Sparre's hand. Whether it was a bittersweet dual suicide by two star-crossed lovers or a murder/suicide by a despondent and destitute Sparre will never be known, but such supposition has only added to the mythology that surrounds their affair. Their story has become a well-known folk tale throughout Scandinavia, and has inspired no fewer than three films, the most memorable of which is Bo Widerberg's 1967 *Elvira Madigan*. Today, the couple rest side by side in the church graveyard at Landet, 3km south of Bregninge.

like a public museum: display cases, cordoning barrier ropes and in-room guards have pretty much been done away with, allowing you to stroll freely among the living spaces and imagine what it might be like to actually live in such a palatial home. All the rooms are stunning in their own right, though be sure to admire the Juel Room, which holds Niels Juel's massive sea chest, in which he stored his most prized military uniforms. The upstairs attic rooms hold an alarming number of stuffed animals, from water buck to wild boar, and a more interesting **ethnographic** collection flaunting the spoils of empire, largely in the form of southern African ritual masks and totems. Outside the main building, two separate wings hold the decent **Museum for Lystsejlads** (Yachting Museum; same hours; 40kr; ⓦwww.lystsejlads .dk), which has a number of finely crafted full-size and scale models of wooden yachts and assorted accoutrements, and the **Legetøjsmuseet** (Toy Museum; same hours; 40kr), which holds a collection of several thousand toys, some dating back to the late nineteenth century. The estate also offers the island's best **eating**: you can snack at the *Æblehaven Kiosk* just outside the castle or go for a full-on meal at the exclusive *Restaurant Valdemars Slot* in the vaulted stone cellars; it's worth timing your trip to coincide with their lunch buffet (summer daily 10am–4pm; winter Tues–Sun 11.30am–2.30pm; 165kr), loaded with Funen delicacies, though the pricey dinner service (Thurs–Sat 6–10pm) is also good.

Once you've had your fill of estate gazing, continue on through the slot's grounds to Nørreskovvej, which leads out to the town of **BREGNINGE**, unremarkable save for the **Tåsinge Museum** (June–Aug daily 10am–5pm; 40kr; ⓦwww.taasinge-museum.dk), a place of mild appeal less for its folkloric collections of agricultural artefacts and nineteenth-century furnishings than for its detailed exhibit on one of Denmark's most beloved and notorious couples, **Sixten Sparre** and **Elvira Madigan** (see box above).

Practicalities

Travelling overland from Svendborg, the only public transport is city **bus** #200 (15kr), which runs to Troense, a ten-minute walk to Valdemars Slot; the Helge **ferry** (see p.226) from Svendborg docks at both Troense and Valdemars Slot. As Tåsinge itself has no **tourist office**, the office in Svendborg (see p.224) deals with enquiries concerning the island. Accommodation options are rather scant, though there are four decent **campsites**: the pick of them is *Vindebyøre Camping* (☎62 22 54 25, ⓦwww.vindebyoere.dk), with a smashing location on the north coast offering access to a beautiful beach, and a number of modern two-person cabins (late June to mid-Aug ❹, rest of the year ❶). The Helge steamer (see p.226) also stops right here. Closer to Troense, 1.5km south of the bridge at Sundbrovej 19, *Carlsberg Camping* (☎62 22 53 84, ⓦwww.carlsberg-camping .dk) is a bit less appealing as it lacks the beachfront, but has cute wooden cabins (❷). The island has just one **hotel**, the *Troense* (☎62 22 54 12, ⓦwww.hotel troense.dk; ❻), Strandgade 5, whose rather boring room interiors are at least offset by their excellent views across the water. On the way into town from the bridge, the tiny thatched home rented out by Erling Larsen (☎62 22 50 03, ⓦwww.ferielejlighed-troense.dk; ❺), Krogvej 4, is a much more bucolic alternative, with a bright and comfy bedroom, a spacious living space, full kitchen and a picnic table out front. The price includes a small breakfast, and there's also a room (❷) for singles in a separate house.

Langeland

The largest of Funen's southern islands, long, thin and fertile **Langeland** lies just off Funen's southeast coast, to which it's connected by road bridge. Langeland is 60km long but only 10km in width at its widest point, and islanders have historically established most of their settlements inland: the climate in the interior is more agreeable and the land drier, making building construction easier and more secure, with coastal forests providing protection from the elements. With several good restaurants, Langeland's capital, **Rudkøbing**, is a good place to visit before exploring the green landscape to the north and south, most easily accessible if you have your own transport. **Cycling** is a perfect way to get around, allowing you to visit the sights – most notably the sculpture gardens of the thirteenth-century **Tranekær Slot** – at your leisure. Southern Langeland holds some interesting out-of-the-way nature spots and archeological finds, but the majority of visitors come to the island for sun, surf and sand. The **beaches** at the southern tip regularly rank in Denmark's top ten, though the north has its share too, and a few excellent camping sites around the island round out the possibilities for lovers of the outdoors.

Arrival and getting around

Frequent **buses** (#910, 37kr) make the half-hour journey from Svendborg to Rudkøbing, dropping you off ten minutes' walk from the town centre at the local school. From here, buses run to all the island's main sites roughly once per hour. Fares are priced by zone: a ticket from Rudkøbing to Tranekær, for example, costs 30kr, while a ride from Rudkøbing to Bagenkop, in the far south, costs 44kr. That said, the best way to get around is either private car or bicycle (see p.236 for rental information). Several of the island's harbour towns (primarily Rudkøbing and Spodsbjerg) have **ferry** services to mainland Denmark, including Ærø (see p.239), Lolland (see p.171) and Omø on Zealand; Rudkøbing tourist office can give specific schedule information. If you plan on

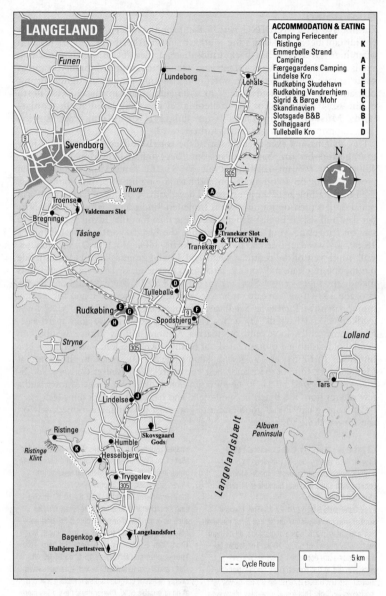

LANGELAND

ACCOMMODATION & EATING

Camping Feriecenter Ristinge	**K**
Emmerbølle Strand Camping	**A**
Færgegardens Camping	**F**
Lindelse Kro	**J**
Rudkøbing Skudehavn	**E**
Rudkøbing Vandrerhjem	**H**
Sigrid & Børge Mohr	**C**
Skandinavien	**G**
Slotsgade B&B	**B**
Solhøjgaard	**I**
Tullebølle Kro	**D**

Funen

Lundeborg

Lohals

Svendborg

Thurø

Troense

Valdemars Slot

Bregninge

Tåsinge

305

Tranekær Slot & TICKON Park

Tranekær

Tullebølle

Rudkøbing

Spodsbjerg

Strynø

Lolland

305

Tars

Lindelse

Langelandsbælt

Ristinge

Albuen Peninsula

Humble

Skovsgaard Gods

Ristinge Klint

Hesselbjerg

Tryggelev

305

Bagenkop

Langelandsfort

Hulbjerg Jættestven

--- Cycle Route

0   5 km

N

visiting during the last weekend in July, book accommodation early, as this is when the annual **Langelands Festival** takes place (ⓦ www.llf.dk). Known as Denmark's largest garden party, this music festival draws close to 30,000 visitors and hosts primarily Scandinavian groups alongside a few international acts – recent years have featured artists such as Runrig, Robin Gibb of the Bee Gees and Sweden's Lisa Ekdahl.

Rudkøbing

Diminutive **RUDKØBING** sits on Langeland's western coast, more or less equidistant between island's the southern and northern tips. There's little on offer here save for a laid-back atmosphere, a pleasant fishing harbour and the bulk of the island's restaurants and accommodation – though you might want to take a look at the renovated old buildings pinned up tightly against one another along Smedegade, Vinkældergade and Ramsherred, just north of the town's **church**, or the archeological relics displayed at the **Lange-lands Museum** (Mon–Thurs 10am–4pm, Fri 10am–1pm; 25kr; ⓦwww .langelandsmuseum.dk), at Jens Winthersvej 12.

The obliging and ever-friendly staff at the **tourist office**, Torvet 5 (mid-June to Aug Mon–Fri 9am–5pm, Sat 9am–3pm; Sept to mid-June Mon–Fri 9.30am–4.30pm, Sat 9.30am–12.30pm; ☏62 51 35 05, ⓦwww.langeland.dk), can provide advice on accommodation and have a long list of private rooms across the island starting at 125kr per person. They also have details of Langeland's bike rental outlets (best option in town is Lapletten, Endredet 1, which charges 50kr per day) and sell an English-language cycling map for 30kr. If you're planning to stay on Langeland, your cheapest option is the island's **youth hostel** (☏62 51 18 30, ⓦwww.danhostel.dk/rudkobing; dorms 140kr, doubles ❸), ten minutes' walk southwest of the centre at Engdraget 11; the grounds are a tad ramshackle but the rooms clean, and you can pitch tents on the grassy lawn for 50kr. **Hotels** include the super-central *Skandinavien* (☏77 78 59 14, ⓦwww.skanhotel.dk; ❻), Brogade 13, whose agreeable rooms look onto the Gåsetorvet; and the slightly more expensive *Rudkøbing Skudehavn*, Havnegade 21 (☏62 51 46 00, ⓦwww .rudkobingskudehavn.dk; ❻), with a large indoor pool and spacious apartment-like rooms which look onto the marina. A more homely choice are the two central old-fashioned rooms rented out by the town's resident jeweller, Inge-Lise Jørgensen (☏62 51 11 19, ⓔvald_j@post.tele.dk; ❸), smack in the centre at Østergade 34. One of the island's best **campsites**, *Færgegårdens Camping*, Spods-bjergvej 335 (☏62 50 11 36, ⓦwww.spodsbjerg.dk), is 9km east of town and a few metres from the beach in Spodsbjerg, and has inexpensive cabins (❷).

Rudkøbing has several good places to **eat**, most of which are immediately off the Torvet, along Østergade.

Cafés and restaurants

City Grillen Østergade 53. The place to go for a quick *pølse*, burger or freshly made sandwich packed with salad and any number of fillings. Mon–Sat 10am–9pm.

Efes Østergade 5 ☏62 51 22 23. This friendly, Kurdish-run corner restaurant serves a full menu of fish and chips, pizza, pasta and salads, all of them reasonably priced, at under 100kr. The tables by the windows are especially good for people-watching out to the Torvet. Daily noon–10pm.

Pichardt's Bystræde 2 ☏62 53 33 53, ⓦwww .housepichardt.dk. This friendly, homely place with an in-house delicatessen is Langeland's newest restaurant, and one of its best. The fusion menu

(mains 160kr–200kr) includes dishes such as fried fillet of mullet with apple compote or a divine quail breast with foie gras and steamed vegetables. Mon–Sat 11.30am–9.30pm.

Slagterpigerne Torvet 6 ☏62 51 10 72. Rudkø-bing's butcher's shop offers take-away snacks such as *smørrebrød* or scrumptious fish and pork *frikadeller* (meatballs) as well as fresh meat. Mon–Thurs 9am–5.30pm, Fri 9am–6pm, Sat 8am–1pm.

Thummelumsen Østergade 15 ☏63 51 00 43. This casual restaurant with tables out front serves twenty different burgers and sandwiches, starting at an affordable 50kr. Dinner dishes are a tad more put-together, with chicken or veal mains starting at 135kr. Mon–Thurs 11am–9pm, Sun 5–9pm.

Tranekær slot and northern Langeland

North of Rudkøbing, farmland and sandy beaches are punctuated only by the occasional village. Langeland's flat topography means that it's become very

△ TICKON Park sculpture

popular amongst cyclists, especially in the far north, where patches of forest break up the occasionally monotonous landscape. The beaches up here are good as well, with the sandbars and shallow waters along the western coast particularly popular with families; best plan is to rent a bike in Rudkøbing and explore at your leisure. Your first stop might be the lovely beach at Stengade, 6km north of Rudkøbing and just east of the roadside town of **TULLEBØLLE** (follow the Stengade Skovvej); dense conifers run all the way to the seashore, and you can swim from thin patches of grassy sand sheltered by towering beech trees. Tullebølle itself has a charming inn, the *Tullebølle Kro* (☎62 50 13 25; Ⓦwww .tulleboellekro.dk) whose restaurant (Mon–Sat 11.30am-8pm) serves traditional Funen standbys like grilled salmon steamed in white wine sauce, and has a particularly large fixed-price lunch for 128kr. They also have small **rooms** upstairs with shared bath (❹). North of Tullebølle, it's 10km along the main road to the village of **Tranekær** and northern Langeland's prime destination: the fairytale thirteenth-century manor house of **Tranekær Slot**, a gorgeous fire-engine red house that maintains its original ramparts, spire, moats and stables, but which is sadly closed to visitors. Other than viewing the manor's magnificent exterior, the real draw here is the surrounding land, occupied by the beautiful **TICKON Park** art and nature centre (June to mid-Sept Mon–Fri 10am–5pm, Sun 1–5pm; 25kr), whose open parkland is dotted with innovative outdoor sculptures made by international artists from natural materials. It's a perfect place for a picnic before rambling around the grounds to admire the artworks or take in the **museums** (same hours; 25kr each): in front of the manor, there's a collection of thousands of kitschy knick-knacks from tourist sights all over the world; the old water mill just opposite has several exhibits covering the history of Tranekær village and the *slot*; while 1km further north on the main road, there's a refurbished **windmill** where, given enough of a breeze, you can see corn being ground. Given the pretty rural surroundings, the Tranekær area is also a great place to try out some of Langeland's popular **bed and breakfast** establishments. Of these, *Slotsgade Bed & Breakfast* (☎62 55

23 25, ⓦwww.slotsgade-bedandbreakfast.dk; ❹) is the most idyllic, set within a pondside annexe just next to the Tranekær Slot. A few kilometres south of here, in a former vicarage just opposite Tranekær town church at Slotsgade 8, Sigrid and Børge Mohr (☎58 35 28 02, ⓔfirmasmohr@post.tele.dk; ❹) rent out several first-class, spacious shared-bath rooms with great landscape views and a large terrace outside. If you're looking to rough it a bit more, head a few kilometres northwest of Tranekær to **Emmerbølle**, where the beachfront *Emmerbølle Strand Camping* (☎62 59 12 26, ⓦwww.emmerbolle.dk), Emmer-bøllevej 24, is easily the best **campsite** on the island, sporting a pool, private beach and a dozen or so four-person cabins (800kr).

North of here, the landscape is largely unremarkable; the island narrows and the coastal forest edges in to take over, providing for a few stretches of lovely road sheltered by the conifers. Continue on to the northernmost tip where Hov Nordstrand beach, in clear weather at least, has excellent views across the Sound to the Storebælt bridge and is a decent place for a quick dip in the blue waters.

Southern Langeland

Southern Langeland is quite a bit more hilly than the north – the local names for the landscape hereabouts are *hætbakke* ("hat hills") and *jomfrubryste* ("virgin breasts") – and holds the island's best beaches as well as a few attractions away from the coast – though as many of the sights are off the main 305 road, having your own transportation is essential if you want to explore. Some 10km south of Rudkøbing, the first reason to turn off the 305 (at the road-side town of Lindelse) is **Skovsgaard Gods** agricultural centre (Mon–Fri 10am–5pm, Sun 11am–5pm, plus Sat 11am–5pm in summer; museum 40kr), located 3km east of Lindelse at Kågårdsvej 12. Run by the Danish Nature Conservancy, the grounds of this post-Renaissance estate contain a museum dedicated to horse-drawn carriages, a renovated windmill, a charming café and 10km of well-kept **trails** that lead through forest and meadow and along the shores of lakes; five pamphlets, available at the entrance, have detailed route maps, though the two-hour guided walks (late June to mid-Aug daily 1pm; in Danish only) are equally enjoyable. After working up an appetite on a hike, you might fancy a meal at the *Lindelse Kro* (☎62 57 24 03, ⓦwww .sikcenter.dk/lindelse-kro), back in Lindelse – their speciality, *æggekage* (98kr), has been made here for over two hundred years, and the classically designed interior and delicious upscale menu make it one of the best **restau-rants** on Langeland; they also have several tidy rooms for rent (❻). If you want to stay on the coast, head just north to Lindelse Nor, where *Solhøjgaard* (☎62 51 22 50, ⓦwww.langeland-a.dk; ❷), Klæsøvej 9, is a small farmhouse with several spacious, modern rooms, as well as a private bathing jetty for swimming, kayaking and rowing in the farm's dinghy.

A few minutes south of here, the hamlet of **HUMBLE** is home to a bookshop, bakery, grocery store and the island's largest church, a pretty late-Romantic brick structure with a fancy mid-nineteenth century altarpiece – making it the largest settlement on southern Langeland, and a good place to stock up on provisions before heading out to the nearby beaches, which are Langeland's best. Of the numerous sandy swathes here, ideal for sunbathing, paddling and swimming, the finest is just west at **Ristinge**, with a wide expanse of sand that's perfect for lazing about; a kiosk here sells ice-creams and refreshments, and it's also a great vantage point from which to view the awe-inspiring cliffs at **Ristinge Klint**, which you can reach via a twenty-minute walk north of the beach. To access both the beach and cliff follow the road to the Ristinge church and turn left onto the small path that reaches the coast; just before you arrive at the boarded walk over the dunes a path leads along the clifftop. If you want to stay in the area, there's the *Camping & Feriecenter Ristinge* (☎62 57 13 29, ⓦwww.ristinge.dk) which has tent pitches, a swimming pool, a café and four-person cabins (450kr).

Another 6km south on the 305, you'll find further respite from beachlife at **BAGENKOP**, a quiet, relatively modern village that revolves around the fishing industry – the lively harbour is appropriately chock-full of trawlers, and you can sample the catch of the day at *Fiski* (Tues–Sat 10am–4pm), a simple kiosk just opposite the entrance to the harbour at Strandgade 4, which sells inexpensive smoked-fish burgers and shrimp salads which you can eat sitting on a bench whilst soaking up the salty atmosphere.

If you fancy something entirely different to beaches and nature, you can head south along the 305 to the **Langelandsfort**, Vognsbjergvej 4b (mid-May to Oct Mon–Fri 10am–5pm, Sun 11am–5pm, plus July & Aug Sat 11am–5pm; 50kr; ⓦwww.langelandsmuseum.dk), a military compound that remained well-hidden for years from nearly everyone. Allegedly, Russian ships spotted off the Langeland coast by the fort's soldiers first alerted President Kennedy to the gravity of the Soviet threat, leading to the Cuban missile crisis; a film inside explains the ordeal. The museum gives an excellent sense of how paranoid the West was about the Russians for so many years; among the various bunkers, uniforms and military paraphernalia, look out for the wooden mine-sweeper and a large-scale submarine – both in use by the Danish military until 2004.

Ærø

Reachable by ferries from Fåborg, Svendborg or Rudkøbing, the pretty island of **ÆRØ** (pronounced AIH-ruh) offers a little more variety than Langeland as well as several charming harbourside villages. The radiant **Ærøskøbing** boasts narrow, cobbled streets lined with exquisitely maintained old timbered and tiled buildings, while the quieter **Marstal** holds an impressive maritime museum. To the south, **Rise Mark** and **Store Rise** are the gateway to some lovely Baltic beaches; the latter is also the home of the world's largest collection of solar panels (around four million); these, alongside the towering wind turbines hereabouts, stand testament to the islanders' attempts to become completely energy self-sufficient. Ærø has become a model for **renewable energy** generation, and looks set to meet its target of using wind and solar power to generate eighty to one hundred percent of its energy by 2008.

Arrival and getting around

Ærø has three separate ferry terminals in each of the major towns. Ærøfærgerne (☎62 52 40 00, ⓦwww.aeroe-ferry.dk) operates **ferries** 5–6 times daily from Svendborg to Ærøskøbing, from Fåborg and Mommark in Jutland to Søby, and from Rudkjøbing in Langeland to Marstal. Tickets for all the routes are sold only on board, and cost 89kr one-way, 145kr return (vehicles 190kr, bikes 25kr, both one-way). Hourly **buses** traverse the island between Søby in the west and Marstal in the east, stopping at Ærøskøbing and passing the outskirts of Store Rise. An unlimited day-pass is available for 70kr, though it's not really necessary unless you plan on trying to cover all the sights on the island in one day – an ill-advised endeavour in any case. Given the more or less linear route of the bus, the best way to see the island is by bike – it's only 35km from the Søby lighthouse on the western tip to Marstal in the east, though you'll need to pedal hard to get up some of the hills. The Ærøskøbing tourist office supplies

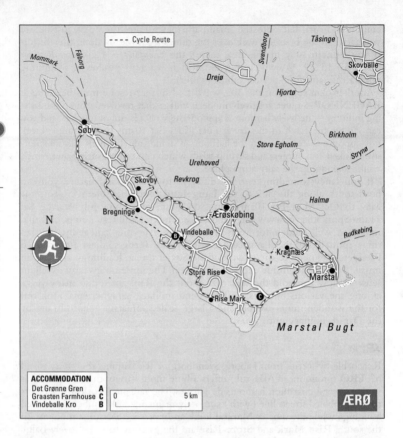

Cycle Route

Mommark

Fåborg

Svendborg

Tåsinge

Drejø

Skovballe

Hjortø

Søby

Birkholm

Store Egholm

Strynø

Urehoved

Revkrog

Skovby

Halmø

N

Bregninge

A

Æerøskøbing

Rudkøbing

B

Vindeballe

Kragnæs

Store Rise

C

Marstal

Rise Mark

Marstal Bugt

ACCOMMODATION

Det Grønne Gren	**A**
Graasten Farmhouse	**C**
Vindeballe Kro	**B**

0   5 km

ÆRØ

free bike maps to help plan your route, and **bicycles** can be rented here for 50kr a day at Pilebækkens Cykler (☎62 52 11 10), Pillebækken 11, in the BP gas station about 200m west of the main marketplace. For a more unusual tour of the island, you can hop onto one of the **aerial tours** offered by Starling Air (☎62 53 33 94, ⓦwww.starling.dk); at 100kr per person for a short flight, it's actually quite affordable.

Æerøskøbing

When passing shipping brought prosperity to Ærø in the nineteenth century, the island split into three divisions: fishermen resided in the windy western tip at Søby; the wealthy shipping magnates and captains resided in Marstal to the east; while the middle classes collected in **ÆRØSKØBING**, still one of Denmark's most idyllic harbourside towns. The locals have long campaigned for recognition and conservation of the town's fine architectural heritage, and though modernization across Denmark during the 1950s and 1960s radically changed the look and feel of many city centres, remote Ærøskøbing has been preserved. Today, its numerous **preserved** and **restored buildings** – the entire town is protected under Danish law – comprise a virtual open-air museum, illustrating the diversity of the country's architectural traditions. The typical Ærøskøbing house sports large front-protruding gables and bays, and an elongated facade that enabled division into individual dwellings, with separate entrances to the street in front and to the courtyard or garden behind. Buildings to look out for include the Prior's House from 1690, with its half-timbered front gable and Hanseatic brown and gold colours – it's now used as a vacation home by the Danish Architects Association. From here, the long and wide Vestergade slopes gently down to the sea, intersecting with the narrower Smedegade, on which a wonderful collection of old terraced houses show a marked variance in height and girth, giving some idea of the relative wealth of the original owners.

The town's architectural and social history is all beautifully described at the **Ærø Museum** (early April to late Oct Mon–Fri 10am–4pm, Sat & Sun 11am–3pm; late Oct to early April Mon–Fri 10am–1pm; 25kr, joint ticket with the Bottle Peter Museum 50kr; ⓦwww.arremus.dk), Brogade 3–5, a simple collection of maps, clothing and housewares culled from island homes. If you're looking for something a bit more unusual, head to Smedegade 22 for the **Flaske-Peters Samling** (Bottle Peter Museum; mid-June to mid-Aug daily 10am–5pm; mid-Aug to late Oct 10am–4pm, late Oct to early April Tues–Fri 1–3pm, Sat & Sun 10am–noon, early April to mid-June 10am–4pm; 25kr, joint ticket with Ærø Museum and Hammerichs Hus 60kr). The Kalundborg-born "Bottle Peter" made over seventeen hundred tiny ships-in-a-bottle throughout his lifetime, all of them meticulously done in rich colours and with amazing attention to detail, and moved here in the 1950s to open a museum to display them. His triumphs include the world's largest bottled ship, elegantly pieced together in front of a tiny, meticulously painted canvas of a Dutch harbour. Another example of the Danes' penchant for amassing various and sundry items is to be found at **Hammerichs Hus** at Gyden 22 (June to mid-Sept daily noon–4pm; 25kr), a riot of woodcarvings, furnishings and timepieces from bygone days. This "museum" is really just the home of an inveterate hoarder who travelled the world to bring back ragtag items like stuffed parrots and ceramic tiles. The low-ceilinged house itself is an interesting example of hermit-like pre-modern Danish homes, but its innards serve primarily as a testament to what can happen when you refuse to throw anything out.

Just southeast of the centre lies the town's **beach**, bordered by a public footpath lined with tall poplars and with a dozen or so tiny, brightly painted **beach huts** fronting the dunes, replete with picturesque verandas, balustrades and shutters. Given the proximity to the harbour, the sand and sea here are surprisingly clean, and the water remains shallow for several hundred metres out; another popular spot for a swim is just north of the harbour at Vesterstrand. Finally, Ærøskøbing's harbour is the jumping-off point for cruises aboard the dual-masted **schooner** *Meta*, which sails on Tuesdays between July and mid-August on two separate trips: one (departing 10am) heads to nearby Strynø island for a four-hour tour (198kr); the other leaves at 7pm for a two-hour sunset trip (138kr). You can try your skills out at the helm or help out raising the mainsail. The same tours sail from Marstal on Wednesdays. To book, ask at the tourist office or at the Maritimt Center in Svendborg (see p.226).

Practicalities

The **Ærø Turistbureau** (mid-June to Aug Mon–Fri 9am–5pm, Sat 9am–2pm, Sun 9.30am–12.30pm; Sept to mid-June Mon–Fri 9am–4pm, Sat 9am–12.30pm; ☎62 52 13 00, ⓦwww.arre.dk), Vestergade 1, is the central point for information about the entire island. Be sure to pick up a copy of the free English-language *Ærø Guide*, which lists summer nature walks (25kr) around the island run by the Ærø Nature and Energy School (☎62 52 25 60).

With numerous interesting choices, Ærøskøbing is a perfect place to **spend the night**, and the town also offers a wide selection of places to **eat**; many are often full during the summer, so it's wise to book ahead. Many of them are quite pricey, but if purse-strings are tight, you could pick up provisions at the Netto supermarket in the town centre. There are also a couple of bars, which comprise the bulk of the island's nightlife.

Accommodation

Ærøskøbing Camping Sygehusvejen 40 ☎62 52 18 54, ⓦwww.aeroecamp.dk. Appealingly situated next to Vesterstrand beach to the north of town, this pleasant campsite features two dozen cabins (❶–❷) in various shapes, sizes and colours. Open May–Sept.

Danhostel Ærøskøbing Smedevejen 15 ☎62 52 10 44, ⓦwww.danhostel.dk/aeroeskoebing. The town youth hostel offers run-of-the-mill rooms (dorms 122kr, shared-bath doubles ❷), but does have ocean views and friendly management. It's located 800m south of the ferry dock on the road to Marstal. Open April to mid-Oct.

Det Lille Hotel Smedegade 33 ☎62 52 23 00, ⓦwww.det-lille-hotel.dk. A good, solid option, with homely, bright rooms that share facilities, and a good restaurant, too. ❹

Pension Vestergade 44 Vestergade 44 ☎62 52 22 98, ⓦwww.pension-vestergade44.dk. An exquisite B&B run by a congenial Brit with eight superb, meticulously decorated rooms that share a bathroom; the gardens out back are perfect for high tea. ❻

Toldbodhus Brogade 8 ☎62 52 18 11, ⓦwww.toldbodhus.com. The four charming rooms in this lovely B&B are painstakingly furnished in a unique style based on a city in which the charming owners have lived – i.e. London (green overlooking a cobbled lane); Amsterdam (deep blue with a four-poster bed); Hong Kong (red with a view of the sea). ❻

Eating and drinking

Arrebo Værtshus Vestergade 4 ☎62 52 28 50. This lively, atmospheric bar, with lots of old maritime photos and portraits on the walls and a few chairs and tables out front, is definitely the most popular place in town, with live music – blues, jazz, country and rock – every evening during the summer. Beer is a bit cheaper (18kr for a bottle) during the day. Daily 10am–5am.

Ærøskøbing Røgeri Havnen 15F. A great place to stop when getting on or off the Svendborg ferry, this harbourside smokehouse offers outstanding fish; the smoked eel fillets (39kr) are highly recommended. Daily: May 10am–5pm; June 10am–6pm; July to late Aug 10am–8pm; late Aug to early Sept 10am–5pm.

Café Aroma Gilleballetofte 2A ☎62 52 40 02. A popular burger and fried-fish joint close to the ferry landing, that also serves salads and tapas dishes until 6pm (69kr–159kr, served). It's essentially a laid-back café, but in the evenings it fills up with dinner guests who come for the airy atmosphere. Summer daily 11am–9.30pm.

Landbogården Vestergade 54 ☎62 52 10 41. Quiet, casual restaurant offering tasty and affordable *dagens ret* dinner menus like fried fish, shellfish pasta and smoked salmon (most from 170kr), and also makes a good stop for an early evening or late-night beer. Daily 10am–late (kitchen closes 10pm).

Mumm Søndergade 12 ☎62 52 12 12. Ærøskøbing's more upscale option, this traditional-looking place is full of character and is popular amongst locals for its tasty American- and Scandinavian-style mains like veal fillet and fried salmon, starting at 150kr. Summer daily noon–2pm & 6.30–9pm; reduced hours off-season.

Marstal

At the eastern end of the island, modern **MARSTAL** doesn't feel nearly as caught in time as Ærøskøbing, and as there's decidedly less to do here, it's a good place to escape the crowds. During the nineteenth century, Marstal's harbour was one of the busiest in Denmark, and today it continues this naval tradition as home to one of Denmark's top sailing schools. The town's seafaring past is covered in immense detail at the superb **Marstal Søfartsmuseum** (Maritime Museum; May & Sept daily 10am–4pm; June & Aug daily 9am–5pm; July daily 9am–8pm; Oct–April Tues–Fri 10am–4pm, Sat 11am–3pm; 40kr; ⓦwww.marstal-maritime-museum.dk), Prinsensgade 1, whose three separate buildings detail several hundred years of nautical history via sundry trappings from ships' galleys and over two hundred large-scale model ships. The courtyard out back has a few abandoned ships for kids to climb onto and explore. Aside from the museum, the only thing to do here is visit is the local **beach**, Ærøshale, a strip of sand lined with colourful beach homes located on a small bit of land jutting out into the sea – it's about twenty minutes' walk east of the town centre.

Marstal is easily reached by bus from Ærøskøbing (or ferry from Rudkøbing in Langeland; see p.236). The town's **tourist office** (mid-June to mid-Sept daily 10am–3pm; ☏62 52 21 00, ⊛www.arre.dk) is just across from the museum at Havnegade 5. **Bikes** can be rented at Nørremark Cykelforretning, Møllevejen 77 (☏62 53 14 77; 50kr per day). **Internet** access is available at Marstal Netcafé, east of the harbour at Havnepladsen 24A (mid-June to Aug daily 10am–1pm & 4–10pm; rest of the year Thurs–Sun 3–10pm); 25kr/30min).

Most people staying here sleep on yachts or in holiday-home rentals, but there are a few budget options, including the **youth hostel** at Færgestræde 29 (☏63 52 63 58, ⊛www.danhostel.dk/marstal; April–Oct), which has dorms (122kr) and doubles (❸), and is conveniently close to the town centre and the harbour. There's also a **campsite**, *Marstal Camping* (☏63 52 63 69, ⊛www .aeroe.dk/marcamp; Easter–Oct), almost on the beach and with a handful of pricey four-person cabins (425kr) whose tiny porches have good sea views. The comfortable *Hotel Marstal* (☏62 53 13 52, ⊛www.hotelmarstal.dk; ❺), near the harbour at Dronningestræde 1A, is the nicest **hotel**, though most of its rooms, while decent in size, are painfully uninspired, and for a water or garden view you have to shell out a few hundred extra kroner.

Of the few good places to **eat** here, many are located on the cobbled main drag of Kirkestræde, though bear in mind that opening hours are severely reduced outside the tourist season. *Den Lille Café* (daily noon–9pm; kitchen closed for meals 3–6pm; ☏62 53 29 01, ⊛www.denlillecafe-marstal.dk), Kirkestræde 15, is an amicable, airy place to have a baguette or coffee, though they also serve more substantial steak meals, too (from 98kr). *Den Gamle Vingård* (daily: May & Sept 5–10pm; June–Aug 9am–10pm; ☏62 53 13 25), Skolegade 15, is nicer still, with walls crammed with memorabilia from Ærø's shipping past, and a menu of sizeable veal, pork and chicken dishes. There is also a pizzeria in the small marina's yacht club (June–Sept only). A good stop for **drinking** is the smoky *Toldbudhus* (Mon–Fri & Sun 8am–2am, Sat 8am–7pm), Prinsengade 7, with a billiards table and plenty of maritime colour. *Cottage Pub* (Sun–Thurs 6pm–5am, Fri & Sat 6pm–midnight), Strandstræde 41, is the island's resident Scottish pub, and draws locals from as far away as Søby.

The rest of the island

The rest of Ærø's towns are less remarkable than Ærøskøbing and Marstal, with a good deal less bustle as well. In the northwest, **Søby** has little going for it other than the waning fishing industry centred around the small harbour, though if you have a bike you'd do well to head out to the pretty Skjoldnæs **lighthouse** (summer daily 7am–7pm) at the far northwestern tip of the island, 5km from the ferry terminal, which affords some lovely views if you climb to the top. If you have to kill time waiting for a boat to Fåborg (see p.228), the terrace at *Arthur's Café*, wedged between the ferry dock and passenger marina, makes a nice place for a snack on a sunny day. South of Ærøskøbing, via Store Rise, the town of **Rise Mark** offers access to what are far and away Ærø's nicest **beaches**, where deep waters are fronted by vast swathes of chalky sand with windmills towering in the distance. Bus services from Ærøskøbing and Marstal drop you off several kilometres from the sand, so you're much better off coming by bike. The rest of the island is speckled with fine **inns** (*kros*) and working farms, the best of which are *Graasten Farmhouse* (☏62 52 24 25, ⊛www.graastenfarmb-b.com; ❹), Østermarksvej

20 in Lindsbjerg, with classy and colourful rooms; the handsome, year-round *Vindeballe Kro* (☎62 52 16 13 ⓔvindeballekro@mail.dk; ❻),Vindeballevej 1 in Vindeballe, which has quite simple rooms, with and without private bath, and a good restaurant (try the seasoned, pan-fried eel) and bar. In Bregninge, there's *Det Grønne Gren* (☎62 58 20 45, ⓦwww.dengronnegren.dk; ❺), Vester Bregninge 17, whose five newly renovated rooms are a bit cramped but adequate enough.

❹ Bjørnø, Lyø and Avernakø

Just outside the entrance to the Fåborg Fjord, and reachable by ferry from Fåborg itself, **Bjørnø**, **Lyø** and **Avernakø** are the most westerly of the archipelago's inhabited islands, and offer the chance to explore some of Denmark's remote parts on foot or by bicycle (the latter best hired at the Fåborg tourist office – see p.231). All three islands are crisscrossed by walking paths that lead from the towns out into the countryside and to the small, stony beaches (those on the west coast are the best for bathing)

Of the three islets, **BJØRNØ** (Bear Island) is the closest to Fåborg and is also the smallest: in fact, it's one of the smallest inhabited islands in the Baltic, measuring just one and a half square kilometres and providing a home for just forty people. The human residents are far outnumbered by the waterbirds that live in the central marshland, and with zero sights *per se* for the day-tripping visitor, the island is a fine place for simply strolling around, listening to the bird-calls and admiring the swans that patrol the coast. You could take a wander along the high cliffs on the north coast, which are home to hundreds of sandmartins and afford superb views back to the Funen mainland. The ferry docks at the island's tiny main "town", from where a path leads southward across the island to a small camping spot on the beach; you can also **stay** at *Bjørnøgård* (☎62 61 08 12; ❹), a small and simple beachside home. Ferries to Bjørnø (☎20 29 80 50, ⓦwww.bjoernoe-faergen.dk; 40kr return) operate from Fåborg six or seven times a day during the week, and less frequently on weekends; the last return trip during the week is at 4.30pm (6pm Thurs).

Five kilometres to the west, **LYØ** is more populous than Bjørnø and a good deal more popular with Danish tourists, too, who descend en masse in the summer to stay in the multitude of small holiday homes set up along the coast. The ferry harbour is a short walk from the island's town, **Lyø By**, an unprepossessing place surrounded by small ponds and with a few buildings of interest, including a handful of impressive thatched homes and an old church. Paths lead out from town to the rolling green hills in the eastern part of the island, and to the flatter western half, at the end of which is a large *klokkestenen* ("bell stone"), a boulder sitting atop a Stone Age burial chamber which makes a unique bell-like ring when tapped. If you'd like to **stay** overnight, enquire at *Lyø Kro* (☎62 61 87 01; May–October; ❸), next to the island's grocery store at Søndergiden 1; there are a few rather dingy rooms, and a **restaurant** serving standard dishes like beef fillet and schnitzel for around 100kr. Rough camping is allowed along the eastern coast: for the best spot, take 1. vej left out of town; once the asphalt ends follow the grassy path which leads to a small waterside bluff. Ferries from Fåborg (☎62 61 23 07, ⓦwww.oe-faergen.dk; 85kr return) sail daily to Lyø, and some stop over in Avernakø; in the summer, the last return boat is at 8.30pm or 9pm.

Some 4km due east of Lyø, **AVERNAKØ** (ⓦwww.avernak.dk) is twice the size of Lyø and quite a bit hillier, and effectively comprises two separate islands connected by a 700-metre causeway. Ferries arrive 1km outside of

Avernak By, the island's town, where you'll find a well-stocked provisions shop, a café and, just east, the island's small early-sixteenth-century church. As in the neighbouring islands, the sole thing to do here is enjoy the country-side: head east from the town to the Korshavn area, where you'll find woods, wild meadows and undulating moors that lead out to the sea. Just east of the Korshavn harbour at Hovedvejen 79, the friendly Lund Jensen (T62 61 71 21; ⑥) rents out several nice flats; there's also a place to **stay** back in Avernak By, where *Bed & Breakfast Avernakø* (T50 99 56 51; ❷), Skallevej 8, has three basic rooms. Alternatively, you can camp rough at a small site accessible from the path leading northwest out of town. For **food**, there's a small **café** by the ferry landing serving sandwiches and inexpensive Danish dishes (summer only).

Drejø, Skarø and Hjortø

Sitting just offshore of the mouth of the Svendborg Sound, Drejø, Skarø and Hjortø are smaller and less touristy than their trio of western neighbours, though quite popular with weekending boaters from Svendborg. All of the islands are small enough to explore on foot, though you might find it more enjoyable to rent a bicycle in Svendborg and bring it with you on the ferry (20kr charge). Reachable via ferries from Svendborg (T62 21 02 62; 4–5 daily; 75kr), **DREJØ** (Wwww.drejo.dk) is made up of farmsteads and salt marshes that support a population of large, slow-flying marsh harriers as well as a few dozen human residents. Arriving at the ferry terminal, walk one kilometre west to the main settlement of **Drejø By**, much of which burned down on Midsummer's Eve in 1942, when a reveller's outdoor fire took hold and levelled the closely-placed thatched and timbered buildings. Your first stop here should be **Gammel Elmegaard** (June–Aug Mon–Thurs & Sat–Sun 1–6pm; 25kr), an old farmhouse housing a simple museum of island history – look out for the pastel-hued model of the village as it stood before the fire. The town also has a grocery shop and a small inn, *Drejø Kro* (T62 21 47 87; ❹), which hires out two small cabins; there's also rough camping just by the ferry dock, with toilet and shower facilities just 50m away, and a few minutes' walk south of here is a small beach. From Drejø By, you can follow the town road west for some 5km to arrive at Skoven, where a series of high, wind-blown cliffs give some good views out to the other islands in the archipelago.

Despite being closer to Funen, **SKARØ** receives fewer day-trippers now that its café has closed down, though intrepid, experienced kayakers still brave the choppy journey from Svendborg. Some 200m south of the harbour, the main town of **Skarø By** is the starting point for several well-groomed hiking trails – you can walk the entire island in a few hours. Ten minutes' walk south, a trail leads southwest to the island's sandy beach at Kalveodde, where there is a large rough camping site. Ferries to Drejø also stop at Skarø.

Four kilometres due south of Skarø, **HJORTØ** is one of the Baltic's smallest and most untouched islands, and is inhabited by just ten people. It used to be known for its abundant population of hares, but without a church, an inn or a shop, it's characterized by its isolated feel today. You're really on your own here – many visitors arrive and depart on their own boats – and this remoteness is firmly part of its appeal. From the ferry dock on the north coast, head south along the sole road to reach the town of **Hjortø By**, little more than a collection of timbered farms, then continue on through the fields; walking right around the island takes just over two hours. You can camp rough just north of the town, and there's twice-daily ferry transport to Hjortø from Svendborg (T40 97 95 18; 70kr).

Travel details

Trains

Odense to: Århus (2–3 hourly; 1hr 38min); Copenhagen (every 30min; 1hr 30min); Esbjerg (8 daily; 1hr 18min); Nyborg (every 30min; 14min); Svendborg (every 30min; 42min).
Middelfart to: Odense (2–3 hourly; 22–34min).
Nyborg to: Odense (every 30min; 14min).
Svendborg to: Odense (every 30min; 42min).

Buses

Ærøskøbing to: Marstal (hourly; 25min); Søby (hourly; 25min).
Fåborg to: Nyborg (hourly; 1hr–1hr 30min); Odense (hourly; 1hr); Svendborg (Mon–Sat every 30min, Sun hourly; 40min).
Kerteminde to: Nyborg (1–2 hourly; 35min), Odense (3 hourly; 30min).
Middelfart to: Odense (hourly; 1hr).
Odense to: Fåborg (1–2 hourly; 50min–1hr 18min); Kerteminde (every 15min; 33min); Nyborg (every 30min; 54min); Nykøbing Falster (hourly; 3hr 30min); Svendborg (2–3 hourly; 1hr 20min).

Rudkøbing to: Bagenkop (hourly; 35min); Lohals (hourly; 36min); Spodsbjerg (9 daily; 10min); Svendborg (1–5 hourly; 25min).
Svendborg to: Fåborg (Mon–Sat every 30min, Sun hourly; 40min); Rudkøbing (1–5 hourly; 25min); Nyborg (every 30min; 44min).

Ferries

Ferry connections are plentiful around the south coast archipelago. Some sailings continue all year, others only operate during the summer. Frequencies given below are for weekdays; sailings are often reduced on weekends and public holidays.
Bøjden to: Fynshav (6–7 daily; 50min).
Søby to: Mommark (2–5 daily; 1hr).
Fåborg to: Bjørnø (3–7 daily; 30min); Lyø (2–4 daily via Avernakø; 1hr 10min); Søby (2–6 daily; 1hr).
Marstal to: Rudkøbing (3–6 daily; 1hr).
Spodsbjerg to: Tårs (10–22 daily; 45min).
Svendborg to: Ærøskøbing (3–6 daily; 1hr 15min); Drejø (4–5 daily via Skarø; 1hr 15min); Hjortø (1–2 daily; 1hr).

5

South Jutland

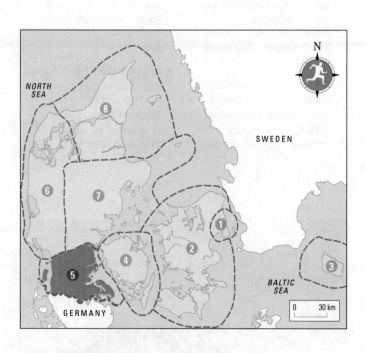

CHAPTER 5

Highlights

✳ **Koldinghus** This thirteenth-century royal castle lay ruined for hundreds of years, and its restoration is nothing short of ingenious. See p.254

✳ **Wadden Sea birdwatching** These huge tidal flats offer some of the best birding in the world, with some of the most easy-access opportunities at Magrethes kog, just west of Tønder. See p.269

✳ **Ribe** The quaint old town centre is ideal for a day's ambling, with beautiful old houses surrounding a grand cathedral. See p.272

✳ **Brundlund Slot** Built by Denmark's first queen, this fortified medieval castle remains surprisingly unchanged. See p.259

✳ **Dybbøl Banke** The moats and trenches here serve as an evocative reminder of the 1864 loss of parts of the south – then north Schleswig – to Prussia and Germany. See p.263

✳ **Lakolk beach** This fabulous and wide sandy beach in the island of Rømø is excellent for all manner of activities as well as swimming. See p.270

△ The Sort Sol, Wadden Sea

South Jutland

Denmark's only point of connection with mainland Europe (by way of a shared border with Germany), **south Jutland** is often overlooked by visitors heading straight to Copenhagen on fast intercity trains. This hasn't always been the case, however, as the region's territorially strategic position has long seen it act as a buffer zone between invaders coming from the south and the rest of Denmark. In fact, southern Jutland represents the country's most hotly disputed land, and the constant struggles for control have left the area littered with the castles and fortifications of its would-be rulers. Until the referendum of 1920, which finally ceded the south back to Denmark and away from German control, the area was part of the Danish **Duchy of Schleswig**; controlled by Danish nobles, but with German as the predominant language toward its south, and Danish to its north. With its strong and abiding affiliation to Schleswig, the region has always stood out slightly. Linguistically, the German-influenced local dialect is almost impossible for many Danes to understand – and though the German-speaking population here, who still maintain Teutonic cultural traditions, remain a minority, there's always an unspoken and nagging doubt as to whether southerners would vote differently should the 1920 referendum take place today.

Most of south Jutland's attractions lie along the two coasts – the interior is primarily agricultural and holds little of interest. The east coast has many reminders of the region's role in national and international conflicts, while the west coast, remote then as now, offers magnificent birdlife and some small but interesting commercial towns. The northern metropolis and gateway to the region, **Kolding** boasts an imaginatively restored castle and a good art museum, while to the south, **Haderslev** is home to a grand cathedral that towers over the medieval townhouses, and **Aabenraa** holds another of the fifteenth-century castles that once defended the region. The country's most devastating defeat on home soil, meanwhile, is engagingly commemorated in and around **Sønderborg**. Interspersed with scenic fjords, the lush rolling hills on the east coast couldn't be more different to the tidal mud flats and marshes of the west, where the **Wadden Sea** area offers fantastic birdwatching, some lovely beaches on the island of **Rømø**, and plenty of possibilities for walking and cycling on neighbouring **Mandø**. Capping the southwest coast, the engaging and well-preserved medieval town of **Ribe** is well worth a day's wander.

Some history

From the beginning of the Viking era up until the 1920 referendum, south Jutland has been a magnet for conflict, and the history of the region is determinedly labyrinthine. Up until the Napoleonic wars in the nineteenth

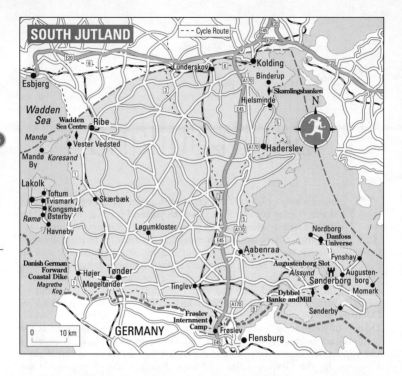

century, the area covered in this chapter (Kolding excepted) was under Danish control as part of the larger **Duchy of Schleswig**, which also comprised a politically significant chunk of modern Germany. It was ruled by a succession of nobles who were often appointed in an attempt to prevent them from meddling with affairs in Copenhagen, but these efforts often backfired – with an eye on the international political climate, the various dukes of Schleswig occasionally stirred things up, at times siding with Prussian or German forces in the hope of taking the Danish throne by force. The rebellious duchy never actually managed to overthrow the Danish crown, and in fact Schleswig was ceded to Prussia during the **war of 1864** (for more on which, see p.263). Leading up to the war, there had been a growing sense of nationalism in Denmark (as there was in the rest of Europe), and the loss of Schleswig (and the neighbouring Holstein) – a third of the country's territory and two-fifths of its population – came as a serious blow to the Danish psyche. It quickly became crucial that the Danish-speaking part of the lost territory retained its Danish cultural identity. Mass meetings were held at places such as Skamlingsbanken (see p.257) to discuss "Danishness" and to keep the national spirit alive; and finally, after Germany lost in World War I, a window of opportunity arrived to reclaim the lost lands. In best democratic tradition, it was decided to hold a **referendum** in order to let the people decide which country they wanted to be part of, and after much debating, Schleswig was divided into two sections, north and south. On February 10, 1920, a 75 percent majority in north Schleswig voted to return to Denmark, and on March 14, 75 percent of south Schleswig's population decided to stay German. But though this was initially seen as the perfect solution to a border conflict, there was still plenty of dissent: all the towns of north Schleswig (bar Haderslev) voted pro-German, and Denmark prevailed only because it had the support of the rural majority that won the vote; conversely, the very pro-Danish city of Flensborg was lost due to the pro-German rural majority around it. Consequently, south Jutland's return to Danish governance was initially problematic, with numerous disputes between the German- and Danish-speaking population in the early years.

Following the reunification of Schleswig with Denmark, an impressive effort was made to minimize future conflict. The area was – in effect – designated as bilingual, and German-language schools, churches, newspapers and social clubs were established with the support of the local and Danish government. Over the years, however, the German influence has gradually subsided, and only one German newspaper, *Der Nord Schleswiger*, now remains. That said, people here are still very clear about their cultural background, although the increasing intermarriage between the two language groups (more the norm these days than the exception) is watering down the differences.

Kolding and around

Handsomely positioned on Kolding Fjord, **KOLDING** is south Jutland's biggest town. Located within easy reach of the bridge from Funen, and with good road connections to Ribe and Tønder as well as motorway and rail links west to Esbjerg and south to German border, it's also the gateway to the region and a convenient place to base yourself while exploring, with a few top-ranking attractions in and around town to boot – from **Kold-inghus castle** and **Trapholt** art museum to the historically significant **Skamlingsbanken**. And though the presence of a massive shopping mall on the outskirts has led to the closure of many of the ancient centre's quirkier shops, most of these have now been replaced by a string of excellent **eating**, **drinking** and **nightlife** venues.

Kolding has a colourful **history** as both a border town and royal seat. First mentioned in 1231 in King Valdemar's court roll (a sort of Danish Domesday Book), the royal castle of Koldinghus was founded about a century later on the north banks of the Kolding Å river – then the border between north Jutland and the rebellious Duchy of Schleswig – to protect Denmark against invasion from the south.

Arrival, information and accommodation

Kolding's centrally located **train** and bus **stations** are next to each other on Mazantigade; conveniently, as many of Kolding's sights and hotels are a fair walk from the centre, city buses stop just outside. These buses are run by two companies; services in and around northern Kolding are run by Vejle Amts Trafikselskab (☎75 82 97 66, ⓦwww.vat.dk), and those to the south by Sydbus (☎70 10 44 10, ⓦwww.sydbus.dk). Central Kolding is covered by one zone, and tickets within this cost 13kr. You can pick up free bus and train timetables which detail all the useful routes and get travel advice at the **tourist office** (July to mid-Aug Mon–Fri 9.30am–7pm, Sat 9.30am–2.30pm; mid-Aug to June Mon–Fri 9.30am–5.30pm, Sat 9.30am–2pm; ☎76 33 21 00, ⓦwww.visitkolding.dk), Akseltorv 8, a short walk from the bus station on the central square. They also have heaps of bumph on local attractions, and useful free maps of the town and region.

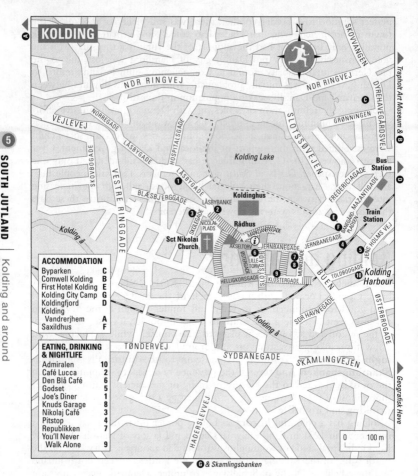

KOLDING

ACCOMMODATION
Byparken	C
Comwell Kolding	B
First Hotel Kolding	E
Kolding City Camp	G
Koldingfjord	D
Kolding Vandrerjhem	A
Saxildhus	F

EATING, DRINKING & NIGHTLIFE
Admiralen	10
Café Lucca	2
Den Blå Café	6
Godset	5
Joe's Diner	1
Knuds Garage	3
Nikolaj Café	8
Pitstop	4
Republikken	7
You'll Never Walk Alone	9

G & Skamlingsbanken

Central Kolding has a fairly limited selection of **accommodation**; many of the options are a short bus ride away from the centre; the tourist office has an extensive list of **private rooms**, mostly in the suburbs or in the surrounding villages. As most places here are geared toward business travellers, rates can drop significantly during weekends and holidays; check websites for offers.

Accommodation

Byparken Grønningen 2 ☎75 53 21 22 ⓦwww
.hotelbyparken.dk. Good-value hotel to the north
of Kolding and adjacent to the city's park, with
views of the centre. The simple rooms are all self-
contained with a small balcony. Buses #1, #2, #3,
#5 and #6 from the bus station all stop here, or
it's a fifteen-minute walk from the station along
Dyrehavegårdsvej. ⓖ

Comwell Kolding Skovbrynet ☎76 34 11 00
ⓦwww.comwell.dk. Large, luxurious hotel next to

a small woodland north of the centre, and offering
fab views of the town. The peaceful, modern rooms
have all mod cons including wireless Internet
and big bathtubs, and the complex has a pristine
indoor swimming pool, sauna and spa, plus a bar
and restaurant. Ten minutes from the centre on
bus #5. ⓑ

First Hotel Kolding Banegårdspladsen 7 ☎76 34
54 00 ⓦwww.firsthotels.dk/kolding. Brand-new
place across from the train station, with a whopping 132 rooms distributed over three floors and

affording views of Kolding Slotsø lake to the back. The tastefully furnished en-suite rooms come with wireless Internet, and there's a bar, restaurant and a small leisure centre in the basement. **⑦**

🏃 **Koldingfjord** Fjordvej 154 ⑦75 51 00 00 ⑩www.koldingfjord.dk. On the wooded banks of Koldingfjord, this majestic hotel with its Neoclassical fjordside facade was built in 1911 as a sanatorium and offers plenty of pure air and tranquillity. The luxurious rooms, a few with large bathtubs, all have wireless Internet. The hotel also has an indoor swimming pool with sauna, a tennis court and a beautifully positioned restaurant overlooking Koldingfjord. It's convenient for Trapholt art museum (see p.255), and a twenty-minute bus ride from the centre (bus #4). **⑨/⑥**

Kolding City Camp Vonsildvej 19 ⑦75 52 13 88 ⑩www.koldingcitycamp.dk. Large, modern campsite 3km south of the centre on the main road to Christiansfelt (take bus #3). Packed with facilities (minigolf, tennis, large play area) plus wireless Internet throughout the grounds, the site also has a range of cabins, from luxurious six-bed affairs

with fully fitted kitchens and private bathrooms (600kr–895kr) to basic 4-bed cabins with beds and a sink (395kr–450kr).

Kolding Vandrerhjem Ørnsborgvej 10 ⑦75 50 91 40 ⑩www.danhostelkolding.dk. Set in a rustic old wooden building on a hillside 1.5km northwest of the centre (take bus #3 towards Albuen and get off at Gøhlmannsvej), and with great views of Koldinghus and Kolding Slotsø lake, Kolding's fully modernized hostel has a range of two- to eight-bed rooms, some sharing bathroom facilities. All can be used as dorms (115kr), or rented privately (two people sharing: **⑧–④**), and there's a fully-equipped guest kitchen. Breakfast costs 48kr.

Saxildhus Hotel Jernbanegade 39 ⑦75 52 12 00 ⑩www.saxildhus.dk. Opposite the train station in a white building from 1910, the beautifully renovated en-suite rooms here come with either antique mahogany four-poster beds and wood-beamed ceilings, or with modern Danish furniture. Downstairs, there's a pub and two restaurants. **⑦**

The town

Kolding's scenic fjordside setting is not something you immediately notice when first arriving at the train or bus station. Instead, it's the compact medieval centre, with its beautiful old townhouses crammed behind the Koldinghus castle hill – and the castle itself – that draw your attention, and rightly so. From the train station, Jernbanegade leads up to Akseltorv, the main town square and a good place to start exploring. Since the Middle Ages, farmers have sold their wares here, and on market days (Tues, Fri and Sat 7am–1pm), locally produced fruit, veg and cheeses are sold by the constantly chattering, coffee-sipping vendors. While on the square, look out for the bullet marks in the town hall's granite bollards, a leftover from the 1849 Battle of Kolding, one of the many conflicts between Denmark and the rebellious Duchy of Schleswig (see p.399). Also on the square, at Akseltorv 2A, is one of the country's finest burgher houses, which dates back to 1595. A crooked, wood-beamed three-storey structure, it's still functioning as an apothecary, with its facade largely intact. If the houses on Akseltorv have whetted your appetite, head a few streets south to Helligkorsgade, parallel to Jernbanegade. At no.18, Kolding's oldest surviving townhouse – from 1589 – was built as a cobbler's workshop and home in Germanic style with the typical crinkly gables; the inscription over the door, which translates as "oh lord, please save our house from fear and danger", seems to have worked. Next door at no.20, on the corner of Slotsgade, the grand yellow-and-black wood-beamed merchant's house from 1632 now houses a restaurant, but the interior bears little semblance to its past glory. Returning to Akseltorv along Bredgade you'll pass **Sct Nikolai Kirke** (Mon–Fri 9am–4pm, Sat 9am–noon, Sun 10am–noon), across from the town hall on Nikolai Plads. Built in 1250, it's Kolding's oldest church, with the nave the only remaining element from the original structure; today's red-brick neo-Gothic exterior stems from a complete renovation in 1886. It's worth a quick peek inside to see the colourful altarpiece from 1590; a gift from Casper Markdanner, the king's vassal at Koldinghus, the discrete figure at the bottom of the right-hand side panel is said to be Caspar himself.

The city's most distinctive building, however, and a prominent feature of the local skyline, **Koldinghus castle** (daily 10am–5pm; 60kr; ⊛www.koldinghus .dk) boasts a lofty hilltop setting at the core of the medieval centre. The castle defended both town and country for more than six hundred years until it was accidentally burnt down in 1808 by resident Spanish forces based here during the Napoleonic wars. Unused to the biting Danish winters, the soldiers stoked a fire so fierce that a chimney caught fire and Koldinghus burnt down overnight. A long period of decline followed, during which the castle became a picturesque and much-painted ruin; by the 1960s, it had become clear that it would soon crumble away completely, and restorers stepped in. The work was completed in 1993, and the remaining original features sit harmoniously with the modern rebuilding. The first structure built on this site was a fortress, raised by King Erik Kipling in 1268 to defend the kingdom – then demarcated by the Kolding Å river to the south of Kolding – from incursions from the rebellious Duchy of Schleswig. None of this original structure remains, and Koldinghus was converted to a royal castle in the fifteenth century by Christian I. Its heyday came in the sixteenth century when King Christian III and wife Dorothea set up permanent residence here – the oldest elements of the current Koldinghus date back to this period. Their grandson – Christian IV, aka the builder king – spent his childhood here and was later responsible for some of Koldinghus' grandest existing features, including the Giants' Tower.

The main entrance into Koldinghus is through the gatehouse in the eastern wing, reachable via a short walk up the hill from Markdannersgade. Approaching from this angle, the modern oak shingle cladding on the outer southern and eastern walls gives a clear idea of which bits of the building have been restored. An important part of the restoration brief was to maintain the building's ruinous look, which is why the original outer walls haven't been rendered and whitewashed, as they were before the fire, and instead retain their raw, weathered, red-brick look. Once inside, a free English-language guide (pick it up at the entrance) will help you find your way around the maze-like **interior**, though if time is short, you might want to concentrate just on the highlights described below. The most dramatic feature is the so-called **Ruin Hall**, where towering modern pillars support the roof and the remaining sections of original brickwork here give a clear impression of the magnitude of the rebuild. Equally impressive is Christian IV's massive **Giants' Tower**, designed to create as imposing an entry point into southern Denmark as Kronborg (see p.135) in the east and affording sweeping views of the surrounding countryside, from Kolding Fjord and the harbour in the east to the fields beyond the city limits. During the fire of 1808, half of the tower collapsed, crashing down onto the Great Hall and Christian IV's chapel underneath. Both were completely destroyed, and today, lamps and chandeliers in the reconstructed **chapel** have been imaginatively used to indicate where vaults and nave once were. The **Great Hall**, meanwhile, is most famous for a masked ball held here in 1711 when the 40-year-old – and married – King Frederik IV openly courted 17-year-old commoner Anna Sophie Reventlow. Soon after, she was abducted from her family home in east Jutland and became the King's consort for ten years, eventually becoming Denmark's queen. On the ground floor of the north wing, the **visitor centre** takes you through the various phases of the building's history, with paintings, display boards and models that make particular (and fascinating) reference to the restoration process. There's a quality **café** in the basement serving delicious, if pricey, home-cooked food.

Around Kolding

Though the castle is central Kolding's main draw, there are a couple of other worthy attractions away from the centre. Some 2km to the southeast, and easily reached by bus #2, the **Geografisk Have** gardens (May–Sept 10am–6pm; 40kr; ⓦ www.geografiskhave.dk) makes for an excellent excursion on a sunny day. Organized into geographic regions – Asia, North America and Europe – the gardens are further sub-divided into smaller sections planted with specimens from individual countries within the regions – the largest sections are China and Japan. It's a stunning, multi-hued place in the summer – look out especially for the **rose garden**, which holds over a hundred different cultivars. There are plenty of open grassy spaces ideal for picnics, and a small café.

If you want to get the full benefit of Kolding's stunning fjordside setting, you'll need to head northeast of the centre on bus #4 from the train station, which also passes the modern **Trapholt** art museum (daily 10am–5pm; 60kr; ⓦ www .trapholt.dk), Æblehaven 23, another of Kolding's highlights. With shrill white interiors and glass walls that flood the place with natural light, the contemporary building is divided into eleven distinct sections, of which about half house outstanding and innovative changing exhibitions centred on modern art, craft and furniture design. The **permanent displays** begin in the long central walkway, where a fine selection of chronologically organized Danish ceramic art lines the walls. This is one of the country's largest collections of so-called **studio pieces** (art that has evolved from functional ceramics): funky, oddly shaped pots that look as if they'd break if you touched them. Turning left off the main corridor into **Room 10**, Danish furniture is represented by classic chairs from some of the country's best-known designers – look for Arne Jacobsen's **myren** ("the ant"), hanging in a rainbow of colours from the ceiling, and Børge Mogensen's stylish "Spanish" chair, a low, robust recliner in oak and leather. Carry on along the main corridor and turn right into **Room 6** for the modern collection, highlights of which include Richard Mortensen's nine massive abstract paintings, *the cow's story*. Upstairs near the café, it's worth seeking out the Franciska Claussen Collection in **Room 8**, which details the life and art of this forgotten Dane, born in Aabenraa in 1899 while south Jutland was still under German rule, and best-known for her surrealist paintings and Art Nouveau advertising posters from Berlin and Paris in the 1920s. Her favourite and most famous painting, *the Screw*, is strategically positioned so you can study it sitting comfortably in the so-called Red-Blue chair, designed by Dutch-born Gerrit Rietveld. The museum's **garden** is also worth a peek, packed with sculptures such as Bjørn Nørgaard's evocative *Homeless Souls*, made in oak, granite, bronze, aluminium, steel and lead, as well as **Arne Jacobsen's summerhouse** (Mon, Wed and Fri–Sun 30min slots at 11am, 1pm & 3pm), accessible from the exit in front of Room 8; a so-called "Kubeflex" house, it's made in cubic modules that can be shifted around whenever the urge takes you. It was considered an architectural gem in design circles, but was never put into production, perhaps because it was too modern for its time.

The central walkway with the ceramic displays culminates in *Café Medina*, a pricey but beautifully positioned café-restaurant overlooking Kolding fjord where you can enjoy coffee and cake or a sandwich. The museum **shop**, at the other end of the walkway by the main entrance, has an expansive selection of functional Danish crafts, design and jewellery.

Eating, drinking and nightlife

Central Kolding has a good selection of **restaurants** and **cafés**, and the city also boasts the region's most active **nightlife** scene, with a wide range of bars, nightclubs and discos. Many of the cafés double as funky clubs at night. We've given a few of the choicer places below.

Cafés, restaurants and bars

Admiralen Toldbogade 14 ☎75 52 04 21, ⓦwww.admiralen.dk. Tucked away behind the harbour and most easily reached via the railway underpass next to the station, this classy restaurant has a simple menu with a handful of delectable fish dishes, as well as a few meat options. The *pièce de résistance* is the bouillabaisse (248kr), though the traditional fried plaice with parsley sauce (168kr) is also out of this world. Mon–Fri 11.30am–2.30pm & 5.50–10pm, Sat 5.30–10pm.

Café Lucca Låsbybanke 4 ☎76 33 39 00, ⓦwww.lucca-kolding.dk. Successful combination of café (with wireless Internet), quality restaurant and trendy nightclub, where the day gently flows between brunch, lunch and dinner – the menu is largely Spanish/Italian. Prices range from 98kr for a delicious home-made cheeseburger to 175kr for the Coq au Vin. The popular nightclub (Fri & Sat; free; over-23s only) offers mostly mainstream sing-along tunes. Mon–Thurs 11am–11pm, Fri & Sat 11am–5am, Sun 11am–6pm.

Den Blå Café Lilletorv, Slotsgade 4 ☎75 50 65 12, ⓦwww.denblaacafe.dk. With outdoor seating on a small cosy square, this is Kolding's best option if you fancy a drink or a light café meal out in the open. In the summer, live bands occasionally play daytime gigs in the square during the day, moving into the Café during the cold months. Mon–Wed 10am to midnight, Thurs–Sat 10am–2am, Sun 11am–10pm.

Joe's Diner Låsbygade 27 ☎75 50 42 78, ⓦwww.joesdiner.dk. Modelled on the American small-town diner, with a jovial atmosphere and a predictable menu featuring the usual array of steaks and spare ribs, and starting at 98kr for a burger. Portions are advertised as being "large enough to satisfy an adult American". Mon–Thurs & Sun 5–10pm, Fri & Sat 5–11pm.

Knuds Garage Munkegade 5. Busy café-bar, packed with trendy, alternative-type young locals and with lots going on, from backgammon and table-football tournaments to live jam sessions on Thursday nights. The usual array of sandwiches and salads (from 65kr) are supplemented by a huge selection of Danish and foreign beers. Wireless Internet access, and an open backyard that gets packed on hot summer days. Daily noon–2am.

Nikolaj Café Skolegade 2, entrance on Blæsbjerggade, ☎75 50 03 02, ⓦwww.film6000.dk. The outstanding café/restaurant at this arthouse cinema is worth a visit even if you're not seeing a movie. It's not the most intimate of places, with bright lights and sparse furnishings, but the compensation is the beautifully prepared food, which ranges from a hugely popular all-you-can-eat weekend brunch buffet (10am–2pm; 125kr) to salads, sandwiches and simple but flavour-packed main courses such as grilled chicken breast with potatoes and ratatouille for 145kr at dinner, and 115kr at lunch. Mon–Fri 11am–11pm, Sat 10am–11pm, Sun 10am–5pm.

Republikken Munkegade 9 ☎75 54 14 40, ⓦwww.republikken.dk. A stone's throw from the train station, the laid-back atmosphere at this café makes it a great first stop when arriving in Kolding. Geared towards a more mature crowd, with focus on beer and beer tastings, there's also a Sunday morning indoor flea market, and bluesy live jazz and 1960s rock a couple of evenings a month. Food is of the light café style including sandwiches, salads and a few pasta dishes, with an excellent value all-you-can-eat buffet brunch for 69kr on weekends. Mon & Sun noon–midnight, Tues & Wed noon–2am, Thurs & Fri noon–3am, Sat 11am–3am.

You'll Never Walk Alone Klostergade 7A. ⓦwww.denengelskepub.dk. Popularly known as the "English Pub", and said to have Denmark's largest selection of beers from around the world. The British owners are staunch Liverpool supporters and Premiership football features heavily on the large screen. Often very packed – and very smoky – with a separate non-smoking lounge bar section and a restaurant section serving basic pub meals. Tues–Thurs 11.30am–10.30pm, Fri & Sat 11.30am–11pm.

Clubs and live music

Godset Jens Holmsvej 3 ☎79 30 10 60 ⓦwww.godset.net. New music venue in the characterful, wooden-beamed setting of the old rail freight terminal behind the train station. Unquestionably the best music venue in the region, with live music three to four times a week, from local pop rock to international blues and jazz. Tickets range from 50kr right up to 300kr depending on the act.

Pit Stop Jernbanegade 54. Kolding's best clubbing venue, with a live band playing one or two nights a week (usually Thurs, sometimes Fri), followed by a DJ playing tunes that lean towards alternative electronica until the early hours. The *Pornobar* lounge, open from 3am onwards, is the only place where the music is subdued enough to have a conversation, and something of a flirting hotspot. Cover charge 30–40kr, or up to 200kr for gigs.

Skamlingsbanken

About 10km south of Kolding, just off the road to Binderup, **Skamlingsbanken**, at 113m, is south Jutland's highest point and affords breathtaking views of the surrounding countryside. During periods of political oppression, this site has been one of the country's most important mass meeting places, and provides an interesting window into an important phase of regional history. The grassy hilltop is criss-crossed by footpaths up to the top, and holds a restaurant as well as a scattering of **monuments** commemorating the region's cultural and spiritual struggle against German dominance in the years between the Napoleonic wars (for more on which, see p.250). Skamlingsbanken served as a mass meeting point during that era, and was the scene of numerous gatherings which focused on the Danish language and cultural identity. Free leaflets are available at the restaurant with English translations of all the inscriptions, some more evocative than others; look out for the one dedicated to N.F.S. Grundtvig (see p.123), who numbered among the many well-known Danes that played a part in the struggle, initiating his Nordic folk high-school movement and offering education to the masses. The 16-metre-high Skamlingsbanken obelisk in front of the restaurant commemorates the champions of the Danish cause in Schleswig and has a unique history. Made of twenty-five blocks of Swedish granite, it was blown to pieces during the 1864 war (see p.263) before it was officially unveiled, and chunks of its valuable stone put up for auction. Two Danish sympathizers bought them all, and the obelisk was reassembled two years later, although with some of its corners missing. If you want to learn more about Skamlingsbanken's history, take a look at the small exhibition hall in the restaurant (April–Sept daily 10am–6pm, March & October Sat & Sun 10am–5pm; ⓦ www.restaurantskamlingsbanken.dk), which also has a small selection of tasty traditional Danish dishes starting at 68kr for the herring platter. The **view** from the top of Skamlingsbanken is absolutely stunning: to the east, the island of Funen stands out clearly, while to the west you can see the backbone of Jutland, a ridge that runs all the way up the length of the peninsula to Skagen. Since 1998, Skamlingsbanken has served as a spectacular setting for a hugely popular open-air **concert** in celebration of its historical significance, with the Royal Danish Opera performing works by Danish and German composers. It's held on the first Sunday of August; ask at Kolding tourist office (p.251) for more information.

Bus #404 (5 daily; 25min), from Kolding bus station towards Hejlsminde, stops at Skamlingen, from where it's a short walk to Skamlingsbanken.

Haderslev and Aabenraa

The east coast fjord towns of Haderslev and Aabenraa have a very similar history. They were both important market towns on the main trade route between southern Schleswig and mainland Denmark, and thrived under the Duchy of Schleswig. After the Napoleonic wars and the battle of 1864 (see box on p.263), the duchy came under German rule and both suffered serious economic and social decline. Neither has since recovered fully, and the main attractions of both are inextricably linked to their former glory. **Haderslev**'s main appeal is its pretty medieval core which stands in dramatic contrast to the enormous cathedral that towers above it; **Aabenraa**'s highlight, meanwhile, is the Brundlund Slot castle, which now houses a modern art gallery. If you find it hard to leave the bright lights, you'll be pleased to learn that it's easy to see both towns on a day-trip from Kolding.

Haderslev

Some 27km south of Kolding, the pretty fjord town of **HADERSLEV** boasts one of Denmark's best-preserved medieval centres, its narrow cobbled streets lined by small, wood-beamed townhouses that lean against each other for support. The obvious place to start your wanderings – it's unmissable from all directions and is a five-minute walk along Nørregade from the bus station – is the enormous **Vor Frue Kirke** (May–Sept Mon–Sat 10am–5pm, Sun 11.30am–5pm; Oct–April daily 10am–3pm; free), which towers up over the centre. From its inception in the eleventh century until the reunification of south Jutland into Denmark in 1920, Vor Frue Kirke was an adjunct of the main Schleswig cathedral – surprising when you consider its enormous size – and only became a cathedral in its own right in 1922, when Haderslev gained Episcopal status. Dating mostly from the fifteenth century, the red-brick Vor Frue has an almost fairytale aspect, with 16-metre-high Gothic windows and a long, narrow tower next to the main entrance. However, it's the building's huge scale (especially acute in comparison to the minute surrounding townhouses) that provides the wow factor. Inside, look out for the four priest's robes and other religious garments designed by the current Queen Margrethe II.

Haderslev's medieval centre spreads out from the cathedral, and if you continue across the square, down Slotsgade, you'll pass some of the town's oldest secular buildings, dating from the fifteenth and sixteenth centuries. The only one you can actually get inside is the timber-framed building at no. 20, built in 1580 and now housing the **Ehlers Samling** (June–Aug Tues–Fri 10am–5pm, Sat & Sun 1–5pm; Sept–May Tues–Sun 1–5pm; 25kr, joint ticket with Haderslev Museum 50kr; Ⓦ www.haderslev-museum.dk), a mildly diverting miscellany of Danish pottery from the Middle Ages until 1940. More interesting, or intriguing, is the building itself: upstairs, look for the meticulously decorated original wooden panelling. The only other thing to do here is take a look at the **Haderslev Museum** (June–Aug Tues–Sun 10am–4pm; Sept–May Tues–Sun 1–4pm; 25kr, joint ticket with Ehler's Collection 50kr; Ⓦ www.haderslev-museum.dk), ten minutes' walk east of the centre via Aastrupvej at Dalgade 7; prize processions are two beautifully decorated Bronze Age bowls found nearby.

Practicalities

From Kolding, Haderslev is reachable by **bus** #34 or via the E170; coming along the E45 take exit 68, for Haderslev V. Of the two **hotels** in town, the most atmospheric is the *Harmonien* (Ⓣ74 52 37 20, Ⓦ www.harmonien.dk; Ⓞ), Gåskærsgade 19, across from the town hall and a stone's throw from the bus station. This grand hotel dates back to 1793, and the cosy rooms have recently been modernized, while the restaurant is the best in town. The more modern *Hotel Norden*, Storegade 55 (Ⓣ74 52 40 30, Ⓦ www.hotel-norden.dk; Ⓞ) is five minutes walk from the centre, with a scenic lakeside setting and Robert Jakobsen paintings adorning the walls. It has a bar/restaurant, a gym with pool, and a sauna/solarium. A more frugal option is the *Haderslev Vandrerhjem* **youth hostel**, Erlevsvej 34 (Ⓣ74 52 13 47, Ⓦ www.danhostel.dk/haderslev), south of Haderslev Dam lake ten minutes' walk from the centre. Apart from standard hostel rooms (dorm beds 122kr, doubles Ⓞ), some with en-suite bathrooms, they also have cute self-contained log cabins sleeping four (450kr for two), and hire out canoes for use on the lake. *Haderslev Camping* is next door (same phone number, Ⓦ www.haderslev-camping.dk).

Aabenraa and around

Continuing south from Haderslev, it's 24km along the E170 to fjordside **AABENRAA**, the most important maritime town on the Lille Bælt coast. Ships have departed from Aabenraa for centuries, bound first for the Baltic and later for the Far East, where local sailors had the dubious honour of being the first Danes to fly the Danish flag. By the middle of the eighteenth century, the booming merchant navy had over a hundred ships registered here, and the fine old houses in the centre stand testament to this prosperity. Today, Aabenraa's harbour remains south Jutland's busiest, and the town is also home to the offices of many large companies and media houses, including the region's only remaining German-language newspaper, *Der Nord Schleswiger*. Commerce apart, it's the medieval castle that makes Aabenraa worth a stop, and if you're happy to see just this, the town can easily be visited in a half-day, though the salty charm here may well make you want to linger longer.

A short walk south of the centre inside a fortified moat off Ved Slottet, **Brundlund Slot** (Tues–Sun 11am–5pm; free; ⓦ www.brundlund-slot.dk) is Denmark's only intact medieval castle. It was founded in an inaccessible bog in the early fifteenth century by the first queen of Denmark, Queen Margrethe I, after she had regained control over south Jutland following prolonged battles with the Duke of Schleswig (see box on p.393) and wanted to make her presence known. She never set foot in the finished castle before her death (from bubonic plague), and instead it became the seat of the king's vassal. The bogs around the castle have long been drained and channelled into the surrounding moat, but the exterior has changed very little, the thick granite walls standing testament to the building's medieval origins. Today the castle houses a **museum of art**, with changing exhibitions of contemporary work from south Jutland, but it's the building itself that's the main draw, and the museum a convenient way of getting inside. Since its main usage has been as a residence for the king's vassal and in later years (until 1996), that of the regional administrator, the interior bears more resemblance to a home than to a castle, an impression that intensifies when you see the parquet

△ Aabenraa

floors and double-glazed windows, the latter affording great views of the museum's sculpture park in the gardens. The basement is only area without a homely feel; the cold and barren dungeon here was used to hold prisoners awaiting trial during the time when the castle served as Aabenraa's court.

Head back into town via Slotsgade, and you'll find **Aabenraa Museum** (June–Aug Tues–Sun 10am–4pm; Sept–May Tues–Sun 1–4pm; free; Ⓦwww .aabenraa-museum.dk) next to the bus station and harbour at H.P. Hansens Gade 33. It documents the town's long maritime history, and exhibits include some quirky relics and souvenirs brought back by sailors from the Far East, Africa, South America and the Pacific, from models to ships in bottles. Of special appeal is room 9, which holds a selection of delicate embroideries made by one Maid Fanny, a native of Aabenraa who, according to legend, was the daughter of Christian VIII, born to his first wife before their marriage. As well as being skilled with her hands, Maid Fanny was also a celebrated medium, whose predictions included the south's loss of territory to Germany and its subsequent return in 1920. In fact, her prophecies were so revered that following the country's reunification, Christian X insisted on carrying out her predictions to the letter by way of crossing the old Kongeåen border on a white horse when returning back into Denmark.

Aabenraa doesn't have much else to offer in terms of sights, but the old centre makes for some pretty wandering, and you can pick up a free leaflet at the tourist office (see below) which describes a town walk that takes you past Maid Fanny's house and a range of other historical homes.

Practicalities

From Kolding, Aabenraa is reachable by **bus** #34 to Haderslev and then bus #23-900X, or via the E170; coming along the E45, take exit 70 and it's 10km from the turn-off. The **tourist office** (mid-June to mid-Aug Mon–Fri 9am–5.30pm, Sat 9am–1pm; mid-Aug to mid-June Mon–Fri 9am–4pm, Sat 9am–noon; Ⓣ74 62 35 00, Ⓦwww.visitaabenraa.dk) is near the bus station at H.P. Hansens Gade 5. Although there isn't much to detain you in Aabenraa, you may well want to **stay**, especially if you're visiting Haderslev and Aabenraa jointly as a day-trip. The priciest option is *Hotel Europa*, H.P. Hansen's Gade 10 (Ⓣ74 62 26 22, Ⓦwww.europahotel.dk; ❼), a business-oriented place between the harbour and the town's long pedestrianized street. More affordable is the deceptively grand-looking *Hotel Royal* (Ⓣ74 62 03 30, Ⓦwww.royal.dk; ❻), Nørretorv 1, with four rooms above a good restaurant (see below), all en suite and excellent value. Finally, *Missionshotellet Aabenraa*, a short walk west at Klinkbjerg 20 (Ⓣ74 63 00 91, Ⓦwww.missionshotel-aabenraa.dk; ❹), is an inexpensive option run in conjunction with the Studio 91 gym, which is free for guests to use. The cheerful, newly renovated rooms either share bathrooms or you can pay slightly more (❺) for an en suite. Breakfast isn't included, but there's a communal kitchen. Reception is through the gym (Mon–Fri 2–9pm, Sat 10am–2pm); call in advance outside these hours.

Two of the best places to **eat** in Aabenraa are within the hotels. The Scottish-run *Fox and Hounds* pub (daily 11am–11pm) at the *Europa* serves mouthwatering spare ribs (portions for 109kr and 139kr) and a selection of real ales; for something more filling, the three-course lunch and dinner menu (128kr) at the *Hotel Royal* restaurant (Mon–Sat 11.45am–11pm, Sun 11.45am–10pm) is excellent value.

Frøslev Internment Camp

About 30km south of Aabenraa and a stone's throw from the German border, tucked away in middle of the Frøslev pine plantation, the **Frøslev Intern-**

ment Camp is a thought-provoking reminder of the German occupation of Denmark during World War II. Denmark was occupied by Germany on the ninth of April 1940. The German forces were initially non-aggressive, in the sense that the Danish government was allowed to govern its own administrative matters as long as the economy was geared toward financing and supplying goods for the Nazi war machine, but the Danish people put up a strong resistance, blowing up trains and bridges to stop arms transportation and smuggling Jews across the Kattegat to Sweden in fishing boats. As the sabotage escalated, Hitler sent in strongman Hermann von Hanneken in 1943 to impose martial law, commandeer the navy and dismiss parliament. This led to a growing number of arrests, and many of those detained were deported to the dreaded concentration camps in Germany. In 1944, a prominent Danish civil servant, Nils Svenningsen, managed to negotiate an agreement to establish an **internment camp** within the country's borders as a means to stop any further deportations and to bring home Danish prisoners from the German camps; by the summer of 1944, Frøslev was completed. Over the next nine months, until the end of the war in spring 1945, more than twelve thousand dissidents and political prisoners were incarcerated here. Although under German command, management of the camp was left to the Danes, and conditions were significantly better than those south of the border – inmates were well fed and relatively free to go about their business. However, the German occupiers didn't keep to their end of the deal, and some 1600 prisoners were sent from Frøslev to prison camps in Germany; 220 never returned.

Today the camp is a national memorial and is always open to visitors. There's a **museum** (mid-June to mid-Aug daily 10am–5pm; Feb to mid-June & mid-Aug to Nov Tues–Fri 9am–4pm, Sat & Sun 10am–5pm; 30kr, Ⓦ www.froeslevlejrensmuseum.dk) in bunker H4 and H6 and in the main watchtower. It shows living conditions during its nine months of operation and there's a section about the history of the camp.

Sønderborg and Als

With its lush green landscapes subsiding gently into a peaceful coastline, Jutland's southeastern corner is most often seen en route to Funen (covered in Chapter 3) – but with a couple of imposing castles and a string of sheltered sandy beaches, the area holds enough appeal to warrant a couple of days' stay in its own right. Laid out along both sides of the Alssund, a narrow but deep channel dividing the island of Als from the Jutland mainland, the lively provincial town of **Sønderborg**, with its sturdy castle, is a convenient base for exploring the surrounding area, including the nearby line of preserved trenches and moats that point to the town's crucial place in Danish history. Despite its expansive size, the rest of Als away from Sønderborg has few designated attractions, and unless the sandy beaches and great seaside campsites tempt you to stay longer, it can easily be visited in one day. If you do decide to stay, consider staying at one of the many excellent beach campsites that line the coast.

Sønderborg

The largest town hereabouts, **SØNDERBORG** is centred around its main attraction of the Sønderborg **Slot**, with its picture-postcard location on the banks of Alssund. It may not be the grandest castle in Denmark, but it's certainly one of the oldest, thought to have been built in 1170 by Valdemar I

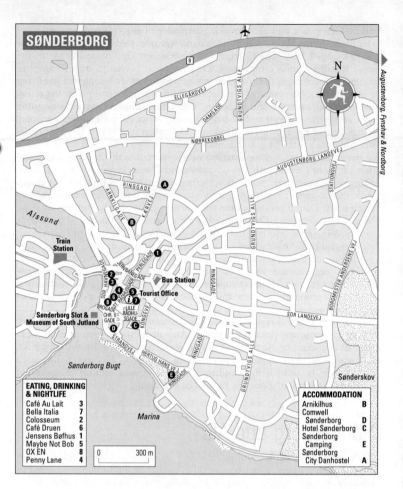

Train Station

Alssund

Bus Station

Tourist Office

Sønderborg Slot & Museum of South Jutland

Sønderborg Bugt

Sønderskov

Marina

0   300 m

EATING, DRINKING & NIGHTLIFE

Café Au Lait	3
Bella Italia	7
Colosseum	2
Café Druen	6
Jensens Bøfhus	1
Maybe Not Bob	5
OX EN	8
Penny Lane	4

ACCOMMODATION

Arnikilhus	B
Comwell Sønderborg	D
Hotel Sønderborg	C
Sønderborg Camping	E
Sønderborg City Danhostel	A

as a defence against the country's two main threats at the time, Wendish pirates from the Baltic and Germanic forces from the south. Almost four hundred years later it was still one of the strongest fortresses in the kingdom, and was used to imprison the deposed Christian II between 1532 and 1549 (see p.393); he was held in his own apartment and supplied with plenty of food and drink. The castle's quadrangular shape stems from the era of his successor, Christian III, whose dowager queen Dorothea lived here after his death, and who built the castle chapel. After her departure, Sønderborg fell into disrepair, but in the eighteenth century, the dilapidated building was restored before being used as a military hospital during the Napoleonic and Danish–German wars. During the latter, it was tossed back and forth between the Danish kings and the dukes of Schleswig, and served as barracks for the Prussian infantry before it was finally handed back to Denmark following the referendum in 1920. A year later it became the **Museum of South Jutland** (May–Sept daily 10am–5pm; April Tues–Sun 10am–4pm; Oct–March Tues–Sun 1–4pm; 30kr), largely to commemorate the former Duchy of Schleswig, and it's still the most substantial collection of local history in south Jutland. The first floor has detailed displays on the various conflicts during the Schleswig era (for more on which, see p.392) which eventually led to the referendum of 1920 and reunification of the region with Denmark. In amongst the uniforms and weaponry, look out for the section devoted to the short-lived Als Republic of 1918, born as the German Reich's dissenting northern ports rebelled against the Kaiser and, in emulation of the then-recent Russian revolution, raised a red banner over the town's barracks – their stand lasted only three days. The second floor provides some welcome relief from the battle scenes below, with culturally oriented displays such as a collection of the sought-after silver vinaigrette produced locally; holding a sponge infused with scented water, they were an important status symbol amongst the ladies of Denmark. Accessed via a dark, uninviting guard room from the late 1300s, the ground floor covers the history of the castle itself, with four reconstructed models illustrating its various stages of development.

Sønderborg and Als

Dybbøl Banke and Mill

There are a couple of good reasons to cross back over the bridge to the mainland (Jutland) side of Sønderborg: site of the last major battle on Danish soil during the War of 1864 against the Prussians, **Dybbøl Banke** holds the informative Battlefield Centre and the strategically crucial Dybbøl Mill, both of which sit amidst a plethora of moats and grassed-over trenches left over from the conflict. Bus #1 from the Sønderborg bus station will take you there in fifteen minutes, but the 3km walk is a much nicer way of getting here; head left on the old gendarme path that runs along the water's edge from the bridge,

The definitive battle of 1864

Ask any Dane what happened in **1864**, and they'll probably answer that this was the year when Malebrok died in the war, paraphrasing a macabre nursery rhyme in the same vein as England's *Ring-a-ring-a-roses*, a natty little children's song about dying from bubonic plague. Nobody knows who Malebrok was, but the continuing prevalence of the nursery rhyme gives an indication of the enduring effect of the war on the Danish psyche. Although Danes were not unused to defeats, the 1864 trouncing was a major blow: a third of Danish territory was lost to Germany and two-fifths of the population suddenly became German.

Leading up to the war, construction of a new defence line at Dannevirke in south Schleswig to deter attacks from the south had given the Danes a false sense of security – and when well-equipped and highly organized Prussian forces backed by Austria and the new German association of states began to make their way north-wards on February 1, they realised that the unfinished Dannevirke line wouldn't hold. Five days later, Danish troops were withdrawn from Dannevirke and marched up to **Dybbøl**, where they were quickly mustered to finish the construction of a new defence line to protect Sønderborg and Als; it was finally completed on March 15. On the same afternoon, the Prussians began their bombardments, using fluted cannons whose range was far greater than anything the Danes had seen before, and slowly worked their way towards the Danish defence line. The final battle at Dybbøl started at 10am on April 18, with Prussian troops attacking the heavily damaged trenches; two hours later, the Danish counterattack collapsed and a truce was called. A final **peace agreement** was reached in August: Holstein and Schleswig became part of the new German federation and remained so up until the referendum of 1920 (see p.400).

passing trenches and memorials for fallen soldiers; turn left right by the stone for lieutenant W.B. Jespersen for the Battlefield Centre. During the final clash of the 1864 War, which took place on April 18, the remains of medieval Sønderborg were all but destroyed when the town was bombarded from the south by Prussian forces. The defeat resulted in the loss of the Schleswig and Holstein duchies to Germany; most of the trenches and moats you see here today are solid German constructions built to protect their newly acquired stronghold against the threat of invading French forces who, in the event, never made it this far. If the trenches have made you curious about what happened here on that fateful day, you can get the lowdown at the **Battlefield Centre** (mid-April to Sept daily 10am–5pm; 45kr, mid-June to mid-Aug 55kr; ⓦwww.1864.dk), on the main road from Sønderborg, with military kit, rebuilt trenches and moats, and multimedia displays that trace the battle in minutest detail.

Heading back towards Sønderborg on the main road, and strategically located behind the Danish entrenchments, **Dybbøl Mill** (mid-April to Oct daily 10am–5pm; 25kr) gained national importance when it was used by Danish troops (aided by the miller) as a hiding place, lookout point and signalling post in the run-up to the final battle. Some of the most intense fighting took place here, and the mill has since become a national symbol, for both Danes and Germans, in memory of the atrocities of the war and of the bravery of the miller. The story is recounted inside with pictures and maps, though the text is in Danish and German only.

Practicalities

Although the bulk of Sønderborg lies across the Alssund on Als, **trains** go no further than the town's mainland section on the Jutland side of the water, a short walk from the graceful modern road bridge. Long-distance **buses** continue across the bridge to the bus station at the northern fringe of the centre on Jernbanegade. Sønderborg **airport**, 7km north of the centre, has regular **flights** to and from Copenhagen; bus #2 runs from here to the bus station four times a day to coincide with the flight timetable. The **tourist office** (mid-June to mid-Aug Mon–Fri 9.30am–6pm, Sat 9.30am–1pm; mid-Aug to mid-June Mon–Fri 9.30am–5pm, Sat 9.30am–1pm; ☏74 42 35 55, ⓦwww.visitsonderborg.com) is just downhill from the bus station at Rådhustorvet 7 and has a list of private accommodation in the area. Otherwise Sønderborg has a good range of **accommodation** options within easy walking distance of the town centre; the hostel is a short bus ride away.

Choosing where to **eat** in Sønderborg is a relatively uncomplicated affair as most of the best places are within a small area in the town centre and along the waterfront. The centre takes on a Mediterranean air on warm evenings as smartly dressed Danes stroll from bar to bar; locals often begin a weekend by shopping at the Perlegade end, then eating their way down to the other end of the street. There's a branch of the ubiquitous *Jensens Bøfhus* steakhouse chain at Perlegade 36; *Café Druen*, at Store Rådhusgade 1, has low-cost snacks, and next door there are good evening meals at English-style pub *Penny Lane* – both sometimes host live jazz and other music. Nearby on Brogade 2, ♣ *OX EN* offers sublime Argentinean steaks with all the trimmings for from 149kr, while *Bella Italia*, on Lille Rådhusstræde 31, has filling Italian meals. By the harbour, on Søndre Havnegade 22, *Café au Lait* is good for drinks and light meals, as is the *Colosseum* next door. **Nightlife** is limited: along Store Rådhusgade, *Penny Lane* at no. 12 (with beers from all over the world), or *Café Druen* at no.1, are your best options. *Maybe Not Bob*, Rådhustorvet 5, is a slightly noisier place, popular with young locals.

Accommodation

Arnkilhus Arnkilgade 13 ☎74 42 23 36, ⓦwww.arnkilhus.dk. Five minutes' walk north of the centre, this good-value red-brick bungalow is easily mistaken for a private home – look out for the sign. The fourteen comfortable rooms are all different (some have private bathrooms), and there's a large terrace at the back. ⑥
Comwell Sønderborg Rosengade 2 ☎74 42 19 00, ⓦwww.comwell.com The grandest hotel in town, this is a business-oriented place on the seafront around the corner from Sønderborg slot, with a lovely swimming pool and good restaurant. Prices plummet by almost half during summer. ⑨
Sønderborg Kongevej 96 ☎74 42 34 33, ⓦwww.hotelsoenderborg.dk. Good middle-ground option which looks straight out of the Addams Family. It's close to the centre yet near beautiful woodlands and the south-coast beaches, and the rooms are all self-contained and comfortable. ⑥
Sønderborg City Danhostel Kærvej 70 ☎74 42 31 12, ⓦwww.sonderborgdanhostel.dk. Shiny, modern youth hostel twenty minutes' walk north of the centre, via Perlegade and Kærvej (or take bus #6 from the bus station), which has dorms June to Sept only (200kr) and doubles (⑤) all year.
Sønderborg Camping Ringgade 7 ☎74 42 41 89, ⓦwww.sonderborgcamping.dk. Beautifully located campsite surrounded by greenery, a short walk from Sønderborg marina and ten minutes' walk from the centre or bus station.

Around Als

Away from Sønderborg, the rest of Als has a couple of attractions to take you away from the string of sheltered sandy beaches dotted around its coastline, both of which are reachable by the hourly bus #13 from Sønderborg bus station. Five kilometres northeast of Sønderborg, and signposted left off the main road to Fynshav (from where a ferry sails to Bøjden on Funen, see p.246), the attractive little village of **Augustenborg** is centred around two main streets, lined by picturesque eighteenth-century townhouses that lead up to the ridiculously grand, Rococo-style **Augustenborg palace**, a great pile which looks somewhat misplaced in relation to the size of the village around it. In 1660 Christian III's great-grandson tore down a village here in order to make room for his new manor house on the banks of Alssund, and named it after his wife Augusta. His grandson, August I, also took his turn and created today's painfully symmetrical three-wing Baroque palace, from which two avenues of trees lead down to Alssund. The palace now houses a psychiatric hospital and the only public access is to the **gatehouse** at the end of Slotsallé, where there's a small exhibit (in Danish) about the palace history; and to the imposing Baroque palace **chapel** (daily 10am–6pm; if locked, pick up a key from the hospital gatehouse), which is built into the palace at the bottom corner of the right wing, and not visibly a chapel from the outside. Inside, the nave is without benches in order to make room for the wide garments worn by the aristocracy at the time, while the elaborate decoration includes an unusual alabaster baptismal font, a present from Czar Alexander the First.

Moving on from Augustenborg and still on the route of the #13 bus, the shallow and child-friendly sandy **beach** at Købingsmark is the main pull on the north coast, and is a lovely spot to sun and swim when the weather's good, and has a decent campsite, *Købingsmark Strand Camping* (☎ & ⓕ74 45 18 70). While you're in the area (and again reachable by the #13 bus), you might want to check out the novel **Danfoss Museum and Adventure Park** (April–June & mid-Aug to Oct daily 10am–6pm; July to mid-Aug daily 10am–7pm; Nov–March Mon–Fri 10am–4pm, Sat & Sun 10am–5pm; Nov–March 60kr, rest of the year 115kr; ⓦwww.danfossuniverse.com), 5km south of Nordborg on the main road from Sønderborg – turn east down Mads Patent Vej. Built and funded by Danfoss, one of Denmark's most successful companies, it's geared mainly towards children, and makes a successful job of explaining the forces of nature and the complex world of technology in a simple, hands-on way. The

Thermolab, housing things like liquid crystals and a wind tunnel in which you battle a gale, is especially popular. It's not nearly as tacky as it sounds, and makes for a fun day out if you're travelling with children.

Two more beaches on the island deserve a mention. On the south coast, close to a dam linking Als with the peninsula of Kegnæs, **Drejby** is a hotspot for wind- and kite-surfing; beginners stay inside the bay, while the more experienced brave the elements on the Baltic side. The long stretch of sand here attracts the crowds during summer, and there's a nudist section to the east of the dam. Good campsites in the area include *Drejby Strand Camping* (T74 40 43 05, W www.drejby.dk), right next to the dam at Kegnæsvej 85; and *Sønderkoppel Camping* (T & F74 40 51 62), past the Kegnæs lighthouse at Piledøppel 2. From Sønderborg bus station, bus #19 runs regularly to the dam. Facing east, and reachable via bus #17, the quiet beach at **Momark** is also a pretty place to chill out, especially if you're waiting for the ferry to Søby on Ærø (see p.239). The only campsite around here is *Solskrænten Camping* (T74 40 74 54, W www.solskraenten.dk), Fiskervej 35, a large, family-oriented site on the coast with a large playground and a swimming pool.

Tønder and around

Tucked away in the bleak, windswept marshes of Jutland's southeastern corner and just short of the border with Germany, **TØNDER** is an intriguing place, first described around 1130 by Arabic geographer Idrisi as a protected anchoring place called Tundira. Despite their inhospitable surroundings, the people of Tønder have always managed to prosper. In the thirteenth century, Franciscan monks set up a monastery here and persuaded King Abel to give the settlement a municipal charter so as to encourage the burgeoning **livestock trade**: horses and cattle were fattened on the rich grass of the marsh meadows and shipped from Tønder's protected harbour to Holland and beyond. Tønder soon became the richest and most important port in south Jutland, possibly even the country. However, to protect the town and surrounding uplands from the frequent tidal floods which devastated Tønder, huge dikes were built in the mid-sixteenth century which blocked access to the sea from the harbour. Facing financial ruin, the people of Tønder determined to find an alternative enterprise and turned to **lace-making**, which became a booming business that employed some twelve thousand local women during its mid- to late eighteenth-century heyday. Tønder is still known as a centre of lace-making, with local work widely revered in modern lace-making circles. Today, the town still maintains many links with its neighbours over the

The Sort Sol

During spring and autumn, over a million migrating starlings pass through the Wadden Sea marshes on their way north for the summer or south for the winter, and the mesmerizing aerial displays that occur just before sunset as they settle down to roost are known locally as the **Sort Sol** ("Black Sun"). The balletic formation movements of the flocks are a sort of collective stance against predators such as hawks or falcons, and the best places to see them in action are Tønder, near Ribe or just outside Skærbæk. Ask at local tourist offices as to where the flocks have last been seen, or join one of the organized tours offered by *Dansk NaturSafari* (T73 72 64 00, W www .natursafari.dk) in Møgeltønder, and *Højer Mølle & Marsk Museum* (T74 78 29 11) in Højer; both cost around 100kr per person, excluding transport.

border; the majority of locals voted for the town to remain part of Germany in the 1920 referendum, and links with Germany remain strong. With a German kindergarten, school, library and a German minister at the Kristkirke church, Tønder feels very much like a north German town, and you'll hear as much German spoken as Danish as you wander the compact centre and check out its brace of absorbing museums.

The area around Tønder is also steeped in history and worth a couple of days' exploration. The frozen-in-time feel of medieval **Møgeltønder** offers a sense of how the king's outposts might have looked two hundred years ago, while to the east, **Højer** is intrinsically linked to the area's attempts at taming the tidal floods of the marshes, most recently with the magnificent Danish-German Forward Coastal Dike, which marks the beginning of the Danish section of the **Wadden Sea**, known internationally for its prolific birdlife.

Tønder

Central **TØNDER** bears clear evidence of the town's former wealth, its cobbled streets containing many ancient gabled buildings built by wealthy merchants. From the bus and train station on Jernbanegade, head towards the pedestrianized street which encircles the compact centre, and whose name changes as you move eastwards from Kongevejen to Vestergade, Storegade and Østergade. Halfway down, at Østergade 1, look out for the former apothecary across from the tourist office (see p.268); dating from 1660, it's a prime example of the lavish houses built on money from the lace trade, with a monumental and beautifully carved sandstone portal that leaves you in little doubt that its owner was very rich indeed. It now houses a bric-à-brac shop, and you can wander inside to see the many old features, including a lovely fireplace decorated with Dutch tiles. Continuing down Storegade, the gabled Drøhses Hus at no.14 dates from 1672 and boasts a similarly impressive entrance. Home to a branch of the **Tønder Museum** (April–Dec Mon–Fri 10am-5pm, Sat 10am–1pm; 20kr), its original features have been fully restored, inside and out. In the basement, changing exhibitions concentrate on various aspects of the lace trade, while the room next door is devoted to beautifully crafted cast-iron stoves; the ground and first floors hold some incredibly intricate and delicate pieces of local lace – the painstaking process of producing it is demonstrated by a working lace-maker during the summer.

Heading back towards the train station, passing the Rococo facade of the so-called Dike Baron's house at Vestergade 9, turn left down Kogade and left again down Skibroen to reach the town's two main museums, both located at Kongevejen 51 and accessed through a central rotunda. To the left, **Tønder Museum** (June–Aug daily 10am–5pm; Sept–May Tues–Sun 10am–5pm; 40kr, includes Kunstmuseum) is accessed by way of a gatehouse, the only remaining part of the sixteenth-century Tønderhus castle. Spread over three floors, the exhibits are primarily devoted to trade in this part of south Jutland and the opulent houses built by local livestock and lace merchants; look out for the displays of elaborately decorated wooden furniture and Tønder silverware and lace. The adjoining **Sønderjyllands Kunstmuseum** (same hours; 40kr, includes Tønder Museum; Ⓦ www.sonkunst.dk) offers changing exhibitions of twentieth-century northern European art, including a significant collection of Danish surrealist works from the 1930s and 1940s. Linked to Tønder Museum by a walkway and run jointly by the two museums (same hours and included in entry fee), the town's former watertower holds a collection of chairs by local boy **Hans J. Wegner** (see p.410), whose designs went on to become internationally recognized. It's worth climbing to the top of the tower to take in the outstanding view of Tønder and the surrounding marshland.

Practicalities

As it's only 4km from the German border, Tønder's **transport** network is mainly geared towards north-south travel, with Ribe (see p.272) being an easy train ride away. There are no direct transport links from Sønderborg; you have to catch a train to Tinglev and then bus #16 to Tønder, or travel back up to Aabenraa and catch the #16 bus. The **tourist office** on Torvet (July to mid-Aug Mon–Fri 10am–5pm, Sat 10am–2pm; mid-Aug to June Mon–Fri 9am–4pm, Sat 9am–noon; ☎74 72 12 20, Ⓦwww.visittonder.dk) has reams of information about Tønder and can help with bicycle hire.

The only plus side to Tønder's limited range of **accommodation** is that it's varied. The most expensive option is the somewhat timewarped *Tønder-hus*, opposite Tønder Museum at Jomfrustien 1 (☎74 72 22 22, Ⓦwww .hoteltoenderhus.dk; ●), a dull-looking red-brick pile built during World War I, and little changed since then; rooms are clean and comfortable, though, and there's a smart new section at the back. A little cheaper and also in the centre is the *Hostrups*, Søndergade 30 (☎74 72 21 29, Ⓦwww.hostrupshotel .dk; ●) overlooking Vidå river and housed in a spacious old villa with creaking floorboards; no two of the tastefully decorated en-suite rooms are the same. The best budget option is the **youth hostel**, *Tønder Vandrerhjem*, Sønder-port 4 (☎74 72 35 00, Ⓦwww.toenderdanhostel.dk; closed mid-Dec to mid-Feb), about 1km west of the train station past Tønder Museum and the river, with dorms (150kr) and doubles (●). There's also a **campsite** at Holmevej 2A (☎74 72 18 49, Ⓦwww.sydvest.dk; April–Sept), with log cabins sleeping four for 2500kr per week.

The best places for **food and drink** include the *Hostrups* hotel (daily noon–9pm), which does good-value traditional Danish meals, and a daily special for 78k; a bit out of the centre on the road to Ribe, the *Bowler Inn*, Landevej 56 (daily 11am–11pm ☎74 72 00 11, Ⓦwww.hotelbowlerinn.dk) is renowned for its draught beers and quality steaks (from 79kr upwards) and has a bowling alley. It's said that Tønder had the world's highest ratio of inhabitants to bars – forty-nine to one – in the eighteenth century, and one of the original spots, the atmospheric ⚑ *Victoria* (Mon–Sat 11.30am–10pm, Sun 2–10pm ☎74 72 00 89, Ⓦwww.cafe-victoria.dk.), Storegade 9, is still going strong and brews delicious beer as well as offering a good selection of substantial burgers (from 75kr), mouthwatering cakes (25kr), and home-made soups (57kr). For something a little more peaceful, ⚑ *Café Engel* (Tues–Fri 11.30am–5pm, Sat 11am–4pm), Gråbrødre Torv (head down Lille Gade from the pedestrianized street), has a lovely array of organic sandwiches, salads and cakes from 49kr upwards. Their Saturday breakfast (11am–1pm; 99kr) of fresh bread, fruit, salad, cheese, and scrambled eggs is out of this world. If you're here in August, don't miss the live jazz and folk of the Tønder Festival (see p.43).

West of Tønder

Just 5km west of Tønder and reachable via bus #66 toward Højer, it's well worth taking time to visit the idyllic medieval-era village of **MØGELTØNDER** which – somewhat unbelievably given its diminutive size – was once the region's main town during the area's maritime era; Tønder was merely its harbour. Since then, time seems to have stood still here, and the village is ideal for an afternoon of peaceful meandering. The village grew up around

Møgeltønderhus – the Danish king's most southerly fortified outpost – which was destroyed and rebuilt in the thirteenth, fifteenth and seventeenth centuries. The town and its ruinous fort were eventually given to Field Marshal Hans Schack as a reward for his war victory over the Swedes at the battle of Nyborg in 1661. He tore down the old ruin and built the current **Schackenborg Castle**, which remained within the Schack family for eleven generations until 1979, when it was handed back to the Danish crown; it's now home to the Queen's youngest son, Prince Joachim. There's no entry to the public, but there are half-hour guided tours of the neatly manicured, moat-enclosed grounds (mid-May to Aug Wed, Thurs & Sat at 11.30am & noon; 25kr) with the possibility, if you're lucky, of a royal sighting; Joachim still farms the land hereabouts. Lined with lime trees, the cobbled Møgeltønder is the village's main street; near the castle end at no.42, the *Schackenborg Slotskro* (daily 11am–10pm; ☎74 73 83 83, ⓦ www.slotskro.dk), is an outstanding (if pricey) restaurant, with a fabulous selection of dishes made from Schackenborg's home-grown produce; it also has luxurious rooms (ⓐ). At the other end of the street, **Møgeltønder Kirke** (daily 8am–4pm) has some nice frescoes dating back to the twelfth century. For information on guided tours of the Tønder marshes or the Wadden Sea (see box, below), visit **Dansk NaturSafari** (☎73 72 64 00, ⓦ www.natursafari.dk) at no. 22.

Some 7km west of Møgeltønder (and on the route of bus #66), the small town of **HØJER** gives an interesting insight into the dramas created by the Tønder coastline. Højer was a seaside town until 1981, when completion of the **Danish-German Forward Coastal Dike** shifted the coastline 2km to the west and reclaimed some twelve hundred hectares of land; the Danish section of this is known as Magrethe Kog. The first dikes were built here as early as the eleventh century, and today's Forward Coastal Dike is the culmination of the long battle to curb the devastating and powerful west coast storm tides. To learn more about the efforts to control the forces of nature, head for the **Højer Mill & Marsh Museum** (April–Oct daily 10am–4pm; 25kr), housed in a restored Dutch windmill that it is impossible to miss. It's entirely devoted to the area's unique history with hundreds of photos depicting seasonal life in the marshes before and after the 1925 drainage system was put in place, and some very scary reminders of the destructive and deadly power of storm tides. Although most of the text is in Danish, the photos provide plenty of insight. Next door, the mill's old grain store is home to the **Højer Mølle Naturvejleder** or "ranger at hand" (☎74 78 29 11), who can answer questions about the area's ecology. The fertile tidal flats along this bit of coast are part of a larger landscape – the **Wadden Sea**

Wadden Sea aquatic birdlife

A 500km coastal strip stretching from Den Helder in Holland to Blåvandshug near Esbjerg in Denmark, the **Wadden Sea** is an essential resting and feeding place for **migratory birds** travelling the so-called East Atlantic Flyway, which sees them heading as far north as Greenland in the summer and as far south as southern Africa in the winter. Each year, more than ten million aquatic birds pass through the Wadden Sea, which is one of the world's most important wetland areas, designated as a protected site under the internationally recognized RAMSAR convention. It covers about 900,000 hectares of marsh, tidal flats, sand banks, beaches and dunes and supports over fifty bird species including a number of specimens designated threatened, from the Kentish plover, dunlin and ruff to the gull-billed and little tern, any of which are regular visitors to the saltwater lake in the reclaimed Magrethe Kog near Højer (see above).

– that stretches from Holland via Germany to Esbjerg, and is one of the world's most valuable habitats for birds. The ranger also offers wildlife tours, including trips to the marshes to see the breathtaking starling roosting displays known as the Black Sun (see box on p.266).

If it's not too windy, you might want to check out the Danish-German Forward Costal Dike and sluice, an easy 3km bike ride west of Højer. The small **tourist office**, next to the mill at Møllegade 12 (☎74 78 29 93; ⓦ www.visithojer.dk) rents out bikes (55kr per day). Follow the signboards past the old dike and sluice at the outskirts of Højer and it's straight ahead to the very Dutch-looking dike, with the reclaimed Magrethe Kog to the left; it's now a protected nature reserve, and a third of its area has been retained as a saltwater lake to serve as home to the area's aquatic birds. The road ends at the dike and the massive Vidå sluice, with its 20m-wide circular tanks and three storm shields; there's an excellent café next to the sluice (daily 10am–8pm), serving traditional Danish seafood dishes (from 89kr). Don't leave town without sampling the delicious **Højer sausage** – actually a salami, and widely acclaimed as Denmark's best. It's available from the butcher's shop at Søndergade 1, across from the church.

Løgumkloster

Another worthy day-trip from Tønder, some 17km to the northeast just off the main road to Kolding and reachable on bus #46, the medieval town of **LØGUMKLOSTER** is worth a quick detour. It's built around the colossal thirteenth-century **Løgumkloster abbey** (Mon–Sat 10am–6pm, Sun noon to 5pm; free), easily visible from all angles as you approach the town. In 1173, at the bidding of the Bishop of Ribe, who chose the site on the basis of its remoteness and fertile soil, Cistercian arrived here to get away from secular temptations and live simple lives of work and prayer. The magnificent church and four-winged abbey was built between 1225 and 1325, and its construction coincided with changing building styles in Europe, from Romanesque to Gothic, as evidenced by the finished building's mish-mash of styles. Only the eastern wing remains today; look out for the beautifully arched chapter hall.

Rømø and Mandø

Just offshore from the Wadden Sea coastal strip lie the neighbouring islands of **Rømø** and **Mandø**. A popular holiday destination for German tourists, Rømø offers some fantastic beaches, while Mandø is less developed and a better example of the Wadden's classic tidal landscapes.

From Skærbæk, twenty-seven kilometres north of Tønder, bus #29 heads across the 9km dam over the Wadden Sea tidal flats to the island of **RØMØ**. Created by the actions of sea, wind and sand over the past two thousand years, Rømø maintains a wild and unkempt appearance, with a duney heathland in its centre, beaches along the western side and marshy tidal flats facing mainland Jutland. In summer, Rømø is a magnet for **beach** lovers, who flock to the west's wide, sandy shores; don't be surprised if things feel crowded at the height of summer. The beaches are divided into sections for designated activities such as windsurfing or kite-buggying (pick up a map at the tourist office), and there's nude bathing at the southwesternmost corners. **Horseback riding** is also very popular here; Rømø Ranch (☎74 75 54 11) on the Lakolk section of the beach offers rides on the beach and across the island, while Kommandørgården on the

5

east coast has Icelandic ponies and, during low tide, offers rides across to Mandø.

If you're interested in Rømø's prolific avian population, head to Tvismark, the first hamlet just south of the causeway. Here, the **Tønnisgård Natur Center** (March–Nov Mon–Fri 10am–6pm; Dec–Feb Mon–Fri 10am–3pm; 15kr; Ⓦwww.tonnisgaard.dk), next door to the tourist office at Havnebyvej 30, organizes birdwatching trips to the Stormengene nature reserve at the island's southeastern tip, where there's a high concentration of migrating birds in spring and autumn. They also have heaps

△ Traditional doorway, Rømø

of material about the island's wildlife and can point you in the right direction if you want to explore on your own, and the centre also has a small exhibit about Rømø's history and distinctive thatched buildings and an informative display about the ecology of the tidal mud flats.

Although beaches and wildlife are Rømø's two top attractions, the island's cultural history is also fairly absorbing. As a typical Wadden Sea island, Rømø has strong seafaring traditions, and the navigation school that once operated here produced many *kommandører*, whaling-ship captains who built grand residences on their return to the island. Just south of Tvismark in Toftum, the handsome **Kommandørgården**, Jurevej 60 (May–Sept Tues–Sun 10am–6pm; Oct–Nov Tues–Sun 10am–3pm; free), was built in 1749 by one Captain Thacken, and its rich interior and elaborate furnishings are a fine illustration of the wealth brought home from the sea. Further down Jurevej, on the right-hand side, look out for the fence made of whale jawbones, the only available building material in 1772 when it was made.

Practicalities

Rømø's **tourist office** (daily 9am–5pm; Ⓣ74 75 51 30, Ⓦwww.romo.dk) is at Havnebyvej 30 in Tvismark, and can help with information about private accommodation (about 250kr per person per day); it's also the island's official holiday letting agency with a long list of pretty cottages. The main village of Havneby holds two good-value **hotels**: *Havneby Kro* (Ⓣ74 75 75 35, Ⓦwww .havneby-kro.dk; ❻), at Skansen 3 near the harbour, with sleek modern rooms atop a quality restaurant; and the inexpensive *Garni* (Ⓣ74 75 54 80, Ⓕ74 75 63 80; ❷), Nørre Frankel 15 (take a right just as you enter town), whose basic rooms share facilities. The most luxurious option is the modern *Kommandørgården* (Ⓣ74 75 51 22, Ⓦwww.kommandoergaarden.dk; ❻), at Havnebyvej 21 in Østerby, a kilometre north of Havneby. Best described as a holiday village, it has the usual double rooms as well as self-contained flats (895kr per day), four-person log cabins (660kr per day) and a **campsite**. Of the island's two other camping options, by far the most popular is *Lakolk* (Ⓣ74 75 52 28, Ⓦwww.lakolkcamping.dk; April to mid-Oct), on the windswept west coast. There's also a **youth hostel** (Ⓣ74 75 51 88, Ⓦwww.romo-vandrerhjem .dk; mid-March to mid-Nov), Lyngvejen 7, in a beautiful old thatched building just north of Havneby; there are doubles (❷) as well as dorms (120kr). **Public** transport on the island is limited to bus #29, which runs four to six times a day between Skærbæk (on the mainland) and Havneby. Alternatively, the *Garni* hotel rents out bicycles for 50kr per day. It's also possible to **cross the border to Germany** from here without returning to the Danish mainland by using the ferry (☎73 75 53 03, ⊛www.romo-sylt.dk; 50min, 49kr) that sails from Havneby to List.

Mandø and the Vadehavscentret

Comprising just eight square kilometres of marshy land, the island of **MANDØ** is tricky to get to – the two roads leading to it are tidal, so it's cut off during high tide – but this relative isolation has left it untouched, and it's an excellent destination for a nature-oriented day-trip. To get here from the mainland, you take the **tractor bus** (daily May–Sept only; 40min, 50kr one way, 60kr same-day return; ☎75 44 51 07, ⊛www.mandoebussen.dk), which leaves from the small town of Vester Vedsted during low tide and returns a couple of hours later. Transport to Vester Vedsted – eighteen kilometres north of Skærbæk – is also tricky as there's no direct bus from Skærbæk; the easiest option is to catch bus #711 from Ribe (see below). If you're travelling under your own steam from Skærbæk, turn left at Råhedevej, and the wiggly road will lead you straight there. The passage over to the island is an experience in itself, and if weather permits, it's worth clambering up to the open roof to take in the views. Once the bus crosses over the flood defences protecting Ribe, the open vista of the Wadden Sea lies flat out in front of you; keep an eye out for the numerous birds feeding on worms, snails and mussels in the muddy sand; if you're lucky, a colony of seals will be basking in the sun to the right of the track just before you reach Mandø. The tractor bus stops at the island's only village, **MANDØ BY**, and near to the **Mandø Center** (May–Sept daily 10am–5pm; free; ☎75 44 53 54, ✆mandoecentret@hotmail.com), where there's a small exhibit describing the island's natural and cultural history and a dozen self-contained rooms (❺) and dorm beds (100kr). Mandø is best explored on foot or by bike. You can bring your own bike over on the tractor bus (60kr) but it's cheaper to hire one on the island (☎75 44 51 07); you'll pay 30kr for the four hours it takes until the tractor bus heads back to the mainland. Whether you're cycling or on foot, the 10km circular route around the island can easily be covered in that time, including plenty of breaks.

If you want to learn more about the area's complex ecology and history, it's well worth visiting the sleek new **Vadehavscentret** (Wadden Sea Centre: April–Sept daily 10am–5pm, mid-Feb to March & Oct daily 10am–4pm, Nov to mid-Feb Tues & Wed 11am–3pm; 60kr; ⊛www.vadehavscentret.dk), in Vester Vedsted next to the tractor bus stop. Storms and tides are explained by way of snazzy, interactive multi-media displays, and there's fascinating film footage of the 1981 flood that left Mandø submerged. It also has an excellent section on bird migration and the global threats to their nesting and feeding habitats. The centre also offers well-organised tours (check their website for a list and prices) of the area, including birdwatching trips into the marshes around Ribe, seal-spotting near Mandø, and treks out onto the Wadden Sea mud flats to look at creepy-crawlies.

Ribe

About fifty minutes north of Tønder by train – and twenty minutes from Skærbæk – lies the exquisitely preserved town of **RIBE**. In 856 bishop Ansgar

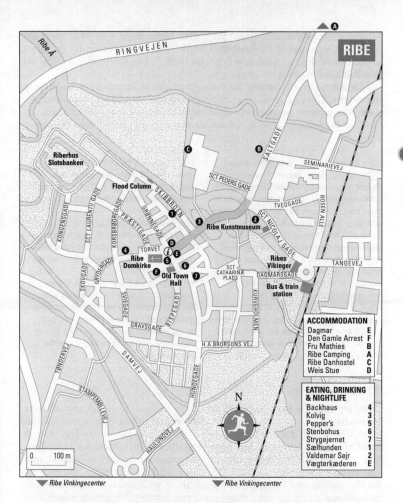

RIBE

Riberhus
Slotsbanken

Flood Column

1

Ribe Kunstmuseum
3
2

Ribes
Vikinger

Ribe
Domkirke
4
TORVET
D
5 E
6
Old Town **F**
Hall
7
SCT
CATHARINÆ
PLADS
DAGMARSGADE

Bus & train
station

RINGVEJEN

Ribe Å

SALTGADE

SEMINARIEVEJ

SCT PEDERS GADE

TVEDGADE

ROSEN ALLE

SCT NICOLAJ GADE

TANGEVEJ

SKIBBROEN

GRØNNEGADE

PRÆSTEGADE

KORSBRØDREGADE

SCT LAURENTI GADE

KONGENSGADE

SKOVGADE

GRYDERGADE

SVIEGADE

BISPEGADE

GRAVSGADE

H.A. BRORSONS VEJ

KURVEHOLMEN

DAMVEJ

TØNDERVEJ

STAMPEMØLLEVEJ

HUNDEGADE

HAULUNDVEJ

N

0   100 m

ACCOMMODATION	
Dagmar	E
Den Gamle Arrest	F
Fru Mathies	B
Ribe Camping	A
Ribe Danhostel	C
Weis Stue	D

EATING, DRINKING & NIGHTLIFE	
Backhaus	4
Kolvig	3
Pepper's	5
Stenbohus	6
Strygejernet	7
Sælhunden	1
Valdemar Sejr	2
Vægterkæderen	E

▼ Ribe Vinkingecenter   ▼ Ribe Vinkingecenter

of Hamburg and Bremen built one of Denmark's first churches here as a base for his missionaries arriving from Germany; a hundred years later the town was a major staging post for pilgrims making their way south to Rome. Ribe's proximity to the sea allowed it to evolve into a significant trading port, but continued expansion was thwarted by the dual blows of the Reformation and the sanding-up of the harbour. Since then, not much appears to have changed. The surrounding marshlands, which have prevented the development of any large-scale industry, and a long-standing conservation programme have enabled Ribe to keep the appearance and size of medieval times, and its old town is a delight to wander in.

Arrival, information and accommodation

From Ribe **train** and **bus stations** on the east side of the river, Dagmarsgade cuts a straight path to the central square, Torvet. Besides the usual services, the **tourist office** (June & Sept Mon–Fri 9am–5pm, Sat 10am–1pm; July & Aug

Mon–Fri 9am–6pm, Sat 10am–5pm, Sun 10am–2pm; Oct–May Mon–Fri 9.30am–4.30pm, Sat 10am–1pm; ☎75 42 15 00, ⓦwww.visitribe.dk), on Torvet to the rear of the cathedral, sells the *Town Walks in Old Ribe* leaflet, a useful aid to self-guided exploration (5kr).

If you intend to stick around for the nightwatchman's tour, you'll need to **stay overnight**. There's a good range of interesting and affordable accommodation, though in summer be sure to book ahead as everything gets packed. The tourist office publishes a list of private rooms that rent for about 200kr per person per night.

Dagmar Torvet ☎75 42 00 33, ⓦwww .hoteldagmar.dk. Wonderful if you can afford it, this beautifully restored place opposite the Domkirke dates from 1581 and claims to be the oldest hotel in Denmark; its gorgeous doubles come with period furniture and loads of character. ❽

Den Gamle Arrest Torvet 11 ☎75 42 37 00, ⓦwww.dengamlearrest.dk. An intriguing option, originally built as a girls' boarding school and which later served as the town's jail. The double rooms are in the former cells, which these days lock from the inside. ❺, en-suite 790kr

Fru Mathies Saltgade 15 ☎75 42 34 20, ⓦwww .frumathies.dk. A short walk from the centre across the river down Nederdammen, this bright yellow pub also has a few comfortable rooms, some of which share bathrooms. 590kr, en-suite ❻

Ribe Camping ☎75 41 07 77, ⓦwww .ribecamping.dk. Some 2km north of Ribe along Farupvej (take bus #771), this pleasant campsite has cabins as well as pitches. Open April–Nov.

Ribe Danhostel Skt Pedersgade 16 ☎75 42 06 20, ⓦwww.danhostel-ribe.dk. An easy walk over the river from the town centre, and with some doubles (❸) as well as dorms (150kr). Open May to mid-Sept.

Weis Stue Torvet 2 ☎75 42 07 00, ⓦwww .weisstue.dk. Attractive doubles sharing bath and toilet facilities in a wonderfully atmospheric teahouse-cum-restaurant, with creaking floorboards and wood-panelled walls; there are only eight rooms, so advance booking is essential year-round. ❻

The centre

Towering over the town and dominating the wetlands for miles around, **Ribe Domkirke** (July to mid-Aug Mon–Sat 10am–5.30pm, Sun noon–5.30pm; May–June & mid-Aug to Sept Mon–Sat 10am–5pm, Sun noon–5pm; Oct & April Mon–Sat 11am–4pm, Sun noon–4pm; Nov–March Mon–Sat 11am–3pm, Sun noon–3pm; 12kr) is the current incarnation of Ansgar's original church. The cathedral was begun around 1150 using tufa rock, a suitably light material for the marshy base which was brought, along with some of the Rhineland's architectural styles, by river from southern Germany. Originally raised on a slight hill, the Domkirke is now a couple of metres below the surrounding streets, their level having risen due to the many centuries' worth of debris accumulated beneath them. The **interior** is not as spectacular as the cathedral's size and long history might suggest, having been stripped of much of its decoration by one Hans Tausen – the reformist Bishop of Ribe who translated the Bible into Danish – during the mid-sixteenth century. The thirteenth-century "Cat's Head Door" on the south side, a good example of the imported Romanesque design, is one of the few early decorative remains. More recent additions that catch the eye are the butcher's-slab altar and the colourful frescoes, mosaics and stained-glass windows by Carl-Henning Pedersen (a member of the CoBrA mid-twentieth-century movement of artists from Copenhagen, Brussels and Amsterdam), added in the mid-1980s. After looking around, climb the 248 steps to peer out from the top of the red-brick **Citizens' Tower**, so named since it doesn't belong to the church but to the people whose taxes pay for its upkeep. The current tower's predecessor toppled into the nave on Christmas morning, 1283.

The nightwatchman of Ribe

At 10pm every evening between May and mid-September – and also at 8pm from June to August – the **Nightwatchman of Ribe** emerges from the bar of the *Weis Stue* inn, Torvet 2, and makes his rounds. Before the advent of gas lighting, a nightwatchman would patrol every town in Denmark to help keep the sleeping populace safe from fire and flood. The last real nightwatchman of Ribe made his final tour in 1902, but thanks to the early development of tourism in the town, the custom had been reintroduced by 1932.

Dressed in a replica of his predecessor's uniform and carrying an original morning-star pike and lantern (the sharp tip doubled as a weapon), the watchman – a role filled for the last thirty years by octogenarian Aage Gran – walks the narrow alleys of Ribe singing songs written by Thomas Kingo (a local priest who lived in Ribe in the mid-eighteenth century), and talking about the town's history while stopping at points of interest. One song tells people to go to bed and to be careful with lighting fires – sensible advice when most of the town's dwellings are built from wood. It's obviously laid on for the tourists, but the tour is free and good fun.

Heading away from the cathedral along Overdammen, you cross three streams, channelled in around 1250 to provide water for a mill. The houses on the right are the best of Ribe's many half-timbered structures. Turn left off Overdammen and walk along the riverside Skibbroen and you'll spot the **Flood Column** (*Stormflodssøjlen*), a stout wooden pole showing the levels of the numerous floods that plagued the town before protective dikes were built a century ago. Continuing along Overdammen, Sct Nicolaj Gade cuts right to the small **Ribe Kunstmuseum** (July–Aug Tues–Sun 11am–5pm; Sept–June Tues–Sun 11am–4pm; 40kr; ⓦwww.ribe-kunstmuseum.dk), housing a reasonable display of works by Danish artists in a chronological progression that takes you from noble portraiture through pre-Raphaelite aestheticism to modern verism. On the first floor the highlight is *The Christening*, by Skagen painter Michael Ancher (see p.374) depicting a host of fellow Skagen painters – including P.S. Krøyer, wife Anna Ancher and himself – at his child's Christening. A handful of accomplished bronze sculptures are supplemented by larger pieces on the back lawn, from where paths and footbridges lead back across the river to the town centre.

Ribe's Viking history – and more – is celebrated at the **Ribes Vikinger** (July & Aug daily 10am–6pm, Wed until 9pm; April–June, Sept & Oct daily 10am–4pm; Nov–March Tues–Sun 10am–4pm; 60kr; ⓦwww.ribesvikinger. dk), further along Skt Nicolaj Gade opposite the train station. The exhibition is centred around Ribe's history, from its Viking beginnings as Scandinavia's oldest known market place on the banks of Ribe Å river, to the flooding in October 1634 when the floor of Ribe Cathedral was submerged under water and the town all but destroyed. Although it's a rather small exhibition, it covers each era succinctly with models, excavated remains and a full-size reconstructed Viking ship.

That's more or less all there is to Ribe, save for the paltry remains of **Ribehus Slotsbanke**, a twenty-minute walk away on the northern side of the town. The twelfth-century castle that stood here was a popular haunt with Danish royalty for a couple of centuries but was already fairly dilapidated when it was demolished by Swedish bombardment in the mid-seventeenth century. The **statue** of Queen Dagmar, a recent addition to the site and standing in bewitching isolation, is the only visible reward for the trek out here.

Denmark's Viking sites

By the time the **Viking** raids finally ceased around the end of the eleventh century, their active cultural, economic and religious heyday had left an enormous mark on the peoples of the Nordic countries, to say nothing of the rest of the world. As Denmark was one of the centres of Viking rule and a strategic stronghold for the regulation of shipping and piracy, there are traces of Viking communities spread all over the country, with a number of artefacts gleaned from the raids still intact. The following comprise Denmark's best-preserved and most notable sites:

Fyrkat, North Jutland This large Viking fortress was most likely built by Harald Bluetooth around 980 AD. See p.352.

Jelling Stone, Jutland This large runic stone was erected more than one thousand years ago by King Gorm the Old, and contains the first written mention of the nation called "Danmark". A second stone, erected by Harald Bluetooth, chronicles the arrival of Christianity in Denmark and the end of the Viking era. See p.311.

Ladbyskibet, Funen Ship burials of important Viking chieftains was a common practice, and this underground tenth-century tomb – the only Viking-ship burial mound ever unearthed in Denmark – contains the remains of a Viking chieftain and his longboat. See p.222.

Lindholm Høje, Jutland The largest Viking burial ground in Scandinavia was found at this peaceful hillside location, where many of the seven hundred graves date as far back as the fifth century. See p.364.

Nationalmuseet, Copenhagen The distinguished collection of Viking artefacts displayed here includes reproductions of the famous Jelling Stone and Bronze Age Sun Chariot. See p.94.

Ribe, Jutland The oldest city in Denmark is home to one of its finest Viking museums, built on the site of an ancient market, while the nearby Ribe Vikingecenter consists of a town, marketplace and farming community populated by costumed interpreters. See p.272 & below.

Trelleborg, Zealand This preserved ring fortress, noted for the mathematical precision of its construction, dates back to 980 AD and the reign of Harald Bluetooth See p.159.

Vikingeskibs Museet, Roskilde Nine Viking ships were discovered during the construction of this spectacular museum, which houses near-complete restorations of the five ships that lay at the bottom of the Roskilde Fjord for hundreds of years See p.148.

Ribe Vikingecenter

If you've not yet had your fill on Vikings, head for the **Ribe Vikingecenter** (July & Aug daily 11am–5pm; May, June & Sept Mon–Fri 10am–3.30pm; 70kr; ⓦ www.ribevikingecenter.dk), 3km south of the centre on Lystrupvej (6min on bus #717). Situated in the grounds of Lystrupholm manor house, it attempts to recreate the Viking lifestyle with costumed attendants demonstrating traditional crafts. It also hosts northern Europe's largest Viking market during the first weekend of May, when "Vikings" from across the globe gather to show off their outfits as well as skills such as archery, fighting and riding. Traditionally prepared food and drink as well as traditional products (leatherwear and jewellery) are sold, and Viking music is played throughout. If the weather's good, it's lots of fun.

Eating, drinking and nightlife

In terms of places **to eat**, the reputable *Vægterkælderen* (Mon–Thurs & Sun 11am–2am, Fri & Sat 11am–3am; ☏75 42 14 00, ⓦ www.hoteldagmar.dk), close to the cathedral in the basement of the *Dagmar* hotel, serves traditional Danish two- (145kr) and three-course (175kr) lunches, and two-course dinners (195kr), plus heavily laden smørrebrød all day; it's also a good spot for evening drinks. *Restaurant Backhaus* (daily 10am–10pm; ℡75 42 11 01, ⓦwww.backhaus-ribe.dk), Grydergade 12, does good-value steaks and burgers; and there's excellent Danish fare at ⌘ *Restaurant Sælhunden* (daily 11am–10pm; ℡75 42 09 46, ⓦwww.saelhunden.dk), set in a wood-beamed listed building overlooking the harbour at Skibroen 13. Nearby *Kolvig* (daily 11am–midnight; ℡75 41 04 88, ⓦwww.kolvig.dk) offers filling, reasonably priced salads and sandwiches in a relaxed riverside setting. For coffee, try *Café Valdemar* (Tues–Wed 1–11pm, Thurs 1pm–2am, Fri & Sat 1pm–5am), next to the art gallery on Skt Nicolaj Gade, which is also a good spot for **drinks** and **music** in the evening, though the beer is cheaper (and the music louder) at the town's two discos, *Pepper's* (Thurs–Sat 8am–late, Fri & Sat DJ midnight–late; ⓦwww.peppers.dk) and *Stenbohus* (Mon–Thurs & Sun 10am–2am, Fri & Sat 10am–5am; ⓦwww.stenbohus.dk), which face each other just up the street; the latter has live blues, folk or rock at least once a week. If you're looking for atmosphere, try the tiny but distinctive ⌘ *Strygejernet* pub (Tues–Weds 3pm–1am, Thurs 3pm–late, Fri & Sat 1pm–5am; ℡75 41 13 51, ⓦwww. strygejernet.dk), Dagmarsgade 1, which serves light meals and snacks during the day and popular draught ales at night.

Travel details

Trains

Kolding to: Århus (hourly; 1hr 25min–1hr 38min); Copenhagen (hourly; 2hrs 18min); Esbjerg (1–2 hourly; 40min–1hr); Fredericia (1–3 hourly; 15min); Tinglev (1–2 hourly; 40min–1hr); Sønderborg (11 daily; 1hr 30min).

Ribe to: Bramming (1–2 hourly; 16–23min); Skærbæk (hourly; 20min); Tønder (hourly; 50min).

Sønderborg to: Kolding (11 daily; 1hr 30min); Tinglev (11 daily; 36min).

Tinglev to: Kolding (1–2 hourly; 40min–1hr); Sønderborg (11 daily; 36min).

Tønder to: Ribe (hourly; 50min); Skærbæk (14 daily; 28min).

Buses

Aabenraa to: Kolding (7 daily; 1hr 5min); Haderslev (hourly; 30–45min); Sønderborg (1–3 hourly; 35–55min); Tønder (15 daily; 50min–1hr 20min).

Haderslev to: Aabenraa (hourly; 30–44min); Kolding (2 hourly; 32–45min); Ribe (5 daily; 1hr 15min).

Kolding to: Aabenraa (7 daily; 1hr 5min); Haderslev (2 hourly; 32–45min).

Ribe to: Haderslev (5 daily; 1hr 15min).

Skærbæk to: Rømø (10 daily; 30–44min).

Sønderborg to: Aabenraa (1–3 hourly; 35–55min).

Tønder to: Aabenraa (15 daily; 50min–1hr 20min); Tinglev (15 daily; 30–50min).

Ferries

Fynshav to: Bøjden (8 daily; 45min).
Mommark to: Søby (2–5 daily; 1hr).

Flights

Sønderborg to: Copenhagen (4–5 daily; 40min).

6

West Jutland

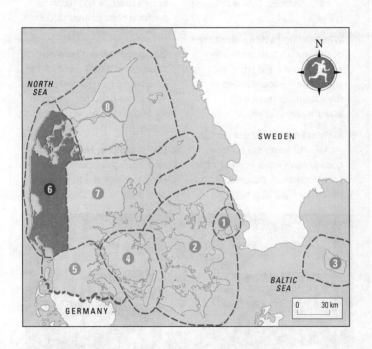

CHAPTER 6   # Highlights

✳ **Stone Age collection, Thisted Museum** The outstanding displays here include an elaborate collection of flint tools and worked-up amber found within the region. See p.284

✳ **Local beers** Please your palate by sampling some of the local brews from the Thisted, Skive or Fur breweries. See p.284, p.289 & p.290

✳ **Windsurfing at Klitmøller** One of the world's top windsurfing spots, and a great place to watch the daredevil antics of the experts or have a go yourself. See p.286

✳ **Moler cliff hikes** The dramatic moler cliffs lining the northern coastlines of Mors and Fur offer some extremely picturesque hiking. See p.288

✳ **Ringkøbing town centre** Sample the great selection of restaurants and cafés lining Ringkøbing's cobbled town square. See p.294

✳ **Hanstholm II battery** This enormous German-built battery from World War II offers a fascinating labyrinth of ammunition stores, crew's quarters and technical sections centred around four huge guns. See p.285

✳ **Birdwatching at Tipperne** Designated a bird sanctuary in its entirety, this marshy peninsula offers great opportunities for spotting local birdlife. See p.296

✳ **Elia sculpture, Herning** This enormous, fire-spurting cast-iron sculpture is a truly magnificent piece of art. See p.293

△ Rinkøbing

6

West Jutland

B attered relentlessly by the thundering waves of the North Sea, Jutland's long western strip, from Hanstholm in the north to Esbjerg in the south, is as windswept and wild as it is desolately beautiful. With its almost unbroken line of sandy beaches and windswept dunes overlooked by an array of pretty summer cottages, the beautiful coastline rightly attracts German tourists in their thousands, but it's the unforgiving westerly winds that characterize the region, and the constant blow from the coast can make the west challenging to explore. To the north is the **Limfjordslandet**, the western portion of the Limfjorden, which wriggles its way inland from the Skagerrak past islands and peninsulas that were carved out during the last Ice Age. On its northern shores, the **Thy** region holds some worthwhile attractions, both in the main towns of **Thisted** and **Hanstholm** and in terms of fjordside beaches and the outstanding windsurfing opportunities on the west coast, while the mid-fjord island of **Mors** and the adjacent **Salling** peninsula offer more bucolic charm and stunning cliffs ideal for hiking. The area south of Limfjordslandet is more desolate, with large expanses of heathland and forest dominating the landscape. **Holstebro** is the main urban draw, currently experiencing a massive cultural revival as a centre for the arts. To the southeast, **Herning** is best known for its textile industry, while to the north, **Struer**, home of renowned hi-fi manufacturers Bang & Olufsen, is one of the country's most important industrial centres. Following the coastline southwards, the ancient harbour town of **Ringkøbing**, with its stunning setting on the banks of the Ringkøbing Fjord, is an ideal base for exploring the area. There are plenty of birdwatching possibilities hereabouts on the Nissum and Ringkøbing fjords, as well as some gorgeous beaches here and in the far south around **Blåvands Huk**, within easy distance of the relatively sizeable town of **Esbjerg**. National cycle route #1 hugs the western coastline, and though public transport connections are decent, a **bike** is by far the best way to explore – though you'll need sturdy legs to cope with the winds.

Limfjordslandet

LIMFJORDSLANDET comprises the area around the western portion of the **Limfjorden**, the body of water that separates northern Jutland from the rest of the peninsula. In around 1100, just as the Viking era was coming to a close, the waters of Limfjorden stopped flowing when the outlet to the Skaggerak at Agger was shut off by sand drifts. The fjord became a brackish lake and its reign

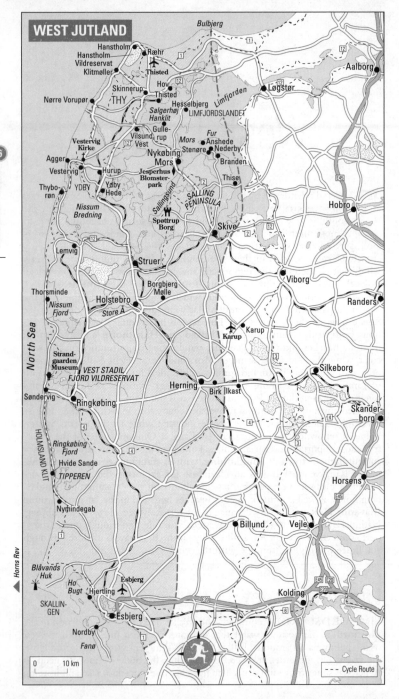

WEST JUTLAND

as the region's main transport artery ended, so destroying the region's trade and isolating it financially and geographically for over eight hundred years. In 1825, a storm reopened the outlet and the waters again started flowing from west to east. Harbours soon sprung up in Limfjordslandet's shore towns and the region's economy flourished, again centred on trade and fishing. In 1862, a new outlet opened a few kilometers to the south at **Thyborøn**, calming the powerful currents that had kept the Agger inlet open and soon closing it off again, as it remains to this day. Today, the Thyborøn inlet is protected by dikes and timber groynes, and Thyborøn itself is a thriving harbour town, connected by ferry to the Agger Tange spit of land on the fjord's northern bank.

The region's isolation following the silting up of the Agger outlet goes some way to explaining why it still feels remote and somewhat disconnected from the rest of Denmark – so making it a wonderful place for a few days of rural exploration. The most visited part of Limfjordslandet is the **Thy** region, which occupies the northwestern corner and boasts both a wild Skagerrak coastline and the more tranquil shores of the Limfjorden itself, a varied and interesting landscape encircled by beautiful beaches on all sides. There are a few interesting sights and museums in Thy's two main towns, **Thisted** and **Hanstholm**, while the Limfjord island of **Mors** and the **Salling** peninsula are both very idyllic, with their main attraction being the dramatic cliffs lining their northern coastlines. Thy's Skagerrak coast attracts legions of northern European tourists in the summer, when it's best to arrange accommodation in advance. At other times, this is a rarely visited part of the country, and it can sometimes feel as if you have the entire place to yourself. Bear in mind, though, that the weather here is unpredictable, with sharp winds blustering in off the sea; and that getting around is difficult: trains only reach to the fringes at Thisted and Skive, so you'll need to rely on buses if you're without your own transport.

Thy

Encircled by water on three sides, with a small sliver of land in the north serving as its only connection with the rest of Jutland, the landscape of the **Thy** region ranges from windswept sand dunes on the west coast to heathland and, in the east, fertile farmlands. This gorgeous variation means that Thy has a lot to offer in terms of the great outdoors, and its few towns hold some interesting attractions, too. Facing east, on the tranquil Limfjorden shores, **Thisted** is a browseable market town with a good museum, while **Hanstholm**, on the fiery west coast, has a ferry terminal, a World War II fortification and a fishing port – and not much more. Further south, the Thy west coast off Klitmøller is the epicentre of Danish windsurfing, nicknamed Hawaii II. Transport to the Thy region is, to put it mildly, limited. There's a local rail line from Struer to Thisted; to get anywhere else you'll have to travel by bus or under your own steam. There's a small ferry connecting Thy with Thyborøn by Nissum Bredning, a bridge following the railway line to Struer and another linking Thy with Mors.

Thisted

Thy's administrative centre and the terminus of the local rail line from Struer, the pleasant market town of **THISTED** is delicately positioned on the banks of Limfjorden, and boasts a large marina and a harbour that fills up to capacity during the annual **Limfjorden Rundt regatta** (ⓦwww.limfjordenrundt.dk), when some fifty traditional wooden sailing ships, from three-masted schooners down to Bermuda rigs, dock here on their way around the fjord. Even if

△ West coast fishing fleet

your visit doesn't coincide with the regatta, it's worth heading down to the waterfront to take in Thisted's magnificent fjordside setting, its entire shoreline blessed with fine **beaches**. You'll find changing facilities and a bathing pier at Søbadet, west of the centre in front of the large Thisted Bryghus brewery, where Henning Wienberg Jensen's *Thisted Pigen* statue of a young girl stares pensively out over the water. Incidentally, Thisted Bryghus produces the delicious, prize-winning Thy Pilsner – among the country's best lagers and definitely worth tasting before you leave. The only other thing worth sticking around for is the outstanding **Thisted Museum** (daily Mon–Fri 10am–4pm, Sat & Sun 1–4pm, Sept–May closed Mon; 30kr; Ⓦ www.thistedmuseum.dk), right in the centre at Jernbanegade 4. The collection includes an elaborate display of flint tools and worked-up amber found within the region, which suggest an usually high population density in the area during the Stone Age. Many of the tools are made from flint mined, from 5000 BC onwards, around what's now the town of Hov, 10km east of Thisted, and the fact that they were exported to Norway also indicates a high degree of social organization. Other ground floor displays include an exhibit illustrating how the region's numerous Bronze Age burial mounds were constructed, alongside glamorous gold and bronze items found inside them. Upstairs, displays are devoted to two of Thisted's famous townsmen: **Christian Kold**, heavily involved in the establishment of the uniquely Danish Folkehøjskole (People's High Schools; see p.123); and **I.P. Jakobsen**, a poet and naturalist who translated Darwin's *Origin of Species* into Danish. Both exhibits are something of a step back in time, with desks and working paraphernalia on display as though Kold and Jakobsen had simply left the room for a minute.

Practicalities

It's an easy **train** journey to Thisted from Struer (see p.291), embarkation point of the regional train service; if you're travelling from northern Jutland, you'll have to catch **bus** #970X from Aalborg. Thisted's bus and train stations are next to each other on Jernbanegade, a stone's throw from the marina and behind Thisted Museum. Thisted airport (ⓦwww.flying.dk), 15km north of town and reached by bus #23, is served by **flights** to and from Copenhagen. Set in the downstairs section of the old town hall at Store Torv 6, the helpful **tourist office** (mid-June to Aug Mon–Fri 9am–5pm, Sat 9am–1pm; Sept to mid-June Mon–Fri 9am–4pm; ⓣ97 92 19 00, ⓦwww.thistedturist.dk), rents out bicycles (60kr per day) – you pick them up at Statoil on Østerbakken 63, five minutes walk up Østerbakken hill from the marina.

With some good places to **eat** and **sleep** – not to mention its beaches – Thisted is an appealing place to stay for a couple of nights. Options include ⚐ *Basses Kro* (ⓣ97 92 16 97; ❺), Vestergade 28A, a small and charming inn on the pedestrianized street with six cosy rooms sharing bathroom facilities and with access to a small kitchen; its restaurant (daily 10am–midnight) serves good-value traditional Danish lunches and dinners such as fried eel or pork chop (from 89kr). Across from the train and bus station at Frederiksgade 16, *Hotel Thisted* (ⓣ97 92 52 00, ⓦwww.hotelthisted.dk; ❼) has stylish en-suite rooms, and its restaurant (daily 11am–10pm) does delicious, heavily laden smørrebrød for lunch (from 45kr a piece) and a good array of French-inspired à la carte options for dinner. The *Thisted Vandrerhjem* **hostel** (ⓣ97 92 50 42, ⓦwww .danhostelnord.dk/thisted; dorms 120kr, doubles ❸), Kongemøllevej 8, is 3km north of Thisted in the village of Skinnerup (bus #23 towards Hanstholm); *Thisted Camping* (ⓣ97 92 16 35, ⓦwww.thisted-camping.dk; April–Oct), Iversensvej 3, is a ten-minute walk east of the centre on the banks of Limfjorden.

Hanstholm

Thy's only other sizeable settlement, the harbour town of **HANSTHOLM** perches on Jutland's most northwesterly point, with the unruly Skagerrak surrounding it on three sides. This strategic position wasn't lost on the Germans during World War II, when the Third Reich constructed a huge fortification here as part of the 5000km **Atlantic Wall** coastal defence, which ran from the French–Spanish border all the way up to Norway via the entire west coast of Denmark, and was designed to destroy Allied craft before they had a chance to drop their bombs or land. The coastline here is still littered with the remains of the Wall's pillboxes, batteries and bunkers, and the largest of these – in fact the most extensive in northern Europe – is the **Hanstholm II battery**, set on a cliff overlooking the harbour and commercial centre. It covers a total of nine square kilometres and, while in operation, was manned by more than three thousand soldiers. Today, an enormous bunker centred around one of the four huge guns has been opened up to the public as the **Museumscenter Hanstholm** (daily: Feb–May & Sept–Oct 10am–4pm; June–Aug 10am–5pm; 50kr; ⓦwww.museumscenterhanstholm.dk). The bunker and surrounding complex are astonishingly big, with a labyrinth of small rooms (the map handed out by the entrance is crucial in order not to get lost) from ammunition stores to the crew's quarters and a technical section all restored to look as they would have when the battery was in operation. The gun pit in the centre once held a 38cm cannon-gun with a maximum range of 55km; alongside a similar battery on the Norwegian coast, it was used to police shipping traffic on the Skaggerak and access to the Baltic – there's a similar cannon-gun by the main entrance. Adjoining the bunker is an exhibition centre displaying German and Italian weaponry and uniforms, as well as the remains of Allied planes shot down here. Sadly, all the labelling in this section is in Danish and German only, though there is some English in the bunker itself. Despite this, the museum is immensely absorbing, not least because of the sheer scale of the place. The hordes of excited Germans that come here every year to see where their parents and grandparents were based during the war also adds to the sense of authenticity.

Apart from the Museumscenter, there's nothing in Hanstholm worth hanging around for, especially since there's no town centre to speak of (most of the action is centred on the harbour); however you may need to stay here if catching an international ferry (see below). The best option – and a great spot for lunch after you've visited the museum – is *Hanstholm Sømandshjem* (☎97 96 11 45, ⓦwww.hshh.dk; ⓪), 150m from the ferry terminals at Kai Lindbergs Gade 71, which has basic en-suite rooms and a downstairs ⌖ **cafeteria** (Mon 7.30–10am & 4.30–8pm, Tues–Fri 6–10am & 4.30–8pm, Sat & Sun 7.30am–2pm & 4.30–8pm) serving outstanding daily specials such as fried plaice, *ribbensteg* or *medisterpølser med rødkål*, always accompanied by a salad buffet (65kr), and a three-slice smørrebrød packed lunch for 30kr.

Bus #23 plies the road between Thisted and Hanstholm and there are **ferry** connections to Egersund, Haugesund and Bergen in Norway with Fjordline (☎97 96 30 00, ⓦwww.fjordline.com), and to Kristiansand in Norway with Master Ferries (☎96 17 87 17, ⓦwww.masterferries.com).

Along the coast

South of Hanstholm, the spectacular **Hanstholm Vildtreservat** wildlife reserve follows the coast south until you reach the windsurfers' paradise at Klitmøller. Before entering the reserve, have a quick peek inside the German-built **Hanstholm I** fortification (no set hours; free) just outside Hanstholm and signposted to the left from the main coast road. It's one of the country's best-preserved coastal batteries, with German motivational slogans still visible on the inside walls. In a bizarre sort of way, it blends in beautifully with the surrounding coastal heathland and, as the battery saw no action, the Germans keeping watch must have considered themselves very lucky given the stunning scenery. Past Hanstholm I, the main road to Klitmøller runs straight through the wildlife reserve and gives a great impression of its vast, windblown open expanse. Most of it is treeless, with coastal dunes to the right of the road, and open heathland to the left. A marshy area to the southeast is inhabited by rare plants such as water crowfoot and bur reed, and supports a significant aquatic bird and otter population; due to its ecological sensitivity, this part of reserve is closed to the public, as is the rest of it between April and mid-June during the breeding season, when up to forty different bird species visit, including the endangered golden plover. Hiking trails go off into the reserve from both sides of the main road, and offer a superb way to take in the gorgeous scenery.

After about ten kilometres, past where the reserve ends, the road branches off to the right to the small beachside town of **KLITMØLLER**, aka Hawaii II in recognition of its optimal windsurfing conditions, with a "wave spot" ideal for jumps and other acrobatics, and less demanding stretches suitable for beginners. If you want to get into the water and give it a try, *Westwind Klitmøller* (☎97 97 56 56), a short walk from the beach at Ørhagevej 151, offer lessons in windsurfing, surf-riding and kite-surfing, and rent out kit too. If you want to linger longer and soak up the surfdude scene, the best place to **stay** is the newly refurbished ⌖ *Klitmøller gl. Kro & Badehotel* (☎97 97 55 20, ⓦwww.klitmollerbadehotel.dk; ⓪), Krovej 15, a friendly, traditional inn with both shared-bath and en-suite rooms, and an outstanding **restaurant** (April–May & Sept Thurs & Fri 6–11pm, Sat & Sun noon–11pm; June–Aug daily noon–11pm; Oct & Nov Fri 6–11pm, Sat & Sun noon–11pm) which does a weekend lunch buffet (noon–3pm; 98kr) featuring herring and a range of local cheeses, and good-value two- and three-course evening meals (168kr and 198kr respectively). **Bus** #22 from Hanstholm passes Klitmøller en route to Thisted.

Continuing south for about 12km (note that only some #22 buses run on past Klitmøller, though the #113 does run here from Thisted), the coast road passes through the fishing village of **NØRRE VORUPØR**, one of the few remaining in Denmark without a proper harbour for its fleet, meaning that boats are still dragged by hand up onto the beach. This puts a definite damper on the boat size, but makes for a pretty, picture-postcard village seafront, with colourful wooden fishing boats lining the shore. The history of fishing and boat building in Nørre Vorupør is engagingly described at **Vorupør Museum** (mid-June to mid-Aug daily 10am–5pm; mid-Aug to mid-June Tues–Sun noon to 4pm; 30kr; ⓦwww.vorupoermuseum.dk), housed in the old village boatyard, a kilometre or so from the beach at Vesterhavsgade 21. The old boat-building machinery is still operational, but it's the village history that's espe-cially intriguing, detailing how the hardship and fears of local fishermen and their families resulted in the birth of a strong evangelical movement along the west coast of Denmark. Just up the road from the museum, the small **Nordsø Akvariet** aquarium (daily: May–June & Sept–Oct 10am–4pm; July–Aug 10am–6pm; 30kr; ⓦwww.north-sea.dk) has touching pools that kids adore.

The main road south of Nørre Vorupør runs through dense pine plantations for some 24km before hitting the small town of **VESTERVIG**, endowed with the enormous, twelfth-century **Vestervig Kirke** (July & Aug Mon–Fri 1–5pm, Sat & Sun 10am–5pm; Sept–June Mon–Fri 10am–5pm; ⓦwww.vestervig-kirke.dk), north Jutland's Episcopal seat during the Middle Ages – its sheer size makes it look surreal in relation to the minute village behind it. From Vestervig you have three options. You can either travel south under your own steam across the rail bridge to Struer (see p.291); catch bus #251 west towards the old Limfjorden inlet town of **Agger** and catch the ferry across the inlet to Thyborøn and Limfjorden's south bank; or east on bus #251 to the railway town of Hurup (trains run south to Struer and north to Thisted), and then catch bus #31 to get to the tiny wooden ferry that crosses over Neessund to the Limfjord island of Mors.

Mors and the Salling peninsula

Though **Mors** is an island and **Salling** a peninsula, they share many similarities, most obviously in their outstandingly beautiful landscapes and unique geology. The northern fringes of both, including the tiny island of Fur just north of Salling, bear witness to the enormously powerful forces of nature that shaped them some sixty million years ago. Their coastlines are lined by dramatic, steep **moler cliffs** – unique to this part of Denmark and characterized by decorative seams of volcanic ash, sedimentary moler is a soft, chalk-like rock that holds numerous fossils and giant crystal formations. Away from the north coasts lies a more sedate landscape of fertile farmland and gentle rolling hills, which holds a few rural sights and an imposing medieval castle.

Mors

Tucked snuggly between Thy and the Salling peninsula, **MORS** (also known as Morsø) is the largest of Limfjorden's islands, with a land area of 368 square kilometers. It's connected to the wider world via bridges to Thy and Salling, and by two rickety wooden ferries that run across Nessund to southern Thy, and across Feggesund to north Jutland, just south of Bulbjerg. Aside from transport to and from the ferry docks to the island's agreeable main town of **NYKØ-BING MORS**, public transport here is pretty dire, and the best way to explore is on foot or by bike (see below for bike rental outlets).

Mors' main attraction are the **moler cliffs** that run along its northern coast, stretching for some 20km between the Vilsund Vest bridge and the Feggesund ferry dock. The coastal path along the clifftop offers outstanding views across to Thisted, but to get the full moler experience it's best to clamber down onto the beach, via one of the many tracks, and take in the spectacular formations from the beach. Some 500m north of the town of Gullerup, the most impressive section, known as **Hanklit**, has a 40m moler band with stripes of dark volcanic ash making beautiful patterns. Mors' highest point is nearby at **Salgerhøj**, an 89m moler cliff that affords stunning views of the island. To learn more about moler and the geology of Mors, head to **Móler Museet** (May–June & mid-Aug to Oct Mon–Fri 10am–4pm, Sat & Sun noon to 4pm; July to mid-Aug daily 10am–5pm; 50kr; ⓦwww.dueholmkloster.dk), Skarrehagevej 8, signposted off the main road just before Feggesund at Hesslebjerg, and reached via bus #32 from Nykøbing Mors to Feggesund. You can dig up fossils at the bottom of a moler pit and museum staff will try to date your finds for you.

Cliffs and geology aside, Mors also has one other attraction worth seeking out. **Jesperhus Blomsterpark** (mid-May to June & mid- to late Aug Mon–Sat 10am–5pm, Sun 10am–6pm; July to mid-Aug daily 10am–8pm; Sept Mon & Wed–Fri 10am–4pm, Sun 10am–5pm; mid-May to Aug 175kr, Sept 140kr; ⓦwww.jesperhus.dk), at Legindved 30, 2km southeast of Nykøbing Mors and 2km from the bridge across the Sallingsund to the Salling peninsula. A theme park-cum-flower garden, it attracts both young and old with blooms galore – including an impressive orchid section in the jungle park – as well as a more mundane mini-zoo and a fancy swimming pool. It's reachable via bus #201 from Nykøbing Mors, or bus #X-B926X from Viborg via Skive, and then a 1km walk

Practicalities

Getting to Mors is straightforward. The main road connecting Viborg and Thy bisects the island, with a state-of-the-art modern bridge linking it to the Salling peninsula in the east, and the older Vildsund bridge connects it to Thy in the west; the fast #X-B926X Viborg to Thisted bus plies this route every hour. In addition, two wooden ferries depart every twenty minutes across Nessund in the south and Feggesund in the north (Sept–May 6.30am–6.10pm, June–Aug 6.30am–10.10pm; 10kr), carrying bus #31 to Hurup in Thy, and bus #32 to Fjerritslev in North Jutland. Mors' **tourist office** (July Mon–Fri 9am–6pm, Sat 9am–3pm; June & Aug Mon–Fri 9am–5pm, Sat 9am–2pm; Sept–May Mon–Fri 9am–4pm, Sat 9am–noon; ☎97 72 04 88; ⓦwww.mors-tourist.dk), Havnen 4, is at the harbour in Nykøbing Mors. They rent out bicycles and sell excellent cycling and hiking maps of Mors.

Although **accommodation** on Mors is limited, there are a few good options. In Nykøbing Mors, best choices are *Pakhuset* on Havnen (☎97 72 33 00, ⓦwww.phr.dk; ❻), a luxurious harbourside converted warehouse with a classy French restaurant (July daily 11.30am–10pm; Aug–June Mon–Sat 11.30am–10pm); and the ⚘ *Nykøbing Mors Vandrerhjem* (☎97 72 06 17, ⓦwww.danhostelnord.dk/mors; dorms 150kr; doubles ❹), Øroddevej 15, a fabulously located hostel on a finger of land jutting out from the town into the Sallingsund sound. Just south of Nykøbing Mors, next to the bridge to Salling, there's the *Sallingsund Færgekro*, Sallingsundvej 106 (☎97 72 00 88, ⓦwww.sallingsund-faergekro.dk; ❻) a traditional inn with forty-odd en-suite rooms, some with balconies overlooking Sallingsund; it also has a basic camp-site. On the opposite side of the island, by the Vilsund Vest bridge to Thy and near the northern moler coastal strip, *Øst Vildsund Gl Færgekro*, Sundbyvej 238 (℡97 74 60 47, Ⓦwww.vildsundkro.dk; ❺–❻) is a similar inn, with en-suite rooms and some with shared bathrooms; it also offers exceptional food (daily 11.30am–9pm), including smørrebrød and local seafood dishes.

The Salling peninsula

Extending northwards up into the Limfjorden, the **Salling peninsula** offers complete rural idyll: field after field, and not much else, all well suited to gentle hiking and biking. On the eastern coast at the foot of the peninsula (and on the rail line between Viborg and Struer), the principal settlement of **SKIVE** is a typical Jutland market town serving a large rural catchment area. Its host of shopping malls and supermarkets make it a good place to stock up and, as the region's transport hub, with bus services to all of Salling's corners, it's a convenient place to base yourself while exploring the area. If you're here in August, you'll find the town overtaken by the Limfjorden Rundt **regatta** (Ⓦwww.limfjordenrundt.dk), which finishes here and sees the scenic harbour filled to capacity with old wooden sailing ships – one of which, the two-masted schooner *Lovise-Moland*, offers boat cruises up and down the Limfjorden. The "Sunset Trip" (July to mid-Aug Mon–Thurs 7–9pm; 229kr) is perhaps the best for scenery, with an evening meal thrown in as well; book via the tourist office (see below). Otherwise, there's not much to do in the town itself, but head 20km or so southwest of Skive and you'll find the **Hjerl Hedes Frilandsmuseum** (April–Oct daily 10am–5pm; July 85kr, Aug 75kr, rest of the year 55kr; Ⓦwww.hjerlhede.dk). One of Denmark's most successful heritage tourism projects, this open-air museum attempts to recreate the development of a local village from the years 1500 to 1900, with a forge, inn, school, mills, a vicarage, a dairy, a grocer's shop and farms, all relocated here from their original sites around Jutland. By far the best time to come is during summer (mid-June to mid-Aug), when the place is brought to life by a hundred or so men, women and children dressed in traditional costumes, who provide demonstrations of the old crafts and farming methods. To get here from Skive, take the train to Vinderup (5–10 daily; 11min; bicycles allowed), from where it's an eight-kilometre walk, taxi- or cycle ride.

Practicalities

Salling is best explored by bike, and you can rent one at Skive's **tourist office** Østerbro 7 (mid-June to Aug Mon–Fri 9.30am–4pm, Sat 9.30am–1pm; Sept to mid-June Mon–Tues & Thurs–Fri 10am–4pm, Wed 10am–1pm, Sat 9.30am to noon, ℡97 52 32 66, Ⓦwww.visitskive.dk). Although Skive's **accommodation** is a bit thin on the ground, there are two good options, both ten minutes' walk from the bus and train stations (themselves south of the centre by the Skive Å river). Closest to the town centre, but near a busy junction at Søndre Boulevard 1, is the grand old *Hotel Gl Skivehus* (℡97 52 11 44, Ⓦwww.skivehus.dk; ❽/ ❻); it also houses the popular ⚜ *Barbara's* restaurant (Mon–Sat 11am–10pm; ℡97 52 16 32, Ⓦwww.barbaras.dk) which has steakhouse and (more expensive) gourmet sections, and a pub where you can try beers produced by the renowned Hancock Bryggerierne microbrewery *Hilltop* (℡97 52 37 11, Ⓦwww.hotel-hilltop.dk; ❻) at Amerikavej 4, around the corner from where Søndre Boulevard crosses Skive Å river is, as the name implies, on a hilltop overlooking the river. Rooms here are a little small and characterless, but the views are fantastic.

Salling's west coast is endowed with some nice pebbly fjord beaches, but the real attraction is the medieval castle of **Spøttrup Borg** (April Tues, Wed & Sun 11am–5pm; May–Aug daily 10am–6pm; Sept daily 10am–5pm; Oct daily 10am–4pm; 45kr; ⓦwww.spottrupborg.dk), Borgen 6A, 2km west of the village of Rødding and reachable via bus #43 from Skive. An imposing four-winged structure surrounded by a double moat, with an adjacent herb garden and wildlife lake, it was restored in 1941 and remains one of the best preserved medieval castles in Denmark, with sparsely furnished rooms that beautifully highlight its many architectural quirks. Salling's east coast is as rural as it gets, characterized by arable land and cattle pastures; appropriately, the main attraction hereabouts is the **Thise Mejer**, Sundørevej 62, in the village of **THISE** (Mon–Thurs & Sat 8.30–11.30am, Fri 8.30am–5pm; ⓦwww.thise.dk; bus #42 to Breum, then #401), one of the country's best dairies and producer of a wide range of flavour-packed organic cheeses, which you can sample if you pop into the adjacent shop – don't be surprised if the queue stretches out onto the street.

Just off Salling's northern tip, yet still considered part of the peninsula, is the tiny island of **Fur**, connected by a ferry between Branden and the main settlement of **STENØRE**. Fur's entire north coast is taken up with dramatic **moler** cliffs, with pebbly fjord beaches at the bottom strewn with mussel shells. The cliffs are best explored on foot, and the **tourist office** in Stenøre (June to mid-Sept Mon–Fri & Sun 10am–4pm, Sat 9am–5pm; ☏97 59 30 53, ⓦwww.fursund.dk) hands out free pamphlets detailing the demarcated hiking trails. They also rent out bikes which, if you don't have your own transport, will come in handy, as the only bus on Fur (no #42 from Skive) merely does a small circuit of the island's southern half. On your ride or hike, head toward **Anshede** on the western tip; just outside the settlement, the Fur Bryghus **microbrewery**, Knudevej 3, offers beer made with water filtered through the volcanic ash and moler, giving it a special and very moreish taste. You can sample the beer in the brewery restaurant (Sun 10am–3pm; ☏97 59 30 60, ⓦwww.furbryghus.dk), which does a delicious Sunday buffet lunch (129kr) using mainly local produce. If the cliffs have sparked an interest in moler and Fur's unique geology, you might want to head over to the east coast to **NEDERBY**, where the **Fur Museum** (April to mid-June & Sept–Oct noon to 4pm, mid-June to Aug 10am–5pm; 25kr; ⓦwww.furmusem.dk), Nederby 28, has a vast collection of rare fossils – plants, fish, birds and insects – and a small exhibit about Fur.

If you decide to spend more time sampling the local beer or hiking along the cliffs and want to **stay** here, try the atmospheric *Fur Færgekro* (☏97 59 30 02, ⓦwww.furkro.dk; ④) ferry inn near Stenøre, which has four good-value rooms, sharing bathroom facilities in the hall. It houses an excellent restaurant (Tues–Sun 5–10pm) serving traditional dishes such as *flæskesteg* and *medisterpølse*, best when washed down with the local brew.

Struer, Holstebro and Herning

Thanks to the presence of hi-fi giant Bang & Olufsen in **Struer** and the country's textile industry in **Herning**, the central portion of western Jutland comprises the island's industrial heartland, but commerce aside, its vast open heathland and pine forests are hardly overrun by development, with the three main towns well spread out. Struer and Herning have little to hold you for long, but **Holstebro**, with its art museum and performing art centres, has become something of a cultural centre for the area. Transport in this region is fairly easy. Fast intercity and slower regional trains (from Vejle and Fredericia respectively) connect the three towns, and there are also regional trains from Thy to Struer.

Struer

Before the arrival of Bang & Olufsen in 1925 (see box, below), **STRUER** was just another fjord town with a pretty harbour. Today, it's a modern, thriving place with a host of sleek buildings – not least Bang & Olufsen's stunning new glass-fronted centre on Hjermvej. That said, the only real reason to visit is to see the snazzy underground glass pyramid extension of the **Struer Museum**, Søndergade 23 (daily 10am–4pm; 50kr; Ⓦ www.struermuseum.dk), entirely devoted to Bang & Olufsen and using lots of fabulous B&O products to detail the company's history and its effect on the town's – and the region's – development. The **tourist office** at Rådhuspladsen (June–Aug Mon–Fri 9.30am–5pm, Sat 9.30am–1pm; Sept–May Mon–Fri 9.30am–4pm; ☎79 85 07 95, Ⓦ www.visitstruer.dk) occasionally organizes tours of the Bang & Olufsen factory, which include the *"BeoLiving"* areas, where luxurious new designs are trialled. You might also amble down towards the harbour to the **Folkets Hus**, Tegltorvet 2 (☎97 85 11 57, Ⓦ www.folketshus.struer.dk; Tues–Fri noon to 10pm, Sat & Sun 10am–3pm), a community centre which hosts concerts and exhibitions, and has a nice café selling coffee and cake, beer, sandwiches (40kr), Iraqi specialities (45kr) and weekend brunch (11am–2pm; 60kr).

There's no real reason to **stay** here, but should you want a bed for the night, the most prestigious option is the *Grand Hotel*, right in the centre at Østergade 24 (☎97 85 04 00, Ⓦ www.struergrandhotel.dk; ❼), a modern red-brick building with stylish rooms fully kitted out with gear from B&O. Much cheaper is *Struer Vandrerhjem*, Fjordvej 12 (☎97 85 53 13, Ⓦ www.struer-vandrerhjem.dk; dorms 105kr, doubles ❷), just off the bridge to Thy and near a child-friendly fjord beach. *Bremdal Camping* (☎97 85 16 50, Ⓦ www.bremdal-camping.dk) is just next door.

Bang & Olufsen

The fantastic audio-visual systems made by **Bang & Olufsen** (B&O; Ⓦ www .bang-olufsen.com) are the epitome of Denmark's tradition of excellence in design, and are world renowned both in terms of their stylistic excellence and their high quality – and, of course, their top-drawer prices. The company has its roots right in Struer, having been first established here in the attic of **Svend Olufsen**'s family home where, in 1925, he and fellow engineer **Peter Bang** designed their first radio, which ran on mains rather than battery power (as was then the norm). From the very beginning the driving force behind their technological innovations was consumer convenience, and the radio was soon followed by the first-ever radio-gramophone, a button-operated mains radio, a radio with pre-set tuning buttons and the world's first stereo record player. All these products were huge commercial successes, and the company went from strength to strength; today Bang & Olufsen is a weighty international player with outlets in more than forty countries. But unlike most other high-tech industries, B&O have opted to keep the major part of their operations in Struer, from the research and development department to the factory, and the company is by far the biggest employer in Struer.

Holstebro

A short train journey south of Struer, **HOLSTEBRO** is the largest town herea-bouts, with an easy-going atmosphere and a small, walkable centre. Whereas Struer and Herning grew up around industry, Holstebro made a name for itself through the arts, something that's immediately obvious in the number of sculp-tures decorating the streets. The tourist office (see below) sells a booklet (20kr) with maps and background info on Hostelbro's public art; look out especially for Bjørn Nørgaard's *People of Holstebro*, at Nørreport, ten figures (modelled on local citizens) standing atop a slab of concrete with water gushing through it. Nørgaard is most famous for the Queen's tapestries in Copenhagen (see p.78), but this sculpture is one of his absolute best. The newly refurbished **Musik-teatret Holstebro**, next to the tourist office at Den Røde Plads 16, is another sign of the town's dedication to the arts. In 1995, renowned dancer Peter Schaufuss was asked to start a dance company and royal ballet school in Holste-bro, and the theatre's stunning facelift is the culmination of his creative efforts (check Ⓦwww.musikteatret.dk for what's on). The town's arty feel is further compounded by the train station, an elaborately decorated red-brick build-ing from 1905 designed by H. Wenck, the man responsible for Copenhagen's Central Station. As you might expect, the commendable **Holstebro Kunst-museum** (Art Museum; July–Aug Tues–Sun 11am–5pm; Sept–June Tues–Fri noon–4pm, Sat & Sun 11am–5pm; 40kr, includes entry to Holstebro Museum; Ⓦwww.holstebrokunstmuseum.dk), in the town park, has a strong contempo-rary Danish collection and some quality international pieces, including works by Matisse and Picasso. In the same building, the **Holstebro Museum** (same hours; 40kr, includes entry to the Art Museum; Ⓦwww.holstebro-museum.dk) has some mildly diverting exhibits on local history.

Hostelbro's **tourist office**, Slotsgade 2 (Mon–Fri 9.30am–5pm, Sat 10am–noon; ☎97 42 57 00, Ⓦwww.holstebro-tourist.dk), sells a booklet (20kr) with maps and details of all of the town's art. Among **accommodation** options, there's yet more art to be had at the modern *Hotel Royal*, across from the tour-ist office at Den Røde Plads 10 (☎97 40 23 33, Ⓦwww.hotel-royal.dk; ❻/❼), with large colourful paintings and sculptures adorning the lobby and main staircase, and simple stylish rooms. *Hotel Schaumburg* (☎97 42 31 11, Ⓦwww.hotel-schaumburg.dk; ❼/❽), on the main pedestrianized street at Nørregade 26, is a different kettle of fish with luxurious, thickly carpeted rooms, and the popular *Fox and Hounds* pub at the front. There's also a **campsite** equipped with cabins and canoes at Birkevej 25 (☎97 42 20 68, Ⓦwww.mejdal.dk). For something completely different head about 12km northeast of town (via bus #27) towards Hjerl Hede to 🍴 *Borbjerg Mølle Kro*, Borbjerg Møllevej 3 (☎97 46 10 10, Ⓦwww.borbjergmill.dk; ❻), a traditional inn with an African slant. Apart from cosy rooms at the inn, there's also an octagonal African-style reed hut with hammocks to sleep in, and a fully equipped, very romantic safari tent. The restaurant (daily 11am–10pm) is very popular, especially for its Sunday coffee buffet (2.30–4.30pm; 65kr), with ten or more delicious home-made cakes.

Herning

About 30km south of Holstebro, the modern conference town of **HERNING** grew to its present size mainly because of its status as epicentre of the Danish textile industry, though the trappings of this – and, consequently, the town's attractions – are pretty much restricted to the suburbs rather than the thriving and compact commercial centre. Just outside the centre (bus #19 or one stop on the train to Århus, get off at Birk Centerpark), the industrial suburb of Birk holds the **Birk Centerpark**, an eldorado for the artistically and architecturally inclined. A long narrow park spanning from the railway tracks in the south to the old Silkeborg highway in the north, it's peppered with sculptures and holds some stunning buildings. Arriving from the Silkeborg road end in the north, the first of these is the **Carl-Henning Pedersen & Else Alfelts Museum** art museum, Birk Centerpark 1 (May–June & Aug–Oct Tues–Sun 10am–5pm; July daily 10am–5pm; Nov–April Tues–Fri 10am–5pm, Sat & Sun noon to 5pm; 50kr for joint ticket with Herning Kunstmuseum; ⓦwww.chpeamuseum.dk), dedicated to two founding members of the CoBRA art movement (see p.127) and displaying only their work; the colourful ceramic tiles by Carl-Henning Pedersen that cover the circular museum building are a good prelude to what is shown inside. Next door, is a large oval white building, from 1965, designed by C.F. Møller for the Angli shirt factory. The factory's founder, Aage Damgaard, was a patron of the arts and invested heavily in local art during the factory's existence. His collection was eventually merged with the local art council's collection to form the collection at the **Herning Kunstmuseum** (Art Museum; May–June & Aug–Oct Tues–Sun 10am–5pm; July daily 10am–5pm; Nov–April Tues–Fri 10am–5pm, Sat & Sun noon to 5pm; 50kr for joint ticket with Carl-Henning Pedersen & Else Alfelts Museum; ⓦwww.herningkunstmuseum.dk), set in part of the old factory building. There's an especially good section on the CoBrA movement, and a large round inner courtyard with Carl-Henning Pedersen's beautiful tiles decorating the entire length and breadth of the circular wall. Behind the museum, the shrub-encircled **sculpture park** was originally designed as a recreational area for the factory workers at Angli, and holds a host of modern pieces. As you move southwards through the park, you'll pass many more stunning buildings and quirky green areas, such as the unusual building at no.10 designed by Jørn Utzon (of Sydney Opera House fame); at the southern end of the park, look out also for the enormous, awe-inspiring cast-iron sculpture, *Elia's dome*, which spurts fire every nineteen days, and has pillars that attract lightning and resonate it back out into the sky – a truly mind-boggling piece.

To learn more about Herning's textile trade, head back to town to the **Textilforum** (Mon–Thurs & Sat–Sun 11am–4pm; 30kr; ⓦwww.herningmuseum.dk), Vestergade 20, housed in a former wool-spinning factory from 1876, and with descriptive exhibits and active workshops displaying everything you could ever want to know about textile production in Herning. Nearby, the **Herning Museum** (July Mon–Fri 10am–4.30pm, Sat & Sun 11am–4.30pm; Aug–June Tues–Fri 10am–4.30pm, Sat & Sun 11am–4.30pm; 30kr; ⓦwww.herningmuseum.dk), Museumsgade 32, details the other side of the coin by way of an interesting section on the harshness of farming the bleak surrounding heathlands.

If you plan to visit most of the places listed above, you can save money by buying a *multipas* card (75kr and 85kr, valid for 24hr and 48hr respectively) that gives you access to a host of places in the greater Herning area, including the ones listed here. They're sold at the **tourist office**, Torvet 8 (Mon–Fri 10am–5pm, Sat 10am–1pm; ☎96 27 22 22, ⓦwww.visitherning.com) on the town's main square, which can also help with canoe rental (250kr per day, plus 100kr to transport canoe back to Herning), should you be tempted by a trip down Store Å through the vast heathlands towards Holstebro and Nissum Fjord (see p.295). Thanks to Herning's status as a conference town there are plenty of places **to stay**, though there's not a huge amount to keep you here, and none of them come cheap. The small *Hotel Vester*, Engdahlsvej 7B (☎97 22 14 22, ⓦwww.hotel-vester.dk; ⑥), is within easy access of Birk Centerpark (bus #19) and exceptionally good value. **Trains** from Århus, Vejle, Skjern and Struer stop at Herning station, south of the centre on Banegårdspladens, and there's a fast motorway linking it with Ikast en route from Silkeborg.

Ringkøbing and around

The ancient fjord town of **Ringkøbing**, on the inner banks of Ringkøbing Fjord, can thank the weather for its somewhat turbulent history. Its first major spout of growth occurred in 1100, when sand drifts closed off Limfjorden's outlet at Agger in the north, halting all transport into Limfjordslandet via the fjord (see p.281) and allowing Ringkøbing (with its narrow outlet from the fjord to the open sea at Nymindegab) a piece of the trade action. The town soon became one of west Jutland's most important harbours, serving uplands as far afield as Holstebro, Lemvig and Viborg, but with wind and weather constantly changing the shape of the coastline, the gap at Nymindegab gradually narrowed and trade moved to Ribe and Hjertling. By 1825, Ringkøbing's role as an export harbour came to a complete halt when the Limfjorden outlet at Agger reopened after a bad storm, and even though a new access point was opened up at Hvide Sande in the early nineteenth century (and protected and regulated with a sluice), Ringkøbing morphed into a market town and hub for the region's tourism. Ringkøbing's narrow **Holmsland Klit** strip of sand attracts visitors – mostly Germans – in their thousands, while the area around **Hvide Sande** is equally popular and a prime territory for watersports. There's also plenty on offer away from the beach, with a couple of lovely wildlife sanctuaries to the north of Ringkøbing,

Ringkøbing

A pretty town with a compact walkable centre and a small harbour, **RINGKØBING** is notable for its absolutely stunning views of the fjord, which looks so vast from here it's hard not to assume that you're looking out at the sea. Despite its long history, it's not a particularly sizeable place, and apart from enjoying the view, there's not much to detain you here for long, though it's a good place to base yourself while exploring this part of the coast, with most public transport hereabouts passing through town. You might want to have a quick look at the **Ringkøbing Museum**, near the harbour at Kongevejen 1 (Jan–June & Sept–Oct Mon–Thurs & Sat–Sun 11am–4pm; July–Aug daily 11am–5pm; Nov & Dec Mon–Thurs & Sat–Sun noon to 4pm; 30kr; ⓦwww.ringmus.dk), where, alongside an informative section on Ringkøbing's turbulent history, there's a small, quirky collection of knick-knacks dating back to the early days of Greenland explorations, and a genuine cast-iron chastity belt.

There is not a huge array of choice when it comes to **accommodation** in Ringkøbing itself as most visitors opt either to rent holiday homes or to stay at one of the beach hotels. The two best places in town, at different ends of the scale, are the romantic *Hotel Ringkøbing*, Torvet 18 (ⓣ97 32 00 11, ⓦwww.hotelringkobing.dk; ⓞ), an old wood-beamed affair on the central town square with a range of atmospheric, newly refurbished rooms; and the *Ringkøbing Vandrerhjem* **hostel**, Kirkevej 28 (ⓣ97 32 24 55, ⓦwww.rofi.dk; dorms 130kr, doubles ⓞ), set within Rofi Centret, a modern sports and training centre on the northern outskirts, off the road to Holstebro (bus #52 then a short walk from Rindum school). The **tourist office** on Torvet (mid-June to Aug Mon–Fri 9am–5pm, Sat 10am–2pm; Sept to mid-June Mon–Fri 9.30am–5pm, Sat 10am–1pm; ⓣ70 22 70 01, ⓦwww.visitvest.dk)

has a long list of agents renting holiday homes. What Ringkøbing lacks in accommodation, it makes up for in good **places to eat**. The harbour is lined by a number of informal and excellent seafood shacks, including the slightly upmarket *Café Kræs*, Ved Fjorden 2B (Mon & Tues 11am–5pm, Wed–Sat 11am–10pm; ☎97 32 42 88), which offers delicious herring platters (69kr) on the lunch menu and mains such as fried plaice with trimmings (148kr) for dinner. Of the more formal cafés and restaurants near Torvet, *Restaurant Borgmestergården* (daily 6–10pm) at *Hotel Ringkøbing* also does fried plaice as part of three- or four-course menus for 245kr and 285kr respectively, while *Café Sif* on the pedestrianized Nygade (daily 11am–9pm) has outdoor seating and a range of delicious salads and sandwiches. For a tasty tipple, 🍴 *Ølgalleriet*, Nørredige 3A at the train station (Mon–Fri 11am–5pm, Sat 10am–1pm; ☎96 74 74 70, ⊛www.oelgalleriet.dk), has beers from most of the country's microbreweries as well as many foreign brands. **Trains** from Esbjerg, Århus and Struer stop at the train station, just northeast of the centre; the regional bus station is further along on the same street.

North of Ringkøbing

North of Ringkøbing, highway 16 skirts along the inland banks of a couple of smaller fjords, the Stadil and Nissum; to get to the smaller road that follows the actual coastline, you have to head west to **Søndervig**, where the road branches north towards Thorminde and south towards Holmsland Klit. From here, the coast road heads north past the flat levels of **Vest Stadil Fjord Vildtreservat** wildlife reserve, set in former reclaimed farmlands which were allowed to revert back to their natural state in the 1990s. This gradual process is still ongoing, but the area has already become an important resting place for migratory barnacle and pink-footed geese, while the reserve itself boasts a beautiful, open landscape crisscrossed by cycling and hiking trails that run along the ridges of the old dike walls. The history of the area is explained fully at the picturesque **Strandgaarden Museum** (July & Aug daily 11am–5pm; May–June & Sept Tues–Thurs & Sat–Sun 11am–4pm; 30kr; ⊛www.gaardmus.dk), in front of the reserve on the coast road at Husby Klitvej 5, which gives an interesting insight into how dune farmers scraped a living through a combination of farming, fishing, hunting and salvaging from stranded ships.

Continuing north along the coast, a narrow strip of sand, in places only just wide enough for the road, separates Nissum Fjord from the sea, and leads to the small village of **THORSMINDE**, built up around the fjord sluice. Here, the **Strandingsmuseum St George**, Vesterhavsgade 1E (Jan–April daily 11am–4pm; May–Oct daily 10am–5pm; Nov & Dec daily 11am–3pm; 40kr; ⊛www.strandmus.dk) is centred around the salvage of the *St George*, which went down outside Thorsminde on December 24 in 1811. Displays feature hundreds of items – guns, china, shoes – rescued from the *St George* and from a host of other ships that have gone down along this wild stretch of coastline – as evidenced by the vast collection of anchors outside. East of Thorsminde, the **Nissum Fjord** is another reclaimed wildlife reserve that's now an important breeding habitat for red shanks, lapwings and oyster catchers, and is a significant resting place for a vast number of migratory birds. You can get a good vista of the fjord and its birdlife from the coastal road just north of town.

South of Ringkøbing

South of Søndervig and lining the coast for some 35km, the **Holmsland klit** dunes separate Ringkøbing Fjord from the North Sea, and though the views along this strip are not nearly as enticing as those around Nissum Fjord to

the north, the landscape still has a magical feel to it, and although you can't
see the North Sea from the road, you clearly sense its presence on the other
side of the sand dune. The holiday feel proper doesn't start until you reach
the town of **Hvide Sande**, built up around the lock that controls the gap
into the fjord. **Watersports** are the order of the day here, from windsurfing and kite-surfing to waterskiing and wave-riding, and you can have a go
either in the calm, shallow waters of the fjord or along the wild west coast.
West Wind (Ⓦ www.westwind.dk) is the best bet for lessons and kit hire (70kr
per hour). They have two outlets on the banks of Ringkøbing Fjord, south
of the sluice at Sønder Klitvej 1 (Ⓣ 97 31 28 99) and north of it at Gytjevej
15 (Ⓣ 97 31 25 99).

South of Hvide Sande, the coast road takes you past the southern end of
the marshy **Tipperne** peninsula, which pokes up into Ringkøbing Fjord and
has been designated a bird sanctuary in its entirety. To cause the least possible
disturbance to the birds, it's open to the public only for a few hours on Sundays
outside the breeding season (Sun: Feb–March & Sept–Nov 10am to noon;
April–Aug 8–10am; free), and you're not allowed to stop on the road leading
to the large birdwatchers' observation tower by the fjord. From here, there's a
2km signposted circular hiking trail through the marshes. Although the hours
are awkward, it's well worth visiting. The birdlife within the reserve is incredibly
varied, reminiscent of an open zoo, with ruff and dunlin the two most important species breeding here.

Hvide Sand makes a great base if you want to spend a bit of time on the
beach. The basic *Hvide Sande Sømandshjem*, Bredgade 5 (Ⓣ 97 31 10 33,
Ⓦ www.hssh.dk; ⑥) is the best-value place to **stay**, with sparkling en-suite
rooms and an excellent **restaurant** (Mon–Fri 7am–10pm, Sat & Sun 8am–
10pm) serving up smørrebrød at lunch, and a daily special (5–9pm; 95kr) plus
a range of filling mains at dinner. Otherwise, for beautifully prepared fresh
fish, head north of the sluice to 🍴 *Fiske-Restaurant Lygten* (daily noon–3pm
& 5–9pm; Ⓣ 97 31 63 00), Nørregade 53, which doubles as a fishmonger and
candle-maker. **Bus** #58 runs from Ringkøbing to Hvide Sande and Tipperen
along Holmsland klit.

Esbjerg and around

With the advent of budget flights to **ESBJERG** from the UK, west
Jutland's only city has gained something of a reputation as a weekend-break
destination. If this is your first view of the country, bear in mind it's an
entirely untypical one. Esbjerg is a baby by Danish standards: purpose-built as
a deep-water harbour during the nineteenth century, it went on to become
one of the world's biggest fishing ports. Nowadays, it's used as a supply point
for the North Sea oil industry and holds a large fish-oil factory, though
it does maintain an air of its original Victorian-era charm, and handsome
townhouses abound. Since both DFDS Seaways ferries and regular Ryanair
and British Midland flights from the UK arrive here, you may find yourself
staying for a few days. If you do, there are a few places worth a nose, most
notably the **Esbjerg Kunstmuseum** and the **Fiskeri og Søfartsmuseet**.
The city also makes a great base from which to explore the surrounding
area, particularly the superb beaches on the island of **Fanø**, a short ferry ride
away, and the vast open landscapes around **Blåvands Huk**, Denmark's most
westerly point.

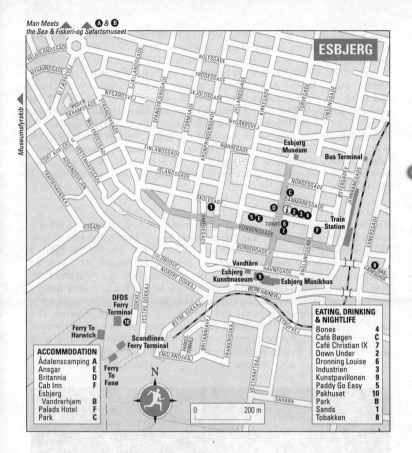

Man Meets the Sea & Fiskeri-og Søfartsmuseet

Ⓐ & Ⓑ

Museumsfyrskib

ESBJERG

HELGOLANDSGADE

NYHAVNSGADE

GL FÆRGEVEJ

PEDER SKRAMSGADE

STRANDBYGADE

FORT ADELERS G

ADGANGSVEJEN

VESTHAVNSGADE

TRAFIKHAVNSKAJ

KOGADE

WILLEMOESGADE

ROLFSGADE

FRODESGADE

SJÆLLANDSGADE

NYGÅRDSVEJ

SPANGSBJERGGADE

SKJOLDSGADE

JYLLANDSGADE

KIRKEGADE

TORVEGADE

FINSENSGADE

NYGÅRDSVEJ

FINLANDSGADE

KRONPRINSENSGADE

NØRREGADE

Esbjerg Museum

Bus Terminal

ISLANDSGADE

STORMGADE

NORGESGADE

ØSTERGADEV

JERNBANEGADE

SKOLEGADE

Ⓒ

DANMARKSGADE

①

Ⓓ

ⓘ②③④

Train Station

SMEDEGADE

⑤Ⓔ

TORVET ⑥

Ⓕ

KONGENSGADE ⑦

EXNERSGADE

BORGERGADE

Vandtårn

HAVNEGADE

Esbjerg Kunstmuseum ⑨

ENGLANDSGADE

Esbjerg Musikhus

ØSTRE HAVNEVEJ

⑧ GAS- VÆRKSGADE

TOLDBODVEJ

NORDRE DOKKAJ

DFDS Ferry Terminal

⑩

DOKVEJ

VESTRE DOKKAJ

ØSTRE DOKKAJ

ESBJUPVEJ

Ferry To Harwich

Scandlines Ferry Terminal

PARKS-TUNNEL

BRITANNIAVEJ

FRANKRISSKAJ

ACCOMMODATION
Ådalenscamping	A
Ansgar	D
Britannia	E
Cab Inn	F
Esbjerg Vandrerhjem	B
Palads Hotel	F
Park	C

Ferry To Fanø

ENGLANDSKAJ

VESTKRAFTKAJ

N

SAHARA

0   200 m

EATING, DRINKING & NIGHTLIFE
Bones	4
Café Bøgen	C
Café Christian IX	7
Down Under	2
Dronning Louise	6
Industrien	3
Kunstpavillonen	9
Paddy Go Easy	5
Pakhuset	10
Park	B
Sands	1
Tobakken	8

Arrival, information and accommodation

The Esbjerg **tourist office**, at Skolegade 33 (mid-June to Aug Mon–Fri 9am–5pm, Sat 9.30am–2.30pm; Sept to mid-June Mon–Fri 10am–5pm, Sat 10am–1pm; ℡75 12 55 99, ⒲www.visitesbjerg.dk), on a corner of the main square, Torvet, can give you all the practical information you might need, as well as leaflets describing a short self-guided walking tour of the city's early twentieth-century buildings, and three longer round-trip cycling routes around the area. The **passenger harbour** is a well-signposted fifteen-minute walk from the centre (bus #5), and trains depart to and from Copenhagen, Århus, Fredericia and Struer via Ringkøbing from the **train station** on Jernbanegade. Long-distance buses arrive at the **bus terminal** further up the road. Esbjerg **airport** (⒲www.esbjerg-lufthavn.dk) is 9km northeast of the city centre. Buses (no number, marked "airport") leave every twenty minutes to and from the train station, and cost 26kr one-way.

   If you're staying, the tourist office has a list of private **accommodation**; otherwise you'll find the cheapest good hotel is the twin-towered 🕸 *Palads Hotel/Cab Inn*, Skolegade 14 (℡75 18 16 00, ⒲www.cabinn.com; ❻), renovated into a mixture of simple, inexpensive cabin-style rooms and more traditional hotel accommodation. Another low-price option is the basic

Park, Torvegade 31 (☎75 12 08 68, ℉75 13 56 99; ❺), where all rooms share bathrooms; while the central *Ansgar*, Skolegade 36 (☎75 12 82 44, ⓦwww .hotelansgar.dk; ❼), is a little more upmarket. The luxurious *Britannia* on Torvet (☎75 13 01 11, ⓦwww.britannia.dk; ❽) has furniture created by Danish design legend Arne Jacobsen in each room – stylish Swan chairs and sofas – as well as free parking and reductions of up to fifty percent on weekend packages. The *Esbjerg Vandrerhjem* **youth hostel**, Gammel Vardevej 80 (☎75 12 42 58, ⓦwww.danhostel.dk/esbjerg; dorms 150kr, doubles ❸; Feb–Nov), is 25 minutes' walk north of the centre, or take a bus (#1, #4, #13, #40 or #41) from Skolegade. There's a well-equipped **campsite** with cabins, *Ådalens Camping*, at Gudenåvej 20 (☎75 15 88 22, ⓦwww.adal.dk), 6km north of Esbjerg along the Sædding Strandvej coast road, and reached by bus #1 from Skolegade.

The city

The best place to get your bearings – and appreciate how small a city Esbjerg is – is from the top of the **Vandtårn** (Water Tower; June to mid-Sept daily 10am–4pm, April–May & mid-Sept to Oct Sat & Sun 10am–4pm; 15kr), a short walk from the harbour towards the centre at Havnegade 22. There are sweeping views of the harbour and surrounding marshes, and on a good day you can see as far as Fanø. A small exhibit inside details the tower's history. Next door at Havnegade 18–20, **Esbjerg Musikhus** (☎76 10 90 00, ⓦwww .mhe.dk) shares a grand entrance and foyer with the town's art museum. The latter houses two concert halls where a wide range of music is performed – from classical to contemporary – and the fascinating modern building is an architectural attraction in itself, designed under the direction of Jørn Utzon, the architect responsible for the Sydney Opera House, and is a fascinating

△ *Man Meets the Sea*

piece of modern architecture, resembling a giant concrete tomb surrounded by massive white flowers. The **Esbjerg Kunstmuseum** next door (daily 10am–4pm; 40kr) includes a modest collection of contemporary pieces whose highlight are some huge steel plates splattered in the blood of their creator, Danish *enfant terrible* Christian Lemmerz. In recent times it also exhibited – to much hand-wringing – Lemmerz's gory collection of dead pigs, and a forum on sex and pornography. As an unusual feature, the museum stores in the basement are open to the public. Filed away in order of purchase (with two boxes of index cards listing what's there) are paintings by Danish modern artists such as Asgar Jorn and Richard Mortensen, which you're free to pull out and study. To get a sense of the city's newness, you might want to drop into the **Esbjerg Museum** (June–Aug daily 10am–4pm; Sept–May Tues–Sun 10am–4pm; 30kr, free Wed; ⓦwww.esbjergmuseum.dk), Torvegade 45, where the meatiest of the few displays recalls the so-called "American period" of the 1890s, when Esbjerg's rapid growth matched that of the US goldrush towns – albeit that the masses came here in search of herring rather than gold. The museum also houses an impressive collection of amber that includes some ancient jewellery.

If the Musikhus has left you in the mood for more aesthetic appreciation, take a bus (#3 or #8 from the train station) out along the coastal road until you arrive at the four 9m-high ghostly, chalk-white figures known as the **Mennesket ved Havet** (*Man Meets the Sea*). Put in place in 1995 by artist Sven Wiig Hansen, this grand piece of public art reflects on Esbjerg's relationship to the sea, with four temple-like rigid figures sitting in a line looking out over the waves. With the beach in the foreground and reflected light from the water making the figures look almost luminous, it provides an excellent photo opportunity. Just around the corner on Tarphagevej is the wonderful **Fiskeri og Søfartsmuseet** (Fisheries and Maritime Museum; daily: July–Aug 10am–6pm; Sept–May 10am–5pm; 75kr; ⓦwww.fimus.dk), where you can cast an eye over the old boats and other vestiges of the early Esbjerg fishing fleet. This is an excellent place to take the kids, not least because of the adjoining Sealarium, part of a seal research centre (feeding times 11am and 2.30pm). Some dark and spooky German wartime bunkers and an old working port – rebuilt brick by brick – make up the rest of this engaging museum.

With an hour to kill before your boat leaves, nip around the harbour to the **Museumsfyrskib** (Lightship Museum: May–Sept daily 10am–4pm; 20kr), which gives a vivid impression of the North Sea lightshipman's lot.

Eating, drinking and nightlife

Esbjerg's **eating** options are fairly limited for those on a tight budget, though the usual run of hot-dog grills and bakeries is scattered throughout the city. In terms of **nightlife**, the city is geared to the thousands of sailors – many of whom are English – that pass through this busy port. There are a run of strip bars on Skolegade, but these can get quite rowdy and aren't recommended for the fainthearted. If you've just arrived from Britain and want to make a more gentle transition to Danish culture (and prices), sip a beer or two at one of the city's pubs, such as the Irish *Paddy Go Easy* (Mon–Thurs & Sun 2pm–1.30am, Fri 1pm–3.30am, Sat noon–3.30am), Skolegade 32, with live music from Thursday to Saturday from 11pm; or the Aussie sports bar *Down Under* (Thurs–Sat 8pm–5am; ⓦwww.downunder.as), Skolegade 31, which shows non-stop live sport on five large screens and converts into a disco after 11pm. For live music, check out what's on at *Tobakken* (☏75 18 00 00, ⓦwww.tobakken.dk), the city's large multifaceted concert venue at Gasværksgade 2; or head for *Industrien* (T75 13 61 66; Mon & Tues 11.30am–midnight, Wed 11.30am–3am, Thurs–Sat 11.30am–5am, Sun 11.30am–5pm), Skolegade 27, which has DJs and live music as well as a bar and café.

Cafés and restaurants

Bones Skolegade 17 T75 13 61 18, Wwww .bones.dk. This dependable chain offers decent value, with dishes such as mouthwatering barbecue ribs for 124kr, burgers for 109kr and steak with all the trimmings from 124kr. Lunchtime prices are substantially cheaper. Mon–Fri & Sun 4.30–9.30pm, Sat noon–10pm.

Café Bøgen Torvegade 14 T75 13 01 11, Wwww.britannia.dk. On the ground floor of Hotel Britannia, this brasserie, bar and café has a large terrace with a popular grill buffet on sunny summer days for 150kr. Otherwise, the two- and three-course menus of southern French-style cuisine go for 188kr and 235kr respectively. Mon–Sat 11am–midnight, Sun 11am–11pm.

Café Christian IX Torvet 17 T75 12 94 00. Popular café on Esbjerg's main square, good for brunch, lunch, salads and sandwiches, or just a cup of coffee. In the evening beer takes centre stage, with DJ's playing in the basement nightclub (Fri & Sat). Mon–Wed 10am–11pm, Thurs 10am–midnight, Fri 10am–3am, Sat 10am–4am, Sun 11am–10pm.

Dronning Louise Torvet 19 T75 13 13 44. A large, glitzy place with outdoor seating on the city's main square, with a good selection of local and imported beers and an extensive café menu that includes a proper English fried breakfast for 75kr; salads and sandwiches and a range of more substantial evening meals (from 139kr) are also

available. Live music every Thursday, and DJs Fri & Sat. Mon–Tues 10am–1am, Wed 10am–2am, Thurs 10am–3am, Fri 10am–5am, Sat 10am–6am, Sun 10am–midnight.

Kunstpavillonen, Havnegade 20 T75 12 64 95 Wwww.josef-kunsten.dk. Set upstairs in the Esbjerg Kunstmuseum building with great views of Esbjerg harbour, specialities here include the excellent lunchtime herring and cheese platter for 125kr; the French-style three-course dinner for 300kr draws in a well-heeled crowd in the evening. The Sunday lunch buffet (11.30am–4pm) with five types of herring and loads of other delicacies costs 125kr. Mon–Fri 11.30am–4pm & 6–9pm, Sun 11.30am–4pm.

Pakhuset Dokvej 3 T75 12 74 55, Wwww .pakhuset-esbjerg.dk. Set in an atmospheric old red-brick warehouse in Esbjerg's dock area, and offering well-prepared local-style fresh fish with all the trimmings for around 225kr. Tues–Sat 5.30–9.30pm.

Park Hotel Torvegade 31. This small, unpretentious hotel offers good-value, traditional Danish meals such as two-course lunch for 74kr. Mon–Fri 6am–8pm.

Sands Skolegade 60 T75 12 02 07, Wwww.sands.dk. Excellent for traditional Danish food and service – try the daily special for 89kr, or the lunchtime smørrebrød platter for 125kr. Mon–Sat 11am–9.30pm.

Around Esbjerg: Fanø and Blåvands Huk

From Esbjerg it's a straightforward ferry trip to **Fanø**, a long, flat island with superb beaches that draw German holidaymakers in droves during the summer. Scandlines ferries (T33 15 15 15, Wwww.scandlines.dk; 30kr return) run frequently between Esbjerg and the island's main village, **Nordby**, where the **tourist office** at the harbour (mid-June to Aug Mon–Fri 8.30am–6pm, Sat & Sun 9am–5pm; Sept to mid-June Mon–Fri 8.30am–5.30pm, Sat 9am–1pm, Sun 11am–1pm; T75 16 26 00, Wwww.fanoeturistbureau.dk) can provide information on accommodation and the few sights (a couple of fairly ordinary local museums and a windmill). Of the island's eight **campsites**, the best is *Feldberg Strand Camping* (T75 16 36 80, Wwww.feldbergcamping.dk), Kirkevej 39, on the west-coast Rindby Strand beach.

The other worthwhile trip out of town is a visit to Denmark's most westerly point, **Blåvands Huk**, some 40km northwest of Esbjerg and reachable by bus #40. The road curves around the Ho Bugt bay area and ends abruptly at the 39m-high Blåvands Huk **lighthouse** (daily 10am–4pm; 15kr), which peers out over the North Sea from its clifftop position. From the top of the lighthouse, you get a stunning view of the desolate surrounding landscape and the unusually wide sandy **beaches** below. To the north are wild windswept west coast beaches and to the southeast, tucked away under a finger of land known as **Skallingen**, are more sedate and shallow child-friendly beaches, protected by the world's largest sea wind turbine park at Horns Rev. Blåvands Huk and Skallingen mark the northernmost reaches of the Wadden Sea tidal flat area stretching down via Germany to Holland and providing essential breeding and nesting ground for birds; on the Ho Bugt side of Skallingen, there's a good chance of spotting dunlin and bartailed godwit, especially during spring and autumn. If you want to **stay** a stone's throw from one of the country's best beaches, the best option is *Blåvand Camping*, Hvidbjerg Strandvej (☎75 27 90 40, ⓦwww .blaavandcamping.dk), on the Skallingen side of the lighthouse.

Travel details

Trains

Esbjerg to: Copenhagen (9 daily; 3hr 11min); Herning (4 daily; 1hr 50min); Holstebro (11 daily; 2hr–2hr 20min); Kolding (1–3 hourly; 42min–1hr); Ribe (1–3 hourly; 33min); Ringkøbing (12 daily; 1hr 17min–1hr 40min); Skive (4 daily; 2hr 47min–2hr 56min); Struer (10 daily; 2hr 12min–2hr 44min); Århus (hourly; 2hr 45min).

Herning to: Copenhagen (9 daily; 3hr 43min); Esbjerg (4 daily; 1hr 48min); Fredericia (hourly; 1hr 16min); Holstebro (1–2 hourly; 35min); Ringkøbing (4 daily; 56min–1hr 7min); Silkeborg (2 hourly; 36min–41min); Struer (1–2 hourly; 44min–1hr); Vejle (hourly; 56min–1hr 6min); Århus (2 hourly; 1hr 30min).

Holstebro to: Copenhagen (9 daily; 4hr 14min); Esbjerg (11 daily; 2hr–2hr 20min); Fredericia (hourly; 1hr 47min); Herning (1–2 hourly; 35min); Ringkøbing (hourly; 39min); Skive (7 daily; 52min); Struer (2–3 hourly; 12min–18min); Vejle (hourly; 1hr 19min–1hr 28min); Århus (8 daily; 2hr 24min–3hr 32min).

Ringkøbing to: Esbjerg (12 daily; 1hr 17min–1hr 40min); Herning (4 daily; 56min–1hr 7min); Holstebro (hourly; 39min); Struer (hourly; 53min); Århus (8 daily; 2hr 49min–3hr 11min).

Struer to: Copenhagen (9 daily; 4hr 28min); Esbjerg (10 daily; 2hr 12min–2hr 44min); Herning (1–2 hourly; 44min–1hr); Holstebro (2–3 hourly; 12min–18min); Hurup (12 daily; 40min–46min); Ringkøbing (hourly; 53min); Skive (1–2 hourly; 25min–30min); Thisted (12 daily; 1hr 15min–1hr 37min); Århus (hourly; 1hr 59min–2hr 14min).

Skive to: Copenhagen (2 daily; 5hr 10min); Esbjerg (4 daily; 2hr 47min–2hr 56min); Holstebro (7 daily; 52min); Struer (1–2 hourly; 25min–30min); Viborg (1–2 hourly; 22min–26min); Århus (hourly; 1hr 36min).

Thisted to: Hurup (12 daily; 34min–37min); Struer (12 daily; 1hr 15min–1hr 37min).

Buses

Esbjerg to: Aalborg via Viborg and Herning (7 weekly; 3hr 40min); Frederikshavn via Herning and Aalborg (2–3 daily; 4 hr 55min); Ribe (11 daily; 32min–55min).

Hanstholm to: Klitmøller (9 daily; 13min); Nørre Vorupør (2 daily; 27min); Thisted (23 daily; 41min–53min).

Hurup to: Agger (14 daily; 18min–25min); Vestervig (14 daily; 8min–15min)

Klitmøller to: Hanstholm (9 daily; 13min); Nørre Vorupør (3 daily; 14min); Thisted (8 daily; 23min–28min).

Nykøbing Mors to: Skive (23 daily; 30min–1hr 5min); Thisted (26 daily; 30min–47min).

Nørre Vorupør to: Hanstholm (2 daily; 27min); Klitmøller (3 daily; 14min).

Ringkøbing to: Hvide Sande (18 daily; 19min–30min).

Skive to: Stenøre, Fur (2 daily; 1hr 5min); Nykøbing Mors (23 daily; 29min–1hr 3min).

Thisted to: Aalborg (8 daily; 1hr 40min); Hanstholm (23 daily; 41min–53min); Klitmøller (8 daily; 23min–28min); Nørre Vorupør (13 daily; 28min–46min).

Flights

Thisted to: Copenhagen (1–2 daily; 55min).

Ferries

Agger to: Thyborøn (10–14 daily; 10min).
Esbjerg to: Nordby, Fanø (12–24 daily; 12min).
Mors to: Thy via Feggesund (20–24 daily; 5min); Thy via Næssund (20–24 daily; 5min).
Salling to: Stenøre, Fur (20–24 daily; 5min).

East Jutland

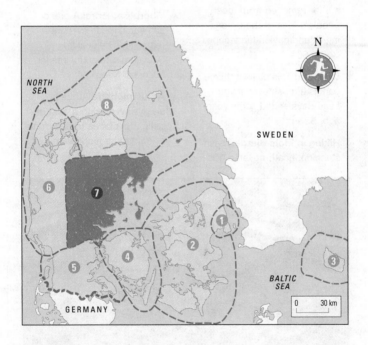

CHAPTER 7

Highlights

* **Grauballemanden, Moesgård Museum** This remarkable peat-preserved remains of a man who lived in 80BC are so well-preserved that you can still see the stubble on his chin. See p.330

* **Djursland beaches** These beautiful sandy beaches are far removed from most people's idea of the unforgiving Scandinavian landscape. See p.334

* **Legoland** This brilliant theme park is a must, even if your Lego days ended some years ago. See p.312

* **Hiking in Mols Bjerge** These stunning, heath-covered hills afford beautiful views of the Ebeltoft bay area and some lovely walks. See p.336

* **Canoeing down the Gudenå** Let the gentle current of Denmark's longest river carry you through some of east Jutland's prettiest countryside. See p.320

* **Viborg Cathedral** A grand cathedral, made even more remarkable by Joakim Skovgård's colourful interior frescoes. See p.342

* **Århus nightlife** Århus is always lively, with a host of delightful places to eat, drink or dance the night away. See p.332

△ Grauballemanden, Moesgård Museum

East Jutland

The most densely populated part of the peninsula, the **east** is also Jutland's most culturally vibrant region. Stretching from the Lillebælt bridge (which connects Jutland with Funen and, ultimately, Zealand and Copenhagen) and up past the grandly named **Lake District** to where the **Djursland** peninsula juts out into the Kattegat, the soft, hilly landscapes of the east are largely moraine formations, created in the aftermath of the last Ice Age when the jagged coastline was carved up by melting ice draining into the sea. These strong forces of nature created an unusually pretty landscape that stands out in an otherwise flat country, and with three national cycle routes

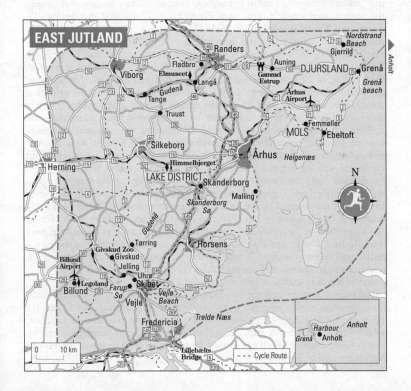

EAST JUTLAND

Nordstrand Beach
Gjerrild
Randers
Fladbro
Viborg   Elmuseet   Langå   Auning   DJURSLAND   Grenå
Gammel Estrup
Gudenå   Århus Airport   Grenå beach
Tange
Truust   Femmøller
MOLS   Ebeltoft
Silkeborg
Århus   Helgenæs
Herning   Himmelbjerget
LAKE DISTRICT   Skanderborg
Malling
Skanderborg Sø
Gudenå
Tørring   Horsens
Givskud Zoo
Billund Airport   Givskud
Jelling
Legoland   Uhre
Billund   Farup Sø   Skibet
Vejle   Vejle Beach
Fredericia   Trelde Næs
Anholt
Harbour   Anholt
Grenå   Anholt
Lillebælts Bridge
--- Cycle Route

0   10 km

N

traversing the area, it's all best seen by bike. The beautiful beaches and pretty rivers are at their most stunning during the summer, when they attract holiday-makers in droves, but you'll get a better appreciation of the area's uniqueness during the quieter months of spring and autumn.

The region's main urban draw, **Århus**, is the country's second city, boasting top-notch museums and a heaving nightlife. Among the coastal towns, **Fredericia** has the oddest history, **Vejle** is home to a few good museums and has an upland packed with historical sights such as the Jelling stone and big-name attractions like Legoland, while **Horsens** has an outstanding and innovative museum of industry, and hosts some of the country's best live gigs. At the heart of the Lake District, **Silkeborg** is inextricably linked to canoeing on the Gudenå river, while the white-sand beaches of **Djursland** leave little to be desired. Slap in the middle of the Kattegat, the tiny island of **Anholt** also does exceedingly well on the beach front, and has the added bonus of a lively night-life. North of Djursland, **Randers'** main offering is its recreated rainforests, steaming under massive domes, while **Viborg** boasts a majestic cathedral and a surrounding countryside that's suffused with history.

Fredericia and around

Set on the east coast overlooking the nearby island of Funen (covered in Chapter 3), **FREDERICIA** is the rail hub for the surrounding area and for trains crossing the Lillebælt bridge to Funen, and with its unique military history (and layout), the town is well worth a quick stop. Fredericia was envisaged by Christian IV during the Thirty Years' War (1618–1647; see history, p.394) as a strategically placed reserve capital and a base from which to defend Jutland, and was eventually founded in 1650 – a year after Christian's death – by his son Frederik III. Three nearby villages were demolished and their inhabitants forced to assist in the building of the new town – and afterwards, they had no choice but to live in it. Military considerations required that Fredericia be built on a strict grid plan, with low buildings enclosed by earthen ramparts reaching up to fifteen metres above street level, and protected further by an encircling moat. More than one million cubic metres of soil was shifted to build the ramparts and nine large bastions. However, seven years after completion, a forceful Swedish army attacked and all but destroyed this supposedly invincible town; most of its citizens fled and Fredericia was left practically deserted. A long and torturous rebuilding process followed, with tax exemptions and promises of religious freedom offered to lure the people back. Catholics, Jews and Huguenots soon arrived from all over Europe, as demonstrated by the town's large Jewish cemetery. The rebuilt fortification was finally completed in 1710, and over the years, until the final defeat in 1864 (see the box on p.263), the town played a significant part in the wars over south Jutland. The fortification was decommissioned in 1909, and turned into a public park a few years later. A military feel still abides to this day, however; the town centre is dotted with memorials to victorious heroes, and Fredericia is home to the only military tattoo still staged in Denmark.

The twenty-minute walk (or five-minute ride on bus #2) along Vesterbrogade from the train station into the town centre takes you through the Danmarks Port, gateway to the most impressive section of the now grassed-over ramparts, which stretch for 4km. A path along the top gives a good perspective on the town's layout, though you'll get an even better view from the top of the **Hvide Vandtårn** (May to mid-June & mid to end-Aug Sat & Sun 10am–4pm;

FREDERICIA

EATING, DRINKING & NIGHTLIFE

Café Carlos	6
Café Filmer	4
Da Isabella	3
Det Bruunske Pakhus	2
Simons Café	5
Ti Trin Ned	1

N

0   200 m

ACCOMMODATION

Fredericia Vandrerhjem	B
Postgården	D
Sømandshjemmet	C
Trelde Næs campsite	A

mid-June to mid-Aug daily 10am–4pm; 10kr), a decommissioned water tower at the Prins Georges Bastion, visible from Danmarks Port and a short walk up the rampart. From here, the straight lines and miniscule size of Fredericia's town centre stand out, as do the tree-covered ramparts that completely encircle the centre. Back down from the ramparts, between the Danmarks and Prinsens Port gateways, the **Den Tapre Landsoldat** ("the brave foot soldier") **statue** by renowned Danish sculptor Bissen epitomizes the local military spirit, its bronze figure holding a rifle in his left hand, a sprig of leaves in his right, and with his foot resting on a captured cannon. The statue commemorates "6 Juli 1849", the day Danish troops secretly assembled in Fredericia to make a momentous (and successful) sortie against the occupying Prussians in the first Schleswig war (see History, p.392). The downside of the battle was the five hundred Danes killed; they lie in a mass grave in the grounds of the town's church, **Trinitatis Kirke**, on Kongensgade. The anniversary of the battle is still celebrated each year as **Fredericia Day**, with memorial ceremonies for the fallen on the evening of July 5, and concerts and fireworks on July 6 – it's a festive affair that's worth sticking around for if you're in the vicinity.

The fortifications around the town centre form the core of Fredericia's appeal. A small booklet (5kr) and free leaflets about the ramparts can be picked up at the tourist office (see below), itself situated in a beautifully renovated building from 1850 that formerly served as Fredericia's prison, town hall and courthouse. Designed by Ferdinand Meldahl (also renowned for his courthouses in Randers and Aalborg), this unique structure boasts heaps of fine detail, its arches and pillars more redolent of Venice than of Denmark. The only other place worth seeking out within the ramparts, and a short walk away along Jyllandsgade, is the **Jewish cemetery** (mid-June to mid-Aug Wed & Sun noon–4pm; outside these hours collect a key at the town museum, see below) on Slesvigsgade 2, near the picturesque white bridge, Hvide Bro, which crosses the moat between Slesvigs and Prinsessens bastions. Though Fredericia's Jewish population was enticed to Fredericia with a promise of religious freedom, the pledge was less a sign of the then-king's open-mindedness than of his desperate need for help in rebuilding the town and fortifications. An interesting memento of this tiny snippet of Danish history, the cemetery holds 550 graves, their tombstones inscribed in meticulous Hebrew writing. The small chapel (same hours; 10kr) houses changing displays depicting different aspects of Jewish history in Fredericia, though Judaism isn't an active religion here today – the last burial took place in 1910.

Just outside the ramparts, on the road leading back to the station from Slesvigs Bastion, the **Bymuseet i Fredericia** (Fredericia Town Museum; Tues–Sun noon–4pm; 20kr), Jernbanegade 10, is, quite predictably, centred around three hundred years of armed conflict via a series of displays in the main building by the entrance. The large, well-presented site also includes typical houses from the seventeenth and eighteenth centuries, moved here from their various locations in town. Keep an eye out for the unusual *soldaterkammeret* (soldier's shack), building 6, an obligatory extension to all townhouses in Fredericia prior to the building of a military barracks in the 1930s, before which all private homes housed soldiers, typically in cold, sparsely furnished shacks at the back of the house. The unusual museum garden is also worth a peek, with crops and flowers that have a historical link with Fredericia. A tobacco section, complete with open drying barn, stems from the Reformed Church members who arrived here from Holland following the promise of religious freedom. Apart from tobacco, they also introduced a range of vegetables to the area including new sorts of potatoes and the Bortfelder turnip.

If it's sunny, you might want to head to the eastern end of Jyllandsgade, where the fine Østerstrand **beach** runs along the entire eastern section of the ramparts, facing Funen on the opposite bank of the Lille Bælt. It has changing facilities, a few bathing piers and a kiosk selling snacks, and tends to be tightly packed in the summer.

Practicalities

Fredericia's **tourist office**, Vendersgade 30D (Mon–Fri 10am–5pm, Sat 10am–1pm; ☎72 11 35 11, ⓦwww.visitfredericia.dk), has an extensive list of private rooms (a 25kr booking fee applies), and a range of cycle maps. Bicycles can be hired at *Cykel Service*, Venusvej 4 (☎75 92 14 09) west of the centre. There are only two **hotels** within Fredericia's ramparts: the good-value *Postgården*, Oldenborggade 4 (☎75 92 18 55, ⓦwww.postgaarden.dk; ❹, en-suite ❺), and the smaller, family-run *Sømandshjemmet* (☎75 92 01 99, ⓦwww.fsh.dk; ❻) on Gothersgade 40, both near the harbour and with good-value restaurants. To the west of the town, outside the ramparts and reachable by bus #2 and #6 from the train station, there's a modern **youth hostel**, *Fredericia Vandrerhjem* (☎75 92 12 87, ⓦwww.fredericia-danhostel.dk; dorms 150kr, doubles ❹), Vestre Ringvej 98, with thirty four-bed rooms that can be rented as doubles; while the *Trelde*

Næs **campsite** (☎75 95 71 83, ⓦwww.supercamp.dk; April–Oct) is beautifully situated at the entry to Vejle fjord, though it's 15km north of town and adjacent to a public beach, so it can get very crowded during fine weather and at holiday times. Take bus #6 from the train station.

For **food**, *Simons Café* on Axeltorv (Mon–Sat noon–3pm & 5–11pm, ☎75 91 49 11, ⓦwww.simons-restaurant.dk) serves well-prepared sandwiches, soups and salads, while *Café Carlos*, Sjællandsgade 56 (Tues–Sat noon–3.30pm & 5–10pm, Sun 5–10pm; winter open evening only; ☎75 92 04 91) has good-value Spanish cuisine. There's also the stylish *Ti Trin Ned*, Norgesgade 3 (Mon–Sat 6pm–9pm; ☎75 93 33 55, ⓦwww.titrinned.dk) serving high-quality food at reasonable prices – just 265kr/310kr for a delicious two- or three-course meal. The friendly, family-run *Da Isabella*, Vendersgade 20 (daily 11.30am–11pm; ☎75 95 44 64) does authentic Mexican and Italian dishes starting at 59kr as well as good Danish steaks. The popular *Det Bruunske Pakhus* at Kirkestræde 3 (☎72 10 67 10, ⓦwww.bruunskepakhus.dk) hosts a range of live bands every weekend from September to June, while *Café Filmer*, Jyllandsgade 20B, offers music, food and drinks, and wireless Internet.

Vejle and around

A twenty-minute train ride north of Fredericia on the mouth of the Vejle fjord, the compact harbour town of **Vejle** is home to the Tulip factory, from where four hundred million sausages a year begin their journey to British breakfast tables. It's also the best base for exploring the contrasting pleasures of the Viking burial mounds at **Jelling**, the **Givskud Zoo** and – rather more famously – the **Legoland** complex at Billund, all within easy reach by bus or train. The less exciting **Horsens**, just north, has an interesting museum devoted to Denmark's industrial history and, in recent years, has made a name for itself as the country's premier international concert venue.

Vejle

With a magnificent backdrop of the slimline E45 motorway bridge as it crosses the fjord behind the town, **VEJLE**'s compact centre offers a couple of diverting and unique attractions. Chief among them, on the central Kirke Torvet, is **Skt Nicolai Kirke** (Mon–Fri 9am–5pm, Sat & Sun 9am–noon) in which a glass-topped coffin holds the peat-preserved body of a woman found in the Haraldskær bog in 1835. Originally, the body was thought to be the corpse of a Viking queen, Gunhilde of Norway, but the claim was disputed and tests carried out in 1977 dated the body to around 450 BC – too old to be a Viking, but nonetheless still the best preserved "bog body" in the country. It's hidden away behind bars in the north transept, but if you want to have a close look, the verger will let you in. Another macabre feature of the church, though you can't see it, are the 23 skulls hidden in sealed holes in the north transept; legend has it that they're the heads of thieves executed in 1630. Not far from the church, and across from the train station at Dæmningen 11, is the less gory and far more contemporary **Økolariet** (Feb–Nov Sat–Thurs 11am–4pm; free; ⓦwww. okolariet.dk). A state-of-the-art educational centre focusing on green issues ("økologisk" translates as "organic"), it illustrates how human consumption affects the planet in various detrimental ways. The main themes are drinking water, waste, energy, and home consumption, and the facts are presented in easy-to-grasp and captivating ways that involve interactive models with buttons to press; if it all gets too depressing, look out for the intriguing and entertaining history of the toilet in the basement.

A short walk west of the centre, on the banks of the partly concealed Vejle Å river, you might also want to check out the outstanding **Vejle Kunstmuseum** (Vejle Museum of Art; Tues–Fri 11am–4pm, Sat & Sun 10am–5pm; free; Ⓦ www.vejlekunstmuseum.dk) at Flegborg 16. It specializes in graphics and drawings, and has an enormous collection of work, mostly from the fifteenth to nineteenth century, of which a changing selection is on display; look out for the remarkable self-portrait by Rembrandt. The museum also houses a less interesting collection of twentieth-century painting and sculpture, and often hosts innovative temporary exhibitions. **Vejle Museum** is slated to reopen at a new location on Vardevej in 2008 or 2009; check at the tourist office for an update. Operated by the museum, and a fabulous destination on a sunny day, is **Vejle Vindmølle** (May–Oct Tues–Sun 11am–4pm; free), a disused windmill which maintains its full complement of ropes, shafts and pinions, displays a through-the-ages account of milling, from Neolithic blocks to modern roller mills, and affords stupendous views across Vejle and its fjord. The site is a ten-minute walk south of the centre via the steep Kiddesvej, which leads off Søndergade.

Practicalities

Vejle's **train station** is just east of the town centre at Banegårds Pladsen 3. All regional and town **buses** stop at the adjacent Vejle Trafikcenter, as does bus #907 (30min; 53kr) from **Billund Airport** (Ⓦ www.billund-airport.dk), some 30km west of Vejle and served by regular flights from Bornholm and Copenhagen. Across from the train station on Banegårds Pladsen 6, the **tourist office** (mid-June to Aug Mon–Fri 9.30am–5.30pm, Sat 9.30am–1.30pm; Sept to mid-June Mon–Thurs 10am–5pm, Fri 10am–4.30pm, Sat 10am–noon; ☎75 82 19 55, Ⓦ www.visitvejle.com) has a range of free cycle maps that come in handy if you choose to explore the region by bike. **Cycle hire** is available at Buhl Jensen, Gormsgade 14 (☎75 82 15 09) as well as at the youth hostel. If you've opted for the five-day canoe trip along the Gudenå river to Silkeborg and beyond (see p.320), catch bus #215 from the Trafikcenter for the starting point at Tørring (25min).

With a host of worthwhile attractions in and around town, Vejle is an appealing place to base yourself while taking in the sights. Unfortunately **accommodation** is fairly limited, though the tourist office has a list of private rooms for 175kr per person per night, but charges a steep 40kr booking fee. A short walk west of the centre, halfway between the train station and the art museum, the friendly *Park* (☎75 82 24 66, Ⓦ www.park-hotel.dk; ❼, 50kr reduction if you pay in cash), Orla Lehmannsgade 5, offers spacious rooms with Rococo-style furnishings, and a bountiful breakfast buffet. *Torvehallerne*, at Kirketorvet 10–16 in the town centre (☎79 42 79 10, Ⓦ www.torvehallerne.dk; ❽), is a more upscale option, housed in a former printing hall across from the church, and with luxurious, minimalist rooms that are slightly on the small side. Perks include a concert venue and a gourmet restaurant. Much less convenient, some 5km west of Vejle in the hamlet of Skibet (bus #207), the four-star *Vejle Vandrerhjem* **youth hostel** (☎75 82 51 88, Ⓦ www.vejle-danhostel.dk), Vardevej 485, has en-suite doubles (❹) as well as dorm beds (120kr). There's also a **campsite** at Helligkildevej 5 (☎75 82 33 35, Ⓦ www.dk-camp.dk/vejlecamp), north of the fjord and close to a popular sandy beach; take bus #10 and get off at the sports grounds.

Central Vejle has plenty of inexpensive **places to eat**. In the courtyard of the wood-beamed Smitskegård, Søndergade 14, *Conrad Café* (daily 11am–midnight;

ⓣ75 72 01 22, ⓦwww.conradcafe.dk) serves substantial salads and smørrebrød through the afternoon, and drinks in the evenings – it sometimes has live music, too. Around the corner, the ⅄ *Brasseriet* (Mon–Thurs & Sun 11am–midnight, Fri & Sat 11am–2am; ⓣ79 42 79 00, ⓦwww.torvehallerne.dk), at *Hotel Torvehallerne*, serves substantial, beautifully prepared meals (two courses for 159kr) in a greenery-filled conservatory supplemented with live jazz every Saturday lunchtime and raucous dance music on Friday and Saturday evenings. Live bands – mostly Danish names – play at the large concert hall in the back. For brunch (daily 11am–2pm; 98kr), inexpensive salads, sandwiches and filling burgers, make for ⅄ *Caféen – Den Gamle Arrest* (Daily 11am–late; ⓣ75 82 93 00, ⓦwww.cafeen.nu), inside the former prison at Klostergade 1, which is also a good place for a drink. Of the number of English-style **pubs** in town, most popular is the *Tartan* at Dæmningen 40.

Jelling and Givskud Zoo

A twelve-kilometer hop northwest of Vejle, the village of **JELLING** is known to have been the site of pagan festivals and celebrations and, on the right hand side of the main road to Tørring, has two **burial mounds** thought to have contained King Gorm, Jutland's tenth-century ruler, and his queen, Tyre. The graves were found in the early twentieth century and, although only one coffin was actually recovered, there is evidence to suggest that the body of Gorm was removed by his son, Harald Bluetooth, and placed in the adjacent church – which Bluetooth himself built around 960 after his conversion to Christianity. In the grounds of the present church are two big **runic stones**, one erected by Gorm to the memory of Tyre, the other raised by Harald Bluetooth in honour of Gorm. The texts hewn into the granite record the era when Denmark began the transition to Christianity. They still provide scholars with lots of unanswered questions, however: on his stone to Gorm, for instance, Harald records that it was he who "won" Denmark. Scholars now believe this refers to a battle at Dannevirke (in present-day Schleswig, Germany) where he regained control over southern Jutland, and not, as was the previous thinking, about uniting the country under one ruler. Across the road from the stones on Gormsgade 23, the modern **Kongernes Jelling Exhibition Centre** (May to mid-June & Sept Tues–Sun 10am–4pm; mid-June to Aug daily 10am–5pm; Oct–April Tues–Sun 1–4pm; 40kr; ⓦ www.kongernesjelling.dk) provides a full breakdown of their history and also about the political rather than religious reasons for Harald's conversion to Christianity.

Train services from Vejle towards Struer and Herning stop at Jelling: both run roughly once an hour on weekdays and less frequently at weekends; **bus** #211 runs hourly to Jelling

△ Rune stone, Jelling

from Vejle bus station. A fun alternative is the **vintage train** between Vejle and Jelling, running every Sunday in July and on the first three Sundays in August (☎75 58 60 60, ⓦwww.klk.dk; 35kr). By **bike**, it's a scenic ride through the hamlet of Uhre and along the shores of Fårup Sø lake. If you want to **stay**, the historic *Jelling Kro*, Gormsgade 16 (☎75 87 10 06, ⓦwww.jellingkro.dk; ❹), has a few pleasant rooms sharing bathroom facilities, and a popular restaurant; or head for *Jelling Camping* (☎75 87 16 53, ⓦwww.jellingcamping.dk; April to mid-Sept), about 1km west of the church on Mølvangsvej. Alternatively there's the more scenic *Faarup Sø Camping*, Fårupvej 58 (☎75 87 13 44, ⓦwww .dkcamp.dk/faarup-soe), a few kilometres out of Jelling on the banks of Fårup Sø lake en route back to Vejle or on to Billund.

Eight kilometres northwest of Jelling, on the road to Herning, the small town of **GIVSKUD** (bus #211 from Vejle via Jelling) is home to the hugely popular **Givskud Zoo** (daily: mid-April to mid-June & mid-Aug to mid-Sept 10am–6pm; mid-June to mid-Aug 10am–8pm; mid-Sept to mid-Oct 10am–5pm; 115kr; ⓦwww.givskudzoo.dk) which, with its thousand-plus animals from around the globe roaming more or less freely on 70ha of parkland, is more of a safari park than a zoo. The idea is that you explore the area in your own car (with wound-up windows if you don't want the monkeys to nick your lunch) or join the safari bus (1.5hr; 20kr), which stops at a parking spot en route, from where you can hike around the immediate area. Animals include lions, zebras, gorillas, elephants and antelopes, but it's the relatively free, natural setting in which they live that makes the zoo a hit, especially with kids.

Legoland and Billund

Twenty kilometres west of Vejle, the village of **BILLUND** has been transformed into a major tourist centre, complete with international airport (see p.310) and rows of pricey hotels. It's all thanks to **Legoland Park** (April–June Mon–Fri 10am–6pm, Sat & Sun 10am–8pm; July to mid-Aug daily 10am–9pm; mid- to end Aug daily 10am–8pm; Sept & Oct Mon, Tues & Fri 10am–6pm, Sat & Sun 10am–8pm; 225kr; ⓦwww.legoland.dk), a theme park celebrating the tiny plastic bricks that have filled many a Christmas stocking since a Danish carpenter, Ole Kirk Christiansen, started making wooden toys collectively named "Lego", from the Danish phrase "*Leg Godt*", or "play well" (which also, by a happy coincidence, means "I study" and "I assemble" in Latin). In 1947, the Lego company began to manufacture its bricks in plastic, becoming the first company in Denmark to use new plastic moulding-injection techniques; the Lego pieces (or "Automatic Binding Bricks", to be perfectly precise) we know today were first created in 1958. The park itself, featuring a cornucopia of elaborate model buildings, animals, planes and many other weird and wonderful things (such as Titania's Palace – home for the queen of the fairies), is aimed chiefly at kids, but anybody whose efforts at Lego construction have resulted in tears of frustration over missing corner bricks might like to discover what can be achieved when someone has 45 million pieces to play with.

Billund's **tourist office** (April, May & Oct Mon–Fri 10am–6pm, Sat & Sun 10am–8pm; June & mid-Aug to Sept daily 10am–8pm; July to mid-Aug daily 10am–9pm; ☎76 50 00 55, ⓦwww.visitbillund.dk) is located by Legoland. If you want to stay, try the modern *Legoland Village* **youth hostel**, a short walk from the airport at Ellehammers Allé (☎75 33 27 77, ⓦwww.legoland-village .dk; doubles ❻). It has no dorms, but a good supply of pricey double rooms and other family accommodation. If you've arrived by bus (from Givskud it's

Denmark's
great outdoors

Although hibernation mode tends to take over during the winter, when most people stay indoors and fend off the cold with hearty food and plenty of warming *gløgg* wine, the mass exodus to the countryside come the first signs of snowmelt will leave you in little doubt that Danes are some of Europe's most enthusiastic lovers of outdoor pursuits. With endless possibilities for hiking, cycling and, perhaps surprisingly, days at the beach, Denmark is a fantastic place to get out and enjoy the great outdoors.

▼ Bornholm coast near Hammershus

Hiking

Walking through open fields, along the coast or up into the undulating, heathy hills is one of the most gratifying ways to explore Denmark, and with a network of waymarked trails criss-crossing the most picturesque parts of the country, hiking here couldn't be easier – you can pick up detailed (free) trail guides in all the tourist offices. Many trails can be walked in half a day, but to really get the flavour of the Danish countryside, you'll need to plan a longer route, overnighting along the way. There are open camping areas (*lejrpladser* or *teltpladser*) in unspoilt, remote spots throughout the country, where you can pitch a tent for free – they're detailed in the *Overnatning i Det Fri* brochure (98kr), available from larger tourist offices. As most of the trails and camping areas are in rural parts, it's a good idea to bring your own food, and it's also fun to add to your meal by sampling the abundant berries – *stikkelsbær* (gooseberries), *hindbær* (raspberries) and *jordbær* (strawberries) – that grow in Denmark's state forests.

Some of the best hikes include the old railway embankment trail from Horsens to Silkeborg in Jutland, a leisurely path that passes through the verdant Gudenå river valley and its pretty country villages; the crags, bluffs and hummocks of Bornholm's northwestern corner, loomed over by the ruins of the thirteenth-century Hammershus citadel; and the half-dozen trails that traverse the quiet farmlands of Rømø island. The Danish Forest Service also maintains dozens of nature trails through woodlands across the country: nearest to Copenhagen are the 1500-hectare Westskoven forest and the Jægersborg Deer Park, the latter once Frederik III's private hunting ground. Elsewhere, the hills of Jutland's Rebild Bakker forest boast a thick and beautiful cover of crowberry, juniper and mountain tobacco – you can amble around for hours without seeing another soul.

Cycling

Bikes are ubiquitous in Denmark. Danes tend to cycle almost as often as they head out on foot, and the cycling paths that navigate the country's picturesque lanes, coastal roads and forests (as well as most towns and cities) make Denmark one of Europe's most cycle-friendly countries. The network of eleven long-distance **national cycle routes** (indicated with large blue signs and marked on the relevant maps within the Guide) cover some 10,000km, and pass by the deep fjords of western Jutland, the flat plains of northern Funen and as far afield as the wide open grassy pastures of Lolland and Falster. One of the most popular is the **Hærvejen** route, from Viborg all the way north to Skagen, passing ancient burial mounds and medieval churches en route; if you're after some coastal riding, head for the **southern Funen archipelago**, whose hundred-odd islands, islets and skerries are wonderfully far-flung, tranquil places to take to two wheels. The most popular place to cycle is the island of **Bornholm**, where a web of well-maintained, secluded cycle routes run along the crisp, clean Baltic shoreline and through coniferous forests.

▲ Cyclists near Tåsinge

Beaches

Most people don't associate Denmark with **beaches**, so it might come as a surprise to learn that the country's 7300km of coastline boasts scores of top-notch swathes of white sand perfect for summer sunning and swimming. And thanks in part to the Danes' staunch respect for the environment, over two hundred of the county's beaches have been given **blue flag** status – the water is pristine and unpolluted almost everywhere, and it's warmer than you might think: around 15° C (59°F) in July and August.

◀ Windsurfers, Skagen

Denmark's top ten beaches

Gudmindrup Lyng Strand, Zealand Regularly heralded as the best beach in the country, this lengthy strand is cleaned every morning and makes a great place to go for a late afternoon swim followed by a spot of sunset-watching. See p.153

Tisvildeleje, Zealand With a decidedly upmarket feel, this sandy swathe boasts ample facilities, family-friendly sandbars and shallows and a host of superb restaurants and cafés. See p.141

Hvide Sande, Jutland This popular beach boasts excellent facilities, and is one of the best places in the country for windsurfing, with plenty of places from which to rent watersports gear. See p.296

Dueodde, Bornholm Easily accessible, with lengthy shallows and the warmest water off Bornholm, the powdery sand at this mid-Baltic gem is said to be some of the finest in Europe. See p.196

Grenå Strand, Jutland Find your own private dune or cove along this clean, quiet 7km strip of silky white sand, backed by some spectacular scenery and very child-friendly. See p.337

Falster Unlike the rest of Scandinavia, nude bathing is allowed at nearly of Denmark's beaches, and is one of the most popular places for a spot of skinny dipping. See p.171

Ristinge, Langeland Sheltered to the north by towering cliffs and dunes, this handsome beachfront is just minutes' walk from a well-placed campsite. See p.238

Klitmøller, Jutland Denmark's largest concentration of beaches lie along Jutland's west coast, and the winds that blow in off the sea here make Klitmøller the perfect spot for a lesson in windsurfing or kitesurfing. See p.286

Amager Strandpark, Zealand Set just south of the capital, this unpretentious beach offers clean water and great views of the Øresunds bridge to Sweden. See p.102

Charlottenlund Strand, Copenhagen Just north of the city centre, this small, secluded beach is very popular and offers great facilities and a designated nude bathing area. See p.125

▲ Sandvig beach, Bornholm

△ Legoland

bus #117, from Jelling you have to return to Vejle and then take #244), it's best to get off at Legoland and walk the remaining 300m to the hostel. The other options in town are even more expensive, and include the modern *Propellen* (☎75 33 81 33, ⓦwww.propellen.dk; ❻), on Nordmarksvej, 500m from the Legoland entrance; and the traditional counterpart *Billund Kro* (☎75 33 26 33, ⓦwww.billund-kro; ❼) near the centre at Buen 6, which also has a fabulous restaurant serving traditional Danish fare.

Horsens

There's every chance you'll pass through the pretty fjord town of **HORSENS**, 30km north of Vejle, when heading north towards Århus and beyond. A like-able if fairly unexciting place, Horsens has recently undergone something of a cultural revival, with huge international music acts along the lines of REM, Robbie Williams, David Bowie, Rolling Stones and Madonna performing regularly in Horsens' two outstanding concert venues. Horsens was also the birthplace, in 1681, of **Vitus Bering**, who discovered what became known as the Bering Strait whilst on a mission on behalf of Peter the Great to find an Asian–American land bridge. A memorial to him stands in the town's park, midway between the train station and the town centre on Kongensgade, which also bears his name.

Kongensgade runs into Søndergade, a long, wide pedestrianized street that later becomes Slotsgade, and which has the harbour at its south end and the Caroline Amalielund park at its north. You can learn more about Vitus Bering at the **Horsens Museum** (July & Aug daily 10am–4pm; Sept–June Tues–Sun 11am–4pm; 30kr; Ⓦwww.horsensmuseum.dk), within the park on Sundvej; it also contains a run-of-the-mill collection of local knick-knacks. Around the corner at Carolinelundsvej 2, the more enticing **Horsens Kunstmuseum** (Art Museum; Tues–Fri 11am–4pm, Sat & Sun 11am–5pm; 30kr; Ⓦwww.horsenskunstmuseum.dk) specializes in art from the 1980s and 1990s and includes an outstanding collection of works by renowned Danish artist Zieler, as well as pieces by Bjørn Nørgaard, best known for the tapestries at the Royal Reception Rooms in Copenhagen (see p.78) There are also some Danish Golden Age masters and an honourable assortment of works by local artists. However, if you only have time for one stop while in Horsens, head for the fascinating **Industrimuseet** (July & Aug daily 10am–4pm; Sept–June Tues–Sun 11am–4pm; 40kr; Ⓦwww.industrimuseet.dk), set in the town's former electricity and gas works, near the harbour at Gasvej 17–19. The museum's aim is to give an insight into how industrialization took place in Denmark from 1860 up until today, and it does so very successfully. The extensive displays include a fully functioning printing press, a collection of the rare Danish Nimbus motorcycles (only fifteen thousand were ever produced), six fully furnished workers homes and a working telephone exchange. There's also a good café, *Gaslight*, which offers inexpensive set menus from the 1950s, 1960s and 1970s.

Although there are plenty of **accommodation** options in Horsens, everywhere fills up quickly when there's a live gig scheduled, and booking months in advance is essential. Most atmospheric option, and the choice of rock stars when they're playing here, is the fancy, peach-coloured ⚜ *Jørgensens Hotel* (Ⓣ75 62 16 00, Ⓦwww.jorgensens-hotel.dk; ➐), housed in an eighteenth-century palace at Søndergade 17, and with a range of rooms offering luxury in varying degrees. Fifteen minutes' walk from the centre (or take bus #9) on the edge of the Nørrestrand nature reserve is the more affordable and scenically located *Horsens Vandrerhjem* **youth hostel**, Flintebakken 150 (Ⓣ75 61 67 77, Ⓦwww .danhostelhorsens.dk; dorms 150kr, doubles ➌), with 27 en-suite rooms as well as dorms and family units. The **tourist office**, Søndergade 26 (mid-June to Aug Mon–Fri 10am–5.30pm, Sat 10am–2pm; Sept to mid-June Mon–Fri 10am–4.30pm, Sat 10am–1pm; Ⓦwww.visithorsens.dk), has a list of **private rooms** (from 260kr per double, plus a 40kr booking fee) and can also help with information about the **nature reserve** around the pretty Nørrestrand freshwater lake, encircled by hiking and cycle trails that provide excellent birdwatching opportunities. Good **cycle routes** in the area also include an old disused railway track up to Silkeborg and national cycle route #5 linking Horsens with Vejle and Århus along rural roads following the coast. The tourist office hires out bicycles. Good-value **restaurants** include ⚜ *Café Dolly* (Mon–Sat 11am–10pm; Ⓣ75 62 34 81, Ⓦwww.cafedolly.dk), Havne Allé 55, which does filling portions of traditional Danish dishes such as *stegt flæsk og persille sovs* for 118kr. For a tasty burger head to *Mackie's* (Mon–Thurs 11am–10pm, Fri & Sat 11am–11pm, Sun noon to 10pm; Ⓣ75 60 16 22, Ⓦwww.mackies-hs.dk), at Graven 2 on the corner of Søndergade near the town's central pedestrian area; while for a romantic Mexican meal, there's the *Tequila Sunrise*, Smedegade 10 (Wed–Sun 5pm–midnight; Ⓣ75 61 65 73, Ⓦwww.tequilasunrise.dk). During summer, bars and cafés in the centre set up chairs and tables outside for alfresco eating and drinking. The best place to head for – and to be seen – is the *Corfitz*

(Mon–Wed & Sun 10am–midnight, Thurs 10am–2am, Sat & Sun 10am–3am; ☎75 62 88 44, ⊛www.corfitz.dk) at Søndergade 23, an elegant place in the heart of town which does light meals throughout the day. For **nightlife**, the smaller *Koks* (Thurs & Sat 6pm–3am, Fri 1pm–3am; ☎75 62 64 62, ⊛www. cafekoks.dk), Nørregade 10, has occasional live bands; while *Paddy's Irish Pub* (Mon–Wed & Sun 4pm–3am, Thurs–Sat 4pm–5am), right in the centre at Torvet 2A; and *Club Etzo* (Fri & Sat 11pm–5am), Graven 12, are the two main clubs, always busy after a live show. The town's two internationally renowned **concert venues** are the intimate Horsens Ny Teater (⊛www.hnt.dk) next to *Jørgensens Hotel* on Teatertorvet, and the grand open-air Horsens Forum (⊛www.forumhorsens.dk) on the sports ground at Langmarksvej 53, a short walk from the youth hostel. Check their websites or ask at the tourist office to find out what's on.

The Lake District: Silkeborg and around

Ensconced in a loose triangle formed by Skanderborg, Århus and Silkeborg, the grandly titled **Lake District** comprises several small lakes amid green, rolling woodlands, and boasts one of the country's highest points, the 147m Himmel-bjerget. If you've only seen Denmark's larger towns, the region is well worth a couple of days' rural exploration, preferably by canoe, and there are innumer-able campsites in which to stay. The north–south rail route passes first through missable Skanderborg, but it's the Lake District's other main town, **Silkeborg**, spreading handsomely across several inlets, which serves as the area's lively centre and is a good base while exploring the region.

Silkeborg

The main reason people flock to **SILKEBORG** is to travel down the Gudenå river by **canoe**, by far the best way to explore the Lake District. If this doesn't tickle your fancy, the weather isn't up for it or if you find yourself in Silkeborg during winter, you'll find some outstanding museums and sights that easily justify a few nights' stay.

The Skanderborg Festival

Although it's difficult to find anything bad to say about the attractive town of Skan-derborg, delicately positioned on the banks of Skanderborg Sø, there's no real reason to visit either – unless, however, you're hereabouts around the second weekend in August, when the beech woods south of the centre are converted into a visually stunning music festival site. Nicknamed the "country's most beautiful festival", for its fabulous setting and positive vibes, the four-day **Skanderborg Festival** (☎87 93 44 44, ⊛www.smukfest.dk) is a lot more laid-back than the Roskilde bash (see p.146), and the general idea is more about enjoying the beautiful surroundings and friendly atmosphere than great musical experiences – although they happen as well. Spread over five stages, music acts in 2006 included top Danish names plus Jamiroquai and Toto headlining as the two main international acts, and DJing by Boy George. **Tickets** cost 1575kr for all four days, and all-day day tickets cost 450kr Thursday, 550kr for Friday, 650kr for Saturday, and 600kr for Sunday. They are available at Billetlugen (☎70 26 32 67, ⊛www.billetlugen.dk) and, until they sell out, at the main entrance.

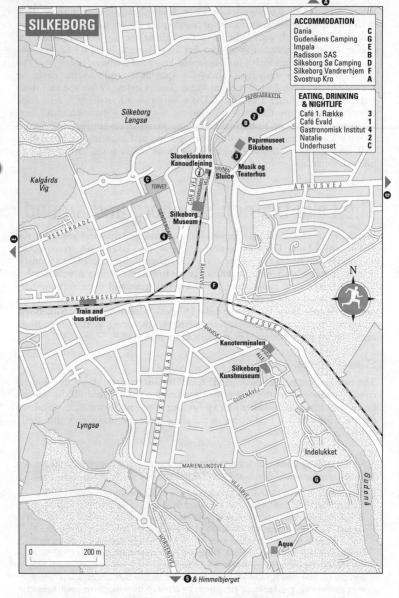

SILKEBORG

Silkeborg Langsø

Kalgårds Vig

PAPIRFABRIKKEN

Papirmuseet Bikuben

Slusekioskens Kanoudlejning

Musik og Teaterhus

Sluice

TORVET

VESTERGADE

Silkeborg Museum

SØNDERGADE

CHR. 8 VEJ

HAVNEN

ÅRHUSVEJ

N

ÅHAVEVEJ

DREWSENSVEJ

Train and bus station

SEJSVEJ

Kanoterminalen

Silkeborg Kunstmuseum

FREDERIKSBERGGADE

RINKE ALLÉ

GUDENÅVEJ

Lyngsø

Indelukket

Gudenå

MARIENLUNDSVEJ

VEJLSØVEJ

HORSENSVEJ

Aqua

0   200 m

& Himmelbjerget

Arrival, information and accommodation

Regional buses and trains arrive at the **train station** on Drewsensvej. From here, it's a ten-minute walk along Christian 8 Vej to the Gudenå river lock, which is the most central point from which to get to grips with the town's offerings. Silkeborg's layout is somewhat complicated. The Gudenå river delineates the edge of the town centre to the east while the Silkeborg lakes separate the residential and industrial suburbs in the north from the old town centre, which has a line of classy patrician villas along the Gudenå riverbank to the south. The three town bus routes (C1, C2 and C3) connect the residential and industrial areas with the town centre and will come in handy if you choose to stay in a private room. The helpful **tourist office**, across from the sluice at Åhavevej 2A (April to mid-June and Sept–Oct Mon–Fri 9am–4pm, Sat 10am–1pm; mid-June to Aug Mon–Fri 9am–5pm, Sat & Sun 9am–2pm; Nov–March Mon–Fri 10am–3pm, Sat 10am–1pm; ☏86 82 19 11, ⓦwww.silkeborg.com) has a lengthy list of affordable rooms, and charges only a 10kr fee per booking. Although **hotels** are plentiful in the Silkeborg area, the region's popularity ensures that they're all relatively expensive. We've listed some of the best options below, as well as a hostel and two campsites.

Hotels and hostels

Dania Torvet 5 ☏86 82 01 11, ⓦwww
.hoteldania.dk. Silkeborg's grand old hotel, which prides itself in having housed H.C. Andersen for a number of years. Though they're full of atmosphere and top-end facilities, the plush en-suite rooms come at a price. ❾

Impala Vestre Ringvej 53 ☏86 82 03 00, ⓦwww.impala.dk. On the northern bank of Silkeborg Langesø lake and a twenty-minute walk from the station, *Impala* has a range of good-value, if somewhat characterless en-suite rooms. ❼

Radisson SAS Papirfabrikken 12 ☏88 82 22 22, ⓦwww.radisson.com. Modern, central hotel in a section of the refurbished paper mill which overlooks the Gudenå river and lock. The en-suite rooms are simple and stylish, but a little on the small side. ❽/❼

🏃 **Silkeborg Vandrerhjem** Åhavevej 55 ☏86 82 36 42, ⓦwww.danhostel.dk/silkeborg. Beautifully situated hostel a short walk from the centre on the banks of Gudenå river, with dorms

(120kr) and affordable triples (488kr) and quads (558kr), though no doubles.

Svostrup Kro Svostrupvej 58 ☏86 87 70 04, ⓦwww.svostrup-kro.dk. A traditional Danish inn, next to the Gudenå river 8km northeast of the centre off the road to Randers. With creaking floorboards and wood-beamed ceilings, this place oozes character and cosiness. ❻

Campsites

Gudenåens Camping Vejlsøvej 7 ☏86 82 22 01, ⓦwww.gudenaaenscamping.dk. Scenically located campsite 2km south of the centre in a wooded area on the banks of the Gudenå river and near Silkeborg Kunstmuseum and Silkeborg Kanocenter. Mid-March to mid-September.

Silkeborg Sø Camping Århusvej 51 ☏86 82 28 24, ⓦwww.seacamp.dk. Some 2km from the centre, just off the main road to Århus on the banks of Silkeborg Langesø lake, and most easily reached via the regional buses to and from Århus. Bicycle hire and canoe hire are ample compensation for its isolation from town. Mid-April to mid-October.

The Town

Silkeborg has little history of its own – it was still a small village in 1845 when the local river was harnessed to power a paper mill that brought a measure of growth and prosperity, something you can learn more about at the **Papirmuseet Bikuben** (Paper Museum; May–Aug daily noon–5pm; 20kr; ⓦwww.papirmuseet.dk), Papirfabrikken 78, housed in the old paper mill by the Gudenå lock, which also holds the town's theatre; entry is through the back. The exhibits explain the process of paper-making, from papyrus to modern methods, in great detail, and to get a flavour of what is involved you get to have a go at making a sheet of paper yourself. The Silkeborg mill was one of the few in the world making paper of high enough quality to be used to print banknotes, and there's an intriguing section about money-making and the various countries' bills that have been produced here.

Following the Gudenå river southwards, sticking to the western bank, takes you past another three interesting attractions. First up, behind the tourist office at Hovedgårdsvej 7, is the **Silkeborg Museum** (May to mid-Oct daily 10am–5pm; mid-Oct to April Sat & Sun noon–4pm; 45kr; ⓦwww.silkeborgmuseum.dk).

In 1938, the discovery of the well-preserved body of an Iron Age woman – the so-called **Elling Girl** – in a bog 15km west of Silkeborg added greatly to the appeal of the town's budding museum. As preserved bodies go, however, it has since been overshadowed by the discovery of the **Tollund Man** in 1950 in the same bog, a corpse of similar vintage whose head – gruesome as it may sound – is in such good condition that it's been deemed the world's best preserved prehistoric body. Housed in a dark, tomb-like room in the museum's new section at the back, Tollund Man lies with stubble still visible on the chin and, according to researchers, the remains of his last meal in his belly, a gruel made of thirty different types of grain and seed, including flax, barley and willow herb. All of this, and much more about how he was discovered and the anticipated situation around his death is thoroughly described on placards in his "room". The rest of the museum's local history exhibits are bit of a mish-mash, and are imminently due for refurbishment.

An equally worthwhile call is the excellent collection of abstract works by Asger Jorn and others in the beautifully situated **Silkeborg Kunstmuseum** (Art Museum; April–Oct Tues–Sun 10am–5pm; Nov–March Tues–Fri noon–4pm, Sat & Sun 10am–5pm; 40kr; ⓦwww.silkeborgkunstmuseum.dk), further along the Gudenå river's west bank, bordering the Indelukket park at Gudenåvej 7. It was to Silkeborg that Jorn, Denmark's leading modern painter and founder member of the influential CoBrA (Copenhagen-Brussels-Amsterdam) group, came to recuperate from tuberculosis. From the 1950s until his death in 1973, Jorn donated an enormous amount of his own and other artists' work to the town, which displays them proudly in this purpose-built museum. If you want to learn more about Jorn – his inspirations and his activities during the Second World War – take in the informative fifteen-minute film shown in the small auditorium just as you enter; ask at reception to have it started. Of the works on display, pieces to look out for include the enormously long and colourful *The Long Voyage* tapestry in Room 13, which Jorn made together with Dutch artist Pierre Wemaëre, and the simple yet powerful sketches given to Jorn by his teacher Fernand Legér in Atelier 1. To top it off, the beautiful grounds around

△ *Hjejle* steamer

the museum are littered with sculptural and ceramic works by Jorn and his contemporaries and shouldn't be missed.

For something less cultural, head for the **Aqua** freshwater aquarium (mid-June to mid-Aug daily 10am–6pm; mid-Aug to mid-June Mon–Fri 10am–4pm, Sat & Sun 10am–5pm; 85kr; ⓦwww.aqua-ferskvandsakvarium.dk), set in the beautiful former tuberculosis sanatorium at Vejlsøvej 15, a fifteen-minute walk south of the art museum through Indelukket park. It has a variety of freshwater fish alongside numerous water birds and mammals, including some cute otters. You can also get here by taking the *Hjejle* steamer (ⓦwww.hjejle.com; 4–6 trips daily; 110kr return), the world's oldest coal-burning paddle steamer, which departs from the lock by Silkeborg Museum. After the aquarium, the steamer carries on along the Gudenå river into Brassø, Borresø and Julsø lakes before reaching the foot of **Himmelbjerget** ("Sky Mountain"), one of Denmark's highest hills; from here the 147m trek to the top takes about thirty minutes, and your reward is some magnificent views of the surrounding area.

Eating, drinking and nightlife

Most of Silkeborg's best places to **eat**, **drink** and be merry are around the lock area and nearby along pedestrianized Søndergade. There are also two music **festivals** to look out for. The Riverboat Jazz Festival (☏86 80 16 17, ⓦwww .riverboat.dk), staged during the last week of June, is one of Scandinavia's biggest jazz festivals and draws musicians from all over the globe for a four-day session of New Orleans and Dixieland jazz as well as more experimental stuff. It's mostly free, with bands playing on squares and stages placed strategically throughout the town (including one by the lock), and the town is alive with atmosphere for the duration. More unusual is the Country Music Festival (☏86 96 70 11, ⓦwww .sccdk.com) held at Indelukket park during the second weekend of August each year where a surprising array of Stetsons and cowboy boots make an appearance. For more information and ticket sales, call or visit the websites.

Restaurants and bars

Café 1.Række Papirfabrikken 80 ☏86 80 59 00, ⓦwww.silkeborg-musikhus.dk. With its open terrace facing the Gudenå river lock, this is Silkeborg's trendiest daytime hangout. The fill-your-plate-once lunch buffet for 40kr, and all-you-can-eat for 98kr, are two sure-fire successes, so it's a good idea to arrive early (service starts at noon) for the widest range of choice. As it's linked to the theatre, the café stays open late on performance nights. Mon–Sat 11am–9pm, Sun noon to 9pm.

Café Evald Papirfabrikken 10B ☏86 80 33 66, ⓦwww.cafe-evald.dk. Brasserie-style café that does great brunch (10am–2pm) and the usual array of burgers, pastas and salads at very reasonable prices, while in the evenings, the large selection of imported draught beer draws in the crowds. The balcony overlooking the Gudenå river gets packed during summer. Mon–Wed 10am–midnight, Thurs–Sat 10am–2am, Sun 10am–11pm.

Gastronomisk Institut Søndergade 20 ☏86 82 40 97, ⓦwww.gastronomiske .dk. A French-style café in the daytime and an up-and-coming gourmet restaurant in the evening,

with a focus on fresh, local produce and careful preparation. Portions aren't huge but quality is high and prices very reasonable for what you get. A four-course menu of rabbit stew, potato-halibut bake, venison and lentil soufflé, and pineapple ravioli costs 299kr. Mon 11.30am–4pm, Thurs–Sat 11.30am–11pm.

Hotel Julsø Julsøvej 14 ☏86 89 80 40, ⓦwww .hotel-julso.dk. At the foot of Himmelbjerget, this picturesque eatery does a fabulous lunch platter of traditional open sandwiches (140kr) and a range of mostly Italian-inspired meals, such as the escalope caprese with mozzarella and fresh basil (85kr). Best way to get here is by canoe or the *Hjejle* steamer (see above). Booking recommended. Mon 11am–4pm, Tues–Sun 11am–11pm.

Natalie Papirfabrikken 10E ☏86 86 10 14, ⓦwww.natalie.dk. Mexican/Italian restaurant offering well-made tacos and burritos or pasta and pizzas as the main staples. The 59kr lunch special and two- or three-course evening meals for 99kr/199kr are extremely good value. Daily 11.30am–10pm.

Underhuset Torvet 7 ☏86 82 37 36, ⓦwww

.underhuset.dk. Popular gastropub specializing in seafood and their trademark plate of oysters. Mains in the restaurant section start at 200kr, while many of the same dishes are available in the pub section for much less. Lunch comprises traditional Danish fare such as *flæskesteg med rødkål*, while dinner is primarily seafood, such as lobster and fried plaice. Daily 10am to midnight.

Canoe trips along the Gudenå

The highlight of a trip to Silkeborg, and the town's main claim to fame among Danish holidaymakers, is a **canoe trip** on the 162km **Gudenå river**, Denmark's longest; best plan is to sign up for one of the many all-in packages offered by the tourist board (see box below). At most points, the water is no more than wading depth, while at others it deepens and is perfect for swimming; and it's hard to imagine anything more peaceful than letting the current gently pull you along while passing through stunning, virtually undisturbed countryside, punctuating your journey at the campsites which are located at regular intervals along the river's course, and range from simple spots with little more than a toilet to full-on affairs. **From Silkeborg**, there are a range of options, including day-trips

Canoe rental

The Silkeborg tourist office (see p.317) organizes a range of **canoe package trips**. The most popular is the Family Tour, which costs 2525kr per canoe for five days, and includes canoe and tent hire as well as campsite fees along the way. The so-called "luxury tours" include overnight stops at traditional inns along the way, and start at 1495kr for two days (one night). If you'd rather have the flexibility **going independently**, we've listed some of the most convenient canoe rental outlets below. Those in Silkeborg will transport the canoe to wherever you want to start your journey, and pick is up again afterwards; with the other three, you must start your journey at the rental outlet, and they pick it up once you've reached your chosen destination. All the operators' prices include a two-person canoe, lifejackets, oars and transport of the canoe to and/or from starting and end points. For a little more you can also hire tents, or have pre-pitched tents waiting for you at the campsites. The tourist office in Silkeborg can store luggage for you while you are away. Note that from Silkeborg, most places also rent canoes by the hour year-round (75kr).

Kanoterminalen Åhave Allé 7, Silkeborg ☏86 80 30 03, ⓦwww.kanoterminalen .dk. From Silkeborg, low-season prices (May to mid-June & mid-Aug to Sept) are 250kr for one day and 1200kr for five days; in high season (mid-June to mid-Aug) it's 300kr for one day or 1350kr for five. From Tørring, five days costs 1450kr, ten days 2100kr.

Slusekioskens Kanoudlejning Havnen, Silkeborg ☏86 80 08 93 ⓦwww .slusekioskenskanoudlejning.dk. From Silkeborg, low-season prices (May to mid-June & mid-Aug to Sept) are 250kr for one day, 1150kr for five; in high season (mid-June to mid-Aug), it's 300kr for one day, 1300kr for five. From Tørring, five days costs 1450kr, ten days 2700kr.

Søhøjlandets Kanoudlejning Trust Camping, Sørkelvej 12, Truust ☏86 87 11 41, ⓦwww.kanoudlejningsilkeborg.dk. In low season (April–June & Aug to mid-Oct), one day costs 290kr, two days 480kr including camping fees but not tents. In high season (July), it's 330kr for one day, 1090kr for five days, including camping fees.

Tørring Kanofart Aagade 33, Tørring ☏75 80 11 63, ⓦwww.kanotur.dk. Canoes cost 275kr per day all year round, plus a 115kr fee to transport each canoe back to base.

Tørring Kanoudlejning Skovhussvinget 7, Tørring ☏75 80 13 01, ⓦwww.kano -udlejning.dk. Three days for 1100kr, five days for 1450kr, ten days 2000kr.

from town – the paddle to Himmelbjerget and back, including a hike up the mountain is very popular – or longer, five-day jaunts downstream to Fladbro by Randers (see p.340), overnighting at campsites or inns along the way. Alternatively, you can start at the source of the Gudenå, just outside **Tørring** by Vejle, and do the five-day journey up to Silkeborg, though this is only possible after mid-June due to the low water levels at Tørring. You can also do the entire river in ten days, or any combination of the above routes. (Note, however, that apart from to Himmelbjerget from Silkeborg, going upstream is illegal.)

As well as taking you through some beautiful scenery, the river also passes a number of museums and attractions that warrant a longer stop. One of the best is the hugely popular **Elmuseet** (mid-April to Oct daily 10am–5pm; 60kr; ⓦwww.elmuseet.dk), on the banks of Tange Sø lake, 20km southeast of Viborg. Housed in ten buildings on the spectacular grounds of the Gudenå hydroelectric power station, the museum deals with all things electric, from Denmark's first wind turbine, which became a prototype for turbines worldwide, to green electricity of the future. Note, however, that during school holidays the river can become a virtual canoe motorway, with only one-way traffic, and this period is probably best avoided.

Århus

Right at the heart of the country geographically, and often regarded as Denmark's cultural capital, **ÅRHUS** typifies all that's good about Danish cities. It's small enough to get to know in a few hours, yet big and lively enough to have plenty to fill both days and nights, and the combination of laid-back atmosphere with a surprising number of sights might keep you around longer than planned. Århus is also something of an architectural showcase, with several notable structures spanning a century of Danish and international design. A number of these buildings form the campus of Århus's **university**, whose students contribute to a nightlife scene that's on a par with that of Copenhagen.

Despite Viking-era origins, the city's present prosperity is due to its long, sheltered bay (on which a harbour was first constructed during the fifteenth century) and the more recent advent of railways, which made Århus a nationally important trade and transport centre. It's easily reached by train from all the country's bigger towns, is linked by sea with Zealand (a fast catamaran service linking Århus with Odden, and a slower ferry linking it with Kalundborg), and also has an international airport with regular connections to Copenhagen.

Arrival, information and city transport

Whichever form of public transport brings you to Århus, you'll be deposited within easy reach of the hotels and main points of interest. **Trains** and **buses** stop at their respective stations on Banegårds Pladsen and Ny Banegårds Gade, both on the southern edge of the city centre. The **tourist office** (May to mid-June Mon–Fri 9.30am–5pm, Sat 10am–1pm; mid-June to Aug Mon–Fri 9.30am–6pm, Sat 9.30am–5pm, Sun 9.30am–1pm; Sept–April Mon–Fri 9.30am–4pm, Sat 10am–1pm; ☏87 31 50 10, ⓦwww.visitaarhus.com) is at Banegårds Pladsen 20. **Ferries** from Zealand dock just east of the centre at the end of Nørreport, a short distance from the heart of old Århus. Buses from the **airport** (ⓦwww.aar.dk), some 45km northeast of the city, arrive at (and leave from) the train station; the one-way fare for the forty-five-minute journey is 85kr.

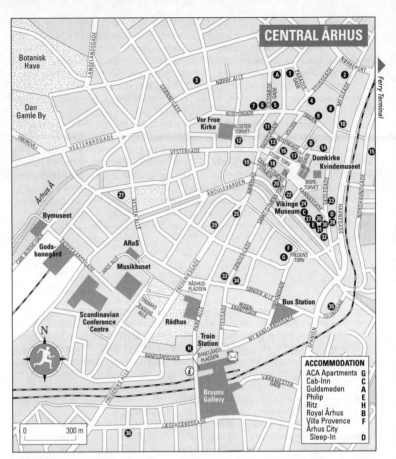

CENTRAL ÅRHUS

ACCOMMODATION

ACA Apartments	G
Cab-Inn	C
Guldsmeden	A
Philip	E
Ritz	H
Royal Århus	B
Villa Provence	F
Århus City Sleep-In	D

EATING, DRINKING & NIGHTLIFE

Athena	16	The Cockney Pub	18	Gyngen & Musikcafeen	2	Royal Århus	B
Bent J	3	Cross Café	19	Herr Bartels	22	Rømer	20
Billabong Bar	26	Den Sidste	1	Jorden	11	Smagløs	12
Bridgewater Pub	32	Dragen	19	Karls Sandwichbar	7	Svej	31
Broen	15	Emmerys	5	Kindrødt	4	Svineriet	8
Bryggeriet Sct Clemens	24	Essens	27	Ministeriet	12	Tir na noq	29
Carlton	13	Fabrikken	6	Pan Klubben	36	Train	35
Casablanca	14	Fatter Eskild	30	Pinden	28	Twist and Shout	25
China Wok House	34	Gaucho-Argentinsk Bøfhus	31	Pinds Café	23	Under Masken	17
Le Coq	9	Globen Flakket	32	Raadhuus Kaféen	33	Voxhall	21
				Ris Ras Filliongongong	10		

Getting around is best done on foot: the city centre is compact and you'll need to use **buses** only if you're venturing out to the University and Moesgård Museum, or the beaches or the woods on the city's outskirts. If you do, note that the transport system divides into four zones: one and two cover the whole central area; three and four reach into the countryside. The basic ticket is the "**billet**", which costs 17kr from machines at the rear of buses and is valid for any number of journeys for up two hours from the time stamped on it. If you're around for several days and doing a lot of bus hopping (or using local trains, on which these tickets are also valid), you have three good options. An **Århus Pass** costs 119kr for 24 hours, 149kr for 48 hours and 206kr for a week, and covers unlimited travel and entrance to most museums, including ARoS Art Museum, as well as sightseeing tours (book at the tourist office). There's also a **multi-ride ticket** (*Klippekort*: 105kr), which is valid for ten trips within the immediate city area and can be used by more than one person at once; or a **24-hour ticket** (55kr), which covers public transport in all four zones for 24 hours. These tickets can be bought at news-stands, campsites and shops displaying the "Århus Sporveje" sign. The driver won't check your ticket but a roving inspector might, and there's an instant fine of 500kr if you're caught travelling without one. You can get **bus information** at Borgerservice (Mon–Wed & Fri 8.30am–5.30pm, Thurs 10am–5.30pm; ☏89 40 10 10, lines open daily 4.30am–1am), at the Rådhus, Rådhuspladsen.

Cycling is another viable way to get around. As part of the very useful citybike scheme (ⓦwww.aarhusbycykel.dk), there are bikes distributed around the city, which you can use for free within the city limits by dropping a 20kr deposit into the slot on the bikes. If you're heading out of the city to Moesgård, for instance, the two most central places to rent a bicycle are Cykelværkstedet Morten Mengel, Mejlgade 41 (☏86 19 29 27, ⓦwww .mmcykler.dk; 65kr per day, 200kr per week) and Bikes4rent, Grønnegade 77C (☏20 26 10 20, ⓦwww.bikes4rent.dk; 75kr per day, 245kr per week).

Accommodation

Århus has some fairly reasonably priced **hotel** and **hostel** options, and the tourist office can help you find affordable **private rooms** (from 350kr a night). The Århus Bed & Breakfast network (☏86 27 51 30, ⓦwww.aarhus-bed-and -breakfast.dk) can also help with rooms for 330kr per night, and self-contained apartments for 650kr per night.

Another option is to stay at the picturesque *Tarskov Mølle* (☏86 94 25 44, ⓦwww.tarskovmolle.dk; ④), Tarskovvej 1 in Harlev, some 15km west of the city and thirty minutes by bus #55. A working farm, it has its own watermill, forest and lake frontage as well as horses for riding. You could also try one of the inns surrounding Århus, such as *Malling Kro*, at Stationspladsen 2 in Malling, 12km south of Århus and half an hour by train towards Odder (☏86 93 10 25, ⓦwww.mallingkro.dk; ③, en-suite ⑤); breakfast costs 50kr. The tourist office has a full list of inns in the Århus area.

Unless otherwise stated, all the options below appear on the Central Århus map, opposite.

Hotels and guesthouses

ACA Apartments Fredensgade 18 ☏40 27 90 30 ⓦwww.hotelaca.dk. Refurbished apartment building a short walk from the bus station, offering great deals if you're staying more than two nights. There's a range of self-contained, modernized rooms and apartments with fully fitted kitchens or kitchenettes. Breakfast is not included in the price. ③/⑤

Cab-Inn Kannikegade 14 ☏86 75 70 00, ⓦwww .cabinn.com. On the banks of the Århus Å river, with its entrance in front of the theatre, the functional cabin-like rooms here (everything folds up and packs away) are very good value. Breakfast is 50kr. ④

Guldsmeden Guldsmedegade 40 ☏86 13 45 56, ⓦwww.hotelguldsmeden.dk. A small, homely hotel in the centre, ten minutes' walk from the station. Rooms are delicately decorated in French colonial style, and no two are the same; some have shared bath. Scrummy organic breakfast buffet included in the rates. ⑦/⑥

Havnehotellet Marselisborg Havnevej 20 (see Around Århus map, p.328) ⓦwww.havnehotellet .dk. Unmanned hotel – hence no phone number – on the Århus marina quay (ten minutes on bus #6 or #19 from the centre), with stunning views of the bay and good restaurants nearby. Checking in to the bright and breezy en-suite rooms, decorated with painting by local Århus artists, happens on a computer in the foyer, and booking is only possible online. Free parking. ⑥

Helnan Marselis Strandvejen 25 (see Around Århus map, p.328) ☎86 14 44 11, ⓦwww .marselis.dk. Bus #6 or #19. Stunningly located beachfront hotel a few kilometres south of the centre. All rooms overlook Århus Bay, and facilities include swimming pool, bar and restaurant, while Marselis woods are at the back door. Good offers on all-inclusive weekend breaks. ⑧

Philip Åboulevarden 28 ☎87 32 14 44, ⓦwww .hotelphilip.dk. Small, exclusive hotel on the banks of Århus Å river, with only eight luxurious suites, a trendy riverside café and a classy restaurant. The tastefully decorated suites are French/Italian-inspired and come with separate living room and a small kitchenette. ⑨

Ritz Banegårds Pladsen 12 ☎86 13 44 44, ⓦwww.hotelritz.dk. As the name implies, this Best Western hotel in front of the train station is both pricey (though with discounts at weekends) and stylish. The elegant rooms all have newly restored en suite bathrooms. ⑦/⑥

Royal Århus Store Torv 4 ☎86 12 00 11, ⓦwww .hotelroyal.dk. The city's grand old four-star hotel, right on the main square and with a beautiful winter garden and the city's only casino under its roof (see p.333). Rooms are elaborately furnished with ornately carved dark mahogany furniture, and the marbled bathrooms are downright luxurious. ⑨

Sportshotellet Stadion Allé 70 (see Around Århus map, p.328) ☎86 14 30 00, ⓦwww.atletion .dk. Bus #19. A functional hotel, part of the fancy sports stadium complex in the Marselisborg forest. The rooms are basic, with two single beds, but all are en-suite, with a kitchenette on each floor, and breakfast served at the stadium café is included in the price. Free parking. ⑤

Villa Provence Fredens Torv 12 ☎86 18 24 00, ⓦwww.villaprovence.dk. Classy, small designer hotel a stone's throw from the bus station. The individualized rooms are all beautifully decorated in light Provencal style, featuring old French-Belgian film posters. ⑦

Sleep-ins and youth hostels

Århus City Sleep-In Havnegade 20 ☎86 19 20 55, ⓦwww.citysleep-in.dk. Bus #3. Near both the city centre and harbour, offering dorm beds (115kr), and doubles with shared or private bathroom (both ③). Guests without their own sleeping bags have to rent sheets and blankets (45kr); facilities include a games room, café and internet access (20kr/hr). Open 24/7.

Århus Vandrerhjem Marienlundsvej 10 (see Around Århus map, p.328) ☎86 16 72 98, ⓦwww .aarhus-danhostel.dk. Bus #1, #6 #8, #9, #16, #56 or #58. Much more peaceful than the central *Sleep-In*, this is 4km northeast of town in the middle of Risskov wood, close to the popular Den Permanente beach. As well as dorms (120kr), it has a hotel-style wing with en-suite doubles (④) and, for a bit less, doubles with shared bathroom.

Campsites

Blommehaven Ørneredevej 35, Højbjerg (see Around Århus map, p.328) ☎86 27 02 07, ⓦwww .camping-blommehaven.dk. Bus #6 or #19. Some 5km south of the city centre, overlooking the bay and with access to a beautiful beach. Open April–Aug.

Århus Nord Randersvej 400, Lisbjerg (see Around Århus map, p.328) ☎86 23 11 33, ⓦwww .aarhusnord.dk. Bus #117 or #118. Around 8km north of the city centre and convenient for the E45 motorway, this campsite is only slightly cheaper than *Blommehaven* above, and not nearly as well situated unless you're arriving from the motorway.

The City

For reasons of simple chronology, Århus divides into two clearly defined parts: even combined, these fill a small and easily walkable area. The **old section**, close to the Domkirke, is a tight cluster of medieval streets with several interesting churches and a couple of museums, as well as the bulk of the city's nightlife. The (relatively) **new sections** of Århus form a collar around the old centre, inevitably with less character, but nonetheless holding plenty that's worth seeing, not least the city's major architectural works.

Århus Domkirke and around

Århus's main street, **Søndergade**, is a pedestrianized strip lined with shops and overpriced snack bars that leads from the train station (where it's initially called Ryesgade), through Sankt Clemens Torv and across Århus Å river into the main town square, Bispetorvet. From here, the streets of the old centre form a web around the **Domkirke** (May–Sept Mon–Sat 9.30am–4pm; Oct–April Mon–Sat 10am–3pm). Take the trouble to push open the cathedral's sturdy doors, not just to appreciate the soccer-pitch length – this is easily the longest church in Denmark – but to take in a couple of features that spruce up the plain Gothic interior, which is mostly a fifteenth-century rebuilding after the original twelfth-century structure was destroyed by fire. At the eastern end, a grand tripartite altarpiece by the noted Bernt Notke is one of few pre-Reformation survivors. Look also for the painted – as opposed to stained – glass window behind the altar, the work of Norwegian Emmanuel Vigeland (brother of Gustav); it's most effective when the sunlight falls directly on it.

From the time of the first settlement here, in the tenth century, the area around the cathedral has been at the core of Århus life. A number of Viking remains have been excavated on Sankt Clemens Torv, across the road from the cathedral, and some of them are now displayed as part of the **Vikinge Museum** (Mon–Fri 10am–4pm, Thurs until 5.30pm; free) in the basement of the Nordea bank at Sankt Clemens Torv 6 (entrance inside the bank on the left). Also on display are sections of the original ramparts around the settlement which was then known as Aros (as explained in the museum's informative accounts of early Århus). Also close to the cathedral, in a former police station on Bispetorvet, the **Kvinde-museet** (Women's Museum; daily: June–Aug 10am–5pm; Sept–May Tues–Sun 10am–4pm; 30kr; ⓦwww.kvindemuseet.dk) is one of Denmark's most innovative, staging temporary exhibitions on aspects of women's lives past and present. After visiting the museums here, you might want to venture into the narrow and enjoyable surrounding streets, lined by innumerable old and well-preserved buildings, many of which now house browseable antique shops, chic boutiques and French-style cafés, the latter some of the city's best drinking spots (see p.332).

West along Vestergade from the Domkirke, behind the Frue Kirke Plads square, the thirteenth-century **Vor Frue Kirke** (May–Aug Mon–Fri 10am–4pm, Sat 10am–2pm; Sept–April Mon–Fri 10am–2pm, Sat 10am–noon) is actually the site of three churches, the most notable of which is the eleventh-century **crypt** (go in through the main church entrance and walk straight ahead), which was discovered, buried beneath several centuries' worth of rubbish, during restoration work on the main building in the 1950s. There's not a lot to see, but the tiny, rough-stone cave, resembling a hollowed-out cave, is strong on atmosphere, especially during the candle-lit Sunday services. Except for Claus Berg's fine altarpiece, there's not much to warrant a look in the main church. However, you can make your way (to the left of the entrance) through the cloister that remains from the pre-Reformation monastery – now an old folks' home – to see the medieval frescoes inside the third church, which depict local working people rather than the more commonly found biblical scenes.

The Rådhus and around

Modern Århus begins as soon as you arrive at the train station which, although from 1927 and not modern in itself, has been integrated into the Bruuns Gallery multi-storey state-of-the-art shopping mall and cinema. From here it's a short walk along Park Allé to one of the modern city's major sights: the functional **Rådhus** on Rådhuspladsen, completed in 1941 and as capable of inciting high passions today – for and against – as it was when it opened. From the outside, it's easy to see why opinions should be so polarized, as the coating of grey Norwegian marble lends a sickly pallor to the facade. But on the inside (enter from Rådhuspladsen), the finer points of architects Arne Jacobsen and Erik Møller's vision make themselves apparent, amid the harmonious open-plan corridors and extravagant quantities of glass. You're free to walk in and look for yourself, but it's worth taking one of the informative **guided tours** (in English, mid-June to early Sept Mon–Fri at 11am; 10kr). You can also tour the bell tower at noon and 2pm daily (same months; 5kr). Inside, above the entrance, hangs Hagedorn Olsen's huge mural, *A Human Society*, symbolically depicting the city emerging from the last war to face the future with optimism. In the council chamber, the lamps appear to hang suspended in mid-air (in fact they're held by almost invisible threads), and the shape of the council leader's chair is a distinctive curved form mirrored in numerous smaller features throughout the building, notably the ashtrays in the lifts – though many of these have been pilfered by visitors. Perhaps most interesting of all, however, if only for the background story, are the walls of the small Civic Room, covered by intricate floral designs in which artist Albert Naur, working during the Nazi occupation, concealed various Allied insignia.

More recent examples of Århus's municipal architecture include the glass-fronted **Musikhuset** (concert hall: daily 11am–9pm; ⓦwww.musikhusetaarhus.dk), a short walk from the Rådhus along Frederiks Allé, which has been the city's main venue for opera and classical music since it opened in 1982. It's worth dropping into, if only for the small café where you might be entertained for free by a string quartet or a lone fiddler. A monthly list of forthcoming concerts and events is available from the box office or the tourist office.

Next door, the large red-brick art museum, **ARoS** (Tues–Sun 10am–5pm, Wed till 10pm; 70kr; ⓦwww.aros.dk), is a remarkable building designed by the same architects as the Black Diamond extension to the Royal Library in Copenhagen (see p.80). Built on a slope, the main entrance is confusingly on the fourth floor, spreading the seven floors of the exhibition over the three floors above and the three below, all connected by a large spiralling staircase and a sleek glass elevator. The collection gives a good overview of the main national trends, from late eighteenth-century formal portraits and landscapes by Jens Juel and finely etched scenes of domestic tension by Jørgen Sonne, through to more internationally renowned names, particularly Vilhelm Hammershoi, represented here by some of his moody interiors. There are lots of worthwhile modern pieces, too. Besides the radiant canvases of Asger Jorn and Richard Mortensen, don't miss Bjørn Nørgård's sculpted version of Christian IV's tomb: the original, in Roskilde Cathedral, is stacked with riches; this one features a coffee cup, an egg and a ballpoint pen. Other highlights include the spookily lifelike five-metre-high sculpture, *Boy*, by Ron Mueck. There's also a good café and a very browseable museum shop, plus magnificent views of the city's skyline from the rooftop terrace.

From ARoS's back ground-floor exit, Aros Allé leads past the building-site of the Musikhus extension and the grand, slimline Scandinavia Conference Centre next door. Turn right down Skovgaardsgade for the **Bymuseet** (City Museum; daily 10am–5pm, Wed until 8pm; 30kr; ⓦwww.bymuseet.dk; bus #18), Carl Blochs Gade 28, housed in the disused Hammel railway station and an ultra-modern extension from 2005. The latest addition to Århus's array of museums, the Bymuseet is still in the process of establishing its collections, which will – and to some extent already do – approach the history of the city from a thematic rather than chronological perspective. Topics like Århus's role in the Danish film industry and Århus as a city of education are imaginatively tackled with old film clips, models, photos and diagrams, as well as in-depth background narratives. The upstairs section of the museum is devoted to changing exhibits along the lines of delicately embroidered flags from local workers' movements in Århus, or the city's hippy scene of the 1960s. There's also a small café, where you're allowed to bring your own food.

Den Gamle By and Botanisk Have

It's just a few minutes' walk from Bymuseet to Viborgvej and the city's best-known attraction, **Den Gamle By** (The Old Town; Jan 11am–3pm; Feb & March 10am–4pm; April–June & Sept–Nov 10am–5pm; July–Aug 9am–6pm; Dec 10am–7pm; 80kr; ⓦwww.dengamleby.dk). An open-air museum of traditional Danish life, it consists of around seventy-five half-timbered townhouses (including a popular Mayor's House of 1597) from all over the country, which have been moved here since the museum's inception in 1914. With many of the buildings used for their original purpose, the overall aim of the place is to give an impression of an old Danish market town, complete with bakers, craftsmen and the like. This is done very convincingly, although sunny summer days bring big crowds and the period flavour is strongest outside high season, when visitors are fewer.

Once you're inside Den Gamle By you're effectively also inside the **Botanisk Have** (Botanical Garden; unrestricted access; free), which Den Gamle By initially was carved out of. The largest and oldest park in Århus, a trip to the botanical garden has been one of the most popular outings for local Århusianere (people from Århus) for generations. Its undulating hills give a great sense of space, while the small, intimate dips provide ideal cover for an afternoon's lazing in the sun (or studying for exams – the gardens' primary use during spring). For the botanically interested, the thousands of plants and trees are all labelled with their Danish and Latin names. Buses #3, #14, #15, #25, #51 and #55 go from the centre to Den Gamle By and Botanisk Have.

Universitetsparken

A fifteen-minute walk from Den Gamle By along Langelandsgade (or five minutes on bus #17 from Vesterbrogade), the **Universitetsparken** (university campus) is a prime example of modern Danish architectural style. Sprawled across a green hillside overlooking the city, the distinctive yellow-brick buildings, mostly designed by C.F. Møller and completed just after World War II, feature white-framed rectangular windows and no decorative touches whatsoever. There are two museums on campus that are worth looking out for. The **Naturhistorisk Museum** (Natural History Museum: July–Aug 10am–5pm; Sept–June 10am–4pm; 40kr; ⓦwww.naturhistoriskmuseum.dk) has an interesting and well-presented exhibition on Danish ecological history (sadly only in Danish), with displays showing bone fragments and sketches of animals that used to inhabit these shores in the time gaps between the ice ages – four in total – such as the woolly rhinoceros and the forest elephant. There's also a large collection of stuffed birds and animals which is due to be reorganized into more user-friendly and educational scenarios based on the ecosystem the creatures were part of. The **Steno Museum** (Tues–Fri 9am–4pm, Sat & Sun 11am–4pm; 40kr; ⓦwww.stenomuseet.dk) is a much grander affair that could easily swallow up an afternoon. Divided into two distinct sections on two sides of a staircase – Medical History and the History of Science – the museum manages to balance itself perfectly between educating and displaying the curious. The **Medical History** section starts downstairs with an insight into hospital wards and operating theatres in the eighteenth century, with some gruesome tools of the trade such as a dentist's torturous foot-operated drill. Upstairs, focus is on the development of medicine over the ages. A plague-doctor's outfit with its hawk-nosed mask – providing room for medicinal herbs to overpower the smell of rot – and Marie Curie's research on radiology are among the exhibits given meticulous attention. Across the staircase landing, you step into a cartographer's paradise, with the **History of Science** section

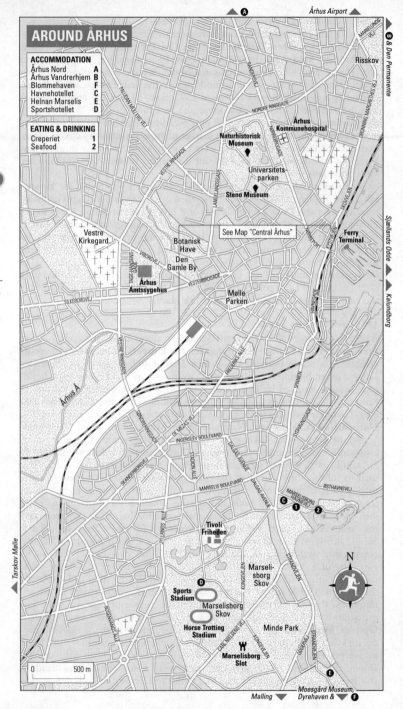

AROUND ÅRHUS

ACCOMMODATION

Århus Nord	A
Århus Vandrerhjem	B
Blommehaven	F
Havnehotellet	C
Helnan Marselis	E
Sportshotellet	D

EATING & DRINKING

Creperiet	1
Seafood	2

Århus Airport

B & Den Permanente

Risskov

Århus Kommunehospital

Naturhistorisk Museum

Universitets-parken

Steno Museum

See Map "Central Århus"

Ferry Terminal

Sjællands Odde

Kalundborg

Vestre Kirkegård

Botanisk Have
Den Gamle By

Århus Amtssygehus

Mølle Parken

Århus Å

Tarskov Mølle

Marselisborg

Østhavnsvej

Tivoli Friheden

Marseli-sborg Skov

Sports Stadium

Marselisborg Skov

Horse Trotting Stadium

Minde Park

Marselisborg Slot

N

Moesgård Museum, Dyrehaven &

Malling

0   500 m

kicking off with maps through the ages, including the astounding upside-down world map by Al-Idrissi from 1154. This is followed, on the first floor, with the history of astrology from the Stone Age via Stonehenge and the Egyptian pyramids through to today. There's also a mind-boggling section on Babylonian sexagisimal maths. The museum also houses a small planetarium (shows only in Danish) and has a herb garden with over three hundred medicinal herbs. To get to the campus from the centre, take bus #2, #3, #11, #14, #54, #56 or #58.

Out from the city

On Sundays, post-brunch Århus resembles a ghost town, with most locals spending the day in the parks, woodlands or beaches on the city's outskirts. If you're around on a Sunday – or, for that matter, any sunny day in the week – you could do much worse than join them. The closest beach (Den Permanente) and woods (Risskov) are just **north of the city** at Risskov, near the *Århus Vandrerhjem* hostel, easily reached on buses #6 or #16, or on any local trains headed for Grenå or Hornslets, some of which halt at the tiny Den Permanente train platform by the beach (but check before boarding, as not all trains stop here). Den Permanente beach is narrow but scenic, with an old-fashioned public bathhouse; and, as it's a Blue Flag beach, the water is sparkling clean. The thick forest behind is criss-crossed with walking and cycling trails, and there are a few ice-cream and hotdog stalls on the beach, but you might be better off taking your own picnic.

For a more varied day, head **south** through the thick Marselisborg Skov forest via the prehistoric museum at Moesgård and on to the hugely popular Blue Flag Moesgård beach (or take bus #19 from the centre). This is also ideal territory for cycling or hiking – see p.323 for details of bicycle rental, and contact the tourist office for maps and suggestions on routes.

Marselisborg Skov and Dyrehaven

Marselisborg Skov, 4km south of the city centre, is a large park that contains the city's sports and horse-trotting stadiums and sees a regular procession of people exercising their dogs. It also holds the **Tivoli Friheden** amusement park (mid-April to mid-June Sat–Mon 11.30am–7pm; mid- to end June & second week of Aug daily 11.30am–8pm; early to mid-July & first week of Aug daily 11.30am–9pm; mid to end July daily 11am–10pm; mid-Aug to mid-Sept Sat & Sun 11.30am–8pm; 60kr, 170kr with tour pass, 110kr after 5pm; ⓦ www.friheden.dk), a child-oriented version of Tivoli in Copenhagen with more than twenty rides plus restaurants and an outdoor stage hosting Danish bands every Friday during summer (free with entry ticket).

Further south, across Carl Nielsen Vej, is the diminutive **Marselisborg Slot**, summer home of the Danish royals, whose landscaped grounds can be visited during daylight hours (free) when they're not in residence (usually at all times outside Easter, Christmas and late June to early Aug); if guards are posted by the gate, they're in and there's a changing of guards at noon. Around the slot, the park turns into a dense forest, criss-crossed with footpaths but still easy to get lost in.

A simpler route to navigate, and one with better views, is along Strandvejen, which runs between the eastern side of the forest and the shore. Unbroken footpaths run along this part of the coast and there are many opportunities to scamper down to rarely crowded (though often pebbly) beaches. Also on this route, near the junction of Ørneredevej and Thorsmøllevej, is the **Dyrehaven** or Deer Park – a protected section of the wood that's home to many deer. The animals can be seen (if you're lucky – they're not the most gregarious of creatures) from the marked paths running through the park from the gate on the main road.

Moesgård Museum

Occupying the buildings and grounds of an old manor house 10km south of Århus city centre, **Moesgård Museum** (April–Sept daily 10am–5pm; Oct–March Tues–Sun 10am–4pm; 45kr; Ⓦ www.moesmus.dk) traces the story of Danish civilizations from the Stone Age onwards via copious finds and easy-to-follow illustrations. It's the Iron Age which is most comprehensively covered and produces the most dramatic single exhibit: the **Grauballe Man**, the remains of a body, dated to 80 BC, which was discovered in a peat bog west of Århus in a state of such excellent preservation that it was possible to discover what the deceased had eaten for breakfast (burnt porridge made from rye and barley) on the day of his death. Also remarkable is the extensive **Illerup Ådal** collection of weapons and military paraphernalia, dating from around 200 BC and recovered, in relatively good condition, from the Ådal bog. Only a roomful of imposing runic stones captures the imagination as powerfully. Bus #6 runs here direct from the city, while bus #19 takes a more scenic route along the edge of Århus Bay, leaving you with a walk of just over two kilometres through woods to the museum.

Outside the museum, the **prehistoric trail** runs from the far corner of the courtyard to the sea and back again (follow the red dots), a distance of about 3km each way, heading past a scattering of reassembled prehistoric dwellings, monuments and burial places – a trail guide is available in English (10kr), and there's a map on the back of your entry ticket. On a fine day, the walk itself is as enjoyable as the actual sights, and you could easily linger for a picnic when you reach the coast, or stop for a coffee and a snack at the small but popular *Skovmøllen* restaurant en route. Bus #19 goes back to the city from a stop about a hundred metres back to the north of the trail's end at the beach.

Eating

Central Århus is loaded with **eating** possibilities and, while nothing is particularly cheap, good and affordable meals can still be found. In general, it's wise to follow locals and students away from the heavily touristed Domkirke and Store Torv to streets such as Mejlgade, Nørre Allé, Vestergade or Skolegade; the latter in particular has a number of unpretentious eateries – so unpretentious, in fact, that they often look closed when they're open. You'll find the best lunch bargains, for around 65kr, simply by cruising the cafés and restaurants of the old city and reading the notices chalked up outside them. If you're prepared to pay a bit more, Åboulevarden – the northern bank of the uncovered section of the Århus Å River – offers a string of trendy eating and drinking venues, and is a good place to head throughout the day for brunch, as well as for lunch or dinner.

If money is tight, or you just want to stock up for a picnic, try the *Frokost-specialisten* outlet at Frederiks Allé 105. For more general food shopping, there's a branch of Brugsen on Søndergade, and a late-opening DSB **supermarket** (8am–midnight) at the train station. There are several other downtown supermarkets of varying quality – try the well-stocked Super Brugsen at Nørre Allé, or the discount supermarket Aldi across the way; at the former, local merchants peddle fruit and vegetables fresh from the fields when in season.

Unless otherwise stated, the places that follow are marked on the Central Århus map. p.322.

Cafés and restaurants

Athena Store Torv 18 ✆86 13 29 15, ⓦwww
.restaurantathena.dk. Good-value first-floor Greek
restaurant overlooking the hustle and bustle of
Store and Little Torv below; try the outstanding
moussaka (125kr). Mon–Sat 4pm–11pm, Sun
5–11pm.

Bryggeriet Sct Clemens Kannikegade 10–12
✆86 13 80 00, ⓦwww.bryggeriet.dk. A popular
brewery-cum-restaurant which does delicious
spare ribs for 125kr, best washed down with
freshly-tapped unfiltered beer; the steaks aren't
bad, either. Lunch ranges from 65kr for dish of the
day to a filling smørrebrød platter for 95kr. Mon–
Wed 11.30am–midnight, Thurs–Sat 11.30am–2am.

China Wok House Sønder Allé 9 ✆86 12 69 23.
As well as standard Chinese fare – predictable but
exceedingly good value – this place also does an
all-you-can-eat buffet (58kr at lunchtime, 109kr
in the evening). Takeaway boxes are sold from the
front window. Mon–Sat 11am–10pm.

Crêperiet Marselisborg Havnevej 24 ✆86 12 13
00, ⓦwww.creperiet.dk. Modern glass-fronted
restaurant with great views of the harbour, serving
crêpes with a choice of twenty-four mouth-watering different fillings (75–112kr), both sweet and
savoury. The beautiful fish soup (105kr) is also
worth trying, and there's a good range of wine.
Take bus #6 from the station. April–August daily
noon–midnight, Jan–March & Sept–Nov Wed–Sun
noon to midnight.

Cross Café Åboulevarden 66 ✆87 31 75 10,
ⓦwww.crosscafe.dk. On the trendy bit of Åboulevarden, overlooking Århus Å river, and serving
up generous brunch platters at 95kr as well
as scrumptious, oversized salmon sandwiches.
Mon–Wed 9am–midnight, Thurs 9am–2am, Fri &
Sat 9am–3am, Sun 9am–11pm.

Dragen Åboulevarden 64 ✆86 13 69 66,
ⓦwww.cafedragen.dk. Stir-fry specialist, where
(for 108kr) you can choose your ingredients from
the wok buffet and have them cooked in front
of you. April–Sept Mon–Sat 10am–11pm, Sun
11am–11pm; Oct–March Mon–Sat 10.30am–
11pm, Sun noon to 11pm.

Emmerys Guldsmedegade 24–26 ✆86 13 04
00, ⓦwww.emmerys.dk. The city's oldest patisserie offers wonderful freshly ground coffee and
delicious home-made bread and cakes, as well
as simple, flavour-packed low-fat breakfasts,
lunches and dinners – but it's the gorgeous cakes
and puddings that make a permanent imprint in
the memory. Mon & Tues 8am–6pm, Wed–Sat
8am–midnight, Sun 8am–4pm.

Gaucho-Argentisk Bøfhus Åboulevarden 20
✆86 13 70 65, ⓦwww.gaucho.dk. Excellent

choice if you're longing for a big, juicy steak,
and despite the riverside location, prices here
are not too bad – a 200g sirloin served with veg
and chips goes for only 149kr. Some of the steak
menus are half-price between 4pm and 5.45pm.
Mon–Thurs & Sun 11.30am–10pm, Fri & Sat
11.30am–11pm.

Globen Flakket Åboulevarden 18 ✆87 31
03 33, ⓦwww.globen-flakket.dk. This large
riverside café, with outdoor seating and a posh
restaurant downstairs, is one of the town's most
popular places for brunch, which starts at 84kr for
the veggie version; don't be surprised if you have
to wait for a table during weekends. There's also
breakfast (22kr) as well as lunch and dinner buffets
(both 78kr) and the usual array of salads and sandwiches. Mon–Thurs 9.30am–midnight, Fri & Sat
9.30am–3.30am, Sun 9.30am–11pm.

Gyngen Mejlgade 53 ✆86 19 22 55, ⓦwww
.gyngen.dk. Good-value organic meat and veggie
dishes served up within the Fronthuset culture
centre. The daily seasonal salad costs 48kr, burgers start at 80kr and main courses at 82kr; local
bands sometimes play after dinner (check website
for listings). Mon 11am–4pm, Tues–Fri 11am–2am,
Sat 5pm–2am.

Karls Sandwichbar Klostergade 32 ✆86 12
98 11, ⓦwww.karlssandwich.dk. Undisputedly
the best burgers in town: huge and home-made,
served with large portions of fries (from 50kr).
Can't beat it. Mon–Wed 11am–9pm, Thurs–Sat
11am–6am, Sun 11am–9pm.

Le Coq Graven 16 ✆86 19 50 74, ⓦwww
.cafe-lecoq.dk. Romantic little restaurant serving
authentic French food such as the mouthwatering
coquelet au vin blanc for 148kr. To work up an
appetite, there's table football at the café-bar at the
front. Mon 4pm–1am, Tues–Thurs & Sat 4pm–2am,
Fri 3pm–2am, Sun 4pm–midnight.

Ministeriet Kloster Torvet 5 ✆86 17 11 88,
ⓦwww.ministeriet.org. Outstanding café-restaurant with outdoor seating on the square, serving
well-prepared meals using mainly seasonal
produce. Food ranges from breakfast (48kr;
until noon) and brunch (from 75kr; until 3pm), to
sandwiches, salads and burgers until 9.30pm,
as well as main meals such as grilled lamb
(from 60kr) or tournedos (140kr) throughout the
day and evening. Great tapas too. Mon–Thurs
9.30am–11pm, Fri & Sat 9.30am–1am, Sun
9.30am–6pm.

Pinden Skolegade 29 ✆86 12 11 02, ⓦwww
.pinden.dk. The speciality here is *stegt flæsk med
persille sovs*; six pieces of *flæsk* with potatoes go
for 78kr, all-you-can-eat 99kr; there's also good
smørrebrød. Mon–Wed 11.30am to midnight,

Thurs–Sat 11.30am–1am.

Pinds Café Skolegade 11 ☎86 12 20 60. Although it often looks deceptively shut, *Pinds* nonetheless opens long hours and does excellent traditional Danish food, including the ubiquitous *stægt flæsk med persille sovs* (90kr) and herring smørrebrød (from 49kr). Tues–Thurs 11.30am–midnight, Fri & Sat 11.30am–3am.

Raadhuus Kaféen Sønder Allé 3 ☎86 12 37 74, ⓦwww.raadhuus-kafeen.dk. Traditional eatery with dark furnishings and wood-panelled walls, offering all-day Danish specials such as *frikadeller* or *flæskeæggekage* for 78kr, and which claims to have the city's longest list of smørrebrød toppings. Daily 11am–11pm.

Seafood Marselisborg Havnevej (see Around Århus map, p.328) 44 ☎86 18 56 55, ⓦwww .seafood-aarhus.dk. A great choice if you're prepared to splash out, with fantastic views of the Århus Bay area and a delectable range of seafood, from Brittany oysters to hake steamed in white wine. Main courses from 215kr. Daily noon–midnight, closed Sun Sept–March.

🏃 **Sivineriet** Mejlgade 35 ☎86 12 30 00, ⓦwww.svineriet.dk. Excellent, laid-back place tucked away in a back yard, serving high quality three- four- and five-course meals (325kr, 375kr and 420kr respectively) using predominantly seasonal products and inspiration from Italian cuisine. Tues–Sat 6pm–midnight.

Drinking and nightlife

Århus is the only place in Denmark with a **nightlife** scene to match that of Copenhagen, offering a diverse assortment of ways to be entertained, enlightened or just inebriated almost every night of the week. And while things sparkle socially all year round, if you visit during the annual **Århus Festival** (*Århus Festuge*), an orgy of arts events held over the first week in September (check what's on with the tourist office or visit ⓦwww.aarhusfestuge.dk), you'll find even more to occupy your time. Equally, during the third week of July, the **Århus Jazz Festival** takes off (ⓦwww.jazzfest.dk), transforming the city to a jazz lover's paradise, with groovy tunes oozing from every street corner.

The city has a wonderful endowment of cafés; many have situated in the medieval streets close to the cathedral, and are among the most popular places to go for a **drink**. There's little to choose between them – each pulls a lively, cosmopolitan crowd and the best plan is simply to wander around and try a few – but we've listed the most enduring options below.

Home to a music school that's produced some of the country's most successful performers, Århus boasts a music scene that's well known throughout Denmark – so if you're looking for **live music**, you won't have to look far. Basic details of all events are available from the tourist office, but a better source for rock music news is Århus Billetbureau, Klostergade 20 (☎86 13 05 44, ⓦwww .aabb.dk), where you can pick up a variety of free local magazines and flyers advertising forthcoming gigs. Århus's **clubbing** scene is equally lively, with both *Voxhall* and *Train* staging club nights when they aren't hosting live bands, and plenty of more mainstream venues providing less achingly cool places to dance. Early in the week, admission to any club is likely to be free; on Thursday, Friday or Saturday, you'll pay 40–60kr. Århus doesn't have the wide network of **gay clubs** you'll find in Copenhagen, though the long-established gay social centre *Pan Klubben*, south of the train station at Jægergårdsgade 42 (☎86 13 43 80, ⓦwww.panclub.dk), has a disco (Fri & Sat 10pm–6am). The second Friday of every month is lesbian-only night; otherwise there's a mixed crowd.

Cafés and bars

Billabong Bar Skolegade 26 ⓦwww.billabongbar .dk. The city's only Aussie bar, full of hardy outback types and serving local and foreign ales. There's a happy hour on weekdays (5–6pm). Mon–Wed 4pm–3am, Thurs, Sat & Sun 2pm–3am, Fri noon–3am.

The Bridgewater Pub Åboulevarden 22 ⓦwww .bridgewater.dk. This riverbank English pub with real ales on tap is the place to go for your football fix, with three large screens and live NFL on Sundays. Mon–Wed & Sun 2pm–midnight, Thurs 2pm–2am, Fri 2pm–4am, Sat noon–4am.

Carlton Rosengade 23 ⓦ www.carlton.dk.
Right in the centre of this quaint, café-heavy
medieval quarter, and always buzzing at night.
The food is slightly pricey, so most people only
come to drink. Mon–Sat 9am–midnight, Sun
noon–midnight.

Casablanca Rosengade 12. A good place to start
the evening, this is Århus's oldest café, with movie-
themed decorations and live jazz on Wednesday
evenings. Mon–Sat 10am–2am.

The Cockney Pub Maren Smeds Gyde 8
ⓦ www.cockneypub.dk. Down a tiny alleyway
from Sankt Clemens Stræde, this popular real-ale
pub features haggis nights and whisky tasting
sessions – and they pride themselves on making
a proper cup of tea. Mon–Thurs 11am–midnight,
Fri & Sat 11am–2am, Sun noon–6pm.

Essens Åboulevarden 30 ⓦ www.cafe-essens.dk.
Hugely trendy café on the Århus Å river serving
colourful cocktails accompanied by chilled lounge
music; wear your designer gear and watch the
riffraff making fools of themselves on the street
outside. Mon–Wed 10am–midnight, Thurs–Sat
10am–3am, Sun 10am–10pm.

Jorden Badstuegade 3 ⓦ www.cafejorden.dk.
Popular café in the medieval cathedral area, which
serves quality brunch until mid-afternoon, and gets
very lively at night when the drinkers arrive. Daily
9.30am–2am.

Kindrødt Studsgade 8. Near the old quarter's
better shopping streets and a great place to rest
your feet and sip a cool drink. Local revellers
liven things up in the evenings. Mon–Wed & Sun
9.30am to midnight, Thurs–Sat 9.30am–2am.

Pinds Café Skolegade 11 ⓦ www.pindscafe.dk.
Fun place to meet the locals, where dancing on the
tables isn't uncommon. Wed & Thurs 11.30am–
5pm, Fri & Sat 11.30am–3am.

Ris Ras Filliongongong Mejlgade 24. Named
after a well-known Danish children's rhyme, this
is a popular student hangout that excels in good
beer and cigars; there's an art gallery in the basement that's well worth checking out, too. Daily
noon–2am.

🏃 **Smagløs** Kloster Torvet 7 ⓦ www
.smagloes.dk. Old-timer of the café scene
that's busy with lunchers during the day and
packed with Århus's students at night; it's especially busy when there's live music a couple of
nights a week. Mon–Thurs 9.30am–1am, Fri & Sat
9.30am–3am, Sun 9.30am–11pm.

Svej Åboulevarden 22 ⓦ www.svej.dk. Tucked in
among the thick row of cafés and bars lining Århus
Å River, with chairs spilling out onto the pavement,
this is *the* place to be seen on sunny summer
evenings. Daily 10am–11pm.

Tir na nog Frederiksgade 40 ⓦ www.tirnanog.dk.
The city's one and only Irish pub, with live Irish folk a
couple of nights a week – and Guinness, of course.
Daily noon–3am.

Under Masken Bispegade 3. Cosy yet quirky bar,
with masks from around the globe decorating the
walls and a wide selection of foreign beers on sale.
Mon–Thurs & Sun 2pm–2am, Fri & Sat noon–2am.

Clubs

Broen Nordhavnsgade 20 ⓦ www.mf-broen.dk.
Set in a boat moored in the harbour and divided
into five separate sections with different decor and
styles of music, from mainstream hip-hop to Frank
Sinatra. Fri & Sat only, changing hours.

Den Sidste Paradisgade 9 ⓦ www.cafeparadis.dk.
Den sidste ("the last") is a lively final stop for all-
night partygoers, who fill the dance floor until the
wee hours of the morning. Fri & Sat 12.30–6am.

Fabriken Klostergade 34 ⓦ www.chokoladefabriken
.dk. The city's coolest club and live music venue
(see p.334), playing the newest, hottest dance tunes.
Massive discounts for students. Over 20s only.
Thurs–Sat 9pm–5am.

Herr Bartels Åboulevarden 46 ⓦ www
.herrbartels.dk. Hugely popular new bar/nightclub
(over 23s only), with a sleek metallic interior and
a long list of cocktails, including a tasty selection
of alcoholic iced teas. The dancefloor is always
packed, so this definitely isn't the place to go if
you need your space. Wed 8pm–1am, Thurs–Sat
8pm–3am.

Royal Århus Store Torv 4 ⓦ www.royal-casino.dk.
Flash hotel basement housing a combined casino/
nightclub that's liveliest early in the week. Smart
dress code applies. Mon–Wed & Sun 2pm–3am,
Thurs–Sat 2pm–4am.

Rømer Åboulevarden 50 ⓦ www.caferomer.dk.
Glitzy riverside café/restaurant that transforms into
popular nightclub during weekends, with a large
dance floor and house, soul and R&B dance tunes
provided by an in-house DJ. On Fridays from 9pm
to 11pm, before the dance tunes set in, it's a lively
cocktail bar. Over 21s only. Fri 9pm–5am and Sat
11pm–5am.

Twist & Shout Frederiksgade 29 ⓦ www.aarhus
.twistandshout.dk. Three storeys of different
music styles: most of it's pretty mainstream, so no
real surprises. Mon–Thurs & Sat 10pm–6am, Fri
7pm–6am.

Live music venues

Bent J Nørre Allé 66 ☏ 86 12 04 92, ⓦ www
.jazzbarbentj.dk. By far the best jazz venue in town,
this smoky, atmospheric pub has free jam sessions
from 4pm on Fridays, and regular performances by

bands (cover 60–100kr). Closed Sunday.

🏃 **Fabriken** Klostergade 34 ☎ 86 76 06 76 Ⓦ www.chokoladefabriken.dk. Hosting up-and-coming local and international bands, from Icelandic folksters to smooth reggae acts, this is the hippest and most experimental place to go for gigs. Also a popular nightclub (see p.333). Tickets cost 60kr.

Fatter Eskild Skolegade 25 ☎ 86 19 44 11, Ⓦ www.fattereskild.dk. Piano bar hosting Danish bar-bands and R&B acts five nights a week. Tues–Thurs 8pm–2am, Fri & Sat 8pm–5am.

Musikcafeen Mejlgade 53 ☎ 86 76 03 44, Ⓦ www.musikcafeen.dk. On the first floor of the Fronthuset cultural centre, this is Århus's main venue for up-and-coming Danish and interna-tional bands, as well as live jazz, rock and the odd techno act. Entrance fee varies between

20kr and 150kr depending on who's playing. Closed Sun.

Musikhuset Thomas Jensens Allé ☎ 86 40 90 50, Ⓦ www.musikhusetaarhus.dk. City-centre concert hall which plays host to classical music, opera and, occasionally, mainstream pop bands.

Train Toldbogade 6 ☎ 86 13 47 22, Ⓦ www.train .dk. Attracting an older crowd and slightly more well-established bands than its rivals *Voxhall* (see below) and *Fabriken* (see left). Gigs take place three or four nights a week; admission runs from 100kr to 350kr, with doors opening at 9pm and the main band starting a couple of hours later.

Voxhall Vester Allé 15 ☎ 87 30 97 97, Ⓦ www .voxhall.dk. Århus's premier venue, hosting the cream of Danish and international independent acts from hip hop to world music. Tickets cost 50–200kr.

Listings

Airlines SAS (domestic and international) ☎ 70 10 20 00, information ☎ 32 32 14 50; Sterling Airlines reservations and flight information ☎ 70 10 84 84; British Airways reservations and flight informa-tion ☎ 86 36 30 60; Ryanair reservations (Ireland) ☎ +353/12 49 77 91.

Bookshops English Books and Secondhand Things, Frederiks Allé 53 (☎ 86 19 54 55, Mon–Fri 11.30am–5.30pm, Sat 11am–2pm), fully lives up to its name.

Bus enquiries Local buses ☎ 89 40 10 10; Abildskou's Århus–Copenhagen coach reservations ☎ 70 21 08 88, Ⓦ www.abildskou.dk.

Car rental Avis, Spanien 63 ☎ 86 19 23 99, and Jens Baggesens Vej 27 ☎ 86 16 10 99, Ⓦ www .avis.dk; Europcar, Sønder Allé 35 ☎ 89 33 11 11, Ⓦ www.europcar.dk.

Doctors Between 4pm and 8pm, call ☎ 86 20 10 22. Outside these hours, contact the Kommunehos-pital (see below).

Ferries and catamarans Mols Linien to either Odden or Kalundborg on Zealand ☎ 70 10 14 18, Ⓦ www.mols-linien.dk.

Hospitals There are 24hr emergency departments at Århus Kommunehospital, Nørrebrogade 44 (☎ 87

31 50 50), and Århus Amtssygehus, Tage-Hansens Gade 2 (☎ 89 49 75 75).

Internet cafés Boomtown, Åboulevarden 21 (Mon–Thurs 10am–2am, Fri & Sat 10am–8am, gates shut at midnight, Sun 11am–midnight; 25kr/hr); Gate 58, Vestergade 58 (daily 10am–midnight; 25kr/hr); Net House, Nørre Allé 66A (daily noon–midnight; 25kr/hr).

Markets There's a fruit, veg and flower market every Wednesday and Saturday on Bispetorvet, beside the cathedral (early morning till noon), though the one on Saturday mornings (10am–2pm) along Ingerslevs Boulevard, south of the centre, is livelier.

Pharmacy Løve Apoteket, Store Torv 5 ☎ 86 12 00 22, is open 24 hours.

Police Århus Politisation, Ridderstræde 1 ☎ 87 31 14 48.

Post office Banegårds Pladsen, by the train station (Mon–Fri 9.30am–6pm, Sat 10am–1pm).

Train enquiries Ⓦ www.dsb.dk has details of all services; you can also call ☎ 89 40 10 10 for info on regional services; ☎ 70 13 14 15 for inter-city services; and ☎ 70 13 14 16 for international trains.

Travel agents Kilroy Travels, Fredensgade 40 ☎ 70 15 40 15, Ⓦ www.kilroytravels.com.

Djursland and east to Randers

East of Århus, the nose-shaped **Djursland** peninsula boasts some of the prettiest landscapes in Denmark, its rolling hills and sandy beaches providing sufficient ingredients for a couple of days' pleasurable exploration. The southern coastal stretch, known as **Mols**, is especially delightful and attracts huge numbers of tourists every year, its heath-covered hills affording some superb views of the Ebeltoft and Kalø bay areas. **Ebeltoft**, the area's pretty urban centre, has a laid-back holiday feel year-round, and has a few interesting attractions should the weather warrant indoor activities. Right on the other side of the peninsula, the beaches of the north coast are second to none, particularly around **Grenå**, itself a departure point for ferries to the dune island of **Anholt**, a sort of micro Ibiza where those in the know return year after year to dance the night away. Heading back inland, **Gammel Estrup Slot** provides an enlightening insight into the life of the landed gentry in times gone by. The large town of **Randers** isn't all that appealing, though it does have its recreated "rainforest" domes and an Elvis museum; and if you're canoeing down the Gudenå from Silkeborg (see p.320), you'll end up at Tørring, just outside town.

Ebeltoft

Easily reached by regular buses from Århus (#123) and Randers (#212), and by frequent ferry services from Odden in Zealand (see p.174), **EBELTOFT** is a cute little town, with pretty timber-framed houses lining the cobbled streets of a compact town centre. A thriving market centre in medieval times, it was sacked by the invading Swedes in 1659 and has only emerged from economic decline thanks to tourism: try to arrive in early summer, before the streets are overrun by (mostly German) tourists shopping for souvenirs. Ebeltoft's main appeal is its proximity to a string of outstanding beaches, which run from its western outskirts along the Ebeltoft Vig bay coastline to Mols Bjerge (see p.336). There are also few good sights in the town itself, and the pretty centre is postcard-perfect enough to deserve a quick stroll, preferably with an ice cream in hand so as not to stand out from the crowds.

Ebeltoft's two best attractions are by the harbour, a short walk from the bus station. The **Fregatten Jylland** (daily: April–June & Sept–Oct 10am–5pm; July–Aug 10am–7pm; Nov–March 10am–4pm; 80kr; Ⓦwww.fregatten-jylland.dk) is a beautifully restored nineteenth-century frigate kitted out with an array of guns and cannons. The last wooden ship to be built in Denmark before the advance of iron (at a time when Denmark was a naval power to be reckoned with), it saw plenty of action, most famously at the 1864 battle of Helgoland, when the Prussian fleet was completely out-manoeuvred and forced to retreat (the victory was short-lived, though, as the Prussians won the war on the ground shortly after). Miniature recreations of famous sea battles are on display in the frigate's exhibition hall, alongside a breakdown of its colourful history – it served as the king's royal yacht at one point – and descriptions of life on board. Nearby at Strandvejen 8, the **Glas Museet** (Glass Museum; daily: April–June & Sept–Oct 10am–5pm; July–Aug 10am–7pm; Nov–March 10am–4pm; 60kr; Ⓦwww.glasmuseet.dk) is a stunning showcase of artworks in glass from all over the world, many housed in a spectacular new waterfront extension. Pieces to look out for include an unusual crystal-shaped blue glass table and a collection of gold-covered Japanese jewellery boxes. If you're feeling flush, there's also a gallery and shop selling some of the items, starting at a mere 700kr for a stylish oval platter and topping at a whopping 124,000kr for an elegant glass sculpture. From April until October (daily 10am–5pm), local artisans demonstrate the art of glass blowing on-site.

From the harbour, Jernbanegade leads up to the cobbled, pedestrianized Adelgade, lined with pretty wood-beamed buildings that, for the most part, house souvenir shops and ice-cream parlours. The one building that stands out is the tiny former town hall from 1789, at Torvet 1 on the town square (turn right down Adelgade when coming from the harbour). It now houses **Ebeltoft**

Museum (mid-June to Aug daily 10am–5pm, May to mid-June & Sept daily 11am–3pm, Oct–April Fri & Sat 11am–3pm; 25kr; ⓦ www.ebeltoftmuseum.dk), which gives a good – albeit brief – insight into the town's history. In the old courtroom, the frail municipal charter from 1301 decorates the wall alongside some interesting oils of Danish kings since 1448 and a curious little exhibit about Ebeltoft's nightwatchmen and police. There are more oddities in the long ochre building next door, at Juelsbakke 3. Here, a small, quirky and mildly diverting **Siamese Collection** (same hours, joint ticket with Ebeltoft Museum), put together by an Ebeltoft-born mining engineer during his years in Siam, features rows of ethnographic paraphernalia and animal skulls – an excellent example of a collector gone overboard.

Ebeltoft's main appeal, its **beaches**, begin on the town's outskirts and continue towards Mols Bjerge, and the sheltered setting on the bay means the shallow water is usually a degree or two higher than elsewhere in Denmark. Unlike the pristine shores of Grenå and the west coast of Jutland, the beaches here are left relatively unkempt, with seaweed and jellyfish sometimes present in abundance – but this doesn't seem to deter the beachgoers. The calm waters here are an ideal place to learn to windsurf or sail a dinghy; lessons and kit hire are available from *Ebeltoft Strand Camping* (see below), which also rents out bikes and is the only place hereabouts with public toilets.

Should you fancy staying in town, the best-value **hotel** is the small, no-frills *Æbeltoft* on Adelgade 44 (ⓣ 86 34 10 90; ❹), where rooms have shared facilities; there's also the *Ebeltoft Vandrerhjem* **youth hostel**, behind the harbour at Søndergade 43 (ⓣ 86 34 20 53, ⓦ www.danhostel.dk/ebeltoft; dorms 130kr, doubles ❷). If you want to stay near the beach, your best bet is the *Ebeltoft Park Hotel*, across the road from beach at Vibæk Strandvej 4 (ⓣ 86 34 32 22, ⓦ www.ebeltoftparkhotel.dk; ❻), which has modern rooms, an outdoor pool and a sauna. Of the several **campsites** along the bay, the one closest to Ebeltoft, and on the beachfront near *Ebeltoft Park* hotel, is *Ebeltoft Strand Camping* (ⓣ 86 34 55 33, ⓦ www.publiccamp.dk), on Nordre Strandvej.

Mols Bjerge

Djursland's beautiful stretch of southern coastline, **MOLS** has been endowed with a bountiful supply of outstanding natural scenery that encompasses pretty highland landscapes, sandy beaches and small, cute villages. The rolling hills here – roughly between Femmøller (7km west of Ebeltoft) and the Helgenæs peninsula – are known collectively as **MOLS BJERGE**, a stunning mosaic of open woodland and heath, carpeted with an explosion of wild flowers in spring and summer supporting rare butterflies and other insects, and with a smattering of Bronze Age burial mounds adorning the highest points. This beautiful highland landscape is slated to become a national park, but until a final decision is made, the Danish nature conservancy agency protects it and maintains a wide network of trails and tracks. The best way to explore the area is on foot or by bike (for rental outlets in Ebeltoft, see above). National cycle routes #2 and #5 run along the northern edge, but the gravel tracks within the protected area are also ideal for cycling (note that the trails are for hikers only). Turn off at **Femmøller**, just after the roadside mill, and the track will take you straight into Mols Bjerge proper. Bus #123, linking Ebeltoft and Århus, stops at Femmøller, from where the marked Den Italienske Sti trail takes you to the heart of the area and to the unmanned **Molbolaboratiorie visitor centre** (open 24/7), where you can pick up free walking maps of the area. At the foot of Mols' so-called mountains, along the heath-covered coastal strip, the tightly packed holiday homes form a buffer between the mountains and the sandy beaches. Unfortunately, if you want easy access to both beaches and the mountains, you'll find that there are very few **accommodation** options. Your best bet is to stay in Ebeltoft, or at the outrageously luxurious *Mols Kroen* inn (☎86 36 22 00, ⓦwww.molskroen. dk; ⓪) at Hovedgaden 16, 2km before Femmøller on the main road from Ebeltoft and right on Femmøller Strand beach. If you want to splash out, the inn's gourmet 🍴 **restaurant** (Sept–March Mon–Sat 11.30am–10pm, April–Aug daily 11.30am–10pm) is worth checking our; main courses mix weird and wonderful ingredients – such as pork, lobster and cabbage in the same dish, for example – and start at 155kr.

Grenå

At Jutland's easternmost point, **GRENÅ** grew up around its harbour in the nineteenth century, and it's still a relatively important port, with frequent ferry services to Varberg in Sweden and the island of Anholt (see below). Though the town centre is pleasant enough, the main draw is the lush, wide and sandy **beach** to the south. Voted second-best Blue Flag beach in the country (out of 211, and surpassed only by Gudmindrup Lyng Strand on Zealand), it offers great facilities (toilets, changing and snacks) as well as beautiful soft, white sand that carries on for miles. One popular attraction, if you get tired of lazing in the sun, or the unthinkable should happen and it starts raining, is the **Kattegatcentret Grenå** (Jan to mid-June & Sept to mid-Dec Mon–Fri 10am–4pm, Sat & Sun 10am–5pm; mid- to end June & mid- to end Aug daily 10am–5pm; July to mid-Aug daily 9.30am–6pm; 110kr; ⓦwww.kattegatcentret.dk) next to the ferry harbour at Færgevej 4. Named after the body of water – the Kattegat – north and east of Djursland, between Denmark and Sweden, this giant aquarium describes itself as a shark centre, with a 550,000-litre tropical seawater tank housing reef, bearded and lemon sharks to name but a few. You can study them from a glass tunnel that runs through the tank, best done – if you're not faint-hearted – around the 2pm feeding time. Among the centre's many other tanks, the most interesting is the Kattegat aquaria, a replica of Kattegat ecosystems, from tidal shoreline to open sea.

The best places to **stay** in Grenå include the yellow *Hotel Grenaa Strand* (☎86 32 68 14, ⓦwww.grenaastrand.dk; ⑥), near the harbour at Havnepladsen 1; alternatively, if you want to be closer to the beach, *Hotel Grenå Havlund* (☎86 32 26 77, ⓦwww.hotelgrenaa.dk; ⑥) at Kystvej 1 (town bus #2 from harbour and centre), is 100m from the water's edge and has a good restaurant. The best of the local **campsites** is *Grenå Strand Camping* (☎86 32 17 18, ⓦwww.grenaastrandcamping.dk; April–Sept; bus #2) at Fulgsangvej 58, 2km south of town in a pine plantation and a stone's throw from the beach. The *Grenå Vandrerhjem* **youth hostel**, Ydesvej 4 (☎86 32 66 22, ⓦwww.danhostel .dk/grenaa; 120kr, doubles ⑥; Feb to mid-Dec dorms), is at the northern edge of the pine plantation and a twenty-minute walk from the beach. Aside from *Havlund* hotel (see above), a good place to **eat** is *Restaurant Stakkels Holm* (☎86 30 08 89, daily 5–9pm) at the marina near Kattegatcentret, which does excellent seafood. Grenå is reachable by train from Århus, bus #214 from Randers, and bus #351 from Ebeltoft.

Anholt

Hidden away in the Kattegat, and equidistant to both Denmark and Sweden, there are two good reasons to visit the tiny island of **Anholt**: its outstanding nature and its never-ending nightlife. The island prides itself on being home to

△ Anholt lighthouse

what's touted as northern Europe's only **desert**, the **Ørken** – actually a rather magical, sandy heathland where over four hundred species of rare lichen thrive in the clean air. Today, this unusual area is protected, and can only be visited on foot. A track leads east from **ANHOLT BY** on the western tip, the island's only town and docking point for the ferry from Grenå. The Ørken's undulating grasses and lichen-covered dunes can be disorientating, and to avoid getting lost, head for the lighthouse at the island's northeastern tip; there's a path back along the northern coast. While at the lighthouse, look out for a large colony of **seals** that have set up permanent residence here – don't get too close, though, as they can be extremely dangerous. The entire island is encircled by a wide strip of beach, whose soft sand and clear waters are great for swimming and undisturbed sunbathing before you sample the **nightlife** (see opposite) in the evening; as there are no facilities, you'll need to bring your own supply of food and water.

Practicalities

Cars are banned from Anholt and **access** to the island in general is very limited. There's a regular ferry connection from the harbour in Grenå, with up to two daily departures in summer, and four weekly departures in winter; booking is essential (☎86 32 36 00, www.anholtfergen.dk). The ferry arrives at the harbour in the Copenhagen neighbourhood of Anholt By, a stone's throw from the town's two excellent music venues (see opposite). In order to get the full island experience – nature as well as nightlife – it's a good idea to stay overnight, though as **accommodation** is in short supply, and booking in advance crucial, you need to plan ahead. The best options are listed below; they're all within Anholt By. A good fifteen minutes' walk from the harbour along Gennem Landet, *Anholt Bed & Breakfast* (☎86 31 91 11, www.anholt-bed-breakfast.dk; ⑥), Nordstrandvej 11B, has nine stylish double rooms sharing facilities; a filling breakfast buffet is included in the rates. Further north along Nordstrandvej, near the beach at no.19, *Anholt Kro* (☎86 31 90 80, www.anholtkro.dk; ⑤, en-suite ⑥; April to mid-November) has eleven comfortable, simply furnished rooms. Nordstrandvej is also home to the island's **campsite** (☎86 31 91 00; www.anholtcamping.dk; mid-May to mid-Sept), with superb pitches in the coastal dunes. For **food**, Anholt By has a small supermarket ideal for stocking up before hitting the beaches, as well as a handful of cafés and restaurants. The two best places to eat are the two music venues (see below). *Casablanca* does excellent pizza, and grills meat and fish on an outdoor barbecue, while *Molevitten* is a little more upscale, with lobster and organic steak dominating the menu.

Anholt's two fantastic and intimate **music venues** are the *Casablanca* (mid-May to Aug daily 3pm–late; T86 31 92 22, Wwww.casablanca.dk) and *Molevitten* (mid-May to Aug daily 5pm–late; T86 31 90 87), around the corner from each other near the ferry harbour. Both have live music most nights from some of Denmark's top bands (this is where musicians go to chill out), with music ranging from jazz, folk and funk to pop, rock and world music; the party tends to carry on until the wee hours of the morning.

The north coast

If it's only beaches you're after, head 10km north of Grenå by local bus #352 to **GJERRILD**, a small and quiet village with an inn, bakery, grocery and a small castle, Sostrup Slot, now a religious retreat run by Cistercian sisters and with a pleasant park open to the public. Continuing 4km north of Gjerrild along Langholmve (no public transport) will take you to the Blue Flag **Nord-stranden beach**, among the best in the country, with miles of soft sand and basic facilities. **Accommodation** is limited to the excellent *Gjerrild Nordstrand Camping* (T86 38 42 00, Wwww.gnc.dk; April to mid-Sept), 500m from the beach, which also has a small shop. Back in Gjerrild, there's also the atmospheric *Gjerrild Vandrerhjem* **youth hostel** (T86 38 41 99, Wwww.danhostel-gjerrild. dk), Dyrehavevej 9, set on the fringes of a woodland in an old railway station, with dorm beds (140kr) and doubles (❸).

Gammel Estrup Slot

An interesting stop en route from Grenå to Randers, a few kilometres after the village of Auning and reachable by bus #214, **Gammel Estrup Slot** is an imposing sixteenth-century pile in Gothic renaissance style. Exactly as you'd imagine a castle to look, it's a commanding three-winged red-brick building with a tower in each corner, surrounded by a moat and with a drawbridge leading through into a cobbled courtyard. The castle complex holds two unusual museums; a joint 70kr ticket covers entry to both. Inside the castle, to the right as you enter the courtyard, the **Jyllands Herregårdsmuseum** (Manor House Museum: April–June & mid-Aug to Oct daily 10am–5pm; July to mid-Aug daily 10am–6pm; Nov–March Tues–Sun 10am–3pm; Wwww.gammelestrup .dk), serves to illustrate the lives of the landed gentry in the eighteenth century. Richly furnished rooms bedecked with family portraits in the upstairs section contrast dramatically with the minute and austere servants' quarters downstairs, while the grand great hall and enormous castle kitchen, with its beautiful vaulted ceiling, give a sense of the size and splendour of the dinner parties held here. The pretty tower room, its walls decorated with painted curtains, offers lovely views of the **grounds**, whose beautiful parkland, orangery and row upon row of carp ponds could easily take up an entire afternoon. Across the stream feeding the carp ponds, the immense **Dansk Landbrugsmuseum** (Danish Agriculture Museum: same hours; Wwww.gl-estrup.dk) occupies the farm buildings and surrounding grounds. Exhibits trace agricultural development in Denmark from the Stone Age until the present, though unless you've a special interest in farming it's not particularly exciting stuff. You might want to check out the reconstructed rural kitchens in the section on farming life or, in the outdoor section, the botanic garden and beehives.

Randers

Strategically located at the point where the Gudenå river narrows and runs into Randers fjord, the town of **RANDERS** came into existence as a place where Vikings crossed the river in the tenth century. A trading and manufacturing base since the thirteenth century, its growth has continued apace over the years, leaving a tiny medieval centre miserably corralled by a bleak new industrial zone. Though it's not the most enthralling of towns, you might well find yourself here to visit one of Jutland's most popular attractions, the **Randers Regnskov** (Randers Rainforest; mid-June to mid-Aug daily 10am–6pm; mid-Aug to mid-June Mon–Fri 10am–4pm, Sat & Sun 10am–5pm; 110kr; Ⓦwww.regnskoven.dk), a recreation of tropical rainforests – African, Asian and South American – set alongside the River Gudenå. Enclosed within three giant domes, you wander through the dense, damp foliage, watching out for the birds, animals and amphibians, which include a number of rare turtles and a flying fox, not to mention a formidable assortment of vipers, boas, pythons, poison frogs and the like. The best part is undoubtedly the dark and spooky "night zoo", located in a dripping stone cave.

Otherwise, Randers holds a few museums that are worth visiting. The Culture Centre, near the bus station on Stenmannsgade 2, holds the **Museet for Dansk Kunst** (Museum of Danish Art: Tues–Sun 11am–5pm; free; Ⓦwww.randerskunstmuseum.dk) on the second floor, with a permanent collection of over two thousand pieces from the late eighteenth century up until today, mostly by Danish artists. You could easily kill a couple of hours here, if only for the wacky glass and mirror installation *Cosmic Space* by the Faroese artist Trondur Patursson. Downstairs, the first floor holds the less captivating **Kulturhistorisk Museum Randers** (Museum of Cultural History: same hours; free; Ⓦwww.khm.dk), which provides a solid if uninspiring historical introduction to the region. A little further down the road, at no. 9C, the **Elvis Unlimited Museum** (Mon–Fri 10am–5pm, Sat 10am–2pm; 30kr; Ⓦwww.elvisunlimited.com) has tons of paraphernalia on display, including the King's personal record collection, two of his guitars, clothes and the Presley archives as collated by the FBI.

Practicalities

Randers' **bus station** is right in the centre at Dytmærsken 12; the **train station** is on the outskirts, ten minutes' walk west of the centre at Jernbanegade 29. First stop should be the **tourist office** (mid-June to mid-Aug Mon–Fri 9.30am–5pm, Sat 10am–1pm; mid-Aug to mid-June Mon–Fri 9.30am–4pm, Sat 9am–1pm; ☏86 42 44 77, Ⓦwww.visitranders.com), at Tørvebryggen 12 on the ring road leading to Randers Regnskov, from where you can get a list of private rooms which rent from 150kr per person per night – but be aware that some of them are a long way outside town. Otherwise, one of the best-value **hotels** is the *Gudenå*, Østervold 42 (☏86 40 44 11, Ⓦwww.hotel-gudenaa.dk; ⑥/⑤), set in the former seamen's hostel overlooking the harbour. More upmarket is the historic *Hotel Randers*, in the centre on Torvegade 11 (☏86 42 34 22, Ⓦwww.hotel-randers.dk; ⑦), whose rates are at the bottom of the price-code range during weekends. The *Randers Vandrerhjem* **youth hostel** (☏86 42 50 44, Ⓦwww.danhostelranders.dk; mid-Feb to Nov; dorms 150kr, doubles ④) is five minutes' walk north of the centre at Gethersvej 1; town bus #6 stops 200m from the front door on Hobrovej. The nearest **campsite**, *Fladbro Camping* (☏86 42 93 61, Ⓦwww.fladbrocamping.dk), with cabins and a swimming pool, is 6km west of Randers at Fladbro, which is also the final staging point for canoe trips down the Gudenå river (see p.320). To get there, take bus #10 to the golf course, from where it's a ten-minute signposted walk. Note that some #10 buses do go all the way to the campsite stop, so ask the driver.

Randers has plenty of relatively inexpensive **restaurants**: try the Greek dishes at *Hellas*, Vester Kirkestræde 3 (daily 5–11pm; ☎86 41 99 11), or the filling traditional Danish lunches at *Maren Knudsen Øl & Vinkælder* on Storegade (☎86 41 88 18; Tues–Thurs 11am–midnight, Fri & Sat 11am–2am, Sun 2pm to midnight). 🍴 *Niels Ebbesens Spisehus* (daily 11.30am–10pm; ☎86 43 32 26, ⓦ www.nielsebbesens.dk), Storegade 13, offers the town's best lunchtime smørrebrød (35kr per piece), and tasty pork tenderloin with all the trimmings for 119kr on the dinner menu. As for **drinking**, Storegade holds a good selection of bars where you can sample the local Thor beer; try the popular 🍴 *Tante Olga*, Søndergade 6 (☎86 41 19 70, ⓦ www.tanteolga.dk; Thurs 8pm–3am, Fri 3pm–5am, Sat 8pm–5am), which has something going on every night, from live blues and rock to whisky-tasting evenings. There's also the marginally more peaceful *Café von Hatten*, Von Hattenstræde 7 (☎86 43 33 18, ⓦ www.vonhatten.dk; Tues & Wed 8pm–1am, Thurs 7pm–2am, Fri & Sat noon–2am).

Viborg and around

Some 40km west of Randers and at the junction of all major roads in Jutland, **VIBORG** was one of the most important communities in the country until the mid-eighteenth century. From Knud in 1027 to Christian V in 1655, every Danish king was crowned here in Viborg; Hans Tausen's Lutheran preaching began in here in 1528, eight years before Denmark's official conversion from Catholicism; and until the early nineteenth century the town was the seat of a provincial assembly. As the national administrative axis shifted towards Zealand, however, Viborg's importance waned, and although it's still home to the high court of West Denmark, it's now primarily a market town, with only its majestic cathedral giving a hint of its past glory days. With its picturesque lakeside setting and a quaint compact centre housing two good museums, Viborg makes for a pleasurable couple of days, and is a good base from which to explore the surrounding countryside. To the south, the tranquil hills of **Dollerup** are steeped in literary and political history, while the **limestone mines** to the east serve as a rather spooky reminder of the harsh lives of miners in times past. Last but not least, the bleak moorlands of **Kongenshus**, smothered in heather during the autumn, offer some great hikes.

Arrival, information and accommodation

Trains and **long-distance buses** arrive at their respective stations on Viborg's western side at Banegårds Pladsen 2 and 4, roughly 1km from the centre. If coming from Århus by train, note that you'll need to change at Langå. The **tourist office** (mid-May to mid-June Mon–Fri 9am–5pm, Sat 9.30am–12.30pm; mid-June to Aug Mon–Fri 9am–5pm, Sat 9am–2pm; Sept to mid-May Mon–Fri 9am–4pm, Sat 9.30am–12.30pm; ☎87 25 30 75, ⓦ www.visitviborg.dk) is close to the cathedral at Nytorv 9; staff have a long list of reasonably priced **private rooms** in and around Viborg, starting at about 125kr per person. Viborg's few **hotels** are all fairly pricey. Best bet is the grand *Palads*, Sct Mathias Gade 5 (☎86 62 37 00, ⓦ www.hotelpalads.dk; ❼), part of the Best Western chain and a short walk from the train station.

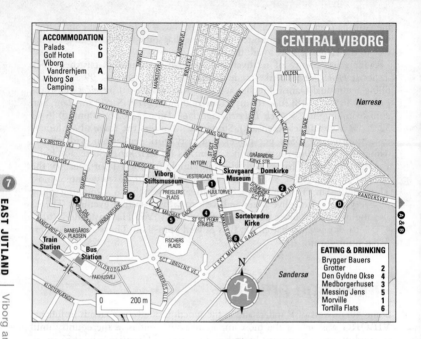

ACCOMMODATION
Palads **C**
Golf Hotel **D**
Viborg
 Vandrerhjem **A**
Viborg Sø
 Camping **B**

CENTRAL VIBORG

Nørresø

Søndersø

EATING & DRINKING
Brygger Bauers
 Grotter **2**
Den Gyldne Okse **4**
Medborgerhuset **3**
Messing Jens **5**
Morville **1**
Tortilla Flats **6**

Even more expensive is the modern *Golf Hotel Viborg*, Randersvej 2 (☎86 61 02 22, ⓦwww.golf-hotel-viborg.dk; ❻), next to a golf course and with a fabulous lake view as well as a swimming pool, sauna and jacuzzi. Also close to the lake, but on the opposite side to the town centre (a 2km walk, or local bus #707), are the *Viborg Vandrerhjem* **youth hostel**, Vinkelvej 36 (☎86 67 17 81, ⓦwww.danhostel.dk/viborg; dorms 125kr, doubles ❷; Feb–Nov); and the *Viborg Sø Camping* **campsite** (☎86 67 13 11, ⓦwww.camping-viborg.dk).

The town

Viborg is cut in half by a lake, named Nørresø in its northern reach, Søndersø to the south and spanned by the Randersvej bridge. Central Viborg is concentrated in a small area, though, and most parts of the old town are within a few minutes' walk of each other. The logical place to start exploring is the **Domkirke** (June–Aug Mon–Sat 10am–5pm, Sun noon–5pm; April, May & Sept Mon–Sat 11am–4pm, Sun noon–4pm; Oct–March Mon–Sat 11am–3pm, Sun noon–3pm), whose twin towers are the town's most visible feature. Built by Bishop Eskil in 1130, the original cathedral was destroyed by fire in 1726 and rebuilt in today's Baroque style in 1860 by one Claus Stallknecht – though he did the job so badly that it had to be closed for two years and refinished. The **interior** is dominated by the brilliant frescoes of **Joakim Skovgaard**, who took twelve years to cover the walls and arches with the entire story of the Bible in an unusually dramatic and colourful style. Look out especially for the angels opening the gates to heaven. Skovgaard is commemorated at the **Skovgaard Museum** (daily: May–Sept 10am–12.30pm & 1.30–5pm; Oct–April 1.30–5pm; 20kr; ⓦwww.skovgaardmuseet.dk), inside the former Rådhus across from the cathedral – a neat building with which Claus Stallknecht made amends for his botched job over the road. There's a good selection of Skovgaard's paintings on display – although they're a little anticlimactic after his splendid work in the cathedral – plus some works by other members of his family.

Two minutes' walk away on Store Sct Mikkels Gade, there's another interesting church in the form of the late-Romanesque **Sortebrødre Kirke**, the sole remains of the cloisters built by Dominican Black Friars, one of four monastic orders in Viborg abolished during the Reformation; you'll need to get the key from the sacristan office next door to get in. Inside the church, the sixteenth-century Belgian altarpiece is the star turn, with 89 gilded oak figures in high relief around the central Crucifixion scene. For a broader – if somewhat dreary – perspective on Viborg's past, head for the **Viborg Stiftsmuseum** (Viborg District Museum: mid-June to Aug daily 11am–5pm; Sept to mid-June Tues–Fri 1–4pm, Sat & Sun 11am–5pm; 25kr; ⓦ www.viborgstiftsmuseum.dk), on the northern side of Hjultorvet between Vestergade and Store Sct Hans Gade. The three well-stocked floors hold everything from prehistoric and archeological artefacts to clothes, furniture and household appliances.

Eating, drinking and nightlife

During the day, you could do worse than pick up some smørrebrød (the best outlet is the *Stjerneskuddet* deli at Jernbanegade 14), and **eat** alfresco in one of the numerous parks or on the banks of the lake. Plenty of reasonably priced eating places can also be found on and around Sct Mathias Gade.

Restaurants and bars

🏂 **Brygger Bauers Grotter** Sct Mathias Gade 61 ☏86 61 44 88 ⓦ www.brygger bauersgrotter.dk. Romantic, candlelit cellar restaurant serving delicacies such as quail baked in orange and port (188kr) for dinner. The lunchtime herring platter (59kr) and salad of the day with freshly made bread (49kr) are also recommended. Daily 11.30am–10.30pm.

Den Gyldne Okse Store Sct Peder Stræde 11 ☏86 62 27 44, ⓦ www.gyldneokse.dk. Small, spotless place serving quality Brazilian steaks from around 100kr and burgers starting at 59kr. Daily 11am–10pm.

Medborgerhuset Vesterbrogade 13 ☏86 62 72 32 ⓦ www.medborgerhuset.dk. Laid-back café in Viborg's community centre, a short walk from the town centre, serving a 45kr *dagens ret* (including a vegetarian option), as well as smørrebrød, sandwiches and inexpensive coffee and cakes. Mon–Thurs 9am–9.30pm, Fri 9am–5pm.

Messing Jens Sct Mathias Gade 48 ☏86 62 02 73, ⓦ www.messingjens.dk. A café-cum-cocktail bar and nightclub, offering simple meals (from 55kr) and funky tunes from the DJ until the early hours of the morning. Mon–Wed 2pm–midnight, Thurs 2pm–3am, Fri noon–5am, Sat 11am–5am.

Morville Hjultorvet 2 ☏86 60 22 11, ⓦ www .cafemorville.dk. A glitzy café-restaurant, with DJs enhancing the mood at night. You can have a cup of coffee or cool beer, as well as mouthwatering main meals such as steak with new potatoes and veg (169kr). Mon–Fri 11am–midnight, Sat 10am–1am, Sun noon–11pm.

Tortilla Flats Store Sct Mikkelsgade 2 ☏86 62 79 97, ⓦ www.tortillaflats-viborg.dk. Lively Mexican restaurant with authentic and affordable Mexican dishes such as a tasty chicken enchilada with green chilli sauce for 99kr. Tues–Sat 5–10pm, Sun 5–9pm.

Around Viborg

The area **around Viborg** is excellent for cycling, with plenty of pleasant spots within easy reach; there's also a decent local bus service. Leaving Viborg, heading south on Koldingvej and turning west towards Herning brings you into **Dollerup Bakker**, a beautiful area of soft hills and meadows on the shores of **Hald Sø** lake. For all its peace, the district's history is a violent one. This is where Niels Bugge led a rebellion of Jutland squires against the king in 1351, and where the Catholic bishop, Jorgen Friis, was besieged by Viborgers at the

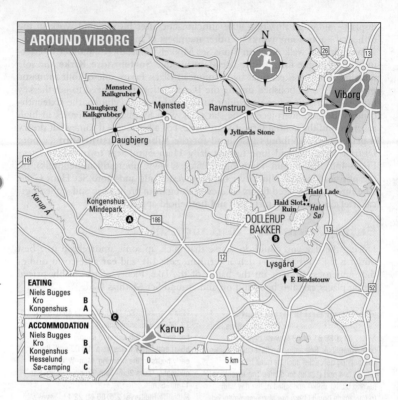

N

Viborg

26   13

Mønsted
Kalkgruber

Daugbjerg
Kalkgrubber   Mønsted   Ravnstrup

16

Jyllands Stone

Daugbjerg

16

Karup Å

Kongenshus
Mindepark   A   186

Hald Lade

Hald Slot Hald
Ruin   Sø

DOLLERUP
BAKKER   B   13

12

Lysgård

E Bindstouw

52

EATING
Niels Bugges
  Kro   **B**
Kongenshus   **A**

ACCOMMODATION
Niels Bugges
  Kro   **B**
Kongenshus   **A**
Hesselund
  Sø-camping   **C**

C

Karup

0   5 km

time of the Reformation. Much of the action took place around the manor houses that once stood here, such as Hald Slot, the ruin which can be reached by following the **footpath** that runs along Hald Sø's western shore. The path starts close to **Hald Lade**, a restored barn by the side of the road, where an exhibition (June–Aug daily noon–6pm; Sept–May Sat & Sun noon–6pm; free) details the history and geology of the area, and the more recent battle against the pollution poisoning Hald Sø. All the text is in Danish, but the many photos are worth a peek. From June to August, rowing boats are available for rent from the historic *Niels Bugges Kro*, by the lakeside just downhill from Hald Lade, which also does good meals and has four comfortable rooms (☎86 63 80 11, Ⓦwww.niels-bugges-kro.dk; ⓪). Just to the south of here, a road leads from the village of Dollerup to **LYSGÅRD**, home to **E Bindstouw** (June–Aug Tues–Sun 10am–5pm; 20kr), the old schoolhouse where **Steen Steensen Blicher** recorded his famous stories. His melancholy novels and poems were centred around rural life in the area's barren heath-covered landscape, and during his lifetime, Blicher was better known in Denmark than contemporaries such as H.C. Andersen and Søren Kierkegaard. He would sit at E Bindstouw in the evenings while poor locals wove socks beside the stove and told folk tales, and note them down for posterity. The small wood-beamed building still contains the fixtures and fittings of Blicher's time, including his writing board, stove, and even a few socks. To get here from Viborg, take the #54 bus from the bus station.

The limestone mines and Kongenshus Mindepark

About 11km west of Viborg are the **Mønsted Kalkgruber** (Mønsted Lime-stone Mines: April–Oct daily 10am–5pm; 50kr; ⓦwww.monsted-kalkgruber.dk), which wind underground for some sixty kilometres and stay at a constant temperature, regardless of external weather. Wandering around their cool, damp innards can be magically atmospheric – although a century ago, conditions for the workers here were so horrific that when Frederik IV visited he was suffi-ciently appalled to bring about reforms; the mines were subsequently known as "Frederik's Quarries" or, more venomously, "The King's Graves". The site closes in winter, when the mines are taken over by an enormous colony of hibernat-ing bats. Bus #28 runs here from Viborg. En route – some 9km from Viborg, between Mønsted and Raunstrup – a lay-by to the left holds the **Jutlands Stone**, an inscribed rock surrounded by lots of cigarette ends, which marks the precise geographical centre of Jutland.

Just beyond Mønsted (and also served by bus #28) is another set of limestone mines, **Daugbjerg Kalkgruber** (daily: June 10am–4pm; July to mid-Aug 10am–6pm; mid-Aug to Oct & end March to May 11am–4pm; 45kr; ⓦwww.daugbjerg-kalkgruber.dk), unlit and much narrower than those at Mønsted, and therefore quite spooky. The entrance was found by chance fifty years ago and no one has yet charted the full extent of the passages; it's said that work began here at the time of Gorm den Gamle, the tenth-century King of Jutland, and that the tunnels were used as hideouts by bandits.

A marked contrast to the rugged landscape around the limestone mines and the rolling hills of Dollerup Bakker, **Kongenshus Mindepark** (early May to mid-Sept daily 10am–6pm; 12kr, cars 30kr excluding passengers; ⓦwww.kongenshus.dk) is a vast, open and windswept moorland which serves as a memorial to the desperate lives of the heath farmers who have attempted to cultivate this area since the mid-eighteenth century. Given the desperately poor soil here, all their attempts failed, and as the wind howls around this stark, inhospitable heath, you can only marvel at their determination. But while the area isn't well-placed for farming, it does offer some great **walking**, especially during autumn, when heather covers the landscape with a carpet of purple; you can pick up a free map of trails at the car park. The grand former home of one of the settlers, who tried to keep sheep here and was rewarded for his efforts by a grant from Frederik V, has now been opened up as the *Kongenshus* **hotel** (ⓣ97 54 81 25, ⓦwww.kongenshushotel.dk; ❹); its delightful restaurant does fine Danish food, such as a smørrebrød lunch platter for 135kr. Of the many **campsites** nearby, *Hessellund Sø-Camping* (ⓣ97 10 16 04, ⓦwww.hessellund-camping.dk; April to mid-Sept), to the south on the banks of Karup Å near Karup, is the closest and best. There's no public transport to the park, so if you want to visit, you'll need a car, bike or sturdy feet to cover the (signposted) three-kilometre walk from Daugbjerg.

Travel details

Trains

Århus to: Aalborg (2 hourly; 1hr 15min–1hr 35min); Copenhagen (3 hourly; 2hr 48min–3hr 15min); Fredericia (4 hourly; 59min–1hr 18min); Grenå (hourly; 1hr 25min); Horsens (4 hourly; 26min–38min); Randers (2 hourly; 29min–40min); Silkeborg (2 hourly; 50min); Skjern (13 daily; 2hr 20min); Vejle (4 hourly; 44min–54min); Viborg (2 hourly; 1hr 5min–1hr 14min).

Fredericia to: Århus (4 hourly; 59min–1hr 18min); Copenhagen (2 hourly; 1hr 44min–2hr 7min); Hors-ens (2–3 hourly; 31min–44min); Vejle (3 hourly; 14min–20min).

Grenå to: Århus (hourly; 1hr 25min).

Horsens to: Århus (4 hourly; 26min–38min); Copenhagen (hourly; 2hr 22min–3hr); Fredericia (2–3 hourly; 31min–44min); Vejle (3 hourly; 15min–22min).

Randers to: Aalborg (2 hourly; 50min–59min); Århus (2 hourly; 29min–40min); Copenhagen (2 hourly; 3hr 28min–3hr 58min); Viborg (hourly; 1hr 6min).

Silkeborg to: Århus (2 hourly; 50min); Skjern (14 daily; 1hr 30min).

Vejle to: Århus (4 hourly; 44min–54min); Copenhagen (hourly; 2hr–2hr 26min); Fredericia (3 hourly; 14min–20min); Horsens (3 hourly; 15min–22min).

Viborg to: Århus (2 hourly; 1hr 5min–1hr 14min); Copenhagen (hourly; 4hr 26min); Randers (hourly; 1hr 6min).

Buses

Århus to: Copenhagen (4–5 daily; 2hr 55min); Ebeltoft (hourly; 1hr 15min); Grenå (10 daily; 1hr 25min); Randers (2 hourly; 50min–1hr); Silkeborg (11 daily; 1hr 15min); Viborg (9 daily; 1hr 45min).

Ebeltoft to: Århus (hourly; 1hr 15min); Copenhagen (2–4 daily; 2hr 55min); Grenå (10 daily; 1hr).

Grenå to: Århus (10 daily; 1hr 25min); Copenhagen (2–3 daily; 3hr 35min); Ebeltoft (10 daily; 1hr); Randers (hourly; 90min).

Horsens to: Silkeborg (13 daily; 1hr–1hr 15min).

Randers to: Århus (2 hourly; 50min–1hr); Copenhagen (3–4 daily; 3hr 55min); Grenå (hourly; 90min); Silkeborg (hourly; 1hr 35min); Viborg (17 daily; 45min–1hr 10min).

Silkeborg to: Århus (11 daily; 1hr 15min); Copenhagen (2 daily; 4hr); Horsens (13 daily; 1hr–1hr 15min); Randers (hourly; 1hr 35min); Viborg (20 daily; 45min–1hr 2min).

Viborg to: Århus (9 daily; 1hr 45min); Randers (17 daily; 45min–1hr 10min); Silkeborg (20 daily; 45min–1hr 2min).

Ferries

Århus to: Kalundborg (1–5 daily; 2hr 40min); Sjællands Odde (5–10 daily; 1hr 5min).

Ebeltoft to: Sjællands Odde (6–7 daily; 45min).

Grenå to: Anholt (4–7 times weekly; 2hr 45min).

Flights

Århus to: Copenhagen (5 daily; 35min).

Billund to: Copenhagen (4–6 daily; 45min); Rønne (June–Sept 2 weekly; 1hr).

8

North Jutland

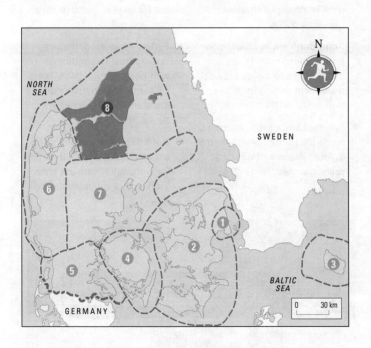

CHAPTER 8 # Highlights

✳ **Meeting of the seas, Grenen**
Stand with one foot in the
Kattegat and another in the
Skagerrak, and watch the
waves clashing over your toes.
See p.375

✳ **Harbourside dining, Skagen**
The outstanding restaurants
here offer fresh fish and fine
wine in atmospheric surroundings. See p.378

✳ **Sand dune walks, Sandmilen
and Råbjerg mile** These vast
migrating sand dunes provide
a stunning setting for a hike.
See p.376 & 377

✳ **Salt-making, Læsø** Watch salt
made the traditional way on this
isolated island with its scenic
saline marshes. See p.371

✳ **Gamle Skagen sunset** This
lovely beach is legendary as
a romantic sunset-watching
spot. See p.376

✳ **Aalborg nightlife** Home of
the wildest nightlife for miles
around, Aalborg's Jomfru Ane
Gade holds some brilliant
drinking spots and is a great
bet for an unforgettable night
out. See p.364

✳ **Fyrkat** Impressive, perfectly
symmetrical Viking fortification,
with beautiful tribute to Viking
craftsmanship in the reconstructed longhouse nearby.
See p.352

✳ **Rold Skov** The country's largest forest, the beech and conifer woodlands here are ideal
for hiking or mountain biking.
See p.353

△ Grenen

8

North Jutland

orth Jutland is the furthest you'll get from the bright lights of Copenhagen, both geographically and in terms of the area's remote feel. Though it does have a few bright lights of its own in the shape of Aalborg, the country's fourth largest city, north Jutland has a distinctly no-nonsense, rural flavour; its population, meanwhile, are known for keeping themselves to themselves – understatement is the prevailing philosophy, and a modest smile here equates to what would be a raucous laugh in other parts of the country. The area is bisected by the **Limfjorden**, the body of water which connects the Skagerrak and Kattegat seas, and which served as the region's main transport artery for centuries until the western outlet at Agger (for more on which, see Chapter 6) was blocked off by sand drifts in 1100 (it reopened again in 1825). To the south of the Limfjorden and north of the much smaller Mariager fjord, the **Himmerland** area holds some remarkable remnants of the Viking era, most notable of which are the fortifications at **Fyrkat** and **Aggersborg**. More contemporary history comes to the fore at the country's largest forest, Rold Skov, where the tree-smothered hills of **Rebild Bakker** play host to the largest American Independence celebrations outside of the US each July; at other (quieter) times, Rold Skov – and specifically Rebild Bakker – offer some superb hiking and mountain-biking. Sitting snugly on the banks of Limfjorden, **Aalborg** is a convenient place to base yourself while exploring the region, with some great places to eat and party, and a few outstanding museums, too. To the north of the Limfjorden, the highlight of the **Vendsyssel** region is **Skagen**, a uniquely atmospheric town on the northern tip of Denmark, whose unusual natural light has long attracted artists. To the south, ferries from the east-coast port of **Frederikshavn** head out to the windswept island of **Læsø**, which offers an unusual history and an intriguing landscape. Southwest of Skagen, the **Jammerbugt** bay is graced with a string of excellent beaches and their accompanying line of holiday towns, which have served as the Danes' top vacation spots for decades. Here, **Løkken** is the destination of choice for party-hungry Danish teens and, unless you choose to join them, is best avoided.

Himmerland

North of Randers (covered in Chapter 7), you enter into Himmerland through **Hobro**, the only town of any size in a region which is largely devoid of major urban settlements. Himmerland's main asset is the **Rold Skov** forest, laced with some excellent hiking and mountain-biking trails. In the middle of the

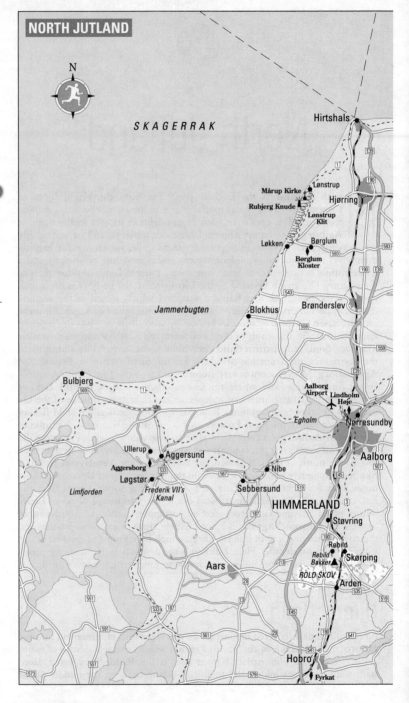

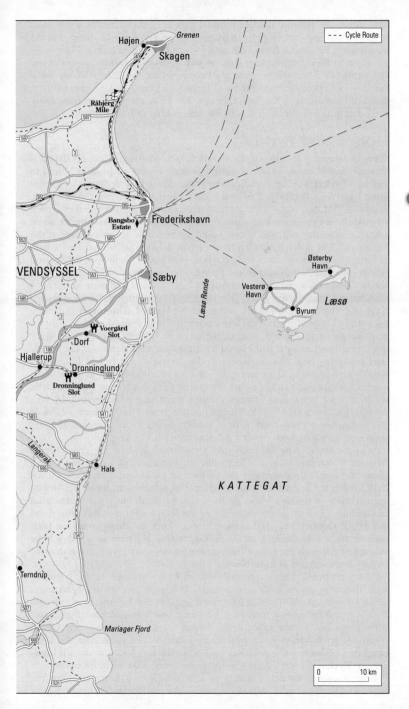

--- Cycle Route

Højen *Grenen*

Skagen

40

Råbjerg
Mile

597

597

3

35

40

35

Bangsbo
Estate

Frederikshavn

553

585

Østerby
Havn

180

VENDSYSSEL

553

Sæby

Vesterø
Havn

Læsø Rende

Læsø

585

541

Byrum

3

5

Voergård
Slot

Dorf

Hjallerup

180

Dronninglund

559

Dronninglund
Slot

583

541

Langerak

583

595

12

Hals

KATTEGAT

541

Terndrup

507

555

Mariager Fjord

0   10 km

531

woodlands, the **Rebild Bakker** national park is characterized by the host of museums and souvenir shops by its main entrance. The park was donated to the government by Danish Americans, and today, US-based "pilgrims" flock in to get close to their Danish roots and, on July 4, descend en masse to celebrate Independence. The other main draws hereabouts are the unique Viking fortifications of Fyrkat, on the outskirts of Hobro; and those at Aggersborg on the banks of Limfjorden, by the small fishing town of Løgstør – both amazing structures that give an interesting insight into the politics of the Viking era.

Hobro and Fyrkat

With its stunning location at the mouth of the Mariager fjord, **HOBRO** is an appealing place for an idle wander, but main reason for heading here is to visit the **Fyrkat Viking fortification** (daily: April–May & Sept–Oct 10am–4pm; June–Aug 10am–5pm; 55kr for joint ticket with Vikingecenter Fyrkat; ⓦwww.fyrkat.dk), some 3km southwest of the centre. What makes Fyrkat remarkable is the astounding symmetry of its perfectly round rampart, some 120m in diameter and with access points set precisely at each corner of the "compass". The construction has been carbon dated to 980–81, the same date as three similar fortifications at Aggersborg (see p.354), Trelleborg on Zealand (see p.159) and Nonnebakken on Funen. This coincidence – together with the fact that they were all of an unusually high standard and were in use for a maximum of just twenty years – has left researchers somewhat baffled. At the time of construction, Denmark was ruled by **Harald Bluetooth** (for more on whom, see p.389) who, ten years prior, had lost control of the country's main southern stronghold, Dannevirke (now in Schleswig) to the Germans. The prevailing theory is that Harald built the four fortifications as tax collection points to fund the recapture of Dannevirke; the attached longhouses would have been used to store the citizens' contributions (in those days, livestock, crops and the like rather than money). If this is true, then his tactic seems to have worked, as Dannevirke was again under Danish rule by 983. All four fortifications were abandoned not long after Harald's death in 986 or 987 – possibly because then, as now, nobody likes the tax man, and Harald's successor (and son) Sven needed the people behind him.

From the entrance by the main road a small track leads to the grass covered rampart, which on first glance looks like the outer wall of a dike. You can go inside the fortification through any of four access points, each of which has steps leading to the path along the rampart's rim, which provides an awe-inspiring overview of the site. Marks on the ground indicate the strict symmetrical positioning – in four groups of four – of the solid longhouses that once stood within the rampart. On a hill outside, an exact copy of a **longhouse** has been erected; it's a remarkably sturdy building that would have required a huge amount of materials and labour – the timber for this and the ramparts is thought to have been shipped in from Norway.

There's no public transport from Hobro to Fyrkat, though the fairly lengthy walk from the centre is pleasant enough. From the bus station, head south down Brogade and after about 200m turn left into Sønder Allé; this leads into Fyrkatvej and becomes a rural road. Continue past Vikingecentret Fyrkat (see below) and into a river valley, where Fyrkat sits on the banks of the Onsild stream. Alternatively, there's a path leading straight to Fyrkat from the town campsite (see below). On your way back from the site, pop into the **Vikinge-center Fyrkat** (Fyrkat Viking Centre; same hours; 55kr for joint ticket with Fyrkat; ⓦwww.fyrkat.dk), a replica of a wealthy Viking farmstead from the same era which provides a good contrast to the sterility and magnificence of

Fyrkat itself. It consists of nine ramshackle structures, each with separate functions and all much smaller than the Fyrkat longhouses. Most evocative is the 30m furnished longhouse, with separate sections for livestock, sleeping and food preparation. In summer, this is an excellent place to get an impression of life during Bluetooth's era via the demonstrations of traditional Viking activities like bronze casting, spinning and dyeing; at other times, you can wander in and out of houses freely.

To get some background on what you've seen at the sites, head back into town to the **Hobro Museum** (May–Sept daily 11am–4pm; 25kr, or free with Fyrkat/Vikingecenter tickets; ⑭www.sydhimmerlandsmuseum.dk), Vestergade 21. There are displays of the best of the finds from the many archaeological excavations at Fyrkat, including knives, forks and a number of funky little keys which may have opened chests in which tax contributions were stored. Artefacts from a burial ground next to the fortification include gifts and treasures that the dead were to take with them on their final journeys, and indicate that although the Jelling Stone inscriptions (see p.311) suggest that Danes had already been converted to Christianity during Fyrkat's era, the people that died here were all still heathen. This discovery has led to much speculation about how – and from which direction – Christianity was introduced to Denmark – for more on this, see "Contexts", p.389.

Seeing the Fyrkat sites and the museum will easily take up a day, so you might want to spend a night in Hobro. The only **hotel** is the luxurious *Amerika* (⑦98 54 42 00, ⑭www.hotelamerika.dk; ❼), Amerikavej 48, a fifteen-minute walk from Hobro harbour, with a scenic path leading down to the Mariager Fjord. The nearby *Hobro Vandrerhjem* **hostel**, at no.24 (⑦98 52 18 47, ⑭www .danhostelnord.dk/hobro; dorms 150kr, doubles ❸; mid-Jan to mid-Dec) is a much cheaper option. *Hobro Camping* (⑦98 52 32 88, ⑭www.hobrocamping .dk-camp.dk), Skivevej 35, has eight fully-equipped four-person cabins starting at 275kr per day. A 2km path from the campsite leads straight to Fyrkat.

Rold Skov and Rebild Bakker

Some 15km north of Hobro, bands of conifer and beech spreading over the rolling hills mark the beginning of **ROLD SKOV**, a lovely place to spend a leisurely day taking in fresh air and beautiful scenery. Covering some eighty square kilometres, the forest stretches from Arden in the south to the small town of Støvring in the north, and from Terndrup in the east to the E45 motorway in the west – a huge woodland in Danish terms, and one that's associated with innumerable myths and stories such as that of the infamous highway robbers of Rold, who would graciously serve their victims a shot of snaps before robbing them bare. Seventy-five percent of the forest is in private hands, with limited public access, but the remaining state-owned and managed area is open to the public, with some outstanding hiking trails as well as a circular 23km mountain-bike route around the perimeter.

In the middle of Rold Skov and 20km north of Hobro, the small town of **REBILD** is a convenient place to base yourself while exploring the area. It's reachable by train from Aalborg; you need to get off at Skørping, then take bus #104. The town sits at the edge of the pretty, heath-covered **Rebild Bakker** hills, a part of Rold Skov that served as Rebild's common grazing land until 1912, when a group of Danish emigrées living in America purchased the land and presented it as a gift to the Danish government on three conditions: it had to remain in a natural state; it had to be open to the public; and Danish Americans were to be allowed to celebrate American holidays here. Today it's a **national park**, best known as the venue for massive **American**

Independence Day celebrations. Every July 4, festivities are staged at the *Gryden* ("cooking pot") natural amphitheatre – a short walk from the gate into the park in Rebild town – where a number of valleys run together; attendance numbers in 2006 reached the eight thousand mark. Many well-known names have appeared as keynote speakers, from Walt Disney and Danny Kaye (who played Hans Christian Andersen in the film *Wonderful Copenhagen*) to Richard Nixon, Walter Cronkite and Danish-American comedian Viktor Borge. Because of the event's high profile, the area around the entrance to Rebild Bakker has become something of a tourist trap year-round, heaving with elderly Danish-American tourists discovering their "home" country, and awash with souvenir shops and overpriced restaurants. Adjacent to the gates into the park, the tacky **Blokhusmuseet** (daily: June noon–4.30pm; July–Aug 11am–5pm; rest of the year open only on demand; 15kr; ⓦ www.rebildfesten.dk) is a recreation of Abraham Lincoln's log cabin, filled with mundane articles from 49 American states alongside facts about Danish migration to the US. More interesting is the **Spillemands Jagt og Skovbrugs Museet** (Fiddlers, Hunting and Forestry Museum: May–Aug daily 10am–5pm; Sept daily noon–5pm; Oct–April Sun 1–5pm; 25kr; ⓦ www.roldskovmuseerne.dk), also near the main entrance across from a large parking area. It gives an insight into the tough life of loggers and the region's infamous poachers, also known for their prowess as fiddle players. Although all of the labelling is in Danish, the displays give a good impression of the difficult living conditions here, and the region's isolation from the rest of Denmark. There's also a café and, should you fancy a bit of folk dancing, fiddle-accompanied sessions during the summer (July & Aug Wed 7–10.30pm; free).

Thanks to the Independence festivities, there's a surprising number of **places to stay** in diminutive Rebild, and it's the best place to stay whilst exploring the forest. Needless to say, booking on or near July 4 must be done years in advance. Most expensive is the *Comwell Rebild Bakker*, Rebildvej 36 (ⓣ98 39 12 22, ⓦ www.comwell.com; ❽/❻) by the main entrance to Rebild Bakker, which has a swimming pool and a fancy restaurant. Nearby at Rebildvej 23, the quaint, thatch-roofed **youth hostel**, *Rebild Vandrerhjem* (ⓣ98 39 13 40, ⓦ www.rebild-vandrerhjem.net; May–Sept; dorms 150kr, double ❸) has dorms and 21 newly refurbished en-suite rooms. The adjacent **campsite** (ⓣ98 39 11 10, ⓦ www.safari.dk-camp.dk) has four- and six-person cabins (from 400kr per day), and is open year-round. However, the most atmospheric place to stay is ⚑ *Rold Storkro*, Vælderskoven 13 (ⓣ98 37 51 00, ⓦ www.roldstorkro.dk; ❼), a traditional inn a few kilometres down the road towards Hobrovej; its **restaurant** is also especially good, with game in some guise on the menu every day.

Løgstør and Aggersborg

About 50km northwest of Hobro (via highway 29 or bus #57, changing at Aars for #109), the pretty fishing town of **LØGSTØR** sits on the southern bank of Limfjorden. Almost exactly halfway between Limfjorden's Skagerrak inlet to the west and its eastern outlet into the Kattegat, Løgstør is typical of the towns along the Limfjorden, and was established in the sixteenth century when herring fisherman settled here to set up their salting-houses on the beach. Although Løgstør is pretty enough in its own right, it's the area around town that's the real draw, with some interesting historical sites that can all be visited in a day. The highlight, and one of the country's most astonishing Viking remains (and northern Europe's largest), is just across Limfjorden. Bus #108 from Løgstør runs across the Aggersund bridge and along the minor road to Ullerup, going right past **Aggersborg** (no set hours; free), overlooking the Limfjorden from its hillside setting. Although the grassed-very rampart is all that remains, it's the

8

imposing size, symmetry and significant history that makes the site worth seeing. One of four similar structures – Fyrkat (see p.352), Trelleborg (see p.159) and Nonnebakken built by Harald Bluetooth in 980 or 981, Aggersborg is thought to have been another of his short-lived tax collection centres (for more on which, see p.352). Like Fyrkat, it's a perfectly circular complex with four access points, but at 228m wide, Aggersborg is more than double its diameter, and once encompassed an astonishing 48 longhouses in blocks of twelve, as oppose to Fyrkat's four blocks of four. Aggersborg's size, combined with its protected position on the Limfjorden and its ease of access to points west, east and north via the waterways hereabouts suggests that it was both the headquarters for taxation in the region and a political and military base from which relations with Norway and England were maintained. Adjacent to the rampart, a small building (unrestricted access) holds an informative display depicting – via sketches and drawings – what life within might have been like. Next to this, and with its cemetery bordering onto the rampart, is **Aggersborg Kirke** (daily 9.30am–4pm), a cute twelfth-century church with faint runic inscriptions on the walls of the nave and the northern chancel. It's thought to have been predated by a wooden church from the Viking era. The fact that no artefacts were uncovered when the oldest graves were excavated suggests that, unlike the inhabitants of Fyrkat, the people that lived at Aggersborg were Christians, so supporting the theory that Christianity was introduced to Denmark from England via the Limfjorden, rather than from Germany as was earlier though to be the case.

South of Løgstør on the Limforden's west bank, and a ten-minute walk from the centre, a more recent construction warrants a quick visit. Dug in the nineteenth century to replace the Limfjorden's silted-up channels (see p.281) and to allow large vessels to access the Limfjordslandet from Aggersund and Aalborg, the 5km **Frederik VII's Kanal** was only in operation for about fifty years, as the original Limfjorden channels opened up again at the turn of the century. Complete with a lock at each end and a swing bridge across it, the picturesque canal now stands in limbo, waiting to be called into action should the Limfjorden channel sand up again. It's a pretty place to go for a walk, and the canal keeper's house has been converted into **Limfjordsmuseet** (Limfjorden Museum; mid-June to Aug daily 10am–5pm; May to mid-June & Sept–Oct Sat & Sun 10am–5pm; 20kr; ⓦwww .limfjordsmuseet.dk), which focuses on fisheries and navigation on the Limfjorden since the Middle Ages. The highlight is the displays on the Limfjorden tradesmen ("*krejlere*") who, in the days when the fjord was the primary means of transporting goods, sailed up and down the fjord for weeks on end in their flat-bottomed barges, selling their wares in the villages along the banks. If you fancy **staying** in Løgstør, your best bet is the cosy old *Hotel du Nord*, Havnevej 38 (Ⓣ98 67 21 00, ⓦwww.hotel-dunord.dk; ⓞ), a stone's throw from Limfjorden, which has a good restaurant. Alternatively there's a **campsite** at Skovbrynet 1 (Ⓣ98 67 10 51, ⓦwww.logstor-camping.dk; Apr–Nov) five minutes' walk from the centre, which also has en-suite, four-person cabins.

It's a scenic bus ride (#50 or the faster #950X) along Limfjorden from Løgstør to Aalborg. Just before you reach the small town of Nibe, look out for the tiny peninsula of Sebbersund to the left. During the Viking era, this was a hugely important trading site where goods from Norway and England were landed and repacked before redistribution. Excavations on site indicate that this was where the first English missionaries arrived – and carbon dating of a Christian burial site here suggests that they arrived prior to the erection of Harald Bluetooth's Jellinge stone (p.311). This remarkable discovery has questioned the entire understanding of Denmark's conversion to Christianity. There's a small exhibition centre (unrestricted access; free) on site.

Some years ago, it was officially decreed that the Danish double "Aa" would be written as "Å". The mayor of Aalborg and many locals resisted this change, and eventually forced a return to the previous spelling of their city's name – though you may still see some maps and a few road signs using the "Å" form.

Aalborg and around

Hugging the south bank of the Limfjorden, **AALBORG** is the obvious place to spend a few days before venturing out to the wild countryside and stunning beaches of the far north. The profits from the seventeenth-century herring boom briefly made Aalborg the biggest and wealthiest Danish town outside Copenhagen, and much of what remains of the well-preserved **old Aalborg** – chiefly the area within Østerågade (commonly abbreviated to Østerå), Bispensgade, Gravensgade and Algade – dates from that era, standing in stark contrast to the new roads that slice through it to accommodate the traffic using the Limfjorden bridge, which links the old town to the northern suburbs and a couple of notable sights. Today, Aalborg is the main transport terminus for northern Jutland and thanks to the presence of Aalborg University in its outskirts, boasts the liveliest nightlife for miles around.

Arrival, information and city transport

Both long distance and local buses stop at the brand new **bus terminal**, near the **train station** at J.F. Kennedys Plads, ten minutes' walk southwest of the centre and within easy reach of Aalborg's hotels and main attractions. **Aalborg Airport** (Ⓦ www.aal.dk) is 7km northwest, and connected to the centre by metro bus #2 (every 15–30min). Although most of Aalborg is easy to explore on foot, you may find a **bus** easier for some of the outlying sights. Aalborg town buses come in two categories: "metro" (with fast direct links to the suburbs) and "by" (operating within the town centre). The local bus company Nordjyllands Trafikselskab operates a zonal system, with all of Aalborg encompassed within one zone (only the airport is in the next). A single ticket (*billet*; 16kr) is valid for one hour's travel within two zones; a multi-ride ticket (*klippekort*; 104kr) is valid for ten trips in any two zones, and can be used by more than one person at once. A more enjoyable option is to get around by **bike**; the most central rental outlet is Munk's Efterfølger, Løkkegade 25 (Ⓣ 98 12 19 46, Ⓦ www.munk-aalborg.dk). The helpful **tourist office** is centrally located at Østerågade 8 (mid- to end June & Aug Mon–Fri 9am–5.30pm, Sat 10am–1pm; July Mon–Fri 9am–5.30pm, Sat 10am–4pm; Sept to mid-June Mon–Fri 9am–4.30pm, Sat 10am–1pm; Ⓣ 99 30 60 90, Ⓦ www.visitaalborg.com), and has information about the entire north Jutland region including bus and ferry timetables; they also give out excellent free cycling maps of Aalborg and northern Jutland.

Accommodation

If you want **to stay** in Aalborg, be aware that bargain-priced hotels are hard to find. The tourist office has a list of private rooms in the area that go for a fixed rate of 325kr per night (plus a 25kr fee if you want the tourist office to make the booking). For a little more adventure, catch the half-hourly five-minute ferry (Ⓣ 98 11 78 23; 6.30am–11.15pm; 16kr) from near the campsite (bus #13 from the centre) to the small island of **Egholm**, where there's free camping under open-sided shelters. In the twelfth century, the island was King Valdemar's hunting ground; today, it's largely farmed but still virtually uninhabited and criss-crossed by hiking trails. In summer, there's a good restaurant (see p.365) by the small ferry harbour.

Central Aalborg

The places below appear on the Central Aalborg map, p.359.

🏃 **Park Hotel** J.F. Kennedys Plads 41 ☏98 12 31 33, ⓦwww.park-hotel-aalborg.dk. Beautifully renovated old railway hotel across from the bus terminal, with dark wood panelling and soft carpets throughout. Rooms are a little small and come with either a shower or, for 50kr more, a bath tub. There's a popular streetside café out front in the summer. ❼/❻

Park Inn Chagall Vesterbro 36-38 ☏98 12 69 33, ⓦwww.parkinn.com. On a busy thoroughfare leading onto the bridge crossing Limfjorden, this modern hotel is within easy reach of the train station and centre. The comfortable rooms are all colourful with, inevitably, plenty of Chagall reproductions on the walls. Use of the fitness centre in the basement included in the rates. ❼/❻

Prinsen Prinsensgade 14–16 ☏98 13 37 33, ⓦwww.prinsen-hotel.dk. Comfortable (albeit basic) hotel across from the train station, with a range of rooms of different shapes and sizes, a cosy in-house bar and free parking. They also offer reduced rates for the fitness centre across the street. ❻

Radisson SAS Limfjord Ved Stranden 14-16 ☏98 16 43 33, ⓦwww.radisson.com/aalborg.dk. A stone's throw from the centre and overlooking Limfjorden, this is the city's most luxurious hotel, with its own casino and two restaurants. As you'd expect in this price range, rooms are stylishly decorated, with the emphasis on modern Scandinavian design. ❾/❼

Greater Aalborg

The places below appear on the Greater Aalborg map, p.362.

Aalborg Sømandshjem Østerbro 27 ☏98 12 19 00, ⓦwww.hotel-aalborg.com. This family-oriented former seamen's home is among the city's cheapest year-round options. It's rather plain-looking inside and out, but the rooms are fully modernized and clean. Fifteen minutes' walk east of the centre, or take bus #11, #14, #17 or #19. ❻

Aalborg Vandrerhjem Skydebanevej 50 ☏98 11 60 44, ⓦwww.danhostelaalborg.dk. Large youth hostel to the west of the town, beside the marina on the bank of the Limfjorden, which has dorms (150kr), en-suite doubles (❹), doubles sharing facilities (❸) and rustic cabins sleeping up to five (520–600kr). Take bus #16 from the centre to Skydebanevej, from where it's a ten-minute walk.

🏃 **Krogen** Skibstedvej 4 ☏98 12 17 05, ⓦwww.krogen.dk. Homely place, some 2km west of the city centre, with a large leafy garden; some rooms have shared facilities. Buses #15 and #38 run closest to the hotel; get off at Constancevej and continue along it for five minutes. ❺

Strandparken Skydebanevej ☏98 12 76 29, ⓦwww.strandparken.dk. About 300m from the youth hostel and next door to Aalborg's open-air swimming pool, this appealing campsite stretches down to the banks of Limfjorden, and has a dedicated section for potentially noisy teenagers as well as a range of cabins sleeping four to six people (from 550kr per day). Mid-April to mid-Sept.

The old town

The tourist office on Østerågade is as good a place as any to start exploring Aalborg, with one of the town's handsome seventeenth-century structures standing directly opposite. The **Jens Bangs Stenhus** is a grandiose five storeys of Dutch Renaissance style and, incredibly, has functioned as a pharmacy ever since it was built. Jens Bang himself was Aalborg's wealthiest merchant but was not popular with the governing elite, who conspired to keep him off the local council. The host of goblin-like figures carved on the walls allegedly represent the councillors of the time, while another figure, said to be Bang himself, pokes out his tongue towards the former Rådhus, next door, the predecessor to the present eighteenth-century building further down Østerågade.

The commercial roots of the city are further evidenced within **Budolfi Domkirke** (June–Aug Mon–Fri 9am–4pm, Sat 9am–2pm; Sept–May Mon–Fri 9am–3pm, Sat 9am–noon; ⓦwww.aalborgdomkirke.dk), just a few steps behind the Jens Bangs Stenhus and easily located by its bulbous spire. Inside, there's a list (rather than the more customary portraits of nobles) of the town's merchants during the 1660s. A small but elegant specimen of sixteenth-century Gothic, the cathedral itself is built on the site of an eleventh-century wooden church; only a few tombs from the original remain, embedded in the walls close to the altar. Apart from these and the aforementioned list, there's little to see inside, but plenty to hear when the electronically driven bells ring out each hour, sending a cacophonous racket across the old square of **Gammeltorv**, on which the cathedral stands. Across the square from the cathedral, the **Aalborg Historiske Museum** (Tues–Sun 10am–5pm; 20kr; ⓦwww.aahm.dk), Algade 48, offers some solid coverage of Aalborg's unique mercantile history. The prehistoric section is fairly routine, so it's best to head straight for the local collections, which give the lowdown on Aalborg's early prosperity; the Renaissance-era room from 1602, with immaculately carved wooden panels from floor to ceiling, clearly illustrates the immense wealth in Aalborg at the time. You might also want to check out the impressive collection of silverware and glasswork, with examples of the different designs from the various glass-working centres in north Jutland – look out for the funky armadillo-shaped bottle.

On the opposite side of the cathedral square, just off Adelgade, the **Helligånds-kloster** (Monastery of the Holy Ghost) dates from the fifteenth century, before the herring boom. Much of the building now serves as a senior citizens' home, and the remainder can be seen only on one of the informative English-language guided tours (mid-June to mid-Aug Mon & Fri 2pm; 40kr). These take in the refectory, largely unchanged since the monks were thrown out in 1536 during the Reformation, and the small Friars' Room, the only part of the monastery into which nuns (from the adjoining nunnery) were permitted entry. Indeed,

---

Danish emigration to the US

The story of the **Danish emigration** to the New World in the late nineteenth and early twentieth centuries doesn't have any of the desperation of the exodus that followed the Irish potato famine or any of the political and religious connotations of the persecution of Jews and Reformed Church members in Russia and Holland respectively. Rather, it was simply a matter of searching for new opportunities, prompted chiefly by the **US Homestead Act** of 1862, which promised immigrants 160 acres of free prairie land once US citizenship had been granted after five years spent living in the country. Denmark's population was booming at the time, and most of the emigrants enticed to the US were young labourers whose only alternative hope of acquiring agricultural land in Denmark was to drain flooded marshlands or dig up barren heathlands, both extremely laborious options promising very low yields. With such poor opportunities at home, huge numbers of Danes opted to try their luck in pastures new, and it's estimated that some 300,000 people emigrated from Denmark between 1825 and 1930, the majority heading for mid-west American states. Kristian Jensen became Chris Johnson and Poul Hansen, Paul Hansson. While most of the emigrants settled into **farming** life, others carved out more public careers. One of Denmark's more famous emigrants was one **Jakob Riis**, originally from Ribe. A carpenter by trade, he left Denmark penniless in 1870 and settled in New York, where he took up photography and scraped a living as a news reporter, illustrating articles about conditions for the urban poor with his own photos. His ground-breaking photo-journalism work gained him great notoriety, and he later became a good friend of President Theodore Roosevelt, who deemed him "New York's most useful citizen" on account of his endless endeavours. The mass exodus from Denmark had very little negative impact on life at home, and ties between the two countries became strong, as they remain to this day.

CENTRAL AALBORG

0   100 m

Limfjorden

N

NORTH JUTLAND

8

STRANDVEJEN

TOLDBODGADE

VED STRANDEN

STRANDVEJEN

SLOTSPLADSEN

Aalborghus
Slot

VESTERÅ

JOMFRU ANE GADE

KATTESUNDET

HOLBERGSGADE

VESTERBRO

GRAVENSGADE

BISPENSGADE

CW OBELS
PLADS

ØSTERÅGADE

SLOTSGADE

NYTORV

FJORDGADE

Helligåndskloster

ADELGADE

ALGADE

Jens Bangs
Stenhus

Aalborg
Historiske
Museum

GAMMELTORV

Budolfi
Domkirke

ALGADE

BREDEGADE

NØRREGADE

Gråbrødrekloster
Museet

VINGÅRDSGADE

GRØNNE-
GANGEN

JERNBANEGADE

SANKELMARKSGADE

HJELM
ERSTALD

MØLLEÅGADE

MØLLE-
PLADS

ARKIVSTRÆDE

Vor Frue Kirke

Dansk
Udvandrerarkiv

DANMARKSGADE

RANTZAUSGADE

BOULEVARDEN

PRINSENSGADE

CHRISTIANSGADE

Train
station

J.F.
KENNEDYS
PLADS

Bus Station

EATING, DRINKING & NIGHTLIFE

Café 1000 Fryd	6
Café Ministeriet	16
Cube	7
Duus Vinkjælder	12
Fyrtøjet	3
Holles Vinstue	14
Il Restaurante Fellini	2
The Irish House	9
Isbryderen Elbjørn	1
Jensens Bøfhus	11
Kunst og Spaghetti	15
Mortens Kro	17
Pakhuset	5
Provence	4
Rendez-vous	8
Studenterhuset	13
Søgaards Bryghus	10

ACCOMMODATION

Park	D
Park Inn Chagall	B
Prinsen	C
Radisson SAS Limfjord	A

this was one of the few monasteries where monks and nuns were allowed any contact at all, a fact which accounts for the reported hauntings of the Friars' Room – reputedly by the ghost of a nun who got too friendly with a monk, and was buried alive in a basement column as punishment (the monk was beheaded). Most interesting, however, are the **frescoes** of various biblical characters – dramatically posed images of Jesus, Samson, Mary and St John the Baptist amongst others – that cover the entire ceiling of the chapel.

The rest of old Aalborg lies to the east across Østerågade, and is mainly residential, with just a few exceptions. The sixteenth-century **Aalborghus Slot** (grounds daily 8am–9pm; free) is technically a castle but looks much more like a country manor, and has always had an administrative rather than a military function. Aside from the grounds, which make a scenic spot for a picnic, the castle is mainly worth visiting for its severely gloomy **dungeon** (May–Oct Mon–Fri 8am–3pm; free), to the right from the gateway, and the **underground passageways** (daily 8am–9pm; free) that run off it. From the castle, Slotsgade leads to the maze of narrow streets around **Vor Frue Kirke** (Mon–Fri 9am–2pm, Sat 9am–noon; ⓦwww.vorfrue.dk); give the church a miss in favour of a look at the meticulously preserved houses hereabouts, many of which have been turned into upmarket craft shops. The best are along the L-shaped Hjelmerstald: the ungainly bulge around the midriff of no.2 accounts for its nickname of "the pregnant house".

If you're here for the Rebild fest (p.354) and of Danish descent, or particularly interested in Danish social history, you might want to visit the **Dansk Udvandrerarkiv**, nearby at Arkivstræde 1 (Danish Emigration Archives: Mon–Thurs 9am–4pm, Fri 9am–2pm, until 8pm Mon May–Sept; ⓦwww.emiarch.dk). The story of Danish migration overseas is recorded through immense stacks of files and books; given enough background facts, details of individual migrants can be traced.

There is one last point of interest in this part of town. East of Østerågade, at Algade 19, the **Gråbrødrekloster Museet** (Franciscan Friary Museum: Tues–Sun 10am–5pm; 20kr) gives some interesting insight into Aalborg's early history; set below ground, it's entered by way of an elevator where you pay your entrance by inserting a coin into the slot. The remains of the friary were discovered during archaeological excavations in the 1990s, and the foundations and walls that were unearthed, alongside skeletons from nearby graveyards, form the bulk of the display. Models and information panels give an excellent introduction to Aalborg in the Viking and Middle Ages.

Out from the centre

There's a lot more to Aalborg than its old town, with several interesting options reachable by short bus rides from the centre. Among the highlights is **Nordjyllands Kunstmuseum** (North Jutland Art Museum: Tues–Sun 10am–5pm; 40kr, Dec free; ⓦwww.nordjyllandskunstmuseum.dk), south of the centre on Kong Christians Allé and housed in a stunning white marble building designed by the celebrated Finnish architect Alvar Aalto which is worth a look in its own right, with every tiny detail, from door handles to window panes, meticulously chosen to best accentuate the building's pristine lines. Perfectly illuminated with natural light from all sides, the works on show comprise one of the country's better modern art collections, strikingly contemporary in both form and content. Alongside numerous Danish pieces, it features works by Max Ernst, Andy Warhol, Le Corbusier and, imposingly stationed next to the entrance, Claes Oldenburg's wonderful *Fag-ends in a Colossal Ashtray*. After leaving the museum, you can get a Danish pastry and coffee plus a grand view over the city and the Limfjorden by hopping in the lift to the top of the 103m **Aalborgtårn** (Aalborg Tower: July daily 10am–7pm; April–June & Aug to late Oct daily 11am–5pm; 25kr; ⓦwww. aalborgtaarnet.com), on the hill just behind. Built for the Industry Exhibition of 1932, it was meant to have been torn down immediately afterwards, but proved so popular that it stayed. A small exhibit inside tells its story. To get here, take bus #15, or head out on foot along Vesterbro; the walk from the centre will take fifteen minutes.

From the tower, you can see what looks like a set of large concrete bunkers on a hill to the southeast of the city. This is the **Gug Kirke** (Mon–Fri 9am–4pm; ⓦwww.gugkirke.dk) on Nøhr Sørensens Vej 7, designed by Inger and Johannes Exner and completed in the early 1970s. It's one of the most unusual churches in the country: except for the iron crucifix and the wooden bell tower, the whole thing, including the font, pulpit and altar (decorated by a collage of newspapers from the days when porn was legalised in Denmark) is made of concrete. The idea was to blend the church into the mostly high-rise parish it serves, and for it to function as a community centre: the perfectly square interior can be turned into a theatre, while the crypt doubles as a café and youth club. It's unique enough to merit a closer look; take bus #13 from the city centre, or catch #14 from the art museum and change onto #13 at Jyllandsgade.

One kilometre south of the tower, the **Aalborg Zoo** (daily: March 10am–3pm; April & Sept–Oct 10am–4pm; May–Aug 9am–6pm; Nov–Feb 10am–2pm; 95kr; ⓦwww.aalborgzoo.dk), Mølleparkvej 63, is a nice enough place to take kids on a sunny day, although the usual array of caged animals can be a bit depressing. The zoo has made something of a name for itself with its bizarre new acquisition, a depopulated African village, complete with schoolhouse and artificial baobab tree. The "village" is set in a so-called African savannah, and has an indoor section where you can see the newly acquired warthog, and an outdoor section where ostrich, antelope, zebra and giraffe roam semi-freely. Bus #11 goes here from the centre, or it's a ten-minute walk from the tower through the Møllepark.

Aalborg Marine Museum and Forsvars-og Garnisons-Museum

West of the centre, en route to the campsite and hostel, are two museums primarily aimed at military buffs. Closest to the centre, on the banks of the Limfjorden next to the marina at Vestre Fjordvej 81, the **Aalborg Marine Museum** (daily: May–Aug 10am–6pm, Sept–April 10am–4pm; 65kr; ⓦwww.aalborgmarinemuseum.dk) is a collection of top-notch naval paraphernalia

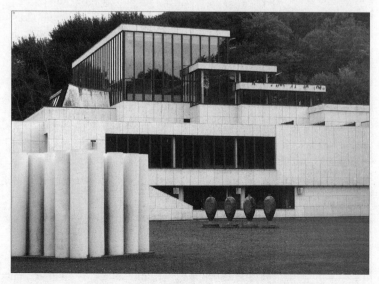

△ Nordjyllands Kunstmuseum

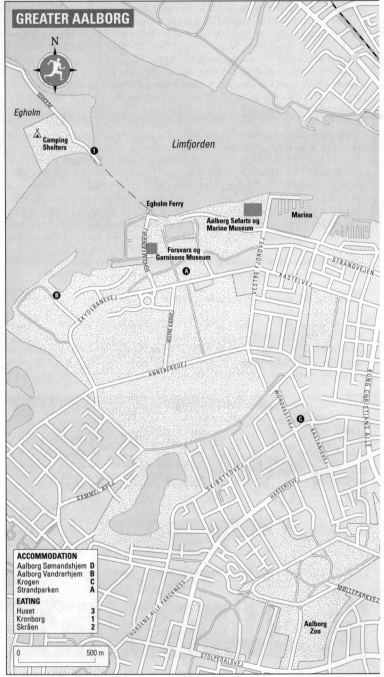

GREATER AALBORG

N

Egholm

Camping
Shelters

Limfjorden

Egholm Ferry

Aalborg Søfarts og
Marine Museum

Marina

Forsvars og
Garnisons Museum

STRANDVEJEN

VESTRE FJORDVEJ

KASTELVEJ

SKYDEBANEVEJ

VESTRE KÆRVEJ

KONG CHRISTIANS ALLE

ANNEBERGVEJ

NORDJESTVEJ

KASTANJEVEJ

SKIBSTEDVEJ

HASSERISVEJ

GAMMEL ALLÉ

MØLLEPARKVEJ

Aalborg
Zoo

THORSENS ALLÉ PARKKNESS

STOLPEDALSVEJ

ACCOMMODATION
Aalborg Sømandshjem   D
Aalborg Vandrerhjem   B
Krogen   C
Strandparken   A

EATING
Huset   3
Kronborg   1
Skråen   2

0   500 m

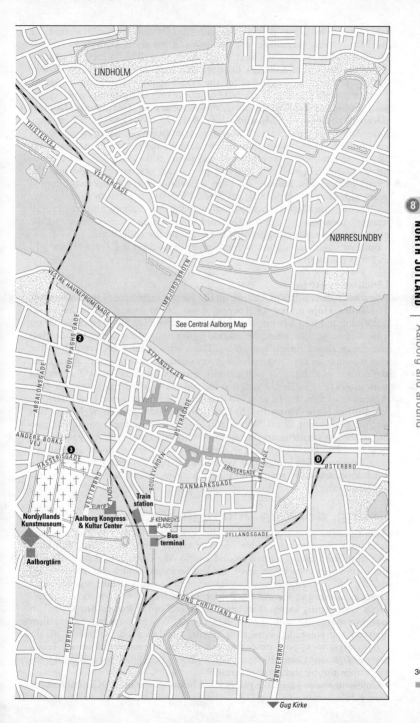

LINDHOLM

THISTEDVEJ

VESTERGADE

NØRRESUNDBY

VESTRE HAVNEPROMENADE

LIMFJORDSBROEN

See Central Aalborg Map

POUL PAGHS GADE

2

STRANDVEJEN

ØSTERÅGADE

ABSALONSGADE

ANDERS BORKS VEJ

3

HASSERISGADE

BOULEVARDEN

SØNDERGADE

LØKKEGADE

D

ØSTERBRO

DANMARKSGADE

VESTERBRO

EUROPA PLADS

Train station

Nordjyllands Kunstmuseum

Aalborg Kongress & Kultur Center

JF KENNEDYS PLADS

Bus terminal

Aalborgtårn

JYLLANDSGADE

HOBROVEJ

KONG CHRISTIANS ALLE

SØNDERBRO

▼ Gug Kirke

put together by a group of enthusiasts. Initially only centered around the last Danish-built submarine, the *Springeren*, it has since expanded to house the world's fastest torpedo boat, the *Søbjørn*, as well as interesting exhibits about the history of Aalborg's boatyard and harbour. You can clamber into both vessels and get a real feel for the claustrophobic conditions on board. Further westwards, past the campsite on the corner of Egeholm Færgevej, the road leading to the Egholm ferry, the **Forsvars-og Garnisons-Museum** (Defence and Garrison Museum; daily: April–May & Oct–Nov 11am–4pm; June–Aug 10am–5pm; 45kr; ⊛www.forsvarsmuseum.dk) has more of a hardcore military flavour, with guns, uniforms, tanks and medals galore. Again, it's all very touchy-feely – you get to crawl inside tanks and jets – and is a real hit with children, while the displays give some interesting insight into the town's military past. Aalborg has been a garrison town for over two hundred years and, since World War II, has housed the largest garrison in the country. During the German occupation of Denmark, Aalborg also had crucial strategic importance, with the Germans constructing three airstrips and the enormous hydroplane hanger that today houses the collection.

Both museums are a good twenty-minute walk from the centre; buses #12 and #13 pass nearby.

Lindholm Høje

A few kilometres north of Aalborg on the Nørresundby side of the Limfjorden, **Lindholm Høje** (unrestricted access) is one of the country's most important late Viking and Iron Age burial grounds; it's a captivating place, especially if you visit at dawn or dusk when the magical light on the south-facing hillside gives the site an almost surreal appearance. There are a number of very rare Viking ship monuments here – cremation graves demarcated with stones arranged in the outline of a ship – as well as more than six hundred burial sites marked with stones or mounds, the oldest at the top of the hill, the newest at the foot. A number of these burial sites and dwellings are reconstructed in the adjacent **Lindholm Høje Museum** (April–Oct daily 10am–5pm; Nov–March Tues & Sun 11am–4pm; 30kr), which also gives some far-reaching insight into life in the site's settlements during the Viking era. From Aalborg, you can get here by metro bus #2 (every 15–30min), or walk there in under an hour: go over the Limfjorden bridge, take Vesterbrogade into Thistedvej, turn right into Viaduktvej, and carry straight on until Vikingvej, which leads to the museum, appears on the left.

Eating, drinking and nightlife

Aalborg comes alive at night, when partygoers from all over northern Jutland (and from near-teetotal Sweden) descend on the city. The **eating**, **drinking** and **nightlife** scene is centred around Jomfru Ane Gade, a small street close to the harbour between Bispensgade and Ved Stranden. Jomfru Ane was a noblewoman and reputed witch who, because of her social standing, was beheaded rather than burnt at the stake – though nowadays, the street is more synonymous with getting legless than headless. Several of the Jomfru Ane Gade bars host live music; just walk along, listen, and decide which appeals. An excellent alternative, if you fancy something grander and less alcohol-oriented, are the international rock, pop, dance, musical and theatre performances at *Aalborg Kongres & Kultur Center*, Europa Plads 4 (☎99 35 55 65, ⊛www.akkc.dk), the city's main theatre and concert venue.

Unless otherwise stated, the places listed below appear on the Central Aalborg map, p.359.

Cafés and restaurants

Café Ministeriet Mølleplads 19 ☎98 19 40 50, ⓦwww.cafeministeriet.dk. Cool, busy new café with a large terrace on Mølleplads, and DJs playing on the square on summer evenings (Fri & Sat). Food starts with breakfast and brunch from 10am until noon (one hot, one cold brunch, both 98kr, neither vegetarian), and continues with the usual array of salads, sandwiches, burgers and snacks, as well as excellent hot meals such as mozzarella-stuffed chicken for 89kr, and baked salmon for 79kr. Mon–Thurs & Sun 10am–midnight, Fri & Sat 10am–2am.

Fyrtøjet Jomfru Ane Gade 17–19 ☎98 13 73 77, ⓦwww.fyrtojet.dk. Of the many eateries along Jomfru Ane Gade, this enduring place is the most reliable, with traditional steak-and-two-veg meals as well as good smørrebrød. The two-course lunch menu is excellent value at 80kr. Daily 11.30am–11pm.

Holles Vinstue Algade 57 ☎98 13 84 88. The city's best smørrebrød, as well as filling traditional Danish meals starting at 45kr. Mon–Fri 11am–8pm, Sat 11am–4pm.

Huset Hasserisgade 10 (see Greater Aalborg map, p.369) ☎96 33 81 00, ⓦwww.huset.dk. A short walk west of the centre, this cultural centre offers outdoor gigs and barbecues in a large courtyard during summer, and an indoor café serving a well-prepared dish of the day (48kr; 5.30–7pm), with a veggie option each Wed. Mon–Fri 12.30–10.30pm.

Il Restorante Fellini Vesterå 13 ☎98 11 34 55, ⓦwww.fellini.dk. Genuine Italian restaurant with good-value pizzas and pastas; the novel Italian brunch (Mon–Sat 11.30–3pm), is a delightful alternative, more of a lunch platter with a selection of Italian cheeses, ham, fresh bread, fruit and cake (99kr including coffee). Mon–Sat 11.30am–11pm, Sun 5–10pm.

Isbryderen Elbjørn Strandvejen 6B ☎43 42 34 34, ⓦwww.isbryderen-elbjorn.dk. Docked across from the *Radisson SAS Limfjorden* hotel, this converted icebreaking ship is the place to head for if you're looking for something different. As well as a top-class seafood restaurant and a lounge bar serving late brunch(Tues—Sat 11am—3pm; 99kr) and a huge range of snaps, there's also an on-board glass blowing artist, a smokehouse and a small exhibit depicting the ship's icy history. Tues–Sat 11am–11pm.

Jensens Bøfhus C.W. Obels Plads 3 ☎98 16 63 33, ⓦwww.jensens.com. The usual steaks and salads, served up in a beautiful half-timbered former merchant's house dating from 1585. Mon–Thurs 11am–10.30pm, Fri & Sat 11am–11.30pm, Sun 11.30am–10.30pm.

Kronborg Egholm 1, Egholm (see Greater Aalborg map, p.362) ☎98 17 27 75, ⓦwww.kronborg-egholm.dk. This quintessentially Danish restaurant on the small island of Egholm (see p.384 for transport details) serves tasty traditional fare such as all-you-can-eat *stegt flæsk* (98kr) for lunch and the speciality fried eel (208kr) for dinner. May–Sept noon to 11pm.

Kunst og Spaghetti Vestebro 65 ☎98 12 63 13, ⓦwww.kunstogspaghetti.dk. Small, friendly place, with changing art exhibits on the walls, serving good-value home-made pizzas and pastas. Daily 5–10pm.

Mortens Kro Mølleå Arkaden, Mølleå 4–6 ☎98 12 48 60, ⓦwww.mortenskro.com. Despite the "kro" in the name, this isn't a traditional inn, but rather a gourmet restaurant set in a temple to modern Scandinavian design. Food comes at a price, starting at 228kr for a dish of fried lemon sole served with shellfish and a veggie gratin, but it's worth every øre. Mon–Sat 5.30pm–11pm.

Provence Ved Stranden 11 ☎98 13 51 33, ⓦwww.restaurant-provence.dk. Around the corner from Jomfru Ane Gade, the tightly packed tables at this romantic French restaurant overlook the Limfjorden. Serving only food from Provence – even the bread is imported – there's an excellent selection of seafood, including a mouth-watering platter for two at 248kr. Book ahead. Mon–Thurs & Sun 5–10pm, Fri & Sat noon–10.30pm.

Søgaards Bryghus C.W. Obels Plads 1A ☎98 16 11 14, ⓦwww.soegaardsbryghus.dk. Excellent combination of microbrewery, restaurant and butcher's shop, offering juicy steaks (from 188kr) and home-made beer; you can also stock up on cold cuts for the picnic basket. Mon–Wed 11am–11pm, Thurs 11am–midnight, Fri & Sat 11am–1.30am.

Bars, clubs and live music venues

Café 1000 Fryd Kattesundet 10 ☎98 13 22 21, ⓦwww.1000fryd.dk. Cultural centre hosting alternative-type international live bands two to three nights a week; also a popular café/bar with a twice-daily happy hour (3–4.30pm & 10–11pm). Tues & Wed 2pm–midnight, Thurs –Sat 2pm–2am.

Cube Jomfru Ane Gade 10 ☎98 10 33 10, ⓦwww.cubeonline.dk. The music at this fun if run-of-the-mill disco is predominantly R&B and house classics, and the dancefloor is packed throughout the night. Not a hangout for sober types. Fri & Sat 11pm–6am.

Duus Vinkjælder Østerågade 9 ☎98 12 50 56. This atmospheric wine bar in the cellar of the Jens Bangs Stenhus is the perfect place for a

quiet evening drink. Mon–Wed 11am–midnight,
Thurs–Sat 11am–2am.

The Irish House Østerågade 25 ☏98 14 18 17,
Ⓦ www.theirishhouse.dk. Atmospheric Irish pub
housed in the former mayoral residence from 1616,
with live music (mostly Irish folk) Thurs–Sat, and a
wide range of beers and whiskies. Traditional Irish
stew is served until 6pm. Mon–Wed noon–midnight,
Thurs–Sat noon–3am, Sun 3pm–midnight.

Pakhuset Ved Stranden 9 ☏98 11 60 22,
Ⓦ www.pakhusetaalborg.dk. Old fashioned nightclub in a wood-beamed, red brick old warehouse
playing sing-along hits from the 1960s and
onwards. Fri & Sat 9pm–5am.

Rendez-vous Jomfru Ane Gade 5 ☏98 16 88 80,
Ⓦ www.rv.dk. A terrace-fronted street-level café,
with a raucous nightclub at weekends on the first
floor. Apart from your standard café-style fare of

brunch, sandwiches and coffee, the café also has
live music most weekends, while the nightclub
(minimum age 22) excels in colourful cocktails and
mainstream R&B, house and pop tunes. Café daily
10am–10pm; nightclub Fri & Sat 10pm–6am.

Skråen Strandvejen 19 (see Greater Aalborg map,
p.362) ☏98 12 21 89, Ⓦ www.skraaen.dk. A short
walk from the centre, this former tobacco factory is
a good place to catch gigs by better-known Danish
rock acts on two stages, the larger hall and the
smaller, more intimate café.

Studenterhuset Gammeltorv 11 ☏98 11 05 22,
Ⓦ www.studenterhuset.dk. The country's largest student-run music venue, with a café (shut
during student holidays) and live up-and-coming
mostly Danish bands and DJs playing three to four
nights a week. Music starts after 9pm. Mon–Sat
11.30am–late.

Listings

Airlines SAS ☏70 10 20 00 or ☏ 98 17 33 11;
Sterling Airlines ☏70 10 84 84; British Airways
☏75 33 15 11; Cimber Air ☏ 70 10 12 18.
Bus enquiries Local buses and regional buses
☏98 11 11 11; Abildskou's Aalborg–Copenhagen
coach reservations ☏70 21 08 88, Ⓦwww
.abildskou.dk.
Car rental Avis, J.F. Kennedys Plads 3 ☏98 13 30
99, and at Aalborg Airport ☏98 17 72 77; Europcar, Jyllandsgade 6 ☏98 13 23 55 and at Aalborg
Airport ☏ 98 17 53 55; Hertz, Jyllandsgade 28
☏ 98 17 15 99, and at Aalborg Airport ☏ 98 17
15 99.
Dentist Lille Borgergade 21, Nørresundby ☏25 20
29 00 (Mon–Fri 8am–3pm).
Doctors Call ☏70 13 00 41 or ask at the tourist
office for details of the doctor on call.
Exchange Bureau Forex, Gravensgade 9 ☏ 98
18 97 00 (Mon–Fri 9am–6pm, Sat 10am–3pm).

Hospitals There's a 24hr emergency department at
Aalborg Sygehus, Hobrovej 18–22 ☏99 32 27 08.
Internet cafés Boomtown, Nytorv 18 (Mon–
Thurs 11am–1am, Fri & Sat 11am–8am, Sun
11am–midnight; 25kr/hr); In the Matrix, J.F.
Kennedyarkaden 1F (daily noon–7am; 15kr/hr).
Markets There's a lively fruit, veg and flower
market every Wed and Sat on Ågade (7am–2pm).
Pharmacy Aalborg Budolfi Apoteket, Algade 60
☏98 12 06 77, is open 24 hours.
Police Politigården i Aalborg, Jyllandsgade 27
☏96 30 14 48.
Post office Algade 42 (Mon–Fri 9.30am–5.30pm,
Sat 9.30am–1pm).
Train enquiries Ⓦwww.dsb.dk has details of
all services; you can also call ☏70 13 14 15 for
regional and inter-city services; and ☏70 13 14 16
for international trains.
Travel agents My Travel, Vesterbro 32 ☏70 10 21
11, Ⓦwww.mytravel.dk.

Vendsyssel

North of Aalborg, the windblown, the triangular shaped **Vendsyssel** region
is roughly delineated by Limfjorden to the south and, to the northeast and
northwest, the two seas that the Limfjorden connects, the Kattegat and Skagerrak. The area is renowned for its infamous **Vendelbo** humour – quietly and
succinctly, without the faintest hint of a smile, you will find your leg pulled
when you least expect it. The region's most noteworthy castles, **Dronninglund**
and **Voergård**, make interesting detours on the way to unappealing **Frederikshavn** on the east coast. As a major transport hub, with ferries to Norway,
Sweden and the scenic island of **Læsø**, Frederikshavn is difficult to avoid. The

highlight of the area is **Skagen**, right at the northern tip, with a magical light reflecting from the two open seas. It's this light that made Skagen the haunt of Danish artists in the late nineteenth century, and today it holds a number of outstanding museums in their memory. To the southwest of Skagen, the wind-swept fishing town of **Hirtshals** marks the beginning of the **Jammerbugten bay** area, where lush green pastures give way to strangely compelling views of bleak moorland and windswept dunes. The main town here, although not on the actual bay itself, is **Hjørring**, a dullish place that's best for stocking up on supplies before heading out to the bay's string of excellent beaches, packed with frisky teenagers during the summer months. Thanks to its good ferry links with Norway and Sweden, both from Frederikshavn and **Hirtshals**, Vendsyssel is trisected by two fast motorways, making travel by car or bus between Aalborg and the major towns here quick and easy. The rail network, on the other hand, has lagged far behind the rest of the country, with the only rail link to Skagen zigzagging via Hjørring and Frederikshavn.

Dronninglund and Voergård

Heading north from Aalborg towards Frederikshavn, there are a few interesting sights en route that warrant a quick detour. First up is **Dronninglund Slot** (tours only: June to mid-July & late July to mid-Aug Mon–Fri & Sun 11am; 25kr; Ⓦwww.dronninglund-slot.dk), 5km off the main Frederikshavn road; turn off at Junction 16 Hjallerup and it's on the right just before the small town of Dronninglund; it's also served by buses #74 and #75 from Aalborg. A grand three-winged, yellow-and-white affair dating back to 1250, it was originally built as the Hundslund Kloster nunnery. Updated and rebuilt a number of times since then, it gained its current name in 1690 when King Christian V's wife, Queen Charlotte Amalie, bought it and lived here (Dronninglund translates as "queen's grove"). The current incarnation is a bit of a mishmash of different building styles, but magnificent nonetheless. If you manage to get on one of the infrequent tours, look out for the modern frescoes in the western tower by Valdemar Andersen, a pioneer within Danish poster-art – these colourful pieces are a rare diversion. The **castle church** (Mon–Fri 9am–4pm) dates from the twelfth century and is also endowed with beautiful frescoes, these from the fifteenth. There's a pricey restaurant in the castle (Mon–Sat from 6pm Ⓣ98 84 33 00, Ⓦwww.dronninglund-slot.dk) specializing in venison and seafood; main courses start at 175kr, and it's an impressive spot for a grand dinner.

Some 10km further up the motorway to Frederikshavn by the village of Voergård (turn right off junction 14), and also reachable via a picturesque back-road direct from Dronninglund that runs through the village of Dorf, the stunning red-brick, Renaissance **Voergård Slot** (mid-April to mid-June & Sept to mid-Oct Sat 1–4pm, Sun 11am–4pm; mid-June to Aug daily 10am–5pm; 65kr; Ⓦwww.voergaardslot.dk), built by the Dutch Renaissance architect Philip Brandin, was the envy of king Christian IV who was himself responsible for a fair few grand constructions. The imposing sandstone **entrance portal**, originally made for Frederiksberg Slot in Copenhagen, is particularly magnificent, with four half-pillars held up by fierce looking lions' heads. It was a gift from Christian's father, Frederik II, to Ingeborg Skeel, a noblewoman who gave the castle its current look, and who's said to still haunt the grounds. Inside, there's an astonishing collection of French furniture and art, with paintings by Rubens, El Greco, Raphael and Goya, and porcelain used by Louis XVI and Marie Antoinette during their captivity at the Temple fortress in Paris, where they stayed before facing the guillotine. These pieces were among a huge cache brought back from France (under much French scrutiny and discontent) by the last resident count, who was married to a French countess. The result is an unusual clash of styles, with the Renaissance building contrasting strangely with its heavy French furnishings.

Frederikshavn and Læsø

Some 65km northeast of Aalborg, **FREDERIKSHAVN** is a major international ferry port, with connections to Larvik and Oslo in Norway, and Göteborg in Sweden, and as such is usually full of Swedes and Norwegians taking advantage of Denmark's liberal drinking laws. Though it's not the most captivating of places, Frederikshavn is the region's transport hub; buses and trains to and from Skagen pass through, and it's also the departure point for ferries to the pretty island of **Læsø**, so you're likely to find yourself here at some point during your travels in north Jutland.

There are a few things worth checking out while here, however. If you only have half an hour to spare, you could make for the squat, white **Krudttårn** tower (June–Aug daily 10am–5pm; 15kr), on Havnepladen near the train station, which has maps detailing the harbour's (now ruined) seventeenth-century fortifications, of which the tower was a part, and a collection of weaponry, uniforms and military paraphernalia from the seventeenth to the nineteenth centuries. With more time on your hands, take the fifteen-minute ride on bus

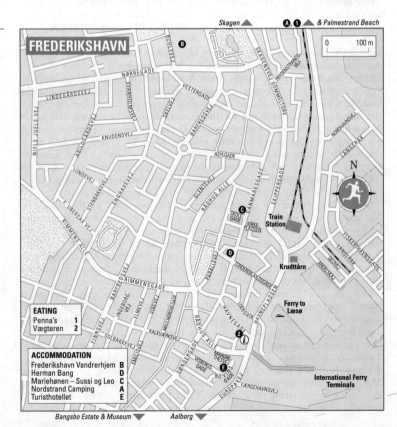

#3 to Møllehuset at the edge of the **Bangsbo Estate**, and walk on through the beautifully groomed botanic gardens to the **Bangsbo Museum** (Tues–Sun 10am–5pm; 40kr; Ⓦwww.bangsbo-museum.dk), set in the manor building on the southern fringe of the estate. Here, comprehensive displays chart the development of Frederikshavn from the 1600s alongside a slightly grotesque, but very engrossing, collection of pictures, bracelets, rings and necklaces made of human hair. The barns and outbuildings store an assortment of maritime articles distinguished only by the twelfth-century *Ellingåskibet*, a ship found north of Frederikshavn, plus a worthwhile exhibition covering the German occupation during World War II and the rise of the Danish resistance movement. The estate also encompasses a large **deer park** and **rock garden** (daily dawn–dusk; free) with various viewpoints and picnic spots. **Bangsbo Fort** at the northern perimeter has cannon and concrete gun emplacements built by the German occupiers during World War II – they never actually hit anything, however. You can experience the claustrophobic living conditions inside the German bunkers at the **Bunker Museum** (June–Aug Tues–Sun 10am–5pm; 30kr; tours at 1pm included in the price) inside the fort. Otherwise, on sunny days, you could do worse than join the rest of Frederikshavn at one of its many child-friendly **beaches**. Most popular is the lush palm tree-endowed Palmestrand, just north of the centre (ten minutes on bus #4), with beach volleyball courts and soft, powdery white sand.

Practicalities

Buses and **trains** terminate at the train station, on the eastern side of town on Skippergade; private trains to Skagen leave from here, too. Crossing Skippergade and walking along Kirkepladsen brings you to the town centre in a couple of minutes. The **ferry** docks, off Havnepladsen, are equally central. The modern, glass-fronted **tourist office**, nearby on the corner of Havnegade and Havnepladsen (July & Aug Mon–Sat 9am–6pm, Sun 9am–2pm; Sept–June Mon–Fri 9am–4pm, Sat 11am–2pm; Ⓣ98 42 32 66, Ⓦwww.frederikshavn-tourist.dk) rents out **bicycles** (75kr/400kr per day/week; book in advance) and can help with **private accommodation**, from 300kr per room per night, plus a 25kr booking fee. With a steady stream of international travellers passing through Frederikshavn there's a wide and surprisingly affordable range of places to stay; we've listed some of the best options below.

There are also a number of good places to **eat out** in Frederikshavn. For fresh fish, marinated herring and the occasional lunchtime jazz session, head for *Penna's* (Ⓣ98 43 82 98, Ⓦwww.pennas.dk; daily noon–3pm), overlooking the marina and just north of the centre at Nordre Strandvej 48. The best dinner option is *Vægteren* (Ⓣ98 42 17 34, Ⓦwww.vaegteren.dk; Tues–Thurs & Sun 5pm–10pm, Fri & Sat 5pm–midnight), Havnegade 8, with Danish/French inspired cuisine; it's also a good bet for a quiet evening **drink**. For a more raucous night out follow the hordes of Norwegians and Swedes, usually to be found drinking their way across town.

Accommodation

Frederikshavn Vandrerhjem Buhlsvej 6 Ⓣ98 42 14 75, Ⓦwww.danhostel.dk/frederikshavn. About 1km north of the centre, this slightly uninspiring hostel has dorms (100kr) and doubles (❷), some en suite. It's two minutes by bus #801 from the station – get off at the corner of Hjørringvej and Vestergade.

Herman Bang Tordenskjoldsgade 3 Ⓣ98 42 21 66, Ⓦwww.hermanbang.dk. Atmospheric old hotel a short walk from the ferry dock, with an array of light and breezy rooms, some sharing bathroom facilities. The in-house wellness centre, with spa, stone massage and much more, makes it an ideal place to regroup, and there's a popular Italian-American restaurant. ❻

Mariehønen – Sussi og Leo Skolegade 2
☎ 98 42 01 22, ⓦ www.hotelmariehoenen.dk. A
short way from the train station, this is a basic
but well-run place with en-suite rooms as
well as some with shared facilities. The owners,
Leo and Sussi, are something of an oddity in
Denmark, both loved and hated as dreadful
entertainers. ⑤

Nordstrand Camping Apholmenvej 40 ☎ 98 42
93 50, ⓦ www.nordstrandcamping.dk. Luxurious
campsite 3km north of the centre (bus #4) near the
marina and Palmestrand beach. April to mid-Oct.
Turisthotellet Margrethesvej 5 ☎ 98 42 90 55,
ⓦ www.turisthotellet.dk. Small, newly renovated
hotel a stone's throw from the ferry harbour; the
en-suite rooms come with a small fridge. ⑥

Læsø

With a total land area of just eighteen square kilometres, **LÆSØ** is not a place
to head for if you're seeking roaring nightlife or cultural stimulation, but if
rural calm in a beautiful setting appeals, then the island will deliver in droves.
Although its livelihood is almost entirely based on tourism, the majority of
the islanders (some 800 in total), would much rather keep the peace and quiet
of their beautiful island to themselves. This says something about both the
island and the islanders. There's no special treatment for tourists here – what
you see is what you get – but if you can accept that, the outstanding beaches,
low-key attractions and distinctly rural Vendelbo vibe make for a memorable
experience.

The ferry from Frederikshavn docks at the town of **VESTERØ HAVN**,
little more than an enlarged village spread around the harbour, which was built
in 1872 with the compensation islanders received when Læsø lost its status as
the last place in Denmark where home distillation of alcohol was legal. Vesterø
Havn is home to Læsø's tourist office (see p.372), and its bike rental outlet
(see p.372) comes in handy if you opt to explore the island by bike in a day
and catch the last ferry back. From Vesterø Havn, bus #840 makes the ten-
minute journey along Byrumvej to the island's main town, **BYRUM**, which
has nothing much to distinguish it other than a few shops and places to eat. It
is, however, just north of **Rønnerne**, a mosaic of tidal mudflats, salt marshes

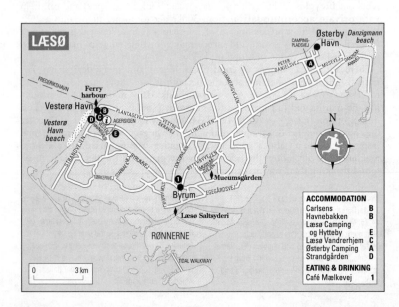

△ Salt shack, Læsø

and coastal heathland which supports significant insect and bird populations, and is perfect for hiking, cycling or horseback riding – keep an eye on the tide, though, as it comes in fast and floods the mudflats. You can also explore Rønnerne by way of an excellent four-hour tractor-bus tour (mid-June to Aug at 1pm; 120kr; ☎98 49 91 56, ⓦwww.roennerbussen.dk), which departs from the main square in Byrum – guides point out all the sights.

Thanks to the high salinity of the marshes, the Rønnerne area was also where the island's **salt manufacturing** industry was established in the early Middle Ages, while Læsø was still the property of the cathedral of Viborg. Within the hundreds of small shacks built here, a large basin of marsh-water was kept under a constant boil, evaporating the water to leave crystallized salt. Unfortunately, the amount of firewood required to keep all the basins bubbling meant that Læsø was soon stripped of all its trees, and by 1652, salt manufacturing had been banned. Today, the area bears clear evidence of its past, with small squares of land sunk into the marshes where the salt shacks once stood. For the sake of tourism, and to keep local history alive, traditional methods have recently been revived on the edge of Rønnerne at **Læsø Saltsyderi** (mid-April to May & mid-Sept to Oct daily 10am–2pm; June to mid-Sept daily 10am–4.30pm; Nov to mid-April Mon–Thurs 10am–2pm, Fri 9am to noon; free; ⓦwww.sydesalt. dk). With three basins on the constant go, the experience is enhanced by a mix of smoky fumes and damp swampy air. The salt produced here is of extremely high quality, and all of Denmark's top restaurants swear by it; you can buy a sample at the small shop on site.

Back in Byrum, a ten-minute bike ride along the road out of town in the opposite (northeast) direction toward Østerby Havn will take you to the **Museumsgården** (mid–April to mid–June Tues–Sun & Sept–Oct 11am–3pm; mid-June to Aug daily 10am–4.30pm; 35kr; ⓦwww.laesoe-museum.dk), Museumsvejen 3, a highlight amongst Læsø's clutch of minor museums. An old seaweed-thatched farmstead, it has been left exactly as it was when the last inhabitant moved out some sixty years ago – and she didn't change it much during her lifetime either. With no electricity and displaying the astounding assortment of gadgets necessary to make absolutely everything from scratch, stepping inside feels like walking into a time capsule – you can almost sense the hard work and misery that dominated life here.

Although it's hard to believe today, given the dense pine plantations of **Læsø Klitplantage**, which dominate the northern half of the island, Læsø was still completely denuded just eighty years ago. Since then, the establishment of the plantations has ensured that there's now enough firewood to feed the southern salt manufacturers and fuel many of the islanders' central heating systems. A positive side-effect of the deforestation, however, was the so-called "desertification". The lack of vegetation meant that the lighter clay and loam content of the island's soil was quickly washed or blown away, leaving only the heavier sand to establish coastal dunes on the island's northern half – and ultimately leading to Læsø's stunning sandy **beaches**, of which **Danzigmann** is one of the best. It's located on the northeastern tip, 4km east of **ØSTERBY HAVN**, the smallest of the island's three towns, but as the entire north coast is one long strip of sand, there's nothing to stop you from picking your own private spot. All the beaches on Læsø are sandy and shallow, and, after stormy days, sprinkled with lumps of amber that make for wonderful beachcombing.

Practicalities

The only way of getting to Læsø is the **ferry** from Frederikshavn (☏98 49 90 22, ⓦwww.laesoe-line.dk; 3–6 daily; 1.5hr); only return tickets are available (130kr), which one could cynically interpret as the islanders' insurance that you'll leave again. Læsø's **tourist office** (April to mid-June & Sept Mon–Fri 9am–2pm, Sat 10am–noon; mid-June to Aug Mon–Fri 9am–4pm, Sat & Sun 10am–3pm; Oct–March Mon–Fri 9am–2pm; ☏98 49 92 42, ⓦwww.laesoe-tourist.dk) is close to the Vesterø Havn ferry terminal at Vesterø Havngade 17, and has useful free maps of the island. All bus transport on Læsø is free; the sole bus route (#840) linking the three main towns departs roughly once an hour from Vesterø Havn, less frequently during weekends and school holidays. However, bikes are easily the best way of **getting around**; you can rent them at Jarvis Ny Cykelservice (☏98 49 94 44), Vesterø Havnegade 29, a short walk from the ferry terminal and tourist office on the main road to Byrum. They're also available at Marina Park Cykleudlejning, at the marina in Østerby Havn (☏40 21 40 03). Should the idea of **horseback riding** on the beach or through Rønnerne grab your fancy, head for Rønnergården, Egegårdsvej 4 (☏98 49 14 39, ⓦwww.naturridning.dk), or Krogbæksgård, Storhavevej 8 (☏98 49 15 05, ⓦwww.rideferie.dk); both are close to Byrum, and offer holiday packages as well as straight rides.

There is a relative abundance of **accommodation** on Læsø, although places are generally small and, thanks to the influx of visitors in the tourist season, often fully booked – it's a good idea to reserve in advance. The tourist office has a list of **private rooms** and **holiday-home rentals**. All of Læsø's hotels double as **restaurants**. *Carlsens Hotel* (daily 11am–11pm) has excellent seafood starting at 135kr for fresh Læsø plaice, while in Byrum, *Café Mælkevej* (Mon–Sat 11am–9pm, Sun 11am–4pm, closed Jan & Feb; ☏98 49 19 01), set in the town's old diary, does traditional Danish meals from 50kr.

Accommodation

Carlsens Havnebakken 8, Vesterø Havn ☏98 49 90 13, ⓦwww.carlsens-hotel.dk. Small hotel, overlooking the harbour and within spitting distance of the ferry terminal; all the rooms have shared facilities. ⑤

Havnebakken Havnebakken 12, Vesterø Havn ☎98 49 90 09, ⓦwww.havnebakken.dk. Atmospheric place next door to *Carlsens*, with a range of different rooms (some sharing bathroom facilities); the more expensive ones overlook the harbour. ⑥

Læsø Camping og Hytteby Agersigen 18, Vesterø Havn ☎98 49 94 95, ⓦwww.laesoe .dk-camp.dk. Appealing campsite, some twenty minutes' walk from the ferry terminal, housing a small village of four-person self-contained log cabins starting at 395kr per day and 2295kr per week. May–Sept.

Læsø Vandrerhjem Lærkevej 6, Vesterø Havn ☎98 49 91 95; ⓦwww.laesoe-vandrerhjem.dk.

Lovely hostel ten minutes' walk from the harbour (follow the signs) with dorm beds (150kr) and doubles (④). May–Sept.

Strandgården Strandvejen 8, Vesterø Havn ☎98 49 90 35, ⓦwww.hotel-strandgaarden. dk. Quaint thatch-roofed hotel near a stunning beach, with a range of different rooms, the cheapest sharing bathroom facilities. Room and dinner packages are available. Mid-April to mid-October. ⑤

Østerby Camping Campingpladsvej 8, Østerby Havn ☎98 49 80 74, ⓦwww.oesterbycamping.dk. Just 200m from a gorgeous beach, with log cabins sleeping six for 350kr per day, and bike rental for residents. Mid-May to Aug.

Skagen and around

Forty kilometres north of Frederikshavn, perched on a narrow peninsula at the very tip of Jutland (and Denmark) **SKAGEN** sits amid a desolate landscape of heather-topped, windswept sand dunes, its houses painted a distinctive bright yellow. Sunlight seems to gain extra brightness as it bounces off the two seas that collide just offshore, a phenomenon that attracted the renowned **Skagen artists** to the area in the late nineteenth century. Their time here, and the work they produced, is the focus of most of Skagen's cultural attractions. The town's tranquil setting, meanwhile, highlighted by the imposing landscapes that surrounds it, has ensured that it has become a popular holiday destination in the summer, when hotels and restaurants are packed to the limits and pre-booking accommodation is essential. Visiting outside the peak period gives you a much better chance of experiencing the area's unique scenery and atmosphere.

The town and around

Skagen was transformed from a small fishing community to the fashionable and popular holiday destination of today by the arrival – and subsequent success – of painters Michael Ancher and P.S. Krøyer, and writer Holger Drachmann during 1873 and 1874. These early pioneers were later joined by Lauritz Tuxen, Carl Locher, Viggo Johansen, Christian Krogh and Oskar Björck, and the group became known as the **Skagen Artists**. They often met in the bar of *Brøndum's Hotel*, off Brøndumsvej, and the then-owner's stepsister, Anna, herself a skilful painter, soon married Michael Ancher. The grounds of the hotel now house the **Skagens Museum** (April–Sept daily 10am–5pm; Oct–March Wed–Sun 10am–3pm; 60kr; ⓦ www.skagensmuseum.dk), which contains the most comprehensive collection of the Skagen artists' work anywhere in the world. The majority of the canvases depict local coastal scenes, capturing subtleties of colour enhanced by the area's strong natural light. Many of the paintings, particularly those of Michael Ancher and Krøyer, are outstanding, but it's the work of Anna Ancher, perhaps the least technically accomplished, which often comes closest to achieving the naturalism that these artists sought. Paintings such as her *Pigen i Køkkenet* ("The Girl in the Kitchen") stand out, with the bright Skagen light shining through yellow curtains onto the central figure.

There's more on the Skagen artists a few strides away at Markvej 2–4, where **Michael & Anna Anchers Hus** (May–Sept daily 10am–5pm; April & Oct daily 11am–3pm; Nov & Feb–March Sat 11am–3pm; 50kr; ⓦ www .anchershus.dk), the Anchers' former home, has been restored with the intention of evoking the atmosphere of their time, but the assortment of squeezed tubes of paint, sketches, paintings, books, ornaments and piles of canvases is not particularly captivating unless you're an avid fan. Equally, you could easily miss the **Drachmanns Hus** (May Sat & Sun 11am–3pm; June–Sept daily 11am–3pm; 25kr; ⓦ www.drachmannshus.dk) on the other

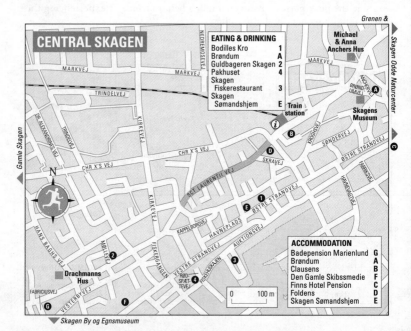

Skagen By og Egnsmuseum

side of town, ten minutes' walk from the centre at Hans Baghs Vej 21, where writer Holger Drachmann lived from 1902. There's a large collection of Drachmann's paintings and sketchbooks, although he was best known for his lyrical poems – at the forefront of the early twentieth-century Danish Neo-Romantic movement. Such was Drachmann's cultural importance that, on his death, the major Danish newspaper *Politiken* devoted most of its front page to him; facsimiles are on display.

Skagen does have more to it than its artistic associations, however, and its prior incarnation as a remote rural fishing community is well documented at the **Skagens By og Egnsmuseum** (Skagen Town and Regional Museum; March–April & Oct Mon–Fri 10am–4pm; May–June & Aug–Sept Mon–Fri 10am–4pm, Sat & Sun 11am–4pm; July Mon–Fri 10am–5pm, Sat & Sun 11am–4pm; Nov–Feb Mon–Fri 11am–3pm; 35kr; ⓦ www.skagen-bymus.dk), P.K. Nielsensvej 8–10, a fifteen-minute walk south of the centre along Sct Laurentii Vej (or the much nicer Vesterbyvej). Built on the now-stabilized sand dune from which local women would watch for their husbands returning from sea during storms, the displays on local fishing techniques are reinforced with photos showing huge numbers of fish strewn along the quay prior to being auctioned. The most interesting displays are set in the auxiliary buildings, where rich and poor fishermen's houses have been reconstructed: the rich house includes a macabre guest room, kept cool to facilitate the storage of bodies washed ashore from wrecks, while the poor man's dwelling makes plain the contrast in lifestyles: it possesses just two rooms to accommodate the fisherman, his wife and fourteen children.

Skagen Odde Naturcenter and Grenen

There are a few more attractions outside Skagen town proper, all of which are anchored around the region's stunning and wild landscape, and well worth seeking out. At the northern outskirts of Skagen, via a half-hour walk along Sct Laurentii Vej or by Skagen Bybus buses from the station during summer, you'll reach Batterivej and the **Skagen Odde Naturcenter** (daily: mid-June to mid-Aug 10am–6pm; mid-Aug to mid-June 10am–4pm; 65kr; ⓦ www.skagen-natur.dk), set in a serene building designed by Danish architect Jørn Utzon, best-known for the Sydney Opera House. The flat concrete structures with black capped roofs blend beautifully into the surrounding heath-covered dunes, and one quickly gets the impression that the exhibit inside is just an excuse to show off the unusual building itself. The displays explore how the natural forces around Skagen – sand, water, wind and light – interact with each other – something that's very evident just outside the centre's concrete walls.

The forces of nature can be further appreciated some 4km north of Skagen (reachable via hourly Skagen Bybus bus during summer) at **Grenen**, the northernmost tip of Denmark and the meeting point of two seas – the Kattegat and Skagerrak. From the bus stop and car park at the end of Fyrvej, the Sandormen tractor-drawn bus (April–Oct; 15kr return) runs regularly along the beach to the tip, though it's nicer to walk the half-kilometre. The spectacle of their clashing waves (the seas flow in opposing directions) is a powerful draw, although only truly dramatic when the winds are strong. At other times, the magical light reflecting off the two seas makes Grenen a beautiful place to relax for a while. On your way back, spare a thought for Holger Drachmann (see opposite), a man so enchanted by the thrashing seas here that he chose to be buried in a dune close to them. His tomb is signposted from the car park. There's a further reference to arts in the adjacent car park, where the **Grenen Kunstmuseum** (daily: May to mid-June 11am–3pm; mid- to end June & mid- to end Aug 11am–4pm; July 10am–5pm; early to mid-Aug 10am–4pm; 40kr; ⓦ www.grenenkunstmuseum.dk) is devoted to more recent Skagen artists such as Axel and Eva Lind, best known for their clunky, almost African-looking sculptures. By the main entrance, Carl Milles' elegant bronze sculpture of a balancing man is even more captivating.

Gamle Skagen

Not to be confused with Skagen, **Gamle Skagen** (known to local elders as **Højen**), is a completely different town with a very different vibe. On the opposite (western) side of the peninsula to Skagen, some 4km distant, Gamle Skagen is endowed with wide sandy beaches that offer some of the best sunset views in the country, and which have long attracted the Danish jet-set. This is almost exclusively the preserve of the rich and famous (including the royal family), and awash with chic holiday homes and posh restaurants. It's a pleasant enough place to cycle to (no buses run here), especially to watch the sun set or to enjoy a slap-up meal, but it can feel a bit contrived and lacks the vital feel of Skagen.

The sand dunes and around

Further down the peninsula from Skagen and Gamle Skagen, and stretching from coast to coast, the **Skagen Klitplantage**, a pine plantation established on the area's dunes at the beginning of the last century to stop the sand from drifting. Crisscrossed by signposted paths, the rolling, tree-covered dunes are an enjoyable place for a hike or bike ride. Off to the right as you enter the Klitplantage from Skagen (follow the red-signposted path), is **Den Tilsandede Kirke**, the "Buried Church" (June–Aug daily 11am–5pm; 10kr), a perfect illustration of why the dunes needed stabilizing. Its name is somewhat misleading, since all that's here is the tower of a fourteenth-century church, built in what was then a minor agricultural area. From the beginning of the sixteenth century, the church was assaulted by vicious sandstorms; by 1775 the congregation could only reach the building with the aid of shovels. In 1810 the nave and most of the fittings were sold, leaving just the tower as a marker to shipping – while not especially tall, its white walls and red roof are easily visible from the sea. The original church floor and cemetery lie buried beneath the sands, though you can go into the unfurnished interior.

The incredible severity of the storms becomes even more obvious 2km south of the church (follow the green path), where the huge **Sandmilen** migratory dune is on the last leg of its travels across the peninsula, blowing sand straight

---

Migratory sand dunes

Migratory dunes have blown across the northern tip of Denmark – from west to east – since time immemorial, constantly changing the shape of the coastline. With every dune that passes, agricultural land underneath is destroyed and unfortunate farmers have to start over again on bare land. About a hundred years ago, the people of Skagen town became so fed up with the town's isolation – there were no rail links and the road was constantly made impassable by sand drifts – that they donated some land and asked the government to stabilize the area in return for a new road and rail link. Plantations were duly established south of Skagen (today's **Skagen Klitplantage**) at Bunkeren; however, a group of local environmentalists felt that it was ethically unacceptable to completely stop these strong forces of nature, and after much debate, **Råbjerg Mile was** left free to make its way slowly across the peninsula.

into the Kattegat. There's a much larger migratory dune, **Råbjerg Mile**, about 17km south of Skagen, midway between the east and west coasts and two stops from Skagen on the Frederikshavn train. A signposted path from the station leads through **Bunken Klitplantage** plantation to the dune. Covering one square kilometre, it's the largest in the country and harbours an enormous destructive force, with its four million cubic metres of sand moving at approximately fifteen metres per year. Råbjerg Mile is at the infancy of its journey across the peninsula – it's estimated that it will reach the Frederikshavn road by 2020, and the Kattegat by 2050, where it will blow out to sea as Sandmilen is doing today. Both dunes are stunning places to go for a walk – though for obvious reasons, there are no trails on either of them.

Practicalities

Privately operated **trains** to Skagen (Scanrail, Eurail and InterRail passholders get half-price fares), leave from Frederikshavn roughly once an hour. **Buses** stop at Skagen's **train station** on Sct Laurentii Vej, which also houses the **tourist office** (April–May & Sept–Oct Mon–Fri 9am–4pm, Sat 10am–2pm; June & Aug Mon–Sat 9am–5pm, Sun 10am–2pm; July Mon–Sat 9am–6pm, Sun 10am–4pm; Nov–March Mon–Fri 10am–4pm, Sat 10am–1pm; ☎98 44 13 77, ⓦwww.skagen-tourist.dk). There's **bicycle** hire next door at Skagen Cykeludlegning (☎98 44 10 70, ⓦwww.skagencykeludlejning.dk), and the Skagen Bybus town bus stops outside.

Staying overnight in Skagen is infinitely preferable to going back to Frederikshavn, and there are a number of options, though none is particularly cheap. **Private accommodation** (from 325kr upwards) can be arranged through the tourist office for a steep 75kr booking fee. All rooms are within a 3km radius of the centre and come without breakfast. There are plenty of **eating** options in Skagen – all of the hotels have good restaurants, though most of them are expensive. We've listed some of the better options below. For **music** and **drinking**, the two quayside restaurants form the core of Skagen's relatively sedate nightlife.

Unless otherwise stated. All of the places below are marked on the Central Skagen map, p.374.

Accommodation

Badepension Marienlund Fabriciusvej 8, Skagen ☎98 44 13 20, ⓦwww.marienlund.dk. Rustic, thatch-roofed farmhouse a short walk from the centre with a small range of rooms; those with a bathroom cost a little more. Closed mid-Nov to Feb. ❼

Brøndum Anchervej 3, Skagen ☎98 44 15 55, ⓦwww.broendums-hotel.dk. Well-known for its association with the Skagen artists, this is by far the most atmospheric spot around; the fact that few of the rooms have their own bathrooms and all are far from luxurious keeps the price of doubles down, but book well ahead in summer. Good food, too. ❼

Clausens Sct Laurentii Vej, Skagen 35 ☎98 45 01 66, ⓦwww.clausenshotel.dk. A traditional yellow-painted Skagen building dating from the nineteenth century, with a range of colourful

rooms, some en suite, some sharing facilities. The rooms are nothing to write home about, but it is centrally located. ❻

Den Gamle Skibssmedie Vestre Strandvej 28, Skagen ☎98 44 67 16, ⓦwww.den-gl-skibssmedie.dk. Set in the old ships' smithy near the harbour, this pretty place is a quieter alternative to the hotels in the town centre. The pleasant, spacious rooms are all en suite. April to mid-Dec. ❼

Finns Hotel Pension Østre Strandvej 63, Skagen ☎98 45 01 55, ⓦwww.finnshotelpension.dk. Just east of the centre, this unusual log cabin used to be a count's holiday home. It now houses five double rooms (and one single), all of which are packed with character; the cheapest has a shared bathroom in the hallway. No children. Closed mid-Oct to March. ❻

Foldens Sct Laurentii Vej 41, Skagen ⊕ 98 44 11 66, ⓦ www.foldens-hotel.dk. Yellow townhouse a stone's throw from the train station and tourist office, with a range of comfortable en-suite rooms – though as there's often live music in the café downstairs, it's not the best choice if you're after peace and quiet. ❼

Grenen Camping Fyrvej (see Around Skagen map, p.373) ⊕ 98 44 25 46, ⓦ www.grenencamping .dk. Right on the beach, on the road to Grenen, with cabins sleeping four at 360kr per day. May to mid-Sept.

Poul Eeg Camping Batterivej 21 (see Around Skagen map, p.373) ⊕ 98 44 14 70, ⓦ www .pouleegcamping.dk. Pretty campsite on the road leading to Skagen Odde Naturcentre, encircled by pine forest. May to mid-Sept.

Skagen Sømandshjem Østre Strandvej 2, Skagen ⊕ 98 44 25 88, ⓦ www.skagenhjem.dk. Next to the harbour, this former seamen's home has a range of basic rooms, some with shared bathrooms. ❻

Skagen Vandrerhjem Rolighedsvej 2 (see Around Skagen map, p.373) ⊕ 98 44 22 00, ⓦ www.skagenvandrerhjem.dk. West of the town centre, a short walk from Frederikshavnvej train station (the last stop before Skagen) with dorms (150kr) and doubles (❺), some en suite and others sharing bathroom facilities. Mid-Feb–Nov.

Eating, drinking and nightlife

Bodilles Kro Østre Strandvej 11, Skagen ⊕ 98 44 33 00, ⓦ www.bodilles.com. Cosy inn serving traditional Danish fare including outstanding seafood buffet lunches and dinners (159kr). Other specialities include a mean *bøf med løg*. Daily 10am–11pm

Brøndum Anchervej 3, Skagen ⊕ 98 44 15 55, ⓦ www.broendums-hotel.dk. With seating inside and in the beautiful hotel garden, and offering a legendary lunchtime herring platter (80kr). There's also a good selection of elaborately decorated smørrebrød (from 50kr a piece), and fresh fish on the evening menu (from 160kr). Daily 11.30am–10.30pm.

De 2 Have Fyrvej 42, Grenen (see Around Skagen map, p.373) ⊕ 98 44 24 35, ⓦ www .restaurantde2have.dk. In the same building as Grenen Kunstmuseum, with stunning views of both Skagerrak and Kattegat, this is a fine place for a bite of lunch after dipping your toes in both seas. The outstanding lunchtime platter with portions of herring, fried place, a beef burger and a selection of cheeses (129kr) is especially

recommended, as is the open prawn sandwich on fresh crusty bread for 79kr. Steak, fish and chicken dominate the dinner menu (from 159kr). May–Sept daily 11am–9.30pm.

Guldbageren Skagen Sct Laurentii Vej, Skagen 104 ⊕ 98 31 12 06. Bakery and café offering superb Danish pastries, sandwiches and fresh bread. You can either eat in, at tables in the adjacent room, or take out and enjoy the delights al fresco. Tues–Sun 7am–5pm.

Pakhuset Rødspættevej 6, Skagen ⊕ 98 44 20 00, ⓦ www.pakhuset-skagen.dk. Set in a former frozen fish warehouse, this seafood-oriented place has an upstairs restaurant offering great harbour views, and a café with outdoor seating downstairs. Fish at both is always fresh and the menu upstairs changes daily. If you're hungry and feeling flush, the three-course restaurant menu (345kr) is good value, including delights such as like lemon thyme grilled brill, or prawn bisque with wild mushrooms. The café does excellent pickled herring; there are also more substantial meals, but its speciality is *fiskefrikadeller* with rémoulade and cucumber (72kr), and there's live music most weekends. Feb–May & Sept–Dec 11am–midnight; June–Aug daily 10am–2am.

Ruths Gourmet og Brasserie Hans Ruths Vej 1, Gammel Skagen (see Around Skagen map, p.373) ⊕ 98 44 11 24, ⓦ www.ruths-hotel.dk. Set in the exclusive locale of Gammel Skagen, this French restaurant and brasserie with an award-winning chef offers some very fine food. Booking is essential in the "Gourmet" section, where fried turbot in escargot sauce costs 325kr, and a plate of strawberries with ice cream will set you back an astounding 150kr. There's no booking in the brasserie, and prices are a little more affordable: a salad Lyonnaise goes for 105kr. Daily 9.30am–midnight.

🏃 **Skagen Fiskerestaurant** Fiskehuskajen 13, Skagen ⊕ 98 44 35 44, ⓦ www .skagen-fiskerestaurant.dk. The superb fish dishes served up at this red wooden shack by the harbour are probably the best in Skagen, if not the entire country. The upstairs restaurant does oysters, lobster, bouillabaisse and the like, all freshly caught, starting at 255kr. Equally delicious are the fishy delights in the less formal downstairs *barstue*, with herring platters (78kr), smoked eel (95kr), fried plaice (85kr) and an array of other traditional fish dishes served for lunch and dinner, either inside or out on the quayside. The *barstue* is also a fine place for evening drinks, with live music every night in the summer. Restaurant: April Fri & Sat 6pm–midnight; May to mid-June & mid-Aug to Sept Thurs–Sat 6pm–midnight; mid-June

During the last weekend of June or the first weekend of July – generally on the same weekend as Zealand's Roskilde Festival (see p.146) – the entire town of Skagen becomes one big festival site. Although the dates of the two festivals coincide, there's never any competition between the two, as the **Skagen Festival** caters for a completely different audience. Since its inauguration in 1971, the event has drawn folk music lovers of all ages and, in the genre's tradition, it's a laid-back affair with emphasis on good music and good beer. Unlike most other festivals, tickets are sold for an evening at a venue, although concerts at the two large stages at the harbour and the town square are free. Musicians are mostly Danish, with a sprinkling of northern European and North American folk bands. Tickets cost between 75kr and 285kr – check ⓦ www.skagen-festival.dk for more details. Accommodation in Skagen during the festival is booked to the hilt, so you'll need to reserve well in advance.

to mid-Aug daily 6pm–midnight. Barstue: March, Oct & Dec Thurs–Sat 11am–10pm; April daily 11am–10pm; May–June & Sept daily 10am–11pm; July & Aug daily 9am–1am.
Skagen Sømandshjem Østre Strandvej 2, Skagen Ⓣ 98 44 25 88, ⓦ www.skagenhjem.dk. Good-

value café in the downstairs section of *Skagens Sømandshjem*, which does a filling breakfast buffet (68kr) and bargain meals throughout the day, including a special for 59kr, and homemade *biksemad* for 49kr. Mon–Fri 6.15am–8.30pm, Sat & Sun 7.30am–8.30pm.

The Jammerbugt coast and Hjørring

From Skagen, a minor road leads for about 25km from the east-coast town of Ålbæk and across to **Hirtshals**, which marks the beginning of the windswept, west-coast **Jammerbugt bay** area. Stretching down to Bulbjerg point, the bay's wide, sandy beaches attract holidaymakers in droves every summer. A little inland, the market town of **Hjørring** is the only settlement of any size hereabouts, and a great place to stock up on supplies before hitting the beaches. Thanks to centuries of sand drifts and migratory dunes blowing inland from the west, no roads run along the coastline here, so the best way of exploring is to hop on a bike – the relatively flat national cycle route #1 hugs the coastline.

Hirtshals

First and foremost a modern port town with huge international ferries departing to three destinations in Norway, **HIRTSHALS**' rugged charm lies mainly in its tough seafaring history, which has impacted deeply on the feel of the place. It took the locals over one hundred years to get permission from the Danish government to build today's harbour, which has served as Hirtshals' lifeblood since its completion in 1930, and is now one of the country's most active fishing ports. Prior to its construction, fishermen dragged their boats up onto the shore, something you can learn more about at the tiny **Hirtshals Museum** (mid-June to mid-Sept Mon–Fri 10am–4pm, Sat 10am–2pm; mid-Sept to mid-June Mon–Thurs 10am–4pm, Fri 10am–1pm; 20kr, ⓦ www.vhm.dk), housed in an old fishing cottage behind the harbour at Sophus Thomsensgade 6. With furnishings from 1912, its focus is on the harsh working conditions of the area's fishermen. You can learn more about why the waters here offer such rich pickings to the trawlermen at the **Nordsømuseet** (North Sea Museum: July & Aug 10am–6pm; Sept–June 10am–5pm; 110kr; ⓦ www.north-sea-museum.dk), Willemoesvej, a few kilometres east of the centre and a short (signposted) walk from Lilleheden station, which is two stops on the train back towards Hjørring (see p.383). Devoted to North Sea marine life and filled with aquaria and educational displays, its *pièce de résistance* is an impressive and enormous 4.5 million litre tank, a so-called oceanarium, where you can watch schools of North Sea fish swim around relatively freely. Outside, there's another huge tank housing grey and harbour seals, who have plenty of space to swim and frolic.

Although it's only 50km from Skagen to Hirtshals, it takes an astounding 2hr 30min and three trains (via Frederikshavn and Hjørring) to get here; the train station is next to the ferry harbour. Hirtshals' **tourist office** (mid-June to Aug Mon–Fri 9.30am–3.30pm, Sat 9am–5pm; Sept to mid-June Mon–Fri 10am–3pm, Sat 9am–2pm; ☎98 94 22 20, Ⓦwww.visithirtshals.com), Nørregade 40, is in the centre by the main roundabout, and has a list of private rooms and holiday homes for rent. Other **accommodation** options include the good-value, family-run *Hotel Skagerak* (☎98 94 60 40; Ⓦwww.hotelskagerak. dk; ❺), down the road from the tourist office at Nørregade 4B, while the stylish new *Hotel Hirtshals* by the harbour at Havnegade 2 (☎98 94 20 77, Ⓦwww .hotelhirtshals.dk; ❻) has elegant rooms, some with large windows overlooking the harbour. The *Hirtshals Vandrerhjem* youth hostel (☎98 94 12 48, Ⓦwww .danhostelnord.dk/hirtshals; dorm beds 150kr, doubles ❸–❹), Kystvejen 53, is a short walk west of the centre and near the beach; note that dorm beds are only available between June and August. A bit further along the same road at no.6, near the lighthouse, is the scenic ⚑ *Hirtshals Camping* (☎98 94 25 35, Ⓦwww .dk-camp.dk/hirtshals).

Along the Jammerbugt coastline

Hirtshals marks the beginning of the **JAMMERBUGT** coastline, endowed with a succession of holiday towns and beautiful sandy beaches – though note that the prevailing westerly winds and strong currents can mean that swimming is dangerous – ask around before you venture in. The strip of **beaches** begins at the outskirts of Hirtshals, a short walk from the hostel (see above). Continue along the beach for about 50m and you reach the pretty **lighthouse**, which is surrounded by German concrete **bunkers** and a battery from World War II, built as part of the Atlantic Wall defence line (for more on which, see p.285); you can wander in and out freely. About 15km further south, one long strip of sand, mirrored by national cycle route #1, lines the coast. Just inland, and 13km west of Hjørring (see p.383), the small fishing village of **Lønstrup** gained some uneasy notoriety in 1877 when, following an unusually heavy downpour, a mudslide washed six houses into the sea, to the great surprise of homeward-bound local fishermen who spotted the wooden buildings bobbing up and down in the water – fortunately, there were no fatalities. You'll find further evidence of just how strong the forces of nature are in these parts if you head south of town to the imposing **Lønstrup Klit** cliffs, which line the coast for 15km as far as Løkken (see opposite). Between twenty and a hundred metres high, they provide a scenic backdrop to the popular sandy beaches below, and the cycle route that runs parallel to the cliff edge offers some lovely perspectives over the bay. Driven by the unrelenting westerly winds, the crashing sea eats away a couple of metres of cliff each year, something that's very obvious just south of Lønstrup, where the pretty medieval church of **Mårup Kirke** is balanced delicately on the cliff's edge, having been built in the thirteenth century in the centre of a settlement which has long since dispersed. There's little of interest in the church itself, but among the tombstones in the churchyard are the graves of 33 of the 226 British sailors who perished when their frigate, *The Crescent*, was shipwrecked just offshore during a storm in 1808. Some 2km further south along the cliffs, the **Rubjerg Knude** lighthouse

△ Rubjerg Knude lighthouse

provides yet more proof of the destructive force of the westerly winds. When first built in 1900, it was 60m above sea level and 200m inland; by 1968, the wind-whipped sand drift had become so high that it was no longer visible from the sea, and it was decommissioned. It was then opened up as a museum on the dunes but, by 2002, even this had to be closed, as the drifting sand had blocked the door and made it impossible to get in and out. Today, it offers a superb photo opportunity, with the force of the wind incessantly changing the shape of the massive dunes in front.

At the southern end of Lønstrup Klit, where the cliffs melt into the beach, the small seaside resort town of **LØKKEN** is destination of choice for Danish teenagers on their first holiday away from mum and dad. Expect noisy all-night partying, especially during school holidays, when the town is completely geared towards making big bucks from the not-so-innocent teens. However, the host of **activities** available on Løkken's wide sandy beaches during the day – including kite flying, windsurfing, paragliding, beach volleyball and surfing – make them among the country's most lively, attracting even a post-teenage crowd who disappear into the many holiday homes once the sun has set. There are a host of places offering lessons and renting out kit within the Løkken town and at the campsites.

South of Løkken, the white sandy beaches continue in an uninterrupted strip to **BLOKHUS**, made up almost entirely of holiday homes, which line the beach and mean that the sand gets a bit overrun during the summer, though it feels impossibly desolate and remote during the rest of the year. It's some forty kilometres from Blokhus down to the limestone hillock at **Bulbjerg**, which marks the end of the Jammerbugt coast and provides a home to vast colonies of birds. National cycle route #1 runs inland slightly along this stretch of coast, through numerous pine plantations that have been established on the dunes to hold on to the shifting sands, and which offer a peaceful place to go for a walk.

Practicalities

There are no direct **bus** connections between Jammerbugten's coastal towns, so unless you have a car or are riding along national cycle route #1, you'll inevitably have to go inland in order to catch a bus along the coast. To get from Hirtshals to Lønstrup by public transport, catch the train back to Hjørring, and then bus #740 to Lønstrup. From Lønstrup to Løkken, it's bus #740 back to Hjørring, and then the #71 towards Aalborg. From Løkken to Blokhus, catch bus #71 to Pandrup, and then bus #200 from Aalborg to Blokhus. The only way to reach Bulbjerg is under your own steam, via cycle route #1 or the main road from Fjerritslev.

There's a good range of **accommodation** along the coast between Hirtshals and Løkken, and we've listed some of the better options below. The entire coastline is also **holiday home** territory; these are available for a minimum of a week's rental only, and if you want to stay in one during the holiday season, you'll need to book months in advance. Agencies such as Nordvestkysten (☎ 96 67 09 00, ⓦ www.nordvestkysten.dk) and Jammerbugtens Feriehusudlejning (☎ 98 24 66 00, ⓦ www.jammerbugten.com) have extensive lists of houses for rent starting at around 2500kr per week. In terms of standard accommodation, try the *Badehotel Lønstruphus* (☎ 98 96 00 66, ⓦ www.loenstruphus.dk; ⓿), Rubjergvej 2, an old-style beach hotel with basic, adequate rooms; it's halfway between Lønstrup town centre and Mårup Kirke, and a short walk from the cliffs and beach. Otherwise, Løkken is probably the most convenient place to base yourself while exploring the Jammerbugt coast – if you can stomach the nightlife, that is. In the centre, the *Klitbakken* (☎ 98 99 11 66, ⓔ hotel.klitbakken@privat.dk; ⓿), Nørregade 3, has balconied rooms and a popular café/bar downstairs. There's also the cheaper and more atmospheric *Villa Vendel* (☎ 98 99 14 56, ⓦ www.villavendel.dk; ⓿) in the town's old merchant's house at Harald Fischersvej 12, with five rustic rooms. However, if you want to join the teenage invasion, your best bet is to head for one of the town's **campsites**. *Løkken Campingcenter & Hytteby* (☎ 98 99 17 67, ⓦ www.loekken-hytteby.dk; June to mid-Sept) is a short walk from both the beach and town centre at Søndergade 69; ask to be dropped off at Junivej if you're arriving on bus #71. It has fully-equipped cabins sleeping four and starting at a whopping 3790kr per week. If you'd rather be right on the beach, *Løkken Strand Camping* (☎ 98

99 18 04, ⓦwww.loekkencamping.dk; mid-April to mid-Sept), 1km north of the centre at Furreby Kirkevej 97, has cabins sleeping five and six starting at 3000kr and 3500kr per week respectively. From mid-April to mid-June they're rented out on a daily basis for 125kr and 150kr respectively, plus a 65kr fee per person.

There are plenty of **eating options** in the towns along the coast. In Lønstrup, the best bet is *Caféen Lønstrup* (Tues–Thurs & Sun 11.30am–11pm, Fri & Sat 11.30am–1am; ⓣ 98 96 08 84, ⓦwww.cafeenloenstrup.dk) offering a range of well-prepared burgers, fish dishes and sandwiches (from 78kr) at lunch, and steaks galore for dinner. The café also hosts live bands most evenings in the holiday season, and has a good selection of foreign and local beers. *Restaurant Løkken Badehotel* (daily 11am–10pm; ⓣ 98 99 22 00, ⓦwww .restaurantlb.dk), on Løkken's central square at Torvet 8, has outdoor seating in the summer, and is a good bet for delicious lunchtime salads and sandwiches (from 75kr), and full three-course affairs at dinner. In terms of Løkken's infamous **nightlife**, there's plenty to choose from. During July, the building at the back of *Klitbakken* is converted into the *Crazy Daisy Beach Club* (ⓣ98 99 15 57, ⓦwww.daisy-lokken.dk; 11pm–late), a nightclub with sand-covered floors and a total of five bars plying the youngsters with booze until the early hours of the morning. There's also the hugely popular *Action House* (ⓣ99 67 67 10, ⓦwww.actionhouse.dk; mid-June to mid-Sept daily 11am–5am), on the outskirts of town at Industrivej 1, which has paintballing, go-carting and bowling as well as a nightclub, *Diskotek New York*, the largest in northern Jutland and occasionally used for international pop/rock concerts.

Hjørring

Moving inland from the beaches, some 20km southeast of Hirtshals and 25km northeast of Løkken, the pretty market town of **HJØRRING** has less of a holiday feel that the coastal towns, and though you're most likely to come here to stock up on supplies, a stroll around the centre makes a nice break from the sunblock-slathered sunbathers. A short walk from the train station along Dronningensgade, three imposing churches demarcate the old centre and indicate Hjørring's regional importance through the ages. The oldest, thought to date back to the eleventh century, is **Sct Olai Kirke** (Mon–Fri 8am–4pm), a Romanesque granite building with a white late-Gothic porch. Inside, on the north wall, there's an interesting painting – formerly part of the altarpiece – of a conversation between Jesus and a pensive Nikodemus, who doesn't appear completely to be persuaded by Jesus' arguments. A few hundred metres away, across to the western side of Nørregade (Mon–Fri 8am–4pm) is the largest and prettiest of the three, with a 1612 altarpiece tucked away into a deep, round vault that gives the building a cosy, cellar-like feel. Above the entrance, there's a beautiful fresco from around 1350 depicting St Christopher carrying a young Jesus on his shoulder, who in turn is holding the world in his hands. Across Store Kirkestræde, **Sct Catharinæ Kirke** (Mon–Fri 9am–4pm, Sat 9am to noon; ⓦwww.catharinae.dk) is believed to be the youngest of the three churches, dating from around 1250; it serves as Hjørring's parish church these days. It has been altered and rebuilt a number of times, most recently in the 1920s, but has still retained some medieval aspects in the shape and structure of its transept. Highlights inside include the gilded Jesus on the crucifix from 1275 and, hanging from the ceiling, a model of the three-masted wooden training ship *Danmark* which, for over seventy years, has sailed around the world crewed by children from troubled or disadvantaged backgrounds, as a means of inspiring them to find their feet in life. To learn more about the churches and the role they've played in the development of Hjørring from the Middle Ages up until today, head to the informative and mildly diverting **Vendsyssel Historiske Museum** (June–Sept daily 10am–5pm; Oct–May Tues–Sat 10am–4pm; 35kr; ⊛www.vhm.dk), a short walk down Lille Kirkestræde at Museumsgade 3, and housed in the old deanery and former school buildings. The region's distinctive windblown landscapes are depicted beautifully in the works on show at **Vendsyssel Kunstmuseum** (Tues–Sun 11am–4pm; 40kr; ⊛www.vkm.dk), P. Nørkjærs Plads 15, a short walk from the train station at the end of Jernbanegade. Recently rehoused in its impressive new premises, a large and totally revamped former factory, the collection of modern regional art includes some great pieces by Sven Egelund and Johannes Hoffmeister, whose landscape paintings beautifully portray the wide skies and that special light that Vendsyssel is famous for.

Once you've seen all the sights, you might be in the mood for a spot of **lunch**. An excellent option is the 🍴 *Blomstercafeen* (☎98 90 08 44; Tues–Sun 11am–3pm), at P. Nørkjærs Plads 16 near the art museum; if the sandwiches and light meals don't grab you, the mouthwatering pastries most certainly will. If you want to stock up on supplies before heading back to the beaches, the huge Føtex superstore is just around the corner at Springvandspladsen. Otherwise Østergade, the pedestrianized street that runs from Springvandspladsen, is lined with a wide assortment of shops.

Travel details

Trains

Aalborg to: Århus (2 hourly; 1hr 15min–1hr 35min); Copenhagen (2 hourly; 4hr 30min–5hr 9min); Frederikshavn (hourly; 1hr 8min–1hr 26min); Hjørring (hourly; 40min–46min); Hobro (2 hourly; 29min–40min); Randers (2 hourly; 47min–58min); Skørping (2 hourly; 22min–25min).

Frederikshavn to: Aalborg (hourly; 1hr 8min–1hr 26min); Copenhagen (9 daily; 5hr 47min–5hr 52min); Hjørring (hourly; 23min–33min); Skagen (hourly; 35min–40min); Århus (10 daily; 2hr 39min–2hr 44min).

Hirtshals to: Hjørring (hourly; 22min).

Hjørring to: Aalborg (hourly; 40min–46min); Frederikshavn (hourly; 23min–33min); Hirtshals (hourly; 22min).

Hobro to: Aalborg (2 hourly; 29min–40min); Randers (2 hourly; 16min); Skørping (hourly; 16min); Århus (2 hourly; 52min–56min).

Skagen to: Frederikshavn (hourly; 35min–40min).

Skørping to: Aalborg (2 hourly; 22min–25min); Hobro (hourly; 16min); Randers (hourly; 35min); Århus (hourly; 1hr 14min).

Buses

Aalborg to: Blokhus (hourly; 56min–59min); Copenhagen (3 daily; 4hr 45min); Dronninglund (hourly; 40min–52min); Esbjerg via Viborg and Herning (7 weekly; 3hr 40min); Løgstør (25 daily; 49min–1hr 11min); Løkken (hourly; 56min–1hr 8min); Odense via Hobro, Randers and Århus (4 weekly; 4hr) and via Hobro, Randers, Århus, Vejle and Kolding (1–2 daily; 4hr 20min); Thisted (8 daily; 1hr 40min).

Frederikshavn to: Esbjerg via Aalborg, Viborg and Herning (2–3 daily; 5hr 5min).

Hobro to: Løgstør (hourly; 1hr 32min–1hr 41min).

Hjørring to: Esbjerg via Aalborg, Viborg and Herning (3 weekly; 4hr 45min); Lønstrup (hourly; 25min–30min); Løkken (hourly; 25min–29min).

Skørping to: Rebild (hourly; 6min).

Ferries

Aalborg to: Egholm (2 hourly; 5min).
Frederikshavn to: Læsø (2–5 daily; 1hr 30min).
Læsø to: Frederikshavn (2–5 daily; 1hr 30min).

Flights

Aalborg to: Copenhagen (18 daily; 50min).

Contexts

Contexts

A brief history of Denmark

Spend any significant time in Denmark and it'll soon strike you that the country's history is entirely disproportionate to its size. Nowadays a small – and often overlooked – nation, Denmark ("Danmark") and the long line of monarchs who have ruled it have nonetheless played a central role in key periods of European history, firstly as the home of the Vikings, later as a medieval superpower and, most recently, as one of the wealthiest members of the EU. Markers to the past, from prehistory to the wartime resistance movement, are never hard to find, and equally easy to spot are the benefits stemming from one of the earliest welfare state systems and some of western Europe's most liberal social policies, advantages and conveniences that are nonetheless threatened, some feel, by governmental tendencies towards the extreme right – most notably in some of the most conservative policies on immigration, assimilation and mixed marriage in modern Europe.

Earliest settlements

While a handful of tools found in modern-day Denmark suggest that *Homo sapien* was roaming the foothills of Europe as early as 120,000 years ago, the earliest reliable archeological evidence of **human habitation** dates to a period some 50,000 years ago with the leftovers of a meal eaten near a lake in central Jutland – some fragments of deer bones that had been prised open for marrow – though it's unlikely that any settlements of this time were permanent, as much of the land was still covered by ice. From around 14,000 BC, things began to warm up, ushering in the end of the Ice Age, the melting ice creating the Baltic Sea – once a landscape of troughs, rifts and river valleys. By 11,000 BC the ice had completely gone and the warmer climate had enabled the growth of vast swathes of dense woodland and forest across Jutland, which soon became populated by herds of reindeer, elk and giant deer. Tribes from more southerly parts of Europe arrived during the summers to hunt reindeer for their meat and antlers, which provided raw material for axes and other tools. The hunters established the first permanent settlements and, as the climate continued to warm and the reindeer were pushed further north, small **Stone Age societies** began to crop up across southern Scandinavia; before long, advances in agriculture and husbandry methods led to farming communities covering much of the country. Arguably the most significant change in early Danish history occurred during the Neolithic period (3000–1500 BC), during which forests were cleared and land cultivation and livestock-herding became a staple of human life. A correspondingly more organized approach to society and religion soon followed, with farmers and herders living in villages, surviving on subsistence amounts of meat and wheat and barley products, and tempering their hard lives with a multitude of rituals and religious practices. They buried their dead in dolmens – great **megalithic tombs** – and made regular sacrifices to their agriculturally omnipotent gods in the form of flint tools, axes, amber beads, and pots filled with food. An astonishing number of these objects have survived, including clay vessels and some of the more solid flint tools, preserved in the peat bogs where they were first offered up to the deities.

△ Engraving of Odin on his throne

The earliest metal and bronze finds date from 1800 BC, the result of new trade with merchant communities in southern Europe. Foreign trade flourished during the Bronze Age, with bronze objects becoming a particularly desirable commodity: most notable among them is the Solvognen ("**Sun Chariot**"), a miniature bronze chariot and horse discovered in the Trundholm Bog and now held in Copenhagen's Nationalmuseet (see p.94). The splendour of such pieces suggests that Danish traders had extensive awareness of, if not contact with, the Mediterranean societies of Crete and Mycenae. Other excavations from this period have unearthed several *lur* – an S-shaped wooden horn blown to announce village meetings – and the preserved coffin of Egtved girl, a blonde teenage girl who lived around 1370 BC, found in a barrow in southeast Jutland (see p.94).

Iron made its first appearance towards the end of the Bronze Age, and by 500 BC it had come to replace bronze as the primary raw material for tools. At this time, conflicts between neighbouring communities became common as villages saught to secure more territory by plundering the land of others. But it was the threat of the advancing Roman Empire, which had launched an offensive into northern Germany in 5 AD, that galvanized these hitherto ad-hoc fighting units into groups that more resembled small armies, equipped with horsemen, archers, soldiers and sophisticated weaponry.

The Viking era

The need to fight the Romans never arose, as they were beaten back to beyond the Rhine by Germanic tribes before they could advance into Jutland. But internal battles for control over individual areas had seen the emergence of a ruling warrior class. Around 500 AD, a tribe from Sweden calling themselves *Dani* ("**Danes**") migrated southwards and took control of what became known as **Danmark**, an area of land that at that time included Jutland, Funen and Zealand, as well as Skåne in southern Sweden and the region surrounding the Oslofjord in Norway. The majority of people who lived on this land were farmers: the less wealthy paid taxes to the king, and those who owned large tracts of land provided the monarch with military forces. In time, a **noble class** emerged, receiving privileges from the king in return for their support, while law-making became the responsibility of the regional *ting*, a type of governing assembly consisting of district noblemen. Above the district *ting* there was a provincial *ting*, charged with the election of the king, the candidate for which could be any member of the royal family, a provision that nonetheless led to a high level of feuding and bloodshed.

The **Viking era** officially began in 780, when merchants and skilled peasant sailors from Viken, a small bit of land flanking the Oslofjord – they were known as *Víkingar* ("Vikings") on account of this provenance – began leading quick raids to the coasts of places like the Hebrides, Brittany and Frisia. Such merchants had become disgruntled when Scandinavian rulers began exacting large tariffs on the sales and purchases of goods that came through Danish waters, and rather than accept overlordship, they opted to follow the trading routes to the source of all wealth entering the country. Their contact with Western European traders had familiarized them with ship-building techniques and given them glimpses of the many internal conflicts plaguing numerous European kingdoms – political feuds and schisms that they were later able to exploit and profit from - although the earliest **Viking raids** were further afield, to places such as Iceland, Greenland, North Africa and, later, Constantinople and markets on the Caspian Sea. While common conceptions of the Vikings locate them as burly, helmeted barbarians ruthlessly engaging in bloody battle, raiding churches, kidnapping local women and generally wreaking havoc, such depictions tend to disregard the **enduring influence** they had on trade, language, and the political and cultural institutions of the countries and peoples with whom they came into contact.

Back on the home front, the **first Danish state** had been established by King Godfred around 800, though a century later the Norwegian chieftain **Harthacnut** conquered Jutland and began to expand eastwards over the rest of Denmark, establishing the foundations of the modern Danish nation – the oldest in Europe. The present Danish monarchy can be traced back to his son, Gorm the Old. There remains some speculation on exactly how and when Christianity arrived in Denmark: the evidence from the Jellinge Stone (see p.311) suggests that it arrived via Germany, but the presence of Viking burial sites in North Jutland would seem to indicate that it first came from Britain. Benedictine monks had come to Denmark as early as 826, but it wasn't until the baptism of **Harald Blåtand**, commonly known to the rest of the world as **Bluetooth,** that Christianity became the state religion, even if his reasons for doing so (to stave off imminent invasion by French and Germans) weren't entirely spiritual. Nonetheless, Harald gave permission to a Frankish monk, **Ansgar**, to build the **first Danish church**, and Ansgar went on to take control of missionary activity throughout Scandinavia. The death of Harald – he was mortally wounded in battle at Helgenæs in 986 fighting against a rebellion led by his son **Sweyn I** ("Forkbeard") – precipitated the construction of Denmark's four Viking ring fortresses, which served as administrative centres and led to the loss (and later recapture) of the Dannevirke, then Denmark's most southerly border, a sturdy wooden 15km wall that would serve to thwart numerous invasions over the next nine hundred years. Though a pagan, Sweyn tolerated Christianity, despite suspecting the missionaries of bringing a German influence to bear in Danish affairs. But maintaining the strategically important mouth to the Baltic – at the point where it meets the North Sea just off the Jutland coast – did not come without its perils, and Denmark was continuously faced with threats from advancing nations who sought to capture its strongholds. Following Charlemagne's conquest of the Saxons in Germany, the Franks began to threaten Danish territory, but the Danes easily defeated them, and in 990 Sweyn joined the Norwegians in attacks on Britain, whose puppet king at the time was the aptly-named Ethelred "the Unready". The attacks were seen to be primarily economic in motive: a severe reduction in the availability of silver from Arabia had marked a shift in focus to England as a potential source of income through the exaction of tribute. By the time of Sweyn's death in 1014, England was all but under Danish rule, though it took a further two years of warring on the part of Sweyn's son, **Knud** (Canute), before he was installed as King of England, marrying Ethelred's widow into the bargain. By 1033, the Danes thus controlled a sizeable empire around the North Sea, including all of England and Normandy, most of southern Sweden and, of course, Denmark itself, dominating trade in the Baltic. This was the zenith of Viking power, and it's from this period that we get the first historical record of the small fishing village of Havn (literally "Haven" or "Harbour"), later to become København or **Copenhagen**, when it was mentioned in 1043 after King Magnus sought refuge there following his defeat in a sea battle in the Øresund.

The last major Viking expedition took place in 1066, with Harald Hardrádi losing to the king of England at the battle of Stamford Bridge. Hardrádi's successors in Norway subsequently abandoned their expansionist policies and focused instead on maintaining domestic order and ruling over the Norse islands of the Faroes, the Hebrides and Iceland, while Denmark and Sweden went on to experience new periods of prosperity by pursuing expansion into pockets of the Baltic.

The rise of the Church

During the eleventh and twelfth centuries, Denmark was weakened by violent **internal struggles**, not only between different would-be rulers but also among the Church, nobility and monarchy. Following the death of Sweyn II in 1074, two of his four sons, Knud and Harald, fought for the throne, with Harald (supported by the peasantry and the Church) emerging victorious. A mild and introspective individual, Harald III was nonetheless a competent monarch, his crowning achievement being the introduction of the first real Danish currency. He was constantly derided by Knud and his allies, however, and after his death in 1080 his brother became King Knud II. He made generous donations to the Church, but his introduction of higher taxes and the absorption of all unclaimed land into the realm enraged the nobility. The farmers of north Jutland revolted in 1086, forcing Knud to flee to Odense, where he was slain on the high altar of Skt Albani Kirke. The ten-year period of poor harvests that ensued was taken by many to be divine wrath, and there were reports of miracles occurring in Knud's tomb, leading to the murdered king's canonization in 1101.

The battles for power continued, and eventually, in 1131, a two-decade **civil war** broke out, with various claimants to the throne and their offspring slugging it out with the support of either the Church or nobility. During this time the power of the clergy escalated dramatically thanks to **Bishop Eskil**, who enjoyed a persuasive influence on the eventual successor, Erik III. Following Erik's death in 1143, the disputes went on, leading to the division of the kingdom between two potential rulers, Sweyn and Knud. Sweyn's repeated acts of tyranny resulted in the death of Knud in Roskilde, but Knud's wounded aide, Valdemar, managed to escape and raise the Jutlanders in revolt at the **battle of Grathe Heath**, south of Viborg.

The Valdemar era

It wasn't until the accession of Knud's right-hand man, **Valdemar I** (the Great), in 1157 that the country was once again united and freed of factional bickering. Valdemar strengthened the crown by ending the elective function of the *ting*, and shifting the power of election of the monarch to the Church. Technically, the *ting* still influenced the choice of king, but in practice hereditary succession became the rule. After Bishop Eskil's retirement, **Bishop Absalon** became Archbishop of Denmark, erecting a fortress at the fishing village of Havn (in 1254, it would become København, or "merchants' harbour") to counter the Wendish pirates, German-based groups that had previously raided the coast with impunity. Besides being a zealous churchman, Absalon possessed a sharp military mind and came to greatly influence Valdemar I and his successor, Knud IV. During this period, Denmark saw some of its best years, expanding to the south and east, and taking advantage of internal strife within Germany, with Havn seeing rapid economic and social development. In time, after Absalon's death and the succession of **Valdemar II**, Denmark controlled all trade along the south coast of the Baltic and in the North Sea west of the Ejder. Valdemar II was also responsible for subjugating Norway, and in 1219 he set out to conquer Estonia and take charge of Russian trade routes through the Gulf of Finland. (According to Danish legend, the red-and-white crossed *Dannebrog* – the world's oldest state flag – fell down from heaven during a battle in Estonia in that same year.) However, in 1223 Valdemar II was kidnapped by Count Henry of Schwerin (a Danish vassal) and forced to give up many Danish possessions, though Denmark gained some land in the south when the southern boundary of Jutland was redrawn, causing the Danish population of the region to be joined by a large number of Saxons from Holstein.

Within Denmark, the years of expansion had brought great prosperity. The rules of the *ting* were written down as the **Jutlandic Code**, thus unifying laws all over the country – an act that concentrated the powers of justice in the monarch, rather than the more disparate *ting*. The king could still easily be brought to account, though: **Erik V**'s powers were limited by a *håndfæstning*, or charter, that included an undertaking for annual consultation with the **Danehof**, or Council of the Danish Realm – an institutional forum that assured the nobility a deciding voice in government, and one that was to survive as a major influence in the Danish government until 1660 and in 1319, **Christoffer II** became king only after agreeing to an even sterner charter, which allowed for daily consultations with a *råd* – a council of nobles. In 1326, in lieu of a debt that Christoffer had no hope of repaying, **Count Gerd of Holstein** occupied a large portion of Jutland. Christoffer fled to Mecklenburg, and Gerd installed the twelve-year-old Valdemar, Duke of Schleswig, as a puppet king.

In 1332, Skåne, the richest Danish province, inflicted a final insult on Christoffer when its inhabitants revolted and transferred their allegiance to the Swedish king, Magnus. By the time Gerd was murdered in 1340, the years of turmoil had taken their toll on all sections of Danish society: from Christoffer's death in 1332, the country had been without a monarch and re-establishing the crown was seen to be essential for restoring stability. The throne was given to **Valdemar IV** and the monarchy strengthened by the reclaiming of former crown lands that had been handed out to nobles. Within twenty years Denmark had regained its former territory, with German forces driven back across the Ejder, the only loss being Estonia, a Danish possession since 1219, which was sold to the Order of Teutonic Knights. In 1361, the buoyant king attacked and conquered Gotland, much to the annoyance of the Hanseatic League, a powerful Lübeck-based group of tradesmen who were using it as a Baltic trading base; they, in turn, took Copenhagen in 1369, dismantling Absalon's castle brick by brick, with the intention of ending Danish control of the Øresund once and for all. A number of anti-Danish alliances sprang up and the rest of the country was slowly plundered until peace was agreed in 1370 under the **Treaty of Stralsund**, guaranteeing trade for the Hanseatic partners by granting them control of castles along the west coast of Skåne for fifteen years and stipulating that the election of the Danish monarch had to be approved by the Hanseatic League – the peak of their power.

The Kalmar Union

Despite these temporary losses, Denmark's fortunes continued to prosper. Valdemar's daughter **Margrethe I** forced the election of her five-year-old son, Olaf as king in 1375, installing herself as regent several years later. Following his untimely death after only a seven-year reign, the shrewd Margrethe became Queen of Denmark and Norway, and later of Sweden as well – the first ruler of a united Scandinavia. Her moment of glory came in 1397 when she formed the **Kalmar Union**, an alliance between the three nations aimed at countering the Hanseatic League's influence on regional trade which allowed for a Scandinavian federation sharing the same monarch and foreign policy, while alloting each country its own domestic legislation. It became evident that Denmark was to be the dominant partner within the union, however, when Margrethe placed Danish nobles in civic positions in Norway and Sweden but failed to reciprocate the gesture in Denmark. She promptly saw to it that her grand-nephew, **Erik VII** ("of Pomerania") was crowned king in 1396, though as he was only 15, she continued to play a major role in the affairs of the country until her death in 1412. Erik, determined to remove the Counts of Holstein who had taken possession of Schleswig in northern Germany during his mother's reign, persuaded a meeting of the *Danehof* in 1413 to declare the whole of Schleswig to be crown property, and three years later war broke out with the German-influenced nobility of the region. Unhappy with the Holstein privateers who were interfering with their trade, the Hanseatic League initially supported the king. But Erik also introduced important economic reforms within Denmark, ensuring that foreign goods reached Danish people through Danish merchants instead of coming directly from Hanseatic traders. This led to a war with the League, after which, in 1429, Erik imposed the **Sound Toll** (*Øresundstolden*) on shipping passing through the narrow strip of sea off the coast of Helsingør. The toll became an endless source of revenue that would underpin Denmark's fortunes for the next four centuries.

For the time being, however, the conflicts with the Holsteiners and the Hanseatic League had badly drained financial resources. Denmark still relied on outsourced armies to do its fighting, and the burden of taxation had caused widespread dissatisfaction, particularly in Sweden. With the Holstein forces gaining ground in Jutland, Erik fled to Gotland, and in 1439 Swedish and Danish nobles elected in his place **Christoffer III**, a judicious king who acquiesced to the nobles' demands and ensured peace with the Hanseatic League by granting them exemption from the Sound Toll. Copenhagen was crowned the Danish capital in 1443, shifting the balance of power away from the former capital and ecclesiastical centre of Roskilde, and revenues from the toll allowed the city's merchants and taxmen to seize growing amounts of trade from the declining ports of the Hanseatic League and to establish itself as the principal harbour in the Baltic. The construction of Scandinavia's first **university** helped to establish the city as a cultural as well as administrative hub. Around the same time, the **Kronborg Slot**, just north at Helsingør, was built to control the Øresund and enforce payment of the toll, further entrenching Copenhagen's pre-eminence in the region.

Christoffer's sudden death in 1448 left – after internal struggle – **Christian I** to take the Danish throne. Following the death of his uncle and ally, the Count of Holstein, he united Schleswig and Holstein at Ribe in 1460 and became Count of Holstein and Duke of Schleswig. In Denmark itself he also instigated the *stændermøde*, a council of merchants, clergy, freehold peasants and nobility, forging a powerful position for the crown – a policy that was continued by his successor, John. John died in 1513 and **Christian II** came to the throne, seeking to re-establish the power of the Kalmar Union and reduce the trading dominance of the Hanseatic League. He invaded Sweden in 1520 under the guise of protecting the Church, but soon crowned himself King of Sweden at a ceremony attended by the cream of the Swedish nobility, clergy and the merchant class – an amnesty being granted to those who had opposed him. It was, however, a trick. Once inside the castle, 82 of the "guests" were arrested on charges of heresy, sentenced to death and executed – an event that became known as the **Stockholm Blood-bath**. This was supposed to subdue Swedish hostility to the Danish monarch but in fact had the opposite effect, as Gustavus Vasa, previously one of six Swedish hostages held by Christian in Denmark, became the leader of a revolt that ended Christian's reign in Sweden and ultimately finished the Kalmar Union. Internally, too, Christian faced a revolt, to which he responded with more brutality. At the end of 1522, a group of Jutish nobles banded together with the intention of overthrowing him, joining up with Duke Frederik of Holstein-Gottorp (heir to half of Schleswig-Holstein), who also regarded the Danish king with disfavour. The following January, the nobles renounced their royal oaths and, with the support of forces from Holstein, gained control of all of Jutland and Funen. As they prepared to invade Zealand, Christian fled to Holland, hoping to assemble an army and return; in his absence, Frederik of Holstein-Gottorp became **Frederik I**.

The Reformation

At the time of Frederik's acquisition of the crown in 1523 there was a growing unease with the role of the Church in Denmark, especially with the power – and wealth – of its bishops. Frederik, while decidedly a Catholic, refused to take sides in religious disputes and did nothing to prevent the destruction of churches, well aware as he was of the groundswell of peasant support for Lutheranism. When he died in 1533, the fate of the **Reformation** hinged on which of his two sons would succeed him. The elder and more obvious choice was Christian, but his open support for Lutheranism set the bishops and nobles against him, while the younger son Hans, just 12 years old, was favoured by the Church and the aristocracy. The three-year **civil war** that thus ensued saw peasant uprisings across the country and a year-long siege of Copenhagen. Though the city's defensive ramparts held firm, many of its citizens starved to death or died of disease. The war ended in 1536 with Christian III on the throne, presiding over the new **Danish Lutheran Church**, with a constitution locating the king at its head and Lutheranism installed as the official state religion.

Danish–Swedish conflicts

New trading routes across the Atlantic had reduced the power of the Hanseatic League, and Christian's young and ambitious successor, **Frederik II**, saw this as a chance to extend the borders of the Danish kingdom. Sweden, however, had its own expansionist designs, and the resulting **Seven Years' War** (1563–1570) between the two countries caused widespread devastation and plunged the Danish economy into crisis. The predicament turned out to be short-lived: price rises in the south of Europe led to increasing Danish affluence, reflected in the rebuilding of Krogen fortress in Helsingør as the magnificent renaissance castle of Kronborg. By the time a ten-year-old **Christian IV** came to the throne in 1596, Denmark was a solvent and powerful nation, its capital now home to the largest naval force in Europe, with Sound Toll revenue providing a consistent source of income for royal purses. Known as the "Great Builder", Christian characterized his sixty-year reign with bold new town layouts and great architectural works, nearly doubling the size of Copenhagen by expanding the defensive fortifications to the north and reclaiming the island of Christianshavn to the east, helping the city to become a major European capital.

But the architectural vision of Christian was not matched by his political astuteness. As arch-rival Sweden's military strength grew, the Danes' steadily weakened, and in 1625 Christian IV took Denmark into the unsuccessful **Thirty Years' War**, defeat leading to increased taxes and rampant inflation.

In 1657, during the reign of **Frederik III**, Sweden occupied Jutland, and soon after marched across the frozen sea to Funen with the intention of storming the capital. Hostilities ceased with the signing of the **Treaty of Roskilde**, under which Denmark finally lost all its Swedish provinces. Sweden, however, was still suspicious of possible Danish involvement in Germany, and broke the terms of the treaty, commencing an advance through Zealand. The Dutch, to whom the Swedes had been allied, regarded this as a move towards total Swedish control of commercial traffic through the Øresund and sent a fleet to protect Copenhagen. The **Treaty of Copenhagen**, signed in 1660, acknowledged Swedish defeat but allowed the country to retain the Sound provinces acquired under the Treaty of Roskilde, so preventing either side from monopolizing Baltic trade.

Absolute monarchy

The conflict with Sweden and the loss of former territory left Denmark heavily in **debt**, and, with the financial and political power of the nobles of the

Danehof slowly fading, the city's burghers decided that everyone, including the nobility, should pay the taxes needed. The nobles lost further power when, in 1660, Frederik III compelled them to sign a charter reinstating the king as absolute monarch, and removing all powers from the *Danehof*, while a **new**

Danish colonies

Like many European nations, the discovery and development of trade routes with Asia, and the European settling of the Americas in the fifteenth century, inspired Denmark to establish and maintain a number of foreign **colonies**, from as early as the seventeenth century. Denmark's interest in the Indian subcontinent goes back to the existence of the **Danish East India Company** in 1616, and **Danish India** was established as a crown colony just over a century later. Danish properties in and around the Indian subcontinent included the Nicobar Islands in the eastern Indian Ocean, first colonised in 1620 and administered from the Danish headquarters at **Tranquebar**, then a thriving South Indian port city. The Danes left some noteworthy remains of their presence in several of the larger colonial settlements, including fortresses, colonial estates, churches, cemeteries and most notably, Tranquebar's grand sandstone Dansborg Fort – Denmark's second-largest fortress after Kronborg. Danish involvement in India ended in 1868, when the rights to Denmark's holdings were sold to the British, who integrated them into the Raj. Denmark also maintained a few settlements along the **West African Gold Coast**, the largest of which was at **Accra**, where the impressive white Christianborg fortress (Osu Castle), built in 1661, still stands today. Across the Atlantic, Denmark had established early colonial holdings in the **Caribbean** on St Thomas (1671) and St John (1718), in addition to purchasing St Croix from France in 1733. The colonies were lucrative centres of the **slave trade** in which Danish manufacturers exchanged purchase of African slaves for sugar cane to transport back to Denmark. The United States purchased the islands from Denmark in 1917 for $25 million after the abolition of slavery had sent many of them into economic ruin.

In the **North Sea**, several remote masses of land have been an integral part of Danish history for centuries. With the 1814 **Treaty of Kiel** control of Norway passed to Sweden, while independent Denmark retained control of the Faroe Islands, Greenland and Iceland, the latter of which existed under Danish rule until 1918, when it won its sovereignty, though many Icelanders still learn Danish in school. The **Faroe Islands**, a group of eighteen islands 350km north of Scotland, have maintained the status of autonomous region under the Danish crown since 1948, which provides them with a high degree of self-governance on most matters, as well as a generous annual subsidy of about €115 million from the Danish government. The 46,000 inhabitants voted to opt out of Denmark's decision to join the EC in 1973, and these days the islanders are generally split on the question of independence from Denmark.

Greenland (*Kalaallit Nunaat*, or "land of men" in Greenlandic) is the largest island in the world, a colossal land mass of 840,000 square miles, of which the Greenland ice sheet covers 81 percent; the coastline itself is nearly 25,000 miles long, approximately same as of the Earth's circumference at the Equator. It was famously discovered by Erik the Red, who took up residence there and named it *Grønland* ("Greenland") in order to encourage further settlement, since which time it became a Norwegian Crown colony, then a Dano-Norwegian holding, before finally being officially integrated into Denmark in 1953 as a dependency. The island was granted home rule in 1978, and the newly established parliament opted out of membership in the EU. Today, Greenland is home to 57,000 Inuit who largely maintain traditional ways of life, although a small percentage of the population is also made up of ethnic Danes, and Danish shares official language status with Greenlandic. Both the Faroes and Greenland can be visited via regular **flights** from Copenhagen; for more information, visit ⓦwww.faroeislands.com and ⓦwww.greenland.com.

constitution bound the king to two sole stipulations: to uphold the Lutheran faith and ensure the unity of the kingdom. The king proceeded to rule, aided by a Privy Council in which seats were drawn mainly from the top posts within the civil service. With noble influence on royal decision-making drastically reduced, Copenhagen was made a free city, with commoners accorded the same privileges as nobles. Frederik III began a rebuild of the military forces and, following three minor wars with Sweden, managed to bring a more or less peaceful coexistence to Denmark.

In 1699, **Frederik IV** set about creating a Danish militia to make the country less dependent on foreign mercenaries. While Sweden turned its allegiances towards Britain and Holland, Denmark re-established relations with the French, a situation that culminated in the **Great Northern War** (1709–1720). By the time the conflict had ended, Russia had emerged as a dominant force in the region, Denmark held a strong position in Schleswig, and Sweden's exemption from the Sound Toll was ended. The two decades of peace that followed saw the arrival of **Pietism**, a form of Lutheranism that strove to renew the devotional ideal. Frederik embraced the doctrine towards the end of his life, and it was adopted in full by his son, **Christian VI**, who took the throne in 1730. He prohibited entertainment on Sunday, closed down Det Kongelige Teater, and made court life a sombre affair: attendance at church on Sundays became compulsory and confirmation obligatory. Meanwhile, in 1711, bubonic plague wiped out a third of Copenhagen's population, while two devastating **fires** in 1728 and 1795 forced the reconstruction of most of the city, during which the basis of the present-day street plan was established.

The Enlightenment

Despite the orthodox beliefs of Christian VI, Pietism was never widely popular, and by the 1740s its influence had waned considerably. The reign of his successor **Frederik V**, who took the throne in 1746, saw a great cultural awakening: grand buildings such as Amalienborg and Frederikskirke were erected in Copenhagen, and there was a new flourishing of the arts, noted in part by the founding of the Det Kongelige Danske Kunstakademi ("The Royal Danish Academy of Art") in 1754. The king, perhaps as a reaction to the puritanism of his father, devoted himself to a life of pleasure and allowed control of the nation effectively to pass to the civil service. Political life enjoyed a period of relative stability, and, with their international influence significantly reduced by the ravages of the Great Northern War, the Danes adopted a position of **neutrality** – a position that saw the economy benefit as a consequence.

In 1766, **Christian VII** took the crown, but his unpredictable mental state and moods soon prevented him from carrying out even the bare minimum of official duties. The king's council, filled by a fresh generation of ambitious young men, insisted that the king effect his own will – under their guidance – and disregard the suggestions of his older advisers. Decision-making became dominated by a young German court physician, **Johann Friedrich Struensee**, who combined personal arrogance with a sympathy for many of the ideas then fashionable elsewhere in Europe; he spoke no Danish (German was the court language) and had no concern for Danish traditions. Through him a number of sweeping **reforms** were executed: the Privy Council was stamped out, the Treasury became the supreme administrative organ, the death penalty was abolished and the press was freed from censorship.

Progressive though such moves may have seemed compared to other parts of Western Europe at the time, there was opposition from several quarters: merchants complained about the freeing of trade, and the burghers of Copenhagen were unhappy with their city losing its autonomy. In addition, there were well-founded ribald rumours about the relationship between Struensee and the queen. Since nothing was known outside the court of the king's mental state, it was assumed that the monarch was being held prisoner, and Struensee was forced to reintroduce censorship of the press as their editorials began to mount attacks on him. The Royal Guards mutinied when their disbandment was ordered, and a **coup** was plotted by Frederik V's second wife, Juliane Marie of Brunswick, and her son, Frederik. In 1772, Struensee was arrested, tried and, soon after, beheaded, drawn and quartered, while the dazed king was paraded before his cheering subjects. The court came under the control – in ascending order of influence – of Frederik, Juliane, and a minister, **Ove Høegh-Guldberg**. All those who had been appointed to office by Struensee were dismissed, and while Høegh-Guldberg eventually incurred the wrath of officials by operating in much the same arrogant fashion as Struensee had, he recognized – and exploited – the anti-German feelings that had been growing for some time. Danish became the language of command in the army and later the court language, and in 1776 it was declared that no foreigner should be given a position in royal office.

The Napoleonic Wars

In the wider sphere, the country prospered through its dealings in the Far East, with Copenhagen consolidating its role as the new centre of Baltic trade, and the outbreak of the American War of Independence provided neutral Denmark with fresh commercial opportunities. But despite its improving domestic position, the country found itself once again embroiled in the mire of international power struggles with the outbreak of the **Napoleonic Wars** (1796–1815), reluctantly siding at first with the **League of Armed Neutrality** (Russia, Prussia and Sweden) in an attempt to stay out of the conflict between expansionist Britain and revolutionary France. Although this move initially had the effect of maintaining trading links across the Atlantic until the end of the war, the British, considering the league potentially hostile and fearing Danish sympathy with Napoleon's continental blockade, sent a fleet under Admiral Nelson to Copenhagen in 1801, damaging the powerful Danish navy and obliging them to withdraw from the agreement. The pact between France and Russia left Denmark in a difficult situation: to oppose this alliance would leave them exposed to a French invasion of Jutland, but to oppose the British and join with the French would adversely affect trade. In 1807, the British returned, worried that Napoleon's advancing armies would take over the newly rebuilt Danish fleet if they didn't, occupying Zealand and commencing a murderous three-day bombardment of Copenhagen that saw many of its finest buildings heavily damaged, before towing away what was left of the Danish fleet. Sweden had aligned with the British and was demanding the ceding of Norway if Denmark were to be defeated – which, under the **Treaty of Kiel**, was exactly what happened. With the loss of the Norwegian minority, the Danes had for the first time in several hundred years become a majority in their own country.

The Age of Liberalism

The Napoleonic Wars had destroyed Denmark's international prestige and left the country bankrupt, and the period up until 1830 was spent in recovery. Yet despite such an inauspicious beginning to the new century, Denmark managed to pull itself up by its bootstraps rather quickly, nowhere more noticeably than in areas of cultural production, where a **national Romantic movement** had gained pace, under which for two decades the Danish arts flourished as they never had before (or since). **Hans Christian Andersen** (see p.208) charmed the children (and adults) of the world with his colourful fairytales about unfortunate and forgotten characters, while **Søren Kierkegaard** (see p.98) scandalized it with his philosophical works. At the same time, the nation's visual media reached new heights under the auspices of sculptor **Bertel Thorvaldsen** (see p.79), and C.W. Eckersberg, who led the emergence of the first entirely Danish school of painting. Social changes were in the air, too: in 1810, the theologian **N.F.S. Grundtvig** developed a new form of Christianity that was free of dogma and drew on the virtues espoused by the heroes of Norse mythology. In 1825, he left the intellectual circles of Copenhagen and travelled the rural areas to guide a religious revival, eventually modifying his earlier ideas in favour of a new faith in the wisdom of "the people" – something that was to colour the future liberal movement.

On the political front, there was trouble brewing in Danish-speaking **Schleswig** and German-speaking **Holstein**, which, in response to the wave of nationalism in France and Germany, were demanding their independence. The Treaty of Kiel had compelled Denmark to relinquish Holstein to the Confederation of German States – although, confusingly, the Danish king remained duke of the province. In Copenhagen, a group of scholars proffered the idea that Schleswig be brought closer to Danish affairs, and in pursuit of this they formed the Liberal Party and brought pressure to bear for a new liberal constitution. As the government wavered in its response, the liberal movement grew and its **first newspaper**, *Fædrelandet* ("The Fatherland"), appeared in 1834. In 1837, the crown agreed to the introduction of elected town councils and, four years later, to elected bodies in parishes and counties. In 1839, **Christian VIII** came to the throne. Having introduced a liberal constitution during his brief tenure in power in Norway's short transition phase from Danish to Swedish rule, he surprised Danish liberals by not agreeing to a similar constitution at home. By 1848, when Christian was succeeded by his son **Frederik VII**, the liberals had organized themselves into the **National Liberal Party**, and the king signed a **new constitution** that made Denmark the most democratic country in Europe, guaranteeing freedom of speech, freedom of religious worship, and many other civil liberties. Legislation was to be put in the hands of a *Rigsdag* (parliament), elected by popular vote and consisting of two chambers: the lower *Folketing* and upper *Landsting*. The king gave up the powers of an absolute monarch, but he could still select his own ministers, and his signature was required before bills approved by the *Rigsdag* could become law.

Within Schleswig-Holstein, however, there was little faith that the equality granted to the people in the constitution would be upheld, and the bickering between the disgruntled Danish royals who ruled the region and the Danish rulers in power in Copenhagen became emblematic of such conflicts between centre and periphery. A delegation from the duchies went to Copenhagen to call for Schleswig to be combined with Holstein within the German

Confederation, but when the Danes proposed a compromise suggesting a free constitution for Holstein with Schleswig remaining as part of Denmark, albeit with its own legislature and autonomy in its internal administration, the Schleswig-Holsteiners promptly rejected it, packing their bags and forming a provisional government in Kiel. Continuing strife over the duchies saw a series of small but disastrous wars in 1864, and, when Bismarck proposed a withdrawal of Prussian support for Denmark, the result was a defeat for the duchies, ultimately marking the end of National Liberalism in Denmark. The Danish prime minister, C.C. Hall, drew up a fresh constitution that excluded Holstein from Denmark. Frederik died before he could give the royal assent and it fell to **Christian IX** to put his name to the document that would almost certainly trigger another war. As a result of the eventual treaty, Denmark ceded both Schleswig and Holstein to Germany, leaving the country smaller than it had been for centuries and dealing a substantial blow to Danish morale. The ramifications of this historical move should not be underestimated: with the loss of such territory, Denmark became for the first time in its history an **ethnically homogenous country**, and the nation began to assuage its sense of defeat by developing the ethos of being a proudly close-knit socio-cultural community.

The new constitution following the election of 1866 retained the procedure for election to the *Folketing*, but made the *Landsting* franchise dependent on land and money and allowed twelve of the 64 members to be selected by the king. The landowners worked in limited cooperation with the National Liberals and the Centre Party (a more conservative version of the National Liberals). In opposition, a number of interests, encompassing everything from leftist radicals to followers of Grundtvig, were shortly combined into the **United Left**, which put forward the first political manifesto seen in Denmark. It called for equal taxation, universal suffrage in local elections and more freedom for the farmers, and contained a vague demand for closer links with the other Scandinavian countries. The United Left became the majority within the *Folketing* in 1872.

The ideas of **revolutionary socialism** had begun percolating through the country in 1871 via a series of pamphlets edited by Louis Pio, who attempted to organize a Danish Internationale. In April 1872, Pio led twelve hundred bricklayers into a strike, but his call for a country-wide meeting was blocked by the government, which had Pio arrested and sentenced to five years in prison. The workers, meanwhile, had already begun to band together, forming trade unions and workers' associations, while the intellectual Left also began to mobilize. A series of lectures delivered by Georg Brandes in Copenhagen cited Danish culture, in particular its literature, as dull and lifeless compared to that of other countries and called for fresh works that questioned and examined society, instigating a bout of literary attacks on institutions such as marriage, chastity and the family, and sparking a conservative backlash as factioned groups in the government formed themselves into the **United Right**, under Prime Minister **J.B.S. Estrup**. The elections of 1890 improved the Left's position in the *Folketing*, and also saw the election of two **Social Democrats**. With this, the left moved further towards moderation and compromise with the right. The trade unions' membership escalated in proportion to the numbers employed in the new industries, and were united as the Association of Trade Unions in 1898, while the Social Democratic Party grew stronger with the support of the industrial workers.

The Danish capital, meanwhile, had been undergoing a massive transformation. In 1851, Copenhagen's external fortifications were demolished, finally allowing the cramped city to expand beyond its medieval limits and sowing the seeds for the new industrial era. Railways, factories and shipyards began to change the face of the city, which was gradually developing into a thriving **manufacturing centre**, while the new working–class districts of Nørrebro and Vesterbro were flung up, with Copenhagen's workers packed into slum tenements that would subsequently become hotbeds of left-wing political activity. The second half of the nineteenth century also saw the establishment of the Carlsberg Brewery, the rapid growth of the Royal Danish Porcelain factory and the founding of a number of recreational possibilities for the city's aspiring bourgeoisie, from the city's two main department stores, the Magasin du Nord and Illums Bolighus, to Det Kongelige Teater and the City Zoo.

Parliamentary democracy, World War I and the Easter Crisis

By the end of the nineteenth century the power of the right was in severe decline. The elections of 1901, under the new conditions of a secret ballot, saw them reduced to the smallest group within the *Folketing* and heralded the beginning of **parliamentary democracy**, the government quickly ushering in a number of reforms, most notably a sliding-scale income tax and free schooling beyond the primary level. As the years went by, Social Democrat support increased, while the left, such as it was, became increasingly conservative. In 1905, a breakaway group formed the **Radical Left** (*Det Radikale Venstre*), politically similar to the English Liberals, whose alliance with the Social Democrats enabled the two parties to gain a large majority in the *Folketing* in the election of 1913, and a year later conservative control of the *Landsting* was ended. Social advances were made, but further domestic progress was halted by international events as Europe prepared for war.

Denmark had enjoyed good trading relations with both Germany and Britain in the years preceding **World War I**, and was keen not to be seen to favour either side in the hostilities. On the announcement of German mobilization, the now Radical-led cabinet, with the support of all the other parties, issued a **statement of neutrality** and was able to remain clear of direct involvement in the conflict. At the conclusion of the war, attention was turned again towards Schleswig-Holstein, and under the **Treaty of Versailles** it was decided that Schleswig should be divided into two zones for a referendum – in the northern zone a return to unification with Denmark was favoured by a large percentage, while the southern zone elected to remain part of Germany – and a new German–Danish border was drawn up just north of Flensburg. As many of the towns that remained in Denmark kept their large bilingual, pro-German minority – especially places such as Tønder and Åbenrå – strong German identities persisted, resulting in the growth of German-language schools and newspapers in the region.

High rates of unemployment and the success of the Russian Bolsheviks led to a series of strikes and demonstrations, the unrest coming to a head with the **Easter Crisis** of 1920. During March of that year, a change in the electoral system towards greater proportional representation was agreed in the *Folketing* but the prime minister, **Carl Theodore Zahle**, whose Radicals stood to lose support through the change, refused to implement it. The king, Christian X, responded by dismissing him and asking **Otto Liebe** to form a caretaker government to oversee the changes. The royal intervention, while technically legal, incensed the Social Democrats and the trade unions; the latter were already facing a national lockout by employers in response to demands for improved pay rates, and saw the king's act as an affront to the idea of a democratic parliamentary system. Perceiving the threat of a right-wing coup, the unions began organizing a general strike to begin after the Easter holiday, with a large republican demonstration held outside Amalienborg. On Easter Saturday, urgent negotiations between the king and the existing government concluded with an agreement that a mutually acceptable caretaker government would oversee the electoral change and a fresh election would immediately follow. Employers, fearful of the power the workers had shown, met many of the demands for higher wages.

The next government, dominated by the Radical Left, fortified existing social policies, and increased state contributions to union unemployment funds. But a general economic depression continued, and there was widespread industrial unrest as the krone declined in value and living standards fell. A month-long **general strike** followed, and a workers' demonstration in Randers was subdued by the army. Venstre (the Radical Left) and the Social Democrats jostled for position over the next decade, though under the new electoral system no one party could achieve enough power to undertake major reform. The economy did improve, however, and state influence spread further through Danish society than ever before. Enlightened reforms were put on the agenda, too, making a deliberately clean break with the moral standpoints of the past – notably on abortion and illegitimacy – and major public works were funded, such as the bridge between Funen and Jutland over the Lille Bælt, and the Stormstrømsbro, linking Zealand to Falster.

The Nazi occupation and World War II

When **World War II** broke out, Denmark again made efforts to remain neutral, this time in vain. While the country itself had little military significance for the Nazis, the sea off Norway was being used to transport iron ore from Sweden to Britain, and the fjords offered good shelter for a fleet engaged in a naval war in the Atlantic. To gain access to Norway, the Nazis planned an **invasion of Denmark**. At 4am on April 9, 1940, the German ambassador in Copenhagen informed Prime Minister Stauning that German troops were preparing to cross the Danish border and issued the ultimatum that unless Denmark agreed that the country could be used as a German military base – keeping control of its own affairs – Copenhagen would be bombed. To reject the demand was considered a postponement of the inevitable, and to save Danish bloodshed the government acquiesced at 6am. "They took us by telephone," lamented one Danish minister.

A national coalition government was formed that behaved according to protocol but gave no unnecessary concessions to the Germans. Censorship of the press and a ban on demonstrations were imposed, ostensibly intended to prevent the Nazis spreading propaganda. But these measures, like the swiftness of the initial agreement, were viewed by some Danes as capitulation and were to be a thorn in the side of the Social Democrats for years to come.

The government was reshuffled to include non-parliamentary experts, one of whom, **Erik Scavenius**, a former foreign minister, conceived an ill-fated plan to gain the confidence of the Germans. He issued a statement outlining the government's friendly attitude to the occupying power, and even praised the German military victory – which upset the Danish public and astonished the Germans, who asked whether Denmark would like to enter into commercial agreement immediately rather than wait until the end of the war. By that point, Scavenius was powerless to do anything other than agree, and a deal was signed within days. Under its terms, the krone was to be phased out and German currency made legal tender.

Public reaction was naturally hostile, and Scavenius was, not surprisingly, regarded as a traitor. Groups of Danes began a systematic display of **antipathy to the Germans**. Children wore red, white and blue "RAF caps", Danish customers walked out of cafés when Germans entered, and the ban on demonstrations was flouted by groups who gathered to sing patriotic songs. On September 1, 1940, an estimated 740,000 Danes around the country gathered to sing the same song simultaneously. The king demonstrated his continued presence by riding on horseback each morning through Copenhagen. For its part, the Danish government continued its balancing act, knowing that failure to co-operate at least to some degree would lead to a complete Nazi takeover; it was with this in mind that Denmark signed the Anti-Comintern Pact, which made Communism illegal but allowed only Danish police to arrest Danish Communists. **Vilhelm Buhl**, who was appointed prime minister on May 3, 1942, had been an outspoken opponent of the signing of the Anti-Comintern Pact and it was thought he might end the apparent appeasement. Instead, the tension between occupiers and occupied was to climax with Hitler's anger at the curt note received from Christian X in response to the Führer's birthday telegram. Although it was the king's standard reply, Hitler took the mere "thank you" as an insult and immediately replaced his functionaries in Denmark with hardliners who demanded a new pro-German government. Scavenius took control and, in 1943, elections were called in an attempt to show that freedom of political expression could exist under German occupation. The government asked the public to demonstrate faith in national unity by voting for any one of the four parties in the coalition, and received overwhelming support in the largest-ever turnout for a Danish election.

Awareness that German defeat was becoming inevitable stimulated a wave of strikes throughout the country. Berlin declared a state of emergency in Denmark, and demanded that the Danish government comply – which it refused to do. Germany took over administration of the country, interning many politicians and requiring the king to appoint a cabinet from outside the *Folketing*. For the first time in Denmark, Germans were free to round up Danish Jews. A resistance movement was organized under the leadership of the **Danish Freedom Council**. Sabotage was carefully co-ordinated, and an underground army, soon comprising over 43,000 patriots, prepared to assist in the Allied invasion. In June 1944, rising anti-Nazi violence led to a curfew being imposed in Copenhagen and assemblies of more than five people being banned, to which workers responded with a spontaneous general strike. German plans to starve the city's inhabitants had to be abandoned after five days, and Copenhagen itself largely escaped the devastation suffered by other European cities. Denmark's two moments of glory during the war came with the **smuggling of seven thousand Jews to Sweden** to avoid their deportation to concentration camps, and later, during a British air raid on the Nazi headquarters at Rådhuspladsen, when many of the captured members of the Danish resistance were momentarily able to escape. Only 481 Danish Jews were sent to the prison camp at Theresienstadt, many of whom actually survived due to action on the part of both the Danish government and Church organizations. Moreover, unlike in other European countries, when the Jews returned to Denmark, they found their homes, pets, gardens and personal belongings had been cared for by their neighbours.

The postwar period

After the German surrender in May 1945, a **liberation government** was created, composed equally of pre-war politicians and members of the Danish Freedom Council, with Vilhelm Buhl as prime minister. On the whole, Denmark had been spared the infrastructural damage and devastation seen elsewhere in Europe, but it did find itself besieged with massive economic problems and it soon became apparent that the liberation government, whose internal differences earned it the nickname "the debating club", could not function as such. In the ensuing election there was a swing to the Communists, and a minority Venstre government was formed.

Domestic issues soon came to be overshadowed by the international situation as the **Cold War** began. Denmark had unreservedly joined the United Nations in 1945, and had joined the IMF and World Bank to gain financial help in restoring its economy, with Marshall Plan aid bringing further assistance in 1947. As world power became polarized between East and West, the Danish government at first tried to remain impartial, but in 1947 agreed to join NATO – a total break with the established concept of Danish neutrality (though to this day, the Danes remain opposed to nuclear weapons).

The years after the war were marked by much political manoeuvring among the Radicals, Social Democrats and Conservatives, resulting in many hastily called elections and a number of ineffectual compromise coalitions distinguished mainly by the level of their infighting. Working-class support for the Social Democrats steadily eroded, and support for the Communists was largely transferred to the new, more revisionist, **Socialist People's Party**. In spite of political wrangling, Denmark succeeded in creating one of the world's most successful **welfare states**, with a comprehensive programme of cradle-to-grave benefits, and a quality of life that soon ranked among the highest in the world. Social reforms, meanwhile, continued apace, not least in the 1960s, with the abandoning of all forms of censorship and the institution of cost-free abortion. Such measures are typical of more recent social policy, though Denmark's odd position between Scandinavia and the rest of mainland Europe still remains a niggling concern. In 1972, Denmark became the first Scandinavian member of the EC – Sweden, the second, didn't join until 1995 – though public enthusiasm remained lukewarm.

The 1970s and 1980s

Copenhagen itself became the centre of attention when, in 1971, the old military base on the eastern side of Christianshavn was taken over by squatters, who created the "Free City" of **Christiania**. Initial, unsuccessful attempts by the police to clear the squatters were followed by a twelve-year trial period, after which the city was legally recognized, even to the point where "Pusherstreet" is now marked on official maps. Perhaps the biggest change in the 1970s, however, was the foundation – and subsequent influence – of the new **Progress Party** (*Fremskridtspartiet*), headed by Mogens Glistrup, who claimed to have an income of over a million kroner but to be paying no income tax through manipulation of the tax laws. The Progress Party stood on a ticket of immigration curbs and drastic tax cuts, and Glistrup went on to compare tax avoidance with the sabotaging of Nazi railway lines during the war. He also announced that if elected he would replace the Danish defence force with an answering machine saying "we surrender" in Russian. He was eventually imprisoned after an investigation by the Danish tax office; released in 1985, he set himself up as a tax consultant.

The success of the Progress Party pointed to dissatisfaction with both the economy and the established parties' strategies for dealing with its problems. In September 1982, **Poul Schlüter** became the country's first Conservative prime minister of the twentieth century, leading the widest-ranging coalition yet seen – including Conservatives, the Venstre, Centre Democrats and Christian People's Party. In keeping with the prevailing political climate in the rest of Europe, the prescription for Denmark's economic malaise was seen to be spending cuts, not sparing the social services, and with an extension of taxation into areas such as pension funds. These policies continued until the snap election of 1987, which resulted in a significant swing to the left. Nevertheless, Schlüter was asked to form a new government, which he did in conjunction with the Progress Party in order to gain a single-seat working majority. A further election, in May 1988, largely served to affirm the new Schlüter-led government, if only because of the apparent lack of any workable alternative.

The urban landscape of the capital also began to experience significant change during the 1980s, when the city government initiated attempts at cleaning up the run-down neighbourhoods of Nørrebro and Vesterbro. First came the disastrous demolition of a number of ramshackle but character-rich buildings in Nørrebro and their replacement with ugly modernist concrete housing estates. The city's population protested, and the remaining buildings there and in Vesterbro were spared demolition and restored, after which the value of the buildings soared and the former working-class inhabitants were pushed out into the suburbs. At the same time, concerns arose about the culture and character of Denmark – the very face of Danish citizens, in fact. The arrival since the 1960s of substantial numbers of immigrants – the so-called **new Danes** – began to raise questions about the future of the country. Guest workers, mostly from Yugoslavia and Turkey, brought in during the boom years of the 1960s to fill lower-paid jobs, became suddenly less welcome in the 1970s, as unemployment rates began to rise and the ugly face of racism reared its head.

Towards the new millennium

Since the 1970s and 1980s, the major barometer of national sentiment in Denmark has been how people have perceived the country's role in Europe. In January 1993, Schlüter's government was forced to resign over a political scandal (it was revealed that asylum had been denied to Sri Lankan Tamil refugees in the late 1980s and early 1990s, in contravention of Danish law). The Social Democrats, led by **Poul Nyrup Rasmussen**, took power in 1994 and formed a four-party coalition. For the first time in ten years Denmark was ruled by a majority government – a centre-left majority coalition that came under attack for its weak policies on tax reform, the welfare state and the thorny issue of **European union**. Though traditionally a reluctant member of the EC, Denmark was carried into the European **Exchange Rate Mechanism** (or ERM, then viewed as the first step towards a single European currency) by Schlüter at the start of the 1990s, a move that transformed the Danish economy into one of the strongest in Europe and made its inflation rate the lowest of any EC member. The price for this, however, was soaring unemployment and further cuts in public spending.

The outcome of the referendum on the **Maastricht Treaty** (the blueprint for European political and monetary union) in June 1992, however, provided an unexpected upset to the Schlüter applecart. Despite calls for a "yes" vote not only from the government but also from the opposition Social Democrats, over fifty percent of Danes rejected the treaty – severely embarrassing the prime minister and sending shivers down the spine of every western European government. The government and other pro-Europe parties didn't give up, however, but set to work on a revised version of the Maastricht Treaty, with the emphasis on protecting national interests – it included a pledge allowing the Danish people to reject citizenship of a united Europe. A **second referendum** in May 1993 was a triumph for the government, with almost 57 percent of the Danish population voting in favour of the new treaty. Anti-European feelings, already intense, reached boiling point, and the night after the referendum young left-wingers and anarchists came together in central Copenhagen to declare the area an "EU-free zone". The police moved in to break up the demonstration, battles with the demonstrators ensued, and, for the first time in history, the Danish police opened fire against a crowd of civilians. Fortunately nobody died, but the incident sparked off a major investigation into the actions of the police, and while Denmark avoided the risk of economic isolation in an increasingly integrated European community, doubts among the Danish people remain, along with a continuing dissatisfaction at the way the "yes" vote was achieved.

Rasmussen and the Social Democrats retained the largest share of the vote in subsequent elections in 1998 and, as the millennium dawned, the country was well placed for life in a new Europe. Danes were ranked at the top of the newly created "European Future Readiness Index", which measures social costs and problems such as environmental quality, healthcare costs, poverty and unemployment, while the organization Transparency International revealed that Denmark had been chosen as the world's **least corrupt nation**: of 99 countries surveyed, only Denmark received a perfect score on its "Anti-Corruption Index". All was not absolutely well, however. In 1999, crime and poverty in Copenhagen were becoming a serious worry for the first time in many years, and decade-long tensions about the growing number of immigrants in the city finally reaching boiling point in November 1999 when **riots** in Nørrebro protested the extradition of a second-generation Turkish immigrant, with police using tear gas to quell more than one hundred protesters – the first such disturbance since the 1993 anti-Maastricht demonstrations.

Into the twenty-first century

In September 2000, the Danish people returned an unexpected "no" vote in the referendum held to decide if the country should finally enter the **Eurozone**. In spite of strong governmental support and many sound economic arguments for membership, 47 percent of the population voted against adopting the euro, leaving Denmark and the UK as the only two EU countries retaining a national currency. Support for the rejection came from the two political extremes, with the nationalist right wanting to retain "Danishness" in all its forms, and the far Left seeking a less centralized government away from Brussels. Although financial doom was predicted as a consequence of the "no" vote, no major negative implications materialized and the Danish economy remained solid. That same year, the landscape of Copenhagen and its environs changed forever with the opening of the **Øresund Bridge**, a road-and-rail link connecting the capital with southwest Sweden. In addition to significantly enhancing the city's connections with the rest of Scandinavia, it has brought the nearby Swedish city of Malmö within thirty minutes of central Copenhagen; while as an economic initiative the bridge itself may have proved something of a flop – steep tolls have kept the number of cars using the bridge far below expected figures – the Øresund region as a whole is booming, with a network of Danish and Swedish universities, cross-border migration and an influx of biotech, medical and food companies employing nearly thirty thousand people.

In November 2001, the political tide changed once again when Poul Nyrup Rasmussen and the centre-left coalition lost the election to a right-wing coalition led by **Anders Fogh Rasmussen**, which immediately passed strict laws curbing immigration. This radical shift reflected the global move to the political right that followed the September 11 attack in America; a feeling of growing resentment against refugees and second-generation Danes (mainly from Turkey) had already been nurtured by the right-wing, anti-elitist Pia Kærsgård, and after the World Trade Center tragedy, people started listening. As well as taking a hostile position toward "foreigners", the new government marked itself as anti-environment (by way of massive scaling down of energy-saving initiatives); anti-development (through cuts in overseas aid) and anti-culture (via the slashing of financial support to alternative types of entertainment). Fogh Rasmussen also upped the military budget and supported the invasion of Iraq, sending troops (and a much-ridiculed submarine) to the Gulf. Though significant anti-war demonstrations ensued, the election of February 2005 gave a second term to Fogh Rasmussen's conservative coalition, with the Folkeparti, the Danish People's Party, taking 24 seats out of 179; the victory, however, was seen more as a reaction against Social Democrat leader **Mogens Lykketoft**'s lack of charisma than as a mark of support for Rasmussen's political platform, and the failure to engage the electorate has left the average Dane feeling increasingly disconnected from politics.

Marriage rights

In a move against what it termed "marriages of convenience", the Danish government enacted legislation in 2002 discouraging **mixed marriages** between Danes and foreign-born citizens, with strict financial and housing requirements and an age stipulation that requires both partners to be at least 24 years old. While the new laws swiftly reduced the number of family reunification permits by more than 75 percent, many such couples have since sought to outmanoeuvre Danish laws via passage to more liberal Sweden, which grants citizenship to Danes after only two years of residence. With a Swedish passport, a Dane can then safely return to Denmark with his or her foreign spouse under the protection of European Union regulations. Since 2002, thousands of mixed-marriage couples have crossed the Øresund – nicknamed by some as "the bridge of love" – to **settle in Sweden**, but many have still adamantly refused to return permanently to Denmark until the right-wing party leaves the coalition. The government has since relaxed such laws because of increasing pressure from human rights groups, but they remain a thorn in the side of many who find love beyond Denmark's national borders.

The Danish cartoons

In early October 2005, the regional Danish newspaper *Jyllands-Posten* published a series of twelve **cartoons** with various depictions of the **Prophet Mohammad**, several of which portrayed him as a radical fundamentalist with a bomb drawn into his turban, angering many Muslims. The ambassadors to Denmark of eleven Muslim countries called the cartoons a "provocation" and demanded an immediate apology, but *Jyllands-Posten*, for its part, stood by its right to freedom of expression. A **diplomatic storm** ensued: Muslim protesters marched on the street of Danish cities, a *fatwa* was issued against the cartoonists and a Danish minister's car was firebombed. The situation escalated when several European newspapers picked up the story and republished the cartoons – some as part of their coverage of the controversy and others to affirm their right to print content even if it offended religious views – a turn that further angered many Muslims, stirring up the heated debate over European immigration policies. Danes around the world were urged to evacuate Muslim countries as Libya and Saudi Arabia recalled their ambassadors from Copenhagen, the Danish (and Norwegian) embassies in Beirut and Damascus were attacked and "Danish" foods were subsequently boycotted by numerous Muslims.

The situation eventually blew over, but not before drawing attention to the convictions of the current Danish government, a regime that has introduced some of the toughest restrictions on immigration of any country in Europe. Under particular criticism are the **Folkeparti**, Denmark's third largest political party, members of which have lashed out with vitriolic remarks against the Muslim community, including one prominent deputy who has made comparisons between Muslim women who wear headscarves and bikers who sport swastikas. The party's popularity rose dramatically in opinion polls following the cartoons controversy, with applications for membership rising some 1700 percent – not a huge amount in numerical terms but indicative nevertheless of the conservative bent of the Danish population. Meanwhile, Denmark's share of asylum applications among the three Scandinavian countries has fallen by sixty percent, while those to both Sweden and Norway have risen.

Denmark today

In recent years, Denmark has repeatedly found itself in the international headlines, a testament to its ability to still wield a disproportionately large amount of influence. The modicum of national joy that came from the birth of the new crown prince to Crown Prince Frederik and his Australian-born wife Mary in October 2005 was quickly tempered by the global uproar over what many saw to be **anti-Muslim cartoons** printed in Danish newspapers that soon followed (see box above), a dark episode in modern Danish history that tested political allegiances, challenged tenets of freedom of speech and heightened tensions over Denmark's treatment of its immigrant population, approximately 150,000 of which are Muslim.

To make matters worse, one of the social experiments that had proven emblematic of Danish liberalism and tolerance has begun to go sour. In 2002, as part of a crackdown on drug dealers, 53 arrests were made in **Christiania**, home to over a thousand artists, activists, hippies and misfits – two-thirds of whom either live on social welfare or have no reported income – and a locale that once attracted up to half a million tourists annually (although admittedly many of them came to buy cheap marijuana). Residents who had previously been granted free use of the land were now required to negotiate with the state and to pay a fixed monthly fee upwards of 1000kr for utilities and services. As of 2006, Christiania no longer maintained its special status, and many believe that it's only a matter of time before the city kicks out the current residents and begins to develop on the land – eighty acres of prime waterfront real estate.

In many senses, Denmark has evolved as a tenuous, **modern-day dichotomy**: a socially progressive liberal democracy with cradle-to-grave care whose government's policies are often perceived as xenophobic, and which observes a liberal outlook towards gay matrimony – it was the first country in the world to legalize gay and lesbian partnerships – and yet imposes draconian regulations on marriages between Danes and foreigners. The Folkeparti has made its intentions clear with a manifesto proclaiming that "Denmark belongs to the Danes and its citizens must be able to live in a secure community ... developing only along the lines of Danish culture" – and though these somewhat brazen statements only reflect the views of a small percentage of the population, support is growing. More positively, Denmark's economy is faring better than it has in many years, with close to zero unemployment in most regions. Though Danes are concerned with the state's conservative leanings and the fact that Danish troops are stationed in Iraq and Afghanistan, most look to the government's generally positive achievements over the last decade, and seem fairly positive about the future.

Danish design

While Finns, Swedes, Norwegians and Icelanders might well beg to differ, the founding concepts of **Scandinavian design** – the cool, crisp, organic style that has since spread to draughtboards and furniture showrooms far outside northern Europe – were decidedly Danish, emerging from the prototypes created across Danish design studios during the first half of the twentieth century.

Danish designers have always been good at syncretism: with such a small population and territory, it was a necessity of survival to be adept at applying skilled craftsmanship to forge foreign paradigms within a local context, and the earliest of Danish designers – Stone Age hunters and carvers and, later, Viking shipbuilders – relied upon an intimate **relationship with their environment** and the skill to make efficient use of available materials such as clay, wood and leather. Attributes of utility and durability took pride of place over any frill or embellishment, an approach that led to the trademark simplicity of design and prioritizing of function over form that characterizes Danish design.

Early aesthetics

As early as the 1820s, Empire-style architect-designer **Gustav Friedrich Hetsch** remarked that "the object of everything relating to interior design and architecture, large or small, must be that it answers its purpose and meets two main conditions: usability and suitability … beauty must always depend on usefulness because without this no satisfaction can be gained for the eye or the spirit." Such a call for **functional design** in household objects and public spaces thereafter became an inherent property of Danish design.

Following the ornate, elaborate constructions of Renaissance and Baroque castles that typified Denmark's rural landscape before the eighteenth century, **Rococo** came into fashion in many upper-class households, with light-hearted motifs such as Chinoiserie borrowed from the French court. At the beginning of the nineteenth century, **Neo-Classicism** was the style of the moment, with sophisticated urban interiors that looked away from grandeur and opulence and towards simple and clean geometric lines in details such as cornice mouldings, plaster relief and slender, hanging lamps. In the 1860s, the Neo-Classical style was dethroned by **Romanticism**, which culled its properties from a variety of heterogeneous sources. Most notable among such works were those of skilled Danish cabinetmakers, prized for their sophisticated detail in fine, untreated wood surfaces.

Towards Modernism

In the 1920s and 1930s, the work of designer **Kaare Klint** marked a critical turn for Denmark's design tradition. In contrast to the Bauhaus designers, who had rejected **Modernism** by creating objects that had little relation to the everyday lives of people, Klint embraced it, espousing an in-depth understanding of modern materials, exacting proportions and measurements and respecting the strong tradition of classical furniture-making. Klint's works were based on his tireless research into the proportions of the human form and the measurement of bodily features: in arriving at a set of common physical proportions for all human beings, Klint had hoped to design the most comfortable and most pragmatic shapes, becoming the forefather of modern ergonomic design in the process. Klint's productions range from the classical, woven *Faaborg* chair (1914) and the *Red* chair (1927) to more exotic *Safari* and *Deck* chairs (1933, 1936). But his concepts were never mass-produced, since they relied on careful precision techniques unavailable in furniture design during that era, and they required much time and financial investment on the part of the designer – commodities which, in the new industrial age, were becoming more and more scarce.

As modernization occurred comparatively late in Denmark, appreciation of traditional handmade craft and building methods remained strong throughout the country. When industrialization overtook the largely agricultural Danish economy in the 1950s, those notions of superior-quality craftsmanship and attention to detail were implemented in industrial manufacturing and design – most memorably in the work of designers such as **Poul Henningsen** (known sometimes simply as **PH**), the best-known innovator of early Danish lighting design, whose constructions, including the *PH Lamp* (1926), employed different shades of coloured glass with frosted surfaces that radiated golden hues. Contemporaries of Henningsen continued his tradition of user-friendly simplicity, like **Kay Bojesen** and his *Bastik* cutlery for Faadvad (1938) and streamlined teak salad bowl and servers; teak became one of the most fashionable hardwoods, with the work of **Finn Juhl** and **Peter Hvidt** helping to codify the popular "Teak Style". At the same time, forward-thinking studios like those of **Fritz Hansen** sought to capitalize on the new processes facilitated by industrialization, producing in the 1930s a bevy of high-volume furniture items that maintained a delicate simplicity.

Later mid-century furniture makers such as **Børge Mogensen** and **Hans Wegner** advocated the ideas of Klint through their modern interpretations of classic furniture pieces, with works like Mogensen's *Shaker* chair (1944), featuring a simple, curved back, beech-frame construction and paper-cord seat, and Wegner's more eccentric *Chinese* chair (1943) and the supremely comfortable and elegant *Peacock* chair (1947). With more than five hundred single chair designs credited to his name, Wegner, in particular, has done more – bar possibly Arne Jakobsen – for the international image of Danish design than anyone else. His big breakthrough came in 1949, when his *Round* chair was hailed by critics as "the world's most beautiful chair", and it rose to even further stardom when it was used in the televised debates between Kennedy and Nixon in the 1960s, after which it became referred to, quite matter-of-factly, as "*The Chair*". Wegner's designs went on to win worldwide critical acclaim during the 1950s and 1960s, and his pieces are now found in the permanent collections of museums all over the world.

Postwar to the present

During the 1950s, the earliest of Denmark's "modern" designers sought influence from as far afield as the traditions of the Japanese and the American Shakers, builders who paid homage to their natural environment through simple designs. Such organic construction is most visible in the work of **Arne Jacobsen**, who vies with Wegner as Denmark's most renowned designer. Equally

△ Jacobsen's Swan Chairs, the *Square* hotel, Copenhagen

adept as both architect and interior designer, among his works of note are the *Ant* chair (1951), an elegant three-legged piece with a narrow waist whose minimalist artistic design marked a distinctive break from traditional approaches to designing furniture, and his *Model No. 3107* chair (1955), which went on to become one of the best-selling chairs ever. Jacobsen's finest and most elegant work is the *SAS Royal Hotel* in Copenhagen (1960), in which he designed everything from the elegant curtained structure itself all the way down to the silverware for the hotel's restaurant. The hotel also became a showcase for his iconic fibre-and-leather *Swan* and *Egg* chairs (1957).

After the early success of Jacobsen, Danish designers began to make use of the shapes afforded by new synthetic materials like fiberglass and foam, a development evident nowhere more than in the work of **Verner Panton**. Panton, for long the *enfant terrible* of Danish furniture design – his style was cricitized by many as being far too eccentric– came up with playful shapes in bold colours that employed new materials to forge a fresh idiom for the role of such objects in public spaces during the latter half of the twentieth century. His best-known piece is the iconic *Panton* chair, or *Stacking* chair (1959), a durable, cantilevered one-piece that has since been regularly produced by Vitra for several decades.

Though a global recession in the early 1970s effected a drop in interest in pricier, design-heavy furniture, Danish design firms like **Bang & Olufsen** (see p.291), **Stelton** and **Georg Jensen** countered this by reaffirming the production of very pragmatic household objects. The hi-tech stereos of Bang & Olufsen – the *Beosystem 2500* (1990), for example – can be found in households across the country, and their streamlined, futuristic look and feel is well-known the world over. This hi-tech style has since been co-opted by furniture makers such as **Niels Jørgen Haugesen**, whose *X-line* chair (1977) employs similar lines.

Since then, Denmark has witnessed a merger of product and graphic design, ranging from the modern industrial design of groups such as **Danfoss** and **Louis Poulsen** to the more consumer-focused **Jacob Jensen** and **Dissing+Weitling**, but the hallmarks of traditional Danish design – attention to detail, user-friendly functionality and the utilization of natural, organic forms – are still very much in evidence today.

Cinema

While admittedly a "minor" European cinema, Danish film these days is a burgeoning industry, with a half-dozen or so very accomplished directors producing several exportable hits each year, and Danish productions are certainly giving the neighbouring Swedes a run for their money.

Early days

The first film screening in Denmark took place outdoors on the Rådhuspladsen in Copenhagen in 1896, and from early on the Danish film industry exported many of its earliest productions of silent fictional and documentary films abroad. The first Danish film, *Travel with Greenlandic Dogs* (1897), was a documentary on life in the colonies by photographer Peter Elfelt, and the Danish production studio **Nordisk Film** was founded several years later, the first major European studio to devote itself to full-length features; it is still the largest producer and distributor of films in the region. Most early Danish films were newsreel-length documentaries and short erotic melodramas such as *The Abyss* (1910), which launched the career of the great Danish silent-film star Asta Nielsen. Denmark's film industry soon lost its early footing, however, once other European directors branched out into feature-length films, a knock compounded by the progression from silent intertitles to the spoken – more often than not English – word.

Carl Theodore Dreyer

Although Danish cinema didn't really recover until the end of the century, it did produce one prominent international wunderkind in its early years. **Carl Theodore Dreyer** made a few early films in Denmark – including *The Master of the House* (1925) – but soon after headed to Germany and France, where he honed his skills, and quickly achieved international renown with his most famous film, *The Passion of Joan of Arc* (1928), a stark and barren picture of emotional intensity about the trial and death of the French saint; the lead role, played by Maria Falconetti, is often considered to be one of the single greatest film performances ever. Dreyer produced nine silent films and six spoken features – slow-paced, passionate studies of human psychology that explore the lives of people experiencing severe personal or religious cri-

△ Still from Dreyer's *Passion of Joan of Arc*

ses. His later works include *Vampyr* (1932) and *The Day of Wrath* (1943), a film about the hypocrisy in witchhunts that addressed themes of oppressed sensuality and love in a discontented society; the film was interpreted by many to be an allegory of the German occupation of Denmark. Among film buffs, Dreyer is perhaps best known for his later productions such as *The Word* (1955), a penetrating story about power and love in a Jutland parish and *Gertrud* (1964), his last film, an exploration into the tragedy of a woman who leaves her flaccid marriage in search of ideal love. Despite his later renown, Dreyer remained a bit of a loner outside the Danish film establishment, as *Joan of Arc* had labelled him a director of religious-themed, cerebral art-house films, a categorization that has unfortunately confined much of his work to film studies classes and the back of the Indie rental shop. But his once hard-to-find films have recently been restored, resubtitled and re-released on DVD by Criterion (Ⓦwww.criterion.com) and BFI (Ⓦwww.bfi.org.uk).

Mid-century film

The **German occupation** was a boon to the Danish film industry since a ban on film imports from the Allied countries created a new appetite for domestic films. Several films from that period stand out, most notably *The Red Horses* (1950), an adaptation of one of Danish writer Morten Korch's novels, a huge success that was followed by adaptations of eighteen other Korch works. Around this same time the genre of popular comedy gained new ground among Danish filmmakers, who also emerged with an increased number of art-house films, stimulated further by the New Wave cinema in Europe in the 1960s. Directors like **Astrid Henning-Jensen**, **Palle Kjærulff-Schmidt** and **Henning Carlsen** explored the new language of realism in film, with productions such as *Weekend* (1962) and *Once There Was a War* (1966), both based on scripts by famed Danish writer Klaus Rifbjerg, and *Hunger* (1966), an interpretation of Norwegian novelist Knut Hamsun's acclaimed novel. In the 1970s, amidst an increase in interest in film production among younger generations, the **Danish Film Institute** was established to provide grants and subsidies for up-and-coming filmmakers, since when nearly all Danish films have been made with at least some state support.

The New Danish Cinema

While Danish cinema remained largely off the map for much of the twentieth century– Dreyer's work being one of the few exceptions – the films of several prominent directors since the late 1980s have managed to transform Danish filmmaking into one of the more vibrant in European cinema, sparking a resurgence in both the number and quality of films produced within the country and a boom in global critical acclaim – and box-office numbers. During the late 1980s, two screenplays adapted from popular Danish novels provided renewed recognition abroad when, in a feat of near statistical impossibility, Denmark won the Academy Award for Best Foreign Film two years in a row, first in 1987 with **Gabriel Axel**'s interpretation of Karen Blixen's *Babette's Feast*, and the following year with **Bille August**'s *Pelle the Conqueror*, a haunting film based on the first part of a trilogy of novels by Martin Andersen Nexø.

Dreyer's legacy as Denmark's most famous filmmaker was further challenged towards the end of the twentieth century with the advent of writer-director **Lars von Trier**. Born in Copenhagen in 1956 and easily the most ambitious and stylistically unique Danish filmmaker since Dreyer, von Trier (the "von" was added to his name while in film school as an homage to director Josef von Sternberg) maintains the mantra that "film should be like a stone in your shoe", and his array of regular international public and critical successes often tackle themes of mercy and ethics. As one of the founding proponents of the **Dogme95 movement** (see box on p.116), von Trier has also become its most successful member, and his films are testaments to how much can be accomplished by simply relying on a strong storyline, talented actors and expert direction. Following the 1991 *Europa* (*Zentropa* in the US), a post-apocalyptic tale set in 1945 Germany, von Trier released *The Idiots* (1998), possibly his most disturbing film, a mockumentary about a group of friends who feign mental retardation in public, inciting unrest wherever they roam. Following *Idiots*, he made a trilogy of successful slow-paced, emotionally charged character studies of women, the first of which was the devastating *Breaking the Waves* (1996), a dark melodramatic tale about sex and religion set in northern Scotland that starred Emily Watson and won the jury prize at Cannes. That was followed up with *Dancer in the Dark* (2000), a beautiful and penetrating portrayal of a factory worker in small-town America who is going blind and who sacrifices herself to ensure that the same fate doesn't befall her son; hailed as a triumphant revival of the musical film, it starred Bjork and Catherine Deneuve. *Dogville* (2003) is another dark story about a woman, this time set in the *mafioso* world of the 1930s, and starring Nicole Kidman. In popular Bergman-esque tradition (and in violation of several Dogme stipulations) *Dogville* was shot entirely in studio with a minimum of props, making deft use of light and sound to augment the film's dramatic tension.

As the driving force behind what's been hailed as the **New Danish Cinema**, von Trier regularly steals the spotlight from other contemporary Danish directors, but several of his colleagues have experienced notable success both domestically and abroad. Most memorable are **Thomas Vinterberg**'s *The Celebration* (1998), a family drama about suicide that plays out over a weekend reunion, and two romantic comedies: **Søren Kragh-Jacobsen**'s *Mifune* (1999) and **Lone Scherfig**'s *Italian for Beginners* (2000) – both offering humorous insights into Danish society and making a splash on screens abroad. Sherfig's quirky English-language *Wilbur Wants to Kill Himself* (2002) was a superb amalgam of dark humour and deep sadness. Other recent Danish films of note include **Lasse Spang Olsen**'s *In China They Eat Dogs* and *Old Men in New Cars* (1999, 2002), **Annette K. Olesen**'s *Minor Mishaps* (2002), **Anders Thomas Jensen**'s *The Green Butchers* (2003), **Simon Staho**'s *Day and Night* (2004) and **Lotte Svendsen**'s *What's Wrong With This Picture* (2004). Most recently, *Dear Wendy* (2005), a collaboration between von Trier as screenwriter and Vinterberg as director, was intended to make a reactionary statement about the liberal licensing of guns in America, though its pretensions to pacifism failed to impress most critics and viewers anywhere outside of Denmark.

Books

Although the amount of English-language books on Denmark is nowhere near that of many other European countries, we've compiled some of the better titles out there. In terms of **history** and **society**, the sheer volume of books on the Vikings leaves you with the impression that historians on the region consider it the only period worth writing about. The outlook for **literary fiction** is a bit more promising, as the past few years have seen a marked rise in North American and British public appreciation of contemporary Danish authors – due in no small part to the phenomenal international success of novelist **Peter Høeg** – and a resultant increase in the number of English-language translations of their better known works, as well as reissues of some of the classics. The most recent information on who's been published where in English translation can be found at ⊛www.literaturenet.dk. Not every work we've listed will be on the shelves of your local bookshop, though if you can't order it there, you most certainly can on ⊛www.amazon.com, or, failing that, through the publishers themselves. For books currently in print, the publisher in the UK is listed in parentheses first, followed by the US publisher. If the UK and US editions are the same, we've given the publisher's name only once, and if the title is available in one country only, we've specified the country. The few books listed that are no longer in print are indicated with "o/p"; these still shouldn't be too difficult to track down, either at larger libraries or through online secondhand resellers. Those marked with a 🏃 indicate titles that are particularly recommended.

Viking history and Norse mythology

Kevin Crossley-Holland *Penguin Book of Norse Myths: Gods of the Vikings* (Penguin). A superb collection of over thirty separate prose translations of the seminal Scandinavian myths, filled with fighting gods, mystical magicians and tales of love, deceit and destruction.

Tom Cunliffe *Topsail and Battleaxe* (Sheridan House). The intertwined stories of the tenth-century Vikings who sailed from Norway, past the Faroes and Iceland to North America, and the author's parallel trip in 1983 – made in a 75-year-old pilot cutter. Enthusiastically written, and illustrated with terrific photos.

🏃 Gwyn Jones *A History of the Vikings* (Oxford). The most

thorough of any of the Viking histories, this well-written, painstakingly-documented chronological account includes a number of drawings, maps and photographs that complement the pop-academic tone of the book.

Else Roesdahl *The Vikings* (Penguin) The most overtly ethnographic of Viking histories, this paperback outlines social aspects of Viking life – trade, language, art and poetry – painting a vivid picture of their day-to-day lives. Included is a lengthy chapter on their influence in England. The tone is less academic and quite a bit more concise than other volumes, making it a quick read and an excellent introduction.

Peter Sawyer (ed) *Oxford Illustrated History of the Vikings* (OUP). One of the newer overviews of the Vikings, this glossy, heavily-illustrated title consists of a dozen contemporary essays on various aspects of Viking society and culture, including a superbly-written and informative piece by Simon Keynes on the Vikings in England.

Snorri Sturluson *Prose Edda, King Harald's Saga* (Penguin). Classics of Norse mythology, these historical tales were composed in the early thirteenth century – the pagan religious traditions of Scandinavia are all but extinct – and are the most extensive source for modern knowledge about the period. Newly translated by an American scholar of archeology, this is exceptional, invigorating reading.

Modern history, philosophy and politics

W. H. Auden (ed) *The Living Thoughts of Kierkegaard* (New York Review of Books). In this bold new anthology of the Danish philosopher's work, the celebrated poet Auden has selected his favourite Kierkegaard essays and written a sparkling introductory essay contextualizing his writings and ideas.

Andrew Buckser *After the Rescue: Jewish Identity and Community in Contemporary Denmark* (Palgrave). A comprehensive account about one of Europe's less understood Diaspora communities that melds historical documentation with the author's personal interviews and observations. A tad academic, though not cumbersome in its language, this ethnography is a fascinating read for anyone interested in modern "minority" communities.

Jane Chamberlain & Jonathan Ree (eds) *The Kierkegaard Reader* (Blackwell). A comprehensive collection of Kierkegaard's most famous writings that includes his own explanations of their significance, as well as insightful forewords to each of the texts written by the editors/translators. By far the best and most accessible introduction to this notoriously difficult nineteenth-century philosopher and writer.

John Robert Christianson *On Tycho's Island: Tycho Brahe, Science, and Culture in the Sixteenth Century* (Cambridge UP). This pioneering study chronicles how Danish-born Brahe – chemist, philosopher and poet – used his charismatic personality to influence a number of contemporaries, reforming European thought ultimately to usher in the Scientific Revolution, marking the birth of modern science.

T.K. Derry *History of Scandinavia* (Minnesota UP). Despite being dated – it was published in 1979, though a brief epilogue covers the end of the twentieth century – this comprehensive volume is an exceptionally well-written account of how the five Scandinavian nations developed along similar paths from pre-Viking times through to modernization. It is especially noteworthy for what it says about how early pan-Scandinavian sentiment intersected with the nationalisms of the individual countries.

Tony Griffiths *Scandinavia: At War With Trolls* (Hurst & Co.) A concise and witty cultural history of modern Scandinavia and the contributions of its great thinkers, artists and musicians from the eighteenth century to today, this short book provides insight into the people and ideas that have helped shape the Scandinavian psyche. One of the best contemporary histories out there.

Knud Jespersen *A History of Denmark* (Palgrave). The only modern history of Denmark available in English, this short book provides a wealth of information on royalty, the Church, economics and politics, as well as some interesting insights into what has created a specific Danish cultural identity. The clipped style makes it a very quick read.

W. Glyn Jones *Denmark: A Modern History* (o/p). A valuable account of the twentieth century (up until 1984), with a commendable outline of pre-twentieth-century Danish history. Strong on politics, useful on social history and the arts, but disappointingly brief on recent grassroots movements.

Søren Kierkegaard *Either/ Or* (Penguin). Kierkegaard's most important work (and his most approachable), a monumental philosophical tract packed with wry and wise musings on love, life and death in nineteenth-century Danish society. The collection includes the (in)famous "*Seducer's Diary*", the disturbing narrative of a man who explores

his sense of detachment by deliberately arousing the passion of a young society girl. Inspired by events in Kierkegaard's own life still shrouded in mystery – at age 28 he decided that marriage was incompatible with his solitary nature – the story is a vivid exploration of the complex psychology of cruelty and love.

Alan Palmer *Northern Shores: A History of the Baltic Sea and Its Peoples* (John Murray). A fascinating history about a tumultuous body of water and the nations whose survival has depended on it, from the Baltic's role as a basin for Viking warships through to its present function for transport and tourism. The focus is on the people – from St Bridget to Lech Walesa – whose lives were intertwined with the historical ebb and flow of the countries that border it.

Emmy E. Werner *A Conspiracy of Decency* (Westview). A short, well-written account detailing how the Danish people were able to rescue nearly all of the country's Jews from deportation – and death – by hiding them and granting them asylum. The author, a developmental psychologist, uses first-hand accounts of eyewitnesses to the heroic acts, making for quite compelling reading.

Biography

Jens Andersen *Hans Christian Andersen: A New Life* (Overlook). Hans Christian's 200th birthday in 2005 inspired a spate of reissues and new translations of his classic fairy tales, as well as new scholarship into his life and influences. This biography by Andersen (no relation) leaves out HC's earliest days to focus on the parts of his life that most affected him, and like many such bios,

explore his sex life (or lack thereof) in great detail. Packed with facts and footnotes, the iconic style makes it a rewarding read.

Jean and Dale D. Drum *My Only Great Passion: The Life and Films of Carl Theodore Dreyer* (Scarecrow Press). The only full-length English-language biography of the Danish film great, this is a comprehensive look into the complex mind of the man who created some of the greatest European films of the pre-colour era.

Joakim Garff *Søren Kierkegaard: A Biography* (Princeton UP). The most comprehensive book on Kierkegaard's life to date, this 800-page tome is surprisingly readable, due in part to its masterful translation into English. It's less an assessment of the influence of Kierkegaard's ideas than it is an investigation into the often-tortured world of a great intellectual through examining the minutiae of his everyday-life experiences.

Frantz Leander Hansen *Aristocratic Universe of Karen Blixen* (Sussex). One of the best presentations around of Blixen's work, with ample references to world literature with which her writing has clear connections. There is an especially good analysis of *Babette's Feast*.

Jack Stevenson *Lars Von Trier* (BFI). The biographical aspects of this compact tome focus on von Trier's formation as a cutting-edge director and emphasizes exactly who and what has influenced his work.

Judith Thurman *Isak Dinesen: The Life of Karen Blixen* (Picador). The most penetrating biography of Blixen, elucidating details of the farm period not found in the two "Africa" books.

Jackie Wullschlager *Hans Christian Andersen: The Life of a Storyteller* (Penguin; Chicago UP). Published in 2002, this finely documented work examines the misery of Andersen's childhood, his subsequent rapid success and his troubled sexuality, arguing that it was the shock and power of these experiences that fuelled many of his mournful tales.

Literature pre-World War II

Hans Christian Andersen *Hans Andersen's Fairy Tales* (OUP). Still the most internationally prominent figure of Danish literature, Andersen's fairy tales are so widely translated and read that the full clout of their allegorical content is often overlooked: interestingly, his first collection of such tales (published in 1835) was condemned by many critics for its "violence and questionable morals". *Travels* (Green Integer, US only) is a small collection of his accounts while travelling in Europe and the Mediterranean, stories that offer a unique insight into Andersen's powers of observation and social critique. His autobiography, *The Fairy Tale of My Life* (Cooper Square), is an interesting perspective on the author's life. It makes a fine alternative to the half-dozen or so modern biographical portraits now available

– though don't expect too much exploration into the author's darker sides.

Karen Blixen (Isak Dinesen) *Out of Africa* (Vintage). This account of Blixen's attempts to run a coffee farm in Kenya after divorce from her husband is a lyrical and moving tale, and was turned into an Oscar winner by Sydney Pollack. But it's in *Seven Gothic Tales* (Vintage) that Blixen's fiction was at its zenith: a flawlessly executed, weird, emotive work, full of twists in plot and strange, ambiguous characterization.

Tove Ditlevsen *Complete Freedom* (Curbstone Press). A selection of short stories by one of Denmark's first feminist writers that explores themes of greed, family relationships and anti-Semitism. A second work, *Early Spring* (o/p), is an autobiographical novel of growing up in the working-class Vesterbro district of Copenhagen during the 1930s; as an evocation of childhood and early adulthood, it's totally captivating.

Per Olov Enquist *The Visit of the Royal Physician* (Simon and Schuster; Vintage). A gripping, racy and witty historical novel by one of Sweden's most beloved novelists, set in King Christian VII's Danish court in the 1760s: the king is a half-wit, the queen is horrendously duplicitous and the forces of the Enlightenment are arranged against the reactionaries. The narrative charts the power struggles of the various weasly courtiers who manipulate the young and mentally unstable king, including his German doctor, the charismatic Johann Struensee, who took the queen as his mistress. Great stuff.

Ludvig Holberg *The Journey Of Niels Klim To The World Underground* (Bison Books). Ludvig Holberg (1684–1754) was a well-known Danish-Norwegian historian, philosopher and playwright. This work, written in Latin in 1741, was his only novel and is of special interest to those interested in early science fiction and social satire: it maintains strong parallels to Jules Verne and Robinson Crusoe, and is said to have influenced Tolkien in his writing. Includes an informative preface by Peter Fitting.

Johannes V. Jensen *The Fall of the King* (o/p). 1944 Nobel Prize-winner Jensen's masterpiece vividly depicts an overlooked period of Danish history covering the tumultuous reign of Christian II (1513–23) and his many years in captivity at Sønderborg Slot, superbly described through the eyes of his servant and friend, Mikkel Thøgersen.

Martin Andersen Nexø *Pelle the Conqueror* (Mondial). Though the novel became more popular abroad after it was made into an Academy Award-winning film by Bille August in 1989, this moving tale about life as an immigrant has been a classic in Denmark for years. Nexø, one of eleven children born in the slums of Copenhagen in the late nineteenth century, was himself no foreigner to the harsh reality of poverty, accounting for his poignant, unsentimentalised character descriptions.

Hans Scherfig *Stolen Spring* (o/p). A group of Copenhagen youths studying for their high-school exams feel they're missing out on the most important spring of their lives. A classic novel, mandatory reading for all Danish school students.

Literature post-World War II

Suzanne Brøgger *A Fighting Pig Too Tough To Eat* (Norvik). A collection of assorted writings – some fiction, some social commentary – by one of the more daring and polemical authors writing in Denmark. Brøgger is one of the few female members of the Danish Academy.

Inger Christiansen *Alphabet* (Bloodaxe; New Directions Press), *Butterfly Valley* (Dedalus). Christiansen, born in 1935, is one of Denmark's most beloved poets and is widely known around the world. The translation in this bilingual edition of *Butterfly Valley*, considered an integral part of the canon of modern Danish literature, does justice to her powerful, visionary sonnets on life, death, art and love.

Stig Dalager *Journey in Blue: A Novel about Hans Christian Andersen* (Peter Owen). Dalager has become one of the most renowned Scandinavian authors of the past few decades. In this novel, he reimagines the musings and words of Andersen through experiences and scenes of his life, providing interesting insight into what caused Andersen's strong sense of alienation and how this fuelled his search for literary validation in the same world that shunned him.

Leif Davidson *Lime's Photograph* (Vintage). An intelligent and compelling thriller involving a fiftysomething alcoholic *papparazzo*; the English of the translation is especially astute. Davidson's most recent crime novel, *The Serbian Dane* (Arcadia), involves a *fatwa* on an Iranian author, a murder conspiracy involving the Danish parliament and a hired assassin hailing from Serbia.

Jakob Ejersbo *Nordkraft* (McArthur & Co). *Nordkraft* is journalist Ejersbo's first novel; a story about three going-nowhere, hash-smoking youths struggling to survive in the city of Aalborg, the book is also an exploration into how Danes perceive ethnic and cultural difference. The author's raw style of writing has drawn comparisons to early Irvine Welsh.

Michael Frayn *Copenhagen* (Anchor). Frayn's devastating, beautifully written play re-examines the reasons and tensions behind the mysterious visit in 1941 to Nazi-occupied Copenhagen by the German atomic physicist, Werner Heisenberg, to see his counterpart Niels Bohr, formerly a close colleague and friend, now working for the opposite side in the race to develop the atomic bomb.

Jens Christian Grøndahl *Silence in October* (Canongate) One of Europe's most widely read

contemporary authors, Grøndahl already has over a dozen novels under his belt, several of which have recently been made available in English translation. *Silence* is his ninth, a stream-of-consciousness tale in which an art critic tries to come to terms with the unexpected death of his wife. The author delicately weaves the relationships between time, space and form as a metaphor for comprehending human emotion.

Peter Høeg *Miss Smilla's Feeling for Snow* (Vintage). Høeg is easily Denmark's most famous modern author. A worldwide bestseller and Høeg's best known work, this compelling thriller deals with Danish colonialism in Greenland and the issue of cultural identity. Other acclaimed books include *Borderliners* (Harvill; Delta) and his most recent novel, *The Silent Girl* (Harvill; FSG), about a world-famous circus artist whose former pupil, a ten-year-old girl, is kidnapped.

Christian Jungersen *The Exception* (Weidenfeld and Nicholson). A bestseller all across Europe, and second novel for Jungersen (who draws regular comparisons to Peter Høeg), this thrilling tale follows the lives of four women who receive threatening emails at the centre for genocide studies where they work. The book deeply considers moral ambiguity as it explores the ethical dilemmas that confront these women, and Jungersen's exacting style keeps you turning the pages without ever letting you guess the ending.

Thomas E. Kennedy *Kerrigan's Copenhagen: A Love Story* (o/p). The Danish capital co-stars in this witty, erudite, Joycean-style tale of an American writer attempting to come to terms with his past through the help of Copenhagen's many bars. Each chapter is devoted to a different watering hole, with the loveable if frustrating hero encountering a host of characters, and musing on topics like city life, beer, books, jazz, sex, cigars and architecture, among other things.

Svend Åge Madsen *Days with Diam* (Norvik). Madsen has written over twenty books (two of which have been translated into English), most of them humorous works that play with perceptions of reality, employing characters who experience an existential transformation after undergoing some extreme situation. *Days with Diam* is an experimental novel in which the narrator encounters himself in a number of different guises.

Ib Michael *The Prince* (FSG). This period novel by one of Denmark's most prominent authors of magical realism is set in the nineteenth century and follows the adventures of a twelve-year-old boy beginning to explore the secrets of the world. The author's trilogy of novels – *The Vanilla Girl*, *The Midnight Soldier* and *Letter to the Moon* – is regarded as the greatest achievement of Danish literature during the 1990s, though none of these have yet been translated into English.

Inge Pedersen *The Thirteenth Month* (Oberlin College). Jutland-born Pedersen has been one of the country's most acclaimed poets for several decades, with touching poems that make use of oft-read Scandinavian themes of light and cold weather. This book, winner of the 2005 Scandinavian-American translation prize, is a compilation of some of the best verses from five volumes of her works.

Morten Ramsland *Dog's Head* (Transworld). Ramsland, a self-described "anarchist writer" who was once declared unfit for grammar school, won the prestigious Golden Laurel prize in 2006, and is just now beginning to achieve acclaim in Denmark and reach European audiences. This quirky debut novel follows a Danish expat who returns home to deal with ghosts from his family's past.

Hanne Marie Svendsen *Under the Sun* (Norvik) A modern fairy tale that follows the life of a lighthouse keeper's daughter in a northern Danish fishing community.

Pia Tafdrup *Queen's Gate* (Bloodaxe). A superb collection of poems that employ water as a metaphor to explore the complexities of the body and soul, with imagery that resonates with the landscape of Scandinavia.

Janne Teller *Odin's Island* (Atlantic Books). Released in English translation in 2006, this debut novel follows the fantastical story of Odin, an ancient man who turns up lost one Christmas Eve on a mystery Scandinavian island, only to be claimed by modern warring religious factions as their prophet. The timing of this novel, part magical adventure and part biting social satire, is impeccable, and Teller's playful style has fun with modern notions of political and religious diplomacy.

Rose Tremain *Music and Silence* (Vintage). Captivating historical novel that follows the lives of Christian IV, his consort, his English lutenist and their lovers. Life in the many castles around Denmark is brilliantly described, and the novel provides a fascinating insight into Danish aspirations and superstitions during the period.

Anthropology, culture and society

CONTEXTS | Books

Andrew S. Buckser *Communities of Faith: Sectarianism, Identity and Social Change on a Danish Island* (Berghahn). An academic monograph that explores the role of religion in modern society by tracing the rise of three religious groups on a Jutland island and assessing the role they play in Danish social and cultural life. Less jargony and theoretical than most ethnographies, making it more approachable for the non-specialist.

Christer Elfving & Petra de Hamer *New Scandinavian Cooking* (mo' media). A cook's tour through Scandinavia's capital cities, mixing history, culinary trends and tips on the hottest chefs and restaurants with delicious modern recipes.

Stefan Hestnes *Funen's Temptations: A Culinary Journey* (Svendborgtryk). A charming, locally produced cookbook that is heavy on appetizers and dessert dishes native to Funen, such as marzipan-flavoured raspberry flutes and a traditional Funen stewed apple tart.

Mette Hjort *Small Nation, Global Cinema* (Minnesota UP). A must for anyone interested in modern Danish cinema, this book looks at the emerging success of the New Danish Cinema, focusing on themes of nationalism, cultural diffusion and representation of ethnic minorities, with emphasis on the Dogme 95 movement. Though it's a decidedly academic publication, the language still makes it very accessible to most readers.

Mette Hjort & Ib Bondebjerg *The Danish Directors* (Intellect). A book of informed interviews with nearly two dozen Danish filmmakers including Lars von Trier, Bille August and Thomas Vinterberg, as well as a number of less-established directors. The interviews cover everything from early influences to filming techniques, though the focus is on the individual directors' self-analyses of their films.

Richard Kelly *The Name of this Book is Dogme 95* (Faber and Faber). Offering excellent insights into the whole Dogme movement, this diary-style account of the making of a documentary on Dogme features interviews with the founders and an in-depth look at some of the seminal films.

G. Prakash Reddy *Danes are like that! Perspectives of an Indian Anthropologist on the Danish Society* (o/p). This now-out-of-print ethnography offers some interesting insights into Danish society, and its style is very accessible to non-anthropologists.

Andreas Viestad *Kitchen of Light* (Artisan). A gorgeous cookbook in which the detailed seafood and meat recipes are interspersed with breathtaking photographs of Nordic coastal life and personal narratives by the author-chef. Though he is Norwegian, his nouveau dishes are decidedly pan-Scandinavian, making use of ingredients and cooking styles that would be familiar to any Dane comfortable in his (or her) kitchen.

Design and architecture

Michael Ellison and Leslie Piña *Designed for Life: Scandinavian Modern Furnishings 1930–1970* (Bushwood; Schiffer). Superbly photographed title detailing the major pieces of Scandinavian furniture – the majority of them Danish works – with descriptions and price estimates, as well as information on retail outlets and auction houses in the US and Europe where you can pick them up.

Magnus Englund & Chrystina Schmidt *Scandinavian Modern* (Ryland Peters & Small). The photographs in this smallish coffee-table book are a roving eye into some of the most spectacular homes in Scandinavia, providing design insight and suggestions for giving your own home some Nordic pizazz.

Charlotte and Peter Fiell *Scandinavian Design* (Taschen). This Taschen classic is a massive, voluminous reference tome of large glossy photographs and informative accompanying text covering every major Scandinavian designer of the twentieth century – from Aalto to Wirkkala.

Jørgen Sestoft, Jørgen Hegner Christiansen & Kim Dirkinck-Holmfeld *Guide to Danish Architecture* (Danish Architectural Press) Great for architecture aficionados, this compact, two-volume set provides a solid overview of all of Denmark's major constructions of the last millennium. Also includes a large fold-out country map detailing where you can find the mentioned works.

Anja Llorella Oriol *New Scandinavian Design* (teNeues). Published in late 2005 in a compact format, this is the most *au courant* assessment of recent trends in Scandinavian architecture, furniture and product design.

Bradley Quinn *Scandinavian Style* (Conran Octopus). There's lots of eye candy in this bright coffee-table book, which highlights contemporary interior and furniture design as much as the influential Baroque, Gustavian and Nordic Classicist styles that still figure prominently in many of the region's older homes.

Carsten Thau & Kjeld Vindum *Arne Jacobsen* (Danish Architectural Press) A gargantuan, descriptive compendium featuring loads of full-page colour photographs and detailed commentaries on the works of Jacobsen, Denmark's most famous designer, from his iconic Ant and Swan chairs to lesser-known works such as his sleek, matte cutlery and rural, modernist schoolhouses.

Frederik Sieck *Danish Furniture Design* (Nyt Nordisk Forlag). A concise but comprehensive overview of the major works of every major twentieth-century furniture designer in Denmark.

Language

Language

Language

T hough similar to German in some respects, **Danish** has significant differences in pronunciation, with Danes tending to swallow the ending of many words and leaving certain letters silent. In general, English is widely understood throughout Denmark, as is German, and young people especially often speak both fluently. However, even with little need to resort to Danish, learning a few phrases will surprise and delight any Danes you meet. If you can speak Swedish or Norwegian, then you should have little problem making yourself understood – all three languages share the same root.

The language section below will equip you with the bare essentials, but if you want something more comprehensive, the Berlitz Danish–English Dictionary and *Berlitz Danish Phrase Book* are good reference guides. If you're planning to really get to grips with the language, the best teach-yourself book is *Colloquial Danish* (W. Glyn Jones and Kirsten Gade). For serious students of the language, the *Danish Dictionary* (Anna Garde and W. Glyn Jones, eds) is excellent; while for grammar, you can't do better than *Danish: A Comprehensive Grammar* (Philip Holmes, Robin Allan and Tom Lundskær-Nielsen).

Words and phrases

Basics

Danish **pronunciation** is a confusing affair, so for the phrases below we've explained in brackets how to pronounce them.

Taler de engelsk? (tayla dee ENgellsg)	Do you speak English?	Hvor er? (voa ea?)	Where is?
Ja (ya)	Yes	Hvor meget? (voa maYETH?)	How much?
Nej (nye)	No	Hvad koster det? (vath kosta day?)	How much does it cost?
Jeg forstår det ikke (yai fusTO day igge)	I don't understand	Jeg vil gerne ha... (yai vay GERna ha)	I'd like...
Værså venlig (verso venli)	Please	Hvor er toiletterne? (Voa ea toalettaneh?)	Where are the toilets?
Tak (tagg)	Thank you	Et bord til ... (et boa te...)	A table for...
Undskyld (unsgul)	Excuse me		
Hi (hye)	Hello/Hi	Må jeg bede om regningen? (moah yai beyde uhm RYningan?)	Can I have the bill/check, please?
Godmorgen (goMORN)	Good morning		
Goddag (goDA)	Good afternoon		
Godnat (goNAD)	Goodnight		
Farvel (faVELL)	Goodbye	Billet (bill-led)	Ticket

Numbers

Nul	0	Atten	18
En	1	Nitten	19
To	2	Tyve	20
Tre	3	Enogtyve	21
Fire	4	Tredive	30
Fem	5	Fyrre	40
Seks	6	Halvtreds	50
Syv	7	Tres	60
Otte	8	Halvfjerds	70
Ni	9	Firs	80
Ti	10	Halvfems	90
Elleve	11	Hundrede	100
Tolv	12	Hundrede og et	101
Tretten	13	Hundrede og enoghalvtreds	151
Fjorten	14		
Femten	15	To hundrede	200
Seksten	16	Tusind	1000
Sytten	17		

Days and months

Mandag	Monday	Marts	March
Tirsdag	Tuesday	April	April
Onsdag	Wednesday	Maj	May
Torsdag	Thursday	Juni	June
Fredag	Friday	Juli	July
Lørdag	Saturday	August	August
Søndag	Sunday	September	September
		Oktober	October
Januar	January	November	November
Februar	February	December	December

Some signs

Indgang	Entrance	Lukket	Closed
Udgang	Exit	Ankomst	Arrival
Skub/træk	Push/pull	Afgang	Departure
Fare	Danger	Politi	Police
Herrer	Gentlemen	Rygning forbudt/ Ikke rygere	No smoking
Damer	Ladies		
Åben	Open	Ingen adgang	No entry

Food and drink

Basics

Kniv	Knife	Ost	Cheese
Gaffel	Fork	Bøfsandwich	Hamburger
Ske	Spoon	Pølser	Frankfurters/ sausages
Tallerken	Plate		
Kop	Cup	Smørrebrød	Open sandwiches
Glas	Glass	Det kolde bord	Help-yourself cold buffet
Salt	Salt		
Peber	Pepper	Pålæg	Open sandwich toppings, typically cold cuts
Sukker	Sugar		
Nudler	Noodles		
Ris	Rice	Sildebord	A selection of spiced and marinated herring
Brød	Bread		
Rundstykke	Crispy roll	Spegesild	Salted and marinated herring
Fuldkornsbrød	Wholemeal bread		
Rugbrød	Rye bread	Leverpostej	Liver paté
Småkage	Cookie	Spegepølse	Salami
Kiks	Biscuits	Rémoulade	Mayonnaise-based condiment with chopped pickles
Wienerbrød	"Danish" pastry		
Mælk	Milk		
Skummetmælk	Skimmed milk	Ristede løg	Crisp roasted onions
Smør	Butter	Rulepølse	Rolled pork belly with herbs
Is	Ice cream		

Egg (Æg) dishes

Kogt æg	Boiled egg	Røræg	Scrambled eggs
Omelet	Omelette	Spejlæg	Fried eggs

Fish (Fisk)

Ål	Eel	Rejer	Shrimp
Forel	Trout	Rogn	Roe
Gedde	Pike	Rødspætte	Plaice
Helleflynder	Halibut	Røget sild	Smoked herring
Hummer	Lobster	Sardiner	Sardines
Karpe	Carp	Sild	Herring
Klipfisk	Salt cod	Søtunge	Sole
Krabbe	Crab	Stør	Sturgeon
Krebs	Crayfish	Store rejer	Prawns
Laks	Salmon	Torsk	Cod
Makrel	Mackerel		

Meat (*Køad*)

And(ung)	Duck(ling)	Kanin	Rabbit
Oksekød	Beef	Kylling	Chicken
Dyresteg	Venison	Lammekød	Lamb
Fasan	Pheasant	Lever	Liver
Gås	Goose	Skinke	Ham
Hare	Hare	Svinekød	Pork
Kalkun	Turkey	Vildt	Venison

Vegetables (*Grøntsager*)

Ærter	Peas	Løg	Onions
Agurk	Cucumber	Majs	Sweetcorn
Artiskokker	Artichokes	Majskolbe	Corn on the cob
Asparges	Asparagus	Peberfrugt	Peppers
Blomkål	Cauliflower	Persille	Parsley
Bønner	Beans	Porrer	Leeks
Champignoner	Mushrooms	Ris	Rice
Grønne bønner	Runner beans	Rødbeder	Beetroot
Gulerødder	Carrots	Rødkål	Red cabbage
Brune bønner	Kidney beans	Rosenkål	Brussels sprouts
Hvidløg	Garlic	Salat	Lettuce, salad
Julesalat	Chicory	Selleri	Celery
Kål	Cabbage	Spinat	Spinach
Kartofler	Potatoes	Søde kartofler	Sweet potatoes
Linser	Lentils	Turnips	Turnips

Fruit (*Frugt*)

Æbler	Apples	Hyldebær	Elderberries
Abrikoser	Apricots	Jordbær	Strawberries
Ananas	Pineapple	Kirsebær	Cherries
Appelsiner	Oranges	Mandariner	Tangerines
Bananer	Bananas	Melon	Melon
Blommer	Plums	Pærer	Pears
Blåbær	Blueberries	Rabarber	Rhubarb
Brombær	Blackberries	Rosiner	Raisins
Citron	Lemon	Solbær	Blackcurrants
Ferskner	Peaches	Stikkelsbær	Gooseberries
Grapefrugt	Grapefruit	Svesker	Prunes
Hindbær	Raspberries	Vindruer	Grapes

Danish specialities

Æbleflæsk	Smoked bacon with onions and sautéed apple rings	Æggekage	Scrambled eggs with onions, chives, potatoes and bacon pieces

Biksemad	Diced leftover roast pork fried with onion and potatoes and eaten with pickled beetroot	**Medisterpølse**	A spiced pork sausage, usually served with boiled potatoes or stewed vegetables
Boller i karry	Meatballs in curry sauce served with rice	**Røget sild**	Smoked herring
		Sild i karry	Herring in hot curry sauce
Brune kartofler	Small boiled potatoes glazed in buttery sugar	**Skidne æg**	Poached or hard-boiled eggs in a cream sauce, spiced with fish mustard and served with rye bread, garnished with sliced bacon and chives
Flæskesteg	A hunk of roasted pork with crackling, hot pickled red cabbage, boiled potatoes and gravy		
Fiske frikadeller	Fish meatballs	**Skipper labskovs**	Sailor's stew: small squares of beef boiled with potatoes, peppercorns and bay leaves
Frikadeller	Pork meatballs		
Grillstegt kylling	Grilled chicken		
Bøf med bløde løg	Thick minced-beef burgers fried with onions		
		Stegt flæsk med persille sovs	Thinly sliced fried pork with boiled potatoes and a thick creamy parsley sauce
Kalvebryst i frikasseé	Veal boiled with vegetables and served in a white sauce with peas and carrots		
		Stegt ål med stuvede kartofler	Fried eel with diced potatoes and white sauce
Kogt torsk	Poached cod in mustard sauce with boiled potatoes		

Drink (*Drikke*)

Vand	Water	**Citronvand**	Lemonade
Kaffe (med fløde)	Coffee (with cream)	**Eksport-Øl**	Export beer (very strong lager)
Te	Tea		
Chokolade (varm)	Chocolate (hot)	**Øl**	Beer
Mælk	Milk	**Fadøl**	Draught beer
Sødmælk	Full-fat milk	**Guldøl**	Strong beer
Letmælk	Semi-skimmed milk	**Vin**	Wine
Kærnemælk	Buttermilk	**Husets vin**	House wine
Appelsinjuice	Orange juice	**Hvidvin**	White wine
Æblemost	Apple juice	**Rødvin**	Red wine
Tomatjuice	Tomato juice	**Mineralvand or Danskvand**	Soda water/ mineral water
Appelsinvand	Orangeade		

Glossary

Båd	Boat
Bakke	Hill
Banegård	Train station
Borg	Fortified castle
Bro	Bridge
By	Town
-et/-en	suffixes denoting "the"
Fælled	Common (as in "communal ground")
Færge	Ferry
Folkeafstemning	Referendum
Dansk Folkekirke	Organization of the Danish state church
Folketing	Danish Parliament
Gade	Street
Gammel	Old
Genbrug	Recycling
Gård	Yard
Have	Garden
Havn	Harbour
Hus	House
Kanal	Canal
Kirke	Church
Klint	Cliff
Klit	Dune
Kongens	King's, royal

Kyst	Coast
Landsby	Village
Lille	Little, small
Lufthavn	Airport
Museet	Museum
Nørre	Northern
Ny	New
Ø	Island
Øster	Eastern
Plads	Square
Port	Gate
Rutebilstation	Long-distance bus station
Rådhus	Town Hall
Sankt/Skt/Sct	Saint
Skov	Forrest, wood
Slot	Castle
Sø	Lake, sea
Sønder	Southern
Stor	Big
Stræde	Street
Strand	Beach or shore
Tårn	Tower
Tog	Train
Torv	Square
Vandrerhjem	Youth hostel
Vej	Road
Vester	Western

Travel store

D: Rough Guide
DIRECTIONS for
short breaks

Available from all good bookstores

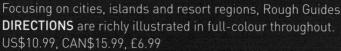

NOTES

Small print and
Index

A Rough Guide to Rough Guides

Published in 1982, the first Rough Guide – to Greece – was a student scheme that became a publishing phenomenon. Mark Ellingham, a recent graduate in English from Bristol University, had been travelling in Greece the previous summer and couldn't find the right guidebook. With a small group of friends he wrote his own guide, combining a highly contemporary, journalistic style with a thoroughly practical approach to travellers' needs.

The immediate success of the book spawned a series that rapidly covered dozens of destinations. And, in addition to impecunious backpackers, Rough Guides soon acquired a much broader and older readership that relished the guides' wit and inquisitiveness as much as their enthusiastic, critical approach and value-for-money ethos.

These days, Rough Guides include recommendations from shoestring to luxury and cover more than 200 destinations around the globe, including almost every country in the Americas and Europe, more than half of Africa and most of Asia and Australasia. Our ever-growing team of authors and photographers is spread all over the world, particularly in Europe, the USA and Australia.

In the early 1990s, Rough Guides branched out of travel, with the publication of Rough Guides to World Music, Classical Music and the Internet. All three have become benchmark titles in their fields, spearheading the publication of a wide range of books under the Rough Guide name.

Including the travel series, Rough Guides now number more than 350 titles, covering: phrasebooks, waterproof maps, music guides from Opera to Heavy Metal, reference works as diverse as Conspiracy Theories and Shakespeare, and popular culture books from iPods to Poker. Rough Guides also produce a series of more than 120 World Music CDs in partnership with World Music Network.

Visit www.roughguides.com to see our latest publications.

Rough Guide travel images are available for commercial licensing at www.roughguidespictures.com

Rough Guide credits

Text editors: Polly Thomas, Keith Drew
Layout: Pradeep Thapliyal
Cartography: Rajesh Chhibber, Athokpam Jotinkumar
Picture editor: Nicole Newman
Production: Aimee Hampson
Proofreader: Stewart Wild
Cover design: Chloë Roberts
Photographer: Helena Smith

....

Editorial: London Kate Berens, Claire Saunders, Ruth Blackmore, Polly Thomas, Richard Lim, Alison Murchie, Karoline Densley, Andy Turner, Keith Drew, Edward Aves, Nikki Birrell, Alice Park, Sarah Eno, Lucy White, Jo Kirby, Sam Cook, James Smart, Natasha Foges, Roisin Cameron, Joe Staines, Duncan Clark, Peter Buckley, Matthew Milton, Tracy Hopkins, Ruth Tidball; **New York** Andrew Rosenberg, Steven Horak, AnneLise Sorensen, Amy Hegarty, April Isaacs, Ella Steim, Anna Owens, Joseph Petta, Sean Mahoney
Design & Pictures: London Scott Stickland, Dan May, Diana Jarvis, Mark Thomas, Jj Luck, Harriet Mills, Chloë Roberts,; **Delhi** Umesh Aggarwal, Ajay Verma, Jessica Subramanian, Ankur Guha,

Sachin Tanwar, Anita Singh, Madhavi Singh, Karen d'Souza
Production: Katherine Owers
Cartography: London Maxine Repath, Ed Wright, Katie Lloyd-Jones; **Delhi** Jai Prakash Mishra, Ashutosh Bharti, Rajesh Mishra, Animesh Pathak, Jasbir Sandhu, Karobi Gogoi, Amod Singh, Alakananda Bhattacharya
Online: New York Jennifer Gold, Kristin Mingrone; **Delhi** Manik Chauhan, Narender Kumar, Rakesh Kumar, Amit Kumar, Amit Verma, Rahul Kumar, Ganesh Sharma, Debojit Borah
Marketing & Publicity: London Liz Statham, Niki Hanmer, Louise Maher, Jess Carter, Vanessa Godden, Anna Paynton, Rachel Sprackett; **New York** Geoff Colquitt, Megan Kennedy, Katy Ball; **Delhi** Reem Khokhar
Special Projects Editor: Philippa Hopkins
Manager India: Punita Singh
Series Editor: Mark Ellingham
Reference Director: Andrew Lockett
Publishing Coordinator: Megan McIntyre
Publishing Director: Martin Dunford

Publishing information

This first edition published April 2007
by **Rough Guides Ltd**,
80 Strand, London WC2R 0RL
345 Hudson St, 4th Floor,
New York, NY 10014, USA
14 Local Shopping Centre, Panchsheel Park,
New Delhi 110017, India
Distributed by the Penguin Group
Penguin Books Ltd,
80 Strand, London WC2R 0RL
Penguin Group (USA)
375 Hudson Street, NY 10014, USA
Penguin Group (Australia)
250 Camberwell Road, Camberwell,
Victoria 3124, Australia
Penguin Books Canada Ltd,
10 Alcorn Avenue, Toronto, Ontario,
Canada M4V 1E4
Penguin Group (NZ)
67 Apollo Drive, Mairangi Bay, Auckland 1310,
New Zealand

Cover concept by Peter Dyer.
Typeset in Bembo and Helvetica to an original design by Henry Iles.
Printed in Italy by LegoPrint SpA

© Rough Guides 2007

456pp includes index

A catalogue record for this book is available from the British Library

ISBN: 978-1-84353-717-5

The publishers and authors have done their best to ensure the accuracy and currency of all the information in **The Rough Guide to xxx**, however, they can accept no responsibility for any loss, injury, or inconvenience sustained by any traveller as a result of information or advice contained in the guide.

1 3 5 7 9 8 6 4 2

Help us update

We've gone to a lot of trouble to ensure that this first edition of the **Rough Guide to Denmark** is accurate and up-to-date. However, things change – places get "discovered", opening hours are notoriously fickle, restaurants and rooms raise prices or lower standards. If you feel we've got it wrong or left something out, we'd like to know, and if you can remember the address, the price, the time and the phone number, but all the better.

We'll credit any contributions, and send a copy of the next edition (or any other Rough Guide if you prefer) for the best letters. Everyone who writes to us and isn't already a subscriber will receive a copy of our full-colour thrice-yearly newsletter. Please mark letters **"Rough Guide to Denmark Update"** and send to: Rough Guides, 80 Strand, London WC2R 0RL, or Rough Guides, 4th Floor, 345 Hudson St, New York, NY 10014. Or send an email to mail@roughguides.com.

Have your questions answered and tell others about your trip at www.roughguides.atinfopop.com

Acknowledgements

Lone Mouritsen would like to thank co-writers Caroline and Roger for being real team players, always ready to step in whenever the shit was close to hitting the fan. Also a big thank you to our editor Polly, who took on the unenviable task of cracking the whip, without which this book would not have been finished on time. Lone would also like to thank the people at Natural England in Cornwall who have given true meaning to the term "flexible working". In Denmark, she would like to thank the Dalls and Egelunds for their in-depth breakdown of what's happening in Århus; the Riise family for the lowdown on Kolding nightlife; mor and Paul for housing and feeding her while in south Jutland; and far and Ingjerd for providing her with a pleasant base on Mols. Last but not least, she'd like to thank Mette and Nina for their in-depth knowledge of canoeing in Denmark and all things fun for children.

Roger Norum wishes to thank the following people, without whom the book would have been much less enjoyable to work on: Lone and Caroline for all their comments and critiques and for making co-writing such a memorable experience; Polly for being such a discerning, thorough and helpful editor; Kate Berens for considering me; and Nicole Newman for such gorgeous photos. Hélène Niveau-Kringelbach, Helle Riis Henriksen, Trine Hartvig Hansen, Rie Poulsen, Lars (Knud) Funch Hansen, Peter and Pernille Funch and Søren Nissen were all super-helpful with my research and are the most hospitable, friendly and hyggelig Danes I know. I'd never have made it through Roskilde without Katrine Sonne, Juan Hein, Sine Hansen, Mettine and the ever-helpful Dea Franka at the Roskilde Festival press office. Thanks also goes to Wilfred Gachau; Lars Kelstrup at Sorø Akademi; Mai Seidelin at the Copenhagen Jazz Festival; Mette Vestergård at Danhostel; Henrik at Rent-A-Wreck; Allan Hansen at the Nørrevang Hotel; Gitte Frank at Marielyst Tourist Office; Barbara Whitmarsh at Odense Tourist Office; Heidi Karlsen, Gitte Rahbek and Pia Hartmann at Rudkøbing Tourist Office; and Allan Sørensen at VisitDenmark, London. Neil Smith at Norvik Press offered much assistance with Danish literature, as did Kirsty McHugh at Oxford University Press; Jon Mulvaney at Criterion; Alex Bowler at Random House UK; Anna-Lisa Sandstrum at Canongate; and Jenny Dean and Thi Dinh at Penguin. Finally, thanks to Patrick Alexander for keeping me laughing; Ania Szatkowska for putting up so lovingly with my regular plaints and gripes; and my adopted family in Oxford – Adrian, Kate and Olivia Mourby – who provided tireless friendship, support and just the right amount of white wine to make the writing happen.

Caroline Osborne would like to thank Roy and Lise for all their help and hospitality in Denmark over the years; Roger and Lone for being great co-authors; and Martin and Daisy for being wonderful research companions.

SMALL PRINT

Selected images from our guidebooks are available for licensing from:

ROUGH GUIDES PICTURES.COM

ROUGH GUIDES

SMALL PRINT

Index

Map entries are in colour.

V

W

Z

Map symbols

maps are listed in the full index using coloured text

‑‑‑‑·	International border	⊞	Hospital
‑‑‑	Chapter boundary	@	Internet access
▬▬	Expressway	ⓘ	Information office
═══	Major road	⊠	Post office
───	Minor road	⟟	Fountain/gardens
▭▭	Pedestrianized street	⚑	Golf Course
⊞⊞⊞	Steps	⌣	Boats
‿	Bridge	✡	Synagogue
‑‑‑‑‑	Path/cycle route	Ⓜ	Metro station
━●━	Railway	Ⓢ	S-Tog station
───	Coastline/river	★	Bus stop
─ ─	Ferry route	🄿	Parking
ᛖᚱᛁᚨᚾ	Rocks	⸸	Church (regional maps)
▲	Peak	⊠—⊠	Gate/entrance
⛉	Light house	▭	Market
✈	Airport	▬	Building
◆	Point of interest	⊞	Church (town maps)
♖	Castle/fort	⬭	Stadium
🏛	Stately home/palace	⊡	Cemetery
♀	Museum	▦	Park
🌾	Windmill	▨	Forest
◉	Accomodation	▩	Beach
⚕	Campsite